Rodney

I.   Admiral Lord Rodney

from an oil painting of 1784–9 by Sir Joshua Reynolds

Rodney

DAVID SPINNEY

*This book is published and distributed
in the United States by the*

UNITED STATES NAVAL INSTITUTE

Annapolis, Maryland 21402

SBN 04 920022 4

PRINTED IN GREAT BRITAIN
in Plantin type
BY UNWIN BROTHERS LIMITED
WOKING AND LONDON

Acknowledgement

My first thanks must be to the staffs of the Public Record Office where most of the research for this work was done, and of the National Maritime Museum. I must also acknowledge my gratitude to the following authorities and individuals for permission to quote from manuscripts and typescripts in their possession: to the trustees of the National Maritime Museum for the *Duff Papers* and much Rodney material; to the Council of the Royal United Service Institution for two Rodney letters, and to the Hon. David Erskine for transcribing them; to the Northamptonshire Record Office for much material relating to the 1768 election; to the Staffordshire Record Office for the *Drakeford MSS.*, and to the trustees of the Lichfield estates for some of Rodney's letters to Anson; to the William L. Clements Library, University of Michigan and to its curator of manuscripts W. S. Ewing, for the *Sir John Vaughan Papers*; to the Earl of Lonsdale and Maldwin Drummond Esq., for their ready assistance and for the use of various letters in their possession; to Lord Herbert and Jonathan Cape Ltd for permission to quote from the *Pembroke Papers*. In particular my thanks are due to the Marquess of Northampton for allowing me to examine and make use of the important papers at Castle Ashby, to the Hon. Simon Rodney for such Rodney papers as have not found their way to the Public Record Office, and to Victor Montagu, Esq., for giving me access to all the papers of the Fourth Earl of Sandwich.

Among the many who have so generously assisted me with their time and their knowledge I must first record my great obligation to the late Sir Lewis Namier, to Doctor F. H. W. Sheppard, and to Professor E. K. Waterhouse. Eugene Finch, V. A. Hatley, Piers Mackesy, and R. F. Mackay have drawn my attention to much that I might otherwise have missed. For the genealogical background I owe much to Anthony Camp, and in particular to Miss Freda Podmore. I must record my warm thanks to Mrs Carolyn Maxwell and to her late husband Wing Commander G. Constable Maxwell MC, DFC, AFC, for making me free of Rodney's old home at Alresford.

The frontispiece is reproduced by gracious permission of Her Majesty the Queen. The other plates have been reproduced by kind permission of the trustees of the National Maritime Museum (Plates II, IV, VIII, XII, XIII, XV, and XVII), the trustees of the Holburne Menstrie Museum of

7

Art, Bath (Plates III and IX), the Royal College of Physicians (Plate XIV), the Earl of Rosebery (Plate XVI), the National Trust and Lady Cawley (Plate XI), Lord Egremont (Plate V), the Hon. Simon Rodney (Plates VI and XVIII), and Lieutenant-Colonel P. L. Thorne (Plate VII).

Lastly to John Brooke, for reading the whole manuscript and suggesting so much for its improvement, and to Lieutenant-Commander G. P. B. Naish and A. W. H. Pearsall of the National Maritime Museum for similar service, I must record a special indebtedness. Without their kindly criticism and correction this work would be far more imperfect than it is. Such shortcomings as remain are my own.

Iwerne Minster, J. D. SPINNEY

May 1967.

Contents

A*   9

Illustrations

Plates *continued*

Maps

Diagrams

Genealogical Tables

Introduction

Rodney's name has always evoked a curious mixture of admiration and antipathy. As a man of action and a fighter he is universally accepted. The image of a resolute and successful sea-officer has always been clearly and correctly recognized. But misconception and prejudice have combined to give it some unlikeable features.

It was his misfortune to be much criticized in his lifetime by disgruntled, but not always disinterested subordinates, many of whose letters have since been published and, in the writer's submission, rather too readily accepted at their face value. Political prejudice, from an age when politics have seldom been more bitter, and the complaints of a highly resentful business community whose activities he had good reason to curb, have contributed to swell the chorus of condemnation. These hostile voices have never been silenced, or even answered. For nearly two centuries the Admiral's case has gone by default.

In any case he was too much a man of his time for the historians of the nineteenth century. They could not forgive him for his gambling and his Tory sympathies, the aristocratic hauteur which, as they supposed, put him at loggerheads with his officers, and his hostility to the American colonists. There was an aura of dissipation about him which they did not like, and more than a whiff of corruption. Above all, there were his debts and his degrading obsession (as they would have it) with money. So, while acknowledging his fighting achievements, they pursed their lips over his supposed shortcomings and turned with relief to brighter figures with whom they found themselves more in sympathy.

All this has been grievous for his fame. Not only has it led to the uncritical acceptance of much to his disadvantage, however suspect the source; but it has inclined later writers to colour their interpretation of his actions unfavourably.

Thus David Hannay's short life, which appeared at the end of the nineteenth century,* is smugly censorious. It is the nineteenth century sitting in judgement on the eighteenth. In his introduction to the Hood papers† Hannay writes penetratingly and well, but even so he makes the suggestion, with no supporting evidence whatever, that Rodney died 'a

---

* English men of action series, Macmillan, London, 1891.
† *Letters of Sir Samuel Hood*, Navy Records Society, 1895.

near imbecile'. The point may or may not be important but there is excellent evidence to the contrary.

More serious, because of the writer's eminence, is Sir Julian Corbett's damaging account of how Captain Rodney, while on an urgent mission to North America, wasted a vital fortnight pursuing and securing a valuable prize.* This story, although disproved by his ship's journal, conformed too closely to the accepted picture of unscrupulous avarice for Corbett to check. Instead he boldly set it down with all its damning implications and headed his page 'Rodney's abberation', thus making a new contribution to the legend. After this it is hardly surprising to find him, a few chapters later, suggesting that Rear-Admiral Rodney deliberately disobeyed orders by sending his ships to hunt for prizes when he should have held them in readiness for another flag-officer, a point highly disputable to say the least.

Enough has been said to suggest that truth has been over long in clearing the Admiral's name. Rodney was never an incarnation of all the virtues, least of all those of modesty and prudence. But he has yet to be judged on the facts, rather than on the partial testimony of old enemies and rivals; and by the standards of his own day rather than those of ours. For the rest, his story is that of a sea-officer. The sea-service was, to him, 'the profession I have always had most at heart',† and therefore this book is largely concerned with details of ships and service. The brightness may be a little tarnished in places, and certain weaknesses too patent to be overlooked. But with the smears and stains removed the picture, like his last great portrait by Reynolds, compels respect and even, perhaps, a measure of sympathy.

* *England in the Seven Years War*, Longmans, London, 1907.
† Rodney to Lord Sandwich, December 1, 1777. *Sandwich Papers* (unpublished).

Chapter 1

Rodneys and Bridges

'*Non generant Aquilae Columbas*'

I N the reign of King George I, when the great war of the succession in Spain was still a fairly recent memory, and a prosperous and triumphant Britain was trying to get used to her new line of kings from Germany, a retired captain of Marines lived with his wife and family at Walton-on-Thames. This was Captain Harry Rodney, Admiral Rodney's father. The family was ancient and honourable but no longer rich. Monuments in the church of Rodney Stoke in Somerset still testify, in stone and marble, to its virtues and eminence under the Tudors and the early Stuarts; and before this the names of other Rodneys stretch back and back until the family roots disappear beyond the gaze of even the most credulous genealogist sometime in the thirteenth century. But when our story opens, the tree that had flourished and proliferated so grandly for 400 years had, in large measure, withered and decayed. Rodney Stoke and other manors once held by the family in the west country had passed to other hands. No longer landowners or local magnates, many Rodneys chose to follow the profession of arms. Each generation seems to have two or three good fighting men to demonstrate, in the Low Countries and Tangier, in Spain or at sea, the truth of their own motto, that 'Eagles do not beget Doves'. Honourable service in the armed forces seems to have become a family tradition by the time Captain Harry Rodney settled at Walton; also in the family tradition was an unfortunate propensity to be unlucky in money matters.

Tracing the family one generation back from the retired captain at Walton, we see its characteristic virtues and misfortunes well exemplified in the careers of four typical Rodneys, the brothers George and Anthony, and their cousins Caesar and William. Of this quartet Caesar was the most hardly used. A colonel in the Guards at Whitehall in the reign of King

Charles II, and later with the Tangier garrison, he then fell upon evil days and languished for eleven years in the Fleet prison and for eighteen months in the Marshalsea. On his release, his only provision was a small allowance from his son, until the latter was killed at the storming of Lille in 1708 after which there was no provision at all for the old and broken officer his father; from the pathetic and moving petition he wrote at the end of his life,[1] it seems he was very little removed from having to beg his bread. His brother William was the exception to prove the rule, a Rodney who not only preserved his skin but prospered too. Sailing from Bristol with William Penn in 1682 he became the first Speaker of the Delaware Assembly, and founded a line of American Rodneys of whom, in later years, it is unlikely that the illustrious Admiral would have cared to be reminded. Of the other two, George Rodney, true to tradition, served in a Marine regiment, rose to the rank of captain, and died in 1700. His brother Anthony was also a soldier but, as the father of our retired captain at Walton and therefore the Admiral's grandfather, he deserves a rather more detailed notice.

A cornet in Charles II's reign, serving with the regiment of the Earl of Peterborough, and then a captain with the Tangier garrison, Anthony's career was not spoilt by debts or any of the hazards which jeopardized an officer's prospects during the Glorious Revolution. He served King William and was present in the King's camp before Namur in 1695, by which time his son Harry was old enough to serve. The Rodneys were always careful for the next generation so it is not surprising to find this young man, at about fourteen years of age, commissioned in his father's regiment. Together they assisted in the Dutch King's only triumph when Namur fell. Soon England was fighting France again over the Spanish succession. Anthony Rodney was now a lieutenant-colonel in Holt's regiment of Marines and young Harry a second lieutenant in the same regiment. They served together in Spain where Anthony, a full colonel in 1704, was present under his old patron Peterborough at the famous siege of Barcelona. Here, in 1705, his successful career came to an abrupt end. He quarrelled with one of his brother officers; they fought, and Colonel Rodney was killed.

It may be that his father's death prevented Harry Rodney advancing any further in the service. He was a captain by that time, but a captain he remained, and when the war ended he retired and settled down on a few acres at Walton-on-Thames. Before the war ended he had married Mary Newton, daughter of Sir Henry Newton, a distinguished diplomat and a judge of the High Court of Admiralty, a union which provided some useful family connections. Mary Rodney, as she became, was the Admiral's mother, and although she remains a shadowy figure it is probable that she brought to the home at Walton something of the great world of affairs in which her family moved. Her father had been Envoy Extraordinary to the Court of Tuscany and the Republic of Genoa during Queen Anne's reign, and her sister Catherine had taken as her second husband Lord Aubrey Beauclerck, son of the Duke of St Albans and grandson of King Charles II. Lord Aubrey was himself a gallant sea-officer, while his brother Lord Vere was a future Lord of the Admiralty. Here were pledges for the future to be taken up when the time was ripe.

The union of Harry Rodney and Mary Newton was fruitful. There was a daughter, Maria Constantia, a second daughter, Catherine, who died in infancy, and the first son, Henry, who was born in 1714. The future Admiral was the fourth child and appeared some time at the end of 1717 or the beginning of 1718. The exact date of his birth is unknown. All that one can be sure about is that he was baptized in the church of St Giles-in-the-Fields in the county of Middlesex on February 13, 1718 (new style), and named George Bridges. If Captain and Mrs Rodney waited until the new baby was six weeks old or more before taking him to church, then he was born in 1717; a shorter interval and the year would have been 1718. One more boy, James, followed in 1724.

A curious legend has survived about the names chosen for the future Admiral. It relates how, at the time he was born, his father, the retired Captain of Marines, was commanding one of the royal yachts conveying King George I to Holland, and that in gracious recognition of the happy event His Majesty consented to stand sponsor along with James Bridges, Duke of Chandos (a distant Rodney connection of whom more will be said later) thus jointly contributing to a baptismal total of George Bridges. It is a flattering story, but difficult to accept. Even if we allow Captain Harry Rodney merely to have been in attendance on His Majesty, for it is inconceivable that a land-officer could command a royal yacht, there is no record of George I going abroad in 1717 or 1718, while the Duke of Chandos did not receive his ducal title until 1719. One of the Admiral's godfathers, beyond any shadow of doubt, was his kinsman (later his guardian), George Bridges of Avington, which seems sufficient explanation for both his names.*

* It is perhaps noteworthy that the Admiral himself never spelt his second name any other way than with an 'i'—'Bridges'.

19

To return to Walton-on-Thames. While the future Admiral was still a baby a shadow fell across the household, of a sort that he himself was to know only too well in later years. The unfortunate tendency of the Rodneys to mismanage their money has already been noted. Captain Harry Rodney was no exception to this, and after 1720 his affairs became seriously embarrassed.

After two and a half centuries the details are blurred, but in the records of the King's Bench his name appears petitioning for release from a Bond of £1,800 advanced, so far as one can gather, for the purpose of dealing in South Sea Stock.[2] Evidently the captain was more of a gambler than a businessman, for the date of the Bond is September 30, 1720, by which time no one with a grain of business sense would have dreamed of having anything to do with the South Sea Company. The famous Bubble was bursting even as Captain Rodney made his ill-judged incursion into the financial jungle, and of course he burnt his fingers. Probably the family home was involved, for the King's Bench records mention property at Walton and four and a half acres of land there. All this passed, after a series of bewildering transactions, into the hands of strangers.

The years which follow provide glimpses of the Captain's legal battles, in a nightmare world of money-lenders and attorneys, trying to recover a little of what he had lost. Suit followed suit, and the wretched business dragged on until his death in 1737, when his affairs were still heavily involved. The retired officer with a growing family and a diminished income is a familiar figure in every age. Rashness and inexperience committed Captain Harry Rodney to his creditors for the rest of his life. His young family can hardly have remained unaware of the cloud darkening their home, and things being what they were, their prospects would not in the ordinary way have seemed very promising. But fortunately there were affluent connections who were prepared to show an interest and do their duty by the hard-pressed Rodneys, and to these wealthy and benevolent collaterals we must now turn.

The link, which in this time of need brought aid and succour, had been forged three generations earlier when Anne Rodney, first cousin as it happened to George, Anthony, Caesar and William, married Sir Thomas Bridges. The Bridges were active and important men of affairs, tending more towards the court and politics, just as the Rodneys tended towards the fighting services, and infinitely more prosperous. The son of Anne Rodney and Sir Thomas Bridges was George Rodeney Bridges who resided at Avington near Winchester on land acquired by his family after the dissolution of the monasteries, and who transformed the old manor house into the splendid mansion which still stands. He had been high in favour with Charles II, he had prospered exceedingly under William III, and when he died in 1714 he left a noble estate to his son George Bridges. It might be thought that the degree of kinship between the affluent country gentleman in Hampshire and the necessitous Captain of Marines at Walton-on-Thames was not very close, but the world was smaller in those days and family ties marked and respected more, perhaps, than they are now. They were close enough for George Bridges to stand sponsor for the captain's fourth child at his baptism; they were now to prove sufficiently close for much more.

There was another connection, more remote than the Bridges of Avington but even more magnificent, and this was the superbly successful head of the Bridges family. While the Rodneys fought on land and sea and shed their blood, and while the Bridges of Avington sat in Parliament and dispensed local justice, James Bridges, ninth Baron Chandos, built up a princely fortune during the War of the Spanish Succession and became a duke. Of his title, his magnificence and his palatial establishment at Canons, nothing now remains except the legend and a few relics.* But so splendid a kinsman must have loomed large on the horizons at Avington and Walton. The Duke knew his cousin George Bridges well. His second wife, for he was a much married man, died while staying with Mrs Bridges in 1735, and quite early in the story he was probably aware of the existence of his rather more distant kinsman George Bridges Rodney.

To return to the family at Walton. After the South Sea Bubble burst, the wealthier and probably wiser relatives stepped in to provide for the older children. Maria Constantia said of herself many years later, when the days of poverty had returned, that she had been 'brought up in splendour',[3] which may have meant Canons or Avington or possibly a place at Court in the establishment of the Princess of Wales, but which can hardly have been her parents' home. For Henry, the eldest son, there was an Exhibition at Balliol College, Oxford, on the nomination of the Duke of Chandos; and for George there was his godfather at Avington who, if family legend and the earliest reports speak true, undertook all responsibility for him at this crisis of the family fortunes and brought him up. James, the youngest, may have remained with his parents. He certainly retained an interest in Walton all his life and is buried there.

---

* One of these, the organ from his private chapel upon which G. F. Handel played and composed, is now in Trinity Church, Gosport.

THE BRIDGES CONNECTION

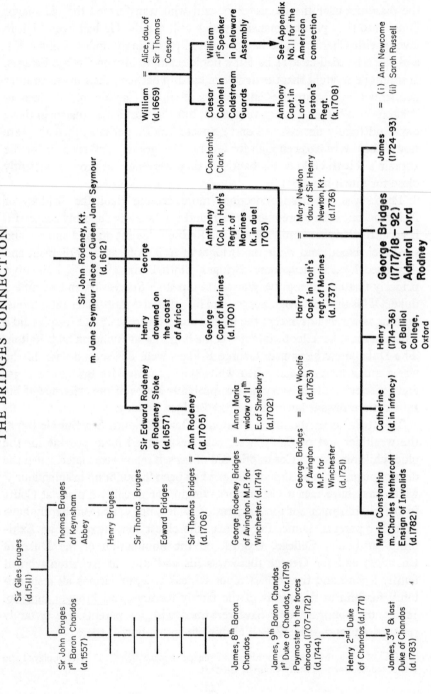

So it was that young George Rodney moved from the family home, with its shadow of debts and disappointment, to an easier and more spacious world; and one of his most lasting impressions must have been the contrast between the sad figure of his father and the affluence and assurance of his guardian. For the establishment of George Bridges was very handsome indeed.

The visitor today can still see Avington Park much as young Rodney saw it when he went to live there in the seventeen-twenties. A symmetrical façade of mellow, red brick, low and spreading but of pleasing proportions, looks west across the broad parkland, and reflects the setting sun from tall windows put in at the end of Charles II's reign, when George Rodeney Bridges rebuilt the old house in the simple but elegant style of Sir Christopher Wren. Money had been plentiful for that rebuilding. Everything was on a lavish scale, from the stabling and outbuildings to the marble stairway and the great ballroom on the first floor where, it was said, Verrio had worked for seven years painting the ceiling. Avington was one of the greatest houses in Hampshire, certainly the greatest within a day's ride of Winchester.

All round spread the lush meadow land of the Itchen valley, with that most delightful of Hampshire rivers winding through the grounds and past the house. Already most of the trees would have been planted which grace the estate today. Beyond it the pleasant Hampshire landscape stretched away to Old Alresford, four miles distant, where one day a successful sea-officer who had learnt to love that part of the country would build his own house; and in the other direction, to Winchester, the centre of local society. A topographer writing at this time described the region as 'one of the finest sporting countries in the kingdom'.[4]

Of George Bridges and his wife it is hard to speak with certainty. Mr Bridges seems to have been a kindly soul, fond of the country and his dogs, and he certainly took to young Rodney for in his will he made him his residuary legatee.[5] Mrs Bridges on the other hand seems to have been something of a Tartar, a capable woman with a good head for business and a will of her own, who survived her husband many years and favoured James Rodney at the expense of his elder brother. Mr Bridges was Member of Parliament for Winchester, so the interests of the household extended beyond the management of the estate, and the sporting life of the countryside. Young Rodney can hardly have escaped having to listen to some talk, probably a great deal, about politics and current affairs. There would have been visits to London for the meetings of Parliament, and the occasional election, a fairly safe affair for Mr Bridges had held the seat ever since the death of his father.

But Avington as young Rodney knew it was much more than the comfortable residence of his kindly guardian. It was rich in memories of a glamorous past, when George Rodeney Bridges and his wife, who had been the notorious Countess of Shrewsbury, used to entertain King Charles II and Nell Gwynne in the days when Sovereigns had been affable and gracious, and the court a magnet for all that was brilliant and ambitious. There were reminders everywhere. The former countess may not have been quite so wicked as some suppose, but a mulberry tree behind the house is still shown as the fatal spot where her first husband fought the Duke of Buckingham; and although one may have doubts about the mulberry tree, there is no doubt whatever about the £1,600 a year that the King granted her out of the Irish revenue, an income which she enjoyed for many years and which probably paid for rebuilding Avington after her second marriage. When, towards the end of his reign, King Charles came down to Winchester to see how his new palace was progressing, he would stop at the Park, and as the cathedral authorities would not have Nell Gwynne at the deanery, perhaps she really did occupy the bedroom and dressing-room at Avington which still bear her name. A bathing-pool and an avenue of lime trees are associated with her too, and a banqueting-hall of Charles II once stood but stands no longer. Rodney's guardian had been seven years old when Charles II died, so he might well have retained some childhood memories of those royal occasions; but in any case he would have had plenty to tell, and the servants too, of his mother's régime, for the former countess did not die until 1702. Life had been quieter at Avington since those days, but such memories and traditions lose nothing in the telling.

This is all we have, not much perhaps, but enough to reveal a little of George Rodney's childhood and early environment in that long-forgotten family circle. The unlucky father with his tales of the wars and his load of debts; the kindly guardian with his great estate and his strong-minded wife; the privileged existence in that lovely part of Hampshire with great affairs and the business of the nation never very far away. All this would provide much material upon which a bright, eager, determined boy might ponder.

At a suitable age the young man went to Harrow. The great days of the English public schools were still to come, but Eton and Westminster had long been patronized by the well-connected, and by the beginning of the eighteenth century John Lyon's foundation ten miles from London was becoming popular too. Although the school records do not go back far enough to include the name of George Bridges Rodney, tradition of the most respectable antiquity* claims him as an Harrovian. The Duke of Chandos, who had interested himself sufficiently in the family to nominate Henry Rodney to an Exhibition at Oxford, was a governor of the school at this time, and might well have extended his influence on behalf of Henry's younger brother. Public school ages in those days would range from the youngest at seven or eight to perhaps fifteen or sixteen, so if we accept the tradition, young Rodney would have been at Harrow some time between 1725 and 1732.

Life at a public school in the eighteenth century was brutal and hard. Latin and Greek took up most of the curriculum, flogging and fisticuffs added their contribution to the toughening process, and drinking was not unknown. A few years at a public school were excellent preparation for life in the Royal Navy. The parents of several illustrious admirals seem to have understood this for Vernon and Keppel went to Westminster, Howe tried Westminster first and then Eton, while there is a possibility that one of the Hoods also went to Harrow at about this time. So it is probable that before the sea claimed him young Rodney went to Harrow on the recommendation of the Duke of Chandos, that he learnt his lessons in the great panelled form-room in the old brick building at the top of the Hill, and that he may have fought his first fight in the historic milling-ground close by. Canons was within easy riding distance, so there may have been visits. One more suggestion may cautiously be put forward, which is that young Rodney remembered Harrow with affection. He certainly sent his son there, and a third generation followed.

'. . . my Idea from a School-boy,' he wrote many years later, 'has allways been to think my life at all times to be exposed in the service of my country',[6] but why he chose the sea rather than the land service is obscure. His aunt, Lady Aubrey Beauclerck, for whom he had a special affection, was married to a very gallant sea-officer, and the influence may have been here; or perhaps it came from that Captain William Bridges who served at sea under Queen Anne. On July 7, 1732, the name 'Geo. Rodney' appears on the ship's books of H.M.S. *Sunderland*, one of the guardships lying at the Nore. His quality is described as 'Vol. per Ord.', which means 'Volunteer per Order', and he was discharged exactly a

---

* The earliest printed reference to Admiral Lord Rodney having been a boy at Harrow is in Ackermann's *History of the Public Schools* (1816). Ackermann's informant was a highly respected Harrovian and native of Harrow, Doctor Parr, who entered the school in 1752. None of Parr's other ascriptions has been contradicted, so he is probably a reliable witness.

month later with no indication why or where save the unhelpful note 'pr. list'.[7] Such is the earliest recorded entry of the career that was to end in a blaze of glory exactly fifty years later.

These cryptic entries need to be explained. There were at this time two ways into the Navy for a young man who aspired to an officer's commission. He might enter under the protection of a friendly captain as a 'Captain's Servant' (the rating had no menial significance) until he knew whether he liked the sea service or not, and most officers started like this. Alternatively he might be launched into the Navy through what amounted to an Admiralty nomination. Armed with a letter from the King (which was in fact the nomination in question) the young volunteer could present himself on board the ship chosen by their Lordships, and the captain of that ship would have to take him whether he liked it or not because the young man was a 'Volunteer per *Order*'. Those who entered like this were known (unofficially) as 'King's Letter Boys'. Young Rodney was one of the last to enter by this system before it was changed.

Who obtained his nomination for him? One can only guess. Perhaps the Duke of Chandos whispered a word in the ear of one of the Lords of the Admiralty; or George Bridges exerted some of his Parliamentary influence; or it may have been that naval uncle already mentioned, or some friend of the family who remembered his grandfather's service in Spain. But whoever it was, the right strings were pulled to produce those terse entries in the books of H.M.S. *Sunderland*. The young man had chosen the sea service and if, besides serving his King, he desired a life of action and adventure, with the chance of great riches and high distinction, he had made a good choice. But it was a bold one.

The great tradition was already strong with memories of the Spanish Armada, the hard fighting of the Dutch wars, the glories of la Hogue, and stirring stories of brave Benbow in the West Indies. The highest distinction had been conferred on the Navy by the later Stuart kings, and since Royalty had condescended to serve, the nobility and gentry were prepared to learn the seaman's trade too; and no one in the service, be he gentle or simple, could be unmindful of the prize-money. A lucky officer might win it in plenty, and turn it into broad acres or government stock at 7 per cent. Men still spoke with bated breath of Admiral Wager's wealth, and of the riches which fell to the captors when the Vigo ships were taken. Spanish prizes in particular had a fabulous reputation, often with good reason; and a Spanish war was very much a possibility at the time when young Rodney elected to go to sea.

But setting aside youthful dreams, the Navy, even in peace time, could offer excellent prospects of employment for a man of spirit. The government of Sir Robert Walpole had the shrewdest understanding where the nation's best interests lay, and whenever these were threatened money was always forthcoming to fit out the fleet and sent it where needed. Then there were pirates to be put down, fisheries to be protected, and colonial governors to be sustained, while in the Mediterranean a watchful eye had to be kept on the coast of Barbary. An active officer with influence behind him need never lack opportunities.

The other side of the medal would not daunt a lad of spirit, although in truth it was daunting enough, for no career offered greater hardship or discomfort—or more hazards. 'No man,' said Doctor Johnson, 'will be a sailor who has contrivance enough to get himself into a jail; for being in a ship is being in a jail, with the chance of being drowned. . . .' If the Doctor had been speaking from first-hand knowledge he might have painted the picture even blacker, for the chance of being drowned was much less likely than the chance of dying most unpleasantly by disease. Young Rodney could not know the full horrors which awaited him, but even as a schoolboy he must have heard about ship-fever, scurvy, yellow-jack, and how, when the fleet lay off Porto Bello in 1727, the unwholesome climate carried off two admirals, ten captains, fifty lieutenants and about 4,000 inferior officers and seamen.[8] Only the strongest constitution could survive conditions on board a King's ship, but what young man on the threshold of a career would give much thought to this? If he thought about it at all, it would be to reflect that things had always been so; otherwise promotion would be even more uncertain than it was.

This brings us to perhaps the most daunting aspect of the sea service— the uncertainty of advancement. Ability, energy and good health were not enough to ensure success. An officer also needed that essential thing called interest, which meant influential backing. Without it all his courage and capacity, his zeal and his patriotism might, and probably would, go for nothing. Interest was needed to start a young man in the service and smooth his path to the rank of lieutenant; interest could obtain a captain's commission for the veriest young duffer, over the heads of hundreds of capable and experienced lieutenants; interest could then send him to cruise where easy conditions and rich pickings might be expected. Without interest an officer, unless he had more than average luck, would probably remain a mere lieutenant all his life.

Young Rodney belonged to the privileged class, and in the early stages of

27

his career at least might count on more than his fair share of this intangible but essential commodity. But the Navy was a responsible service, and although it might be riddled with every form of patronage and political string-pulling, there were limits to the influence these could exert. Ability and zeal would generally be needed to ensure their continuance, for to take a simple parallel from the race-course, no patron in his senses would back a poor performer for long; and this applied with increasing force as the higher ranks were reached.

On the day his name appeared on the books of the *Sunderland* young Rodney's naval career may be said to have begun. But although, by the standard of those times, he was quite old enough to go to sea, it is unlikely that he did; it is doubtful if he even set foot on board the *Sunderland*. She was a guard-ship, dividing her time between Sheerness and the Nore, and the column in her muster-book to indicate the date of Mr Rodney's appearance on board is suspiciously blank. This introduces another aspect of service in the old Navy, the fact that a flying start might be made in acquiring seniority by the early entry of the volunteer's name on the books of some ship. Many years before, an eminent Secretary to the Admiralty, Mr Samuel Pepys, had decreed that three years' service was necessary before a young gentleman could qualify for midshipman. Our ancestors, while recognizing the wisdom of such regulations, were not above getting round them when they could, and here it was generally accepted that the qualifying period began on the date the volunteer's name was entered, and that officialdom would not enquire too strictly (particularly if influential persons were involved), by how many weeks, months, or even years, the book entry ante-dated the actual appearance on board. On the peacetime establishment of a guard-ship it is doubtful if the young man would have learnt much. Probably George Bridges sent him back to Harrow after his nomination, with the approval of everyone concerned. After all he was only fourteen.

Chapter 2

Young Mr Rodney

(1733–1740)

'. . . bred in ye Fore Top as well as ye Quarter-deck,
as you and I were some 50 years ago in our
Youthfull Days.'
(Lord Northesk to Lord Rodney, May 1, 1783.)[1]

THE plans to send young George Rodney to sea went forward. On May 1, 1733, his name was entered in the books of His Majesty's ship *Dreadnaught* of 60 guns,[2] Captain Alexander Geddes; on that same day he presented himself on board as she lay at Spithead; and in the *Dreadnaught* he remained for the next four years.

The day was overcast and windy when young Mr Rodney joined, so he would have had a wet trip from the Sally Port, or Portsmouth Point, or wherever it was he embarked. We may imagine, if we will, a Hogarthian waterfront and a slim youth with blue eyes, probably a blue coat, and certainly a sea-chest. But after his boat has taken him out to the *Dreadnaught*, and his figure has disappeared through the entry-port into the mysterious wooden world of the Georgian Navy, speculation must cease. The light of future genius is seldom obvious on the brow of a young volunteer aged fifteen and a half, and is likely to be even less so if he has been foisted on a captain who had not asked for him, and who probably did not want him. Volunteers berthed on the orlop deck, a dark and noisome region below the waterline where, according to one sardonic observer: 'He that can chose to live contentedly need never trouble his head what Lodgings are chalked out for him in the other World'.[3] If the young man from Avington Park viewed the cockpit of a man-of-war with dismay, he would not have been the first to do so.

The *Dreadnaught* was one of the Portsmouth guard-ships, and busy completing to full complement. Two or three guard-ships were always stationed at Portsmouth, Plymouth, and Sheerness, with reduced crews. Whenever a cloud appeared on the international horizon they could be brought forward with no more delay than was caused by the need to complete their complement and stores; and whether there was a cloud or not, some were brought forward for a few months each summer.

So young Rodney could start learning his profession at once. He was rated 'able-seaman', and had he ventured a startled protest there was a perfectly rational and satisfactory explanation. As a mere 'volunteer', there was no scale of pay to which he was entitled. But as an able-seaman he could draw twenty-six shillings a month, although out of this he would have, like everyone else, to contribute to Greenwich Hospital and the Chatham Chest. So, as an able-seaman (for administrative reasons) his professional education began, and in a manner more curious and varied than anything Harrow could provide. If he was on board on July 5th he might have seen nearly two hundredweight of condemned cheese thrown overboard; and on August 6th there was the spectacle of a seaman being flogged from ship to ship, a punishment much less common at that time than at the end of the century.

It would be wrong to suppose that a young sea-officer in the eighteenth century did not have plenty to learn on the academic side. The *Dreadnaught*'s complement included a schoolmaster, Mr George Kennedy, to instruct in the rudiments of geometry and navigation. From him, young Rodney would have learnt something of the theory and use of the backstaff, a cumbersome instrument used at that time to determine latitude. Together they may have discussed the new quadrant just invented by Mr Hadley for the same purpose, and shaken their heads, with every mariner since the art of navigation began, over the impossibility of determining longitude at sea for want of an accurate timekeeper. A reward of £20,000 had been going begging since 1714, but no one had yet been able to make a chronometer sufficiently accurate to claim it, and some said that no one ever would.

His eyes would have been opened to yet another aspect of his profession at the end of the year when the *Dreadnaught* went up harbour to 'clear' for the dock. This was a tiresome but essential business involving a great deal of heavy manual labour. In the *Dreadnaught*'s case, 60 guns, each weighing about 3 tons, had to be swung off onto lighters alongside, followed by most of the ammunition and stores, and some of the ballast; and at the same time most of the intricate web of spars and rigging had to come down. Such work demanded leadership, perfect familiarity with the ship's organization and fittings, and good practical knowledge of what could be done with blocks and tackle. A young officer could not start familiarizing himself with these matters too early.

On this occasion there was an atmosphere of purpose about the operation, for the *Dreadnaught* was to be used more actively in the new year. Spain, always the potential enemy and trouble-maker in Rodney's youth, had been interfering with British ships on the Spanish main, and there was also concern for the safety and independence of Britain's ancient ally Portugal. At the beginning of 1734 the government offered a bounty for volunteers. The *Dreadnaught* came out of dock and lumbered up channel to the Downs to press seamen for the fleet; and with this first modest excursion to sea there opened a new and exciting chapter in young Rodney's education.

In the whole world there was no place like the Downs for seeing so many sorts of ship. From the opulent Indiamen to the humblest coasters, colliers and fishing-smacks, every vessel using the North Sea, almost, one might say, every vessel using the ports of Northern Europe, would sooner or later fetch up in the Downs. On one side of them stretched fifteen miles of Kentish coast, and on the other the cruel sands which have ensnared ships and sucked them down ever since the days of Earl Godwin. Between was that wonderful stretch of water where whole fleets of merchantmen would sometimes lie for weeks.

Here the coastal traffic would await the next favouring slant of wind, and with it would be other vessels, arrived through stress of weather or for the simple need to communicate with the shore. Hundreds of ships might be seen tossing endlessly up and down and swinging with the tide, their numbers increasing daily; and among them, all day and every day, plied the skilful seamen from Ramsgate, Sandwich, and Deal, in their luggers, cutters, and beach-boats. Then would come the long-awaited shift of wind to set them all working at capstan and windlass, and in a matter of an hour or less the whole vast area would empty. To complete the picture there were generally a few of the King's ships stationed in the Downs, to keep the peace, protect shipping, and, if need be, to press seamen for the fleet. This was now the *Dreadnaught*'s business. Here she lay from February to August 1734, her boats continually away after men from the merchantmen, and it is unlikely that the young gentlemen who were on board to learn their profession missed much of what was going on.

The impress duty demanded common-sense, resolution, and experience; its officers might expect evasion, concealment, and sometimes violence, but never a welcome unless the merchant skipper had a man he wished to be rid of; in this business an alert, intelligent boy of sixteen could learn a lot. Care must be taken to respect the 'Protections' issued to ship's officers, apprentices, watermen on the London River, and certain other categories of seafarers. A merchantman must not be left with insufficient men to continue her voyage although, if she was homeward bound, a few reliable hands might be lent her from a King's ship to work her in. So the system operated and it is unlikely that many people in that insensitive age gave much thought to the feelings of the seamen. No one would deny that it might be hard for a man just back from an Indian voyage of over a year to be pressed for the fleet within sight of England's shore. But in time of need the requirements of the fleet must come first: otherwise the trade could not sail with safety. And most seamen were feckless creatures anyway. Few of them were bread-winners, and in most cases their impressment would merely mean a deferment of the debauchery they had promised themselves on shore, and a transference from the squalid misery of a merchantman's forecastle to the rigour and discipline, less squalid but probably no less miserable, of the gun-deck.

As the summer months passed and Spain's attitude towards Portugal became more and more threatening, the British lion began to flex his muscles. More and more ships were brought forward, and Admiral Sir John Norris, who had been hurrying things along at the Nore, took command of all the men-of-war in the Downs, including the *Dreadnaught*, and carried them with him to Spithead where his flag continued to fly. That autumn the concentration was allowed to disperse a little and the seamen were given a month's leave. Britain was relaxed but still watchful. Sir John continued as commander-in-chief.

In November, Captain Geddes left the *Dreadnaught*, taking with him six of his midshipmen and some fifty seamen, and in his place came Captain Henry Medley, fresh from an interesting commission on the American coast. Geddes seems to have taken little notice of young Rodney who remained an able-seaman throughout his period of command. Medley advanced him to midshipman within twenty-four hours of his arrival on board. The new captain was to continue as he had begun, and he was a friend worth having for he had made his own way in the Navy under the protection of the Commander-in-Chief himself. So the auspices became as favourable as any young officer had the right to expect; and to crown the happy prospect there was now every chance of the fleet being ordered to sea in the new year.

For Spain's attitude towards Portugal did not improve and the government was listening with increasing sympathy to Portugal's plea for support. In the spring of 1735 there were at Spithead thirty-five of the line, with Sir John flying his flag in the *Britannia*. Every ship was under-manned except the flagship.[4] The *Dreadnaught* was 84 short out of 400. But fully manned or not the government decided that the appearance of a British fleet in the Tagus would have a most beneficial effect, so Sir John received his orders.

Rodney's Commander-in-Chief was such an exceptional man that he deserves more than a passing reference. He was now over sixty years of age, with a length of service and experience that went back to the time of King Charles II. He had commanded ships in the famous actions of King William's reign. He had been knighted by Queen Anne and commanded her fleet in the Mediterranean years before Rodney was born. Having outlived nearly all his contemporaries, he towered in seniority over every officer in the fleet. The admiration and respect for such a venerable figure can be imagined. To a young midshipman he must have seemed immeasurably remote, a giant from an earlier and more heroic age. All the same, young Rodney's shrewdness would have reminded him that the system which had raised Sir John Norris so high, and which had enabled Sir John to advance Captain Medley, might bring others forward in their turn, however lowly they were at present.

The fleet received its orders in May but the Commander-in-Chief had not reached his position without learning a thing or two, and until the commissioners came down and paid the men, he would not sail. By May 25th £8,000 had been disbursed, but the wise old man was still not to be hurried, and as more money was reported on the road he did not give the order to unmoor until the 27th. On that day young Rodney, from his post of duty on board the *Dreadnaught*, witnessed an impressive demonstration of seapower when twenty-five ships of the line, his own included, with many smaller vessels, weighed anchor and proceeded to sea.*

The fleet made a good passage of only fourteen days and the *Dreadnaught* anchored above Belem castle on June 10th. The ships received a rapturous welcome and the country all round Lisbon was scoured to provide beef, mutton, and poultry, oranges, lemons, and greenstuff. Many years later Rodney used to say that the warm weather countries, particularly Spain and Portugal, were always his favourites,[5] and who can doubt but that some of his pleasurable recollections stem from this time? It was high

* For list of ships see Appendix 1.

summer. He was just seventeen, and this was his first sight of foreign parts.

Lisbon, before the great earthquake of 1755, was a city to see and admire from the waterside. The medieval jumble of houses and narrow streets spread up the sides of the hills in picturesque squalor, sprinkled with the towers and spires of over forty churches and about ninety convents. But the river-front was impressive. The splendid Renaissance palace built for Philip II fronted the river with the palace of the Corte Real on one side of it and the great square, the Terreiro do Paco, on the other. Ships docked almost below the royal windows, and above and below all this architectural magnificence stretched the wharves, warehouses and business premises of the merchants. The country might be poor but the capital was famous for the contents of its palaces and churches, and even more famous for the concentration of wealth in those warehouses along the quays. The very powerful British factory in Lisbon had its grip on Portuguese commerce and largely controlled the flow of Brazilian gold. Here, more than anywhere else, is the reason for the coming of Sir John Norris's fleet.

The British ships lay in the Tagus for nearly two years while the Court of Spain digested the implications of their presence, but the *Dreadnaught* was spared much of this inactivity. So much confidence had the Commander-in-Chief in Captain Medley that whenever any particular service was required, the *Dreadnaught* was generally the ship to be sent. After only a fortnight she was off to Cadiz, returning in July. There followed six weeks swinging round her anchors and then she was off again, this time up the Mediterranean to Genoa where she stayed six days before proceeding by way of Leghorn to Minorca.

To an intelligent young officer, keen on his profession, Minorca, with its famous harbour, was of greater interest even than Lisbon. Captured in 1708, and confirmed to Great Britain five years later, it gave the Royal Navy two priceless assets—an island base in the Mediterranean 600 miles east of Gibraltar, and a harbour safe from every wind that blew. As the *Dreadnaught* passed through the narrow entrance and warped up the long, narrow harbour, the old hands would have pointed out the naval hospital on Bloody Island, built by Admiral Jennings, and then, as they came into sight, the squadron of unbelievably shabby and dilapidated hulks that had once been part of the Spanish fleet off Cape Passaro, taken by Sir George Byng in 1718 and still awaiting a decision as to their fate. Finally, at the top of the harbour was the new town of Mahon, astonishingly English in appearance, with the dockyard and the naval storehouses. A new military road, one more example of the expensive work undertaken since the British occupation, ran from the town to St Philip's castle at the entrance of the harbour. Minorca had its governor and a garrison. The *Dreadnaught* lay there from September 30th to November 15, 1735.

She returned to Lisbon before the end of the year to pass another three weeks with the rest of the fleet. Then all through 1736, while Sir John busied himself with the Court of Portugal and the other ships swung endlessly at their moorings, the *Dreadnaught*'s agreeable routine of peacetime cruising continued. Gibraltar, Cadiz and Lisbon were her commonest ports of call, although sometimes she stretched across to the Barbary coast where delicate negotiations were going on with the King of Morocco, a wily potentate with whom Captain Medley had had dealings before.

Fortune had been kind to Rodney in sending him with the fleet to Lisbon, and kinder still in putting him on board the only ship that did any interesting seatime after they arrived. But although so often away on particular service, the *Dreadnaught* spent more than fourteen months at Lisbon, long enough for a personable young man to make friends on shore. The English colony had every reason for welcoming the British fleet and many doors were open. In this, Fortune was preparing for Rodney the greatest of all her favours.

The British Minister at Lisbon at this time was the Hon. Charles Compton, brother of the fifth Earl of Northampton and therefore pre-eminent in the English colony as much by his social as by his official position. Mr Compton was amiable and hospitable. With his wife and family he had lived in the country for many years, but the arrival of Sir John Norris's fleet was by far the greatest event of his official life, and so long as the ships lay at Lisbon his home seems to have been something of a social centre. The Commander-in-Chief would have had plenty of business with the Minister anyway; there would have been the captains whom Sir John presented; and it is not stretching imagination too far to suppose that the Compton hospitality might sometimes be extended to include some of the young gentlemen whom their captains brought ashore with them. Medley was an old follower of the Commander-in-Chief, the *Dreadnaught* was a favoured ship, and when one notes that two of her midshipmen later married two of Mr Compton's daughters one may draw one's own conclusion. There were four Compton girls, still children at this time but probably glad enough to entertain and be entertained by presentable midshipmen. With Rodney's background and upbringing what more

35

natural than that he should have been a welcome visitor? Indeed, a reference some years later to the old days at Lisbon[6] makes it quite clear that he was: and Arthur Scott, the fellow midshipman and shipmate who also married a Compton, must have been another. So, between intervals of seagoing, agreeable memories were laid up, and perhaps even at this early date pledges given for the future.

After twenty-one months at Lisbon the Commander-in-Chief wrote home in March 1737 desiring the Admiralty Secretary to acquaint their Lordships that 'the disputes between Portugal and Spain are now brought to a happy conclusion ...'.[7] He intended to bring his ships home as soon as possible but went on to say that he would leave the *Dreadnaught*, with certain small craft, 'to attend to the service of the Court of Barbary'. So Sir John and his great fleet sailed out of the Tagus and out of this story, and before the end of April they were back at St Helen's.

The *Dreadnaught* was busy for six months longer on her special duties. When all seemed quiet on the Barbary coast she turned her bows homeward and anchored at Spithead on September 3, 1737. Rodney had joined her as a boy of sixteen. He was nearly twenty when he returned to England. Avington was less than a day's journey from Portsmouth and no doubt leave was forthcoming.

All was well at his guardian's, but his homecoming was saddened by the narrowing of the family circle at Walton. During his absence his elder brother had died, and before his return his mother died too. Henry Rodney had been the scholar of the family. How his sailor brother cherished his memory is shown by an MS. book of Latin verses and heroic couplets, all signed 'H. Rodney', which he kept until the end of his own long and busy life. Mary Rodney died in January 1737. Her husband was still alive when his son returned home, but before the year ended he too went to his grave in Walton churchyard. The retired captain of Marines never recovered from his disastrous speculation in South Sea stock, and after his death the administration of his goods and chattels was granted to one of his creditors, none of his family objecting.[8] During the next six months after his return Rodney's name stood on the books of the 70-gun *Berwick*,[9] but with no indication that he ever appeared on board. The nominal entry was probably a technicality intended to hasten the day when he could qualify for lieutenant. Six years' service was required before a young gentleman could do this, and Rodney, whose service had begun (officially at any rate) in 1732, would soon be eligible to take the examination.

From the melancholy circumstances of his first home leave he was recalled to service in the spring of 1738 under the happiest auspices. Captain Medley had been given the *Romney*, a 50-gun ship intended for the Newfoundland station, and was willing to take Rodney with him. Nothing could have been better. Medley was an old friend, the new ship carried a capable schoolmaster, well qualified to prepare him for the lieutenant's examination, and the new station would reveal aspects of the service as different as possible from any so far experienced.

The Newfoundland station owed its existence to the cod fishery, a most important line of the nation's business. During August and September every year the season's catch (which would keep most of Catholic Europe in salt-fish for the next twelve months) was salted down and stowed on remote beaches far from civilization or any responsible authority. Some sort of control was essential, and this was best exercised by a sea-officer who could keep order among the fishermen, and deal with any foreign interference. So two or three ships were always stationed there at the height of the season, and the senior officer was officially recognized as governor and vested with special powers. In 1738 it was to be Captain Vanbrugh of the *Chatham* who would fly the broad pendant of a commodore. The routine was for the governor's ship, and perhaps the others, to proceed down channel in early summer, collecting from Poole and the ports further west any vessels desiring their protection to Newfoundland. The governor would be on the station during August and September and then, before winter closed in, he would sail with the trade for Lisbon where the catch would find a good market. What happened after Lisbon depended on the current situation. Another convoy might be needed up the Mediterranean, but if the warships were lucky they would be back in England by the end of the year; then, after four months refitting, they would do the same round again.

Rodney joined the *Romney* on May 2, 1738, and found her smaller than the *Dreadnaught*. Fifty-gun ships were quite big enough in waters where pilotage could be extremely intricate. In her midshipman's berth were two other future admirals, John Byron who became his lifelong friend, and George Edgcumbe, a friend and political associate for twenty years. The *Romney*'s schoolmaster Mr Harding who, in a moment of perhaps prophetic inspiration had been given the baptismal name of Ichabod, but who nevertheless did so well by the three future admirals under his instruction, deserves a special mention. The fact that Captain Medley knew something about conditions in North America, having been iced up for three months at Annapolis a few years before, may or may not have encouraged confidence on board. With the *Chatham* the *Romney* sailed from Spithead on June 26th.

Nothing very notable happened during Rodney's first visit to Newfoundland, where later he was himself to be governor. Three weeks after taking her departure from the Rame head the *Romney* encountered fog, and for nine tedious days she drifted through a white blanket, sounding and firing guns, while the moisture dripped from the sails and the watch on deck shivered. They arrived at St John's on August 7th, and after an interval for setting up the rigging sailed to perform the routine duties of the station. They crept in and out of the creeks and inlets, and visited the settlements on the coast, settling disputes and collecting facts about the fisheries for the governor's report. A junior officer on this service could learn a lot. Then, after two months of exacting duty, the *Romney* sailed for Lisbon, a welcome release from fogs and fishermen to society and sunshine. She lay in the Tagus from November 3rd to December 9th, which allowed ample time for visiting old friends. Then at the end of the year she was rolling up channel before a December gale, to drop anchor at Spithead on December 26th. Thence she proceeded to the Nore, and so to the sheer-hulk at Woolwich.

Very few personal details have survived about Rodney's early service at sea, but a gleam of light is thrown on his time in the *Romney*. Sixteen years later Mr Harding wrote to Captain Rodney for a testimonial. The Captain's reply[10] does credit to them both:

'Having been educated under Mr Ichabod Harding in the different branches of the Mathematicks, I can not refuse his earnest request in giving him a testimonial to their Lordships, of the character I have known him bear for sixteen years past, part of which time I have sailed in the same ship with him.

'I must beg leave to assure their Lordships that Mr Harding was remarkable for his diligence, and keeping a proper discipline among the young Gentlemen entrusted to his care, being himself an example to them of morality, Patience, and even temper, and has always been so happy as to gain the esteem of every officer under whom he has served.'

A young fellow could not go very far wrong in a ship like the *Romney*, and under men like Captain Medley and Mr Harding.

Rodney remained in the ship all through the arduous business of

clearing for the dock and preparing for the new season. But although
Medley returned to the station in 1739 as governor, Rodney did not sail
with him again. It seems that his uncle Lord Aubrey Beauclerck was now
prepared to take a direct interest in his nephew's career. Lord Aubrey

THE BEAUCLERCK CONNECTION

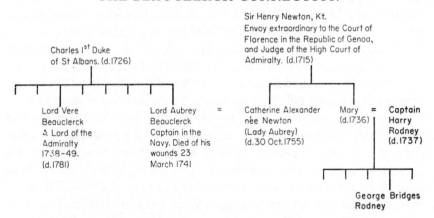

commanded a small frigate in the Mediterranean. Few would not have
preferred this station to Newfoundland, but the new appointment offered
more than blue water and sunshine. In the Mediterranean there were now
good prospects of active service.

For Spain and her *guarda-costas* were again threatening the peace. Since
the return of Sir John Norris from Lisbon that country had returned to her
old, bellicose ways. Sir Robert Walpole and his government took a
detached and balanced view, but the opposition in Parliament and the
nation as a whole did not. The ear of a certain Captain Jenkins had been
produced with dramatic effect in the House of Commons, and although
the grisly relic had actually been cut off some years earlier in circumstances
which have never been clearly established, the nation was pleased to
regard it as the final *casus belli*. Walpole continued to pursue his sensible
negotiations with the Court of Madrid, and hope for the best; but he
resolved all the same to reinforce the Mediterranean. So it came about that
in July 1739 Rodney's name appears in the books of the *Somerset*,[11] flagship
of Rear-Admiral Haddock, for the passage out to join his uncle's ship.

Lord Aubrey commanded the *Dolphin* of 24 guns (and small ones at that)
with a crew of 130. One of the shortcomings of the Navy at this time was
that all the frigates were small. There was nothing between little ships like

39

the *Dolphin* and vessels of nearly double their force mounting 40 guns on two decks, and as these were clumsy and slow, their smaller sisters usually had more than their fair share of work. The *Dolphin* was the smallest ship in which Rodney ever served. Conditions on board may be judged by the fact that there was only 4 ft 6 in headroom beneath the beams on the main deck. But for Rodney this might have mattered less as he was no longer a midshipman. He was borne in the *Dolphin* as 'acting officer' which, besides other advantages, entitled him to a minute cabin.

His status on board is interesting. He is described as 'Supernumerary, borne as an acting officer by order of Nicholas Haddock Esquire, Rear-Admiral of the Red and Commander-in-Chief, bearing date October 30, 1739, for victualling only'.[12] This meant he was not one of the *Dolphin*'s lieutenants officially and would receive no pay, but that his uncle was prepared to find room for him on board, with the approval of a complaisant commander-in-chief. Why Rodney had not yet received his lieutenant's commission is obscure. Probably his uncle, while glad to have him, would not allow one of his own lieutenants to be displaced. The point is unimportant and was soon put right. What was important was that, with war almost certain, Rodney was out in the Mediterranean where there would be the best opportunities of advancement.

What had not been anticipated was that the Admiralty would be so inconsiderate as to order the *Dolphin* home soon after he joined. For a few weeks in November and December 1739 she was on convoy duty, and busy collecting invalids from various ports in the western Mediterranean. On December 4th, as she lay in Gibraltar bay, the declaration of war against Spain was publicly read on board, but five days later she sailed for England with her invalids, one distinguished passenger, Lord George Graham,* and a convoy of twenty-three sail. She arrived safely in February 1740, Lord Aubrey left her, and to replace him came Captain Francis Holburne. The new captain took over on February 18th and Rodney's commission as lieutenant bears the same date. So Lord Aubrey passes from this story while his nephew remained in the *Dolphin* under the new captain. The apprenticeship was over.

---

* Although the naval fame of this officer is small, he and his retinue have achieved another sort of immortality. Hogarth's portrait of him in his cabin deserves attention as the best contemporary evidence of the easy style of living to which fortune's favourites might aspire in the Georgian Navy.

Chapter 3

The Fortunate Lieutenant

(1740–1742)

'. . . you shall sometimes stumble upon a Lieutenant . . .
who, as they have been born to, and bred up in the
Principles of Honour and Virtue, so they would not,
for all the Plunder got at Alicant, stoop to
anything beneath their Birth and Character.'
(Ned Ward, *The Wooden World dissected*, 1751.)

THE *Dolphin*'s new captain was a Lowland Scot, and one of the few survivors from Hosier's disastrous expedition to Porto Bello. He was a capable and considerate officer, and to Rodney he was to prove a staunch friend. As soon as he assumed command he took the *Dolphin* round to Sheerness to prepare for channel service, which meant the usual unrigging and docking, and at the same time he took the opportunity to obtain ten days' leave for the men who had been so long in the Mediterranean. Then followed a colourful interlude escorting the King to Holland. These little expeditions were fairly frequent under the first two Georges. A very senior admiral (usually the Admiral of the Fleet if still sufficiently mobile) commanded the escort, and the royal yachts with their gilding and their gorgeous appointments made a brave show, although most of them were only for the retinue or the royal baggage. On this occasion Sir Charles Wager, First Lord of the Admiralty and aged seventy-four, commanded the squadron. At half past ten on March 24th the *Dolphin* was working into Hellevoetsluys; at eleven His Majesty landed to a salute of twenty-one guns; and next day all the ships returned to England.

In May the *Dolphin* was ordered to Plymouth to put herself under Captain Fox of the *Newcastle*. The two ships were to cruise off Ferrol and report any movements by Spanish warships, but all that summer the enemy never stirred. Plenty of Frenchmen were examined as they navigated by Finisterre, but never a Spaniard came their way until the *Dolphin* encountered a little 10-gun brigantine with a crew of 40 which she sent in to Plymouth. During the next 42 years Rodney was to see prizes of every size, shape and nationality, but this little Spaniard was the first. She was the *Dolphin*'s only success before returning to Plymouth in September. So far the year had passed without anything exceptional: ten men down with scurvy, the result of their summer cruise, was nothing unusual. But now Rodney's ship was to undergo an ordeal which no one on board would ever forget.

From Plymouth they were ordered to Leith to protect the trade and raise seamen for the fleet. The *Dolphin* proceeded up channel, sailed from the Nore on October 20th, and at once ran into dirty weather. Winter came early to the east coast in 1740. A north-westerly gale with icy rain and sleet turning to snow made conditions so bad that Captain Holburne decided to put into Yarmouth roads and wait, rather than go on beating the seas to no purpose. Here they found many light colliers bound north like themselves, and here they waited eight days. On the 29th the wind backed westerly and the whole fleet hove up and proceeded, only to be driven back into the roads as it veered northerly again. Then at about midnight it backed once more, and this time the *Dolphin* and all the colliers were able to get clear on their way.

All of Thursday, October 30th, the ships wallowed up the coast, past the Wash with its dangerous outlying shoals and the Humber estuary, but on Friday the 31st the wind veered north-westerly again. At this point the great head of Flamborough offers protection from any bad weather from that quarter, and Captain Holburne decided to anchor in Bridlington bay. Here the *Dolphin* found some sixty northbound colliers sheltering under the lee of the land, and she was followed in by two brigantines, one Dutch and one Swedish. Looking round after they dropped anchor it struck the captain that a few more men might be pressed from some of the ships close by. All the colliers had protections but he was able to press six men out of the brigantines, lending them six of his own in lieu, and if those men came on board the frigate cursing their luck they were to be thankful later. They found all hands snugging her down, top-gallant masts and yards on deck, and the rigging being set up afresh. Captain Holburne was taking no chances.

At about ten o'clock that evening the wind suddenly backed to the south-west, blowing fresh and true, and every northbound vessel got under way once more. It carried them all along until nine o'clock next morning (November 1st), by which time the *Dolphin* and most of the shipping were off Hartlepool, the colliers close under the lee of the land and the frigate, luckily for herself, a little further to seaward but not much. . . . Then it died away completely, leaving them all tossing uneasily in the swell with sails flapping and spars swinging in all directions. It was a pause heavy with menace.

Then, without warning and suddenly, the treacherous wind piped up again. It came at them out of the opposite quarter. It caught them on the wrong tack, pinning them down on a lee-shore, and in no time at all was shrieking at gale force and still increasing. The clumsy, undermanned colliers never had a chance. In a matter of minutes they were smashed to matchwood in the breakers, a whole fleet cast away. The *Dolphin*, further to seaward, was better placed, but she had to fight for her life. They managed to get her round on the other tack—not a moment too soon—and then to take in the topsails as she staggered away to the south-east, the only direction in which she could sail. The wind blew harder and harder. 'I think I never was in such a storm of wind', wrote Captain Holburne later. And now, as she laboured on, pressed down by her courses which could be neither reefed nor furled, a new danger threatened—Whitby rock under her lee bow.

Until clear of this the ship could not be eased in any way. She was almost on her beam-ends, her hatches under water, her masts almost parallel to the surface, and all her people up on the weather side, clinging on for dear life. Masts, rigging and canvas were strained almost beyond endurance; deck gear began to fetch adrift; water was pouring through the hatches. But there was nothing to be done for the moment except keep her on course and trust in Providence. The *Dolphin* was a good ship and exceptionally well maintained, for everything held. Pressed down and down by that awful, merciless pressure, battered by the seas and groaning and complaining in every part, she cleared the rock by less than a mile, her hatches under water the whole way.

Now, as she pounded on into the North Sea, a new danger threatened. One of the anchors broke loose (it was the best bower weighing some twenty-five hundredweight) and it turned itself into a terrifyingly destructive weapon by dropping under the forechains. This was no time to consider costly government property. A party of determined men with axes was able to cut it away before it knocked a hole in the ship. Some cable went with it, and there followed a chilly and exhausting struggle in the wet darkness forward to plug the hawse-hole. A lot more water poured into the ship before this could be done.

So much water had now entered the ship, through the straining sides, the hatches and the hawse-hole, that she was becoming noticeably sluggish. The ballast was washing over to leeward with other things in the hold, the pumps were no longer holding their own, and unless she could be lightened there was every chance of her settling lower and lower until she surrendered to the sea. The situation was serious with the storm still at its height, but there was one possible remedy. Captain Holburne consulted his officers—a wet and anxious conference it must have been—and all agreed the only thing to do was to heave some guns overboard, if they could.

So another fierce struggle followed with these awkward, inanimate objects each weighing a ton and a half. There were eleven on the starboard side and the men could get at only six of them; but these they managed to propel through the ports one by one. This eased the ship considerably.

The gale had struck at about nine. The *Dolphin* had been fighting it for four hours and it was now one o'clock. Dinner was impossible with the fires out and everything either soaked or inaccessible, but luckily Captain Holburne had some brandy in his cabin with which to fortify his exhausted men before the next task. This was an attempt to shorten sail. But they soon found that the wind was much too strong to permit any liberties with the canvas. No sooner had they hauled up the fore-course and got down the yard than the sail took charge, whipped itself to rags and blew away—'and glad I was to see it go'—confessed the captain afterwards. So the *Dolphin* laboured on under her main-course only; there could be no question of meddling with this, for had it gone they could never have set another, and for the rest of Saturday and all Sunday that devoted piece of canvas held, and carried them clear of danger. At last, in the small hours of Monday morning the wind began to ease. But for two days and two nights the crew of the *Dolphin* had not a dry thread on, no sleep, and no refreshment whatever except the captain's brandy.

When dawn broke on Monday November 3rd, it was possible to get up a new fore-course and haul in for the shore. Night fell before any land appeared, but next morning the east coast was in sight and at noon they identified Orfordness. There could be no question of continuing the voyage. Besides six guns and one anchor the *Dolphin* had lost three courses, two cables, a long-boat and everything that had been on deck—topgallant masts and yards, studding-sail booms, spare spars and much more. The hold needed re-stowing, much ballast had been pumped out and lost, and if all this was not enough there was the possibility that the hull had been strained. So they made their way cautiously down the Swin, deducing from the quantities of wreckage and debris sighted that many had been less fortunate than themselves, and in the afternoon of November 5th were back at Sheerness.

The *Dolphin* with Lieutenant Rodney on board had come through one of the worst gales of the century. All round the coast reports were soon coming in of destruction and loss of life. 'Shipping suffered more than it has done in any one time for twenty years past', was a report from Yarmouth, where the shore was covered with dead bodies and wreckage. Eight ships were reported wrecked near Cromer, about sixty altogether between Lynn and Yarmouth, while on the other side of the channel nine were ashore between Ostend and Calais, and a fine Dutch East Indiaman off Boulogne. At the Nore the *Catherine* (yacht) drove down on the *Royal Escape* and put her ashore, while the *Rupert* (60), victualling at Blackstakes, was so damaged she was ordered back to Chatham where she had just been refitted. Away to the westward the great fleet of Sir Challoner Ogle, five days out from St Helen's with the expeditionary force for Cartagena, was so buffeted that one ship of the line had to return to Spithead and two others needed an escort into Lisbon.[1] On land there was much more than the usual destruction. At about 8 p.m. on the Saturday, according to the *London Evening Post*, one of the spires of Westminster Abbey was blown down; another spire that went was St Margaret's at King's Lynn; and at about the same time a prodigious quantity of lead was stripped from the roof of Greenwich Hospital, and part of the wall of Hyde Park collapsed. Their Lordships in London can have been left in no uncertainty as to the severity of the *Dolphin*'s ordeal.

So Captain Holburne's return was fully approved. More than this, when he seized the auspicious moment to put in a plea for his crew who had behaved so well, and whose pay was in many cases fifteen months overdue, the order was immediately given for the *Dolphin*'s books to be made up until the end of June, which meant twelve months' back-pay for nearly everyone. This should have put the ship's company in the best of humours as they made good the damage and prepared for sea once more.

They sailed three weeks later, reached Leith without any more adventures, and settled down to the unheroic business for which they had been sent. It is hard to suppose that anyone enjoyed it. The weather in December and January 1741 was atrocious, and despite the good Scots background of the *Dolphin's* captain, his compatriots showed great unwillingness to volunteer for the King's service; only a handful of starved landsmen came forward. There were plenty of unprotected seamen working the passenger boats from Edinburgh, so Captain Holburne stationed a tender off the North Ferry to catch them; and if he failed to catch them, he argued, he would stop them plying their trade and so 'starve them out'. But this only infuriated the Scots. The *Dolphin's* tender made herself so hated along the coast that when she put into Dundee a little later, her only boat was torn to pieces by a waterside mob and she was prevented from sailing, to the great humiliation of Rodney's unfortunate mess-mate Lieutenant Cow. Service like this offered no prospects for an ambitious young officer, which may be why Rodney left the *Dolphin* fairly soon. On February 21, 1741, while he was still in the Edinburgh Firth, he was transferred to the *Essex*, a 70-gun battleship fitting for the Mediterranean.

At first sight the new appointment appeared as dreary and unpromising as the old one. The *Essex* lay at Woolwich, desperately shorthanded, and in view of the difficulty of getting men and the rather ineffectual gentleman who commanded her, it looked as if she might be there for some time. But Woolwich was closer to London than Leith roads, an important point if one had friends in high places. Meanwhile a keen young officer owed it to the service as well as to himself to make the best of things.

Captain Nicholas Robinson, Rodney's new captain, seems from his letters to have been a pathetically inadequate creature, and by no means a favourite with their Lordships. They had allowed him the use of a small tender called the *Prince William* to assist in raising men and were understandably annoyed when they discovered that after nearly three weeks of delay she was not yet out on the job. This was just before Rodney joined. Poor Captain Robinson, when called upon to explain, could only plead that the master of the tender was 'indolent', but the arrival of his new lieutenant enabled him to conclude a very lame reply with the hopeful statement that 'Mr Rodney has constantly attended her to get her ready for the service'. One has the impression that the captain rather hoped he might placate their Lordships by mentioning him.

A month later, but still very short of men, the *Essex* had struggled down as far as the Hope where we are able to observe the alert and dependable Mr Rodney in action. On May 30th he went ashore at Tilbury, spotted an obvious seaman without a protection, and had him impressed at once. The man swore that he belonged to a collier called the *Amity* and was protected. Off went Lieutenant Rodney to verify this, and on board the *Amity*, although he found no protection he found two more seamen whom he also sent on board the *Essex*. However, before nightfall along came the master of the *Amity* with three protections in his pocket to claim his men back, and an odd scene followed with the collier captain taking his stand on the protections and refusing to be denied; Lieutenant Rodney resolutely opposed; and poor Captain Robinson dithering between the two and so incapable of making up his mind that he ended by sitting down and writing to their Lordships for a ruling. Service under such a captain must have damped the keenest spirit. In June the *Essex* was struggling round the North Foreland but still very shorthanded for Captain Robinson ventured another characteristic bleat to the Admiralty. 'I have a great many landsmen on board,' he complained, 'and the Marines being very indifferent, weak, poor creatures, some being boys and the others decayed old men, unfit to serve their country, I hope their Lordships will indulge me to keep the few able seamen I have.' This request could not be granted, so the *Essex* was still no further than St Helen's four months later when Rodney left her, one would suppose with profound relief. There were some good officers on board. Another of her lieutenants was Hugh Palliser whose time just overlapped Rodney's. But she was a hopeless ship, and her depressing story continues as far as Lisbon where eventually she arrived, her scanty crew further thinned by disease and desertion, and her hull so foul she could scarcely move through the water. In Lisbon her captain consulted his officers what they ought to do, and they reached the conclusion they could proceed no further. So in Lisbon she stopped until the unhappy Robinson got himself into trouble over some irregularity in the purchase of wine and was dismissed. Rodney was well out of such a ship.

For him a very different prospect was opening. He was now a lieutenant of some twenty months' standing. Most of the officers in the Navy were lieutenants, many of them had been lieutenants before he was born, and the vast majority would never be anything else but lieutenants. Between them and the exalted eminence of a post-captain (or even a master and commander) there was a great gulf fixed, only to be crossed by the influential or the exceptionally fortunate. But Rodney was one of these. His interest had been sufficiently good to remove him from the *Dolphin* and then from the *Essex*. It was now to give him the opportunity for further promotion so coveted by every lieutenant. But before he approaches the rungs of that exclusive ladder by which the higher ranks of the Navy might be reached, a brief digression is necessary to explain how the jealously guarded system worked.

The essence of promotion beyond lieutenant was that it was promotion *to command a ship*. Indeed, it would be correct to say that because the lieutenant had been given a ship he was advanced in rank. If she were a small ship of 20 guns or less he would be made master and commander, and might hope for advancement to a larger ship one day. But if he were very fortunate indeed he might be promoted into a large ship direct, in which case he would go over the heads of all the lieutenants senior to him, the master and commanders as well, and be placed with definite seniority in the list of post-captains. No one could jump over his head now, and he would move slowly up the list until due for his flag.

The great snag was of course that there were so many more aspiring lieutenants than there were ships to give them. At home the First Lord of the Admiralty decided the appointments, and in a world where political pressure was usually so strong and the First Lord himself more often a politician than a sea-officer, it may seem remarkable that any good appointments were made at all. But there was another and less direct way by which a lieutenant might reach post rank. A situation might arise on a foreign station or far from home when one of His Majesty's ships might be deprived of her captain. In such circumstances, with the Admiralty too far off to be consulted, it was the recognized privilege of the local commander-in-chief to appoint to the vacancy, the Admiralty confirming his choice. The commander-in-chief would almost certainly appoint a lieutenant he knew, almost always the senior lieutenant from his own flagship, and when that favoured individual had entered into his inheritance, the 2nd, 3rd, 4th and 5th lieutenants in the flagship would all move up one place with heightened expectations of favours to come. The post of lieutenant in a flagship was therefore well worth having. It might not be a bed of roses, but it was a fairly certain path to promotion so long as the officer avoided falling foul of his admiral.

In March 1742 the *Namur*, a three-decker of 90 guns, was fitting out at Portsmouth for the Mediterranean, to be the flagship of the new Commander-in-Chief, Vice-Admiral Thomas Mathews. Rodney had left the *Essex* the previous October. During the weeks which followed influences were at work to obtain for him one of the coveted lieutenants' appointments in the *Namur*. Who pulled the strings, it is again impossible to say. It could not have been Lord Aubrey Beauclerck, now dead at Cartagena, but it might have been his brother Lord Vere Beauclerck who was a Lord of the Admiralty. On March 5, 1742, he was appointed fifth lieutenant of the new flagship 'at the request of' Vice-Admiral Mathews.[2] His friends had applied their influence where it would do most good. Provided he lasted the course, advancement was fairly certain.

Mathews had not been to sea for eighteen years. His last appointment had been Commissioner at Chatham, since when he had retired to his large estate in Wales and occupied himself with the usual pursuits of a country gentleman. He was a robust Tory, hot-tempered, intolerant and exacting, and strongly given to likes and dislikes. His officers had every reason to expect that their admiral would be 'difficult', and he was. But Mathews was also brave, warm-hearted and generous, and it is possible that his bark was much worse than his bite. His chief faults seem to have been his inability to delegate authority and a quite abnormal propensity to make complaints. He came on board the *Namur* on April 11th and lost no time in expressing his displeasure with everything that he saw and found.

It must be admitted that he had much to complain about. He was to bring out to the Mediterranean reinforcements and storeships, but very little was ready. The dockyard was inefficient and corrupt, or so he inferred, and he knew something about dockyards; the supply of seamen was almost exhausted; but what roused him to the highest pitch of exasperation was that so many officers were inexplicably absent. Day after day he bombarded the Admiralty and the Navy Office with his complaints. The *Torbay* was a typical case. Her purser was incapable of performing his duty and as her *only* lieutenant was laid up with the gout all the work devolved on her captain which, for an 80-gun battleship due to sail on foreign service in wartime, was disquieting, to say the least. 'I have long since given her up', grumbled the Vice-Admiral at the end of a particularly notable broadside. The *Russell* lacked four of her officers and the gunner of the *Dolphin* was 'none knows where'. Most of the newly pressed men 'would desert at the very first opportunity', and the fleet's resentment about arrears of pay was not removed when money came down without the necessary pay-books for its distribution; a fine wind was wasted while waiting for these, which did not sweeten the Vice-Admiral's temper, and when at last the fleet weighed anchor, the wind dropped. All the way to Gibraltar the stream of complaints continued. '. . . greatly detained on my Passage by some very heavy sailing ships, particularly by one belonging to the Ordnance', wrote Mathews, aiming a shaft at another government department, and then, on the subject of the men's health: 'Our sick lists are chiefly owing to Gin: I hope, as that pernicious liquor is now not to be got, they will soon recover'. Once in the Mediterranean his rage returned to his favourite target, the dockyards. 'Never was any place so destitute in all manner of conveniences . . . as I found Minorca and Gibraltar', he expostulated, and the shortcomings of his own flagship were the subject of a notable communication, concluding: 'As to what relates to the fitting of my apartments I shall only say that never in my life had any ship so scandalously fitted. . . .'

Admirals have ways of making their displeasure felt which are denied to ordinary mortals, but the interesting thing about Mathews' fulminations is that although they were loud and continuous, all the lieutenants of his flagship seem to have survived with their careers unscathed. One of them, it is true, was discharged at his own request, and there may be a story behind this; and the atmosphere on board the flagship may have been sultry at times. But eventually all, with the one exception, gained their flagship promotions. The *Namur*'s muster-book during the next eight months records their upward progress until each, as the vacancies occurred, attained independent command.

Rodney had started in the lowly position of fifth lieutenant, but he had been on board only ten days when the promotion and departure of the first lieutenant moved all the others up one place and he became number 4. The next upward step was at Gibraltar, two months later, and the unconscious instrument of it was his future father-in-law Mr Charles Compton who, in his capacity as Envoy Extraordinary, wrote to the Commander-in-Chief from Lisbon to report the death of the captain of the *Greyhound*. The result was that Mathews posted the commander of the *Drake* (sloop) into the *Greyhound* and promoted John Stringer, first of the *Namur*, into the *Drake* as master and commander. All the other lieutenants in the flagship moved up another place so that Rodney, from fourth lieutenant, now found himself the third. Only fourteen days later another blessing was vouchsafed when a vacancy occurred in the *Salamander* (bomb). This went to Merrick de l'Angle of the flagship who, only thirteen days before, had succeeded Stringer as first lieutenant. Rodney stepped into de l'Angle's shoes as the flagship's number 2.

On July 24th the pieces moved again. Captain Watson of the *Feversham* had to be invalided home. The lucky de l'Angle was posted from the *Salamander* into the *Feversham* and James MacKay, the latest first of the flagship, went to the *Salamander* and became a master and commander in his turn. And so, by this absorbing lottery which made the health of every commanding officer in the fleet the object of endless speculation among the flagship's lieutenants, Rodney at last became number 1 of the *Namur* and the next man of destiny. The climb had taken him less than five months: but then followed weeks and months of impatience and anxiety with never another vacancy anywhere. The pause enables us to leave Lieutenant Rodney and his ambitions for a moment, to consider the no less important matter of the war in the Mediterranean.

By the summer of 1742 what had begun as a maritime quarrel between England and Spain had widened considerably. The campaign on land had spread to north Italy where the forces of England's allies the Queen of Hungary and the King of Sardinia were facing a Spanish-Neapolitan army.

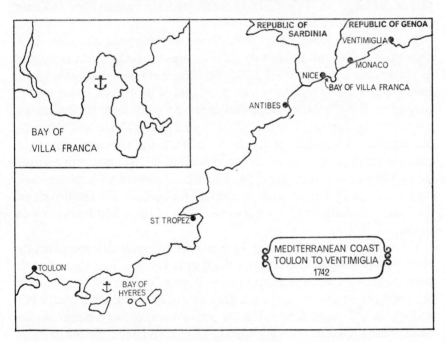

The first duty of our ships in the Mediterranean was to prevent reinforcements from Spain reaching this theatre, a duty which became increasingly complicated as the attitude of France became increasingly hostile. Spanish troops were already in Provence, transports for them were waiting at Antibes, and a Franco-Spanish fleet glared menacingly out of Toulon. No one expected France to remain neutral much longer. This is why Mathews had come out with reinforcements.

As a very young officer under Medley, Rodney had seen something of how a sea-officer might sometimes have to turn diplomat. As the first lieutenant of the *Namur* in the summer of 1742 he now saw this at rather closer quarters and at a very much higher level, for Mathews enjoyed the status of a plenipotentiary, receiving his instructions from the Secretary of State and communicating with him direct; and being outspoken to the verge of indiscretion it is unlikely that his officers were left in much doubt as to what was going on.

Disregarding French feelings the new Commander-in-Chief boldly appropriated the sheltered waters inside the island of Hyères as his fleet anchorage. He despatched a squadron to argue with the Neapolitans. He then proceeded with his flagship to Villa Franca (Villefranche), at this time part of the kingdom of Sardinia, to confer with the commanders on shore and open communications with Turin.

The Franco-Spanish army in Provence was the great problem. If it attempted to reach north Italy by sea there was the British fleet to dispute its passage but if, as was much more probable, it attempted to come by the coast road, Villa Franca lay in its path, and Villa Franca could not be allowed to fall. So Mathews landed men and guns from the *Namur* to strengthen its defences. Beyond Villa Franca was Monaco and the supposedly neutral Republic of Genoa. Fellucas, balancelles and other light craft were plying continuously between Antibes and Monaco with military stores, while in Genoa the far-sighted business community was giving itself over to the most blatant and un-neutral stock piling, for the benefit of the Franco-Spanish army when it came. None of this could be allowed to go on.

The coastal traffic, which kept well inshore and generally proceeded by night, was difficult to intercept, for the fleet lacked the right kind of small craft. Mathews found the answer in the shape of a powerful twenty-eight oar row-boat which he purchased. He manned her from his flagship, put Rodney in charge, and sent him to patrol inshore every night. It can hardly have been the sort of command he had been hoping for but he must have tackled his task with zeal and efficiency for the results were excellent. This row-boat was named the *Hester*. There is no indication why.

The *Hester* was a partial answer to the problem, but however efficiently she patrolled, there were already large quantities of military stores in the magazines at Genoa. Mr Birtles, the very capable British consul, kept Mathews fully informed about this. They consisted mostly of corn and barley (without which an invading army would starve in that country) and straw, a seemingly innocuous commodity but one without which no Spanish soldier (or at any rate no Spanish officer) could be expected to sleep comfortably while on cpamaign. Mathews fulminated in his best style against the Genoese. 'We are not dealt with upon the square', he complained to Birtles on August 8th. '. . . if the Republic does not forth-with give their orders to prevent any magazines being erected within their territory, you may assure them from me that I will make them a proper visit, and also that this is the last warning I shall give them.'[3] As the Republic paid no attention the Commander-in-Chief resolved to make good his words. But to teach the Genoese a lesson without provoking them into open hostility (for his orders were emphatic about this) would be a delicate operation. Whoever he put in charge would have to be adroit and discreet, as well as resourceful and resolute. If things went wrong the Commander-in-Chief's reputation at home would certainly suffer. It is therefore all the more significant that the man he chose was Lieutenant Rodney.

What he wanted Rodney to do is best described in his own orders to him.[4]

'Whereas I have received certain Intelligence that Don Philip, at the head of a Spanish army, is determined to force his passage through the territories of the King of Sardinia into the River Genes, in whose terri-tories there are Magazines of Straw and Barley erected for the use of the Spanish army, particularly at Vintimelia, and it being of the utmost conse-quence to the common cause to prevent if possible the said Don Philip's army from not only forcing their passage but likewise their receiving subsistence of any kind in their passage. . . . You are therefore directed and required forthwith to proceed with H.M. row-boat under your Command to Vintimelia where you are to land and march directly to the Magazines of Straw . . . and put fire to them; but in regard that the Magazines of Barley can not be easily destroyed by fire, you are to carry and throw it into the Sea; and in case you should be anyways opposed in the execution of these my Orders, You are hereby directed to make use of your whole force, and repulse Force by Force, till you have actually demolished all the Magazines of any kind of Grain shewn you to be erected for the Service of the Spanish army. . . . Dated on board the *Namur* in Villa France Harbour, the 12 August 1742.   *THOMAS MATHEWS*.

'To Lieutenant Rodney, Commander of His Majesty's Row Boat the *Hester*, for the present intended Expedition.'

In case there was any trouble Mathews had a frigate at hand to send reinforcements, but this precaution was not necessary. Rodney burnt the magazine of straw and the house in which it was hidden, and threw into the river all the ground and unground corn which he found in the mill. It was not a particularly glorious exploit but it earned him a mention in the despatch Mathews wrote home a few days later to the Secretary of State, the Duke of Newcastle. Usually so ready to complain, the Commander-in-Chief was positively enthusiastic about this affair. It had been conducted, he said, 'with Prudence and Discretion, and without the least Disturbance'.[5] In this auspicious way Newcastle became officially aware of how Lieutenant Rodney was conducting himself in the Mediterranean; and Newcastle's protection and interest were well worth having.

In the weeks which followed, the Spanish commander had second thoughts about reaching northern Italy by the coast route and instead directed his thrust inland where it need no longer concern us. Mathews rejoined his fleet at Hyères and busied himself with the endless problems of administration. The French were still technically neutral, and the whole *tempo* of the war slowed down as winter approached. This was the time to send home such ships as could not be repaired on the station. Mathews studied the monthly reports in which the defects of all his ships were revealed with depressing candour. Against the name of the 60-gun *Plymouth* he noted on October 24th: 'Very bad in all respects and must be sent home the first ship.'[6]

Rodney had been first of the *Namur* longer than any of his predecessors and would have been scarcely human if he had not felt that the next flagship promotion was somewhat overdue. But now his exacting and critical chief took the condition of the *Plymouth* into consideration, in order to make a suitable vacancy. Captain Curtis Barnett of the *Dragon* was going home, but the *Dragon* would remain in the Mediterranean. To her Mathews now transferred Captain Watson of the worn-out *Plymouth*, thus making a vacancy in the latter for his first lieutenant, even if it was only for the passage home to an English dockyard.

And so, ten years after his name first appeared on the books of the *Sunderland*, and while he was still only twenty-four, Rodney was promoted by Mathews over the heads of every lieutenant senior to him, and every master and commander, and placed at the bottom of the captain's list. He signed his Commission for the *Plymouth* on November 9, 1742.

Chapter 4

Junior Captain

(1742–1745)

'November 9. Tuesday. This day I was appointed to command
His Majesty's ship *Plymouth*, by Commission from
Thomas Mathews Esq., Vice Admiral of the Red, and
Commander in Chief.'
(Captain's Journal, H.M.S. *Plymouth*.)

THE *Plymouth* was lying in the bay of Hyères when her new captain
came on board. Service custom decreed that all work should
cease and the ship's company assemble to hear him read his
Commission. On this day then—it was November 9th—we may
picture the scene on the quarter-deck, with every officer and man present
from the old and grizzled to the youthful and aspiring, and the centre of
attention, 'more elegant than seemed to become his rough profession',[1]
Captain Rodney. All uncover and the Commission is read.*

'*By Thomas Mathews Esquire*, Vice Admiral of the Red Squadron of His
Majesty's fleet and Commander in Chief of His Majesty's ships and
vessels employed and to be employed in and about the Mediterranean.

'To Mr G. B. Rodney, hereby appointed Captain of His Majesty's ship
Plymouth.

'By virtue of the Power and Authority to me given, I do hereby constitute
and appoint you Captain of His Majesty's ship *Plymouth*, willing and
requiring you forthwith to repair on board and take upon you the Charge
and Command of Captain in her accordingly; strictly charging and
commanding all the Officers and Company of the said ship to behave
themselves jointly and severally in their respective employments with all

---

* Rodney's Commission for the *Plymouth* has not survived, but in the above I have
repeated the wording used by Mathews's secretary for other Commissions at this time.

due Respect and Obedience to you their said Captain; and you likewise to observe and execute the general printed Instructions and such Orders and Directions as you shall from time to time receive from me, or any other your Superior Officers for His Majesty's service. Hereof, nor you nor any of you may fail, as you will answer the Contrary at your Peril. And for so doing, this shall be your Warrant.

'Given under my hand and Seal this 9th Day of November 1742, in the sixteenth year of His Majesty's Reign.

'(signed) *THOS. MATHEWS.*'

The intoxicating moment over, Captain Rodney would have to come down to earth. The *Plymouth* was very leaky, she needed sails and cordage, her foretopmast had been condemned, and she had not been docked for more than eighteen months. The young man who was to sail her back to England in winter time might find his hands full.

To add to his responsibilities she was to take home the invalids from the fleet. Sixty-seven of these came on board on the same day as the new captain. Docking was impossible before she sailed, but she obtained a rough topmast from the *Kingston* in exchange for her own mainyard which was much too good to be allowed to go home; and for the same reason all her Marines were transferred to another ship. On January 10, 1743, she was ready. With three victuallers in convoy she proceeded cautiously to Port Mahon to pick up more invalids and have her main-beam secured. Gibraltar was the next port of call, but before she sighted the Rock she engaged in a brief but noisy diversion which can only be explained by her new captain's eagerness to fire off his guns.

Off Almeria a small Spanish coaster was sighted, and Rodney could not resist taking the *Plymouth* into action. The coaster must have been uncommonly slow, or very badly handled, not to have shown a clean pair of heels to a crazy old 60-gun ship which had no business to go chasing her anyway. Rodney's men blazed away for all they were worth. They fired 6 times with the big 24-pounders on the lower deck, 36 times with the small 6-pounders on the quarter-deck, and 88 times with the 9-pounders. It must have been quite an experience for the invalids. But the expenditure of ammunition was justified for the coaster, perhaps because of a lucky hit, perhaps out of sheer terror, ran herself on the beach. The *Plymouth* anchored half a mile off-shore and Rodney sent away a boat, manned and armed. But finding their victim full of water and her Spanish crew sniping at them from the sand-dunes, the boat-crew returned empty handed. The adventure had been expensive in terms of powder and shot, besides which the *Plymouth*'s barge was stove as they hoisted her in; but the fillip to morale in a ship that had been so long without a smell of powder must have been considerable. Two days later they reached Gibraltar.

Then came Lisbon, last visited by Rodney when a midshipman in the *Romney*. To return, after less than five years, as the captain of a battleship would have sweetened the social round considerably. The Comptons were still there with Mr Charles no longer a mere consul but, in consequence of the war, an Envoy Extraordinary. His principal factotum for affairs, and the business of the port, was a certain John Clies, a Lisbon merchant, whose lively little daughter Henrietta was much in evidence at the Comptons' house. She was the same age as Mr Compton's second daughter Jane who had just celebrated her thirteenth birthday. It is more than probable that Mr Rodney's return as a dazzling young captain left an unforgettable impression on both young ladies.

From Lisbon he wrote to the Admiralty to report his movements. Every commanding officer was expected to do this, but in his formal communication of February 15th he made no mention of that expensive engagement with the coaster: after all, his Commission had not yet been confirmed. His orders were to collect any of the Lisbon trade that wanted an escort home. Nine merchantmen responded to his signal, and before he sailed he took on board the *Plymouth* for passage to England a distressed British seaman with an interesting story. This was a certain Lewis Ledger who claimed to have sailed to the South Seas with Commodore Anson, of whom next to nothing had been heard since he disappeared round the Horn some time in 1741. Two of his squadron had returned, but beyond this all was doubtful report and unsubstantiated rumour. Now, from the Pacific coast of Mexico appeared this man, who had been Anson's cook. He had been captured while ashore and had taken ten months to reach Lisbon by way of Havana and Lagos. The Admiralty and the Government too, would be extremely glad to have his information.

March is not the best of months in the Bay of Biscay and the Channel. Any captain sailing from Lisbon at this time of year would take every precaution, particularly with a ship like the *Plymouth*, and a Commission not yet confirmed. Rodney's letter reporting his arrival describes with becoming reticence what must have been a most unpleasant passage:

'*Sir*, Spitthead, March 31st 1743.

'Please to acquaint their Lordships that this day I arrived at Spitthead with His Majesty's ship under my command in 25 days from Lisbon, having nine sail of merchantships under convoy, most of whom lost company by excessive bad weather which laid us under a reefed mainsail 14 days, and was succeeded by as hard a gale at south-west which brought us into the Channel under a reefed foresail with two sail of the convoy, but it proving such bad weather, could not press their hands. The ship is in a very bad condition, most of the rigging and sails being quite unfit for service, besides the main, fore, and orlop beams being sprung and the cheeks of the head and bows very rotten. The rudder likewise is very loose and works prodigiously att sea.

'As their Lordships might be glad to hear news concerning Commandore [sic] Anson, I have brought home his cook who was taken prisoner in the South Seas and came to Lagos in the *Princessa* galleon lately arrived at that place. I shall send him up to London forthwith in order for their Lordship's examination, meantime refer them to the enclosed.*

> '*I am, Sir,*
> '*Your most humble servant,*
> '*G. B. RODNEY.*'

This most correct and acceptable communication, clear evidence, if their Lordships would but note, of how well fitted Mr G. B. Rodney was to hold post-rank, was followed two days later by another, of infinite consequence: 'Enclosed I send my Commission for H.M.S. *Plymouth*, granted me by Vice Admiral Mathews, which I hope their Lordships will be so good as to confirm. . . .' He need not have worried. A satisfactory answer came by return. His last duty as captain of the *Plymouth* was to take her round to the west-country port whose name she bore and put her out of commission. This was done on April 23rd, and he came on shore.

There followed five months of unemployment. How he occupied them may be surmised with confidence. All his life he was never backward in pressing for what he wanted, and in this summer of 1743 the height and summit of his ambition could only have been a ship. With Lord Vere Beauclerck still at the Admiralty, and now the Duke of Newcastle to be reminded of the young officer who had acted so capably at Vintimilia, his interest was better than ever. No doubt he cultivated it to the full. Apart from this, opportunities would not have been lacking for agreeable dalliance. He was young, good-looking, with an eye for a pretty face, and unlike a

---

* This was a 650-word report by Ledger of the adventures of Anson's squadron between January 1741 and April 1742.

mere lieutenant who only had hopes, he was a post-captain with prospects. Finally there were Mr and Mrs Bridges down in Hampshire, in the midst of one of the finest sporting countries in the kingdom. So the summer probably passed, and in September he was appointed to command the *Sheerness* of 24 guns.

Certainly his interest had been good, for the *Sheerness* was a brand-new ship of improved design, and the sort of command any young captain would covet. The Navy had not yet developed the fast, powerful frigates of a later date, and still had to make do with an inadequate number of little ships, usually too small for their duties. But the new class to which the *Sheerness* belonged was a step in the right direction. She carried the same number of guns as the *Dolphin*, but was nearly 100 tons larger and had more men.

His new command was still on the building slip at Rotherhithe, and after the first appraisal Rodney's spirits may well have sunk at the thought of all that needed doing before she would be ready. It would be his business to get her rigged and stored, and to get all the guns and ammunition on board. This would entail endless dealings with the various officials of the dockyard, a suspicious and obstructive fraternity who owed allegiance, not to the Admiralty but to the Navy Board; and even if these gentlemen proved co-operative and helpful he would still be powerless until he had some men. Manning was the bugbear of every commanding officer in the Navy.

The Admiralty had promised him eighty men from the *Ruby* (half of the number he needed) and would of course appoint the commissioned and warrant officers; but beyond these Rodney would have to fend for himself. He would have to send one of his officers away in a tender to press from the shipping along the coast, or set up a recruiting rendezvous ashore. On October 5th only six from the *Ruby* had appeared and he was still without a boatswain, a carpenter and a purser. Then, for a few days, he went sick himself.

On the 8th the *Sheerness* was launched and warped down to Deptford. Four days later her lower masts were in, her ballast was going in, and twenty-two of the *Ruby*'s men had appeared. Where to accommodate them was now the problem. The painters were at work in the *Sheerness* making her quite uninhabitable and there was as yet no cook-room* capable of functioning. So the men had to live on board the tender, and as there were no partitions up in the *Sheerness* for cabins some of the officers may have

---

* As this is the term used by Rodney himself it seems correct to use it here.

had to live on board the tender too. This of course prevented her being employed on her proper purpose and further held up the manning. A week later the men were still living on board the tender when Rodney received a tart enquiry from the Secretary to the Admiralty to know why that vessel had not yet sailed. He got his men on board the *Sheerness* as soon as she was habitable and then hurried the tender off under Leaver, his first lieutenant, to scour the east coast for men. But no sooner was she away than a message came down that Leaver had been re-appointed and was wanted at Portsmouth at once for a ship under sailing orders. Fortunately the tender was beyond recall.

Things may have been better after November 15th when a very capable nineteen-year-old midshipman, Mr Samuel Hood, joined. With assistance from the yachts, because she was still so short of men, the *Sheerness* moved down from Deptford to Long Reach on the 19th for her guns. Then a heavy storeship came crashing into her on the flood tide, damaging jib-boom and spritsail yard after which, to add to Rodney's worries, the tender with Leaver and the pressed men on board became overdue. December came with no news, and the young captain wrote anxiously to the Admiralty that he feared some accident had befallen her.

But amid so much that was vexatious and frustrating, one small episode at the beginning of December may have brought encouragement. Four seamen, supernumeraries in the *Princess Royal*, petitioned the Admiralty to serve in the *Sheerness* under Captain Rodney.[2] Sailors are quick to perceive the qualities, good and bad, in their officers, and later in Rodney's career such petitions recur with pleasing frequency. But it is interesting that he should have made his mark so soon. To cut the story short, the missing tender appeared on December 8th and the *Sheerness* reached the Nore on the 11th, still short of men but otherwise ready for sea. She was urgently needed, for the war was entering a new phase.

For the last four years Spain had been the only enemy, and although the most lenient critic of the government could hardly say that the war had been conducted with conspicuous efficiency and success, yet at least it had been conducted at a safe distance from home and without danger to the British Isles. All this was now to change. France, whose behaviour in the Mediterranean was still giving Vice-Admiral Mathews concern, was about to come in on her own account. Naval preparations in Brest were too advanced to be disregarded, and to heighten apprehension there were reports of a formidable concentration of troops and transports at Dunkirk. Everything pointed to invasion.

This indeed was the French intention. The ships from Brest were to come up channel and cover an attempt by the Dunkirk troops under Marshal Saxe to land in the Thames estuary, all without a declaration of war. At the same time the usual swarm of privateers would be let loose on British shipping. On December 22nd the Cabinet took alarm and ordered all ships in the home ports to be brought up to four months' supply of provisions, and four days later there was a hot press.* All round the coast of Great Britain the authorities were alert and watchful. This was the situation in December 1743 when Rodney received his orders.

He was to cruise in the Soundings (i.e. the Channel approaches), an assignment which promised plenty of unpleasant weather off the south-west of Ireland. Here he would be well placed to intercept some of the illicit trade between the south Irish ports and Spain, and if France entered the war there would be the British trade to protect and the Brest fleet to report on. For a month the *Sheerness* cruised on her station and endured a succession of January gales. The water poured in through her badly caulked topsides and through her row-ports, an antique survival on which the Navy Board still insisted; the pumps worked continuously and her men began to go sick. But all she caught was one French merchantman, the *Prudence*, with 1,140 barrels of Irish beef ostensibly for Marseilles but more probably for the Spaniards, which Rodney sent in for examination. In Cork he managed to press 11 men and learnt from the captain of the *Squirrell* that the latter had seen 21 sail, almost certainly the Brest fleet, only a few days before off the Lizard. Then he received orders for Dublin.

At first rumour said that they were to escort the Duke of Devonshire's baggage to England. Then it was not ducal baggage, but some of the Irish foot regiments to Ostend. But when Rodney waited on His Grace he was simply told to await further orders. If the Brest fleet was at sea this was no time to send troops to Ostend. For a few days there was uncertainty in high quarters.

The Brest fleet had sailed on January 26th, and on the same day Prince Charles Edward Stuart, the Young Pretender, landed in France, a sinister development of which the British Cabinet was soon aware. The crisis was imminent and Sir John Norris was ordered to proceed to Portsmouth and take command of the fleet. Then a number of factors intervened to spoil the French design and the British response. The Cabinet, which thought itself wiser than its Commander-in-Chief, directed Sir John to quit his anchorage

* I.e. the press-gangs were out along the waterfronts, and official protection was withdrawn from certain categories of seamen.

at St Helen's and station himself in the Downs, thus depriving him of his best chance of catching the French; at the same time the poor seamanship of the latter as they beat up channel gave them second thoughts as to the feasibility of their project. However, the Brest ships were off Brighton on February 22nd and off Dungeness on the 25th, by which time some 7,000 troops had embarked at Dunkirk.

All of which explains why Captain Rodney was kept waiting at Dublin. His orders, when they came, were to escort the Irish foot regiments, not to Ostend but to England, with all possible speed and land them either at Chester or Bristol, whichever was best served by the wind. He landed them at Chester on February 19th and for three weeks was weather-bound while the French invasion project petered out ignominiously. The Brest fleet was almost within Sir John's clutches when the same gale that held the *Sheerness* at Chester drove it in confusion down channel, and wreaked havoc among the French transports at Dunkirk. This was the end of the crisis.

In this inauspicious way France entered the war. Her official declaration came on March 25th, by which time the *Sheerness* was on her way up channel to be docked at Portsmouth. Rodney had managed to press 22 more seamen out of the merchantmen at Chester and now had a muster of 137 out of a complement of 160 which was fairly satisfactory. But he had been without a gunner since the commission began and now had to report the death of his boatswain. Life was hard in these small ships at the best of times, and worse than hard in winter. The strain on the captain, with two warrant officers short, must have been considerable.

There was now no safety for unescorted British shipping in home waters, so as soon as the *Sheerness* was out of dock she sailed with a channel convoy to the Nore. Convoy duty was arduous and generally thankless. Rodney had plenty of it in the summer of 1744. From the Nore, at the beginning of May, he took the north-bound trade as far as Tynemouth where he found upwards of 200 ships waiting for a fair wind south. Half were colliers and most of the remainder were bound for the Dutch ports. It is uncertain whether all desired to sail in convoy but Rodney left them in no doubt at all. During the interval of waiting, before the wind came fair, he collected the particulars of 185 ships, for the detailed list that the regulations required. Then he took this enormous convoy under his charge, kept it closed up all down the east coast, frightened away a small privateer off Lowestoft, released the colliers off the Thames, and then bore away for Holland with the remainder. On May 22nd he safely delivered 103 merchantmen, most of them loaded with corn, at Hellevoetsluys.

The *Sheerness* brought back 30 merchantmen from the Dutch port and at the beginning of June sailed again with 35, most of them with corn and tobacco, for Amsterdam and Rotterdam. This convoy, like the others, sustained no losses. Indeed, Rodney might be said to have returned with a bonus, for off the Texel the *Sheerness* recaptured an English merchantman lately taken by the French. In August she was ordered to cruise between the Orkneys and Shetlands. Many ships, and particularly the valuable East Indiamen, now went round that way and the authorities were acutely sensitive about their safety. For a month she patrolled those northern waters without incident. Then, at the end of her allotted time, the weather deteriorated, a September gale laid her under double-reefed topsails, and while she was thus snugged down and riding the seas comfortably a mastless hulk was sighted in dire distress. Rodney bore down on her and discovered that she was the *Montford*, East Indiaman, homeward bound from Madras and Bengal. During her long voyage she had buried most of her crew and the remainder, weakened by disease, were in no condition to fight the gale. She had been dismasted off the Shetlands and was now drifting helplessly with all the life beaten out of her.

Rodney sent across a working party with some spare gear, stood by her down the east coast, and on September 12th brought her safely in to Yarmouth roads. Usually an Indiaman, at the end of her voyage, had plenty of men to be pressed, but the poor, battered *Montford* had only thirteen worth taking. However, while they were still in Yarmouth roads, there appeared another Indiaman, the *Salisbury*, in rather better shape, and Rodney sent three boats across at once to try his luck with her. The *Salisbury*'s men saw the boats coming and would not allow anyone on board. It is possible that Rodney sympathized with them. But duty was duty and men were men, so he unmoored the *Sheerness* and fell alongside the Indiamen. Then, in his own words:

'I went myself on board and told them the consequences that might happen by my boarding them with my ship, and that it would be much better for them to enter voluntarily as His Majesty had such an urgent occasion for men, whereupon they unanimously agreed to enter, hoping their Lordships would permit them to stay some little time on shore to see their friends, having been three years out of England. . . .'

It is a pleasant picture, the brisk young captain talking to the sailors in their own language and the loyal fellows agreeing unanimously to enter the service. But it is doubtful if they got their run ashore. To the unemotional men at Whitehall (and perhaps to the reader too) the guns of the *Sheerness* would have been too obviously the deciding factor in clinching Rodney's argument. Nevertheless he handled the situation with humanity and skill, and at the same time obtained fifty good men for the Navy.

From Yarmouth to the Thames the *Sheerness* had the *Montford* in tow. At noon on September 20th all three ships anchored at the Nore. The *Montford* and *Salisbury* fired a 13-gun salute which the *Sheerness* returned. Then the two Indiamen went up to their moorings off Erith[3] while Rodney turned to the correspondence which was waiting for him, and learnt that he would command the *Sheerness* no longer. He was to exchange with Captain Gordon into the *Ludlow Castle*.

This was a mark of their Lordship's favour. The *Ludlow Castle* was a new ship and bigger than the *Sheerness* while Gordon, who was nine months Rodney's junior, could have no grounds for complaint. Rodney's last letter from the *Sheerness*, dated September 28th after Gordon had appeared, happily illustrates the relations between a good captain and his men:

'. . . As I am informed that many of the men that their Lordships were pleased to turn over on board the *Ludlow Castle* are very desirous to go with Captain Gordon, and at the same time many men belonging to the *Sheerness* are willing to take their fortunes with me, I must take the liberty to beg their Lordships will permit us to change man for man. . . .'

So he quitted the little *Sheerness*, after twelve months of exemplary command. Among those who elected to follow him to the new ship was Mr Samuel Hood.

The *Ludlow Castle* was fitting at Deptford and wanted as soon as possible, so there could be no leave for her new captain. She was one of a new class of two-deckers, the smallest ever built for the Navy and, according to one eminent authority, the worst.* The intention of the design was a small ship with an exceptionally heavy broadside, so she carried 20 18-pounders on the lower deck and 20 9-pounders on the upper deck, making 40 guns altogether. But this was too much metal for her tonnage and the result was a rather stumpy and top-heavy little ship, crowded and uncomfortable at all times, and unable to use her lower deck guns in the slightest swell because the ports were so close to the water—less than five feet amidships. Some twenty-five of this class were built and they soon had a

* 'Certainly the worst vessels which at that time composed any part of the British Navy.' Charnock, *Marine Architecture*, 1802, Vol. III, p. 158.

bad reputation. However, as the *Ludlow Castle* counted as a fifth rate, Rodney received more pay for commanding her (8 shillings a day, as against 6 in the *Sheerness*); and no doubt the prestige of two complete gun decks counted for something. This may be why James Rodney, at the age of twenty, decided to try his chances at sea with his sailor brother. He entered as a volunteer on October 2nd. If he valued his comfort and safety he made an unlucky choice when he chose to go to sea in the *Ludlow Castle*.

All October they were fitting for sea and trying to scrape together a ship's company. The manning situation was as bad as ever. Rodney felt he was being unfairly treated and ventured a tactful protest: 'I with pleasure submitted to their Lordship's regulations in having one third landmen and two thirds seamen but out of 56 men that came from the *Royal Sovereign*, many of them were landmen and the greater part far from seamen. It has always been my endeavour to avoid troubling their Lordships in regard to men, but as the safety of His Majesty's ship under my command, and the honour and reputation of those that serve in her might suffer by her being so ill-manned, [I] beg their Lordships will indulge me with a few of the *Kent*'s men . . . now on board the *Royal Sovereign*.' This was the way to approach their Lordships. Rodney got what he wanted, which was fortunate for some rough experiences lay ahead.

The orders were to escort the trade to Holland, with particular attention to a transport in the convoy carrying a present of six valuable horses from King George II to the Prince Royal of Denmark. On the return a south-westerly gale drove the *Ludlow Castle* northward, beyond Flamborough, into a part of the North Sea beyond the knowledge of her pilot, although not perhaps of her captain if he recalled his experiences in the *Dolphin*. Then it went round and blew really hard from the north with snow and hail so that, for ten black days, the *Ludlow Castle* laboured under her topsails only, without any sight of land. Water poured in continuously through decks and upperworks. How her men must have cursed builders and dockyard that sent such a badly designed and badly caulked ship to sea. They went sick in scores until some eighty of them were huddled below, wet and miserable, for it was impossible for any man to lie dry in his hammock. Cautiously they felt their way towards Yarmouth, and on the morning of November 24th sighted land and ran in towards the roads. Then, with the anchorage before them, the ship struck the sand so violently that there was a very real danger of her masts going by the board. Relentlessly she ground and bumped over the Standford shoal. The masts stood, contrary to expectations, although none could say what damage was being done below. Then she drove clear and was able to anchor in safety. Nothing like this had happened in the little *Sheerness* and the result was that the *Ludlow Castle* spent most of December in dock.

Rodney was so dissatisfied with his men's living conditions that he ventured some suggestions of his own for improving them. It was sheer presumption of course and unlikely to succeed, but with a quarter of his ship's company still sick he could not keep silent; so he begged leave 'to give their Lordships my sentiments upon the occasion'.

His first point was that the *Ludlow Castle* was a very wet ship. The watch on deck was never dry, health suffered, and the remedy, simple and practical, would be 'an awning' on the quarter-deck (i.e. a continuation of the poop-deck forward beyond the cabin) to protect the after-guard from the weather. Secondly, she was an overcrowded ship. There would be room against the taffrail at the after end of the poop to build two small cabins for the first lieutenant and the master and thus release more room between decks for the men. But their Lordships had no intention of rebuilding a brand-new ship to the specifications of a junior captain. They instructed the Secretary to inform Captain Rodney that they were sorry for the sick, but that they did not think it proper for the alterations to be made. All Rodney could do was accommodate his men on board a hulk and have the inside of the *Ludlow Castle* washed several times with vinegar and thoroughly dried. Nevertheless, some form of sickness, which he called a fever, continued to lay his men low at the rate of three or four a day until well on in January, and all that time the *Ludlow Castle* lay at Sheerness.

Another of his attempts to improve the amenities of his ship, this time for his midshipmen, was treated in much the same way. He requested the appointment of a schoolmaster for their instruction, but was given clearly to understand that the Lords of the Admiralty had other things to do than find schoolmasters for midshipmen. 'Let him know,' one of them condescended to explain, 'that he must look out for one and recommend him.' There was no queue of applicants for teaching posts in the Georgian Navy.

1745 was another year of crisis, but for the *Ludlow Castle*, as soon as the sick were recovered and the ship at sea again, the first six months passed pleasantly enough. Medley, Rodney's old patron and now a rear-admiral, was going out to fly his flag in the Mediterranean and would take with him reinforcements for the fleet, and at the same time all the trade for Lisbon, Oporto, the Mediterranean ports and the East Indies. The *Ludlow Castle* escorted some of these down channel to join the main concentration and sailed with the convoy, which numbered 116 sail, at the beginning of April. It was light duty. November gales in the North Sea could be forgotten for the time being. On the 22nd she brought the Lisbon section safely into the Tagus. The homeward trade not being ready, Rodney cruised off the Rock of Lisbon for a fortnight and then, on June 2nd, sailed for England with a convoy of sixty-seven. Besides these he was entrusted with a considerable sum of money by the Lisbon merchants who allowed him one per cent of its value for carrying it home. This was his first taste of 'freight-money', a cherished perquisite enjoyed only by captains, although sometimes flag-officers got their cut. It made him richer by £441 16s 6d.[4] The *Ludlow Castle* arrived safely in the Downs after a twenty-six-day passage, and here Mr Samuel Hood left her to rejoin his old patron Commodore Smith.

That summer, the French launched an attack on the Austrian Nether-lands. Ghent fell on the day the *Ludlow Castle* arrived in the Downs. Evacuation was in the air and she was sent across at once to stand by. On July 25th Rodney sent back a detailed report from Ostend on the military situation and six days later, when the French advance works were within half a musket shot of the town's outer defences, he sailed with the first convoy of evacuated troops, landing them at Dover and returning at once with empty transports. Then the *Ludlow Castle* joined the escort bringing His Majesty back from Holland.

On his return in mid-August Rodney found a large concentration of shipping in the Downs with Admiral Vernon flying his flag in the *St George*. The Stuart Pretender had landed in Scotland and Vernon was disposing his forces to intercept any movement from the Continent. He had a light squadron under Rear-Admiral Byng watching the French coast, but being of opinion that the best means for preventing foreign aid reaching the rebels would be 'a nimble squadron of ships and small vessels to watch their entrance into Edinburgh Firth or any of the ports on the Eastern coast of Scotland', he had given Byng discretionary orders to stretch across to Scotland if necessary. The *Ludlow Castle* was not nimble, and was by now so foul that her convoys had often out-sailed her. Never-theless, she was one of the ships sent to join Byng, and in due course found herself patrolling the shores of the northern kingdom.

Rodney was a staunch supporter of the House of Hanover and had no sympathy with the Jacobites. ''Tis everyman's business at this critical juncture to do his duty to the Utmost of his Powers, in the service of his

King and Country', he wrote in October, when the Jacobite hopes were at their highest. In this spirit he was cruising that November between Montrose and Buchanness when a brigantine from Dundee passed a report that a French dogger had landed some ammunition at Montrose only a few days before, and that several of the fishing-boats from John's Haven nearby had actively welcomed her, and indeed towed her in. Being then only two miles from John's Haven Rodney decided to test the loyalty of its inhabitants, and perhaps teach them a lesson. Hoisting French colours and taking the brigantine with him, he sailed quietly in and signalled for a boat. The bait was taken at once. Out came a reception committee of fifteen men: nor did they realize their mistake until some of them had climbed on board and found themselves under arrest.

Rodney's command of the *Ludlow Castle* ended as dangerously and uncomfortably as it began. In December 1745 she joined the light squadron stationed off Harwich under Commodore Smith. On the 21st she was cruising offshore in blowy weather under double-reefed topsails. The visibility was poor, and Harwich was somewhere in the murk to leeward, but no danger was apprehended. Suddenly, without warning, she ran hard on a shoal and began to beat violently. The local pilot, a good man and well known to Rodney, had put her on the Whiting Sand. It was a much more serious calamity than when she grounded on the Standgate. The strong wind pinned her down on the shoal with no hope of getting clear, and from 1 p.m. until 4, as the tide rose, she bumped and crashed her way further on to it with extreme violence.

The only hope, and it was a slender one, was to lighten the ship so that she might drive over it, and to this end Rodney ordered the beer and water to be started. By this simple but effective measure the butts and barrels were emptied into the bilges which were then pumped out in the usual way. The lofty spars were a source of danger so he ordered the topmasts to be cut away. Before long the *Ludlow Castle* presented a deplorable spectacle, floundering and crashing helplessly in the shoal water, her crew pumping continuously, and nothing above her upper deck except the three lower masts. For three hours the ordeal went on. The rudder was smashed, and Rodney was about to cut away the lower masts as well when they bumped for the last time, drove clear of the shoal, and found themselves in deep water again. Thankfully they dropped anchor and began to take stock. Because of her stout construction the ship still floated. But she was making about four feet of water a watch, and Rodney feared that part of her keel was gone as well as the rudder.

Next morning, vessels came out from Harwich to assist. The remains of the rudder were sent ashore for a new one to be made, and within less than a week the *Ludlow Castle* was patched sufficiently to limp down to Sheerness. At this time, when coastal navigation depended so much on local knowledge, the responsibility for a misadventure like this was the pilot's. The reaction of their Lordships, as soon as they heard of the affair, was to order him into confinement, although the real culprit was the leadsman who had given an incorrect sounding of seven fathoms just before they struck. Rodney came to the pilot's defence in a characteristically generous letter which explained all the circumstances. Justice apart, the man was an excellent pilot; Rodney had often employed him before so he stood by him now. He also pressed for a buoy to the east of the Whiting sand, and a buoy was placed there a few years later. But the happy sequel to the misadventure was that Rodney left the *Ludlow Castle*. While she was still in dock at Sheerness he learnt that he was to be relieved, and that their Lordships had something better for him.

Chapter 5

The *Eagle*

(1746–1748)

'. . . Captain Rodney, a young seaman who has made a
fortune by very gallant behaviour during the war.'
(Horace Walpole to Sir Horace Mann, December 26, 1748.)

THE new ship was the *Eagle* of 60 guns building at Harwich, and
Rodney's appointment to her a well-deserved compliment for
which he lost no time in writing to thank the Duke of Bedford.[1]
Then, on January 7, 1746, he hurried down to Harwich and
found her already launched and with her lower masts in. But to obtain the
400 men she needed was, at this stage of the war, beyond even his power.
He got as many as he could from ships paying off, and after a tussle with
his successor in the *Ludlow Castle* he made sure of most of his followers
from that ship, although they did not include James Rodney; fourteen
months in the *Ludlow Castle* had been quite enough for that gentleman,
and although his brother had already advanced him to midshipman and
master's mate, James now decided to quit and try his luck on shore. The
lieutenants went cruising, but collected only thirty men, so that when the
Eagle sailed she was still one-fifth short of complement. However, many
ships were much worse off, and this time Rodney *did* win his battle for
more accommodation under the poop. He also got his awning for the
afterguard. Indeed, he seems to have caught their Lordships in an indulgent
mood because, by the same letter which approved the better accommodation, he also obtain his first and second lieutenants out of the *Ludlow
Castle*. So altogether the prospects were encouraging and the *Eagle* was a
command worth having. She had twice the gunpower of the little *Sheerness*,
and as it turned out, everything in the way of speed and seagoing qualities
that the *Ludlow Castle* lacked. In the next two years she was to bring him
fame and fortune.

70

They came to sail for the first time on February 26th, and proceeded to Ostend where, for seven unexciting weeks from March to April, they blockaded the port, lying for most of the time at anchor. It was poor work for a fine new ship but the rebellion was still active in Scotland, reinforcements from Ostend had been slipping across, and the government was taking no chances. Then came the news of the Pretender's defeat at Culloden which Rodney as a loyal Hanoverian celebrated with a 21-gun salute, after which the *Eagle* and a great many other ships were available for service elsewhere.

A new and important development was about to take place in the war at sea. This was the creation of a powerful squadron to cruise continuously between Cape Finisterre and the western approaches of the Channel. Enlightened naval opinion, as voiced by Norris and Vernon, had long advocated this as the keystone of our naval disposition in a war against France, but ignorant politicians had paid them little heed. However, at the beginning of 1745 there was a new Board of Admiralty with Sir George Anson as its most influential naval member, and the idea was tried with a degree of success which encouraged its wider application as soon as more ships were available. That time had now come and Anson would shortly go to sea to take command himself. However, the squadron that the great Admiral conceived and the rest of the Board was prepared to send out, could not be assembled in the matter of a few days, or even weeks, and a fine new ship like the *Eagle* could not lie idle. With another 60-gun ship, the *Nottingham* (Captain Philip Saumarez), and the *Falcon* (sloop), she was sent to cruise in the south-western approaches, and remarkable good hunting the three ships enjoyed that summer among the enemy privateers.

The *Eagle* took her first prize on May 24th while proceeding to her station. She sighted a sail to the north-west at 3 p.m. and gave chase. After four hours she had overhauled sufficiently to open fire with her bow guns, and the pursuit went on for another four hours until 11 p.m., when the quarry abandoned hope of escape and surrendered. Rodney ranged up alongside and learnt that she was the *Esperance* of St Sebastian, a Spanish privateer of 16 guns with a crew of 136. A damaged ship crowded with cutthroats was something of a problem. He sent a lieutenant across with twenty men, and next morning took her in tow for Kinsale.

The *Eagle* was with the *Nottingham* and *Falcon* for her next adventure. At 8 a.m. on June 13th a suspicious sail was sighted to the north-east. After seven hours of light airs and calms they were within three miles of her when the wind dropped completely. The chase got out sweeps and began to row. The *Eagle* and the *Nottingham* sent their boats across to tow the *Falcon*, and for the next hour there was an exhausting contest of muscles under the hot sun as the sloop slowly overhauled the stranger, which gave up at four in the afternoon. This time it was a French privateer out of Morlaix called the *Ponté Quarré*, with 12 guns and 138 men.

A month later the three ships sighted first a sail to the northward, and then another to the south-west. The *Eagle* separated from her consorts to chase the second vessel, and was up with her after five hours. Only two shots were necessary before the French brigantine *Joseph Louis* of Bordeaux, with 4 carriage guns and twenty-four men, struck her colours and brought to. A week after this the three hunters chased a sail to the eastward for six hours. The *Falcon* was up with her as darkness fell, and the two exchanged broadsides for half an hour until the arrival of the larger ships brought the quarry to her senses. This time it was another Spaniard, the *Neustra Señora del Carmen*, with 26 guns and 148 men.

What is remarkable is the way the *Eagle* overhauled her victims. Usually a privateer might expect to make rings round a heavy 60-gun ship, but not if that ship was Captain Rodney's *Eagle*. At the end of July the three hunters lay together in Kinsale harbour, and with them lay a whole squadron of small victims, French and Spanish. With cheerful thoughts of prize-money the *Eagle*'s crew hove her down to scrub as far below the waterline as could be reached; they set up the rigging afresh and caulked the decks. Then, as smart as zeal and enthusiasm could make her, she sailed for Plymouth with her two consorts to join the new Western Squadron.

The Admiral had seventeen of the line and six fifties, with a free hand to use them as he thought best. All September and October he sought the enemy. The ships stretched across the Bay of Biscay to Finisterre and then down to the latitude of Cape St Vincent, and all the time the training went on. There was no place on any quarter-deck for the political favourite or the mere fighting blockhead, unless he could sharpen his wits and learn his business afresh. Under the Admiral's eye they practised the attack, made and shortened sail, exercised the great guns, and performed every evolution that might be needed in battle. Day after day the *Eagle*'s journal records their ceaseless activity. From Anson's captains in the Western Squadron were to come most of the successful admirals and squadron commanders of the next generation, with professional standards hitherto undreamed of.

Whenever a strange sail showed over the horizon the Admiral detached a fast ship to chase her. This brought Rodney several more opportunities. There was a little Spaniard unexpectedly named the *Prudent Sarah* with

8 guns and forty men, which yielded, among other goods, forty-two bales of snuff. Most memorable of all, however, was the *Shoreham*.

The squadron had been seven weeks at sea and was some 100 miles south-west of the Scillies on October 28th when two sails were sighted at about 6.30 in the evening. Darkness had fallen before Rodney received Anson's signal to investigate, but he confidently shook out a reef and set a course for the night most likely to bring him up with them in the morning. To do this successfully required luck as well as judgement, but he possessed both in those days, and when dawn broke they were not merely in sight but close enough for a gun to be fired at one of them. It must have been the shock of their lives when the *Eagle* swooped out of the morning mist.

Both bore away at once and scudded to the westward, and on board the *Eagle* they settled down to the familiar experience of a long stern-chase. Soon the smaller of the two hauled her wind and disappeared to the southward, but the other continued to run to the westward under all the sail she could carry. All day the wind strengthened, which was to the heavier ship's advantage. Slowly the *Eagle* overhauled her quarry. At 5 p.m. she opened fire.

The chase hung on gamely, with the obvious hope of escaping under cover of darkness, but this she was not permitted to do. At 9 p.m. the *Eagle* ranged up alongside and fired several shots and at last, as though admitting defeat, the other began to shorten sail. But this was not the end. As soon as the artful Frenchmen observed the *Eagle* to be shortening too they loosened their gaskets, hauled their sheets, and were off again into the night. It was exasperating. For another hour and a half she struggled to get away, and when at 10.30 the *Eagle* was on top of her once more Rodney ordered a full broadside. Only then did the Frenchman bring to properly.

But still it was not the end. She would not strike her colours, and when Rodney sent a boat across no amount of shouting would make her accept it. All that could be understood on board the *Eagle* was something about 'not until the morning', and this was the answer when a second boat was sent. So another hour and a half passed, with the two ships drifting to leeward, guns run out and crews glaring at each other. One o'clock in the morning came, and still the French colours flew. The only solution was another broadside, and this Rodney let them have. The Frenchman replied in like manner *pour l'honneur du pavillon* and then struck. The whole business had lasted thirty hours.

She was a French privateer, the *Shoreham*, of 22 guns with a crew of

C*

260, less than forty-eight hours out from Morlaix. Rodney took all the prisoners on board the *Eagle*, put a lieutenant and thirty men into the prize, and then under very easy sail (for his broadsides had left their mark) escorted her to Crookhaven where they arrived on November 3rd. Here they lay for six days. After two months at sea the *Eagle*'s stores were low, but the *Shoreham* was well stocked and the opportunity too good to be missed. Then they struggled round to Kinsale and put the prisoners on shore, but here they were weatherbound for a month. The *Eagle* did not get back to Plymouth until December 16th when Rodney learnt that Anson and the squadron had already sailed, and that he was to follow with all possible speed. This he did, two days before Christmas.

The winter cruise was chiefly directed to the interception of some unhappy French ships which were staggering back from North America, riddled with sickness and disease. They missed them in a succession of hard gales and had a most uncomfortable time themselves, but the bad weather did not affect the *Eagle*'s luck. On January 2, 1747, she took *le Grand Comte*, a Rochefort privateer on 20 guns and seventy-seven men.* Then, on February 3rd, when in company with the *Edinburgh* and *Nottingham*, she took the *Bellona* of Nantes, a very formidable privateer indeed, mounting 36 guns and with a crew of 310. In a westerly gale which drove the rest of the squadron up channel the *Eagle* and *Nottingham* escorted this ship to Plymouth.

Ships and men were now exhausted and a merciful respite followed. Their latest prize, it appeared, was a famous, almost a notorious vessel, and soon the record of her activities, as well as her size, set all tongues wagging. She was the enemy that had recently fought the British frigate *Greyhound*, beaten her off and escaped; she had been extremely active in the late rebellion, and after Culloden had brought away some of the leading Jacobites, Lochiel himself it was said, and Lord Elcho. But besides this there had been a darker side to her record which her conscientious captors ferreted out and then reported to the Admiralty.

'*Eagle*, Plymouth Sound, 7 April 1747.

'... H.M.S. the *Eagle* and *Nottingham* under our commands, in company with the *Edinburgh*, having on our last cruise taken a privateer of 36 guns called the *Bellona* whose officers and men are now in this port, having lately heard of such an act of inhumanity committed by her captain as we can not,

* This vessel, with her prize-crew, was unfortunately recaptured a few days later.

without a breach of our Duty, omit acquainting their Lordships with; that in the course of their cruise an English merchant ship called the *Elenor* from London, whose cargo chiefly consisted of mules and horses, having sprung a leak and almost foundering were obliged to have recourse for relief to the first ship they saw which proved to be the privateer . . . and having surrendered fondly flattered themselves with the hope of having saved their lives at the expense of their Liberty. But the captain of the *Bellona* . . . instead of the generous enemy acted the rapacious Pirate, and having Plundered them, refused admitting them on board and even forcibly turned them back into the merchant ship where they perished. . . . What still if possible aggrivates this tragical accident were the entreaties of a gentleman and his lady who, with their servants were passengers in the ship and earnestly implored him to receive them on board but were, with the like barbarity, refused, and perished with the ship.

'. . . . As there appears to us strong presumption that this un-natural treatment of His Majesty's subjects will, on proper examination, be fully proved, we have taken the liberty to lay it before their Lordships whom, we are persuaded, will punish such a flagrant violation of the Law of Nations and Arms as the heinousnes of the Crime deserves.

'G. B. RODNEY.
'PHILIP SAUMAREZ.'

In April came news from the French ports which hurried the Western Squadron to sea and Rodney, with his usual luck, snapped up a St Malo privateer, the *Mary Magdalen* of 22 guns and 170 men, only two days after sailing. But then came a twist of apparent ill-fortune. On April 21st the *Eagle* was detached to cruise independently for fourteen days. She took another privateer on May 1st and then fell in with some belated reinforcements for the Admiral under Commodore Fox who took her under his command. Meanwhile, on May 3rd, which was before the *Eagle* and Fox's reinforcements could rejoin, Sir George Anson and the Western Squadron met the French under M. de la Jonquière and won the first decisive naval success of the war. In the ordinary way, Rodney and most of Fox's captains would have been beside themselves with mortification at missing this action. However, Fortune had not forgotten them.

Besides the *Eagle* Fox had with him the *Kent* (64), *Hampton Court* (64), *Lyon* (60), *Chester* (50), *Hector* (44), and two fireships the *Dolphin* (Rodney's old ship now much come down in the world), and the *Pluto*.

Until June 15th they cruised unsuccessfully between Cape Ortegal and Cape Finisterre and then, as water was getting low, they began to work back to the northward. Shortly before dawn on Saturday June 20th, they sighted strangers.

At first, in the faint morning light, only a small group of ships could be seen in the obscurity to the northward. Then, as the light increased, more and more became visible until there was an immense fleet filling a quarter of the horizon from north to east. It was the great French convoy from St Domingo, laden with coffee, sugar and indigo, plodding slowly towards the Biscay ports like a great flock of sheep. From the *Eagle* her enraptured seamen counted 132 ships—and who could say how many more might be beyond these? The only escort in sight were three of the line and a frigate. Here was wealth sufficient to make every man rich for life.

Unfortunately the convoy was some ten or fifteen miles dead to windward. Fox's ships shook out their reefs and crowded on all the sail they could set, but it was soon clear that on their north-westerly course they would pass astern of the quarry so, at 8 a.m. Fox ordered his squadron to tack. All that Saturday they had the convoy before their eyes but could not touch it. A few French stragglers tacked to the north-west and disappeared out of sight, but except for these every ship was on the same course, with the clumsy French merchantmen sagging to leeward and the British drawing up slowly. The French escort formed line astern of their charges but the distance was too great for any shots to be exchanged. Then night fell and all was lost in the darkness.

Next day, Sunday June 21st, was cloudy and overcast with occasional showers of rain and little wind. Fox's ships, most of which were foul, moved sluggishly over the water, but the convoy was much closer. Over 100 merchantmen were still in sight, some to the north-west on the other tack but the great mass of them to the north-east; a few were already to the south-east and to leeward of the *Lyon*, the leading British ship. Of the French escort there was now no sign.

Rodney surveyed the scene and decided to take a line of his own. While the commodore and the others continued to the eastward, he tacked at 5 a.m. and went after that part of the convoy to the north-west. He turned a blind eye to Fox's signal of recall, and when at 7 a.m. the commodore fired two guns, these also failed to gain his attention.[2] By noon, the rest of the squadron was out of sight from the *Eagle*, but she was coming up on the first French straggler, a small schooner called the *Ste Claire*. At about 2 p.m. Rodney was able to put a midshipman and six men on board who found that she was loaded with sugar, coffee and indigo for St Malo. At about 3 p.m. the *Kent* took her first prize, and, before dark, another was taken by the *Lyon*; but this was all the squadron took that day.

Monday was a different story. During the forenoon there was so little wind that the clumsy French merchantmen could hardly move. The warships crept up on them, but even in these favourable conditions the stragglers were so widely dispersed and it took so long to approach them and take possession that the number of victims was but a small proportion of the whole convoy. In the afternoon the wind freshened and backed westerly. The merchantmen eased their sheets and fled before it until the darkness saved them. The result of this day's work as far as the *Eagle* was concerned, was four ships, two large ones, the *Europa* and *St Malo*, and two small, the *Esperance* and *Charlotta*, but all immensely valuable. It was a humane and comparatively civilized form of warfare. The sailors might expect a speedy exchange, while owners and part owners had nobody but themselves to blame if they were not covered by insurance, which was generally placed in London. Rodney put an officer with a handful of men on board each prize and ordered them to keep company with the *Eagle* as far as the Downs. Then, without any further regard for Commodore Fox he proceeded homeward with his small convoy. On the 26th he snapped up one more straggler, the *Maréchal de Saxe*, and on the 30th he anchored in the Downs with his six prizes. The commodore, with sixteen, had arrived in Spithead two days before.

Altogether forty-eight ships were taken in this famous encounter with the Domingo fleet, and Rodney's participation in their capture laid the foundation of his fortune. The particulars of his own prizes are as follows:

			Sugar	Coffee	Indigo
St Malo	370 tons	36 men	510 Hogsheads	38 Barrels	30 Barrels
Europa	350 tons	30 men	480 Hogsheads	54 Barrels	26 Barrels
Charlotta	150 tons	24 men	174 Hogsheads	38 Barrels	34 Barrels
Esperance	120 tons	20 men	100 Hogsheads	5 Barrels	30 Barrels
M. de Saxe	120 tons	22 men	200 Hogsheads		6 Barrels
Ste Claire	100 tons	20 men	180 Hogsheads	6 Barrels	6 Barrels

The *Charlotta* also had 200 bags of cotton and 300 hides.

When they had been valued and sold and the necessary divisions and

THE DOMINGO FLEET

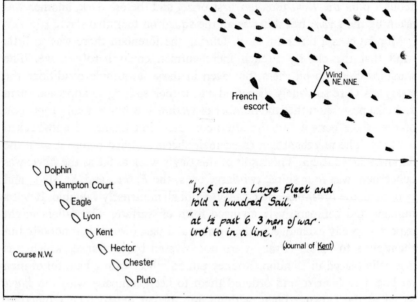

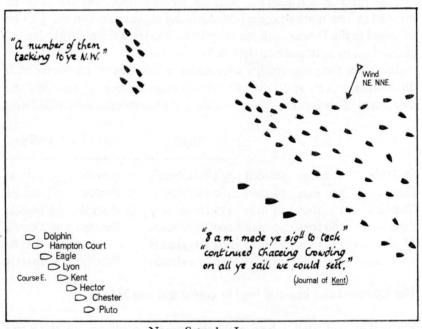

7.30 a.m., Saturday June 20

Noon, Saturday June 20

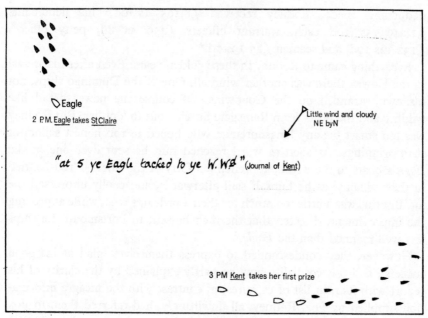

Eagle

2 P.M. Eagle takes St Claire

Little wind and cloudy
NE byN

"at 5 ye Eagle tacked to ye W.Wᵈ" (Journal of Kent)

3 PM Kent takes her first prize

Sunday June 21

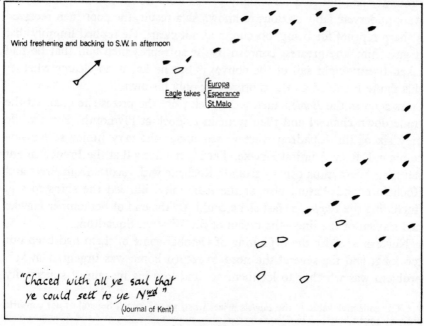

Wind freshening and backing to S.W. in afternoon

Eagle takes { Europa
Esperance
St.Malo

"Chaced with all ye saul that
ye could sett to ye Nʷᵈ"
(Journal of Kent)

Monday June 22

deductions made, Rodney received £8,165 1s 0d,[3] his lieutenants £1,049 15s 10d each, warrant officers £459 5s 8d, petty officers £132 12s 10d, and seamen £25 19s 0d.*

Everything came to Rodney in these golden years. Even after his arrival in the Downs there was another windfall. One of the Domingo ships, not his own, stranded on the Goodwins. Of course the news spread like wildfire and the boats from Ramsgate hurried out to loot her. But Rodney was too smart for any longshoreman who hoped to rob honest sailors of their winnings. As soon as word reached him he sent over one of the *Eagle*'s boats to the wreck, apprehended forty of the thieves, 'red-handed in their villainy' as he himself said afterwards, and coolly impressed the lot. But this was a little too much for their Lordships who, while approving the impressment, directed that the men be sent to Portsmouth for ships less well manned than the *Eagle*.[4]

However, they condescended to express themselves 'glad at his good success', and this cordiality may be partly explained by the clarity of his report with its neat list of captures, in contrast with the meagre information supplied by Fox. Rodney, all unwittingly, had referred them to Fox for the full details of the encounter but the latter, in spite of great prolixity, had not said how many prizes were taken, and this the Lords were understandably anxious to know. As a result, the poor man received a sharp reproof for being 'obscure and not clear'. He replied humbly that it gave him 'the greatest concern' to be so represented and that he had taken twenty-eight sail of the convoy;[5] but he left it no clearer whether this figure included all the captures, or only his own.

As soon as the *Eagle*'s men were back from the prizes she escorted the trade down channel and then went in to dock at Plymouth. For a while only six of the squadron were at sea under the very junior second-in-command, Rear-Admiral Hawke. Then came news that the French might sail their West India convoy from la Rochelle with escorts from Brest and Rochefort, and Anson, now at the Admiralty, hurried the ships to sea, (including the *Eagle*), as fast as he could. By the end of September Hawke had sixteen of the line—the cream of the Western Squadron.

Nevertheless, by the beginning of October some of them had been out too long, and for several the need to return home was urgent. Hawke's problem was whether to let them go, and lose his margin of superiority

---

* The collective value of the *Eagle*'s prizes was £37,798 8s 2d. Several of her consorts did very much better. The *Pluto*'s prizes came to over £78,000, and the *Kent*'s to over £70,000.

just when he might need it, or to share out the provisions and water from the latest arrivals and so be able to keep them all with him a little longer. He chose the latter. It was a gamble because eventually the whole squadron would have to return home instead of only a few. But it was the right decision. At daylight on October 14th, when the squadron was some sixty miles west of Finisterre, the *Edinburgh* made the signal that she had sighted seven ships in the south-west.

It was indeed the French West India convoy, escorted by eight of the line and a 60-gun ship of the Compagnie des Indes. Hawke at once signalled a general chase, reefs were shaken out, and by 9 a.m. a great fleet was in sight standing to the westward. The wind came fresh and true from the south-south-east, broad on the beam for hunters and hunted. There could be no delay or uncertainty about an issue. The only question was how would the commander of the French escort meet the challenge.

Hawke's ships came up rapidly. By 10 o'clock the Rear-Admiral could see enough to appraise the situation. He stopped the general chase, made the signal for the line of battle, and there followed a period of backing and filling as his ships sorted themselves out and fell into their correct stations. Wherever the *Eagle* had been in the chase (and as she had recently been cleaned it is easy to guess) she now had to take the last position but one in the line. Meanwhile, it became clear what the enemy was doing. The great mass of merchantmen was squaring away to the north-west before the wind under all the sail they could carry, while the eight battleships of the escort were forming up to cover their flight. De l'Etanduère, the French Admiral, had decided to sacrifice his warships to save the convoy. With the odds at nearly two to one it was a brave decision.*

In formal line the British ships no longer gained on the enemy, so Hawke cancelled the order and signalled to resume the chase. The battle therefore developed into a succession of individual combats as each of his ships in turn came up with the enemy and engaged. Except for Fox's ship, the *Kent*, which was out on the *Eagle*'s weather beam, and the 44-gun *Hector* which was too small for the line and lay astern, every ship in the squadron was ahead of Rodney as the engagement opened. From the *Eagle* they could see in the distance the leading British ships closing on the French rear. The sound of gunfire came back across the water.

At 11.30 the *Lyon* overhauled the rearmost French ship, the 70-gun *Neptune*, engaged her to leeward at a respectful distance, and passed on to engage the *Fougueux*, the *Severn* and the *Monarque*. After her came the

* For details of the British and French squadrons see Appendix 2.

Princess Louisa, the *Monmouth* and the *Gloucester*. In succession the British ships passed up the French line until some of them reached its head and were able to double back. Much powder and shot had therefore been expended before the rearmost British ships, the *Eagle* and *Kent*, began to engage.

This was a little after noon. The two were sailing roughly level with each other, the *Kent* slightly ahead and to windward, and together they were overhauling the French 70-gun *Neptune*. Now a French 70-gun ship

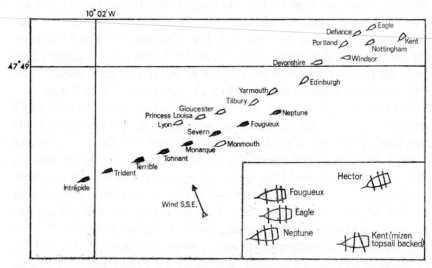

Second Battle of Finisterre, October 14, 1747; beginning of the attack, about 11.45 a.m. Inset: *Eagle* engaging *Neptune* and *Fougueux* a little later

was a formidable antagonist for a British 60. It was not just that she was 10 guns stronger. Her artillery, besides being more numerous, was heavier, with proportionately greater smashing power. The weight of her broadside might be more than half as much again as that of a 60-gun ship.

Rodney was well aware of the *Neptune's* strength and as the *Eagle* came up he observed to John Harrison, his First Lieutenant, that he thought it would be prudent if both *Kent* and *Eagle* stuck close to her until she struck.[6] With this intention he steered directly for the *Neptune's* lee quarter, but the latter's sails took the *Eagle's* wind as she approached and prevented her coming up broadside to broadside as Rodney intended. The best he could do was to place his ship on the *Neptune's* lee quarter at pistol-shot range, and from this position a fierce action developed. As for the *Kent*, the last Rodney saw of her before he luffed up to engage was that she seemed to be backing her mizen-topsail for some inexplicable reason, thus allowing the *Eagle* to shoot ahead.

Eagle and *Neptune* had been exchanging broadsides for about thirty minutes when Rodney, from the quarter-deck, observed a French 64 with her quarters painted red, coming in on his disengaged side. This was the *Fougueux* which had already been hammered by some of the leading British ships but which still had some fight left in her. His first reaction was to send down to warn Harrison on the upper deck to divide his guns' crews, as they would soon be busy on the starboard side. Then he hurried to his cabin and passed through to the stern-gallery to see where the *Kent* was. What he saw brought him little comfort. Fox's ship was still lagging astern with her mizen-topsail backed. No support could be expected from her (see Diagram 5).

With an antagonist on each side the *Eagle* was now very heavily engaged indeed. Harrison cheerily encouraged his sweating gun-crews by promising that a British 64 would soon come to their aid; but whenever he could spare a moment to snatch a glance through a gun-port, there was the *Kent* still some way off. Two broadsides the hard-pressed *Eagle* gave the *Fougueux*, receiving the same in return. Then the Frenchman drifted astern, disabled, and a little later Rodney through his stern window saw her strike to the *Hector*.

Eagle and *Neptune* had been fighting each other for more than an hour when a French broadside smashed the *Eagle*'s steering-wheel, killing every man at it. With masts, rigging and sails much cut up, and now no rudder to hold her to the wind, the *Eagle* drifted clear of her antagonist. She drifted down on Hawke's flagship the *Devonshire* which was coming to her assistance. Twice the two ships fell together with a great splintering of woodwork and parting of cordage, and the *Eagle* lost her jib-boom and some gear forward before she got clear. After this, Rodney and his men were too busy repairing damages to pay much attention to what was going on elsewhere.

By the time the *Eagle* was manœuvrable again it was late afternoon. Dusk was falling and the fighting was almost over. A few ships still lay barking at each other in a desultory way but the majority were repairing damages and several of the French battleships were now mastless hulks in possession of their captors. But de l'Etanduère's flagship, the 80-gun *Tonnant*, still flew the flag of France, and now there appeared the almost undamaged *Kent*. From the *Eagle* they watched her approach the *Tonnant*, and Rodney remarked sourly that he hoped she would stick close by her and regain the honour she had lost. Hawke saw her from the *Devonshire* and threw out a signal to engage. The *Nottingham* cheered her into action, and the *Kent* cheered back.

But for the second time that day this ship disappointed expectations. She merely edged up to rake the *Tonnant* at long range and then sheered away to leeward until clear of her fire. 'My God,' cried Captain Saumarez of the *Nottingham*. 'Why does she shoot ahead?' He might well ask. Comment on board the *Eagle* may be imagined.

As darkness fell on that October evening, the *Tonnant* and the *Intrépide*, the only survivors of the French squadron, set what sails they could and stole away. All their consorts had struck, and retreat was the only course left. But the *Eagle* was again a fighting unit and Rodney thirsted for more action. So did Saunders of the *Yarmouth* and Saumarez of the *Nottingham*. Despite their exhausted crews, these three squared away after the two Frenchmen, and until nearly ten o'clock that night the sounds of their gunfire in the darkness told the rest of the squadron that the battle was not yet over. But the only result of their persistence was a sad one. When they returned they brought the melancholy news that the gallant Saumarez had fallen to almost the last shot of the engagement. He had been one of Anson's favourites, with a future as bright as any captain in the Western Squadron.

Next morning Hawke summoned a council of war. The other captains came on board the *Devonshire* bitter and resentful against Fox of the *Kent* and there was an embarrassing scene when they all turned their backs on him. Not one of them would rank with him or sit at the same table with him. They would have nothing to do with him until his character was cleared. So the unhappy man returned to his ship while the others sat down with the Rear Admiral to decide what to do.

By every reasonable argument the most sensible course was to return home. They had six prizes on their hands, the *Monarque* (74), *Terrible* (74), *Neptune* (70), *Trident* (64), *Fougueux* (64), and *Severn* (50).* All had taken a terrible hammering. Four were completely dismasted and the other two were left with a foremast each. The British ships, although in much better shape, were in no state to keep the sea, and it was late in the season. But (and it was a very big but) there was a French convoy of immense size, considerable value, and quite unprotected, not very far beyond the western horizon.

* This ship had been taken by the French on October 16, 1746, almost exactly a year earlier.

The voice of prudence prevailed. But a warning was sent to Commodore Pocock at the Leeward Islands to look out for the convoy, with the result that a month later most of the merchantmen fell into the hands of that most fortunate officer. For the next two days victors and vanquished tossed up and down off Finisterre repairing damages. The *Eagle*'s casualties were sixteen killed and fifty-two wounded. Four of the squadron had suffered more heavily, but most of the others considerably less.* On board the *Kent* only one man was killed. The weather was kind and in due course all the prizes were carried in to Portsmouth.

The *Eagle* came in to Plymouth on October 29th with her masts fished and her rigging full of long-splices.† A week later her guns sounded again as she, and all the ships in the Hamoaze, saluted the body of Captain Philip Saumarez. Active seagoing was over for the year and for a while Rodney was free to enjoy the pleasures of the land and to discover that he now had a reputation as well as a fortune; for the second battle of Finisterre, as it came to be called, had been a notable affair. From Anson came one of that great man's rare letters.[7]

'Admiralty, the 10 November 1747.

'Dear Sir,

'I find you have dropped me as a Corrispondent because I have not been punctual in answering your letters; don't ascribe it to anything but the reall cause, indolence, and an aversion to writing, for nobody can esteem you more than I do, nor has felt a more sensible satisfaction in the share of honour which you have gained in the late action, which has raised the reputation of our fleet to the highest pitch; may the same success attend your attack on shore, which I find was the reason I had not the satisfaction of seeing [you] at Portsmouth where it was intended yr ship should have cleaned.

'I was extreamly flatter'd by the remembrance of the Western Squadron in appointing my Secretary Agent for their prizes. I should be glad of any opportunity of showing them how much I think myself obliged by it as it was done unask'd, and beg you will make my compliments to them upon the occasion, as I can not write to them all by this post; I have just parted with yr freind Keppill who perseveres in yr old scheme and I suppose will

---

* For British casualties, see Appendix 2.
† Makeshift repairs to masts and rigging necessitated by battle damage.

come off no better than usual before he leaves the town; your example may make a sober, discreet man of him.   *I am,*

'*Your obedient, humble servant,*

'*ANSON.*'

Praise from Anson was praise indeed. The reference to an 'attack on shore' is intriguing, and it is to be regretted that Rodney was much too deferential in his reply[8] to respond to the great man's allusion. 'Yr freind Keppill', otherwise Captain the Hon. Augustus Keppel, was already a notable figure in the Navy, and an engaging character. Having sailed on the great voyage he was very much in the Anson circle, along with such bright stars as Charles Saunders and the late Philip Saumarez. Rodney was on the friendliest terms with all three, but his friendship with Keppel, which may have begun when their ships were together in Kinsale in July 1746, was to last forty years and to survive some astonishing political stresses.

During these winter months Rodney was able to turn his attention to his finances and it was time he did so for, as his man of business Mr Francis Magnus put it in the pleasant way bankers have when their clients are doing well, Neptune was filling his coffers fast.[9] The captain's share of the prize-money, two-eighths of the value of all ships and cargoes taken, was the main source of his enrichment, and so fortunate had he been that by the end of 1747 there was more than £10,000 to his credit.* It was a fortune in those days and he laid out most of it in land. Annuities and government stock were all very well and he made substantial purchases of both, but a stake in the country commanded respect and conferred prestige in a way that nothing else did, and for this reason it was, for George Bridges Rodney, the best investment of all. Mr and Mrs Bridges looked after most of the purchasing formalities for him. By November enough money was available for Mr Magnus to pay Mr Bridges £5,000 on Captain Rodney's

---

* Here, when all deductions had been made, are the principal sums Rodney received when a junior captain.[10]

Ship *Providence* and her cargo of coal, retaken by the *Sheerness*, June 1744.	£17 1s 9d
Freight (at one per cent), from Lisbon in the *Ludlow Castle*, July 1745.	£441 16s 6d
The *Ponté Quarré* (privateer), taken June 13, 1746, in company with the *Nottingham* and *Falcon*	£61 14s 6d
Neustra Señora del Carmen taken July 17, 1746	£360 2s 3d
The *Shoreham* (privateer) taken October 6, 1746	£422 4s 0d
The *Bellone* (privateer) taken February 3, 1747	£337 2s 6d
The *Mary Magdalen* (privateer) taken April 11, 1747	£137 18s 6d
The St Domingo prizes taken June 1747	£8,165 1s 1d
'The October fleet', prizes of October 14, 1747	£341 0s 0d

behalf. So it came about that under his old guardian's direction the French and Spanish prizes, the coffee, sugar, and indigo from the Domingo fleet, and the head-money* resulting from the action of October 14, 1747, were transmuted into farms and copy-holdings in Hampshire. They lay round the small hamlet of Old Alresford, five miles from Avington. In exactly five years the penniless captain had become one of the landed gentry; and although influence and luck had certainly helped, he had worked extremely hard to deserve them.

In the easy circumstances he was now enjoying, Rodney could indulge his taste for expensive living. When he fitted out the *Eagle* he bought an expensive carpet for his cabin, a fine mahogany table, and enough crockery to suggest that he entertained fairly lavishly. After the windfall of the Domingo prizes he had his own chaise built for more than £50. He paid £189 9s 0d for a chest of plate and nearly £40 for books which were sent down to him at Plymouth.[11] The golden harvest would soon recommence, but before the *Eagle* sailed again there was one very distasteful business to be settled—the court martial on Captain Fox for his conduct on October 14th. This was held at Portsmouth and lasted, with adjournments, from November 25th to December 20th.

The Navy was sick and tired of sensational courts martial. Mathews's command in the Mediterranean had ended with a whole series of them. Admiral Osborn, opening the proceedings against Fox, probably spoke for the whole service when he said: 'It is my ardent wish that this trial may be the last known in the British Navy.' One by one the officers of the Western Squadron gave their evidence. Captain Rodney's was described by the prisoner as 'very circumstantial', and that of Harrison his First Lieutenant as 'pointed with a good deal of rancour'. Day after day the probing went on. For a moment we may hear Rodney give his evidence in the great cabin of the *Duke*.

Q. 'How far do you think the *Kent* was from the *Neptune* when you began to attack her?'
A. 'Upon my word I can't tell for I minded only the *Neptune* for a little while.'
Q. 'Can you tell where the *Kent* was when you was attacked both sides?'
A. 'I frequently saw her through my stern.'

* This was £5 a head allowed for every man alive on board a captured enemy warship at the beginning of an action, the sum being shared by the captors in the same proportion as with prize-money.

Q. 'How long engaged with the *Neptune* before the next ship attacked you?'
A. 'About half an hour.'
Q. 'Who did the *Neptune* strike to?'
A. 'I don't know—not to me.'

    The prisoner's defence was detailed but unsatisfactory. Fox had backed his mizen-topsail on the advice of the master to avoid fouling the *Eagle*; it had remained backed longer than intended as the crew of the gun under the gangway had unrove the cross-jack brace which was in their way; the Rear-Admiral's signal to engage the *Tonnant* had been misinterpreted to him by his officers. The picture that emerges is that of a weak man misled by untrustworthy subordinates. He was found guilty of misconduct and dismissed his command, not from want of courage the court was careful to point out, but 'from his listening to the persuasions of his first lieutenant and master, and giving way to them'. Keppel, who was a member of the court, said later that Fox was in no way to blame but that he seemed to have been 'in the hands of his first lieutenant and master—two damned bad fellows'.[12] Others less charitable hinted that the wealth from the Domingo prizes had made some people gun-shy. What is certain is that he was no longer the man to command a ship in the Western Squadron.*

    Rodney detested courts martial,[13] and as he also took a poor view of the society in sea-port towns he can not have enjoyed his enforced attendance at Portsmouth. But early in the new year the Western Squadron was at sea again. It had more than justified its existence, and the plan for 1748 was to extend its range to cover the Atlantic routes to Cadiz. In February, the main body was once more on the old beat, while further south a detached squadron under Commodore Cotes of the *Edinburgh* cruised between Cape Cantin and Cape St Vincent. The victories of Anson and Hawke had left the French with little heart for any new enterprise, but from Cadiz came reports of several ships of the line ready for sea, and rumours of a convoy soon to sail. Cotes's station therefore offered the best prospects of action, and the *Eagle* was sent to strengthen it as soon as her new masts were in. By the end of the month Rodney was with the commodore off Cape St Vincent. Cotes's squadron consisted of the *Edinburgh* (70), *Princess Louisa* (60), *Eagle* (60), *Windsor* (60) and *Inverness* (sloop).

* Fox was later placed on the rear-admirals' half-pay list. He died on February 7, 1763.

The Spaniards did not keep them waiting long. In the early morning of March 7th the *Eagle* was scouting ahead of the squadron to the north-west when she sighted a mass of shipping on the horizon and passed back the news. Cotes's ships crowded on all possible sail and another enthusiastic chase began. At 7 o'clock the *Eagle* came up with the first straggler and Rodney learnt that the Cadiz convoy, four days out, was almost within their grasp—almost but not quite, for he also learnt that it was escorted by nine of the line which, if true, altered the picture considerably. The only thing to do was to press on and see. Soon nine large ships were observed to detach themselves from the main body. Before long their lower deck gun-ports could be seen and it was evident that there could be no holocaust among the Spaniards after all.

Rodney, who seems to have been handling the *Eagle* like a reconnaissance frigate, signalled this information back to Cotes and then, on rejoining, hailed the *Princess Louisa* with the useful news that several stragglers to leeward of the escort might be cut off. As a result, four more prizes, three of them valuable register ships, were snapped up before noon. But this was all. The Spanish escort was too strong for a repetition of Hawke's tactics of October 14th, and behind its protective shield the rest of the convoy made off unscathed to the westward. After dark, Cotes detached the *Eagle* and *Windsor* to shadow them and do what they could, but there were no more pickings, although they followed hopefully until Madeira was sighted. Only then did they turn back for the rendezvous at Lisbon. Cotes and the rest of the squadron came in a few days later with the five prizes. It was the last success before the war ended.

Never can Rodney have brought his ship into the Tagus under happier auspices. Lisbon was always a place of pleasant associations. There were plenty of old friends to entertain the squadron, and to dispose of the prizes too, for the agents who remitted Rodney's share—some £5,000—to Mr Magnus in London, were Messrs Medley and Clies. A little later Keppel arrived and the two friends had an exhilarating reunion, if a subsequent reference in one of Keppel's letters means anything. Writing to Anson on April 12th he concluded: '. . . Cotes sailed two days ago with the *Eagle*, *Windsor* and *Louisa*. Rodney is very well and in his usual good spirits.'[14]

Who can doubt it? Neptune's last contribution to his overflowing coffers had been most handsome and the war, which had begun nine years before, was ending in a blaze of glory for the Navy. 'I shall never live to see so well disciplined and compleat a Squadron as we have to the West-ward',[15] wrote Anson at this time. In May came orders to cease hostilities

Chapter 6

The *Rainbow*

(1749–1752)

'. . . you . . . who so well know how to keep good order
and Government amongst us.'
(Whitshed Keene to Commodore Rodney, St John's,
November 22, 1749.)[1]

EUROPE was to have peace for the next eight years. In England the
ships were paid off, the seamen returned thankfully to the
merchant service, and such officers as were entitled went on
half-pay to enjoy, so far as their means allowed, the blessings
of the land. Captain Rodney, late of the *Eagle*, repaired to Bath to restore
his health and to indulge his taste for society. Gossip (admittedly of a
later date) has linked his name with that of the Princess Amelia,[2] one of the
daughters of George II, and if there is any substance in the rumour this
could have been the time when some such affair might have begun. But
Bath, with all its social delights, did not hold him for long. Ambition was
still the spur. The sea-service, which had carried him so far already,
might carry him a great way further, and he very much intended that it
should.

The war had given a new sense of unity and importance to the corps of
sea-officers. There was impatience with the old, rather haphazard system
of the past, a wish to improve their status, and above all a desire to emphasize professional standards and qualifications. All this, and many technical
matters too, was now the deep concern of the great body of weatherbeaten
professionals who came on shore at the end of the war.

One manifestation of this fresh wind blowing through the Navy was the
introduction of an official pattern uniform for officers. The first move had
been in February 1745, when the Board of Admiralty had received an
address drawn up by a committee of captains on this subject. Four years

91

passed during which the Royal opinion, whenever it had been reminded of the matter, had tended perilously towards the military red although most sea-officers, to judge from their portraits, favoured blue. However, the happiest of solutions was eventually reached as the result, if the popular story is true, of His Majesty catching sight of the attractive riding-habit (blue with white facings) worn by the Duchess of Bedford. This providential creation so pleased the royal eye that a decision was reached on the spot; and if Reynolds's early portrait of Keppel is any guide, one would suppose that the uniform coat first put on by Rodney and his fellow captains in 1749 was well received.

Very different, however, was the reception accorded to another proposed reform of this year—a measure 'for amending, explaining and reducing to one Act of Parliament the laws relating to the government of H.M. ships, vessels and forces by sea'. In essentials this was no more than administrative streamlining. But what set the senior ranks of the Navy by the ears was Article 39, which provided for the subjection of sea-officers to naval discipline *at all times*, even if they were on half-pay. This was new.[3]

The corps of sea-officers was extremely aware that employment in their profession could be desirable, or very much the opposite. An officer with interest might expect to enjoy more than his fair share of the good appointments while one without would, more often than not, be given what was disagreeable, unhealthy (the West Indies was notoriously a station to be avoided) and unremunerative. All the more important, therefore, was his right, particularly if he lacked interest, to refuse an appointment he did not care for. Ten years earlier a group of stern individualists had formed 'The Sea Club', their purpose being 'to oppose all illegal innovations, secure justice in all grievances, and maintain their liberties as subjects 'tho' they be officers'. Article 39 violated one of the Club's most cherished principles, and when the news got round, members prepared for battle.

On Sunday February 12, 1749, thirty-one of them met to discuss the matter. Rodney sided with the small minority who saw no harm in the new article. Keppel and Saunders, both of course Anson men, thought the same. But the general voice was against them. No decision was reached except to meet again in three days' time, not at the Club's usual meeting place, Will's Coffee House, but at the King's Arms in Palace Yard, Westminster, a venue sufficiently close to the House of Commons to leave members in no doubt what was in the wind. Here on Wednesday February 15th, the obnoxious article was hotly discussed by forty-two officers. The Anson group still considered it neither harmful nor dangerous; but the majority, while never for one moment denying the government's right to their services while they were on full pay, were adamant on the subject of their freedom while unemployed. The spirit of Vernon, who had plagued the government with his pamphlets and defied the whole Board of Admiralty, pervaded the assembly so that it was resolved to pursue the matter further, take counsel's opinion, and hear him at 9 o'clock on the following Friday.

During the next two days both sides whipped up all the support they could, so that when the Club met on Friday morning seventy-nine officers were present. The dissidents had persuaded the venerable Admiral of the Fleet Sir John Norris to lend the great weight of his unique authority and prestige to their cause. Ranged with him were two of Rodney's former captains, Holburne and Robinson, and others whose names will appear later in these pages. Some no doubt sincerely believed that they were making a stand against official tyranny. But it is possible that there were others who, whatever they may have felt about liberty, were equally if not more interested in making trouble for the government. For it was a politically-minded age.

On the other side were those supporting the whole Bill, 'ministerial lackeys' as their opponents might call them (and probably did), who had nothing to fear if they lost their liberty because they had friends in high places. Their number included Keppel, Saunders, Piercy Brett, Peter Dennis, all Anson men, and Rodney himself. In the heat generated by the controversy, the point that discipline and efficiency would be greatly improved by the new article was less important to its opponents than the fact that an active officer would henceforth have to go where he was sent, and no longer be able to disregard Admiralty direction if he felt like it. The Anson group thought differently. The learned counsel was heard and then a vote was taken, whether or not to petition against the Bill. Fifty officers wished to do so and twenty-nine, including Rodney, did not. The dissidents left the King's Arms in triumph and no doubt due notice was taken in the Palace of Westminster across the way. So matters stood over the weekend.

On Tuesday the 21st a deputation, led by Captain the Hon. Augustus Hervey, attended the Board of Admiralty. High words passed, and the deputation came away with their ears stinging. But all the same they had won their victory for the government had decided to retreat. By Thursday, the 23rd, after a second deputation led by the more diplomatic Captain Geary had attended the Board, it was known that the obnoxious article would be withdrawn. Tempers subsided and before nightfall ninety-seven officers, including many who, like Sir Edward Hawke and the Hon. John Byng, had sat firmly on the fence, had subscribed their names to a grateful effusion thanking their Lordships 'for the honour done us by communicating the intended alteration in the proposed Articles'.[4] From this, the names of the leading dissidents were conspicuously absent.

On Friday the 24th, the last, ironic scene took place when the aged Sir John Norris, supported by four admirals and fifty-two captains, delivered the petition, already out of date, to the House, and received all the necessary assurances. The stir over this Bill foreshadows the baleful intrusion of politics into naval affairs which was to do such harm in Rodney's later years. Why he supported the government is fairly clear. It was his nature to side with lawfully constituted authority, and discipline was important; also Anson was his patron while the rest of the group were his intimate friends. But there were some hard feelings at the time. Edward Boscawen, another rising star in the Navy, never forgave him for the part he played, although the exact cause of his resentment is obscure. But any breach there may have been with Holburne or Hervey was quickly healed and the government was not ungrateful. Keppel had already been chosen for a command in the Mediterranean and sailed a few weeks later. As for Rodney, it can hardly be coincidence that only eight days after the petition to the House he received his Commission to command the 50-gun *Rainbow*, an appointment carrying with it the government of Newfoundland; and if tongues wagged and some malicious things were said, no fair-minded person could deny that a young and active captain, with a brilliant record and previous experience on the station, was as good a choice as any and better than most.

His appointment as Governor of Newfoundland was as good as settled when his Commission for the *Rainbow* was signed on March 3rd, but as that government was a Crown appointment, and lay particularly within the province of the Commissioners for Trade and Plantations, much interdepartmental red tape had to be observed before it was confirmed. Thus on April 7th the Board of Admiralty (Lords Sandwich, Anson and Duncannon) resolved that a letter be written to the Secretary of State (the Duke of Bedford), 'to desire that he will obtain His Majesty's Commission for Captain Rodney to be Governor of Newfoundland'.[5] His Grace, whose acquaintance with Rodney has already been noted, wrote to the Commissioners for Trade and Plantations on the 10th, indicating His Majesty's pleasure. The Commissioners (whose number included the Earl of

Halifax, Mr John Pitt and Mr Grenville) received the Duke's letter two days later and ordered a draft of the Commission to be prepared. On the 14th they approved it and by the 20th it had been transcribed and signed. So the cumbersome wheels of government revolved, and the reader will note how many illustrious persons must by this time have become aware of Captain Rodney's existence. The formalities were not complete until the Commission and the Board's instructions had been approved by an Order in Council on May 2nd, by which time of course the *Rainbow* was almost ready for sea. For Rodney, true to his nature, had been down to his new ship at the earliest possible moment, to hurry things along and make sure of getting what he wanted done to her.

She was very like the *Romney* of his first visit to Newfoundland, and like several of his previous commands, stupidly deficient in accommodation. She had another more serious shortcoming too, and after a word with his predecessor Rodney wrote to the Admiralty.

'Woolwich, 17 March 1748/49.

'H.M.S. *Rainbow* under my command, being in the dock and Captain Baird her late commander having informed me that the ship was very leewardly, he had intended to have apply'd to their Lordships in order to remedy it had not the ship been paid off; and consulting since with Mr. Allen, the Surveyor, he is of opinion that if an addition of 6 or 8 inches be added to the false keel to angle to nothing at the Gripe, it would make her hold a better wind and likewise forereach; if their Lordships approve of this addition Mr. Allen assures me it can be done in proper time so that the ship can come out of dock this Spring.

'As a few additions to the inside of the ship are necessary, and what I shall request being very little expense to the Government, I hope their Lordships will indulge me with them, Viz: A steerage before the Great Cabbin at the bulkhead of which a small office for my clerk to keep my books and accounts in; a cabbin on the quarter-deck for the officers, the Taffrail being of a sufficient height to admit it; and a slight awning to the mizen-mast as the voyage to Newfoundland will require the peoples being sheltered from the Fogs and bad weather incident to those parts.'

He found the Lords much more sympathetic to such requests than in the past. Everything he asked for was approved—if time permitted. His surgeon and purser were old followers from the *Eagle*. A suitably qualified schoolmaster was found for the young gentlemen among whom was the captain's godson, Richard Rodney Bligh, aged twelve. There followed the routine he had first known in the *Romney*. They dropped down to Long Reach for their guns. Then, with the *Mercury* (20), Captain F. W. Drake, they proceeded to Spithead at the end of May, and thence to Plymouth. The *Mercury* called at Poole, Weymouth, Topsham and Dartmouth to enquire for any trade bound for Newfoundland, and Rodney wrote the usual letter to the mayors of the ports further west in the same sense.

Although the *Rainbow* was smaller than the *Eagle*, being indeed not much more than an improved version of the *Ludlow Castle*, the status of her captain was much more eminent. With three of His Majesty's ships under his command—*Rainbow*, *Mercury* and *Saltash* (sloop), the last already on the station—he was allowed to wear a broad pennant and assume the rank of commodore. As Governor of Newfoundland he was entitled (although not perhaps very often) to the honorific 'Excellency'. Lastly, and this probably the most gratifying of all, he was, by virtue of his appointment, in confidential relations with the ministers. For the Newfoundland command was now much more complicated and important than in Medley's time. The French in North America had never been easy neighbours, and now they were pushing forward into regions where they had no business to be. Just before the *Rainbow* sailed from Plymouth, Rodney was honoured with a private communication from the First Lord.[6]

'Admiralty, June 7 1749.

'*Dear Sir*,

'By the last accounts we have received from Governor Cornwallis, we learn that the French have possessed themselves by force of all that part of Nova Scotia that lies on the other side of the Bay of Fundi, and have burnt Beaubassin to ashes, and carried away the inhabitants with their goods and effects. M. le Corne, a French officer from Canada is at the head of a body of 2,500 men, French and Indians, and publickly avows his design to maintain himself where he now is settled. Proper representations have been made to the Court of France upon this extraordinary proceeding; but as it seems possible some time may be taken up in discussion between the two Courts before the final instructions are given in this affair, and that M. le Corne may still continue his outrages, to the great detriment of the new settlement, I think it necessary to inform you that if Governor Cornwallis should have occasion to apply to you for succour, and send to you for that purpose to Newfoundland, it would be approved by Government if you should comply with his request. It is judged improper as yet to send any publick order upon a business of so delicate a nature, which is the reason of my writing to you in this manner, and I am satisfied that your prudence is such as will not suffer you to make any injudicious use of the information you now receive. There are some people that can not be trusted with any but publick orders; but I have too good an opinion of you to rank you among them, and shall think this important affair entirely safe under your management and secrecy.

'*I am, with great truth,*
'*Yours etc., etc.*

'To Commodore Rodney   *SANDWICH.*'

Ministers do not often write in such flattering terms to comparatively junior officers, but in his expressions of regard Lord Sandwich was probably sincere. He was a shrewd judge of men, keenly interested in his department, and for many years was to look after Rodney's interests in a way that the latter sometimes took too much for granted. So the *Rainbow* took her departure from Plymouth on July 1st and had the usual tedious passage across the Atlantic. There were gales and headwinds until they approached the Banks. Then the wind fell, the fog closed in, and for the last week they groped westward sounding continuously, while the crew shivered and cursed, until hooks and lines were issued and they all fell to fishing* while Commodore Rodney, it is more than likely, shivered too and thought enviously of Keppel in the Mediterranean. After more than a month at sea, Cape St Francis was sighted and on August 4th the *Rainbow* warped into St John's harbour to the sound of a 15-gun salute in honour of the new Governor.

Rodney found the merchants of St John's a prosperous community, but all had a depressing tale to tell of conditions on the island. It was not only the intolerable concession which allowed French fishermen the best beaches for their salting and drying, and which had always been a sore point. A new and disquieting problem was the increasing number of Irish papists, disaffected spirits who refused to abjure either the Pope or the Pretender and who bore no love for England. With the French so close, and Louisbourg on Cape Breton Island so strong, this element might one day be a very real danger. But apart from the resident magistrate, Whitshed Keene, in whom he found a kindred spirit, it is unlikely that Rodney cared much for the society he found at St John's. Its prosperity did not come

---

* This seems the only possible explanation for an entry in the Master's Journal on July 28th: 'Served hook and lines to ship's company.'

only from the fish trade. Much of the building material for Louisbourg as well as the victuals for its garrison, was supplied by these same protesting patriots at a substantial profit. Nor did they fail to take advantage of the fact that there was no custom's house at St John's.

But little as he may have liked the local inhabitants, he liked the American merchants from Boston who traded with them even less. He did his best to be civil and to entertain them, but when he found himself compelled to listen to republican sentiments, brazenly avowed at his own table, he gave up. Behaviour that was merely ill-bred he might have endured, but not open sedition. Eventually he declined to have any social intercourse whatever with these Bostonians. Twenty-five years later the memory of them still rankled.*

However, if he had to close his eyes to some things and turn his back on others, his own job was a different matter. The fishing was much as it had been on his last visit eleven years before. In the spring the sack-ships arrived from London, Bristol, and elsewhere, loaded with goods for barter, and crowded with temporary labour for the season. All the summer the larger ships worked the banks as much as 200 miles from the coast, while the by-boats and shore fishers launched from the beaches. As the season wore on, salting down and stowing, barter and exchange, turned every beach and settlement into a roaring camp where the fishermen admirals exercised a sort of rough justice, backed by the authority of the naval governor. Then, by the beginning of October, the ships sailed for the markets of northern Europe and the Mediterranean, the naval governor took his departure, and the island settled down once more to the long winter under one of the resident magistrates.

The rich abundance of cod made Newfoundland a source of wealth, but the home government valued it no less as a nursery for seamen, and was determined to keep it so. To this end settlement was discouraged, but every ship bringing men from England for the fishing had to include one fresh man in every five, and bring the same number home. A jealous interest was maintained over every detail of the island's population and productivity, of which the naval governor was expected each season to render an elaborate statistical report. As he was there only from the end of July to the beginning of October, he had plenty to do.

* Writing to Lord George Germain in 1775 he said: 'The Boston merchants who traded at Newfoundland when I had the honour of being Governor of that Island in the years 49, 50, and 51, had the insolence at my table to avow such principles, which gave me such disgust that I never after permitted them to have the least connection with me further than as my duty as Governor Obliged me.' P.R.O. 30/20/26.

From the many complaints he received, Rodney judged that the more remote settlements had been much neglected by his predecessors and supposed this to be because even the smallest naval vessels were always too large to approach them. When he also heard something of the illegal practices that had grown up in consequence he hired two small vessels, put a lieutenant and sufficient men in each, and sent them off to assist the *Mercury* and the *Saltash*. The Newfoundlanders were impressed. Among the illegal practices condoned, if not introduced, by some of his predecessors had been the granting of scandalously oppressive monopolies. One individual enjoyed the sole right of drawing bait on a certain beach, a concession which threatened ruin to all his neighbours. Commodore Rodney had a short way with abuses like this.

On October 6th, after the usual two months, the *Rainbow* sailed for Lisbon. Snow and sleet were falling as she got under way, a great swell was running outside the harbour, and within a few hours she was scudding before a full gale under foresail only. Gone were the dignity and consequence that had sustained her in St John's harbour. Great seas swept the long-boat overboard and much deck gear. As she lurched and staggered, her seams began to open. All the way across the Atlantic the pumps clanked continuously.

Lisbon no doubt made amends. After the fogs and cold, the provincial society and the seditious talk, Rodney was once more among old friends and in the warmth that he loved. Lisbon too might have some freight for him. All that Newfoundland offered in this way was an opportunity to participate in the fish trade, and he had already taken a half share in a cargo of salt cod, although there is no record that he made any profit on it.* But freight from Lisbon was different. It was one of the sweets of office that the Naval Governor of Newfoundland expected. Nor was he disappointed. The *Rainbow* lay in the Tagus for a month being recaulked, and when at last she sailed for England, Rodney had enough freight from the merchants to bring him a commission of £570 17s 6d.

They made a quick passage home and dropped anchor in Long Reach on December 21st. The usual orders came down for the ship to go up to Woolwich and clear for the dock, with the usual admonition to her captain 'to give constant attendance at the ship'. But Commodore Rodney had other ideas and applied for leave to come to town. What he was busy about may be deduced from the letter with which he startled the Lords a few days later.[7]

---

* He paid £591 for his half share which was shipped in the *Two Friends*, Dan Lander, master.

'London, 18 January 1749/50.

'*Sir*,

'Whereas I have a prospect of getting a seat in Parliament, which is inconsistent with the Government of Newfoundland, I therefore hope their Lordships will represent this to His Majesty that he may be graciously pleased to grant me leave to resign the said Government. . . .'

Evidently some patron had offered him a seat, and there is no mystery who that patron was. The Duke of Bedford, the same whom Rodney had thanked for giving him command of the *Eagle*, was not satisfied with his position in the government and on the point of resigning. He had his own following in the House of Commons, the larger that following was the more influence he could exert, and it was now his hope to make sure of the borough of Lauceston in the west country with Commodore Rodney as his candidate. For such a prize the latter was willing even to resign his Newfoundland government.

A seat in Parliament was the goal of every ambitious officer. A member had opportunities of obliging his friends, opportunities of showing himself worthy of ministerial favour, and of course far better opportunities of employment in his own profession. He stood on an assured footing where wealth, elegance, influence and authority intermingled at the centre of the nation's life. To a man of Rodney's urbane and, it must be admitted, not unworldly nature, a seat in Parliament offered the key to nearly all that made life worth living. However, although he did resign his government to Captain Drake of the *Mercury*, he never stood as the Bedford candidate for Lauceston.

It is not suggested that the ministers were seriously alarmed by the fear that the Bedford group might gain so valuable a recruit as Commodore Rodney. But it does seem that this possibility stimulated them to take him more seriously as a candidate for a government seat as soon as one could be found. For besides the boroughs cultivated and dominated by local magnates there were others where the authority of the Treasury or the Admiralty carried all before it, and for which a distinguished and dependable serving officer was particularly suitable. That they now had him seriously in mind is shown in the conclusion of a letter from Anson which sped him on his way before he sailed again for Newfoundland. 'I heartily wish you health and all kinds of prosperity in your voyage; if any vacancy in Parliament happens in your absence I will not fail to remind your friends of you.'[8] Nevertheless, Rodney did not abandon his intention to visit Lauceston and see the Duke's agent if he could, before he made his final departure.[9]

So, with encouraging words ringing in his ears, he prepared for a second season in Newfoundland. For there was no question of resigning his command of the *Rainbow*. Drake might hold the titular rank of governor, and did, but Rodney would continue to command on the station. A little before he sailed for this second season a letter arrived from Keppel which deserves to be quoted for the light it sheds on their friendship.[10]

'Gibraltar, *Centurion*, Dec. 22 1749.

'*My Dear George*,

'I am much Obliged to you for the fish you sent me. I flattered myself with the hopes of either seeing or hearing from you, but since that has not been my fortune I must return you my thanks for your tenderness in regard to my station; you have Always shown your Inclination to a friendship with me and the Older I grow the more I find it. I hope you'l never find it otherwise in me: indeed I may say as yet it has been but a very poor thing the troubles of the country has kept me from making the Advantages I might otherwise have made; Proby tells me you got me chose for young Whites. I thank you for it but I am a very unworthy member as I don't play for sixpence: win, if I could afford, I don't believe I should; pray have Mercy upon Charles Saunders this year and don't let them get the Income of his Estate from him.

'The Captains of this select Squadron has beg'd me to send for a H.Hd. apiece of Claret. I fear it will be giving you a cursed deal of trouble. If you find it so only remember we can not drink the damn'd stuff that is sent to the Garrison for Claret. I shall by but a H.Hd. for myself as I am still strong in wine if they don't spoil before I drink them. I have been very ill of a Clap and after that a Violent Ague and fever, so that I am as yet a Milksop but I am very well again.

> '*My Compliments to all friends and believe me*
> *dear George what you will allways find most*
> *sincerely yours,*

'*A. KEPPEL.*'

The *Rainbow*'s first duty in 1750, after refitting, was to join the squadron escorting His Majesty to Holland. Immediately afterwards she proceeded down channel *en route* for Newfoundland. The second season was very like the first except that Governor Cornwallis, uneasy about his French neighbours, invoked Rodney's assistance to hurry two companies to Halifax.[11] On the Banks the fishing was good. On shore Rodney busied himself with the building of a hospital, and the clearing of ten acres of land to grow garden produce for the ship's company, and provide pasture for the cattle belonging to the men-of-war. The work kept his sailors out of the town, and he wondered that none of his predecessors had thought of it.[12] At the end of the season the *Rainbow* was ordered to Cadiz where she arrived on October 23rd. Here Rodney found the punctilious Spaniards seething with indignation at the recent behaviour of some visiting British warships whose captains, for some reason best known to themselves (perhaps an untimely sense of humour) had made a point of returning all salutes in the harbour, even those meant for the governor. This had made a deplorable impression. The local inhabitants had been deafened and the authorities made to look ridiculous. Rodney, who detested uncouth behaviour, hastened to smooth the Spaniards down. Later, reporting the matter to Anson, he commented stiffly: '... the dislike the Spaniards have generally expressed to English officers has proceeded from these sort of things. For my part I perceive nothing but the greatest civility ... and if other gentlemen have met with different usage I can not help thinking it has proceeded from their not appearing in a proper character.'[13]

Luckily, before he sailed for England he was able to do his hosts a service. Some Cadiz merchants approached him with a request that he would escort two valuable register-ships for the first stage of their voyage. This was down the pirate-infested coast of Morocco, and as the ships and their cargoes belonged partly to British subjects, Rodney readily agreed. So the little convoy plodded south-west for a fortnight until the sharp peak of Tenerife broke the southern horizon. It was as far south as his sea-going had yet taken him. This duty done the *Rainbow* turned back for Cadiz where she lay for another fortnight before sailing for home. On December 29, 1750, she dropped anchor in Plymouth Sound and a few days later was once more at Woolwich clearing for the dock.

There was as yet no news of a seat in Parliament, but some interesting developments were taking place in Rodney's private life. He was building himself a house on the land he had bought at Old Alresford; and other matters of an even more personal matter were occupying his attention too.

A start had been made on the house before his first season at Newfoundland. Mrs Bridges looked after the business side of it in his absence, and during 1750 and 1751 she paid the builder and sub-contractors over £1,000 of Rodney's money.[14] Costs were still moderate then and he could afford to do himself handsomely, with a third storey to the main block and several expensive chimney-pieces at £100 each by Mr John Cheere. It still stands, close by Old Alresford church, a substantial Georgian mansion, typical of its period, severe in outward appearance but lacking nothing in solid dignity. Cheere's marble chimney-pieces and nearly all the original content have long disappeared, but in the centre of the library ceiling may still be seen, impressively moulded in the plaster, an eagle discharging thunderbolts in all directions. So Rodney preserved the memory of his old ship and her fine gunnery. Friends who knew what was going on at Old Alresford may well have wondered how much longer he would remain a bachelor. There is not much to indicate that he had any particular attachments at this time; but attachments there certainly were.

Readers will not have forgotten the agreeable Compton family who received young Rodney into their Lisbon home when the *Dreadnaught* was lying in the Tagus. They had returned to London in the autumn of 1745 and were now established in Grosvenor Street. Mr Compton had a small post in the government, the two boys, Charles and Spenser, were at school, but Jenny, Kitty, and Bet were all living at home and of marriageable age though not yet married. The attraction of such a household for a bachelor sailor is easily understood and one may suppose that whenever the *Rainbow* was at Woolwich or Deptford her captain came up pretty frequently.

At first he was attracted by the beautiful and lively Kitty. But before long he was equally smitten by the quieter and more serious Jenny. Both young ladies adored him—others had observed this if Rodney had not—but which to choose was the problem. Kitty had the good looks. She was a beauty while Jenny was almost plain. But Jenny had greater depth of character, and he was becoming increasingly aware of this, while for all Kitty's radiant loveliness—was there anything more to her than a pretty face? He could not be sure.

The weeks were speeding by. Soon he would have to sail again for Newfoundland and when he returned his new house would be ready. He could not leave England without reaching a decision. In his perplexity he wrote to his aunt, Lady Aubrey Beauclerck, widow of his late captain in the *Dolphin*, who occupied a very special place in his affections, and who knew the Compton girls well. To Lady Aubrey then, the Governor of Newfoundland poured out his heart and asked what he should do. Then he turned his full attention to the final stages of preparing the *Rainbow* for sea.

The 1751 season, Rodney's last on the station, was the longest, the busiest, and the most exhausting of all. In April, when he was worrying himself ill over Kitty and Jenny, and at the same time battling with the Navy Office to obtain fresh meat and greens for his men, he learnt that he was to be entrusted with two new scientific inventions, for trials at sea. They were a highly sensitive compass designed by the ingenious Dr Knight of the Royal Society, and his new 'magnetical bars' for magnetizing it. Before he sailed the Lords wished him to wait on the doctor and acquaint himself with their principles. They also wished him to search, on his way across the Atlantic, for a mysterious island which the master of a merchant ship supposed himself to have sighted two years before. It was most unlikely that any such island really existed, but the man had been examined by Trinity House and sworn to a length of six or seven leagues, with waves breaking over the rocks, and a bluff like Dunnose, and trees visible too, and been altogether so detailed that the matter had to be settled.[15]

Before he sailed there was yet one more infliction—a visit from the whole Board of Admiralty. Periodic inspections of ships and dockyards was another of the reforms introduced by Lord Sandwich and Lord Anson. One may picture the *Rainbow* on that 12th of May when they all came on board. She was just out of dock, her topsides newly paid with tar and red ochre, and as one of the few battleships in full commission something of a showpiece. The appropriate salute of 17 guns thundered over the waters of Long Reach as Commodore Rodney received his illustrious visitors, Lord Sandwich, Lord Anson, Lord Barrington and the rest. Two days later Anson brought down the Secretary of State, Lord Holdernesse, and two days after this, on the 16th, the Duke of Kingston and the Earls of Waldegrave and Ashburnham came on board. Rodney's star was in the ascendant and to crown all, in the middle of this junketing came the news, not unexpected, that he had been returned to Parliament in the Saltash by-election.

Saltash in Cornwall was the safest of Admiralty seats, held for years by the veteran Secretary to the Admiralty, Thomas Corbett. Many flag-officers and captains would have been glad to step into Corbett's shoes, but on his death the nomination went to Rodney. He cannot possibly have attended the poll for it took place during that busy week when so many notables visited the *Rainbow*, but such a seat is unlikely to have been contested. The commodore's good fortune and his parliamentary future, as well as Dr Knight's compass and the prospect of adding a new island to the British Empire, would have been obvious subjects for discussion and congratulation as he entertained his distinguished visitors. But the problem of Jenny or Kitty had not yet been settled for Lady Aubrey had not yet answered his letter.

At Spithead a week later private affairs again took charge. Letters there were with family news in plenty. First, Lady Aubrey who was most sympathetic.[16] 'I am sensible of your situation,' she wrote, 'know it, feel it. . . .' But she was much too wise to tell her nephew in so many words whom she thought he ought to marry. However, she knew a good deal more than she was prepared to admit openly and she dropped a hint. 'If you like both better than all the World beside,' she went on, 'I'm of opinion both return the Compliment. Both likes but one Loves. The Elder sees it, I'm persuaded knows, for her poor innocent, artless heart can not desguise it. I love them both but whichever loves you best, may She be best beloved when Fortune favours. . . .' Lady Aubrey's style is a little confusing but Jenny was the elder, and Rodney would have been blind indeed not to have perceived his aunt's drift. Always the man of action he replied at once, to tell her that as soon as he returned to England he would make Jenny, and Jenny only, the object of his serious intentions; and four years later, when happily married, he was able to write: 'Thank God that enabled me to see the difference, and to prefer Merit and every amiable Virtue, to Beauty. . . .'

But there was sad news from Avington. On May 16th, the day Rodney entertained his last party in Long Reach, his old guardian fell into the river near his home and was drowned. The circumstances were pathetic. The old gentleman, who was seventy-two and partly paralysed, was trying to pull a favourite dog out of the water and slipped. George Bridges is a shadowy figure in Rodney's life, scarcely less so than his father, but the evidence of his will points to a considerable measure of intimacy and regard. The real estate, with the great house at Avington, reverted to the head of the Bridges family, the Duke of Chandos, but all leasehold and copyhold estates in the parish of Old Alresford, after being held in trust until the death of Mrs Bridges, went to Rodney; and the old man further directed that the rest and residue of his personal estate, after the death of his wife, was 'to be Paid to my Godson George Bridges Rodney for his use and benefit'.[17] The *Rainbow* did not sail from Spithead until June 7th so there would have been time for Rodney to make a flying visit to his old home.

At Plymouth, where the *Rainbow* made her usual call, there was another letter from Lady Aubrey.[18]

'Milford June ye 15. [1751]

'*Dearest Sir,*

'I'm truly sorry I could not have the pleasure of seeing you at Milford. My servants saw you pass the Needles. I should have had no pleasure had I seen the ship and supposed it yours. Your brother made me a visit the next day, staid till Monday from whence he returned to Avington. . . . He says you complain of your Stomach and frequently take Vomits. Let me entreat you to be cautious. . . .'

After a request for some seashells, should the mysterious Atlantic island be found, there follows a surprising disclosure.

'You are very good to wish me to leave Milford, but being allways used to a home tis too late in life to be without one. Tis true you offer me yours in the most friendly manner but believe me my Dear Sir, twill be better to meet sometimes than to live constantly together. Two familys never do quite well together for a continuance, and tho I love and relish my Friends conversation, a natural fondness for retirement makes it sometimes necessary for my happyness. Your kindness is most estimable and [I] hope we shall meet and be happy often at Alresford, Milford, and London. Tho mine is only a cottage, if you can bear it I shall be allways sincerely glad I see you, so you leave your Dogs at home for I dread those Gentry for fear of my Catts.

'But all this while I say nothing of the chief Article in your former letter, and your important intention on your return. The Blow I fear will be a bitter one, therefore lett me conjure you to suffer only one of them to hope . . . that by the entire removal of all expectations from the other, time and absence may recover her spirits and fix her (if possible at least encline her) somewhere else before your return. Unless you do this I shan't have the least courage to come to Town . . . because I imagine from my own observation a scene I could not support. . . .'

All this, with much more in the same strain, the kind lady directed (under seal) to Jenny herself, to be forwarded. The young lady's covering note is a model of demure propriety:[19]

'London, june ye 17th.

'*Sir,*

'Just before I sat down to dinner today I was favoured with a letter from Lady Aubrey. She gives me a strict charge not to miss a post but send you the enclosed, for that you are to sail very soon. I should not trouble you with this but that she writes me that you desired your Compliments to us and we had no other way of returning ours, as likewise of telling you that my Sisters join (in wishing you a good voyage and safe return) with your most

'*Humble Servant*,
'*J. C.*

'To George Bridges Rodney Esq, Commanding His Majesty's ship the *Rainbow* at Plymouth.'

Thus fortified in resolution, Rodney sailed from Plymouth on June 22, 1751, to rule the Newfoundland fishermen for the last time.

At sea the magnetic bars were a great success. They not only retained their magnetism but they charmed all the *Rainbow*'s compasses (which usually differed considerably) into exact agreement which was just as well, for Doctor Knight's own compass proved impossibly lively in anything but a flat calm. 'Impossible to steer by' was Rodney's verdict. As for the mysterious island, the *Rainbow* and her consort spread to a distance of six miles and made a succession of long zig-zags to north-west and south-west for several days, but all they found was a little drift-wood, and no bottom at 200 fathoms. Then came the usual fog as they approached the Banks, and before they dropped anchor in Aqua Fortis harbour a topman fell from the yard and was drowned. The voyage had taken much longer than usual.

As in the previous season there was the same arrangement between Rodney and Captain Drake. In later years Rodney used to say that he had been for three years Governor of Newfoundland, and no doubt in essentials he was; but Drake was officially the Governor in 1751, as he had been in 1750. However, the work went on just the same. The hired craft cruised where larger ships could not, the usual 'Scheme of the Fisheries' was sent in by Rodney, and this year the *Rainbow* herself, instead of lying all the time in St John's, cruised for a fortnight along the northern settlements. Then, on September 20th, earlier than usual, she sailed for Lisbon.

Rodney's three years' government (*de jure* and *de facto*) was over. On the records that exist it is hard to judge how he compares with the other capable and conscientious men who served on this dull and unrewarding station. The naval governors were sometimes criticized by the regular officials and officers of the island for their ignorance and gullibility, and a certain Captain Griffiths Williams of the Artillery, who was stationed there for fourteen years and presumably knew what he was talking about, was particularly scathing. But this cantankerous soldier, who saw so many naval governors come and go, commends Rodney (he mentions no one else) for his suppression of abuses. That Rodney was more active, better informed and less easily imposed on than many of the naval governors is something one readily accepts.

The remainder of his time in the *Rainbow* was a weariness to the flesh and a vexation to the spirit. An old sailor would have said there was a Jonah on board. The ship leaked badly on passage, and as soon as she finished re-caulking at Lisbon contrary winds held her up for a month before she could sail for Cadiz. On her return to Lisbon, contrary winds kept her beating to and fro for a week (from January 5th to 12th), before she could enter the river; the crew were jaded and sickly and small-pox appeared.

Still there were no welcome orders for home. An ugly squabble had broken out between the gentlemen of the British factory at Lisbon and the Portuguese government, over the export of specie. There had been incidents. The situation was explosive and to complicate matters the British consul had just died. The British community entreated Rodney to delay his departure, and there was a letter from the Secretary of State[20] directing him to do so until a special envoy arrived from England. So, for the rest of January and all February, they lay in the Tagus with all the ingredients for a serious international quarrel simmering round them. Then Lord Tyrawly arrived, and at last the *Rainbow* with her tired captain and her sickly crew was free to go home. They reached Spithead on March 18, 1752, but even here misfortune continued, for a hard gale compelled them to strike yards and topmasts and blew so strongly that it was impossible to weigh anchor. Rodney was now so exhausted that he could not carry on. After eight days with the gale howling round them and no sign of a lull he could endure it no longer and wrote to the Admiralty.

'Portsmouth, 26 March 1752.

'I am sorry my ill-health forces me to be so troublesome to their Lordships as to request the favour of them to suffer the *Rainbow* to be carried round by the First Lieutenant. I was in hopes to have been able (if the weather had permitted), to have proceeded agreeable to their Orders, but finding myself much worse, being confined to my bed and attended by a Physician, obliges me to acquaint their Lordships therewith.'

This was to be a regular feature of his seagoing for the rest of his life. Prolonged exertion was nearly always followed by a breakdown in health and near collapse. The Lords were sorry for his indisposition and agreed to his request. So ended Rodney's connection with the *Rainbow* and Newfoundland, apart from the remaining paper work which was considerable, and which he conducted from his lodgings in Conduit Street. When he came on shore he was a very sick man. The human frame could not continue at full stretch indefinitely, Nature had given her warning, and he was now thirty-four. The time had come to relax and allow, for a while at any rate, those urgent impulses which drove him to die down. His fine new house was ready. Only a wife was lacking.

Chapter 7

Jenny

(1752–1757)

'My dearest Jenny perceives that I can not pass
a post without letting her hear from me.'
(Captain Rodney to Mrs Rodney, February 18, 1755.)

FOR the next ten months Rodney was unemployed, but not inactive. There was his property in Hampshire, there were his Parliamentary duties, and there were his visits to the Hot Springs at Bristol and to Bath where, as one observer noted in August 1752, his stay coincided with that of the Princess Amelia.[1] But if there ever had been anything between the handsome Captain Rodney and the somewhat flighty daughter of King George II, this was probably the end of it. For his great preoccupation was with the Compton household.

It is hard to suppose that his courting met with much opposition. To Mr Compton he was the boy they had first known in the old days at Lisbon, now a distinguished officer and a fellow Member of Parliament. To the ladies in Grosvenor Street he was the dashing sailor, sociable, able to sing a good song, and never backward (if reports are true) when there was a girl to be kissed. Small wonder if they were all swept off their feet. But Jenny's heart was his from the first. Before the end of 1752 everything was settled. The old gentleman gave his blessing; the lawyers drew up the settlement; and on January 31, 1753, in the Oxford Chapel in Vere Street in the parish of St Marylebone, he and Jenny became man and wife.[2]

But for all his domestic bliss, Rodney had no wish to give up the Navy. Prolonged seagoing was not to be thought of, but a guard-ship, preferably at Portsmouth, was a different matter. Such commands were keenly sought, but with Anson at the Admiralty no application from Captain Rodney was likely to go unheeded. On January 16, 1753, he received his Commission to command the 60-gun *Kent* at Portsmouth,[3] the same ship that had played such a dubious part in the action off Finisterre. His twelve months in her are notable for nothing whatever except the long and frequent periods of leave he enjoyed.

For already his roots were down at Old Alresford. Here he and Jenny set up house soon after they were married, and here they were to live for most of their short married life. There was society of a sort. Winchester was seven miles away and just down the road lived the Rev. Doctor Hoadley, one of the bishop's sons, in a new rectory nearly as big as the Rodneys' house. Old Mrs Bridges, increasingly cantankerous, still reigned at Avington five miles away; James Rodney and his wife lived at nearby Hambledon when they were not at Avington; and Rodney's sister with her not very satisfactory husband were at Alton.

In the country, living was cheap but the company perhaps a little dull. In London, whither the Rodneys repaired for the meeting of Parliament, it was very much the other way round. At Grosvenor Street there was of course Mr Charles Compton and the rest of the family. The old gentleman was most assiduous in his attendance at the House. Two formidable, unmarried sisters of Mr Charles, the Ladies Penelope and Margaret Compton, lived close by in Bruton Street: their relations with the Rodneys seem to have been distinctly cool. Intimate friends included Lord George Sackville and Lady Betty Germain, and from the naval side the Keppels, Edgcumbes and Byrons, Charles Saunders and Augustus Hervey. To Rodney, so well fitted to enjoy the civilized amenities of his time, the release from the servitude of the sea must have afforded immense satisfaction, and whatever pleased her dearest Captain Rodney was also agreeable to his adoring wife—always excepting his addiction to late nights over the card table. Before a year had gone by, Jenny's first child was born—George, later the second Lord Rodney—on Christmas Day, 1753,[4] and Rodney began to discover, if he had not known it already, how much he adored children. Mr Charles Compton, no less delighted, contributed ten guineas to his grandson's christening a few weeks later.[5]

The year 1754 followed much the same pattern at London and Alresford, with occasional spells of duty at Portsmouth. But now Fortune who had smiled for so long had two disappointments for him. In January the *Kent* was required for the East Indies and after turning over to her new captain there was no other guard-ship available—only the promise of one. Much worse than this, in April Parliament was dissolved and Rodney was mortified to learn that there would be no seat for him in the new election. It does not seem that he was particularly out of favour but simply that his

Saltash seat was wanted for Admiral Clinton, and there was nothing else available. Old Lord Edgcumbe came out strongly on his behalf for the borough of Grampound and wrote twice to the Duke of Newcastle, but to no avail.[6] Nothing could be done by either Admiralty or Treasury, not even if Captain Rodney (as he was quite ready to do) paid all his election expenses himself.

A seat in Parliament was not to be forfeited without a struggle. If the government would not or could not help him there was one very eminent nobleman who might—the Duke of Bedford. So it was that the ministers learnt that there would be some opposition down at Camelford; that the election there might be more expensive than anticipated; and that the interloper, fighting in the Bedford interest, was Captain Rodney. Anson confided to his father-in-law Lord Hardwicke that this venture might be the result of 'pique' on Captain Rodney's part, and the Duke of Newcastle assured the King that despite the great sums offered by the opposition Camelford would be safe for the government.[7] He was right, and the venture cost Rodney and his backer some £3,000 with nothing to show for it. However, some consolation followed in May in the shape of another Portsmouth guard-ship, this time the *Fougueux*, one of the Finisterre prizes. The additional pay enabled the Rodneys to acquire a town house on the north side of Hill Street, where London's westward spread was reaching out towards Hyde Park. That summer Mr Compton came down to enjoy the country air of Hampshire as the very welcome guest of his son-in-law and daughter, and from October onwards Rodney was more than usually persistent in his requests for leave. Jenny was expecting another child. Their second son, whom they named James, was born that autumn.

But before the year ended there were signs that the halcyon days of married life might be numbered. Shots had been fired by British and French in America. The French, in defiance of the recent treaty, had established themselves at the headwaters of the Ohio, and a column of Virginians under a certain George Washington had been compelled to surrender at Fort Necessity. That October the Cabinet in London resolved, as a precautionary measure, to send out some regular troops, and on December 23rd Keppel sailed for America with General Braddock and 1,500 men.

Early in 1755 the prospects worsened. The French, who had obtained a copy of Braddock's orders, prepared to reinforce their own colonists on an even larger scale. A vigilant Admiralty could not disregard the reports from Paris and Brest, and soon the war clouds which had appeared some 3,000 miles away over the New World began to threaten the domestic tranquillity of Alresford and Hill Street. Following Keppel's departure the order went out for more ships to be brought forward. Captain Rodney could be spared from his duty no longer.

January saw the *Fougueux* fitting for sea. There was every prospect of her sailing and her captain with her. Down at Portsmouth, in the midst of his preparations, Rodney poured out his heart in a revealing letter.

'Portsmouth, January 30 1755.

'*My Dearest Jenny*,

'I was made happy by the receipt of yours last night. Believe me my love, the greatest pleasure I have in this world, (next to seeing you), is to hear from you. That Happyness let me often enjoy since at present Cruel Necessity parts us.

'I sincerely wish I had quitted before this Bustle came on. However, I will be wise for the future and learn to live without a Guard-ship—'tis but staying so much longer in the country to make up the difference in expense. I now learn, when 'tis too late, that Ambition has lost its Charms to met and that to have a Wife and Children ingroses all our attention, and tha, where ones Heart is, there the Mind is also, for whatever I am about or doing, I think of nothing but Hill Street and the dear Pledges I left there with you. . . .'

He was still confident that the war scare was no more than in his own words, 'a Spithead affair'. Jenny, writing from Hill Street on the same day, was less hopeful.

'Your kind indulgence, my dearest Captain Rodney, in letting me hear so often from you, is beyond what I could expect. You make me by it as happy as I can be without you. I am very glad you find all quiet and hope in God we shall have Peace and quietness while I live, for was you to be obliged to go abroad Misery to me must ensue; I have not Philosophy enough to support so severe a tryal, nor would your coming home loaded with Riches make up for my sufferings during your absence. With what we have I am content provided you are with me, but without you life is not worth my care, nor would millions make me Happy. . . . I hope you will then, as soon as you possibly can, give up that vile ship that causes us both so much pain. . . .'

And this is exactly what Jenny's devoted husband was preparing to do. He replied on February 1st.

'For God's sake my Dearest, do not grieve at what is unavoidable. Our Separation can not be long. . . . To convince you that I do not intend going abroad in case the *Fougueux* should be ordered to sea I have this day desired my Lord Anson to remove me into a ship of Ninety guns that is in this Harbour and which it will be impossible to be ready for the sea at least a year—long before which I hope all this storm will blow over. . . .'

Jenny replied on the 4th, overjoyed. 'Last night about 10 o'clock Papa brought me my dear Cap. Rod's letter. He say'd he thought by bringing it he made himself doubly welcome and indeed it was very true for I was a little uneasy at not hearing. You made me very happy in having wrote for a ship not likely to go abroad soon. . . . Papa was surprised at your asking for so large a ship. He wishes you a cruiser. I did not tell him the kind reason you are so good as to give me for it. For God's sake don't let him dissuade you from it.' After a budget of news about the children—'Georgy is eating his pudding and looks as Beautiful as a Little Angel'—Jenny concluded: '. . . . am extremely glad your Cold has left you. The good hours you keep I doubt are not thro' inclination but compel'd to them by having no Whist Partys, so you see I am not willing to allow you any merit in it. I have given your love to Jocky . . . my constant guard and companion. Sancho chuses to take up his residence in Grosvenor Street at which I am a small matter offended. . . .'

But the Admiralty was slow in replying to his application for the larger ship and for the next ten days Rodney was so busy with the *Fougueux* he had no time to write. Then:

'. . . My delay proves intirely from emulation in getting the *Fougueux* to Spithead as soon as other people, than no reflexions may be cast upon my conduct at a time when every person is observed weither they are dilligent or not. And I am sure, sanguine as you are to see me, you could not bear to hear me spoke slightingly of. My ship will be ready for Spithead tomorrow. The moment she is there I will set out for town since my dear Girl will have it so. . . .'

The *Fougueux* went out to Spithead next day, but before Jenny saw her husband she received yet another letter.

'Portsmouth, 14 February 1755.

'My dear Girl will be surprised to receive this letter instead of seeing me, but she will find thereby that Love will get the better of Interest, and that her Influence has induced me to change the best sailing ship in the world for the *Prince George* of 90 guns, of which there is not the least likelyhood that she will ever go to sea. But I beg you will not let your father know of it as he certainly will laugh at me.

'Last night (after I had bespoke four horses to be in my Chaise at daylight), I had a letter from the Admiralty to acquaint me that I might have the *Prince George* if I pleased, and that they must have an answer by the return of the Post. So that it was lucky I had not left this place in the morning. I have by this Post accepted the ship and suppose that my Commission will be down on Tuesday, so that my dear Girl may now be easy in her mind and depend upon seeing me some day next week, and has not now the least occasion to dread my going abroad. I expect that this will raise your spirits—but don't betray me Hussy. I must stay to deliver the *Fougueux* to the new captain and make up my books. . . . Now my Dearest, I will bring you down with me, and if we can but prevail with one of your sisters to accompany you, I shall be happy.'

Alas for these cheerful hopes. Jenny, with her father so active in the House of Commons, was probably better placed than her husband to know the latest news, and it was not reassuring. Three weeks later, and still at Hill Street, she wrote in deep depression: 'I can assure you I shall chuse to remain at Alresford if you must go abroad, for I am sincere when I assure my dear Captain Rodney I have no pleasure without him and it will be better for the children to be in the country. . . . I hate the thought of the sea or a ship and yet can't help enquiring the News. In that way I wish you had been a Parson or anything but a Sailor. Then I had not known the uneasyness of being parted from him I love better than life.'

On March 11th appeared the Royal Proclamation offering a bounty for service in the Navy. Exactly a week later the Cabinet resolved that the French reinforcements to Canada must be intercepted, and on the 24th, when Parliament met, His Majesty outlined the dangers threatening the Realm and asked for a proper augmentation of supplies. It was not yet war, but it looked as if it very soon would be.

The nightmare of separation threatened: the problem was to postpone it to the last possible moment. The Rodneys solved it in a way only too familiar to serving officers and their wives. Before the end of March he wrote to her resignedly: 'I am going today to look at a lodging and hope it will do tho' I am much afraid before I see it. However, at this place we must not expect Pallaces.' 'This place' was Alverstoke (called Stoke then), and in lodgings here poor Jenny waited and worried for the next three months, while her husband went through the hectic nightmare of preparing a three-decked line of battleship for sea. On April 8th the *Prince George* sailed out of Portsmouth Harbour and anchored at Spithead. But for the time being, other ships had first claim on the men coming in, and the *Prince George* was still swinging round her moorings on April 27th when Rear-Admiral Boscawen sailed to intercept the French (if he could), before they reached Canada. On May 11th another squadron was off under Rear-Admiral Holburne, Rodney's old captain, to reinforce Boscawen. The *Prince George* was to join the Channel Squadron under Sir Edward Hawke when there were enough men to man the ships, and when the Cabinet could decide what orders to give Sir Edward. But men were coming in very slowly and the Cabinet was perplexed and divided so for the rest of May and all June the *Prince George* lay at Spithead in plain view to poor Jenny as she walked on the beach.

During this time Rodney was involved in a rather worrying business over impressment. The *Prince George*'s tender was away on this duty under one of the lieutenants, a Mr Robert Sax. Sax fell in with a ship called the *Britannia* off Portland whose crew, having no wish to be pressed at the end of their voyage, tried to make off. Heavily laden she was no match for the tender which bore down on her again with peremptory orders to bring to. This was answered with defiance from the merchantman so Sax sent a boat, which was beaten off. Then one of the *Britannia*'s small cannon was seen to be trained on the tender at which Sax felt justified in ordering his men to fire a volley. This cowed the men in the *Britannia*, and small wonder, for when the naval party boarded her they found that three of them had been shot dead.

Here was a pretty kettle of fish. If the bodies were brought ashore for burial a Coroner's jury must be summoned with every chance of a verdict of murder against Lieutenant Sax. But when Rodney reported the matter. Sir Edward Hawke had a very simple solution. Rodney was to put enough reliable men in the *Britannia* to carry her round to London, and heave the bodies overboard off St Helen's, by which highly practical expedient the case was kept from the lawyers and much trouble avoided.*

* Sax was later brought before a naval court martial, acquitted, and remained in the *Prince George.*

A few days after this, on June 4th, the ships at Spithead were visited by Royalty, with the Lords of the Admiralty in attendance. Not all of the harassed captains may have appreciated the honour done them by H.R.H. the Duke of Cumberland, but whatever their feelings every one of them, including Captain Rodney, had to put on full dress uniform and, with Sir Edward Hawke at their head, wait on Lord Anson at the coffee-house on the Parade at 8 a.m. Then, after the presentations, the whole company embarked at the Sally Port to row round the fleet. Ships were manned to cheer His Royal Highness as he passed, with officers drawn up on the gangways and drums beating a march. The procession of barges must have taken a long time and the expenditure of saluting powder would have been considerable. But the significance of the ceremony was clear. Great Britain was about to resume her ancient sway over her watery realm, and Royalty had come to speed the ships on their way. But this was small consolation to a captain's wife watching the distant ships from across the water.

The rest of June passed and most of July before the dreaded moment of departure came. On July 22nd, when at last the *Prince George* weighed from Spithead, poor Jenny was in despair.

'. . . I was very sorry I had not greater command of myself yesterday, but when the time approached that you (who are far more dear to me than my own life) was to leave me, I could not support it with the patience I am afraid I ought. I trust in God I shall not have longer than six weeks to lament your absence, which time shall be intirely devoted to the care of our little ones, and praying for your preservation. They are both very well. If you leave St. Helen's tomorrow I shall set out for Alresford but can not leave this place till you are out of sight, tho' I have not the least hopes of seeing you.

'As your watch does not go, think it will be of no use to you and therefore send my own.

'I must not detain the man so my Dearest Love, Adieu. God bless and preserve you and send you safe to her who is, with the most faithfull love your most affectionate wife,

'J. RODNEY.

'Charles is gone to Portsmouth to hear what news.'

The *Prince George* sailed with Hawke's squadron on the 25th, but before she weighed her captain was able to reply:

117

'. . . the returning of my long-boat which I can not take to sea gives me this oppertunity of letting you hear from me. My Captain of Marines tells me he saw Charles yesterday. For God's sake don't part with him but if possible spend a month at Bourne in case your father presses you, as the time there will not hang so heavy on your hands as it must do at Alresford.* P.S. Thanks for your watch, but I can not bear to think that you should be without one. Let Charles take mine to a watchmaker and see what it wants.'

And so Sir Edward Hawke's squadron sailed with a fair wind down channel, and poor Jenny with a heavy heart made her way back to Alresford, and thence to her father's house at Eastbourne after a tedious journey during which little George 'made an excellent traveller—Jemmy as bad'. Here she found a large family party for August, her father and Charles much absorbed by the Lewes races, her sister Kitty pursued by young George Medley, and the Ladies Penelope and Margaret Compton, 'tollerable, yet bitter against me on account of my dogs—wish I had left them both at Alresford'. News had come of Boscawen's taking two French warships off Newfoundland and most of the country was jubilant although wiser heads suggested that, as there was still official peace between England and France, Boscawen had either done too little or a great deal too much.

But before the month of August was over, two letters, both written on the same day, brought news of the *Prince George*.

'Off Cape Finisterre on the Coast of Spain, August 3 1755.

'I take the oppertunity by one of our small ships that goes for Plymouth tomorrow morning to tell my dearest Jenny that thank God I am very well but not in the least satisfied with being at sea as, to my great mortification, I have seen several French ships which politely put themselves in our possession, but it seems our orders would not allow us to detain them. For my part I don't understand this method of proceeding for I imagine the people of England expect that this noble Fleet has sailed with an intention of distressing France, but they will find themselves deceived in their imagination when they hear that we let the French Trade pass by us unmolested. . . . I hope they will send us proper orders for I desire not to have been sent on a Fool's errand. So much for sea-news.

'I must now enquire about what more nearly and tenderly concerns

* By 'Bourne' Rodney meant Compton House, Eastbourne, then used by old Mr Compton. 'Charles', Jenny's brother, was later the sixth Earl of Northampton.

myself which is of the Wellfare of my Dear Girl and Dear little ones. I was a stranger even to myself in what I should feel in being absent from them but I can most sincerely assure you, both waking and sleeping, they are ever in my mind and present themselves to my imagination as the Dearest Blessings Heaven could bestow upon me. Supremely happy should I be if I could be assured you was in health and could bear my Absence with that resignation which your Virtue and Education should indicate to you. Trust, my Jenny, in Providence, and depend upon that Being who has so often conducted me with safety through so many Perils and brought me to the highest pitch of human Happyness by bestowing on me a woman of Virtue and one that I love preferable to the whole World besides. Kiss my dear babys and pray take care that Georgy don't forget to know me when I arrive, which I think cannot be long as I certainly think they will not keep these Great Ships out above a month longer. . . .

'I send this to Bourne in hopes you are there, but have sent another to Alresford for fear this might miscarry.'

The Alresford duplicate, although similar in substance, was more cheerful in tone. After complaining about letting the French trade pass, he continued: '[I] long to hear that you are easy in mind and find yourself happy at Bourne, and that Georgy does not take the liberty of doing his occasions in every room of the house to your great Disgrace and to the offence of the Good Company. Tell the young Rogue if I hear any complaints I shall certainly exert my authority and confine him to his nursery when he longs to abroad. I know when you read this you will call me Old Fool and say to yourself 'tis I spoil him most and am most foolishly fond of him, and that I have no business to trouble my head about him till he is 10 years Old. My love to Kitty and all at Bourne, and tell her I shall be very angry if I don't hear she is on the brink of matrimony.'

Jenny replied to this on August 25th, properly indignant about letting the French trade pass: '. . . I am vexed and provoked to a degree to have you sent out upon such a fool's errand . . . they should not, had I a Commission, have it in their power to serve me so a second time. I suppose you must pocket it (least should you show a proper Spirit People might say you quarrelled with your bread and butter). . . . They will not consent to my leaving Bourne till I hear your ship is arrived.

'Georgy is just gone to bed. He gave me a kiss to send to Papa. I think he will not soon forget you. He here stands a fair chance to be spoiled. Grand Papa, Aunts and Great Aunts all strive which shall have the greatest share in making him a saucy boy, but the Lady Comptons go away in a week, and in 10 days Papa sets out for Northampton races, so they won't have much longer to spoil him. Jemmy improves daily and grows extravagantly fond of me, but I dare not have him much as it makes Georgy very jealous. All here desire to be remembered to you. Kitty most particularly sends her love. . . .'

The next news from the *Prince George* was that they were now at liberty to take the French ships although Rodney sorrowfully commented: '. . . had we had these orders sooner we should have been in possession of 50 sail at least'. Two posts later he wrote to his father-in-law.[8]

'I can not let slip this oppertunity that I have by sending in some of our Prizes, to return you thanks, and to assure you how infinitely I think myself obliged to you for being troubled with my Baggage and her Brats, which I am afraid are more troublesome to you than you expected, as George is very apt to behave in the manner that Henny Clies used to do at Lisbon; but as you have been used to bear with patience all the foibles of children, I hope mine will not be too troublesome especially as I flatter myself Jenny has taught my eldest boy to get the blind side of you as she used to do herself. I should be very happy if I knew she was in health (as I did not think her so when I sailed), being still so very unfashionable as to be absurd enough to love my wife preferably to the whole world, notwithstanding I have been acquainted with her so long. . . .'

To Jenny he confided: 'We have taken several Prizes of considerable value and hope we shall bring more in with us 'tho many have escaped our hands in a hard gale of wind we lately had. . . . Nothing in Nature is so disagreeable as bad weather at sea.' His letter concluded wistfully: '. . . I shall never think myself happy till I can for a certainly spend all my Days . . . undisturbed and unmolested with Warships or any other thing that makes the World so busy, being but too certain that Happyness can never be found but in company with those who love so dearly as we do. . . .'

Mercifully it is not given to poor humans to know the future. But the *Prince George* was not to be much longer at sea. On September 14th her captain sat down to write the letter his wife was so eagerly awaiting: '. . . in 8 or 10 days at furthest we shall certainly be for making our best way to Spithead . . . contrive to go to Alresford as soon as you can after the receipt of this letter . . . we have taken about 30 ships and daily I hope shall make capture of more if they are so obliging to come in our way.

They are all sent to England and I suppose by this time war is declared that we may make our captures legal Prizes.' On September 29th the *Prince George* anchored at Spithead. She went up harbour a week later and did not go to sea again that year.

Ship's business and such tiresome duties as sitting on courts martial, which he detested, kept Rodney at Portsmouth most of October, but the *Prince George* saw little of him from November onwards. Mr Charles Compton had been in failing health for some time and that November he fell seriously ill at Bath. Rodney now learnt from Robert Andrews, an old friend and family lawyer, that he could not live many more days and that he had made him the sole executor of his will and guardian of all his children under age; and if this was not enough Andrews (who was one of the Duke of Newcastle's political managers) also hinted how glad his Grace would be to see Captain Rodney succeed Mr Compton as the Member for Northampton.[9]

Rodney had applied for leave to go to Bath before he received Andrews' letter, but he was not present when Mr Compton died on November 20th. He now found himself burdened with the execution of a long and complicated will[10] and the guardian of Charles and Spencer Compton, aged respectively eighteen and seventeen. Their fortune was considerable, as he explained to the Admiralty in a letter from Grosvenor Street dated December 1st, requesting an extension of leave. The Lords, knowing there would be no employment for the *Prince George* until the spring, granted him another month.

While still in London on this business he received a perplexed and worried letter from Jenny at Alresford. 'I was very much surprised today,' she wrote, 'to receive an order to deliver your horse, and am still very uneasy but think I must not detain it as the order is from the Admiralty. . . . They say it is offered to His Majesty and if he nor Lord Anson do not like him he is then to go to the King of France.' The animal in question, a superb Arab from Senegal, had come out of one of the French prizes. How it found its way into Rodney's stables at Alresford should not, perhaps, be enquired into too closely, but it was destined for an influential French nobleman, and as war with France was not, even yet, officially declared, it had become the subject of diplomatic representation at the highest level. No wonder Jenny was puzzled.[11]

Not until May 18, 1756, was war formally declared, the immediate cause being the news of a French landing on the island of Minorca. This came as a shock both to the country and the Ministers. While most of Britain's

Navy was guarding her southern shore the enemy had struck elsewhere, and although tardy reinforcements were on their way to the Mediterranean under Admiral Byng and all might yet be well, more were needed without delay. One result of this was that Rodney left the *Prince George*. She was now wanted to go out with all speed under Commodore Broderick who would have four other ships with him and take out a batallion of infantry. For Rodney another ship was found at once, the *Monarch* then lying unrigged at Plymouth. So, while all England was buzzing with news of the attack and hoping to hear soon of some success by Byng, he hurried back to Alresford for a few last days with Jenny before setting out for the west country. When the time came she was loath to let him go and he so far yielded to her entreaties as to linger one night longer, slipping from her side at first light, to be well on his way before she woke. Bitterly did she reproach herself.

'Alresford, May ye 28.

'When James brought me word you were roused up at 4 in the morn how vexed was I to think I was the cause of your being so hurry'd. It has made me resolve never to let selfishness so far get the better as to prevail on you to stay an hour longer with me than the time you fix. . . .'

From Plymouth Rodney replied as usual reassuringly: he was confident 'the Bustle' could not last long, and he was pleased with the *Monarch*. There was no port admiral at Plymouth in those days but there were thirteen ships in varying stages of unreadiness (including the *Sheerness*, *Ludlow Castle* and *Eagle*) and he was the senior officer of the port. So, in addition to his job of preparing the *Monarch* for sea (and she was without masts and needed 400 men), he found the whole business of Plymouth dockyard devolving on him.

If this is why the Admiralty sent him there they had speedy evidence of his ability and willingness to cope. From his first official letter dated June 1, 1756: 'Being the Senior Officer at present in this Port I think it my duty to acquaint their Lordships . . .', his energy and competence are impressive. Every day the port orders, 'By George Bridges Rodney, commander of His Majesty's ship *Monarch*, etc., etc.' streamed forth. All through June and July the work went on; discharging, receiving and entering men; tedious correspondence with the Board of Ordnance and the Commissioners for the Sick and Hurt; demands for stores; and interminable wrangles over pay and allowances. Probably he was working harder than he had ever worked in his life, and all that summer the weather was vile. But as the days passed and the ships completed their fitting and sailed to play their part in the war, more and more disquieting reports came in about Admiral Byng in the Mediterranean. They are echoed in his correspondence with Jenny.

At first, being from French sources, they were received with proper scepticism. 'I don't believe a word of the French news concerning Mr. Byng,' he wrote on June 6th, and she replied a week later: 'I lose all patience upon hearing Sir Edward Hawke is ordered to supercede Mr. Byng for I can not believe he has behaved as represented by the French.' But before long the facts became all too plain. Distant though he was from London, Rodney had his own sources of news: 'I am sorry to hear that Mr. Byng's retreat causes such confusion, Hatred, and uneasyness among the Great Men in London', he wrote on June 15th. 'Why did they not send him with a superior Force?' It was a question all England was asking. Three days later, again to Jenny, he commented sourly: 'Our Ministers are very quick in their superceding of Admirals before they know what Mr. Byng has done.' Byng was a friend and Hill Street neighbour—yet as the facts became clearer even the partisans began to waver.

But with Jenny most of their correspondence was naturally of a more personal nature. She longed to be with him at Plymouth. '. . . cruelly tantalising to be parted when you are ashore', she wrote; and again: 'O my Rodney, what pain and anxiety does your absence cause me. . . .' It was dull at Alresford, she was sick and fractious, their third child was on the way, and all that June and July the rain fell endlessly which made for eternal mowing in the garden; sometimes it was so cold they were glad of a fire. But the children were thriving. 'I am persuaded you must be a long time absent before Georgy will forget you', she wrote soon after Rodney's departure. 'He calls for Papa perpetually and seem'd vastly delighted when I told him I had heard from you and that you sent your Blessing to him. I give you my word he echoed Papa round the room and still continues to look for you when he comes to me in the morning and cries "Papa, Papa— No, No?" You may depend on my often talking of you to him as well as to comply with your request as to gratify my own inclination on dwelling on the most pleasing subject to me in life.'

Indeed, the Rodneys' home was a happy one. 'Our dear boys are very well,' she wrote on another occasion, 'and look the picture of health. The kitchen garden is kept locked as the strawberries begin to look tempting. They have not yet spied out the gooseberries, which I wonder at.' There were other inmates of the household to be reported on: 'Your dog and Parrots are well, your green one very troublesome for there is no keeping him in his cage and he often chuses to get top of the curtain in the red Parlour for which he and I quarrel. . . . Jockey is the most faithfull of all dogs.'

To all of this Rodney replies as an affectionate husband should. Another interest was the enlargement of his estate. Land could be a good invest-ment, but not as Rodney was generally prepared to buy it. Jenny saw the danger with business-like good sense. 'I think it a pity it should be said that you are so desirous of enlarging your estate round here and that you will give more than other people, for by that means you are likely to be much imposed upon. . . .' She knew her husband. But ever the dutiful wife she continued: 'however, if you see it in a different light to what I do I shall very readily submit'. So Pingleston and Lanham Farms were bought, and then came an opportunity to acquire the Bishop of Winchester's great pond which covered many acres south of the house. 'As 'tis so very much my interest to have the pond,' he wrote on June 1st, 'I can not answer it to myself or Children not to purchase it, especially as the reeds only will pay me the interest of the money and I may never again have such an opportunity of showing our Mercy in not suffering the poor birds to be shot at—not to mention the oppertunity of always having what fish we please.' The pond was bought and, although smaller now than it was, is alive with birds and fish to this day.

Early in July the *Monarch* was ready and orders came for her to join the Channel fleet under Vice-Admiral Boscawen. One letter survives from her brief cruise.

'July 30 1756. At sea.

'Captain Keppel has this moment sent me word that I may have an Oppertunity of writing to my dearest Jenny as he has received orders to go for Portsmouth tomorrow morning, and will take perticular care that my letter is sent to you immediately on his arrival. We are now prodigiously strong having been joyn'd this morning by another 1st Rate which makes us sufficient strong to cope with the whole Naval power of France.

'The songs upon Mr. Byng occasion some mirth to those who are glad to trip up his heels, but I hope he will be able to give sufficient reasons for his conduct when he comes home, though I must own I cannot perceive the least glimpse in his favour. His not landing the troops after the battle is inexcusable, as likewise his not sending a boat on shore to St. Philip's to acquaint them with the occasion of his retreat. I suppose I shall be plagued with being one of his Judges next Winter. You know I abhor Court Martials.

'I hope my dear Girl and her little ones enjoy fine weather and that Alresford daily improves in beauty and that Georgy and Jamy can play all day long without doors. . . . If you have gained their hearts from me I will certainly be revenged on you for you know Georgy has sense sufficient to know that I can protect him against anybody, notwithstanding somebody scolds him. . . .'

Soon after receiving this letter, Jenny learnt that her husband's ship had arrived unexpectedly at Portsmouth. Three days after he wrote, it became apparent that several things were very wrong with the *Monarch*. The knee of the head (or, put in simpler terms, the heavy bow bracket sweeping up from the cutwater to the figurehead) was working loose. With this were developing other defects so alarming that, with extreme reluctance, Rodney felt obliged to report her condition to the Vice-Admiral. Boscawen, besides being no friend, was a Lord of the Admiralty, an important matter for a senior captain who might hope to hoist his own flag before long. But the *Monarch*'s defects were no fault of his and Boscawen ordered her to Spithead at once. She arrived on August 12th, went up harbour a few days later, and remained there.

Waiting for Rodney at Portsmouth was a letter from that shrewd judge of men and naval affairs Lord Sandwich.[12] His Lordship, writing from Hinchingbrooke on August 1st, supposed him still with Boscawen. After wishing him every success he added significantly: 'I wish such men as you may fight for us whenever a future opportunity shall happen. I believe they are not plenty and therefore are the more to be esteemed.' A great many Englishmen were feeling the same about the scarcity of good fighting men for the unhappy Byng was back, and the clamour against him louder every day. But Rodney was to have no opportunity of showing his metal in 1756. The *Monarch*'s defects were even worse than had been supposed, although her captain would not have been himself if he had not attempted to take advantage of the prolonged docking to introduce some practical improvements of his own.

His popularity as a good commander was shown that September by a remarkable incident that took place while the *Monarch* was in Portsmouth. Seven seamen who had served under him before, and were anxious to do so again, were so foolish as to desert their own ship for this purpose. They delivered a petition to Lord Anson himself, betook themselves to Portsmouth without any orders, and were of course arrested as deserters. The moment Rodney heard about it he wrote to the Admiralty.

'. . . As the men have served many years under my command and allways behaved remarkably well I can not help concerning myself on their behalf, and shall take it as a particular favour if you will sollicit their Lordships that their present crime be forgiven as they have erred more through their regard for their Old Captain than any premeditated intention of deserting. I can not expect to have the men myself though I would willingly give ten of the best men of my ship's company for them. My friend Keppel would be made very happy could he get them, and I will answer for the men that for the future they will never deserve punishment. You will oblige me much if you can possibly prevent their punishment which must give me great uneasyness, as 'twas through their regard for me that they have offended. . . .'

The Lords, although at this time almost overwhelmed by the Minorca crisis, were not men of stone. Against Rodney's letter the Secretary wrote: 'Admiral Osborn to send these men to serve on board the *Swiftsure*. Let Mr. Rodney know it.' The *Swiftsure* was Keppel's ship.

That autumn saw the birth of a daughter to Jenny. The occasion was less joyful than it might have been as it brought about a further decline in Jenny's health. In the ordinary way Rodney would have been enchanted by such an event, but there is hardly a reference to his third child in all his papers. Poor little Jane Rodney only lived for eighteen months and but for the entries of her baptism and burial in the Alresford parish register we would not even know her name. It seems probable that her mother never recovered from the birth. The sad references in her later letters to the symptoms of her illness leave the question in very little doubt. Until the end of the year she lingered on at Alresford, and while the shades closed about her the compulsive demands of her husband's political connections drew him from her side, more and more frequently to London.

For although he no longer sat in the Commons, the great men had not forgotten him. Since the fall of Minorca, the Duke of Newcastle's government had lost what little popular confidence it had ever possessed, and now the voice of the Nation was calling loudly for Mr Pitt. Mr Pitt was very ready to take up the task if he could form a government, and in the delicate negotiations to that end Captain Rodney was called on to play a part.

Clearly he was no mere go-between but a trusted envoy, high in the confidence of that powerful political group sometimes known as 'the Cousinhood', which included Mr Pitt, George Grenville and Earl Temple. Writing to Jenny from London on November 4th to explain why he could not be back until the beginning of next week, he told her: 'I must go to Woburn tomorrow to try what my Rhetoric will do with the Duke of B . . . d, to make him take upon himself the care of Naval affairs, as I hear Lord A. must certainly go out. There never was such confusion as at present and it seems allmost impossible for the Great to agree among themselves. However, tomorrow or next day I hear it will certainly be settled. I hope it will as I should be glad to make my interest with the First Lord now I am in Town, which will save me a second jaunt. . . .'

But Captain Rodney's 'Rhetoric' was not enough to persuade his old patron to take the Admiralty. When the dust settled the Duke of Devonshire stood forth at the head of the new administration with Mr Pitt. Anson's great services counted for little against the loss of Minorca and he was replaced by Lord Temple. As for Rodney, his incessant activity, the excitement of the political crisis, and perhaps the late hours he kept, were wearing him out. During these last weeks of 1756, while Jenny continued to decline at Alresford, he went sick too in their house in Hill Street.

At once Jenny was filled with alarm. '. . . for God's sake let me come to town to take care of you till you go out again. . . . I hope, if you are not really well I shall tomorrow receive your leave to go to town, for I never can be easy while the Dearest Person to me on earth is ill, and I from him, he nursed by a Common Housemaid or man-servant . . . poor George raves for Papa and was near crying when I told him you would not be home today. . . .'

This is the last of Jenny's letters: although near death herself all her thoughts were for him. The illness threatening her husband he kept at bay a little longer. In his reply from Hill Street, reassuringly superscribed: 'ten o'clock, you see what early hours I keep', he said, '. . . I only stay'd at home out of precaution as the weather has been exceeding Cold, and am now going to Court to see the new Ministers kiss hands. They all take their places tomorrow. I can assure my dear Girl that I stand the best with them of any person in the Navy and am assured from the First Lord that I shall have whatever ship I please, and has likewise done me the honour to assure me that my advice shall go a great way with him in conducting Naval affairs, so you find I am a great gainer by the exchange. . . .

'Assure my dear babys they shall see me soon and to make you happy I

II.   Vice-Admiral Thomas Mathews
from an oil painting of c. 1743 by C. Arnulphy

III.   Captain Francis Holburne
from an oil painting of c. 1750 by an unknown artist

IV.   Captain the Hon. Augustus Keppel
from an oil painting of 1749 by Joshua Reynolds

V.   Rear-Admiral Rodney
from an oil painting of 1756–9 by Joshua Reynolds

VI. The Bombardment of Havre, July 1759
from an oil painting of 1760 by R. Paton

VII. Admiral Sir George Pocock
from an oil painting by T. Hudson

VIII. John, Fourth Earl of Sandwich
from an oil painting of 1783 by Thomas Gainsborough

IX.   Vice-Admiral Sir George Rodney
from an oil painting of c. 1770 attributed to Tilly Kettle

Paris May 5*th* 1778

I have received from his Excellency
Marshall, Duke D Byron, the Sum
of Twenty four Thousand Livres France
which I promise to pay, on Demand,

X.   Facsimile of Sir George Rodney's note of hand to the Marshal de Biron

XI.   The *Sandwich* on April 17, 1780
from an oil painting by T. Luny

XII.   Rear-Admiral Lord Hood
from an oil painting of 1783 by J. Northcote

XIII.   Vice-Admiral Marriot Arbuthnot
from a mezzotint by C. H. Hodges after J. Rising, 1792

XIV.   Doctor Gilbert Blane
from an unfinished oil painting by J. Archer Shee

XV.   Comte de Grasse
from a mezzotint by J. Walker after Miller, 1782

XVI. Admiral Lord Rodney
from an oil painting of 1783–7 by Thomas Gainsborough

XVII.   Admiral Lord Rodney
from an oil painting of 1789 by J. L. Mosnier

XVIII.   George, Second Lord Rodney
from an oil painting by an unknown artist

believe I shall scarce go to sea this Winter. Adieu my Jenny, and as you love me take care of yourself and little ones. . . .'

'Adieu my Jenny.' There is no need to speculate on what may have passed between Rodney and Lord Temple, for the sickness now struck down both husband and wife, and from the valley of the shadows only one of them was to return. There is no knowing how the next weeks went by. Perhaps he brought Jenny up to London for the best attention the capital could provide and they lay ill in the house in Hill Street together. It is too heart-rending to imagine them apart as Jenny's days drew to a close. The Admiralty files draw aside the curtain a little. On December 12th Rodney wrote from Hill Street: 'Being afflicted with a Violent Bilious Cholick I desire you will please to represent the same to their Lordships and hope they will indulge me with as long a time as the nature of the service I am ordered on will admit, and hope a short time will enable me to execute any commands they are pleased to honour me with.' The Lords were pleased to give him the leave he asked but warned him that as he would, in a few days, receive a summons to attend the court martial on Admiral Byng he must take care to be at Portsmouth by the day it was to be held. But Rodney's health did not improve and twelve days later, on December 24th, he wrote again from Hill Street: 'I beg you will acquaint Lord Temple that I am under the greatest concern that my health still continues so bad as to render it impossible for me to set out for Portsmouth, not having been out of doors since I had the honour to see his Lordship last, and constantly attended by a physician, as Mrs. Rodney is by three. I beg you will acquaint his Lordship that if he thinks it necessary he will dispose of the *Monarch* as he pleases, and I hope by the time the new ships are launched I shall be able to execute any orders he pleases to honour me with.'

Then, for a month, the curtain falls completely. The trial of Admiral Byng began on December 28th, but without Captain Rodney. At Hill Street the battle went on, and for Jenny the end came on January 29th, two days short of the fourth anniversary of her happy marriage. She was buried at Alresford on February 7th. To her memory in the little church her husband put up a lavish monument in carved marble. The portrait bust shows a young woman whose features indicate amiability and good sense. The tablet below concludes the record of her virtues with the words: 'An honour to her Family and the Delight of all that knew her.'

Chapter 8

The *Dublin*

(1757–1758)

'Captain Rodney . . . resolved not to lose a moment's
time in getting away.'
(General Amherst to the Rt Hon. Mr Pitt,
March 15, 1758.)[1]

THE year 1757 which opened so sadly for Rodney, marked the beginning of a new phase in his life. Following his marriage the tempo had slackened; there had been talk of quitting the service, or at any rate of living without a guard-ship. Now, with Jenny dead, what was there remaining *but* his career? The war had brought new political figures to the front, men with whom he had already established himself, and the country was quickening under their leadership. Opportunity beckoned once more. In the active pursuit of glory and advancement in his chosen profession there might be some compensation for what he had lost.

But first there were the children to be considered. Looming before poor Jenny's tortured imagination as she lay dying had been the picture of the neglected nursery, her husband away at sea, and their beloved babies left to the care of underlings and servants. A few days before she died she desired all to leave the room except her sister Kitty. Then, too weak to hold a pen, she whispered her last request, to be communicated to her husband after her death; and the pathetic letter in which Kitty set all down,[2] was written a few hours after her sister died.

Always practical, Jenny's idea was that Mrs Clies, who had first known the Compton sisters in the far off childhood days at Lisbon, should be taken into the house to superintend the servants in the care of the children, although she added that if her husband knew any woman better to be trusted, she would not pretend to control his opinion. The Clies had been for many years associated with the English factory at Lisbon, and the late Mr Clies had acted as a sort of confidential agent and general factotum for Mr Charles Compton when he was consul and envoy. In those days the family, and their little daughter Henrietta, whom they called Henny, must have been familiar figures to young Rodney when he visited the Comptons. Probably Mrs Clies returned to England with Henny after her husband's death, when the friendship with the Comptons was resumed. Thereafter, to an increasing extent, she figures in the Rodney story, always on affectionate terms with Mr Compton's daughters, often present at sick-beds and confinements, and, on the evidence of some of the house accounts, by no means averse from her glass of port and her pinch of snuff. Evidently she was a very old friend, capable and trustworthy, but still a dependent; Jenny had specially asked that the charge, if she undertook it, should be made worth her while.

So it was arranged. Mrs Clies came to run the house and look after the children, and there is no reason to suppose she ever caused Rodney to regret it. Henny, who would have been seventeen at this time, probably came with her. Jenny's sisters, particularly Bet, were anxious to do their duty as aunts, and make their contributions to the children's upbringing. So when Captain Rodney returned to face the world the home front, although grievously breached, was reasonably secure.

Towards the end of February he was about again in London, a London that could talk of little else but the sentence just passed on Admiral Byng. Enlightened service opinion, while condemning Byng's failure, was aghast at the idea of shooting him, and there was a movement afoot for a reprieve. Captain the Hon. Augustus Hervey, an officer who stood out even in that age of individualists, was Byng's most active champion. He and Rodney had been opponents over the Navy Bill, but they were as one over the miscarriage of justice which threatened. They conferred together, bustled about London canvassing Members of Parliament, and in the little time left strove to stir up some sort of petition.[3] That Byng died was through no want of activity on Rodney's part. The line he took was generous and disinterested, as was always his way when his sympathies were aroused. Afterwards, he and Hervey were friends until the latter's death.

Meanwhile, at the Admiralty, Lord Temple was ready to keep his promise about a ship. There was no question of a return to the unsatisfactory *Monarch*. Since Rodney left her she had accommodated the unhappy Byng, and upon her quarterdeck the last act of his tragedy had been played. For her there was to be no more active employment, and she was broken up before the war ended. Lord Temple now offered Rodney a new battleship, the *Dublin*, of 74 guns. She was still on the building slip at Deptford when, on April 4th, he picked his way through the dockyard and climbed on board to read his Commission.

In giving Rodney the *Dublin*, Lord Temple probably saw her as no more than the next suitable ship that was available. But the appointment is of interest to ship lovers because she was one of the first, perhaps *the* first, of England's seventy-fours, those two-deckers of medium size, which were thenceforward to form the backbone of every battle-line until the era of the sailing ship ended. Warship design in England had been criticized during the late war with France and Spain. Our ships were said to be slower than foreign contemporaries, unable to fight their lower deck guns in bad weather, of too many types, and too often over-gunned for their tonnage. One of the reforms associated with Lord Anson's period at the Admiralty is the development of fewer types along more efficient lines. It is an exaggeration to say that in thinking out and developing the seventy-four Anson and his surveyors, by deliberation and intent, evolved the perfect battleship; the compromise they hit on just happened to be the one best suited for development. But it is arguable that of this famous type Rodney's *Dublin* was the first, and as such a notable ship.

Her captain still had to man her, but Rodney was an old hand at this game. He had his Impress Warrant made out and his rendezvous set up in London while his ship was still on the stocks. His own popularity was a great asset. 'Very desirous of being on board under so good a Commander' is noted against a number of the *Dublin*'s entries, while a word to Lord Temple enabled him to recover several of his old followers, petty officers and key ratings. And so, although the men came in slowly enough, and the merchantmen coming up the river had all been picked clean long before they reached Deptford, he probably had less difficulty than most captains at this time.

The *Dublin* was launched on Friday May 6th, at 3 p.m. Her lower masts and bowsprit were stepped the following Tuesday. Then came her ballast and here Rodney had a brush with the master-attendant of the dockyard. From time immemorial the old wooden ships had ballasted with shingle, and the *Dublin* was due to take 189 tons of it. Rodney had no objection to this. But he did object most strongly to 70 tons of pig-iron as well, arguing as a practical seaman that it would make his ship 'laboursome'. The master-attendant took refuge behind Mr Slade, Surveyor of the Navy,

who backed him up and insisted that the *Dublin* took the pig-iron, whereupon Rodney protested to the Admiralty.

It was the familiar conflict between the theoretical expert and the
practical seaman, but by appealing to the Admiralty, Rodney must greatly
have displeased the Navy Board, within whose province all matters of
design and equipment fell. In this case the Lords could hardly do anything
but back up their experts, and they informed Captain Rodney that as the
Dublin was a new ship the opinion of her designer must prevail. So,
grumbling no doubt, he had to watch those 70 tons of pig-iron go on board.
But he did not intend to accept the situation. Not he. Where his ship was
concerned he would defer to no shore-going expert, be it the Surveyor of
the Navy himself.

Deptford dockyard rigged the *Dublin*, ballasted her as we have seen, and
filled her hold with everything needful, by eighteenth-century standards,
for her safety and the sustenance of her crew. On July 1st she was carried
down to Long Reach and by the 12th her hold was properly stowed and
her decks clear for the guns. Getting these on board took another three
days. Then, on July 26th she came to sail for the first time and anchored at
the Nore. At last it was possible to deal with that important matter of the
ballast. There was no further correspondence on the subject, but as soon
as the anchor was down, the hold, newly stowed, was partly cleared to get at
it (a two-day job), and 30 tons of the shingle went overboard. Unfortunately the iron pigs could not be disposed of so summarily, but 20 tons of
them were extracted too and unobtrusively returned to the dockyard. The
Dublin was now 50 tons lighter, but even so not light enough, for Rodney
dumped 10 more tons of shingle after his first cruise, after which he seems
to have been satisfied. One more new battleship was now ready for service.

It will be remembered that Britain's dispute with France had arisen
largely over the question of territorial sovereignty in America; but much
had happened since Keppel sailed with those inadequate reinforcements in
December 1755, and very little of it to Britain's advantage. Hostilities had
spread to the Continent of Europe, Minorca had been taken from us, and
now the great Mr Pitt was in power, and hoping to keep the French so busy
in Europe that they would be in no state to withstand us in America and
Canada. But success was a long way off in the summer of 1757. The French
had been passing ships and men across the Atlantic more expeditiously than
the British, while on the Continent they were driving His Royal Highness
the Duke of Cumberland and his army of observation before them, and
were soon to enter his father's electorate of Hanover. A vigorous response

was called for, and the great Minister was planning to relieve the pressure on Cumberland's army by a descent in force upon the coast of France. British regiments in the United Kingdom were to be used; transports and escorting warships in large numbers would be required, and the Admiralty was being ruthlessly hustled to provide them. The objective was to be the Biscay port of Rochefort and the *Dublin* would be required to take part.

This welcome news was followed by orders for the *Dublin* to take on board, as part of her complement, two complete companies of Lord Effingham's regiment which, when they arrived, turned out to be no more than caricatures of soldiers, 'either very old men or meer boys, unacquainted with the use of arms and without spirit or discipline', as their disillusioned host described them. Worse than this, they brought with them, from the gaols and slums where most had probably been recruited, an 'Epidemic Feaver' almost certainly typhus, which was to infect the *Dublin* all the time Rodney had her. It was a heavy infliction on a new and untried ship.

There now ensued three weeks of waiting in the Downs. The *Dublin* lay there most of August while the sickness took hold. After six days Rodney himself went down and slipped ashore to recuperate as much as possible before they sailed. Early in September the order came to join the great armada of transports and warships at Spithead, and on the 8th the expedition sailed.

The enterprise makes depressing reading. From the first the military commanders were pessimistic, almost defeatist; all the way down channel the ships were attended by baffling winds and fog; they were not off their destination until evening of the 20th and then, instead of dashing in at once after the manner of Drake, Sir Edward Hawke showed himself most uncharacteristically hesitant and fumbling.

Owing either to bad staff work or bad navigation it was much too late when they arrived off the isle of Oleron to make an entry that night. Next day the only pilot who knew the approaches could not be obtained until after noon, and by the time he was available not enough day remained to complete the entry; the fleet only managed to get itself halfway in and then had to anchor. Ahead now lay the fortified Isle of Aix, guarding the mouth of the Charente and the approaches to Rochefort itself.

Next morning, the 23rd, they completed their entry and the fleet smelt gunpowder. Vice-Admiral Knowles directed his squadron against the Aix forts and the *Dublin* led the way. But the hero of the attack was Captain Lord Howe of the *Magnanime* who laid his ship within fifty yards of the forts and then, in Rodney's own words, 'kept so terrible and continuous a fire for 35 minutes as drove them from their batteries and obliged them to submit'.[4] Officers in the Georgian Navy were rarely moved to praise each other, least of all to influential politicians, but Rodney was writing to George Grenville, Treasurer of the Navy and brother-in-law to the great Mr Pitt. 'Cool and steady Resolution as has (most justly) gained him the universal applause of both Navy and Army', was another of his generous tributes to a brother officer of whom, in later years, he could find little good to say.

Nothing now prevented the troops from landing and taking Rochefort. Hawke, who had shaken off his hesitation, sent his Vice-Admiral, with three captains, to choose a landing place. Rodney, continuing his letter to Grenville, was optimistic about the prospects. But at this point the generals began to baulk, and on the return of Hawke's officers, full of the promising landing place they had discovered, they requested a Council of War before they would commit themselves to anything. It was too late to have it that day, but in order to lose no time on the morrow Hawke began to move the transports closer inshore.

The Council of War which met on the morning of September 25th and sat for most of that day, must have been one of the most remarkable ever held. As Rodney himself took part we may pass with him into the great cabin of the *Neptune* and attend the proceedings. Facing each other across the table were the three admirals, Hawke, Knowles and Broderick, and the three generals, Mordaunt, Conway and Cornwallis, at whose request the Council had been convened. An army colonel and Captain Rodney were the junior members, bringing the total up to eight.[5]

Lieutenant-General Sir John Mordaunt, Commander-in-Chief of the land forces, was a veteran of sixty, who had served for a quarter of a century before he first saw active service at Culloden in 1746. That had been eleven years ago and he was now in poor health, distrustful of himself, and more pessimistic than ever about the chances of success. With the accumulation of delays any hope of taking the enemy by surprise had long been lost, and this weighed heavily on him. His second, Major-General Conway, had seen more service but was young, only thirty-six, vacillating, irresolute, and the last man to stiffen his hesitant and dispirited chief. Hawke, one imagines, was brusque, impatient and perhaps a little contemptuous. The best soldier with the expedition, a certain Colonel James Wolfe, was not present.

The land-officers were dubious whether the walls of Rochefort could be carried by escalade. There would be a ditch. If it were dry an assault might be practicable, but if it were wet the town must be reckoned impregnable. That was their professional opinion which the sea-officers were in no position to dispute. But whether the all-important ditch was wet or dry was uncertain. Reports conflicted, nobody could be sure, and so the Council shied away from Rochefort altogether, and began to look round for an alternative objective. However, nothing could be agreed on although Rodney complained later that he had been very ready with suggestions for annoying the enemy, which had been ignored. The astonishing upshot, after a whole day had been wasted, was a unanimous decision by the Council—unanimous only because the sea-officers felt they must defer to military opinion on military matters—that to attack the town was 'neither advisable nor practicable'. Afterwards Hawke protested that he only signed the decision as a matter of form, and Rodney excused himself to Grenville by saying that he was obliged to depend on the judgement of those 'who were supposed to be masters of their profession'.[6] So this remarkable Council broke up with nothing resolved, and all the while the Rochefort defences had given themselves up for lost.

For the next two days the armament lay in the Basque roads doing nothing. On shore the French, from far and wide, were flocking to the defence of the town, while on board warships and transports 9,000 troops wondered at their inaction. On the third day the unhappy commander of the land forces requested another council of war, this time with a view to attacking the forts at the river entrance. The same sea-officers attended as before, but this time they did not stop long. Sir Edward Hawke had three points to make. Firstly, he held as strongly as ever that a landing should be made; secondly—as to what should be attempted—this was for the land-officers to decide; and thirdly, he was ready to carry out, to the utmost of his power, any decision his military colleagues might reach. Having delivered this broadside he withdrew, taking the other sea-officers with him, and as might be expected, a reaction was not long in coming. The soldiers were unanimous for a landing that very night.

But now the weather took a hand. A strong off-shore wind piped up that evening so that there would be small chance of the first wave of troops getting ashore before daylight, several hours might pass before the second wave could arrive to support them, and there was small chance of the men from the more distant transports getting ashore at all. Again the military hesitated, and next morning Hawke lost all patience. 'Sir,' he wrote to his military colleague, 'should the officers of the troops have no further operations to propose considerable enough to authorise my detaining the squadron under my command longer here, I beg leave to acquaint you that I intend to proceed to England without loss of time.' It was September 29th and they had been in the Basque Roads for over a week. This was the end of the enterprise. The expedition sailed for home in an atmosphere best left to the imagination and the *Dublin* anchored at Spithead on October 7th.

It had been a shocking fiasco. The country was indignant, Pitt furious, and Mordaunt's career was finished for good. What Rodney thought about it we can only guess. His letters to Grenville are sensibly discreet, but inwardly he must have been fuming. 'On my return,' he said at the end of his last from the Basque Roads, 'I hope to see you, when you shall know the whole of this unhappy affair.'[7] And perhaps, down at Wootton or in town, a report was made in swift, vehement sentences, to give the Minister much food for thought. Two things above all else had been lacking in the expedition—adequate planning beforehand and cordial co-operation and understanding between the services. Martinique was to show, four years later, how these lessons were taken to heart by at least one member of the Council of War.

The dismal affair was just one more disappointment in a vexatious and unhappy year. The war was going worse than ever. Our attempt to take Louisbourg had been called off, and in Germany the Duke of Cumberland had capitulated to the French. In England there were riots and demonstrations against the new Militia Bill. Even the *Dublin* was not all she might have been, with her mounting list of defects for which the dockyard could not find time, and those sickly soldiers of Lord Effingham's regiment. Rodney had lost one of his best petty officers overboard returning from Rochefort but the wretched soldiers, he now learnt, would be with him for the next cruise.

Then there was disturbing news about young Spencer Compton, his second ward. Hitherto, this young man had been no particular trouble, apart from his inclination to get into debt and a reluctance to write letters. While Jenny was alive, he had passed much of his time at Alresford, and he had just been commissioned in the Army. He was nineteen, and his guardian now learnt that he had thrown up his Commission and run away to Edinburgh with 'an admired Beauty of Northampton',[8] eleven years his senior, whom he had married on July 23rd. His elder brother disapproved and so probably did the rest of the Compton family. For a guardian so conscientious as Rodney it was vexatious in the extreme.

Lastly there is reason to suppose that he was disappointed with Sir Edward Hawke. Rochefort may have had something to do with this, but that is not the complaint he made to George Grenville. After the expedition, Knowles and Broderick had been replaced by Boscawen, which meant that the fleet now had only one junior admiral instead of two. The discreditable reason behind this, as Rodney was at pains to point out,[9] was so that there would be fewer to share the flag-officer's prize-money. One is sorry to find him writing a letter of this nature. It is out of character and seems to be the only occasion when he behaved in such a way. A more respectable grievance, probably shared with most other captains, was the fear that there might be less employment for junior admirals if Hawke could manage with only one.

But the frustrations and disappointments of this unlucky year were not yet over. On October 21st the fleet sailed to intercept the French returning from Louisbourg, and for the next six weeks it patrolled the bay of Biscay, between Finisterre and the Soundings. The weather was vile, wearing out ships and men, and with never a sign of the returning Frenchmen.

On board the *Dublin* the sick-list mounted daily. A manually-operated ventilator, recently installed, worked continuously, and the walls were swabbed with vinegar. But the sick-lists continued to mount until 150 men were down. At the same time the stormy weather began to find out the weak places in a new ship.

Something was very wrong with the *Dublin*'s rudder. Twice the tiller broke in the rudder-head, an unusual sort of accident, but one which might have the most serious consequences. The end of this wretched cruise, as far as the *Dublin* was concerned, came on November 25th when a third tiller broke. A strong S.S.W. gale was blowing at the time and the fleet was some seventy leagues west of Ushant. With his ship temporarily out of control all Rodney could do was fire two guns as a signal of distress, although the sea was too high for any consort to send assistance. The *Alcide*, also in trouble at this time, signalled that she could not keep company and bore away for England, and Hawke, remembering the sickly state of the *Dublin*, directed her to follow. The two casualties reached Spithead safely three days later, by which time there were 165 men on the *Dublin*'s sick-list.

Hawke remained on his beat until sheer exhaustion of ships and men drove him in a few weeks later. On the other side of the Atlantic, Holburne's ships, which had been watching Louisbourg, had been scattered and mostly dismasted by a furious hurricane which struck them on September 24th. In their absence the French ships emerged and staggered back across the Atlantic. They eluded Hawke, but reached Brest so riddled with scurvy and putrid fever that neither they, nor the port which they rapidly infected, were to be capable of further part in the war for many months to come. So, by the end of this bitter and disappointing year, all the principal fleets were off the board, and the dockyards of Europe overflowed with ships requiring attention. In England the great War Minister, up to his ears in work, planned for next year's campaign.

The *Dublin* went up harbour and into dock where her rudder was the first concern. Among other things it was found to be too big ('too wide aloft'). Deptford had made a poor job altogether of her steering-gear (despite Rodney's protests at the time). The wheel was so far aft that the helmsman could not see any sail at all, and it had no index to show how much helm was on.[10] All this the Navy Board directed be made good, as well as the strengthening of the poop-deck which had shown a disconcerting tendency to rise with the pull of the mizen topsail-sheets. Rodney had also requested a new type of pump, of a kind he had seen the Indiamen use,[11] and an extension of the *Dublin*'s quarter-deck as far forward as the main-mast, but these were not possible in the time. By mid-January 1758, she was out at Spithead again, and ready to play her part in the War Minister's new projects.

These projects were mainly directed against French power in North America. Canada was the main objective, and the key to the heart of Canada was the great fortified harbour of Louisbourg. Situated on the bleak north-east tip of Cape Breton Island, and closed in the winter months by ice, it commanded the approaches to the St Lawrence River with its direct access to Quebec and the interior. Well aware of its importance, the French had made it the strongest fortress in the New World. In 1757 they had rushed ships and men to its defence so promptly as to defeat Britain's more deliberate preparations. Pitt was determined that this would not happen again, and the first troop convoy was due to leave England in January.

On January 29, 1758, the *Dublin* again came to sail, to escort an advance force of eighteen transports bound for Halifax to a point 200 leagues south-west from Scilly. She parted company with her charges on February 9th and was back at Spithead in time to see the departure, on the 19th, of Boscawen with the main body of transports. There were no new orders for her as yet, but on the evening of the day that Boscawen sailed they witnessed from her decks an episode which was to decide the *Dublin*'s part in the 1758 campaign. This was the destruction of the battleship *Invincible* which drove on to the Dean sand to become a total loss. The *Invincible* was intended to carry the military Commander-in-Chief of the expedition against Louisbourg, Major-General Jeffrey Amherst. In consequence of her loss the *Dublin* was now chosen by Pitt to take her place.

Amherst was very different from Sir John Mordaunt. Only a year older than Rodney, he had demonstrated his abilities as a staff officer in two wars, and after the disgrace of Cumberland had attracted the attention of Pitt. Promotion, and the new command in America had followed. On March 14th he came on board with his staff. Delay to his baggage kept the ship waiting another day, during which time Rodney, who had several things on his mind, wrote a letter to Mr Pitt. It is perhaps of sufficient interest to be quoted in full.[12]

'*Dublin*, at Spithead, March 15th 1758.

'*Sir*,

'The Liberty I take in troubling you with this letter will I hope meet with your Pardon when you know it proceeds from a Heart warm in your Interests and desirous to contribute his Mite towards rendering your Administration what every Honest Man wishes it to be.

'The Moment I heard twas your desire that the *Dublin* should supply the Place of the *Invincible*, with Chearfullness and Alarcrity I got her ready for the Sea and have waited some time for the General who came Yesterday, and when his Baggage (which is hourly expected) arrives, if the Wind permits I shall get under sail and lose not a moment's time in proceeding to the place of Destination.

'As I presume you are acquainted with the Great Concern I am intrusted with for the Compton Family the Heir of which comes of Age the latter end of the Summer, give me leave to beg your assistance that the *Dublin*, when the Service on which she is sent is over, may be ordered to return with the First Ships that are sent home.

'I beg you will permit me to assure you that I am, with the utmost respect, Sir,

'*Your most obedient and most humble Servant*,

'*G. B. RODNEY*.

'To the Rt. Hon. William Pitt.'

With young Spencer's escapade so recent, one can understand Rodney's concern with his responsibilities as a guardian, and in the past he had not hesitated to beg leave from the Admiralty, or even the Duke of Newcastle, whenever they appeared to conflict with his duty on board. But to bother the great War Minister about them, and at such a time, is surprising. Of course there was more to his request than he liked to disclose to Pitt. The truth was that Boscawen had a nine-year grudge against him over the Navy Bill, and Rodney had no wish to serve in North America under that formidable figure, a day longer than he must. Writing by the same post to George Grenville, after repeating what he had said to Pitt about his responsibility as trustee and guardian, and requesting Grenville's interest with 'our common Friend' to get the *Dublin* ordered home as early as possible, he went on: 'I need not acquaint you with my reasons for desiring the Commander-in-Chief may have such orders. You know him: you remember the Navy Bill, you know his Resentment, and in case a squadron should be ordered to Winter in that part of the World, if he thinks it will be disagreeable to me I know, if left to him, my ship will be the one that stays.'[13] As for Charles Compton, he would come of age on July 22nd, which did not leave much time for the capture of the strongest fortress of the New World. The sooner Rodney could land the General at Halifax the better. But as things turned out the voyage was tedious and protracted beyond all expectations.

However, the adverse wind which laid the *Dublin* on a long tack to the south-westward after rounding Ushant, brought her a most acceptable windfall when six days out. A gale was blowing at the time, with rain, when a French Indiaman was sighted, lying to with all sails furled. Her crew, after four months at sea, were in no state to fight the elements, and as Lorient lay some twenty-five leagues to leeward she was comfortably drifting down in its direction with her head under her wing. When the *Dublin* bore down on her she hoisted British colours, but Rodney had no hesitation whatever in declaring her to be French, and sure enough, a moment later, she set a few scraps of canvas and scudded off before the wind, compelling the *Dublin* to chase her for an hour before she struck. She was the *Montmartel*, with 200,000 lbs. of coffee from the Isle of Bourbon, and a prize all the more to be rejoiced over because the *Dublin* was sailing under Admiralty orders, so no admiral could claim his eighth share.* Nevertheless, she was something of an embarrassment. If sent back to England with a prize-crew she might well be recaptured by a French privateer; but she could hardly accompany the *Dublin* to Halifax as most

---

* This did not prevent Boscawen from putting in his claim from North America when he heard of the capture. (See *High Court of Admiralty, Ed. Boscawen against G. B. Rodney*, H.C.A. 32/221).

of her people were down with scurvy. To abandon her was unthinkable so she plodded on across the bay with her captor, and so into the neutral port of Vigo.

How, it may be asked, could Rodney allow even such a prize as this to delay him for a single moment from his mission? But the eighteenth century was tolerant in such matters and no contemporary, not even Amherst, seems to have complained. Prize-money was almost as much a sailor's right as his pay, the whole ship's company of the *Dublin* shared the claim, and the *Montmartel* was the first prize to come their way.

In any case the delay was small. Vigo was no great diversion from the *Dublin*'s course and she was there for only two days (March 29th–31st). By a lucky chance the *Peregrine* (sloop) commanded by an old friend, Captain Logie, arrived in Vigo the same day, and Rodney had no qualms about ordering his prize home under the *Peregrine*'s protection, to be delivered to James Rodney Esq., Mr Francis Magnus, merchant, and Philip Stephens Esq., Agents. In describing the capture to George Grenville, he took some credit to himself for resisting the wish of his officers to run back with the prize to Plymouth, and Amherst, who sent off a report to Pitt,[14] made no complaint of any delay, only expressing the hope that the later part of their voyage would be more expeditious than the first.

In this he was to be disappointed. For ten days after leaving Vigo there were light airs and contrary winds, and in these exasperating conditions the *Dublin* drifted southward towards Madeira. After ten days of calm came ten of storm and headwinds, so that after five weeks at sea she was further from her destination than when she sailed. Even by eighteenth-century standards the voyage promised to be a long one. Slowly she worked her way westward, and as the tedious voyage spun itself out the ugly legacy of Lord Effingham's regiment reappeared: men fell sick and began to die.

On May 17th a ship, homeward bound, hailed her to take off survivors rescued the day before from a Bristol privateer. Rodney and Amherst both took the opportunity to send letters home. Rodney reported 130 of his men now sick. Amherst concluded with the hope that they would see Halifax 'Tomorrow or the Next Day'.

It was high time they did. Nine weeks had passed since the *Dublin* sailed. For nine weeks Captain Rodney and Major-General Amherst had kept each other company in the great cabin, and all topics of conversation must long have been exhausted. It is to be doubted if either of them in after years can have recalled their voyage together with much pleasure. Amherst in particular must have been chafing to get to his command. The first of his troops had started across the Atlantic in January; the main body had sailed with Boscawen in February; but three months later their Commander-in-Chief was still at sea.

But the *Dublin* now sailed into another area of fogs and calms and ten more days passed. She was at last off the coast of Nova Scotia, had even sighted land, but then came three more days of thick fog. However, most of Amherst's anxieties ended on May 28th. The fog cleared and Rodney was feeling his way in towards the land again, when the whole of Boscawen's fleet with all the transports came in sight, sailing out of Halifax harbour. The commanders had at last decided they could wait no longer, and the whole expedition was under way. Amherst lost no time in transferring himself and his baggage, and the *Dublin* sailed on into Halifax.

Here, for the next three weeks, Rodney enjoyed the congenial role of senior officer. His first demand on the dockyard was for a shed capable of accommodating 200 sick, but this, at Halifax in 1758, was beyond even his powers to obtain, and his men had to recover as best they could under canvas.

Meanwhile, 300 miles to the north-east, the attack on the strongest fortress in the New World had begun. This was an almost entirely military operation, the fleet taking little part, once the soldiers had been put ashore. Boscawen landed some cannon, but he considered the harbour too strongly defended to be forced from the sea, so while the soldiers fought it out, the warships and transports lay in Gabarus Bay and a squadron under Sir Charles Hardy rolled at anchor in the Atlantic swell outside the harbour mouth.

By the time the *Dublin* arrived on the scene at the end of June with her crew partly recovered, the siege had been going on for nearly a month. Boscawen's ships were still in Gabarus Bay, and General Wolfe's artillery was banging away at the French warships inside the harbour. The *Dublin* joined Hardy's squadron, and for nearly all of July she had her anchor down outside the entrance. Her crew listened to the firing by day and watched the flashes by night. They busied themselves making wads for the gunners ashore and landed seventy barrels of powder for them and some guns. Their only chance of action came on July 16th when a French frigate tried to escape. The squadron got under sail and captured her. Then it returned to anchor.

The siege was lasting much longer than expected, and the French warships in the harbour were making a contribution to the defence out of all proportion to their number and size. But on July 21st a bomb destroyed one of them, and from her the fire spread to two more. The remaining two, Boscawen decided, might be cut out. Altogether some 600 seamen were involved. On the night of the 25th this force dashed into the harbour, and watchers on board the *Dublin* soon heard a violent firing of small arms and some cannon. At four in the morning they could see one of the French warships in flames, and a little later the other being safely towed up the north-east arm of the harbour. So the last defences fell, and the French commander surrendered the next day. Three days after this the *Dublin* entered to land her sick men.

Louisbourg's stubborn defence ruled out any chance of Rodney being home for Charles Compton's coming of age. That event took place three days before the fortress fell. However, Rodney's wish that his ship might be among the first to be sent home was fulfilled. She was much too sickly to be any use on the station and for this reason, grudge or no grudge, would probably have been chosen for the first returning convoy anyway. So it was that on August 15th Rodney sailed for the last time, and probably without regrets, from those foggy northern waters where so much of his early service had been done. Ten transports and their escorts carried the late garrison of Louisbourg and the crews of the French warships. It was an important convoy and Rodney, as the senior officer of the escort, had five battleships under his orders.* In the *Terrible* were the late Governor of Louisbourg and his wife, with most of the officers of the garrison. In the *Dublin* were the French sea-officers.

But his disposition, and the instructions he issued, have no more than academic interest for the only enemy encountered, once the convoy was at sea, was the scurvy. Among captors and captives alike, the sick lists mounted. Rodney went down with it badly, and to add to his worries there was report of a plot by some of the prisoners to seize one of the transports and carry her into a French port.[15] Mercifully, the voyage was not prolonged. On September 14th they were off the Start and here, the wind backing easterly, he directed the transports and their sickly prisoners into Plymouth, thankful to be rid of them. The *Dublin* continued to beat up channel for three more days, to anchor at Spithead on the 17th, by which time her captain was a very sick man indeed. He wrote immediately for leave 'to go into the country for a month for the recovery of my health'. So it had been, returning with the *Rainbow* in 1752, all his vitality and nervous energy draining away as the anchor dropped for the last time.

* *Dublin* (74), *Terrible* (74), *Burford* (70), *Northumberland* (70) and *Kingston* (60).

The Lords granted it as soon as the ship should be in dock, but now those perverse conditions which had bedevilled his command from the first, reappeared. Day after day the wind blew so fresh from the north that no ship could enter the harbour at all. After a week he wrote again in desperation: '. . . my health being very much injured I beg you'll be pleased to move their Lordships that I may have immediate leave to be absent for the recovery thereof'. The reply came back: 'to have leave directly', and soon his chaise was rolling along the rough country road to Alresford.

It is pleasant to imagine a little of that home-coming, with Mrs Clies ready and anxious to minister to every need, and probably Henny, now in her nineteenth year, in attendance. The home comforts, after so many months at sea, the healing attentions of feminine care, all these must have fallen like balm on his sick body and weary spirit. And there would have been his little boys, George now nearly five and Jamy a year younger, to refresh and delight his heart.

But a month was not enough to restore him so, on October 21st, he requested to be excused taking the *Dublin* to sea for the next cruise. After six or eight weeks, he assured the Lords, he would be able to do his duty, but if he went to sea again immediately his scurvy would return with great violence. The Lords were sympathetic, and agreed that the Hon. George Edgcumbe should go as temporary captain. There was no knowing how long that next cruise would last, and in the meanwhile he could recover his health completely and wait upon events. There was a pleasant element of uncertainty about his future. Sixteen years had now passed since that great moment in 1742 when he had stepped on to the quarterdeck of the *Plymouth* to read his Commission, sixteen years, during which his name had been moving steadily up the captains' list. The top of the ladder was in sight. The next batch of promotions might give him his flag. But employment as a rear-admiral would be another matter. Questioning the future, Rodney, like so many officers before and since, must have examined his prospects and taken stock.

He was now forty. He had commanded ships of war as long as any of his contemporaries, and more successfully than most. Perhaps the highlights of his career had been his fighting under Hawke at Finisterre, his record as Governor of Newfoundland, and his efficiency and drive while command-ing at Plymouth in 1756. He cannot have been blind to the fact that he had a considerable reputation, certainly inside the service, and probably beyond it.

Interest also he had in plenty, and that of the best kind. Anson at the

Admiralty had always recognized his merit, George Grenville, Treasurer of the Navy, was his friend and correspondent on naval matters, and Lord Temple had obliged him in the past. There was also the great Secretary of State and War Minister, Mr Pitt, ever on the lookout for men of zeal and ability, the very qualities which Rodney must surely have reckoned himself to possess in some measure. The omens, therefore, were not unfavourable.

As events turned out, Rodney never returned to the *Dublin*. His days as a captain were numbered, and in considering him for the last time in that rank one more of his qualities should be recognized. Zeal and ability are not everything. The efficient and thrustful leader who pleases his superiors by getting things done is often less acceptable to those beneath him. But Rodney was, as we have seen, always a popular captain, and the reasons for his popularity go a long way to explain his success. It was not merely that he was a good fighter under whom a crew might expect to fill their pockets with prize-money, although this of course helped. He was also a most humane and considerate commanding officer. His official correspondence shows, over and over again, how great was his concern for the health and welfare of his men, much greater indeed than that of his superiors at the Admiralty and the Navy Board who so often turned down the suggestions he made on their behalf.

If his newly pressed men came on board in rags, as they often did, Captain Rodney would petition an advance of pay for them, so that they could buy themselves slops at once. He would do his best (although not always with success) to get his ship put on to the most generous scale of victualling at the earliest possible moment. He seems to have had a positive obsession about protecting his after-guard and the watch on deck from bad weather: a short awning on the quarter-deck was his solution, which he failed to have approved for the *Ludlow Castle*, but which he obtained for the *Eagle* and the *Rainbow*. Whenever his ship carried some young gentlemen he did his best to make sure they had a schoolmaster.

He seems to have been equally ready to do his best for his people individually (provided the case was a deserving one). He wrote a heart-warming testimonial for his old schoolmaster in the *Romney*, pleaded urgently for the release of a landsman wrongly impressed by the constable at Poole 'as soon as possible before the poor man should be turned over into some other ship'; and with the same urgency for his former clerk in the *Ludlow Castle*, 'a man that has a wife and two small children in very low circumstances'. Over and over again appear these indications of humanity, consideration and good-nature. One of his longest and most generous letters was on behalf of the pilot who stranded the *Ludlow Castle*.

It is fitting that our last glimpse of Rodney as a captain is an agreeable one. By the oddest of chances the prisoners from Louisbourg, so recently his passengers across the Atlantic, became, a few weeks after landing, his neighbours at Alresford. A government camp for them was set up not far from his home. There was dissatisfaction among the French officers and the captains of the ships of war, who had been his guests in the *Dublin*, begged him to intercede on their behalf with the Admiralty, that their parole might be extended beyond the mile they were allowed. Writing from Alresford on October 1st, Rodney concluded: 'If their Lordships would be pleased to let their liberty extend to 4 or 5 miles, I would answer for their not exceeding that distance.' His request was granted, and it is possible to imagine the household at Alresford entertaining the gallant sea-officers of the French Navy, whom the master of the house had brought to England in the last ship he ever commanded as a captain.

Chapter 9

Channel Command

(1759–1761)

''Tis hot work at Havre. . . . God send good success to Rodney say I.'
(Sir R. Lyttleton to George Grenville, July 7, 1759.)

RODNEY'S promotion to rear-admiral, which came in May 1759, coincided with, and may even have resulted from, a new development in the war with France.

By this time Pitt's strategy of aiming for successes beyond the seas while paying Britain's continental allies to fight the French in Europe was beginning to produce results. After Louisbourg there was little the French could do to save Canada. Their counter-strategy, logical and ingenious, was based on the fact that although Britain might be victorious in North America and apparently invincible on the ocean, she had very few troops at home. Let our perfidious enemy, argued the Marshal de Belleisle, win victories across the Atlantic and elsewhere. They will avail little if we can strike successfully at her unprotected heart. With London occupied, no concession will be too great for her to make, and all France's losses will be recovered in the peace. The scheme was by no means chimerical. A French officer had recently given his opinion that a single French regiment could walk unmolested from one end of England to the other; and only fourteen years earlier a small Scots army had marched as far south as Derby. So plans began to take shape for an invasion in 1759, with a concentration of naval strength to cover the channel crossing.

Pitt's reply was to direct Hawke and Boscawen to blockade Brest and Toulon. It was the best thing to do, although no certain safeguard because wind and weather were as likely to aid our enemies as ourselves. Then, still in the early months of 1759, disturbing reports began to come in about the French port of Havre. The enemy were said to be constructing flat-bottomed boats on the beach, and during April confirmatory details poured in. One hundred and fifty of these vessels were projected, perhaps more, each to carry 100 men or 50 cavalrymen with their horses, and to operate under sail. More than 600 shipwrights and carpenters were being sent from Brest, and the First Commissioner of the Navy, M. le Pellerin, was already there to speed the work. Later reports spoke of great piles of timber and naval stores on the waterside, and the vessels themselves taking shape in plain view from seaward. August was spoken of as the invasion month.

All this was much in the minds of Pitt and Anson at the end of April and the beginning of May. The threat was unmistakable. Poor though security was in those days, French troops would have little difficulty in reaching Havre and embarking before we could learn about it. And then, who could say but that a few hours later, while the main fleet was still watching Brest, they might launch forth. With resolute leaders, a dark night, and a little luck, next morning might see them in their thousands on the Sussex beaches. The distance was less than 100 miles. It was resolved to destroy the French invasion barges using bomb-vessels.

These highly specialized craft were designed to anchor close inshore and throw shells from high-angled mortars placed amidships. The shell, which was simply a hollow metal sphere filled with explosive, had to be fused and the fuse lit before firing. Then away it went in a high parabola to descend (if well aimed) on the target. For the flat-bottomed boats building on the beaches, and for all the workshops, stores and timber-piles crowded behind the fortifications, the bomb-vessel was the perfect weapon.

They would have to anchor in the estuary of the Seine itself; and they would need protection. Frigates would be necessary and a few vessels of force, perhaps some of the small 50- or 60-gun ships; also tenders to carry the ammunition for the bombs and a cutter or two for despatches. All told it would be a sizeable force operating on the enemy's doorstep. So Anson and the Board would have developed the project until they arrived at the delicate question of who should command it. The size of the force would require a rear-admiral rather than a commodore, and the nature of the work would call for an officer of high capacity, cool, resolute, and resourceful.

So we come back to Captain Rodney, now well on the way to recovery from his scurvy but still unemployed. There seems to have been no one else available to whom Pitt and Anson would entrust the new project. His only disqualification was that he was not yet of flag rank, and although this could be remedied, something had to be done first about the two captains above him. One of them, Smith Callis, was a famous character. He had been made post, and received a gold medal and chain, for an exploit with fireships in 1742, and he had the reputation of being one of the best fighting officers in the Navy, and one of the touchiest. Smith Callis could not be shelved or disregarded. But luckily he was serving in the Mediterranean, and although he had to be promoted, there could be no question of bringing him home. The other, John Wickham, had taken post a week before Rodney and remained one place above him on the list ever since. For him it was now superannuation on a rear-admiral's half-pay. So at last, sixteen years after his posting into the *Plymouth*, Rodney became a rear-admiral of the blue, in circumstances which reflect nothing but credit on himself and those who brought him forward. There were no more flag promotions for the next two years.

In May the new Rear-Admiral left his pleasant Hampshire home and repaired to Portsmouth to deputize, with characteristic vigour and efficiency, for his old friend Francis Holburne, the port admiral, on leave in London. There is no indication whether he had any fore-knowledge of what was in store for him. His flag flew in the *Royal Anne*, a very ancient three-decker, but as his letters are addressed simply from Portsmouth, he was probably living ashore.

On June 6th, at half past two in the morning, he was summoned from sleep by the arrival of an express from Lord Anson which informed him officially, and perhaps for the first time, of the task before him. The first emphasis was on the need for secrecy. Nothing could conceal the fact that he would soon be taking a squadron to sea, but the story was to be that its destination was Gibraltar, and to make sure of this deception, false orders for the Mediterranean would be made out in the usual way. Meanwhile, the First Lord wanted to know the state of the bomb-vessels in the dock-yard, and whether there were any flat-bottomed boats fit for use—all of this to be ascertained and reported without delay, but without arousing the attention of the Port-Admiral or anyone else.

As a junior officer Rodney had won approval by his promptness in obeying orders; flag rank had not changed him in this respect. He dressed, and as soon as he decently could, he waited on Admiral Holburne now back from London, with the request for a day's leave to visit Alresford. An hour later, had anyone observed him making his investigations in the dockyard and been bold enough to ask what he was doing, he would have explained that bad weather had after all caused him to postpone his visit home. By 9.30 he had discovered what Lord Anson wanted to know and was writing his report.[1] One bomb, the *Basilisk*, was ready and out at Spithead with her tender; the *Furnace* would be ready in three days, but the tender she lost on the Barbary coast had not yet been replaced; the *Firedrake*, foul and leaky in decks and upperworks, would go into dock that evening; and there were only three serviceable flat-bottomed boats. Although he had aroused no suspicions, he felt bound to point out that service talk was already linking the bombs at Portsmouth with the enemy preparations at Havre. Secrecy would not be easy.

The false orders for Gibraltar arrived on the 9th, and if there was any leakage of information from the Admiralty or elsewhere, they served their purpose, for the French took no measures whatever against the impending attack. But the good people of Portsmouth, who could see the bombs fitting out, and who knew what was preparing at Havre, were not slow putting two and two together, and their answer was *not* Gibraltar. 'Very attentive and inquisitive about what is transacted', Rodney reported uneasily to Mr Secretary Clevland, the day after the false orders arrived. Four days later, with that touch of asperity which became more characteristic in later years, he described them as 'very impertinent in their surmises, particularly in the victualling office'.

Indeed, he must have detested trying to maintain the pretence in the midst of so much knowing speculation. Captain Hollwall of the *Deptford* was probably typical of many when, with an eye cocked for a hint from the Rear-Admiral, he remarked meaningly that he had been ordered to send his observations *on the Normandy coast* to Lord Anson. . . . Rodney, who reported the matter, replied coldly that he hoped the officer sent would be back at his duty before his ship sailed.[2] Hollwall had touched a sore point. In all Rodney's time at sea he had never been on that part of the coast it was intended to attack. But it was difficult to obtain suitable Havre pilots for a squadron supposedly going to Gibraltar.

With or without pilots some sort of reconnaissance was desirable, and on June 15th orders came down for Hollwall with two frigates to blockade Havre and take soundings for the bomb-vessels. The express was nineteen hours on the road, a fact which Rodney did not fail to report disapprovingly to the Admiralty who passed on the complaint to the Postmaster-General; and when reporting Hollwall's departure and the shortcomings of the post-boy, he took the opportunity of reminding the Lords that there was another bomb-vessel in the dockyard, the *Blast*. If she was to join his squadron, as he presumed she was, it would be well if she were put under his direct orders at once; otherwise she would never be ready in time.

His urgency was justified. Some of the French invasion-craft had not only been launched but had already been out under sail. Reports spoke of their excellent performance. One had been tried with cavalry on board and although her decks had proved unequal to the weight, a defect easily put right, she had otherwise come well up to expectations. M. le Pellerin was again expected, this time to witness a practice embarkation. Such was the situation when Hollwall's squadron appeared.

To take soundings off an enemy port is to invite retaliation, but the French in Havre had no ships strong enough to interfere, so the work proceeded uninterrupted. Even within range of the shore batteries the resourceful British sailors achieved their purpose by waiting until an unsuspecting Dutch merchantman appeared, outward bound down the river. Then thirty of them swarmed on board her, to present the French artillerymen with a perplexing problem as they cruised up and down under Dutch colours, sounding as they pleased.[3] By the time the French had recovered their wits and begun to fire warning shots, the work was done. The much abused neutral was allowed to lower her colours and anchor under the batteries, while the survey party made their cheerful escape by boat. With Hollwall on this occasion, and perhaps the author of this ingenious ruse, was Rodney's former midshipman, Samuel Hood, now commanding the frigate *Vestal*.

Meanwhile, Anson had collected a very respectable force for the enterprise. There were six bombs—the *Basilisk*, *Furnace*, *Firedrake* and *Blast*, which were ready or nearly ready at Portsmouth, and the *Mortar* and *Carcass* which were coming round from the Thames. The last three were brand new. To cover the bombardment there would be five small battleships, six frigates and two sloops. Rodney's flag would fly in the *Achilles* (60).

She appeared on the 17th, and three days later was fit to receive him and his retinue. Then, when all should have been ready, Captain Willis of the *Blast* found that the sweep of his mortar-beds was too small, and the bomb-rooms below not properly finished off, all of which, with other deplorable examples of dockyard negligence, would take three more days to put right.

Rodney had a short way with inefficiency of this kind. Bursting with nervous energy he hurried ashore to speak his mind to the store-keeper of the Ordnance, the Commissioner of the dock and anyone else responsible. The result was an undertaking to work night and day, and a promise to have the *Blast* ready in thirty hours. On June 25th she was out at Spithead with the others and he could at last report the whole of his squadron (except for the two bombs from the Thames) ready to proceed.

This was what the Lords (and Mr Pitt) had been waiting for, and Rodney's instructions came back by return. Their rolling periods do full justice to the importance of the occasion:

'Whereas the King has received undoubted intelligence that the enemy are making great preparations for invading these Kingdoms, and particularly that 130 flat-bottomed boats are building at Havre; and it being of the greatest consequence that all possible means should be used to frustrate this design of the enemy, you are hereby required and directed to take under your command the ships and vessels named in the margin* . . . collect all the pilots near at hand acquainted with the said port and its road . . . and . . . so soon as the wind shall prove favourable and the weather appear settled to repair off Havre and having placed the bomb-vessels in the best situation and made a proper disposition of the rest of your force, you are to endeavour, as well by bombardment as by all other means in your power, to destroy the boats building upon the beach and also any Naval or warlike materials that may be there, or any boats, magazines, stores, provisions and materials that may be in the basin, harbour and town of Havre. . . .'

All this eloquence and a great deal more was signed by three Lords of the Admiralty on June 26th, and went down to Portsmouth that night. The endorsement: 'At 9 p.m. by Tranter the messenger', suggests a decision at the end of a long day, and a humble cog in these great affairs clattering off from the dim portals of the Admiralty and galloping through the summer night. Being secret they went to Rodney direct, and not through the port-admiral's office. The Lords were uneasy about this, assuring Admiral Holburne by the same post that no slight was intended, but that 'the Service being of a secret nature is the reason of the instructions to Mr. Rodney not being sent through your hands as usual'.[4]

But now the wind piped up fresh from the north-west. The pilots were positive there would be a great sea and a dangerous lee-shore in the road of Havre, so, for the next four days, the squadron lay at St Helen's, giving the bombs their first opportunity to exercise their mortars. The delay was a

* See Appendix 4.

blessing in disguise if these vessels were to hurt the enemy and not themselves, for there was great ignorance on board all of them. Luckily Rodney
had two highly qualified artillery officers with him, Colonel Desaguliers*
and his very capable assistant Captain Smith, both of whom worked
tirelessly to instruct officers and men in their very specialized work. Two
small Dutch hoys which arrived in the anchorage while the bombs were
exercising were detained in the interests of security. Then, on July 2nd,
the weather improved and the squadron sailed.

The town of Havre (or Havre de Grace as it was better known in 1759)
lay snug within its triple defences. The town itself had its inner ramparts,
a deep moat, and beyond this a complicated system of outworks. Into
this formidable and complex plan a long, narrow arm from the sea made its
way between two enclosing moles to form the harbour; and along the
crowded quays was part of the British target, the stores, rope walks, and
warehouses. But most of the building slips were more accessible than this.
The sudden demand for flat-bottomed boats had far exceeded the town's
ordinary building capacity, and the report that most of them were taking
shape on the sea-shore beyond the walls was true.

No rumour of the intended attack seems to have reached the French.
If they deduced anything from Hollwall's reconnaissance it might have
been the possibility of an armed landing. There had been several the year
before, but as the town was full of troops they had nothing to fear on this
score. But they had no heavy artillery capable of denying the waters outside
the harbour to the British bombs.

Rodney's ships approached the Seine estuary on the morning of Tuesday
July 3rd, with a light breeze from the north-west. They anchored about
1.30 p.m., the two-deckers in the Great Road, the frigates inshore of them,
and the bombs with their tenders further inshore still. On the beaches,
plain for all to see, were the flat-bottomed boats: from the *Firedrake* they
counted 130. At two o'clock Rodney summoned all captains on board the
Achilles.

There had been a slight hitch. It was desirable that the bombs should
be aligned as nearly as possible at right angles to their line of fire, with
one at least able to sight straight down between the pier-heads. And
because enemy retaliation could not be ruled out they must be grouped
together and not scattered. But between them and the shore, as if specially
placed by Nature to make the operation harder, was the *banc de la jambe*,
where faulty pilotage might leave a ship stranded under enemy fire.

* Later Lieut.-General and Colonel Commandant of the Royal Artillery.

Colonel Desaguliers wanted the bombs close in on the edge of the *banc*. No pilot would take the risk. Hence Rodney's council of war on board his flagship. The outcome was that Hollwall of the *Achilles* and his first lieutenant, with Hood of the *Vestal* and Phillips of the *Juno*, all with recently acquired local knowledge, took over the pilot's job and went on board the bombs.

The *Basilisk* and *Firedrake* weighed and edged cautiously in towards the shallow water. They took some time to anchor but between six and seven that evening the *Basilisk* was in position and opened fire. She threw four shells for range and four only: all fell short.

Greater risks would have to be taken so, as darkness closed in, all the bombs weighed and crept still closer to the edge of the shoal. It was after midnight before they were in position, with the *Basilisk* at the northern end of the line in five fathoms, then the *Firedrake* in four, and the *Blast* and *Furnace* in even less. A defence flotilla organized by Hollwall rowed guard round them during the dark hours, but no counter-attack developed, although there was a brief alarm when the *Carcass* and *Mortar* arrived, with the *Chesterfield* (44), and dropped anchor in the outer road. At half-past three in the morning dawn was breaking. The Portsmouth bombs were ready and they opened fire together.

The effect on the inhabitants of Havre was shattering. They heard the explosions. They marked the course of each projectile as it soared gracefully into the morning sky and they waited for it to descend. But they could do nothing in reply except sound the alarm, ring the church bells, and set the soldiers to putting out the fires. Soon the *Carcass* and *Mortar* crept in to join the others and by noon on this Wednesday July 4th, all six bombs were in line before the town and firing steadily. But long before this the Rear-Admiral had gone on board Hood's frigate for a better view. From the *Vestal*, while the morning was still young, he sat down to write his first despatch as a flag-officer.

'On board the *Vestal* in the Road
of Havre de Grace, 4 July 1759.
'*Sir*,
'I have the honour to acquaint their Lordships that yesterday. . . . I anchored in the Road of Havre, and immediately gave orders for placing the bomb-vessels . . . but every pilot I had in the squadron were so totally ignorant of the place that had it not been for the captains of the *Deptford*, *Vestal* and *Juno*, and the first lieutenant of the *Deptford*, I should have

found it extremely difficult and tedious to have anchored the Bombs properly. Those gentlemen having exerted themselves on this Occasion and during the night had placed the *Blast* and *Furnace* in such a situation that every shell they throw either falls among the flat-bottomed boats or into the town, which has already been twice in Blaze.

'The *Mortar* and *Carcass*, with the *Chesterfield*, joined in this Morning. I have hurried them all that was possible and I hope they will be in their station in an hour to two. As I am now on board the *Vestal* (one of the frigates that supports the bombs), I can assure you I have seen several of the shells fall among the Boats and Storehouses.

'The enemy's fire is pretty brisk from 2 or 3 Bomb Batteries, but as yet they have done no harm.

'9 o'clock A.M. All the Bombs but the *Carcass* are now in their stations. She is under sail and will be so in a few minutes. The enemy's fire from their Bomb Batteries are very brisk indeed.'

Brisk the French fire may have been, but it was quite ineffectual. Havre was unprepared for this sort of attack; the range of the British mortars and the quality of the British powder came as a horrifying surprise. But

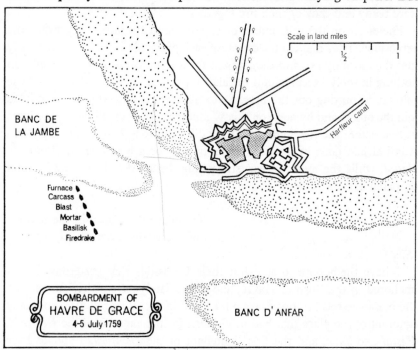

Scale in land miles

BANC DE
LA JAMBE

Harfleur canal

Furnace
Carcass
Blast
Mortar
Basilisk
Firedrake

BOMBARDMENT OF
HAVRE DE GRACE
4-5 July 1759

BANC D'ANFAR

her experiences at first light were nothing to what had to be endured when all the bombs were in position and the rhythm of fire was working smoothly. A French report estimated that 500 shells were fired in twenty-four hours, which, if correct, works out at one shell approximately every fifteen minutes from each of the six bombs.* Considering the complicated fire drill and the elaborate precautions necessary, this ought to have satisfied even Rodney's standards of briskness.

July 4, 1759, marked the climax, so far, of his fighting career. As he surveyed the scene from the *Vestal*, he could see all his force deployed against the enemy. Inshore were the six bombs with their tenders, banging away and covered in smoke; further out, the frigates and sloops, with the squadron's boats, ready at the first sign of movement from the harbour to launch away; and further to seaward his five heavy ships. Before nightfall, unless anything untoward happened, his first despatch would be trotting up to London as fast as horses could carry it, to inform Lord Anson, Mr Pitt, his Grace of Newcastle and possibly His Majesty himself, that Rear-Admiral Rodney's attack had begun well.

He does not seem to have visited any of the bombs. They would have been much too small and crowded to accommodate him and his retinue. But this is no reason why the reader should not be introduced a little more closely to the working of these vessels upon whose performance the whole operation depended.

They lay, as we have seen, about a mile from the shore, anchored bow and stern with their mortars trained to port. To a visitor climbing on board for the first time the massive main-mast just forward of amidships would have been the most striking feature. The 10-inch and 13-inch mortars, the *raison d'être* of the vessels' existence, might at first have escaped notice. They gaped skywards from their bomb-beds, which were slightly below deck level, one forward of and the other abaft the main-mast. Below each bomb-bed was a shell room with fitted racks for forty-eight shells. More than this the crowded little ship could not stow. Further aft the visitor would see the unusually large capstan and then the break of the poop, a small mizen-mast and the ship's wheel. The full complement amounted to some sixty all told.

---

* '*Nous eprouvons depuis 24 heurs toutes les Horreurs de la Guerre. . . . Il est impossible de vous dépeindre la Consternation. On a fait Sortir les femmes, les enfants, et les vieillards. Les Chemins sont remplies de Gens qui fugent avec leurs effets. On n'avoit point imaginé que les Anglois puissent approcher si près pour nous ecraser. . . . Le feu est en différent endroits de la ville et du Port; on nous a jetté 500 bombes dans 24 heurs. . . .' Intelligence Report, 'du Havre le 5 Juillet 1759'. Ad.1/3945.*

Firing regulations were strict. An experienced warrant officer from the Artillery was in charge between decks to supervise the delivery of the fixed, i.e. fused, shells from the racks, all of which must be expended before any came from the tender. On board the latter two artillerymen were employed solely in filling and fixing more shells, and Rodney had two of the squadron's boats attending each bomb to carry them across to her. The powder came from the magazine under the poop, and here the standing orders leave an impression of nerve-racking care and endless precautions against accidental explosion. No powder might be opened or measured out except in the captain's cabin which, with the alleyway approaching it, was kept constantly wet, the door being kept shut all the time and covered with tarred hide. A naval party of eight under a warrant officer assisted at each mortar, and of these the two most reliable were solely employed holding the lighted port-fires or matches in the tubs of water provided.

So if we are to picture the scene on board one of the bombs we should not visualize the wild exhilaration and abandon sometimes associated with a naval action, but instead a tense atmosphere, iron discipline, and a slow and methodical drill carried out with almost pedantic respect for safety precautions. Alert and capable, Colonel Desaguliers and Captain Smith were on board each bomb in turn, advising, correcting, and encouraging.

All that Wednesday the firing went on. The half-built boats on the beaches were the easiest possible target, and when the gunners had disposed of them they ranged beyond, with increased charges, to drop their shells inside the harbour, along the quays, and even in the tidal basin. A hundred shells fell here or in the harbour according to a neutral Spanish captain who claimed to have counted them, and three at least hit the great church. As for the French reply—the *Furnace* recorded the passing of a few shots fired at extreme range, between her masts. That was all.

As evening approached, the fire of the bombs began to slacken. All were beginning to suffer from their exertions. The first to have trouble was the *Basilisk*. At 6 p.m. her poop bulkhead collapsed, leaving her captain's cabin, where the powder was measured out, open to the upper deck. But her captain was a man of resource. Quickly he contrived a screen of wet hides and hammocks nailed across the opening and soon the *Basilisk* was firing again. A little later the 13-inch mortar-bed of the *Carcass* gave way, and her fire-power was halved. After this the progressive deterioration on board the bombs is best followed in a brief timetable.

20.00 *Furnace* in trouble. Bed of 10-inch mortar gives way and the mortar found to be cracked.

21.00 *Carcass* in trouble again. 10-inch mortar found to be flawed. Both guns now unserviceable and ship very leaky.

21.00 *Furnace* in trouble again. 13-inch mortar found to be cracked in several places. (Both *Carcass* and *Furnace* now out of action and haul out from the firing line.)

22.00 *Firedrake* in trouble. 13-inch mortar unserviceable.

So, by the end of that first day, fire-power had been reduced from twelve mortars to seven, with the expectation that the others would break down before long. To nurse his remaining material, Rodney directed the surviving bombs to haul closer in on the rising tide so that they could reduce their charges—but the deterioration continued. At 4 a.m. on Thursday the *Firedrake*'s remaining mortar became unserviceable, and at 6 a.m. the *Mortar* had to give up as well. With her decks badly damaged, one 10-inch mortar out of action and the whole ship very shaky, she followed the *Firedrake* to the outer anchorage, having discharged 102 shells and carcasses in twenty-four hours. Only the *Basilisk* and *Blast*, leaky and shaken but with their mortars still serviceable, remained in the firing line as the second day of bombardment wore on.

But this withdrawal of four of their tormentors brought small consolation to the French for at 6.30 a.m., half an hour after the *Mortar* ceased fire, the greatest disaster of all befell them. A large timber pile in the north-west of the town was set alight.* The conflagration was visible for four hours, and was a more deadly blow to French preparations than the destruction of all the boats on the beaches. By now the town was largely emptied of its old folk and children, and troops were pouring in. But still there was no effective retaliation.

Apart from the great fire, Thursday's bombardment was on a diminishing note. Rodney was again on board the *Vestal*, and the squadron's boats continued to row guard round the bombs, now reduced to two. But still the French counter-attack never came, and at three in the afternoon the *Basilisk* had to give up. She had been the first to open fire, forty-five hours earlier, but her 10-inch mortar was now out of action, and her 13-inch mortar-bed showed signs of collapse. She had fired 19 13-inch carcasses,

---

* French intelligence report specially mentions '*Un magazin de bois entierement brulé*'. Ad.1/3945.

72 13-inch shells, and 91 10-inch shells, a total of 182 projectiles altogether. Now she hauled off.

The *Blast* continued firing with both mortars until 6 p.m., when the spindle below her 13-inch mortar broke, and the weapon itself was found to be cracked. But her 10-inch mortar went on barking at the enemy until midnight, and only when this devoted weapon blew out at the touch-hole was the bombardment of Havre over. Rodney had tried his material to the limit, and although more ammunition was available at Portsmouth, every bomb was now *hors de combat*. This is why the operation stopped when it did.

At nine on Friday morning the Rear-Admiral shifted his flag back to the *Achilles*, and at noon the *Vestal* slipped from the anchorage, the first of the squadron to depart. She took with her Rodney's second despatch, a surprisingly brief document considering the readiness with which he usually put pen to paper, but with it went Colonel Desaguliers, and Faulkner, captain of the *Furnace*, to fill in the details. Most of the other ships followed a few hours later leaving a small squadron to blockade the port. So shaken were the bombs when they arrived at Spithead that they had to go up harbour at once.

From His Majesty downwards the Nation was delighted with the exploit. Rodney's first report of July 4th elicited from Anson another of his rare personal letters.[5]

'Admiralty, 6 July 1759.

'*My Dear Rodney,*

'Yr letter of the 4th inst. gave great satisfaction to everyone here, I have seen the King and all his servants who are extremely pleased with your commencement, and don't doubt but that you will go on and prosper; I take it for granted you will throw all your shells which will convince us of the full operation of a bombardment; if more shells should be wanted you will send some of your bomb tenders to Portsmouth. The D. of Newcastle desires me to send you his compliments, his Grace has secured you a sure seat in Parliament, I hope your good weather will continue which has been very fortunate,

'*Dear Sir,*
'*Your much obliged humble Servant,*
'*ANSON.*'

The Lords collectively were less effusive but expressed themselves as 'very well satisfied with Admiral Rodney's conduct'. They gave him leave to come to town, and desired him to bring the exact bearings, depth of water, etc., from every bomb, a request which caused some of their captains no small embarrassment although they all managed to produce something. A successful sailor, just back from administering some shrewd knocks to the enemy, can always be sure of popular acclaim, particularly if the politicians are behind him to share the credit and for a while the name of Rodney was probably as familiar to the man in the street as that of any admiral since Vernon. A naval cutter was named after him, the first of a long line of notable warships, tongues wagged with approving gusto, and while the bombs in Portsmouth dockyard were being refitted for a new attack, the man of the hour was in London to receive the attentions which were his due.

Before he returned to his command he was able to find the time to pay a visit to the studio of Mr Joshua Reynolds. The result is quite the most sympathetic and agreeable likeness of him which exists. The smooth brow, the candid eyes, the generous mouth—all these belong to the successful young sailor who enjoyed the friendship of Keppel, the approval of Anson and the love of Jane Compton. It may be that Reynolds did the first version of this portrait a few years earlier, before Jenny died. But the fine rear-admiral's coat, worn with a negligent grace which few of his service contemporaries managed to achieve, would have been brand new when Rodney went to the studio in Great Newport Street at one o'clock on July 19th for a single sitting; probably it was the reason for it. So we see him as Reynolds saw him, before he returned to his channel command, and before the trials of later life left their mark.*

But while all rejoiced at the success, the government did not delude itself that the invasion danger was over. On July 25th, Newcastle informed Hardwicke: 'By all Advices the Flat Bottomed Expedition is pushed with more Activity and talked on with more Confidence than ever. I did not see the King yesterday. Mr. Pitt was very grave.'⁶ For once the Duke was correct in his appreciation. The French in Havre, when they had put out the fires and surveyed the damage, decided that the destruction, although severe, might have been a lot worse, and they went on with their project. This is why, in August, Rodney was again at Portsmouth, hastening the preparations for another bombardment, encouraged by the knowledge that

---

* This portrait now hangs at Petworth House. When the Rodney family sold it many years later it was bought by Lord Egremont with the remark: 'You may send me the Admiral: I knew the grandson of Lord Rodney who was like enough the picture to have sat for it.' *Memoirs of the Life of John Constable.* I am indebted to Professor E. K. Waterhouse for this information, and for the details from Reynolds's appointment book.

Mr Pitt himself was being kept informed how his requirements were being met. He wanted more 13-inch mortars, more effective carcasses, of a type he had seen at Woolwich, and more precise regulations for the Train of Artillery. The authorities did what they could.

On August 29th he was off Havre once more with the bombs, with his flag flying in Hollwall's *Deptford*, but this time the cards were stacked against him. The wind began to freshen from the north-west causing a heavy swell. Prudently he kept all his ships out in the great road away from the sands, and it was well he did so for in the night the wind strengthened to gale force putting them all on a dangerous lee shore. Next morning there was a great sea in the road and that evening, while the ships rolled and pitched at anchor, the French showed their teeth. Down the river came two large, ungainly shapes which resolved themselves into two massive floating batteries. They moored in the shallows so as to command the area where the bombs would operate and it became very clear to the British, as they surveyed these monsters through their glasses, that the second bombardment of Havre (if it ever took place at all) would be very different from the first. Next day Rodney boarded one of the cutters to have a closer look. Each mounted four cannon pointing through embrasures, with room behind for a mortar. As they were anchored in the shallows it would be impossible for his frigates to engage them effectually; nor did it look as if the boats of the squadron would be able to attack them either, for each battery was attended by a large flat-bottomed boat crowded with soldiers—and no doubt more would be forthcoming if needed. Batteries and boats all fired briskly on the cutter as she made her reconnaissance. Rodney returned to the *Deptford* in a less hopeful mood.

The weather worsened. On September 4th it blew such a gale that the clumsy bombs had to run for the Downs. The rest stuck it out off Havre until the night of the 5th when, the gale veering northerly, all were in imminent danger of driving on shore. Only the ebb tide coming off with the gale saved them from destruction, and for the next few days they kept a good offing. Not until the 11th did the weather allow them to anchor again, by which time the French defences had been further reinforced. Three floating batteries now commanded the channel between the pierhead and the Anfer bank, while in the shallow water between the pierhead and the *banc de la jambe* were six galleys and two armed vessels. It was check. The batteries would prevent the bombs attacking the town and the galleys would prevent the boats of the squadron attacking the batteries. For a while Rodney toyed with the idea of a night attack, but the French patrols were too good and the shore defences too close. His officers thought the same. 'The Captains of the Squadron,' he wrote regretfully, 'men of gallantry and spirit, are of opinion nothing further can be done by bombardment.' The Lords accepted this and directed that the port be closely blockaded.

This was to be Rodney's service for the rest of his channel command. A close blockade made heavier and more exacting demands than any other form of sea warfare. It called for unremitting vigilance to keep ships seaworthy and to keep them at sea, to keep them on the station and to keep them off the rocks; it meant days and weeks and months of restless, exhausting seagoing, usually in the worst of weathers, with nothing to show for it except lists of defects, lists of men sick, and reports of victuals condemned. By the end of the year Rodney had learnt some hard lessons.

Until the end of September the weather was merely uncomfortably boisterous. Then, with October, the reports of bad food suddenly became a flood—butter 'stinking and unfit to eat', cheese, bread, and beer 'musty, stinking and unfit'—the calamitous chorus swelled from every ship in the squadron. In mid-October the weather worked up to another full gale from the south-west. With great difficulty and no small danger the ships rod it out long enough to witness the withdrawal of the floating-batteries into the harbour. Then the gale worsened, and they were whirled away up channel and scattered. With the *Brilliant* and *Unicorn*, the *Deptford* was driven down to leeward of Beachy Head before she could bear up for the Downs. This was no station from which to blockade Havre, but they could not claw their way back until the 24th, when it was observed that the French troops had struck camp and their tents on the cliff were gone.

The *Deptford* was now impossibly foul, so Rodney shifted his flag to the 50-gun *Norwich*, not that she was much better. The next gale carried away her main topsail-yard and jib-boom and she was lucky to make St Helen's safely. During the stormy weeks in mid-November only the *Unicorn* and the cutters held out on the station.

The *Norwich* was off Havre again on the 19th when all seemed quiet. There were no flat-bottomed boats on the beaches, although a neutral reported 200 hauled up between Caudebec and Rouen, and 150 on the south bank. However, within twenty-four hours the invasion danger vanished altogether, for on the evening of the 20th, some 350 miles to the westward, Sir Edward Hawke drove the main fleet of France to destruction among the rocks of Quiberon Bay. But this made no difference to Rodney's orders. The close blockade had to go on, and the famous year of victories continued tempestuous to the end. When he could he stretched across to Havre with the whole squadron; when this was impossible he kept a frigate on the station with a cutter or two; and if the weather became too bad even for a frigate, then only the devoted cutters held their ground. By the end of December the *Norwich* was as bad as the *Deptford* had been, if not worse. She had to be pumped every two hours in fine weather and continuously in bad, and her hull was so foul and ragged as to chafe and spoil the cable whenever she anchored.

During this tempestuous November Rodney was once more returned to Parliament, and to understand how this came about a brief digression must be made. On June 17th the borough of Okehampton fell vacant through the death of its member, Thomas Potter. Within twenty-four hours of this event we find a certain Lieutenant Joseph Hunt with Rodney at Portsmouth, and Rodney writing the same day for permission 'to take him with me as a Volunteer Lieutenant. . . .'[7] In the ordinary way there was nothing remarkable about this for Hunt was an old follower from the *Dublin*.* But he was also a man of influence in Okehampton. Newcastle knew about him and Anson, who hated political jobbery, had blocked his promotion until Thomas Potter's death made this possible no longer.[8] Coming when it did, Rodney's application to take Hunt with him can hardly be coincidence.

The outcome was that Hunt was immediately promoted master and Commander of the *Mortar* (bomb), and at the same time Newcastle became suddenly convinced of Rodney's suitability to represent the electors of Okehampton. When, immediately after the bombardment, Anson passed on the Duke's assurance of 'a safe seat', Rodney must have known very well which it was. The Duke of Bedford's consent had to be obtained as Rodney still owed some sort of allegiance to him, but there was no objection here, and the matter was settled.

There was one slight difficulty, however, for voters liked to see their candidates, if only at election time, and Rodney would almost certainly be at sea. Polling day was fixed for November 24th, and as the date approached, Robert Andrews, Newcastle's agent, and John Luxmore who nursed the borough, expressed some concern about this. But the Duke adroitly turned the circumstances to advantage in a persuasive reply. 'I desire you will represent to our Friends that nothing but the King's immediate Service, which obliges Mr. Rodney to return forthwith with a squadron of His Majesty's ships to block up the French vessels at Havre could have

---

* He was the lieutenant sent home with the *Montmartel*.

prevented him from attending at Okehampton upon this occasion. As soon as His Majesty's service shall permit, he will, I am sure, with the greatest pleasure wait upon the Corporation. In the meanwhile you will be so good as to represent this to Our Friends in such a manner that his Absence (which is unavoidable) may not prejudice his election.'[9]

Who could resist such an appeal? Not the patriotic electors of Oke-hampton, for on November 25th Luxmore was able to inform the Duke of Rodney's unopposed return. Rodney's letter of acknowledgement to his patron, written from the *Norwich* at Spithead on December 2nd, is a model of propriety. 'I beg your Grace will permit me to return you my most sincere thanks for the honour you have bestow'd on me in chusing me a member of Parliament of Okehampton; a steady adherance to your Grace's commands shall ever distinguish me while I have a seat in the House.'[10]

So ended the famous year 1759. Rodney's contribution had made him for a few weeks something of a popular hero, for what that was worth, although the exploit that so attracted public attention was simply a well-conceived technical operation carried out with skill against an unprepared enemy. More worthy of praise was the blockade which followed it, and the long, uncomfortable weeks with winter coming on, until Hawke's victory eased the situation. Two of the Rear-Admiral's flagships were worn out in these months, but of all his ships the cutters kept the seas longest and bore the heaviest burden. To the end of January 1760 he flew his flag in the leaky *Norwich*. Then, on the 28th, he turned over to Captain Darby and came on shore.

For the next four months the records are almost blank, but there would have been the agreeable duty of attending at the House of Commons, and the possibly rather less agreeable duty of waiting on his constituents in remote Okehampton. He may have had another bout of illness. A letter from Hill Street dated May 21st: '. . . confined for several days past with a Violent Cold and Bilious Cholick . . .', strikes a familiar note. Neverthe-less, six days after writing it he again hoisted his flag in the *Deptford*.

There was no question of another bombardment for the floating batteries were already back in position. His orders were simply to blockade the port, intercept coastwise shipping, and sweep the channel for privateers; but there was nothing static or repetitive about the way he interpreted them. Thus Captain Ogle of the *Aquilon* had orders to cruise off Cape Barfleur to intercept coastwise traffic, stretch frequently across to Dunnose to catch privateers, and report to the Rear-Admiral off Havre every ten or twelve days. Captain Jervis of the *Albany* (sloop) was to range along the Sussex coast as far as Beachy Head, cross to Dieppe, and thence return to Havre. Target practice with the great guns gave the men plenty of exercise, and a large French fishing-boat was captured and taken in to service as a useful means of deceiving the enemy. There is an impression of continuous and varied activity.

In July the French began passing some of their flat-bottomed boats along the coast to Brest, not to concentrate for invasion, but as a means of transporting naval and military stores to that remote corner of France. Rodney learnt about this from a disgruntled Spanish captain who, having failed to sell his cargo in Havre, was glad to do the French an ill turn. According to him the boats made their first hop by night across the Seine estuary to Honfleur; then, choosing another dark night, they crept along the coast in small groups, ready to scuttle if attacked; seven had already reached Brest in this way, seven more were waiting at Honfleur, and there were ninety-four up the Seine, ready to go. Rodney duly reported this to the Admiralty and prepared to pounce. His difficulty was that the Seine estuary and the coast from Honfleur westward was so shallow that he could not attack until the quarry was well clear of the river. But he sent his cutters, suitably disguised, to cruise inshore during the dark hours, posted the *Albany* (sloop) and the *Furnace* (bomb), also disguised, west of the Caen river, and remained with the rest of the squadron observantly at anchor.

On July 14th there was a fair wind from the north-east. At noon, five boats emerged from Honfleur and, escorted by one galley, they crept across the estuary exchanging frequent signals with the shore. In the British squadron not a signal was made and not a sail loosened. The enemy carried on past Dives Point and ran as far as the mouth of the Caen river where they could be seen standing backwards and forwards in the river mouth; their intention was to wait until sunset, still an hour away, and then push on under cover of darkness. The moment darkness fell Rodney sent the *Aquilon*, *Tweed* and *Firedrake* after them, remaining himself in the road watching the port. Next morning five more crept out from Honfleur and in the clumsy *Deptford* Rodney weighed and followed them. Of course they kept out of range in the shallows and then slipped up the Caen river.

The first group were less fortunate however. Pressing on through the darkness they were duly intercepted in the small hours by the *Albany* and the *Furnace*. Jervis* of the *Albany* was the last man to miss a chance like

* Later Lord St Vincent.

this, and the five were promptly driven on shore near the village of Port-en-Bessin, twenty miles west of the Caen river. Rodney learnt of this the same morning and pressed on towards the sound of gunfire.

But now the wind fell light, progress became infuriatingly slow, and before Rodney could communicate with his squadron the sound of the firing ceased. At last the little port appeared in sight. There was a cluster of ships off shore and the flat-bottomed boats could be seen on the beach; but there were no signs of any activity and an inexplicable hush hung over

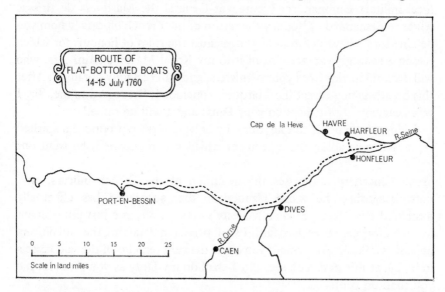

the proceedings. The *Deptford* was hardly moving and the Rear-Admiral had to be patient a little longer until a boat arrived from the *Aquilon*. Captain Ogle, it appeared, had behaved with spirit and humanity.[11] He had silenced the little fort overlooking the roads so that he could close in and smash the flat-bottomed boats on the beach; but when it was seen that some houses would be damaged, he had held his fire and called the French to a parley. The result had been a gentleman's agreement by which the houses would be spared if the French would burn the boats themselves. A wait of more than two hours had followed, at the end of which a Captain de Beaumont of the Regiment of Rohan came on board the *Aquilon* to repudiate the whole agreement. Captain Ogle now awaited his Admiral's orders.

Rodney's reply was characteristic. He expressed the opinion that the whole business was a French manœuvre to gain time; he gave orders for the boats, and of course their valuable cargo, to be destroyed without any more delay; and he directed that the French officer be detained, and with him three others who had come on board for no better reason than curiosity to see a British warship. So, before night fell, the squadron closed in to a range of only 200 yards, and the flat-bottomed boats were very effectively destroyed.

It was not a particularly heroic exploit but it was a useful one, and it certainly annoyed the French. Their irritation was voiced next day by the local military commander, Lieutenant-General the Marquess de Brissac when he demanded of Rodney the return of the French officers 'whom you detained, as I have before told you, against the rules of honour, for which reason I shall give an account of it to my Royal Master's Ministers, who will demand justice from your Ministers, and will certainly obtain it'. After this breath-taking threat the Marquess concluded: 'In regard to me, Sir, I will hear nothing further; do your Duty, and I will do mine.'

Rodney, who never did anything by halves, at once produced a spirited reply. After recalling the agreement which was repudiated, he went on:

'Such Chicanery authorises the detention of the French officers, and, notwithstanding the warm Cannonade that succeeded has effectually destroyed His Most Christian Majesty's vessels, yet, as a just punishment for so Notorious a breach of faith I shall persist in detaining the said officers unless, as a Public Atonement you cause the very remains of the said vessels to be burnt this day. You see, Sir, I shall do my Duty as you acquaint me you shall do yours. . . .'[12]

But with five flat-bottomed boats and three prisoners to his credit, as well as the last word, Rodney could afford to be magnanimous. The fiery de Brissac was only acting under orders from his superior. So tempers returned to normal and the French officers were released. But nothing could put those five flat-bottomed boats together again, nor do the English sources mention any more of them slipping through to Brest.*

The affair off Port-en-Bessin was Rodney's only brush with the enemy in 1760. The rest of the year wore itself out in exhausting and unspectacular blockade duty, with the weather worsening all the time. On August 7th there was a most violent gale during which the squadron was driven from

---

* A French report of July 21st, after calling the episode a 'Catastrophe', speaks of a decision to unload all the rest and send them up to Rouen where they are unlikely to have played any further part in the war.

its anchorage and the bombs were near foundering. The *Deptford* began to leak again. September saw some very hard gales, and at the beginning of October the *Aquilon* was nearly lost on a lee shore. By this time the *Deptford* was no longer seaworthy and the *Nottingham* (60) was ordered round from Plymouth to replace her. She arrived at Portsmouth, her crew unpaid, scantily clad, and followed overland by a mob of seamen's wives, desperate for an issue of pay to their husbands before the ship went on service.

Human problems were always Rodney's concern. As a rear-admiral he could speak with a freedom hardly possible as a mere captain. He made sure the men got their pay, although at the cost of forty hours' delay to the ship, and other demands followed. Plymouth yard had not provided the extra accommodation for a secretary's office so this had to be done at Portsmouth. He was insistent that his quarters should *not* be newly painted, but on the other hand he did insist on the usual admiral's fittings for them, particularly a green floor-cloth on the deck.* An evasive and obstructive stores officer received an exemplary dressing down.

But as he never overlooked what was due to himself, so he never forgot what he owed to even the humblest of his dependants. A letter from four followers, left behind in the *Dublin*, deserves a place on the record.

'*Dublin*, November 13 1759.

'*Most Honbl. Sir*,

'Wee humbly beg leave to lett Your Goodness know that Wee wrote to Yr Honor from Plymouth—and Having this oppertunity again, Wee think it Our Duty to acquaint Your Goodness that Wee Should be Glad to serve His Majesty Undr Your Honr's Command then Any Others in the Navy.

'Therefore, as Your Honor is Certain Wee have been with You in the late War and This Will Not Forgett Us at this Present And will as is our Duty be ever Obedient To

'*Yr Honor's Commands.*

'*JERH. McNAMARA*
'*JOH. MILLER*
'*JOH. PURVIS*
'*FRAS. EMLINGTON.*'

Of course he responded. He had Miller, who had been upwards of twelve years a quartermaster under him, made boatswain of the *Aquilon*.

* Flag-officers were allowed green kersey for this purpose. Captains had red.

But Miller was constantly drunk and absent from duty, so Rodney advanced McNamara in his place, confessing, in his letter to the Admiralty, that he was 'almost ashamed to ask a favour on his behalf after the behaviour of Miller', but recommending him none the less because he had been with him for so many years. Such obligations were paramount.

To return to the *Nottingham*. As soon as she was on the station a really vicious gale caught her and drove her up channel to seek refuge in the Downs. Ten days later, when it had moderated, she escorted 400 merchantmen down channel and was off Havre again by November 1st. But the lull was only temporary. Three weeks later she was once more in the Downs, plunging uncomfortably at her cables with topsail yards on deck. December saw the elements at their worst, beating upon the ships day after day in a crescendo of baffled fury while they lay, as most of them did that month, at Spithead with topmasts housed. Seagoing was pointless; ships and men were being worn out to no purpose, until Rodney himself began to protest: 'Tis excessive absurd to keep us longer off Havre,' he wrote to Robert Andrews on December 19th, in a letter which might perhaps be seen by the Duke of Newcastle, 'as tis not one day in twenty any of my squadron can venture to look upon the coast.'[13] To the Admiralty, on January 10, 1761, he put it more tactfully. '. . . the officers and seamen . . . have suffered much from the severity of the weather . . . it has been with difficulty the ships could be worked, with sails and rigging being so hard frozen.' But all through that bitter January of 1761 the blockade went on.

Under such conditions mistakes could easily happen and they did. Hood, in the *Vestal*, was thrashing out of the roads on January 2nd when he mistook the four British cutters for Frenchmen, beat to quarters, and, to lure the supposed enemy within reach, hoisted French colours. Naturally the cutters fled, with the *Vestal* in hot pursuit. The result of this comedy of errors was that one was 'captured' while the other three reached Portsmouth with the report of a French frigate in the Channel. For the next six days additional ships patrolled between Boulogne and Havre until a report from Hood made all clear.

By the end of January conditions at sea, and perhaps the nervous strain of the last eight months, had become too much for Rodney. On the 24th he requested a fortnight or three weeks' leave 'to recover a sufficient share of health to return to my Duty'. The Lords were sympathetic. Perhaps some of his remarks about the absurdity of the blockade were at last bearing fruit. In any event, three days after his application he was in London.

The rest of the story is soon told. In less than a fortnight he was back at

Portsmouth, not to wear himself out off Havre, but to administer the chief command of the ships and vessels at Spithead, where drive and energy were needed to prepare some reinforcements for Indian waters. But this done, and it did not take long, he was again writing to the Admiralty. There was something else on his mind besides his health.

'Portsmouth, February 23 1761.

'The Dissolution of the Parliament drawing near, and having received by the last Post very pressing letters setting forth the necessity of my appearing personally very soon at Okehampton. . . . I must desire you will please make it my Humble Request to Lord Anson that I may be relieved of the command at this Port. . . .'

The magic word Parliament was an 'Open Sesame' for release. Rear-Admiral Geary was at once ordered to Portsmouth in his place, so that Rodney could at last quit his command and attend to those political interests on shore that always meant so much to him.

Chapter 10

Martinique

(1761–1762)

'I have landed 14,000 brave fellows on Martinique and if they don't reduce the island it will be their own fault but for my part I make not the least doubt of it.'
(Private letter from Rear-Admiral Rodney, Case Navires Bay, January 19, 1762.)[1]

WHEN Rodney quitted his channel command in February 1761, and hurried to London he must have been itching to find out what was going on, for the King had died the previous October and none knew better than he how a sea-officer's prospects might be affected by political changes. Particularly would he wish to know what the Duke of Newcastle intended for him in the new Parliament. As soon as he learnt of the King's death he had been prompt to condole with his patron in a letter in which sorrow for the deceased monarch was not allowed to dim an eye already scanning electoral horizons.[2]

'Portsmouth, Nov. 27 1760.

'My Lord,

'As I have been constantly employed on the coast of Normany, permit me to take the oppertunity of my arrival here, most sincerely to condole with your Grace on the melancholy loss the Nation has sustained in the death of our late most Gracious Sovereign.

'I must beg leave to acknowledge the very great obligations I lay under to your Grace, for all the preferments I have attained in the Navy, obligations which I can never forget, and which now call upon me most humbly to offer what little interest I have in the County of Southampton, to be disposed of at your Grace's pleasure, as 'tis whispered in this County there is a likelyhood of an Opposition at the ensuing Election.

'In all other respects, among your Grace's many friends you shall find none more ready to obey your commands than him who has the honour to be, with most profound respect, humility, and gratitude,

'Your Grace's most obliged and most obedient, humble servant,

'*G. B. RODNEY.*'

Newcastle throve on communications like this, and at the time can have given Rodney no cause to fear for his Okehampton seat; and Luxmore the local manager was so sure he would again be the government candidate that on December 14th he wrote to remind Rodney of his promise to obtain a post ship for that invaluable fellow Joe Hunt, whose borough influence had been so useful in the previous election.[3] As late as February 23, 1761, when he wrote from Portsmouth asking to be relieved of his command, he was still cheerfully confident that he was the government candidate for Okehampton. His horrified surprise on discovering, only a few days later, that he was not, is shown by his anguished appeal to the Secretary to the Treasury, James West.[4]

'27 February 1761.

'A letter I received by last night's post has given me inexpressible concern. Mr. Andrews acquaints me therein that he has received the Duke of N . . . e's commands that Mr. Wenman Coke was to be chosen at Okehampton on Mr. Thomas Pitt's interest. For God's sake, Sir, what have I done to gain his Grace's displeasure? You know full well Sir that it was to serve him that I came into Parliament, and was desirous to continue on no other foundation.

'I must entreat you Sir to represent my case in the humblest manner to his Grace and beg of him not to let me suffer in the eyes of the public as a person obnoxious to him and unworthy of his protection, which I shall infallibly do unless his Grace vouchsafes to let me have a seat in Parliament by his influence.'

It was as if the whole foundation of existence was sinking beneath his feet although his anguish was premature for it had never been Newcastle's intention to drop him. Nevertheless, the Duke was at his wit's end how to fit all the pieces of his political jig-saw together and for a while Rodney was on tenterhooks. At first Newcastle had a mind to put him in as the naval member for Portsmouth, but this would have meant displacing Sir Edward Hawke which would not do at all. A better idea was the small Cornish borough of Penryn, whose members were usually returned on the interests of Lord Falmouth and Lord Edgcumbe. The Edgcumbe seat would be available in the new election and by a happy chance Rodney had been, for many years, on the friendliest terms with the family.* He was therefore particularly suitable for Penryn in the Edgcumbe interest; his willingness to put up £2,000 was of course an additional qualification.

But Falmouths and Edgcumbes were not to have it all their own way in 1761. There was a powerful local interest, with two rival candidates in the field and plenty of money behind them. There could be no avoiding the rigours of the canvass this time, so down to Penryn Rodney had to go. The disturbing developments he found there, and the best way to defeat them, he reported fully to his patron.[5]

'Penryn, March 25th 1761.

'*My Lord,*

'I must beg leave to lay before your Grace the present situation of affairs at this place where I arrived on Sunday last, and hence in company with Lord Falmouth and Mr. Edgcumbe canvassed the town.

'We find at present but a small majority owing to a defection of several Officers of the Customs and Salt Office both here and at Falmouth, as likewise two men belonging to the Pacquets who are all obstinate in opposition. . . . I must therefore join with Lord Falmouth and Mr. Edgcumbe for the Demission of one Charles Robbins a Tydesman etc. at Falmouth, which may have the desired effect on the other officers.

'I must now take the liberty to point out to your Grace a measure which I am sure will infallibly secure the Election, and which I most earnestly entreat may take place immediately, as it will convince the people in general (whose minds have been poisoned with different notions) that I have the honour to be nominated by your Grace as candidate.

'Captain Peard of the *Savage* (sloop of war), a Freeman of this Town whose friends have great influence, has been offer'd by the Adversaries a bond of one thousand pounds and that they will procure him a post ship; he has resisted the temptation and has continued firm.

'If your Grace will make it a Point that it may appear here before the

---

* Rodney had been shipmates with young Edgcumbe in the *Romney*, and in 1754 the old lord had done his best, although without success, to get him chosen for the borough of Grampound.

election that Captain Peard has post, I am sure all difficulties will be removed. My ship, the *Marlborough*, has no captain appointed as yet. . . .'

Of the *Marlborough* more later. Sufficient to say that Captain Peard never took post in her, or in any other ship; perhaps he took the Adversaries' £1,000 instead. The poll was on April 4th and the government candidates just scraped home. Lord Falmouth, reporting this to Lord Bute, commented wryly: 'The place has been expensive.'

If Rodney ever reckoned the cost, which is extremely unlikely, he would probably have considered the money well spent. His Penryn seat would put him in an infinitely stronger position to press his claims to another and better command. This, when all is said and done, is seen as the reason for his political preoccupation at this time. European waters were no longer important. In North America the war was virtually over. But elsewhere, other prospects were opening.

The theatre with the best future now was the West Indies. Guadeloupe had already fallen but there was still Martinique, the most desirable prize of all, and Pitt was determined to have it. Lying in the centre and to windward of that great crescent of islands, the lesser Antilles, it was ideally placed for attacking every British island except Barbados. From its numerous creeks and inlets the privateers swarmed to prey on British trade, and from its plantations (for in Martinique the sugar cane flourished exceedingly) the French exported the molasses and rum which so often undersold the produce of the British islands, sometimes in markets where the French had no business to be at all. As early as January the project had been in the great Minister's mind. At the same time there had been talk of the *Marlborough* for Rodney's new flag-ship. Perhaps even at this early date there had been an understanding or a half promise.

Long before his final orders arrived he must have known unofficially that he would command at Martinique and fly his flag in the *Marlborough*. His own instructions for convoying and disembarking troops were probably composed and seen through the press that summer. In September he was applying from Hill Street for old followers from the *Rainbow* and the *Dublin*.

But as that summer wore on the shadow of Spain loomed larger and increasingly hostile across Britain's path. Spain had many old scores to settle and her young monarch was itching to settle them with the sword. The question facing the Cabinet was whether to try to avert the danger by fair words or strike first and strike hard. Pitt was for the latter. He pointed out that as Spain was only waiting for the arrival of her plate-fleet, Britain should declare war at once. But only Temple supported him. For hours he argued with his colleagues. He alarmed them, he offended them, he united them against himself. But he did not persuade them.

The struggle went on until October. Rodney was near enough to the seat of power to know what was going on. But whatever happened about Spain his appointment to command the sea forces against Martinique was assured. The end of the West Indian hurricane season was near, and soon he would be exchanging the London scene for blue water. At the beginning of October the summons came.[6]

'Admiralty Office, 5 October 1761.

'*Dear Sir,*

'I am commanded by my Lord Anson to acquaint you that the King hath signified his pleasure that you should Command in Chief at the Leeward Islands and proceed thither immediately with the reinforcements and ships that are now very near ready to sail. His Lordship therefore desires you will come to Town as soon as you can, as you can not stay more than twenty-four hours after your arrival, and that you will give all necessary orders to your servants preparatory to your embarking on board the *Marlborough* at Spithead.

'*I am, etc.,*

'PH. STEPHENS.

'P.S. Lord Anson desires you won't fail to be in Town tomorrow.'

It was natural for Anson to desire a last word with a protégé about to command in waters which were strange to him. But there is a note of urgency in the postscript and perhaps a reason for it. In the Orders for Martinique, both naval and military, someone had blundered, and it was important that Rodney should be in no doubt about where the plans might go wrong, and what was expected of him.

The grand total of troops to be employed against Martinique might amount to some 13,000 men. Ten batallions, with engineers and artillery, were coming from America; from Belleisle on the French coast, which had fallen in June, four regiments would proceed direct to the West Indies; and there would be contingents from Antigua, Guadeloupe, Dominica, and Barbados. But there was a certain ambiguity about the rendezvous. Both the American and the European contingents had been directed first to Barbados which, as it lay well to windward of the objective, was an ideal springboard for the assault. But the orders went on to say that if they found no instructions waiting for them there, they were to carry on for Guadeloupe. From here, as any sailor familiar with those waters would know, Martinique would be for all practical purposes inaccessible because of the prevailing wind and current.

How the blunder came to be made need not concern us. Anson, who advised Pitt on naval affairs, was away from the Admiralty in August and part of September which probably had something to do with it. As things turned out Commodore Sir James Douglas, the man on the spot, had already reacted violently to the mention of Guadeloupe and sent a warning to General Amherst that none of the American troops should be directed thither; but Anson would not know this. Among the other subjects he and Rodney would have discussed would have been the possible entry of Spain into the war. Here the only certainty was that the Spaniards would be allowed to choose their own moment to strike, for the Cabinet crisis in London had come to a head. Baulked by his colleagues Pitt intended to resign; indeed, he did so on the same day that Rodney had his last interview with Anson.

The *Marlborough* was already out at Spithead when Rodney hoisted his flag three days later. His retinue included Hollwall, formerly of the *Deptford*, Thomas Atkinson, his official secretary since 1759, and an important newcomer, the Rev. William Pagett, a pushing and ambitious cleric who seems to have found his way on board through his connection with the Northampton family, and who was to be Rodney's chaplain and private secretary for many years. The Rear-Admiral was to bring out with him the *Vanguard* (74), *Modeste* (64), and *Nottingham* (50), with the *Thunder* and *Granado* (bombs); also the *Foudroyant* (80) and the *Dragon* (74) from Plymouth if they were ready. The rest of the squadron was already on the station under Douglas, and it was to be hoped that the troop convoys were by now at sea.

The *Marlborough* was one of the oldest ships in the Navy. She had started life under another name in the reign of Charles II, had twice been rebuilt, and now mounted 68 guns. She was an odd choice for a flagship and in no respect ready to accommodate the Rear-Admiral when he came on board, but the *Foudroyant* would be available if he wished to move, and Anson had expected that he would. However, there were difficulties about this, as will be seen. Discovering that his flagship was extremely leaky, and that water could not drain away properly from the upper-deck where it was usually over the men's shoes, Rodney joined battle with the dockyard in his usual way. The squadron was delayed ten days by foul winds. A gale scattered the ships soon after they cleared the channel, after which the picture of the Rear-Admiral proceeding to his great command reduces to an inconsiderable scale; for when the weather moderated, the *Marlborough* found herself alone on the ocean, except for one of the bomb tenders. Day after day the flagship and her humble companion ploughed on without a sight of the others, but such a situation was not unusual. Dozens of transports and thousands of troops should have been somewhere at sea besides Rodney's scattered squadron, but sooner or later, unless things went very wrong indeed, the wind would waft them all to Barbados. There was nothing the flagship could do except work down to her latitude and sail along it until that island broke the western horizon, which it did on November 21st. A few ships were riding at anchor in Carlisle Bay but none of the missing consorts. Douglas was blockading Martinique. On shore there were 500 whites and 600 blacks raised for the expedition by the Governor. There was no news of troop transports from America, or from anywhere else.

With the curtain about to rise on the new drama half the cast was missing. But this was no excuse for inaction. Still apprehensive about the Guadeloupe rendezvous, Rodney sent a frigate to look out for any troop convoys, with the most positive orders for them to join him *at Barbados*. Short of small craft he hired a number of small armed vessels, pressing their crews with the consent of their owners; and he requested Governor Dalrymple at Guadeloupe to obtain all the maps, charts, and pilots he could for Martinique, and not to haggle over the price.

The truth was that Major-General Monckton and the great troop convoy from New York had only just sailed. They had passed Sandy Hook on November 19th, three days before Rodney reached Barbados, and would not be with him for weeks. But after five days his own ships began to straggle in. The *Foudroyant*, *Modeste*, and *Basilisk* arrived on the 26th, the *Nottingham* and *Thunder* on December 1st, and the *Vanguard* on the 9th. As some of them were already sickly Rodney promptly despatched the *Marlborough*'s tender to Tobago to catch or buy turtles for the invalids, an item of expenditure unlikely to endear him to the Navy Board. All the old, condemned sails from the squadron he directed to be cut up and made into tents for the Marines, soon to be serving on shore. As soon as each ship recovered he sent her off to join Douglas.

At last came news of some troops. Nine crowded and very clumsy transports, with General Lord Rollo and 1,200 men from Dominica, were trying to make the Barbados rendezvous. Wind and current were forcing them to leeward of St Lucia and for a month this unhandy convoy tacked to and fro, while the wretched soldiers went on short rations and the naval Commander-in-Chief fumed. Some very trenchant messages passed before the escort commander, who, by dividing his charges into three groups,[7] eventually brought them into Carlisle Bay. By the time this happened, all the rest of the land forces had appeared.

On December 14th the first convoy arrived with 2,000 troops from Belleisle, escorted by the *Temeraire* and *Actaeon*, and at last the anchorage began to look like the staging point for a great assault. Another week passed. Then came news that the American convoy might be expected hourly. An interlude of bad weather followed with fears of enemy privateers picking up scattered transports. At last, on December 24th, Rodney's heart was gladdened by the report that the whole of the American convoy was in sight.

Very impressive it must have looked, standing into the bay. Escorted by three battleships and a frigate, there were 64 transports, 4 victuallers, and 2 large hospital ships, besides other ancilliary vessels. They brought with them some 7,600 hardened and experienced veterans of the war in North America. For once the troops had travelled in comparative comfort. There had been enough shipping to allocate space in the proportion of 2 tons per man. But they could not be hurled at the enemy immediately. Every transport had to be re-victualled and watered, some troops had to be redistributed, and the commanders had to confer. All this went on over Christmas and into the first days of January 1762.

Rodney was fortunate in his opposite number. Major-General Robert Monckton had been Wolfe's second at Quebec and was experienced in colonial and amphibious warfare. He was also a man of good understanding and equable temper. Throughout the operations which followed, admiral and general remained on excellent terms. In all he had some 13,000 men, to which should be added a number of negro slaves to carry the stores. But Rodney was determined that the sea service should contribute its quota. In the first whirl of activity after arriving at Barbados he had directed that each ship of the line should contribute sixty suitable landsmen to be trained for fighting on shore. Quebec had shown what could be done in inter-service co-operation. There must be no falling short at Martin'que.

Something must now be said about this French island, thirty-five miles long by thirteen across, upon which were to be landed 13,000 of His Majesty's troops. Everywhere Nature would be on the side of the defenders.

Movement on shore would be difficult and over most of the island impossible. To the conventional soldier it would be a campaigning nightmare. The waters round the island were nearly as disagreeable to the sailor as was

DOMINICA CHANNEL

Pearl Rock

LA TRINITÉ

St. PIERRE

FORT
ROYAL

StLUCE

ISLAND OF
MARTINIQUE

Diamond Rock   St.ANNE

Pte Salines

ST. LUCIA CHANNEL

the terrain to the soldier. Coral reefs, shoals and rocky ledges abounded—incompletely charted and often unsuspected. In places sheer cliffs 300 feet high raised an insuperable barrier to soldier and sailor alike.

The heart of Martinique was the splendid bay of Fort Royal, halfway up the western side. Here was the administrative centre, the carenage, and a harbour safe from every wind likely to blow. There was no stronger base anywhere in the Leeward Islands. An invader would have first to pass the outlying defence of Pigeon Island; then, while negotiating the tricky approach, with all the navigational hazards of rock and shoal and the difficulty of tacking against the fluky wind under the land, he would have to endure heavy plunging fire from the citadel. There was no easy way here.

But if the bay of Fort Royal was too difficult, by what other way might its citadel be approached? Fourteen miles to the north was St Pierre, the commercial capital of the island, with an open roadstead and no defences worth mentioning. But so bad were road communications in Martinique that the army siege train, if landed at St Pierre, could never be brought overland to Fort Royal. Otherwise there was la Trinité with a good harbour on the windward side of the island, and St Anne's Bay, sheltered and commodious at the south end, and both poorly defended. But to these the same objections applied. There were also one or two possible landing places much nearer to Fort Royal, one of which had been used in the abortive attempt on the island two years before.

By 5 p.m. on January 6th, 175 sail were moving out from Carlisle Bay. Landing barges, sturdy craft with ten oars a side, able to carry thirty soldiers each or forty at a pinch, were on the decks of the transports or towing astern. On January 7th the high peaks of Martinique rose steadily from the sea, and next day Rodney's great force rounded the south end of the island and came to anchor in St Anne's Bay. Douglas had already silenced the few weakly manned batteries and there was excellent shelter. But already Nature's defences had taken their toll. The 64-gun *Raisonable*, Captain Shuldham's, had stood in too close while engaging a shore battery, and was stranded. Her dejected wreck, with men salving what they could, marked the edge of the shoal water as the armada rounded up for the anchorage.

It is doubtful if Rodney and Monckton ever supposed they could conquer Martinique by landing on the southern end of it, but it was most desirable to keep the defenders in suspense. To this end Rodney also arranged for a demonstration along the coast. Flying an admiral's flag in the splendid *Foudroyant*, Captain Robert Duff, with a small squadron, sailed past the bay of Fort Royal and up as far as St Pierre, to the alarm and confusion of the French. During the night he increased the alarm on shore by a display of pyrotechnics and coloured lights. In Fort Royal the Governor, with fewer than 1,000 regular troops, was trying to animate the island's reluctant militia, but with threatening reports from every quarter these became increasingly wishful to return to their estates, their plantations, and their slaves. Duff's demonstration not only perplexed but demoralized the French colonials.

All the same, there was still the problem of finding a suitable landing place not impossibly far from Fort Royal. St Luce was considered and rejected. The next possibility was the little bay of La Petite Anse d'Arlet, just round the corner as it were from Pigeon Island and the bay of Fort Royal. Monckton thought that from here something might be attempted against Pigeon Island, either with guns from on shore or with boats from

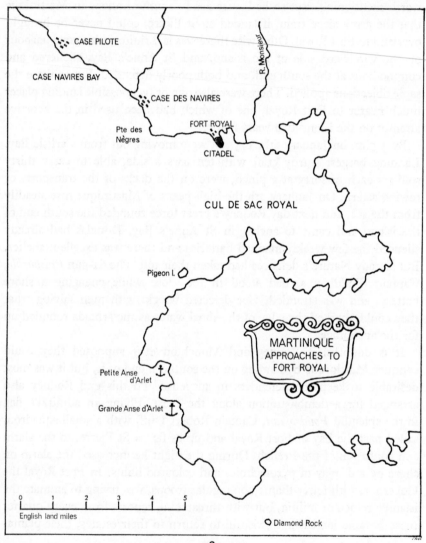

the fleet; it might even be possible to advance on Fort Royal itself. He requested Rodney to land two brigades and see what could be done.

For this exploratory probe Douglas, with five of the line, was detailed to cover the operation, while Commodore Swanton, with four more and a frigate, landed the soldiers. At about 3 p.m. on January 10th the troops under Brigadier Haviland were put ashore without difficulty, and the same afternoon Hervey landed a force of seamen and marines from the *Dragon*, a little further south in La Grande Anse d'Arlet. Forts were captured, guns spiked, and by 7 p.m. the British were in possession of both bays. Early next morning the advance began, but the soldiers soon found that there was no way to Fort Royal from where Swanton had landed them, and no hope of annoying Pigeon Island either. Thus the probe had to be abandoned.

Three years earlier another expedition had disembarked a few miles north-west of Fort Royal at Case Navires Bay. Six thousand troops had stayed on shore just over twenty-four hours, then lost heart and gone on to take Guadeloupe instead. There now seemed no choice but to try again in the same place. Monckton's engineers were dubious, and the General seemed to share their view that the defences would have been strengthened, but Rodney pooh-poohed their fears. He was positive that his ships could silence any shore batteries the French had. He took the general and his staff across the bay in his old ship the *Dublin*. Let them pick any spot they liked between Pte Nègre and the Morne aux Bœufs and he would guarantee to land the whole army without the smallest risk. At this there followed a prolonged consultation between Monckton and his engineers. Eventually they pointed out a small gully about half a mile north of Case Navires. So it was decided.[8] During the next four days (January 12th–15th) the whole force concentrated in the Grande Anse d'Arlet, while the two staffs worked out the details.

By this time all of his captains and everyone else concerned would have familiarized themselves with six printed pages in booklet form, impressively headed:

RULES

*To be observed by that part of His Majesty's Fleet under
the command of Rear Admiral Rodney in Landing
and Re-embarking the Troops.*[9]

Here were orders, lists of signals and details of organization, sufficient to leave no one in any doubt of what he had to do. Nevertheless it is part of the nature of such operations that planning goes on to the last moment. So we may, if we like, picture the flagship's office at this time with Atkinson, Pagett, and one or two clerks adding last-minute corrections, filling in blank spaces, and completing the final details, their work interrupted more frequently perhaps than they liked by visits from officers in red coats or blue, and the occasional peremptory summons to the Rear-Admiral's cabin.

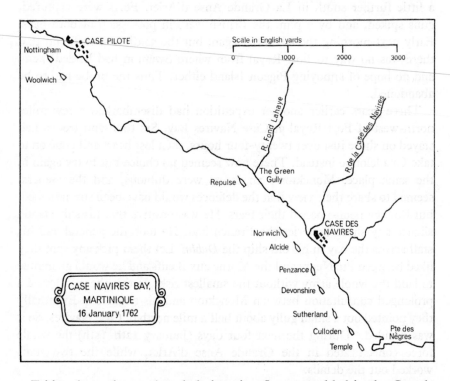

Friday the 15th saw the whole invasion fleet assembled in the Grande Anse d'Arlet. Some of the transports had transferred their troops to battleships, and the ships detailed for the preliminary bombardment had lent most of their boats to those carrying troops. The first move was at 6 p.m. when the bombarding squadron under Captain Barker of the *Culloden* weighed and proceeded to sea.*

At 4.30 next morning (Saturday January 16th) the Rear-Admiral made the signal for all the rest of his force to weigh, and as the great mass of

* For the ships detailed for this duty, and all the others engaged in this operation, see Appendix 5.

shipping hove up and stood across the bare nine miles of water that lay between the anchorage and the landing beach, Barker's squadron could be seen coming in from seaward to take up positions opposite the batteries.

Broadsides of 20 or 30 guns at a range of a quarter of a mile or less were more than the French colonials could stand. The firing began at about 9.30 and at 10.35 the first battery fell silent. The transports were now turning smartly in to the bay, all firmly impressed with the Rear-Admiral's order that they must *not* shorten sail too soon. At 11.30 Rodney signalled his three bombs to engage. At noon the *Granado* opened fire and soon after this, when it was clear there was not much fight left in any of the batteries, he signalled for the troops to be ready. At 1 p.m. came the order for the fleet to anchor, followed an hour later with that for the troops to embark in the boats.

At once every warship sent to collect her quota of landing-barges from the transport specified in her orders, manning each with twenty rowers and a reliable petty officer. Some ships also contributed their own longboats for this purpose. The troops detailed for the first wave then embarked, after which the boats assembled under the sterns of the rendezvous ships to await the next signal. When it came they formed up in three divisions, about a quarter of a mile offshore. Commanding the centre was Swanton of the *Vanguard*, identified by a red flag; on the right was the division of Molyneux Shuldham, late of the *Raisonable*, flying the red cross of St George; and on the left that of Augustus Hervey of the *Dragon*, identified by a blue flag. A slight drizzle was falling. Then Swanton gave the signal and all the boats surged forward as fast as their rowers could drive them, until all were in the breakers. The French were in no condition to resist anything like this, and within five minutes, 5,000 men were ashore and drawn up on the beach. From then until sunset boats plied to and fro, ferrying the remaining redcoats and their gear ashore, not forgetting puncheons of drinking water for them; and all through the night they continued to ply, so that by morning 14,000 men, including two batallions of marines, were safely landed. By this time the first arrivals were attacking the French redoubts inland, the bombs coming close inshore to lob their shells ahead of them as they pushed forward. Rodney was cheerful and sanguine. Completing his first despatch he assured their Lordships: 'No time shall be lost in giving every assistance of every kind which the Army can be in want of, or which may even anticipate their own requests.'

He had good reason to be pleased, for hardly were the troops ashore when an express arrived—only three weeks from Lisbon—with the welcome news that Spain was at last an enemy. Such early intelligence might be worth a gold mine, and it came from Captain George Johnstone of the *Hornet* (sloop), who had learnt from a captured privateer that Spain had ordered the seizure of all British shipping. This, if true, could only mean war. At once he put into Lisbon to get confirmation and then, without delay and on his own responsibility, he manned and victualled his prize and sent her away to warn Rodney. The latter was keenly aware of the possibilities. 'The News coming to me so soon will give me an oppertunity to do them all the Injury I can before the people in this part of the world are acquainted therewith.' However, until the soldiers triumphed on shore, he could not turn his eyes very far elsewhere.

Patience was needed. It was soon evident that the troops had a rough road before them and that Monckton, faced with unusual difficulties, was not to be hurried. Rodney, with his own despatch already written, and with Captain Walsingham waiting to take it home, was on fire to send it off, but the General begged him to hold it until the Army had something material to report, which he did until the 21st when he could wait no longer. In a letter to the Duke of Newcastle,[10] the last before the packet went, he excused himself. 'I have put off the Departure of the ship which brings this News for five days at the General's request, but receiving this day a message from him that he has no despatches as yet to send . . . I thought it absolutely my Duty not to delay a Moment longer. . . .' Six weeks later England learnt that the Navy had put the Army ashore on Martinique, but no more than that. Rodney's despatch came under the august notice of H.R.H. the Duke of Cumberland who commented sourly to Newcastle: 'I will own to you alone I don't like the four days inaction of our Army as Rodney states it—but you know Rodney. . . .'[11] Perhaps memories stirred of some remarks on Rochefort.

To return to the soldiers on shore. The distance to Fort Royal as the crow flies was only three miles, but it was all broken ground, rocky outcrops and thick tropical undergrowth, with the heights of the Morne Tortensen and the Morne Garnier to be stormed before the attackers could point their guns at the citadel. With the heavy train of artillery, progress was bound to be slow: but for Rodney's determination to give the Army all the help he could, it would have been infinitely slower. The sailors of the fleet brought the guns ashore. Then, under the inspiring leadership of Captain O'Brien of the *Temple* who wore himself out by his exertions, they dragged them most of the way to Fort Royal, showing what could be done with blocks and tackles and abundant good will. An infantry officer was amazed.

'You may fancy you know the spirit of these fellows,' he wrote, 'but to see them in action exceeds any idea that can be formed of them. A hundred or two of them, with ropes and pullies, will do more than all your dray-horses in London. Let but their tackle hold and they will draw you a cannon or mortar on its proper carriage up to any height, though the weight be never so great. It is droll enough to see them tugging along with a good 24 pounder at their heels; on they go, huzzaing and hullooing, sometimes up hill sometimes down hill; now sticking fast in the brakes, presently floundering in the mud and mire; swearing, blasting, damning, sinking and as careless of everything but the matter committed to their charge as if death or danger had nothing to do with them. We had a thousand of these brave fellows sent to our assistance by the Admiral; and the service they did us, both on shore and on the water, is incredible.'[12]

These were no starved and resentful slaves but healthy, happy sailors, working under officers whom they respected and in novel conditions which they enjoyed. They were not allowed to exert themselves in the heat of the day, breaking off work at ten in the morning and starting again at three in the afternoon. When they could outflank the defences from the sea these same sailors returned to their native element, and with the marines and the faithful landing-barges (backed by the attendant bombs), rowed along the coast and helped the soldiers break through one position after another. Well might Monckton, in his first despatch, acknowledge 'the harmony that subsists between the Fleet and the Army, and the cordial assistance we have received from Admiral Rodney';[13] and well might the Rear-Admiral, writing at the same time, pay tribute to 'the eager and cheerful activity of the officers and seamen who contributed everything in their power. . . .'

The real strength of Fort Royal had lain in its seaward defences and the difficult terrain. Once these were overcome the French commandant had very little hope of keeping the militia to their duty. At 4 a.m. on January 24th, 1,200 armed seamen landed on Pointe Nègre under the eyes of the Rear-Admiral who was on board the *Temple*. A daylight bombardment followed. The firing stopped. The Army advanced, and by 8 a.m. the Morne Tortensen was occupied and the enemy in full retreat. On January 27th there was a last engagement on the heights after which nothing remained between the British 24-pounders and the citadel. The militia now deserted in scores, dropping down from the walls before the very eyes of their commandant, despite his orders to fire on them, and scampering away before the fortress could be invested.[14] The Governor of Martinique,

Vassor de la Touche, was in no position to send help. His own militia was deserting likewise, and he withdrew to St Pierre to prolong the resistance for a few more days. On February 3rd, the 952 regulars in Fort Royal beat the *chamade*, and that night a naval party (a lieutenant and thirty men from each ship), under Captain O'Brien, slipped quietly up the Monsieur River to cut the garrison's retreat, and were rewarded with the capture of six privateers. Next day the garrison surrendered to Monckton. Pigeon Island followed—on the appearance of Rodney's bombs—with fourteen more privateers. After this the rest of Martinique could be only a matter of time. Two possible centres of resistance remained—the harbour and settlement of La Trinité on the north-east side of the island, and St Pierre itself. Both were more easily reached by sea than by land, so the initiative again passed to Rodney.

La Trinité was already blockaded by the *Penzance* (40) and the *Levant* (28). Hervey now arrived in the *Dragon* (74), with the *Zephyr* (12) and the *Basilisk* (bomb). He landed fifty marines and the French colonials needed no further inducement. 'Success with no loss and only a little trouble', was how he described the business. St Pierre, being a considerable town, might be expected to resist, but the appearance of four British battleships, and the fear that these might soon be joined by the terrible British bombs, was quite enough for the inhabitants, already aware that as neighbouring Guadeloupe had been selling her sugar and molasses much more profitably since surrender,[15] they too might sweeten the bitterness of defeat in the same way. Against this point of view de la Touche was powerless. He was an old officer of the Marine who had fought on board the *Tonnant* on October 14, 1747, and commanded a sixty-four at Quiberon, and although himself from Martinique, he had small sympathy with its civilians. But the colonists were inexorable. So it was that on February 13th his brother appeared on board the *Marlborough* with articles of capitulation 'just in time', as Rodney commented grimly, 'to save the town of St Pierre from destruction.' So Martinique fell. The Rear-Admiral ended his second despatch with another tribute to his men.

'As this great island is now intirely subjected to His Majesty's Obedience, I can only repeat in this publick manner my intire approbation of the conduct of all the Officers and Seamen of that part of His Majesty's fleet which I have the honour to command, all having exerted themselves in their proper stations with an ardour and resolution becoming British Seamen.'

Rodney's official despatches are always impeccable, but in his private communications he is not backward in reminding his patron that the labourer is worthy of his hire. A letter to Newcastle of February 10th[16] has a delicately pointed implication impossible to miss. 'I have likewise great satisfaction,' he purrs smoothly, 'when I consider that this conquest puts it into your Grace's power to oblige many of your friends by the Posts and Employments in your Grace's gift, and which are very lucrative in this island.' And in case the Minister should miss the point he goes on: '. . . if I have the good fortune to continue in your Grace's esteem and that my conduct on this expedition meets with your Grace's approbation, I shall be extreamly happy, as among your Grace's many friends none is more truly, etc., etc.' Critics of a later age, better instructed of how a gentleman should behave, may condemn such brazen soliciting, but Rodney's world thought nothing the worse of a man for pressing his claims, and would probably have thought meanly of him, did he not. Never one to leave anything like this to chance he wrote again on February 27th[17] to remind the Duke that 'the height of my ambition is to prove myself worthy of the patronage your Grace has always bestowed'. Regrettably, he was wasting words as far as Newcastle was concerned. That Minister's long tenure of office was nearly over and he was to resign in May. It is even possible that in the proscription of his adherents which followed, the services of Rear-Admiral Rodney received less attention than they deserved.

But he would not know of this for some time, and whether ministerial favours would be forthcoming or not, there was still work to do. The details of the French capitulation are unimportant for everyone knew that the ultimate fate of Martinique would not be decided until the statesmen met round the peace table. In the meantime a military governor was appointed, and 590 French regulars were sent back to France in two transports. A decision for which Admiral and General were later criticized was their refusal to make terms with the Martinique privateers. Rodney probably persuaded Monckton that the best way to deal with these pests was to seize St Lucia and the sparsely populated neutral islands, and to this task he now addressed himself. Swanton, with six of the line, two frigates, and two bombs* sailed south to blockade, and at discretion capture Grenada. Hervey, with two of the line, three frigates, and one bomb, was to blockade, and at discretion capture St Lucia and St Vincent.

---

* *Vanguard* (70), *Temple* (70), *Devonshire* (64), *Modeste* (64), *Nottingham* (60), *Rochester* (50), *Repulse* (32), *Lizard* (28), *Granado* and *Thunder*. It seems likely that this large force was meant also to attend to the Spanish main where the *Actaeon* (28) had already taken a valuable register ship from Cadiz.

The scene was thus pleasantly set for the victors to enjoy a series of easy conquests with plenty of prizes thrown in. Rodney himself lay at St Pierre, a most agreeable town with shady streets, well-built houses and abundant fresh water, which he found infinitely preferable to the gaunt isolation of Fort Royal. He now had the ambitious and plausible Shuldham, late of the *Raisonable* (called by Hervey 'the Superior of the Jesuits') as his captain, a change which caused some heart-burning among the other captains,[18] and which was probably ill-judged. Congratulations arrived from Amherst in North America, to which he replied as one victorious commander-in-chief to another, thanking him 'for your kind and friendly remembrance of your old Acquaintance'.[19] Much had happened since that tedious passage in the *Dublin*.

During this halcyon period the lively experiences of Hervey deserve notice. St Lucia claimed his attention first. The French commandant would not even consider surrender, but during a parley Hervey had all the opportunity he needed to study the defences, and conceiving a poor opinion of them, he prepared to sail straight in and lay his ship against the fort. The mere threat was enough and a capitulation came out at once. Hervey reported this success and was about to go on to St Vincent when he received the most urgent orders from Rodney. They were dated March 3rd and directed him to destroy all the cannon on the batteries and then rejoin the flag without a moment's loss of time.

Chapter 11

The Coming of Pocock

(1762–1763)

'. . . His Majesty has thought proper to appoint Admiral
Sir George Pocock to be C. in C. of H.M. ships to be
employed in this expedition . . .
. . . we rely on your hearty concurrence. . . .'
(Secret Orders to Rear-Admiral Rodney,
February 5, 1762.)

THE event which shattered the Rear-Admiral's calm was the
arrival of news from Europe. At 11 a.m. on March 5th the
Aquilon (28), Captain Challoner Ogle, dropped anchor at St
Pierre.[1] The information she sent across after her crew had
saluted the *Marlborough* with three cheers, was that a strong French
squadron had sailed from Brest on January 23rd and was probably close
on her heels. For weeks the French had been waiting for the chance to get
their ships away. On January 24th the *Aquilon* had sighted eight of the line
and five frigates in the Bay of Biscay, steering south-west. Ogle bore up to
inform the commodore of the blockading squadron and was despatched at
once to inform Rodney. He had been nearly six weeks on passage and seen
nothing on the way. But if the enemy were bound for the West Indies they
might arrive at any moment. At once the whole character of the operations
in the Leeward Islands changed.

Hervey's force at St Lucia not being large enough to look after itself
was, as we have seen, recalled. Swanton at Grenada would be inferior to the
French, if reports were true, by one ship of the line only and one frigate;
but if they came his way as well they might, the *Falkland* (50) and the
Actaeon (28), both cruising to windward of Grenada, might reasonably be
expected to fall back and reinforce him, thus equalizing the numbers. So to
Swanton Rodney's orders were less urgent. The commodore was to keep a

sharp lookout but to complete the conquest of Grenada. This done he was to rejoin the flag without delay, but should the French appear he must fight.

Meanwhile the frigates cruising to windward were reinforced and the ships still at Fort Royal and St Pierre hastened their preparations for sea. Rodney intended, when Swanton joined him, to dispose one squadron to the north and another to the south of Martinique, both strong enough to fight the enemy; but there was no time for this.

For the French ships under the Chevalier de Blénac were indeed only a few days behind the *Aquilon*. De Blénac had 5,500 troops with him,[2] sufficient to save Martinique if he could put them ashore in time; but he could not know until he arrived whether the island had fallen or not. All he could be sure of was that the British squadron would be stronger than his own, and that if Martinique had already capitulated he could do nothing useful in the lesser Antilles. An approach with an inferior force called for caution, but he had one great advantage. He would be approaching down wind, and Rodney's screen of frigates was so thin that he might break through it unobserved.

It so happened that de Blénac managed to discover the situation on shore before he was sighted. One of his frigates sailing ahead attempted to land an officer near la Trinité during the night of March 8th/9th. His boat was driven off by a party of troops but not before some negroes shouted to it that the island was in British hands.[3] This gave the French Admiral sufficient time to recaste his plans and prepare for a game of hide-and-seek with his opponent, preparatory to breaking through to St Domingo.

Next morning the French squadron was sighted. By an odd chance it was the *Aquilon* herself, hurried out to strengthen the frigate screen, that made the first visual contact with the enemy that she had last seen six weeks earlier. With the *Woolwich* (44) she was proceeding to her station when she sighted thirteen sail, including eight of the line, beating south some fifteen miles to the eastward of la Trinité. This was about 8 a.m. on the 9th. Without wasting a moment the two British ships wore round and crowded on all sail to warn the Rear-Admiral who was still on the other side of the island at St Pierre.

Why it was necessary for two frigates to carry one report is not clear, but their precipitancy played straight into de Blénac's hands. The responsibility lay with Ogle of the *Aquilon* who was the senior captain and who, one would have thought, would have sent the report by one ship and shadowed the enemy with the other. The wind was light and not until eight hours

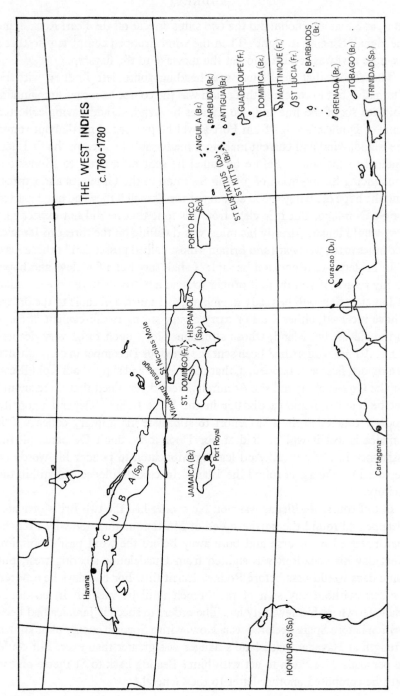

THE WEST INDIES
c.1760-1780

ANGUILA (Br.)
BARBUDA (Br.)
ANTIGUA (Br.)
GUADELOUPE (Fr.)
DOMINICA (Br.)
MARTINIQUE (Fr.)
ST LUCIA (Fr.)
BARBADOS (Br.)
GRENADA (Br.)
TOBAGO (Br.)
TRINIDAD (Sp.)

ST EUSTATIUS (Du.)
ST KITTS (Br.)

PORTO RICO (Sp.)

Curacao (Du.)

St Nicolas Mole
Windward Passage
HISPANIOLA (Sp.)
ST. DOMINGO (Fr.)

JAMAICA (Br.)
Port Royal

C U B A (Sp.)

Havana

Cartagena

HONDURAS (Sp.)

G

later, at 4 that afternoon, did the two ships appear off the Pearl Rock flying the signal, 'Enemy in sight'. Then the wind dropped completely so that a six-mile row was required to get the message to the flagship.

The report that de Blénac was heading south left Rodney with no alternative but to conclude that south was the course he meant to maintain. So, with six of the line and two frigates he weighed, and having collected some of Douglas's ships from Fort Royal he proceeded northabout round the island, wind and current making it inadvisable to attempt the St Lucia channel to the south. Before he sailed he sent off a letter to Monckton, announcing his intention of joining Swanton in the Grenades and expressing the hope of giving a good account of the French if they had not departed for St Domingo. But it is clear from his tone that he did not expect that they would linger. Already his mind was dwelling on the threat to Jamaica 900 miles to the westward and Britain's most valued possession in those seas.

In his letter to Monckton he said: 'I shall stay but a few days and hope, on my return, if you think it proper to send any troops to the preservation of Jamaica, they will be ready to embark, as I must, agreeable to the orders I have received, either send or carry a very strong reinforcement of ships to the aid of that island, whose situation I look upon to be very desperate. . . .' These orders had been sent the previous December in consequence of a report, false as it happened, that the French had slipped out from Brest, for the Government and the Admiralty were determined that there should not be another Minorca disaster in the West Indies. 'Depend upon it,' Rodney concluded, in a last effort to stimulate his military colleague, 'if Jamaica is lost it will be laid at our Door if we don't Despatch all the assistance in our power.' And leaving Monckton to ponder his words he departed to take a cast round the islands in case de Blénac was still in the vicinity.

But of course de Blénac was not. No sooner had the two British frigates disappeared round the northern end of Martinique than the wily Frenchman reversed his course and bore away before the wind past Dominica. Next day his squadron was sighted from Guadeloupe steering west, but some days would pass before Rodney learnt this. For five days he scoured the seas without any sign of the French until he was left in no doubt whatever where his new duty lay. The orders to succour Jamaica had been written before Spain declared war. Now, with a Spanish enemy of unknown strength at Havana, that island's danger was greater than ever. But could he persuade Monckton to act with him? Beating back to St Pierre on the 14th he composed another letter to the General.[4]

'I sincerely wish, Dear Sir, you would consider the importance of that island and what a turn it would give to affairs at Home if it should fall into the enemy's hands . . . it is impossible you can hear in time from England as they can not know the danger of Jamaica, and officers employed in these distant parts must in a very great measure Act according to the intelligence they receive on the Emergence of affairs. . . . I shall be at St Peter's tomorrow and hope we shall then settle all these matters. . . .'

Monckton was awkwardly placed. It was easy for the Rear-Admiral to urge independent action; he had discretionary orders to succour Jamaica in certain circumstances and his duty was plain. But the embarrassed General had no such discretion and while it was one thing for ships and sailors to make free in their own element, it was quite another to launch 13,000 soldiers on such a hazardous and unauthorized adventure. Monckton sympathized with Rodney: but he could not be persuaded to act without orders. There were no acrimonious exchanges. In his report Rodney writes with understanding of Monckton's difficulties; perhaps he even welcomed the opportunity of carrying the whole burden himself.

There is no doubt the situation was one after his own heart. Here was the chance of performing a signal service to his Sovereign, of winning universal acclaim and probably of enjoying unlimited authority too, for the admiral commanding at Jamaica had just died. Besides, if the danger was really pressing, and he was convinced that it was, the Navy without the Army could reach Jamaica much more speedily. So, as soon as the *Marlborough* was back at St Pierre the orders began to fly in all directions. Douglas was to remain in the Leeward Islands with a few 50-gun ships and frigates, while the conquest of the neutral islands would continue; the *Rochester* (50) was to take Brigadier Walsh and his troops for the occupation of St Vincent; the Rear-Admiral himself would proceed to Jamaica with all the rest of his squadron. Basseterre roads in the island of St Kitt's was to be the first rendezvous, and in the next four days most of his ships of the line, frigates and bombs received orders to proceed thither.

With fighting ahead, there was the question of maintenance and repairs. The dockyard at Antigua lay within his command, notorious even in those days for the leisurely tempo of its existence and the questionable ways of its officials. These gentlemen had a rude shock when they suddenly received vast demands for stores—all to be loaded without delay in one of the largest of the transports; worse than this, they were warned to expect the fleet hourly with the Commander-in-Chief in person, and to be ready for all other requirements. A week later he was with them, stirring up the sleepy dockyard as he had stirred the dockyard at Plymouth when the war began. From Antigua, on March 23rd, he wrote encouragingly to Forrest the senior captain at Jamaica, that he might be expected 'hourly' (a favourite expression of his at this time) with thirteen of the line, seven frigates and three bombs.

Clearly he was thirsting for action. '. . . but as I think the best way to defeat the enemy's design will be to attack them, if possible in their own ports . . . [he must have had his bombs in mind] . . . I should be glad if you will join me with all the ships at present under your command off Cape St. Nicolas. . . .' Strategically, such a disposition could not be bettered. Cape St Nicolas, on the western tip of St Domingo, was the French base closest to Jamaica where, as it happened, de Blénac had arrived eight days before. By holding the Windward Passage between St Domingo and Cuba, Rodney could keep French and Spanish from uniting and would be between both and Jamaica. There was also the Admiralty to be informed. After summarizing the sequence of events he concluded: 'I flatter myself their Lordships will not be displeased with me if I take the liberty to construe my instructions in such a manner as to think myself authorised and obliged to succour any of His Majesty's colonies that may be in danger. And shall therefore, without a moment's loss of time, hasten to the succour of Jamaica. . . .'[5]

It was his supreme moment as a young flag-officer. On every count, zeal for the service, promptness of decision, willingness to accept responsibility and soundness of judgement, he touched the heights. Not for him the irresolution and incompetence of poor Byng before Minorca. As his flagship pressed on to the rendezvous a man so sanguine as Rodney would have been less than human if he did not let his mind dwell, for a moment at least, on the entrancing possibilities. This was the opportunity of a lifetime. Within a week or two, a month at most, his niche would be secure.

Three days after writing to Clevland he was lying in Basseterre roads, all his hopes dashed to the ground. The blow had fallen as the *Marlborough* was approaching St Kitt's. A strange frigate, which turned out to be the *Richmond*, signalled that she was express from England with important despatches. These, when they came across, were seen to be signed by the whole Board of Admiralty and dated February 5th. As Rodney read them all his fine hopes faded.

After expressing the hope that by now the operations against Martinique would be finished, their Lordships revealed the government's intention of making 'some signal and effectual impression' on the Spanish colonies in the West Indies; but not under the direction of Rear-Admiral Rodney. That officer was now informed that: 'His Majesty has thought proper to appoint Admiral Sir George Pocock to be Commander-in-Chief . . . not,' their Lordships hastened to reassure him, 'from having the least diffidence of your abilities, but the largeness of the force destined on this important Expedition, and the urgency of the present crisis requiring an officer of High Rank, and one who, by being on the spot to receive the necessary instructions, could be fully apprized of the present views and intentions.' Pocock was four years senior to Rodney, a full admiral and a K.B., with a good record against the French in Indian waters. Whatever the new project might be, Rodney could hardly cavil at his appointment. Moreover, the Board had obviously taken trouble to be conciliatory.

But this was only the beginning. Pocock was expected at Barbados at the beginning of April with the Earl of Albemarle who would command the land forces. Monckton's troops would come under Albemarle, and Rodney was instructed to have 16,000 tons of transports ready for them, victualled for three months. He must also have transports ready for the artillery and ordnance stores, and if any remained, about 15 or 16 hundred tons should be sent down to Jamaica under convoy. But worse than all this, Pocock was authorized to take the best of Rodney's squadron from him, ten ships of the line, with three or four frigates and the bombs, for further service. It would reduce his command to a mere shadow. And to complete his chagrin he was clearly given to understand that everything must yield to the new project. 'Should forces be employed in operations against any other islands or places whatsoever, they do desist from such operations. . . .' So ran the order.

The remaining paragraphs only emphasized Rodney's subordination. The *Richmond* must go on at once to Jamaica. Rodney must concert with General Monckton in choosing a suitable rendezvous where all the troops could embark and the shipping be watered; and this information must be sent to await Pocock at Barbados (duplicated in case of mishap), and with an intelligent officer in case Pocock had any questions to ask. 'Observe the most scrupulous exactness and precision in the Report,' Rodney was admonished, 'marking every circumstance of time and place which may be necessary to fix (beyond all possibility of mistake) the Rendezvous. . . .' These were almost the last orders Anson signed and it is possible that he and the Board may have felt a twinge of uneasiness at demanding so much from the man on the spot. 'We rely,' the order concluded, 'on your hearty Concurrance with His Majesty's land and sea officers employed on this important occasion, not doubting the exertion of your utmost efforts and abilities to forward the Service.'

Although the Order kept silent on the object intended, Rodney cannot have had much doubt what it was. Cuba, the 'Pearl of the Antilles', was Spain's richest possession in the West Indies, and on its northern shore lay the almost legendary port of Havana, through which passed most of her trade and treasure. It was Havana of course—the most splendid trophy any officer could hope to win. Martinique had been well enough, but what was a French sugar island to the magnificent prize now offered to Albemarle and Pocock?

Whatever his private thoughts, the new orders put Rodney in a quandary. They were explicit beyond any possibility of misunderstanding or evasion. Pocock might be expected 'at the beginning of April', and it was already March 26th; all the resources of his command must contribute to the new enterprise, and all other operations whatsoever must give way. If this had been all it would have been a simple, if not particularly agreeable, order to obey. But the situation was complicated by the new development. The orders made no mention whatever of de Blénac's escape, so he had to assume that in London they were not yet aware of it.* Should he then obey them blindly and jeopardize Jamaica? Or should he boldly assume that he was better informed than the Lords and once again construe his orders afresh?

It is unlikely that he hesitated long. Twelve days before, he had instructed Monckton that: 'Officers employed in distant parts must act according to the intelligence they receive upon the Emergence of affairs.' What certainty was there, he must have asked, that Pocock would arrive at the beginning of April? All experience suggested that troops from a distance generally arrived later rather than sooner, and sometimes very much later. It would be small consolation to have obeyed orders if, while tamely waiting for Pocock and organizing his transports, Jamaica was attacked and fell. He was convinced that the island was in imminent danger; he even knew the names of the military commanders who had come out with de Blénac. Byng had been condemned for not doing his utmost: Rodney would never fail in this respect. So, within twenty-four hours of receiving the new order,

---

* Actually the Lords did know. Report reached them on January 28th, a week before Rodney's orders went off. Their apparent neglect to advise him on the new situation is hard to understand.

his mind was made up. The immediate needs of Jamaica must come first. But this need not mean disappointing Pocock.

Some of his squadron, he decided, should carry on as originally intended. He had been ordered to have ten ships of the line with some frigates and the three bombs ready for further service under Pocock. Very well, these would be the ships. Let them wait for Pocock where they might be some use—at Jamaica. With the ships already there, the force would amount to seventeen of the line and thirteen frigates, and the security thus afforded to the island would offset any slight disruption of Pocock's arrangements—at least it was to be hoped so. But there could be no question now of Rodney himself going. Sir James Douglas, as the second in command, would inherit this splendid opportunity, and he would have to be summoned at once. So the *Modeste* was sent off for this purpose, followed by Swanton in the *Vanguard*, who would arrange to have Pocock informed of the best rendezvous (Case Navires Bay where the troops had landed was the most convenient in every way) and start getting his transports ready.

The Rear-Admiral must also turn his back on glory and return to Martinique. But for a few days longer he lay in Basseterre roads surrounded by his splendid force. Twelve ships of the line, seven frigates, and two bombs were there, besides many smaller craft, and all flying the blue ensign in compliment to his rank. Then on April 3rd Douglas arrived to hoist his broad pennant once more on board the *Dublin*. His orders were simply to dispose of his ships in the best manner to protect Jamaica, and be ready for the arrival of Pocock. Soon afterwards he weighed anchor, and within a few hours the best part of Rodney's command was no more than a number of diminishing specks on the southern horizon.*

A week later Rodney was back at Martinique in reduced circumstances very little to his taste. Of the seven battleships which remained to him only three, the *Foudroyant*, *Vanguard* and *Modeste*, were in good condition, while the *Falkland* and *Norwich* were so rotten they had to be earmarked for the next convoy home. The *Marlborough* was also in poor shape. Of Pocock there was still no news. Swanton had started things moving, but reported that there would not be enough transport tonnage to supply the extra 1,600 tons which was to go down to Jamaica. Luckily, Rodney had sent off nearly that amount with Douglas, so this was one problem the fewer. But he was worried about the miserable condition of the landing barges. Since the attack on Martinique they had received little

---

* For security reasons they steered south until out of sight from the Dutch island of St Eustatius. For list of ships sent to Jamaica, see Appendix 5.

attention, but Pocock would certainly want them. There was work here for all the carpenters he had, and all the shipwrights from St Pierre; oars, too, were needed for most of them.

On April 10th, feeling that the *Foudroyant* and *Modeste* could be better employed at sea, Rodney sent them to cruise to windward of Antigua and Tobago, respectively, for the protection of trade. A week later, on the 16th, he sent the *Vanguard* to earn her keep as well, with orders to range down the islands, collect the frigates *Levant* and *Stag*, and cruise upon the Spanish main for a month. Four days after Swanton sailed, Rodney himself went sick. He called it 'a bilious fever', but it was probably the old nervous exhaustion which so often laid him low after prolonged activity at sea. As usual, only the comforts of the land could put him right, so the *Marlborough* sailed up the coast to St Pierre where he was carried on shore.

On the same day that he went sick, Pocock with four of the line* and thirteen transports arrived at Barbados. Here he learnt of the Case Navires rendezvous, and that the ten battleships he had been counting on had gone ahead to Jamaica. If this last item of information caused him any concern he gave no indication in the letter he wrote to Rodney from Barbados.[6] He congratulated him on the taking of Martinique, announced that he would be sailing next morning, and only ventured a mild reminder to his junior of the priority of his own expedition—'all others to yield to this one object'. On April 25th he arrived in Case Navires Bay.

Here he remained ten days. The great concentration for Havana was ready but Albemarle the new and not particularly capable military Commander-in-Chief, wished to redistribute some of the troops already embarked, and some of the empty transports had to be fitted for horses. During all this time Rodney lay sick at St Pierre, and the two flag-officers did not meet. But they corresponded. Hardly had Pocock dropped anchor in the bay than he sent Shuldham to Rodney with the dire news that he intended to take from him his flagship.

Rodney knew better than to argue. 'It gives me real pain', he replied,[7] 'that my ill state of health prevents my paying my respects to you in person. . . . Captain Shuldham informs me that you have an intention to take the *Marlborough* with you. I am sorry the King's service requires it as it will greatly distress me, but in case it is unavoidable I shall be glad you would let me know what ship my Captain, Officers and followers are to be removed on board of. I must beg leave to take notice to you that for the

* *Namur* (90), *Valiant* (74), *Belleisle* (64) and *Hampton Court* (64).

guard of this great range of islands I have but a very few frigates, the *Crescent*, *Actaeon* and *Echo* being at English Harbour, the former condemned as unserviceable and the others only repairable for the voyage home. As I continue still but very weak I must beg leave to refer you to Captain Shuldham for all further particulars.'

Pocock replied with bland politeness:[8] 'Nothing but the real necessity of the very important services expected from the present expedition would induce me to take the *Marlborough*. . . .' He was still 900 miles from his destination with a large convoy of transports to which would soon be added the trade from St Kitt's. Further, the fact that he would have ten escorts fewer than expected cannot have pleased him. But he never questioned Rodney's decision to send those ships ahead to Jamaica; nor, when they came to hear of it, did the Admiralty. He took the *Marlborough* because, in his opinion, the squadron sent ahead under Douglas did not amount to ten full ships of the line, as specified in the Admiralty orders, and he was determined to exact his full pound of flesh. His letter continues: '. . . I am sorry you sent away all the ships of the line, considering that only eight went with Sir James Douglas, as the *Sutherland* can not be reckoned one; and from all accounts I have received the *Culloden* will prove altogether unserviceable for our present purpose; and I find also that the *Cambridge* at Jamaica is in the same condition. . . .'

By 'all the ships of the line' Pocock meant the *Vanguard*, *Foudroyant* and *Modeste*, and it seems that Rodney is to blame for sending them off to cruise, instead of keeping them at hand in case his senior wanted them. Pocock's only possible grievance was that Rodney included among the ships sent with Douglas, the 50-gun *Sutherland*; for the orders had specified ships of the line, and the little 50-gunners no longer fell into this category. But beyond this it is hard to see that Pocock had any other ground for complaint at all; and he certainly had no right to base a claim for any more of Rodney's depleted squadron, on flimsy allegations about ships he had not seen. The *Culloden* was still waiting for new topmasts when Douglas sailed; they reached her safely and she was ready for Pocock at St Kitt's when he arrived there. The *Cambridge*, whatever her state, was sound enough to play her part in the capture of Havana and get back to England afterwards, which is more than can be said for the old *Marlborough* which left her bones in the West Indies. This is the source of the myth, repeated by nearly every historian who has noticed these events, that instead of holding a powerful squadron in readiness for Pocock, Rodney sent his ships to cruise for prizes, thus disobeying orders, jeopardizing Pocock's chances of success, and confirming the legend about himself as a self-centred and rapacious careerist. The facts do not support it very far.

But if Pocock felt he had been the victim of sharpish practice over the *Sutherland*, as perhaps he had, he certainly made his junior pay for it when he deprived him of his flagship; and he might have taken the *Foudroyant*, *Vanguard*, and *Modeste* as well, had they been within reach. As it was he got away with eleven of Rodney's battleships (if one includes the *Sutherland*) instead of the ten prescribed. He also took two frigates, a 14-gun sloop and the last of the bombs.*

On May 6th he sailed with most of the troops from Martinique, and in the empty anchorage Rodney's flag flew from the 50-gun *Rochester*, into which small vessel captain and followers had to crowd themselves before the *Marlborough* sailed. Opportunity had passed them by. They must have been very uncomfortable and very disgruntled. The Rear-Admiral's absence on shore was probably to the satisfaction of all concerned. Meanwhile Pocock passes from this narrative in a blaze of glory. By a brilliant feat of seamanship he took his great armada along the north shore of Hispaniola, through the old Straits of Bahama, and his approach from this unexpected direction sealed Havana's fate. Keppel was with him and Hervey, and all the sea-officers won great renown and wealth which they well deserved. But for those left behind at Martinique the pattern of events was different. It is not surprising that there should have been a feeling of frustration and disappointment. One of its earliest fruits was a first-class row between Rodney and Captain Duff of the *Foudroyant*.

It was hardly to be expected that the Commander-in-Chief at the Leeward Islands would continue to fly his flag in a mere 50-gun ship when his squadron included one of the finest 84-gun ships in the Navy. But it was distinctly unfortunate that the *Foudroyant*'s captain should have been Robert Duff, whose seniority and Scottish dignity made him extremely averse from playing second fiddle to any admiral on board his own ship. He had made this very clear to Rodney at the earliest possible moment, and Rodney had left him alone in the *Foudroyant* until Pocock deprived him of the *Marlborough*. Then as soon as Duff returned from his cruise, Rodney informed him of his intention.

> '*Rochester*, 3 June in St. Pierres
> Bay, Martinique.
>
> 'Sir,
> 'It having been judged absolutely necessary for His Majesty's service

* *Echo* (24), *Rose* (20), *Barbados* (14) and *Basilisk*.

that the *Marlborough* (on board which ship I had my flag) should proceed with Sir George Pocock on the Secret Expedition, I am under the necessity to make choice of the *Foudroyant*, that ship being the most proper of any remaining in these seas for a Flag Officer, Commander-in-Chief.

'And 'tho' My Lord Anson told me in conversation that he expected I should hoist my flag on board the said ship, which supposition was very natural from her being the ship of the greatest force of all those I had the honour to command, yet I never intended to move in to her while the *Marlborough* was in a condition to remain in the West Indies, purely out of the personal regard that I had for you, who had expressed your very great dislike to be an Admiral's Captain upon my mentioning to you the intention of the Admiralty at our first arrival in these seas; to which you was pleased to add that you was too old an Officer to be an Admiral's captain, and had any Admiral in England hoisted his flag on board the *Foudroyant* you would have commanded her no longer than till an Express could have gone to the Admiralty. This open declaration of yours made me conclude that whenever His Majesty's service made it necessary for me to remove in to the *Foudroyant* I could not flatter myself with its being agreeable to you to remain in that ship as my captain. I had therefore provided myself with a captain willing and desirous to go with me in whatever ship should be looked upon as destined for me and for my officers; and agreeable to the Custom practised by all Flag Officers in Foreign Parts, and generally indulged to them by the Admiralty at home, I shall appoint Captain Shuldham to command the *Foudroyant* . . . not from the least disregard to Captain Duff who I know to be as deserving an officer as any in the Navy, and for whom I have the highest esteem and regard, but from the Declaration you was pleased to make to me at Barbados, and my having it in my power to offer you the command of the *Modeste*, a ship of equal Rate (tho' not of equal Force) with the *Foudroyant*, which ship would be ready to proceed to sea in a few days in order to cruise against His Majesty's enemies, into which ship you might remove what officers and followers you thought proper. . . .

'Judge, Sir, how much I was surprised this morning at the warmth wherewith you expressed your unwillingness to command the *Modeste*, declaring to me that you would accept no Commission whatever to command any ship in these seas but that granted you by the Admiralty to command the *Foudroyant*, desiring to remain my Captain in her; a declaration so repugnant to the conversation that passed between us on our first arrival in these seas much astonishes me, as it is impossible you could serve with any satisfaction to yourself. . . .

'But if you persist in your determination not to command the *Modeste*, and as I have all the Deference imagineable for your Service to the Publick, which I acknowledge to be Great, I'm glad I have it in my power to make you another offer (which nothing but the Personal regard I bear you should induce me to), of commanding the *Falkland* bound home with the July convoy.

'I therefore hope you will think cooly and deliberately before your finally resolve upon declining to accept of a Commission; and give a Real Friend leave to tell you that when you dispassionately reflect upon the Occasion that has made these removes necessary, you will own it has always been the Custom of the Commanders-in-Chief to take with them all their officers—and if you think yourself injured, it is better you should return to England as commanding one of His Majesty's ships, than as a passenger, as you will have the same opportunity and with a better Grace may lay your Complaints before the Admiralty, who are ever ready to redress real Grievances, which I can not look upon yours to be.

'You will therefore, Sir, let me have your Answer tomorrow Morning, as I shall no longer defer making those removes I think necessary for His Majesty's service, and unless I had a particular regard for you I should not have condescended to have given you my reasons for the steps I think proper to take on this occasion.

'*I am Sir,*

'*Your most Obedient, etc., etc.,*

'Captain Duff, *Foudroyant*.   *G. B. RODNEY.*'

Duff needed careful handling. He had distinguished himself under Howe in the Channel, he had held the rank of commodore off Brest, and he claimed kinship with the Earls Fife. Rodney's touch was velvet. But the Scots captain remained adamant.

'*Foudroyant*, St. Pierre Roads, 4 June '62.

'. . . What I said to Admiral Rodney then I again repeat, that was I in England I would not serve any longer as an Admiral's captain than an Express could go to the Admiralty and return, being well convinced, from the justice of the Lords Commissioners of the Admiralty (which I have been so happy as to experience), and the gracious manner they were pleased to honour me with the command of the *Foudroyant*, that if they judged it necessary for the Service to make her a Flag-ship, they would appoint me to command another ship equally good. . . .

'But however disagreeable and inconvenient it may be to me to serve as an Admiral's captain, I have the honour to acquaint Admiral Rodney that as captain of the *Foudroyant* I am on all occasions ready to accommodate the Service, and as ready to obey any orders he may please to send me with his Flag. But that I can not accept of a Commission from Admiral Rodney for any other ship as there is none here under his command equal to the ship to which their Lordships did me the honour to appoint me.

'I can not conclude without returning Admiral Rodney my thanks for the High Opinion he is pleased to express of me as an Officer, and it gives me great concern to be under the necessity to complain of one who does me so much honour and has always professed a sincere regard for me.

> '*I am, etc., etc.,*
> '*ROBERT DUFF.*'

So Captain Duff went home in high dudgeon. He took passage in the *Crescent* and beguiled some of the hours at sea composing a formal letter of complaint to the Admiralty with hearsay evidence (unsupported), that it had been Rodney's deliberate intention to injure him.[9] Rodney, in his own report, was more generous: 'I cannot conclude this letter without acquainting their Lordships that Captain Duff diligently executed the Duty of his station during the time he was under my command and I am sorry he has chosen to return a passenger.' The contrast is striking, and both officers enclosed copies of their correspondence for the unfortunate Secretary to pore over. Duff was a good officer, but if he found it 'disagreeable and inconvenient' to be Rodney's captain, and said so publicly, he can hardly have expected Rodney to keep him.

This was only the first of a series of tiresome irritations after Pocock had gone. The war had swept away from the Leeward Islands. No more distinction might be expected, only the necessary tidying up, and the endless pursuit of irregularities and privateers. To all of this Rodney now addressed himself.

His next clashes were with the rather odd collection of civilian followers whom Monckton had brought with him to administer the civil functions of the captured islands. The General had already returned to America but his chief adviser in civil matters, blightingly described by Rodney as 'an apothecary of New York',[10] was very much in the ascendant. This individual had, during the Rear-Admiral's illness, allowed vast quantities of coffee and sugar to be cleared from Martinique, contrary to the terms of the capitulation, the ostensible destination being St Kitt's although it was common knowledge that the consignments were bound for the neutral Dutch island of St Eustatius, the general clearing house of the West Indies. Rodney had little love for the ways of merchants, particularly if they transgressed the Acts laid down by Parliament for the regulation of trade, and his hand came down heavily.

Then another abuse came to his notice, nothing less than a civilian encroachment with Army backing, on the Navy's most cherished perquisite—prize-money. It was Monckton's American followers again—'not any officers or even gentlemen, but the whole a scramble who shall cheat His Majesty most' (this was how Rodney described them), who had 'so much imposed upon the Major-General's understanding' (Rodney's words again), as to induce him to appoint two of them prize-masters, with arbitrary powers to sell all prizes and charge one per cent.[11] Blood pressure in the squadron rose to dangerous heights. The naval agent, Mr Udney, had very properly refused to recognize these 'Vendue Masters', as they were called; they had retaliated by calling in the military, and he had been hauled before Monckton by a file of muskets and threatened with prison.

Prize-money, always a delicate matter, was particularly so at Martinique in 1762 because there was so little of it. The Rear-Admiral, whose own claims would suffer like those of everyone else, was the last man to tolerate an abuse like this, but when he took the matter up with the military, he kept his temper.[12]

'. . . the forcing an Agent for the captors to pay such an unreasonable and unjust demand, directly in contradiction to the encouragement given by His Majesty and the Nation to the seamen, is but a bad return for the share they had in the reduction of this island, and the laying a duty of one per cent without the legal authority of Parliament would sound but ill at home, and is what I can not submit too. . . .' There could be no argument: the new impositions would have to stop forthwith. 'This demand I make, Sir, in the name of all the Officers and Seamen under my command'; and he warned Monckton's successor that he had instructed the naval agents to sue the Vendue Masters. There was no more trouble after this.

In July the Rear-Admiral descended on Antigua. Here he found a sorry state of affairs with the *Woolwich* beyond dockyard aid, the *Repulse* and *Stag*, after nearly two months refitting, almost ready, and the *Virgin*, which had waited as long, still untouched. A long stay meant that half the crew went down sick, and he was particularly incensed to discover that much of the delay was due to the time wasted by carpenters and their crews on ladders, gratings, and fancy work. Rodney had no delusions about dockyards and knew that the impact of a visiting commander-in-chief was usually well cushioned at the time, and soon forgotten after his departure. He left English Harbour with the conclusion that much of the work would be better done in the careenage at Martinique under his own eye.

Privateers still infested the islands. General Rufane, the Governor, looking out from his window on one occasion, saw them at work with his own eyes. Every creek and inlet was a nest for such vermin, and the French inhabitants were of course hand in glove with them. Rodney hired what small craft he could and made sure that captured privateersmen were sent to England as prisoners, so that they could not serve again. In October he paid another visit to Antigua, intending to settle the affairs of English Harbour for good, and was irritated at being recalled almost at once by an alarming express from Rufane who believed he had discovered a dangerous French plot to recapture Martinique; the details included a general insurrection, and the poisoning of the cisterns at Fort Royal. Leaving the affairs of the dockyard still unsettled he hurried back, to discover that Rufane had contracted his quarters to St Pierre and Fort Royal, and abandoned many coastal batteries, thereby greatly easing the operations of the privateers. It was all petty and irritating police work, its inadequacy made embarrassingly obvious by the soaring insurance rates between the islands which, despite all efforts, remained higher than those for the voyage home.

But in spite of disappointments, frustration, and the deterioration in his health, Rodney's good-nature and humanity, and above all his concern for the welfare of his men, remained unchanged. Quotations and instances to illustrate the asperities of high command make good reading, but seldom give the whole picture. When Rodney visited Antigua he made the officials shake in their shoes; but at the same time all his sympathies were aroused by the plight of the sick seamen whom he saw tottering, and sometimes crawling, up to the hospital in the hot sun. This was intolerable, and the agent victualler was ordered to keep a carriage with a cover in constant readiness for their conveyance. The generous testimonials and recommendations for deserving officers flowed as readily as ever from his pen. Nor was his good nature reserved only for followers and favourites. When Captain Keith of the *Amazon* objected to the transfer of one of his officers he received a reprimand which, even for Rodney, was a notable composition; but when, a little later, he applied for shore leave to restore his health, the Rear-Admiral's tone was very different, 'I have experienced too great a share of illness myself,' he replied, 'to desire anybody under my command to go to sea in that condition.'

For a weary man, sick of the sea and craving for the comforts of the land, there can have been few pleasanter spots in the West Indies than St Pierre. Fresh streams ran down the centre of the broad streets; the solid stone houses of the merchants ringed the bay and climbed the hillside; and overlooking these from halfway up the hill stood the fine house of the governor. Here, almost certainly, the naval commander-in-chief took up his abode, and from behind it a noble roadway, made on his direction,[13] swept in magnificent zig-zags up the hill to the lookout post and battery above.

But more and more, as the war drew to its close and the responsibilities of command diminished, Rodney's mind turned towards home. The sea service had, for the time being, fulfilled its purpose. Soon the fruits must be gathered. Nearly all the old landmarks had disappeared from the political scene since he left England, but the prospects were nothing the poorer for at the Admiralty, in place of Anson, was now George Grenville.

Learning of the appointment in December he wrote at once.[14] From the first congratulatory paragraph his letter developed into a detailed description of each one of the Leeward Islands, which he modestly described as 'the plain narrative of a seaman who endeavours to give the best intelligence he can to a Minister and a friend'. It was, in fact, a most valuable first-hand report which any minister would be glad to have. In December also came news of the peace preliminaries being signed at Fontainbleau, and of his own promotion to vice-admiral. His small craft were still harrying the privateers and obtaining some successes, but now, as a further sign of the decline of his command, orders came for him to send all his supernumerary seamen to Keppel, the Rear-Admiral at Jamaica. With the end of hostilities so close he wrote again to Grenville,[15] urging Great Britain's retention of certain islands and putting in his own application for a grant of land on St Vincent. This he supported by some frank revelations. '. . . my reasons for desiring some land in the conquered islands proceeds not only from a desire that my name may be remembered in a part of the world where I was honoured with the chief command of His Majesty's fleet in a prosperous war, but likewise from a desire to gain to my posterity some solid advantage, as Fortune, though so very favourable to me in the execution of His Majesty's commands, has not smiled upon me in other respects, and I believe no conquest was ever made with so little advantage to the Chief.

I can assure you upon my word of honour, that my share on the entire reduction of Martinique and the other islands only amounted to £700 sterling, by which means I was considerably out of pocket by the expense I was obliged to be at, and though I have never suffered any ship to be idle, but have constantly kept them at sea and in those stations most likely to distress the enemy, yet the prizes that have been taken have been but little more than sufficient to maintain the rank and figure I am obliged, by my station to keep up. I may properly say that the conquest of Martinique has been £20,000 loss to me as it deprived all French ships coming in to these seas. . . .'

That he was much out of pocket is quite possible. Only the best was good enough for George Bridges Rodney, and the best in the West Indies could be very expensive indeed. Apart from the Spanish register ship taken by the *Actaeon* (and she was loaded with arms), his cruisers had been unlucky. The ships taken at Fort Royal, St Pierre and the Grenades, with twenty-six prize negroes, produced, when all deductions had been made, £15,475 3s 2d for distribution among the captors. Of this the flag-officer's eighth part came to £1,934 7s 10d which, when shared with Sir James Douglas in the proportion of two to one, brought a mere £1,290 to the Commander-in-Chief.[16] So although Rodney's own figure of £700 should be accepted with reserve, the conquest of Martinique did leave him out of pocket. He would return home with laurels enough, but they would not be tipped with gold.

By the beginning of 1763 there can have been few on the station who did not realize that the greatest of the captured islands would soon be French again. In none of Rodney's letters to Grenville at this time does he suppose there was even a remote possibility of Martinique or Guadeloupe being retained. But he provided the minister with much sound argument for keeping some of the smaller islands, particularly Dominica, St Vincent and Tobago,[17] and retained they were, with Grenada as well. These four islands are the best memorial of Rodney's appointment in the Leeward Islands.

On February 22, 1763, hostilities ceased and residence on shore became impossible. Soon after the cessation of arms he sailed in the *Foudroyant* for Barbados. For six weeks he nursed his health in Bridgetown, and allowed the war organization to run down. The surgeon at the hospital was authorized to discharge the men into merchant ships if they wished it; the agent for the prisoners of war was authorized to let them go.

On May 25th he sailed on the first stage of a leisurely progress northward, along the chain of islands that formed the backbone of his command.

For twenty-four hours the *Foudroyant* lay in her old anchorage at St Pierre, long enough for Rodney to turn over to Swanton, who was there in the *Vanguard*. The second in command would have to attend to the evacuation of the conquered islands, take the remaining ships under his command, and open all public despatches. His chief was no longer capable of transacting business. Prince Rupert's Bay, Dominica, saw the flagship for twenty-four hours, then Guadeloupe, where Hollwall was left to chart and survey an anchorage soon to be returned to France. On June 2nd she arrived at Antigua.

By now he had made up his mind to return to England. The hurricane season was near, so ships that could sail must sail soon. His health was worse. Pagett, writing on June 17th, described him as 'extreamly ill'. News that a French squadron had already arrived at Martinique and demanded possession of Fort Royal cannot have improved anyone's temper or spirits. At the end of June the ships were ready and he laid down the burden of command. On Saturday, July 2nd, he was carried on board the flagship. She was already under way when he wrote his last letter to Swanton:

'July 3rd, off St. Kitt's.

'. . . as neither my health nor spirits will permit me to attend at all to business I herewith transmit to you their Lordship's Additional Instructions . . . and as there is no probability of my recovering my strength here, and it is absolutely necessary for the *Foudroyant* to sail for England, I am hastening there as fast as I can . . . here, or wherever you are, I most sincerely wish you all possible health and happiness.'

The pattern of Rodney's health should by now be familiar. When danger or ambition offered their challenge, the fires burnt at their brightest. But his physique was not robust—in all his portraits there is a suggestion of delicacy—and the subsequent reaction, aggravated by conditions on board ship, always left him prostrate. So it was when he terminated his notable command in the Leeward Islands at the age of forty-five.

The *Foudroyant* took her departure from Anguilla on July 4th and for the next six weeks she and the late Commander-in-Chief were out of all contact with the world on land. But Rodney's friends were thinking of him and some of them were writing letters. A few of these deserve notice for their salty flavour and for the agreeable light they shed on ties with old shipmates. Admiral Holburne wrote[18] to thank his former lieutenant for promoting one of his nephews, 'more than I expected and I am very much obliged to you', but then went on to remind him, in blunt, sailorly terms of a forgotten promise to 'my poor, good woman's nephew who, if you could shove in before you leave the Country to a Command, it would lay me under an everlasting obligation'. It seems that just before Rodney took up his Commission he promised a lieutenant's post in his flagship to the nephew in question, but had then let it go to one of Hervey's recommendations. 'And so Mr. Hervey comes after and talks you out of it when I was not there', grumbled the old seaman. But this was not a grievance to rankle. 'All is well at Alsford,' he concluded, '. . . I wish you well home.'

And Keppel, now a rear-admiral, wrote from the Jamaica station.[19]

'*Valiant* at sea, July 14 1763.

'*Dear Rodney*,

'Your friends at home have assisted you better than mine have me, and you get to England in a favourable season, which I have not the least probability of. The vast space of time I have been without hearing from England, and the critical time for the surrender of our conquest being long elapsed, gives us reason to imagine that the frigate may have sailed, especially as the Spaniards came to us on the last of June with a duplicate of the King's orders to General Keppel. After the embarcation we could not, with propriety and convenience stay in this port, and consequently must go somewhere. The General thought England the only spot to retire to and I furnished him with all my ships. Gladly should I have attended him myself but that appeared to me impossible. I thank you for the assistance you gave me in men. When you yourself was present them you sent were good, but those that came from Antigua by the *Pembroke* were such as would have been sent in time of war home as invalids. The Captains that trifle so with the Service ought to be punished.

'. . . I should have closed the war well if it had not been for the stupid behaviour of a cursed privateer that grew tired of his prisoners and landed them at Cape Francois the very day my ship took a fine Chebrick loaded with Indigo, Fourteen more was to have sailed next day or at furthest three days; when these prisoners told them that the preliminaries were signed, sensibly they immediately embargoed every ship till the time for hostilities ceased. Your share of the little taken in the Moria Passage I now remitt to you by an Order on Adair. I believe the account is stated right. I wish it had been more for both our sakes. I beg my compliments to all friends and am, Dear George,

'*Your very obedient Servant*,
'*A. KEPPEL.*'

Rodney's friends write with a warmth which strikes through the stilted conventions of the time. Even old Admiral Knowles, one of the most difficult and quarrelsome officers of his day, could conclude his letter with the hope for 'a happy sight of you, being most sincerely and affectionately yours. . . .'[20] But these, and others in his post-bag were not to reach him for some time. The *Foudroyant* dropped anchor at Spithead on August 12th, forty days from the Leeward Islands, and on the 15th, at 8.30 a.m., his flag was struck. He was not to hoist it again in war for sixteen years.

Chapter 12

His Majesty's Bounty

(1763-1767)

'Give me leave to take notice to my friend that I am
the only Commander-in-Chief who has returned from a
successful expedition and not (as yet) tasted of
His Majesty's Bounty.'
(Vice-Admiral Rodney to George Grenville,
November 28, 1763.)

I N every dockyard port in England in the summer of 1763 the ships
were paying off. The picture of a sailor of the period with guineas
in his pocket and all his belongings knotted in a handkerchief is
familiar, and there would have been many such footslogging it up
the London Road as the late Commander-in-Chief of the Leeward Islands
drove through Bishop's Waltham and Winchester to Alresford, and thence
to London. Naturally he travelled in style. Two days were needed to get
his things ashore from the *Foudroyant* and two wagons to convey them
to Alresford; three baskets had to be specially bought for the turtles.
His health was sufficiently restored to permit him to press on to London at
once. He was in town only two days after his flag had been struck at
Portsmouth.

Here a bitter disappointment awaited him. The lands which he so much
desired were at the disposal of the Secretary of State, Lord Egremont.
Similar grants to General Monckton had already been confirmed and
Rodney's hopes were high. But Lord Egremont was sick (he died on
August 21st, only five days after Rodney arrived in London), and his
successor, George Grenville, now busied himself with the disposal of all the
territories remaining, and conceived the idea of selling them for the public
benefit. Once determined on this, nothing would change him.

Rodney saw Grenville who was sympathetic but adamant. The decision
about the lands could not be revoked. But Rodney's services merited some

special recognition, and either at this time or shortly afterwards, Grenville offered him the choice from three glittering prizes, when available.[1] They were the governorship of Greenwich Hospital, a Major-Generalcy of Marines, or a seat on the Board of Admiralty. In addition, and as a more immediate reward, he might have the red ribbon of the Bath or a baronetcy, whichever he preferred.

Over the immediate reward he did not hesitate long. The ribbon and star were fine things no doubt and suitable recognition of distinguished services in war. But a baronet took precedence of a knight of the Bath, and his distinction did not die with him, an important consideration for a man who had his posterity in mind. So he chose the baronetcy. But the Herald's Office worked slowly, and 1763 ended with nothing conferred on the captor of Martinique except a deputy-lieutenancy for the County of Southampton, which he received on November 18th.[2] Not until January 1764 was the Patent signed, conferring on him the dignity of a baronetcy of Great Britain. His finances, however, received no immediate benefit.

This made the choice of the more substantial reward all the more important. The Hospital was worth £1,000 a year, with a magnificent residence as well; it would stay with him for life and be a most public recognition of his eminent services. The only drawback was that the present Governor, Admiral Townsend, although in poor health was still alive, and no one could say how long he might keep his successor waiting. The Major-Generalcy of Marines would probably bring the same money as the Hospital, with the same permanency of tenure, but without the residence and without the prestige. There never had been a Major-General of Marines, the rank would have to be created for him, and it is doubtful if Rodney considered it for long. As for the seat on the Board of Admiralty, it was tempting with all its opportunities for authority and patronage, but might be transient, being largely dependent on the political situation. Like the Hospital it would not be immediately available.

For nearly a month Rodney hesitated. Then there were alarming reports about Admiral Townsend's health, and he hesitated no longer. On November 28th he wrote to Grenville from Hill Street: 'I have this moment received a letter from Greenwich acquainting me that Admiral Townsend has been struck with a palsy and is in a dangerous way. Should he die, permit me to depend upon your friendship to succeed him. . . .' The reply was prompt and favourable. If we are to believe what Rodney wrote in a memorial twenty-four years later, he actually kissed hands on the appointment and the thing was as good as settled. Nothing could have prevented him entering upon his inheritance except the recovery of Admiral Townsend, but this is what happened. After the physicians had given him over, the tough old seaman recovered. So, within three months of his return Rodney missed two prizes, the lands on St Vincent by the death of Lord Egremont, and the governorship of the Hospital by the recovery of Admiral Townsend. These disappointments, on top of his eclipse by Pocock and the scarcity of prize-money during his late command, may well have provoked a grumble. England was still intoxicated with victory. At Marylebone gardens, night after night, Mr Thomas Lowe was attracting huge audiences with *Rule Britannia*, *The British Grenadiers*, and above all *Heart of Oak*.

> *Come cheer up my lads, 'tis to Glory we steer,*
> *To add something more to this wonderful Year.*

The disillusioned hero of Martinique, who had added so little to his own store, would hardly share the audience's warmth. In a world where success and standing were closely scrutinized and accurately assessed he desired, above all else, to make a figure and leave an honoured name (a fortune too if possible) to his posterity. In an age not remarkable for delicacy a man was a fool who did not press his claims. However, he had from the King himself a promise of the Hospital as soon as it became available. In the meanwhile the Major-Generalcy was forgotten, but not the seat at the Admiralty.

After so much active service and responsibility it was agreeable to return to the familiar things of home and family, and the years which followed his command in the Leeward Islands, saw the old connections re-established, and the old links renewed. Two figures disappeared from the family circle in the year he returned home. Old Mrs Bridges died at the beginning of 1763, after whittling away much of her late husband's legacy to Rodney, in a series of codicils to his brother James;* and Charles Compton, Rodney's elder ward before he became Earl of Northampton, died in October. The Duke of Chandos now succeeded to the Avington property, and young Spencer Compton became eighth Earl of Northampton. But now a new figure steps forward to occupy the central position in his family circle.

Seven years had passed since Jenny died, during which time Rodney remained a widower. The war which brought him such renown and distinction cannot have brought him much happiness. Now that it was

---

* To George Bridges Rodney she bequeathed £800 'as a Mark of my friendship and being in Charity with him', the last point rather implying that this had not always been the case. (P.C.C. Will Calendars, 1763 (Caesar), Anne Bridges, Southampton, Feb. f. 42.)

THE CLIES CONNECTION

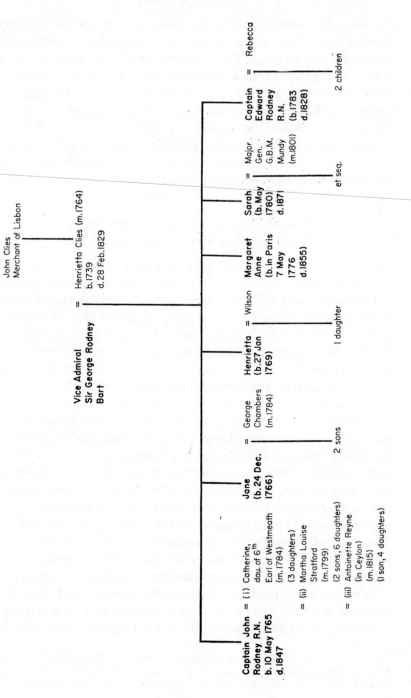

John Clies
Merchant of Lisbon

Vice Admiral = Henrietta Clies (m.1764)
Sir George Rodney   b.1739
Bart   d. 28 Feb.1829

Captain John = (i) Catherine,
Rodney R.N.   dau. of 6th
b. 10 May 1765   Earl of Westmeath
d.1847   (m.1784)
                   (3 daughters)
             = (ii) Martha Louise
                    Stratford
                    (m.1799)
                    (2 sons, 6 daughters)
             = (iii) Antoinette Reyne
                     (in Ceylon)
                     (m.1815)
                     (1 son, 4 daughters)

Jane = George
(b. 24 Dec.   Chambers
1766)   (m.1784)

2 sons

Henrietta = Wilson
(b.27 Jan
1769)

1 daughter

Margaret
Anne
(b. in Paris
7 May
1776
d.1855)

Sarah = Major.
(b. May   Gen.
1780)   G.B.M.
d.1871   Mundy
           (m.1801)

et seq.

Captain = Rebecca
Edward
Rodney
R.N.
(b.1783
d.1828)

2 children

over, and the prospect of further employment remote, his thoughts turned to another wife. In 1764 he married again.

The details of this second marriage are curiously obscure, and readers must draw their own conclusions from the few facts available. Not one reference to it seems to have survived in any of the *Rodney Papers*; no mention of the ceremony has been found in any of the current periodicals; there is no indication where it took place or when.* But there is no uncertainty about the young lady, and it was a union that may have startled some of Rodney's friends. She was none other than the youthful Henrietta, the daughter of the invaluable Mrs Clies whom Rodney took into his household to look after the children after Jenny's death. In the old days at Lisbon the Clies had been in and about the Compton household, and no doubt they were very useful to the family. Later the pattern had repeated itself in England with the Rodneys. But there is no denying that they were dependants, and that for Henrietta to have secured as her husband a Baronet of Great Britain, a Vice-Admiral of the Blue, and a Member of Parliament, was a triumph, to put it mildly. The new Lady Rodney was twenty years younger than her husband.

It was highly proper that something should be spent on decorations and furniture, to mark the accession of a new lady at Alresford, and as nothing but the best was good enough for Sir George Rodney, he went to Henry Webb for the latter.[3] But his original intentions had gone a good deal further than furniture. All over England gentlemen were rebuilding their houses and improving their properties. Sir George, with a new title and a new wife, was not the man to hold back when money was being spent on the symbols of worldly success, and in the same year as his second marriage he had great plans for his country house. These included the building of two large wings and the construction of a new sweeping approach from the other side. There was to be an additional kitchen garden, melon ground, rick-yard, and cow-yard, all on a lavish scale. But the values of 1764 were very different from those of fourteen years earlier when Alresford house was built, prices had risen since the war, Neptune had hardly replenished his coffers at all, and the fine schemes had to be dropped. Nothing came of them in the end except a beautifully executed plan which has survived all the changes of ownership and is still in the house.

* In the pedigree entered in the House of Lords and certified May 15, 1783, by Rodney himself, his second marriage is stated to have taken place at St George's, Hanover Square. (Edmondson's *Baronagium Genealogicum* (1784), 6, p. 101.) But St George's parish register ignores the marriage, so it seems Rodney was not sufficiently interested in accuracy on this point to have the facts stated correctly.

Greenwich Hospital was still as far away as ever, for Admiral Townsend remained obstinately alive, but Sir George made a step in its direction at the end of 1764 when he became one of the governors. There were twenty-four of them, eminent sea-officers, city merchants, and gentlemen, who met two or three times a year. When Sir George attended his first Court of Governors on December 31, 1764, there were present two members of the Board of Admiralty, Lord Egmont who had married his old flame Kitty Compton, and Lord Howe; also Sir George Pocock, wealthy beyond belief after Havana, Swanton, back at last from Martinique, Charles Saunders and Keppel. It was almost an exclusive club, very far removed from the ordinary run of serving officers.

The marriage to Henrietta was soon blessed with a son. John Rodney was born on May 10, 1765, and to a father as indulgent and devoted as Sir George, the event must have brought great joy. The year of John's birth saw also the death of Admiral Townsend on November 21st. The royal promise held good and at long last Sir George entered into his inheritance. His warrant was signed on December 16th. Two days later he was in the House for the great debate on the Stamp Act, and on the 28th he went down to Greenwich. His warrant was read and he attended his first Council of Directors. For the next five years the Hospital, with its superb official residence, was the principal frame and setting in which the world saw him. It is fitting therefore that more should be said about the splendid institution over which he would now preside.

Greenwich Hospital was one of the noblest establishments in Europe. Five miles down the river from London Bridge stood the rich complex of buildings, laid out by Wren in the grand manner, ornamented in lavish style, and dedicated by a not ungrateful Britannia to the security and comfort of her seamen in their declining years. Foreigners in London would visit Greenwich to admire the magnificent proportions, the superb site, the rich excellence of the stonework, and to wonder at the benevolence and wisdom which ordered and sustained such an institution. Seamen passing up and down the river were familiar with the fronts of King Charles and Queen Anne blocks, with their pillars and porticoes of Portland stone, their tall, deep-set windows, the great square nearly one hundred yards wide, that lay between them, and the gilded cupolas of King William and Queen Mary blocks beyond. The natives of Greenwich, who took all this architectural magnificence for granted, knew as part of their daily lives the blue-coated pensioners with their shilling a week for beer, snuff and tobacco, and their endless reminiscences. These ancients had been coming ever since the days of Queen Anne. Some were now so old they could barely crawl across the courtyard. The bed-ridden were cared for by nurses, themselves the widows of seamen. Others, more active, stumped around on their wooden legs, swapped yarns, grumbled, quarrelled, and sat about in the sun. But all of them, whether active and spry or decrepit and senile, had been smart fellows in their day and the humble instruments of Great Britain's prosperity. There were nearly 2,000 of them in 1765.

The Governor's quarters were in King Charles's block, overlooking the river. The size of his establishment may be judged from the fact that he had three coach-houses and stabling for twelve horses; and his style of living from the size of his butcher's bill—£200 for meat in 1767 and the same in 1768.[4] With two establishments to maintain, one of them of exceptional size, Sir George was, at this period of his life, spending a great deal of money.

But there can be no doubt that he relished his position. At Greenwich he was the figure pre-eminent. Few admirals in the long history of the Hospital have been better fitted for the post. Rodney had the grand manner and the distinction. He was nearly as far removed from the captains and subordinate officers as from the pensioners and the gossiping nurses; and yet he was as much of the sea service as any of them, and his assured position made the descent to affable condescension not only easy but acceptable. His achievements were matters of general knowledge, and material for endless reminiscence. His reputation as an exceptionally considerate commander, as well as a hard fighter, would cause old sailors to touch their hats to him as readily as to any officer on the flag-list.

The Governor's duties were not onerous. In theory he was expected to hold a council once a week, to visit the wards frequently, to receive daily an account of the numbers in diet and also of such as were absent or in the infirmary, and to appoint boatswains and their mates. In practice he was much too exalted to exercise anything more than a general supervision over these matters. Day-to-day administration was delegated to the Lieutenant-Governor, an officer of captain's rank who received £400 a year, who presided at the weekly councils, and who was seldom absent from the Hospital.

Captain William Boys, Sir George's first Lieutenant-Governor, was something of a rough diamond, having entered the Navy through the merchant service. Despite this handicap he had attained post-rank and had commanded a squadron off Dunkirk in 1759 with the rank of commodore. He was a man of deep religious conviction. Annually, on July 7th, he observed a strict and solemn fast to commemorate his deliverance from death at sea. He must have been a remarkable character even if he lacked, as he probably did, the polish and distinction of the Governor. Every Monday then, except on the rare occasions when Sir George chose to turn up, Boys presided at the Council of Directors, and in case the reader is tempted to criticize the Governor's almost invariable absence it must be pointed out that the weekly Council was much less distinguished and responsible than its name suggests. It seldom consisted of more than three or four under Boys's chairmanship, and the matters it settled were usually extremely petty. One could hardly expect an eminent figure like Sir George to give his mind to such a problem as whether to mulct a pensioner 6d for a minor misdemeanour, or how long a man should wear a yellow coat as his punishment for swearing. Nevertheless, Sir George did occasionally preside. Every now and then, if any special circumstance warranted it, he would make his lofty appearance.

The first was four months after his appointment on April 25, 1766, and it seems that he came because he had something on his mind. His sense of propriety had been affronted by the condition of the flat, paved walks in King William's Square. Grass and weeds were sprouting between the stones, and the stewards had allowed an unsightly accumulation of old casks to clutter up the approaches to the Painted Hall. This could no longer be tolerated. Having discovered from the minutes of a council twenty-five years before that it had been the custom then for the pensioners to weed the squares, he intended that they should do so again. So the order went forth, with meticulous directions how the work was to be organized; furthermore the steward was to be desired to remove the offending casks at once. Perhaps because it was his first appearance in council the Governor requested that all punishments inflicted that day (except three) should be taken off and all the penitential yellow coats likewise. Having made his impact, more than a year passed before he presided again.

The next occasion was on June 19, 1767, and for a much more serious matter. Too much beer was disappearing from the hospital, even by the easy-going standards of eighteenth-century Greenwich. Sir George had made enquiries and discovered that the hallmen were taking it out of the hall to sell in the town. This was an old custom, hitherto always winked at, so miserable was their remuneration. Sir George was sorry for the hallmen, but also for the pensioners who were not getting their beer. He ordered the wages to be increased and the illicit sales to stop.

The objectionable state of the foreshore beneath the windows of his official residence seems to have caused him concern. There is a story—

unsupported it must be admitted by the Council minutes, but which may well be true—of his directing the more active pensioners to clearing it up. And there is the anecdote related by Mundy of his famous clash with Boys over the pensioners' greatcoats.

It seems that the old gentlemen could obtain these garments by petition to the Council or by application to the Governor, but that in the past they had always been too frightened to approach either, and were resigned to shiver through the cold weather. Then came the first winter of Sir George's appointment when some bold spirits summoned up their courage to test the new Governor's famous good nature. The results so surpassed expectations that some of the council were moved to protest. Boys considered the Governor's interference 'highly reprehensible', and had the effrontery to tell him so. At this Sir George got up and, after expressing surprise at the Lieutenant-Governor's conduct, very calmly said to him:

'I have the greatest respect for you as a man who, by the greatest merit has raised himself from the station of a foremast-man to the rank of an admiral—a circumstance which not only does you the highest honour but would have led me to have expected you as an advocate instead of an opposer to such a necessary indulgence. Many of the poor men at the door have been your shipmates and once your companions. Never hurt a brother sailor. And let me warn you against two things more: the first is in future not to interfere between me and my duty as governor; and the second is not to object to these brave men having great-coats whilst you are so fond of one as to wear it by the side of as good a fire as you are sitting by at present. There are very few young sailors that come to London without paying Greenwich Hospital a visit, and it shall be the rule of my conduct, as far as my authority extends, to render the old men's lives so comfortable that the younger shall say when he goes away: "Who would not be a sailor to live as happy as a prince in his old age?"'

The anecdote may owe something to its editor (certainly Boys was never an admiral), but it brings Sir George's character and personality sharply into focus. 'To do a good-natured thing, repel an intrusion on his authority and remind an officer who had come in through the hawse-hole of the respect he owed his social superior, while fully acknowledging his merit, was quite in the admiral's way.' So commented an earlier biographer* in words which cannot be bettered. The episode has a ring of truth.

* David Hannay, *Rodney*, Macmillan, London, 1891.

Sir George attended the General Court of Governors at the Admiralty much more regularly than the Council of Directors, although it was usually the dullest of routine committee work. The admirals and aldermen would settle such matters as the leases for the farms and lead-mines on the Derwentwater estate,† the raising of the Lieutenant-Governor's salary or the appointment of a third matron at the infirmary. In January 1768, Sir George himself, active as always on behalf of his dependants, had a proposal to put forward. The old dispensary was at last available for conversion back into wards for the pensioners, with room for another lieutenant.

But of course Greenwich was only a part of his life. There was also his family and his Hampshire home, his noble relative at Northampton and his attendance at the House of Commons. There were also his evenings at the card-table. The light that illuminates his affairs during the seventeen sixties is fitful, and the details are curiously assorted. Henrietta, burdened with child-bearing and domesticity remains a name only, but the younger generation is more obtrusive. Young Spencer, the tenth earl, became keen on sailing, bought a yacht and pestered his 'Dear George' for professional advice. There was the children's education to be thought about. Young Georgy went off to his father's old school. References in the years which follow, to turnpike charges to Harrow, to 'mutton pyes and tarts' sent to Harrow and to charges for Master Rodney's board, give tantalizing glimpses of a paternal Sir George doing his duty as a father and an Old Harrovian.[5]

In August 1766, he fell seriously ill at Alresford. The faithful Pagett was at hand, either in his capacity as secretary or simply as an old friend, and provides our information. As it happened, Spencer was at Southampton with his yacht and had young Georgy with him. Naturally they deferred their cruise, while Pagett kept them informed of the patient's progress.[6]

From these daily bulletins, the picture emerges of several physicians attending Sir George and some of them staying in the house; of Lady Rodney standing the anxiety 'amazingly well'; and of old Mrs Clies presiding over the sick-room while Pagett had to wait outside. The combined wisdom of the physicians recommended 'the Bark' (i.e. quinine) as soon as Sir George's fever left him, and on the 15th or 16th Pagett reported that this sat very well on his stomach. But then the patient turned fractious and difficult. On the 19th Pagett reported to Spencer:

'When I came home on Saturday evening I found Sir George had

† The rents from the estate of the attainted Earl of Derwentwater contributed about one-third of the Hospital's income.

desisted from taking the Bark at 4 o'clock, in spite of all that could be said to him, the effect of which I fear he still feels and is sorry for, no ground having been gained since.

'. . . he sent for me this morning and made me promise to tell you, when I went to Southampton, that he should die content in the assurance of your Lordship's protection to his poor girl and children—this he spoke with such a manly firmness (it was) almost too much for me.'

Two days later the picture was a little brighter. The patient had had two hours' good sleep, there was no more talk about dying, and Pagett added a postscript to remind Georgy that he had promised to write to his Papa. Two days after this, on the 23rd, the patient was definitely on the mend and regaining his strength rapidly. The doctors were discharged, Sir George came downstairs, took the air in his coach and Master Rodney's letter came to hand. After this the next report is from the patient himself in a letter to Spencer, without date unfortunately, but addressed surprisingly from Greenwich.[7]

'*My Dear Lord,*

'This is the first day I have attempted to write, and tis only to assure you that the moment I am able to travel ten miles a day I will set out for Ashby which I hope will be on Sunday at furthest. I have only been able to take an airing these three days—My Complaint an Ague and Fever caught at Alresford, which place I have now let for £200 per annum clear of all expenses. . . .'

How can the invalid have reached Greenwich before he was sufficiently recovered to travel ten miles a day? A possible explanation may be that he used Spencer's yacht from Southampton: and after all, why not?

During these years he enjoyed greater liberty to attend the House than at any other time in his life. His temperament inclined him to support a government rather than oppose it (opposition was to him almost synonymous with rebellion); to approve measures that were firm and direct; and above all to pay the greatest deference to the wishes of his Sovereign. When he came home in 1763 the head of the government had been George Grenville whose policy towards the American colonists he certainly approved. There is no record that he voted for the disastrous Stamp Act although it is likely. But it is significant that when Rockingham, Grenville's enlightened successor, repealed the Act Sir George was one of those who, on December 18, 1765, voted with the Opposition for the production of papers on American affairs—an indication that he was not well disposed towards the new government's American policy.[8]

In July 1766, just before he went sick at Alresford, the government changed again and a ministry much more to his taste, led by the great Pitt, now Earl of Chatham, took office. What follows affords a sad illustration of how political considerations were beginning to cut across service interests and old friendships.

The Chatham ministry had been in power for four months when a crisis arose at the Admiralty. The two naval members of the Board were Saunders and Keppel, both, as it happened, survivors from the old administration, and not too happy with the new one. In November both resigned. Party considerations brought these two friends into conflict with the government. A few days later Keppel was deprived of his post of Groom of the Bedchamber.

Sir George, who had never taken his eyes off the Admiralty since his return from Martinique, was on to the opportunity at once, with an application for Keppel's seat on the Board. However, others were before him.

'Tuesday December (2) 1766.

'*Dear Sir*,

'I am honoured with your obliging letter offering your services to the King for the seat at the Admiralty vacated by Mr. Keppel's resignation. His Majesty having already fixed the seats at the Board, where Sir Edward Hawke is to preside with Sir Piercy Brett under him, there remains nothing for me upon this occasion but to assure you of the great Personal Regard and distinguished consideration with which I have the honour to be, Dear Sir,

'*Your most faithful and most obedient humble Servant*,
'*CHATHAM*.'[9]

Correspondence with the great Minister always stimulated Sir George to special flights of literary fervour. 'Nothing,' he replied, 'but a Heart overflowing with Gratitude for the expressions of friendship you have honoured me with, could make me thus intrude upon your time. I am fully conscious of the superior Merit of the Admirals placed at the Board, and am sure there can not be an officer in the Navy but must applaud the choice. I am made Happy by the continuance of your Lordship's regard It shall be my business to deserve it.'[10]

The tone is that of a loyal supporter, a little disappointed perhaps but still hopeful. But the signs were ominous. Politics was beginning to split the Navy, or at least its higher ranks, into bitterly opposed factions. Keppel went out because Saunders did, and because both were Rockingham Whigs. Sir George hoped to step into Keppel's shoes because he was of the opposing faction. Between Rodney and Keppel, friendship was strong enough to survive this evil of their time. But the evil was to play queer tricks on both before it worked itself out.

However, 1766 was not to end on a note of disappointment. Something that would be dearer to him even than a seat on the Admiralty Board was on the way. Henrietta, his beloved Henny as she now was, was expecting another child, and on December 24th she gave birth to a daughter. Ten years before, another daughter had been born, and named after her mother. Neither had lived. But the memory of both was still very dear to Sir George, for the little girl born at this time was also named Jane. She grew up to be a joy and a delight to her father, and the closest to him of all Henny's children.

By the end of 1766 Sir George's life had settled down to a dignified and agreeable pattern. Besides Greenwich there were his visits to Northampton and Bath. London, so easily reached by water, saw him for his attendance at the House and at the Admiralty, while for his diversion there were the occasional race-meetings in the country, and the card-tables at White's, Mrs George Grenville's, and elsewhere. To the world, his position must have seemed unassailable. But in truth it was already undermined and threatened, and by the beginning of 1767 he must have known it.

In January 1767 he signed a note of hand for £2,100, payable in three months at Backwell's, the Pall Mall banker.[11] Either his debts were catching up on him or the payment was part of an arrangement for the next parliamentary election. Of the debts, more will be said later. But it is doubtful if they weighed as heavily on him as the fact that the Parliament in which he sat was approaching the end of its life. Elected in 1761 it could not live beyond the spring of 1768. If he wished to continue as a senator, it was high time he looked about him and made the necessary arrangements.

Chapter 13

The Northampton Election

(1767–1768)

'The most violently contested Election ever
known in this or any other Borough.'
(MSS. account by Joseph Hall, 1785.)

As the end of the old Parliament approached, Sir George would have become increasingly aware how times had changed. The war had receded into the background, and with it his fame. Of his former patrons the Duke of Newcastle had long ceased to count in politics, and George Grenville was out of office. Chatham, now head of the government, was not the man to play the part of a Newcastle and find him a seat. Nevertheless, a seat he was determined to have. It behoved him, therefore, to trim his sails afresh and fortunately (as it must have seemed at the time) just when political connections would serve him no longer, family influence was ready and willing to take their place.

For many years the borough patronage at Northampton had been comfortably shared between the Earls of Northampton and Halifax. From their respective seats at Castle Ashby and Horton the borough was nursed and tended through the years. The succession was not unbroken and it was sometimes contested, but it had been sufficiently continuous for the two families to regard the two seats as their own. Now, with another election impending, where could a better representative be found for one of them than Lord Northampton's brother-in-law and former guardian, particularly when he was a man of Sir George Rodney's stamp? Lord Halifax's candidate for the other was his nephew, Sir George Osborn.

Thus it was that Sir George became involved in the famous Northampton election of 1768, a contest which, even if it did not complete the ruin of three noble families as some have said, helped to complete his own. Hitherto his path to Westminster had been easy, and he had trodden it

226

without much exertion or expense. Camelford, it is true, had been a disappointing exception, but for Saltash and Okehampton he had not even had to attend the poll. Now, for the first time in his life, he had to step right down into the political arena. Eighteenth-century elections could be unscrupulous and rough, and this one was to be more so than most. But before we descend with him, something must first be said about the hard-headed and unsentimental borough which he aspired to represent.

Comptons and Montagus might regard it as their own, but it must be admitted that so far as most of the townsfolk were concerned, robust self-interest rather than any traditional loyalty would decide how the voting went. A large borough with a comparatively independent electorate was always expensive, and every noble family which played with Northampton politics sooner or later burnt its fingers. But there can have been no expectation of any such calamity as the two earls reviewed their prospects before the 1768 election. Not for a generation had their supremacy been seriously challenged, and the new mayor, who would take office in September 1767, was devoted heart and soul to their interest. He was one Thomas Breton, an apothecary. In his capacity as mayor Mr Breton would be the chief returning officer when the time came, and about the most useful ally any faction could have.

At the beginning of September 1767 Sir George was at Bristol, and went to Bath once a week to take the water.[1] From thence he proceeded to Castle Ashby, ostensibly for the Northampton races. Already his name, and that of Sir George Osborn, were being tipped as the prospective candidates, but official confirmation was withheld until the end of the race week. On Michaelmas day (September 24th), the new mayor was to be inaugurated, and that afternoon a large company dined with him and his corporation at the Red Lion—always the Compton headquarters at election time. No single room being big enough for so many, several were taken over for the occasion, and between four and five o'clock, when the repast was finished and belts comfortably loosened, a distinguished procession made its way from room to room. Escorted by the new mayor there appeared the two noblemen best known to the citizens of the town, the Earls of Northampton and Halifax, and with them 'the two Sir Georges', as they soon came to be called. In each room, when silence had been obtained, Lord Halifax presented his nephew and Lord Northampton presented his distinguished brother-in-law and former guardian as their candidates for the borough; and no doubt the usual promises and pro-testations were made and the usual slogans shouted as the announcement was acclaimed by the patriotic company before their betters moved on. One thing only was lacking to complete the satisfaction of the astute electors, a third candidate to raise the bidding and make their votes really worth something. They were not to be disappointed for later that evening Sir James Langham of Cottesbrooke came forward. Canvassing began at once. A committee of between thirty and forty was set up to manage the campaign for the two Sir Georges, of which the most active member was that disinterested official the new mayor.

The next episode reflects little credit on the participants. On October 20th there was another of those enthusiastic dinners at the Red Lion, with the two earls and the two Sir Georges again dining with the mayor and their supporters. Northampton, as befitted one of the great coaching towns of England, possessed an exceptional number of large and commodious inns, of which the Red Lion and the Peacock, almost opposite each other across the market square, were the most notable. The Peacock was the Halifax headquarters. Less well situated, at the corner of Bridge Street, was a third great inn, the George, where Sir James Langham hoped to direct his campaign.

At the Red Lion that evening the company was described as 'very jolly', and at about seven o'clock it was resolved to march round the town 'to animate their friends'. So, with more than 100 links for illumination, the drums and fifes of the militia playing in front, and half a hogshead of ale on a truck following behind, the valiant company sallied forth to the stirring battle cry of 'Northampton and Halifax for ever'.

Led by the two earls, the two Sir Georges, and the indefatigable mayor, they paraded round the town, stopping to howl, groan, and hiss outside the houses of their opponents, and particularly of course outside the George. An interlude followed at the Market Cross. The earls and the candidates drank a mug of ale each in a bumper: 'Success to the town and corporation of Northampton', and after the rest of the company had refreshed themselves, it was decided to make a second demonstration outside the George.

But by now the enemy was on the alert, and the pot-valiant army was met by about sixty or seventy opponents armed with sticks and stones. The mayor, as might be expected, was in the thick of it, and bellowing 'Rodney and Osborn' at the top of his voice when a rude boy attempted, in the mêlée, to set his wig on fire. Realizing that an unusual form of attack was being made on him, the much tried civic dignitary whipped round, the boy disappeared in a flash, and the outraged Mr Breton, mistaking his assailant, turned a regular volley of abuse on one of the bystanders,

228

gnashing his teeth and dashing his hat in his face. But such an affair could not go on for long. Thanks to cooler heads and steadier legs the party from the George prevailed, and their opponents were driven back, breathless and discomforted, to the Red Lion.

Here a debate was held, whether the insult should be endured or revenged, and the result being what might be expected everyone was ordered to arm themselves with brooms and mop-sticks and put a piece of white paper in their hat. However, some cooler head than the majority suggested that the mayor should first go to the George as ambassador to ascertain whether it was to be peace or war.

In the George Mr Breton found the enemy still washing the blood off their faces and bathing their bruises with brandy. Feeling was very high indeed, and his first remark was not conciliatory. 'The Lords desire to know by me,' he began, 'as we are determined to go down Bridge Street, whether we are to go peaceably or fight our way there?' But his hearers were too incensed to give any satisfactory reply, so his embassy came to nothing.

War being declared, the two earls and the two Sir Georges, their forces now swollen to nearly 200, sallied forth once more. Outside the George the enemy were barring the way down Bridge Street. It conforms to the singular pattern of this night's work that the first blow of the new engagement was delivered by Lord Northampton's active and excitable chaplain. Weight of numbers now told. The enemy were beaten back and retreated into the courtyard, closing the gates behind them. The victors then broke all the remaining windows of the George after which, honour being satisfied, they all went home to bed. Next morning Sir George was voted a Freeman of the Borough and three days later, on October 25th, Sir James Langham withdrew from the contest.

The prospect of the two Sir Georges being returned unopposed and reasonably cheaply caused such disappointment in the town that many of the independent voters began at once to look round for another third candidate to make the running. They did not have to look far.

Five miles to the north-west of the town stood Althorp, seat of John, first Earl Spencer, who had long wished to break the monopoly of borough patronage enjoyed by the Earls of Northampton and Halifax. In a minor contest four years earlier over the recordership of Northampton he had managed to win a third of the corporation. Now he was ready for a greater trial of strength. On November 2nd, which was only eight days after Sir James Langham's withdrawal, an innocent insertion appeared in the

Northampton Mercury: 'It is with real pleasure we inform the Publick that the truly generous and good Nobleman Earl Spencer has given £1,000 to the Poor of this Place, to be distributed in Bread, Flour, Coals etc., at the discretion of a Committee appointed to that Purpose.' Public benevolence on such a scale and at such a time could mean only one thing—that 'the truly generous and good Nobleman' was about to throw his hat into the ring; and any doubt was settled exactly a week later when it was publicly announced that the Hon. Thomas Howe would contest the seat in the Spencer interest. On that same day the forces of Lord Spencer made their ceremonial entry into the town with band playing and colours flying. Their candidate was the youngest of a notable family. Riding in the ranks with him was his elder brother, a sea officer whose future fame would one day bear comparison with that of Sir George Rodney himself.

Sir George had left the town soon after that memorable dinner at the Red Lion, his attendance being required at the funeral of H.R.H. the Duke of York and Albany, younger brother of King George III and an admiral of the blue. The prince had died at Monaco. His body was landed at Greenwich on November 2nd and was to be buried in Westminster Abbey on the day (or rather the evening) following, with full naval honours. Such an occasion was much more to Sir George's taste than the vulgar demonstrations at Northampton, and it would have been with sober satisfaction that he put on his uniform coat, with black waistcoat and breeches (as the directions required)[2] to pay his last respects to dead royalty. The funeral over, he returned hot-foot to meet Lord Spencer's challenge.

Mr Howe had made his entry on the 9th and was following it up with a three-day canvass. Sir George managed to get back on the 11th, to be met a mile outside the town by the other Sir George and a crowd of supporters all with orange and blue cockades, and the drums and fifes of the local militia again in attendance. Thus escorted, the ceremonial entry was made that day. After a tour of the town, this time without incident, the whole company drew up on Market Hill. Here the two Sir Georges rode from rank to rank thanking the gentlemen most politely for their attendance and inviting them to partake of a collation at the Peacock, which was later described by the *Northampton Mercury* as 'handsome'.

Polling was still four months off and until then work at Northampton would fall upon the agents, committees, and other party supporters, with the candidates making an occasional appearance from time to time. Then as now, elections could be lost or won long before polling day, and it is instructive, although not particularly edifying, to observe the measures taken by the three wealthy and determined noblemen during this period.

At Northampton the borough franchise was as wide as anywhere in England. All male householders not receiving poor relief could vote, and a poll of over 1,000 might be expected. But what exactly constituted a householder? The general feeling was that so long as he had a separate entrance to his abode and a fireplace to cook his food, his length of residence need not be scrutinized too closely. This liberal interpretation gave ample opportunities to the party organizers. A judicious expenditure on bricks and mortar, the insertion of a door here and a fireplace there in some suitable house, followed by the installation of a complaisant occupant, produced one more voter in the right interest. So it was that from October onwards, if not earlier, all Northampton was ringing to the sound of picks, saws, and hammers as every craftsman plied his trade, knocking out doorways and putting in new fireplaces and windows, at the expense of one or other of the three noblemen. The civic authorities were faintly disturbed about this. Three times in 1767 they took Counsel's opinion on the knotty problem of what exactly constituted a householder—not that any learned opinion would have mattered one halfpenny, the way things were going.

But this was only the beginning. The householders had to be maintained until polling time, and here the local innkeepers reaped a golden harvest. Two square meals a day at the Red Lion, the Peacock, the George, or elsewhere, the account to be sent in to my lord's agent—some such arrangement was essential if these 'occasional voters' as they came to be called, were to be at hand when wanted. There was also the continual drain of miscellaneous disbursements. Such seemingly trivial items as ribbons, candles, and bell-ringers accounted for staggering sums. The printers too were kept busy, and no doubt charged suitably. By December, with polling still three months off, the pace was becoming too hot for Lord Northampton. Ready cash was running short and being replaced by promises. With his noble relative hard-pressed, a man of Sir George's impulsive and open-handed nature might be expected to increase the stakes, and he probably did. So the account mounted, as discretion went to the wind.

With polling still a month off the candidates themselves crossed swords in public. On February 18, 1768, Sir George, then in London, received this card from his opponent:

'Mr. Howe desires that his Pretentions may be decided upon by the genuine and legal Voters of this Town and Borough of Northampton, and as a testimony of the sincerity of these his sentiments, he declares himself not only willing but anxiously desirous that a proper deputation may immediately be formed in order to ascertain the true Constituents; and the Candidates in consequence to conclude themselves by a signed list of them, which will rescue the Returning Officer from all Embarrassment, and protect him against every possible imputation of Partiality.'

This stately proposal, for reasons not hard to guess, was unacceptable to the two baronets whose answer, dated February 20th, reveals a pen well versed in the niceties of official correspondence.

'Sir George Osborn and Sir George Rodney are equally desirous with Mr. Howe that his and their Pretentions may be decided by the genuine and legal Voters of the Town and Borough of Northampton. But as to the deputation Mr. Howe wishes for ascertaining the true Constituents, it might bear the appearance of a Scrutiny before an Election, and be thought an unconstitutional Pre-judgement of the Rights of the Electors.'

The thrust was neatly parried, but it should not be inferred from Mr Howe's proposal that the practice of setting up 'occasional voters' was limited to the two baronets; more probably, their position in this respect was the stronger.

As polling approached we may imagine a frenzy of last-minute arrangements, endless comings and goings at the Red Lion, the Peacock, and the George, and all the time those lists of voters in their various categories of dependability being scrutinized, discussed, and amended. For reasons of convenience it was agreed that polling should be by tallies, which meant that each side in turn should bring up its voters in small groups of a dozen or so. Voters for Rodney would emerge from the Red Lion, and those for Osborn from the Peacock; behind the doors of these strongholds the organizers could assemble and check the tallies, and fortify them for their ordeal, before shepherding them across the square. Lord Spencer, much less well off for headquarters as the George was too far away, had to operate from the house of one Revell, a brasier, on the third side of the square. Voting procedure had nothing of the privacy and impersonality of the modern polling station. On a raised platform in the square, and plain for all to see, sat the three candidates with their respective counsels; also on the platform were the mayor and two bailiffs as returning officers, with the town clerk and constables in attendance. Each voter had to establish his qualification to vote to the satisfaction of all on the platform before he was permitted to do so. What with marshalling and organizing the tallies, producing them at the right time, and arguing each voter's right, one by one, an election could be a slow business.

On March 16th, the day before the poll opened, Sir George Rodney was admitted to the Freedom of Northampton, which had been voted the previous October. Then began a fortnight which the inhabitants of the town would remember for the rest of their lives. As the mayor, attended by the constables, made his way across the Market Square on the first day, scandalized observers noted that all were parading the colours of Osborn and Rodney, and that even the constable's staffs had blue and orange ribbons. All being seated, the Town Clerk read the Act of Parliament against bribery and corruption, after which the mayor and bailiffs took the oath. It was then proposed by Mr Murphy, leading counsel for the two Sir Georges, and agreed by Mr Graham, leading counsel for Mr Howe, *not* to tender the oath against bribery to the electors, after which the whole organization for securing the return to Parliament of the people's choice went into action. On that first day 49 votes were recorded for Howe and 4 rejected; 50 for Rodney and 2 rejected; and 51 for Osborn and 2 rejected.

From March 17th until the 30th, each candidate polled a daily average of about 40 votes. It was a wrangling and often rather discreditable business. A few examples will illustrate the character of the proceedings. The third man up on the first day, one Richard Hedge, was presented by the two baronets, but against him it was argued (by Mr Howe's counsel) that as the parish had paid his rent from Easter until January 30th last, he had been in receipt of charity and therefore might not vote. The parish books confirmed this, and the case against Hedge seemed clear. But according to Messrs. Murphy and Hopper, counsel for the two Sir Georges, the money had been paid, not to Hedge but to his wife, so the husband was eligible to vote after all. This was quite good enough for the partisan mayor. On another occasion a most dubious voter was presented by the two baronets, and was about to be disqualified by the testimony of his landlord. The latter could be seen hurrying across the square when, just before he could set foot on the platform, the alert Mr Breton directed that the vote be recorded. At this there was much clamour and hissing from the Howe side. Again and again tempers rose, but at times laughter broke in as when Thomas Turner, a baker and an 'occasional voter' if there ever was one (he had only taken over his house at Michaelmas) came up to vote in the colours of Osborn and Rodney, and then polled for Howe. The price of a vote rose of course during the fortnight. According to a local chronicler writing seventeen years later, the sum might be from twelve to fourteen guineas at the beginning, and as much as fifty, or even more, at the end. Turner, who voted on the eighth day, probably did well by both sides.

But it should not be thought that all the sharp practice was on behalf of the two Sir Georges. Earl Spencer may not have created so many 'occasional voters', but he had other methods. Weeks before polling began, honest simpletons (but voters all of them), were being hospitably treated at the George, and then remembered nothing more until they woke up next morning at Althorp; and others were carried there by force. Behind Lord Spencer's substantial wall they could roam at will in the park, and they received a guinea a week, with food and drink. But until they were taken to the poll, there they had to remain, and it was only with the greatest difficulty that even their wives could see them. However, in all fairness to Lord Spencer it must be admitted that when the time came, his prisoners were generally taken to the poll in a post-chaise and having voted were (sometimes) gratified with as much as forty guineas.

Reports of Lord Spencer's outrageous behaviour soon reached the headquarters of the two Sir Georges through the victims' wives, and provoked much virtuous indignation. One of the most curious papers surviving from the election is the copy of a letter written by Sir George Rodney himself to one Wilkinson, who had been forceably carried off to Althorp as early as March 4th.

'ffrend John,
'Your wife complains that you were taken away and dettained by force at Althorp. You may depend upon the support of your friends, and that Justice shall be done you. Let me know by her if you are there kept prisoner, and be assured I am,

> *'Your friend and humble servant,*
> *'G. B. RODNEY.'*

Poor Mrs Wilkinson underwent many trials before she could pass the Althorp defences and deliver this letter to her husband. But the end of the story, as far as this voter is concerned, is revealed by the scrap of paper she brought back with her, signed by the man himself and denying any constraint. A clear inference may be drawn.

Day after day the contest went on, with chaises posting between Althorp and the town, the tallies moving obediently across the square, counsels for the candidates wrangling on the platform, and the unblushing Mr Breton weighing the scales for all he was worth. From March 17th until the 30th all three candidates kept roughly level, so that at the end of this, the twelfth day, the figures were:

Rodney 513   Osborn 505   Howe 504.

But the last days would decide the election, and as the tallies came up on March 31st it was obvious that Lord Spencer was throwing in voters he would never have presented if he had anything better. The returning officers took advantage of this to put the two Sir Georges into the lead. Voter after voter for Mr Howe was rejected, while the tallies for the two baronets still issued triumphantly from the Red Lion and the Peacock. Figures at the end of this day were:

Rodney 568   Osborn 563   Howe 536.

April 1st was the last day. The two Sir Georges now threw all their reserves into the conflict, to the number of 60 odd, although 21 were so dubious that even the returning officers had to turn them away. But all Mr Howe could produce was a pathetic Falstaff's army, 22 altogether, of which 20 were rejected. At the end of the day Mr Breton was able to declare Sir George Rodney and Sir George Osborn the successful candidates by a majority of 53 over Mr Howe, the final figures being:

Rodney 611   Osborn 611   Howe 538.

But Lord Spencer was not yet beaten. '. . . let Mr Howe's opponents enjoy their short-lived triumph', he (or one of his minions) thundered in the columns of the *Northampton Mercury*. 'But while they count up the number of Mr Howe's pot-wallers and occasional voters (as they call them), who have been rejected, let them not forget the occasional tenants of Widow's houses who, on their side were admitted; the drummers and Militia sergeants, the barbers, shoe-makers, and weaver's journeymen, the tradesmen from London and other places; and the Day labourers; who have all been fetched from their several habitations for the purpose of this Election.' This revealing attack was followed by a petition to the House of Commons by Mr Howe for an enquiry into the conduct of the election.

Then followed many months of uncertainty and suspense. The hearing did not begin until January 19, 1769, and during the weeks that it lasted a great many people were inconvenienced and embarrassed. Down to London in the cold winter weather came the unhappy returning officers, and with them all the poll-books, ratings and assessment-books, charters, and town records. Down to London also came a crowd of witnesses for Mr Howe, bursting with indignant recollections of the mayor's outrageous behaviour; and at the same time down came many supporters of the two Sir Georges, bitter in their denunciations of Lord Spencer and his methods.

In the end the extreme partiality of the returning officers proved more of a liability than an asset. The committee disallowed as 'grossly fictitious' 193 of Sir George Osborn's votes and 191 of Sir George Rodney's. At the same time 63 of Mr Howe's votes were disallowed, but all the same the amended figures put him at the top of the poll with a majority of more than 50. On February 14, 1769, according to the *Journal of the House of Commons*, he was declared elected *vice* Osborn. A Northampton resident writing seventeen years later,[3] has a pleasant story that for the other seat 'the two Sir Georges tossed five guineas into a hat, which should have it, and Rodney won'. This is in character with the popular picture of Sir George as an open-handed gambler, but the other seat was his by the narrow margin of two votes over his fellow baronet.

Few elections have been fought with such reckless abandon, and few can have left behind such legacies of debts and bitterness. At Castle Ashby there are whole bundles of bills, petitions for payment, and receipts, all indicating the long period of financial embarrassment. One contemporary estimated the amount spent by all three parties as about £160,000, and Sir George Rodney's contribution as £30,000. Accurate or not, the figures show what people were prepared to believe. Castle Ashby was closed, a great deal of timber was cut down, and Lord Northampton with his family departed for Switzerland.[4] Lord Halifax, who reckoned himself the greatest benefactor Northampton ever had, left the district altogether. For Sir George Rodney the success was dearly bought. It is probably true to say that those hectic weeks at Northampton ruined him. The tide of good fortune and worldly success that had swept him upwards with such dignity and consequence had come to the full, could he but have known it, before he contested that fatal election in 1768. Before it, he had his debts, but they were not such as to affect his style of living. Afterwards the position became precarious—as will be seen. The tide of his fortune was now to ebb for ten long years, and the last of these were to be bitter indeed.

But apart from the disturbing considerations of expense, the election would not have been an experience he enjoyed. Patrons, managers, and supporters might throw themselves with ardour and enthusiasm into these contests; local and personal rivalry, and the sheer joy of the combat, had much to do with this. But a candidate like Sir George Rodney would be unlikely to share their zest. In all surviving accounts he is markedly reserved and undemonstrative. The Earls of Northampton and Halifax, Olympian figures though they were, descend to fight and speechify and riot with a right good will among the humbler folk in the Northampton streets. But not Sir George Rodney. Though he is with them, though he attends the dinners, drinks the toasts, rides in the processions and sits on the platform, he is by comparison a very frigid Olympian indeed.

During that last, disreputable fortnight one instance and one instance only is on record of his opening his mouth. On the fourth day of the poll, counsel for Mr Howe was objecting at great length to one William Reynolds as an 'occasional voter', when one of the bailiffs broke in and insisted that he be polled. Counsel solemnly protested that he had not half done and went on speaking, whereupon Sir George leant across and asked him whether, after such a delay, the returning officer ought not to poll the vote. The impression given is not that he was pressing for a decision in his favour, but that the futile and tedious wrangling had become almost more than he could bear.

Chapter 14

The Quicksands

(1769–1771)

'. . . but Sir George, you are not open with any of
your friends, and therefore you put it out of any
their power to serve you.'
(John Marr to Sir George Rodney, October 1, 1774.)[1]

READERS must now brace themselves for what is inevitably a
painful topic—Sir George's debts. From his earliest youth,
surrounded by the splendours of Avington, he had lived
among the wealthy and influential. He loved the great world.
It was the breath of life to him. Naturally his tastes were expensive. These
things had not mattered so much when he was a young captain with coffers
generously filled by Neptune, but it was very different when he returned
from Martinique in 1763, with everything at home so much dearer but no
corresponding increase in his own fortune. It is hard to say when the tide
began to turn against him, but it was probably at the time when he
abandoned the idea of improving his Alresford property. The Northampton
election hastened the crisis, however, and nothing in his character or style
of living made it easy for him to economize.

Had this been all he might still have managed well enough, but it was
not. It must now be admitted that Nature, besides endowing him with so
many admirable qualities, had also cursed him with a weakness for play,
and unfortunately gambling in its most extravagant and reckless form had
never been more prevalent than at this time, and in the circles in which
he moved. At White's Club, where he had been a member for years,
thousands of pounds changed hands on the turn of a card, or on the most
trivial of wagers. Fortunes lost by midnight might be won back before the
light of dawn crept through the drawn curtains, and if they were not, the
day of reckoning could always be postponed with an IOU, while in the

background were those who, on suitable security and at exorbitant interest, would oblige with loans.

This is not to say that he lost an entire fortune at cards or by foolish wagers. But it cannot be overlooked that he loved late nights over the card-table, and that he moved among men who sometimes did lose such large amounts. The high stakes at White's which dismayed Keppel[2] had not dismayed the young captain of the *Eagle*, and as far back as December 1748 we hear of him losing £150 to a professional card-sharper.* Extracts from old letters and account books all point to the same disturbing conclusion, that in the hard, brilliant, spungeing, predatory society of London and Bath, he conducted himself with the same reckless daring and generosity that he showed at sea, but with infinitely less happy results. 'Dear Sir,' wrote the second Duke of Chandos in April 1761, 'pardon the liberty I take and assure yourself that the most pressing Occasion is the reason for it. It will be of the most infinite service if you can lend me one hundred pounds. . . .'[3] Rear-Admiral Rodney, as he then was, sent fifty guineas next day, but his noble kinsman's IOU was never redeemed. Before he sailed for Martinique he owed more money to Mr Richard Rigby over play at White's than that acquisitive careerist owed to the enormously wealthy Sir James Lowther;[4] and he was keeping more dangerous company than Rigby. On April 2, 1760, he made out a bill for £157 10s 0d to a certain Robert Mackreth, and to the same individual on May 14, 1761, another for £147.[5] These are only straws in the wind but they are significant straws; for 'Bob' Mackreth (much patronized by the members of White's) was one of the most notorious usurers in London.

He was a remarkable man was 'Bob', and because of his influence on Sir George's affairs he deserves more than a passing mention. From the humblest origins (he began as a waiter and billiard marker in Arthur's chocolate house) he rose to acquire a huge fortune, a seat in Parliament, and even a title, before dying at the age of ninety-three. When White's Club was established at Arthur's 'Bob', who was shrewd and ruthless but no doubt obliging to the members when it suited him, became manager and general factotum. Then, like the industrious apprentice, he married his master's daughter and inherited everything. Soon he was seeking wider fields. In 1763 he transferred the business to a relative known as the Cherubim and set up in 'Change Alley' as a financier and dealer in landed

---

* Horace Walpole to Sir Horace Mann, December 26, 1748. The sharper, who happened to be a baronet, had Captain Rodney and 'a stupid Irish peer' to dinner, and seems to have beguiled them with the prospect of admission to a Pelham levee. A second meeting and the card game followed. The victims discovered the baronet's character next day.

property, elastic terms which covered most forms of shady dealing from usury to book-making. He combined ruthless energy and brazen self-assurance with an outstanding ability to turn other people's misfortunes to his own advantage. He was a man to keep clear of.

If Sir George was in Mackreth's clutches as early as 1760 it is obvious where some of his money was going, and 'Bob' was not the only usurer in London. If only Jenny had lived the story might have been different. She was a woman of character and background who might have saved him from himself. But poor Henny, so much younger than her splendid husband and possibly a little in awe of him, can have had small influence in this direction; in later life she ran up debts herself and saved nothing. As for all the agents, secretaries, and men of business who served Sir George at one time or another, he never gave his whole confidence to any one of them, and by his wayward determination to take a line of his own, defeated all their attempts to save him from himself.

Perhaps he was too proud, or too independent, or possibly too sanguine about his own business ability to put his affairs completely into the hands of anyone. But it is remarkable how much attachment he inspired. Pagett stood by him for years and laboured devotedly in his interest when all seemed lost; so did John Marr, of whom more later; so did the Drummonds, the Charing Cross bankers, who were also his connections by marriage. But most devoted of all was his London agent, Mr Richard Kee, who managed as much of his patron's affairs as he was allowed to, from the time that he commanded the *Prince George* in 1756. To Kee, Sir George was still the brilliant young officer whom he had so admired in the great days of Mr Pitt's maritime war. Because of his deep attachment, his time, his own credit, his lifelong familiarity with the ways of the Navy Office, and all his energies even when tottering on the edge of the grave, were ever at Rodney's service. Pride it may well have been which caused Sir George to withhold his full confidence from so much loyalty and devotion. Instead, when things became difficult, he turned to 'Bob' Mackreth and others more dangerous still.

In 1769, having weathered the storm of his disputed election, he staved off any immediate financial crisis with a loan of £800 from Sir James Lowther. It was a desperate expedient, for Lowther was one of the most rapacious and unscrupulous men in England, but he must at this time have been at his wit's end for money. There was a whole sheaf of those deadly notes of hand 'payable to bearer on demand'. Among the creditors were the faithful Kee, who was content to wait; Shuldham, his late captain from

Martinique, who (most emphatically and rather unpleasantly) was not; and his brother-in-law Lord Northampton who, so far from being in a position to help, was embarrassed himself. Lowther's £800 can have gone nowhere, but for the short breathing space it gave him, he put himself into the power of one capable of doing him greater harm than Mackreth. Then, if all this was not enough, at least four law-suits were pending for debt,* and others might be on the way. The humiliating situation had been reached in which the Governor of Greenwich Hospital and conqueror of Martinique could no longer meet any of his liabilities, from his debt of honour to Lord Robert Manners to his account with Wizzel, the Greenwich baker;[6] and it was hard to suppose that he would be able to obtain any more credit from anyone.

There comes a time when such embarrassments can no longer be shrugged away with gentlemanly unconcern. Creditors, too long unsatisfied, become abusive; servants, no longer receiving their wages, become insolent, quit their service and are hard to replace; recourse has to be made to evasions and subterfuges, and it becomes harder and harder to put a good face on things. For the year 1770 there is very little indication of Sir George's doings, or where he was. The flow of contemporary references dries up almost completely. He attended a Court of Hospital Governors at the Admiralty on February 8th[7] and in April he wrote from Welbeck Street announcing his intention of going shortly into the country to attend some business in Hampshire, probably the letting of one of the Alresford farms.[8] It was almost as if the Governor of the Hospital was taking care to appear in public as little as he could.

Faced as he was with ruin, Sir George may have reflected bitterly on the ease with which Fortune had come to him as a young captain, and how completely the golden fountain had dried up since. Pocock's luck at Havana (Pocock had now retired from the service after a quarrel with the Admiralty) did not bear thinking of. But in other ways too the world was becoming an increasingly unsatisfactory place. The House of Commons was at odds with the nation over Mr John Wilkes, and some of it was also at odds with the colonists in America while, worst of all, the opposition made no secret of their sympathy with the Americans. Since letting the house at Alresford he no longer had his country seat, but any consolation for the rent which it brought was embittered by the knowledge that his brother James, who had done so well for himself out of old Mrs Bridges, was now

---

*Barlow v. Rodney, Dalrymple v. Rodney, Duncan v. Rodney, and Teasdale v. Rodney. (Chancery Reports C.12/601/21.)

settled in Alresford in a fine house he had built himself only a quarter of a mile down the road. James Rodney had married again in circumstances which had given great offence to his elder brother, and relations between them were not cordial.*

But all this was as nothing compared with the immediate problem of his debts. Short of a miracle the only thing that could save the situation would be a war and a command at sea. Such an appointment would relieve him of immediate problems and probably extend his credit; and if he were fortunate the harrassing shadow might pass. But Europe was sunk in profound peace, the mighty fleet which had been laid up at the end of the Seven Years' War still slumbered in ordinary, and only the smallest detachments of the Royal Navy were in active commission. The only sea-going he was likely to see were the ships passing up and down the river, beneath the tall windows of his official quarters at the Hospital. Then, in the summer of 1770, with his own fortunes at their lowest ebb, a Spanish war suddenly became a possibility.

A disquieting report reached London from our squadron in the West Indies, that the Spanish governor of Buenos Aires had sent an armed force to uproot the small British settlement at Port Egmont in the Falkland Islands. The British Government protested to the Court of Spain and demanded the action of its governor be disavowed; and while the leisurely diplomatic exchange went on between London and Madrid, a burst of activity in all the royal dockyards indicated Britain's intention to resist aggression, if necessary, with armed strength.

For Sir George, racking his brains to keep his creditors at bay, the new situation offered a gleam of hope. The squadron in the West Indies was to be reinforced and a senior officer would go out to Jamaica to relieve Commodore Mackenzie. Here, if war broke out, would be the naval command *par excellence*. The new commander-in-chief, whoever he might be, would have all the wealth of the Indies at the mercy of his skill and enterprise.

It may be imagined how Sir George worked to obtain this supremely desirable appointment, how he lobbied, and canvassed, and pestered ministers, and anyone else likely to be useful. A sense of delicacy had seldom deterred him from pressing a claim, and now it was almost a matter of life and death. By his rank and fighting record he was as well

---

* According to tradition the magnificent plantation of beeches which divides the two properties, was planted by Sir George, so that his sight might not be offended by his brother's prosperity.

qualified as any officer on the flag-list; and as a loyal supporter of the government, who had near ruined himself in the last election, he may have argued that he deserved it, or some such return, for his expenses and exertion. The gambler, with everything hanging on his last throw, could not have been more tense as he weighed his assets against those of his professional rivals. For of course others were also angling for Jamaica; the Hon. Samuel Barrington, backed by H.R.H. the Duke of Cumberland, was his most dangerous rival.[9] Much would depend on the First Lord, but at the head of the Admiralty was Sir Edward Hawke, never noticeably friendly.

But before the year ended, and before a final decision was made, Sir George had new hope. There were to be changes on the Board. Sir Edward was old, and his health was poor, and he had at last been persuaded to quit. He would be replaced by Lord Sandwich, a friend and patron for twenty years. Moreover, with other government changes that were taking place the sentiments of the administration promised to be more in conformity with Sir George's own robust Tory views—and Barrington was a Whig. Twenty years had not lessened Lord Sandwich's high opinion of Sir George's merit in the naval line. It seems that before he took office some sort of understanding was reached (perhaps a promise or a half-promise was actually given), that if and when he took his place at the head of the Board, his old friend's claim would receive first consideration.

Early in 1771 many hopes and fears were resolved. Spain showed no sign of climbing down, so the naval armament went on, and on January 12th Lord Sandwich took charge at the Admiralty. The new First Lord was as good as his word. Sir George's rivals were hardly considered. The Jamaica command was his if he still desired it—but on one condition. Lord Sandwich had made it clear that if ever it was his good fortune to be in a position to serve him in this matter, Sir George must give up the Hospital, and the latter had appeared to acquiesce. But now that the time had come to choose between his stately residence (with £1,000 a year) and the new command Sir George was torn. The new command he must have: but he could not give up the other without a struggle. Only three days after Lord Sandwich took office (so quickly did events move), Sir George sat down and wrote him an eight-page letter urging his claims to retain the Hospital while he was at Jamaica.[10] The Hospital, he argued, had been his reward for services rendered, for which reason he should be allowed to keep it. Historic precedents were on his side. Admirals Aylmer, Jennings, and Balchen, earlier Governors, had all retained it when they had returned to sea. Finally, argued Sir George, he deserved to keep it, if for no other reason because his late command at Martinique had been so unremunerative.

It was an excellent letter, bland, persuasive, and reasonable. He had had a narrow escape, the future promised well, but if he could retain his snug berth at home, so much the better. Lord Sandwich replied at once with admirable patience.

'Privy Garden, January 16 1771.

'*Dear Sir,*

'Your letter surprises me not a little as I concluded that the affair to which it relates was already finally settled, and to your entire satisfaction. What indulgences were shown to Sir John Jennings, Lord Aylmer, etc., I know not, but I am sure it is wrong that a sea-officer should possess such a retirement, and at the same time be in the most honourable, active, and probably lucrative employment that can be given him. I gave you your option: what could I do more? And again I repeat the same offer. But when you have once chosen let me entreat of you not to alter your mind a second time. . . .'[11]

This was final. Jamaica it had to be, and Sir George's Commission as commander-in-chief is dated exactly a week later. The Hospital Lord Sandwich decided to bestow on Sir Francis Holburne, now a very sick man at Bath.

At this stage a new complication arose. Sir George's debts cannot at this time have amounted to less than £4,800 and probably were much more. Within the spacious bounds of the Hospital he had been able to take the air undisturbed by the vulgar intrusion of bailiffs, and still enjoy the respect and deference that were his due. This protection was his no longer. The news that he was going out to Jamaica could not be kept secret, and its effect on those to whom he owed money was electric. He might, if he was lucky, return a very wealthy man: on the other hand he might not return at all. Those who took the latter view were now galvanized to such activity that the Commander-in-Chief designate, preoccupied with all the details of a new and important appointment in distant seas, found himself plagued beyond anything he had known previously; probably he was plagued beyond endurance. This can be the only possible explanation for his next step into the financial quicksands.

Impatient to be relieved once and for all of these importunities, and with the need to lay out a large sum of money on the various necessaries of a commander-in-chief, Sir George now entered into a financial agreement at which his friends, when they came to hear of it, held up their hands in horror. The new appointment had restored his credit up to a point, sufficiently at any rate to persuade such disinterested creatures as Mackreth and Lowther that he might still be a business risk worth gambling on. With the aid of a lawyer called Garforth, one of Lowther's jackals who contrived to run up a staggering bill of charges for his services, these two now offered to come to Sir George's help. They would advance him £6,000, and use it to pay off all his debts: in return he bound himself to pay them an annuity of £800 for an unspecified period of time. The original of this remarkable agreement has not come to light, but at Castle Ashby and at Brizes Park there are what appear to be preliminary drafts, both dated January 25, 1771.* It is almost inconceivable that an enormously wealthy man like Lowther should have joined with an ex-waiter from White's in usurous dealings at exorbitant interest, and harder still to believe that anyone in his senses would have accepted their terms. But the facts are beyond dispute. They are confirmed by many later references, and in the suit which Lord Rodney brought against Lowther and Garforth in 1785.[12]

Why did Sir George accept such terms? It was Kee's belief that he never even read the deed, but this explanation is too easy; Sir George may have been lofty and extravagant, but he was not unbusinesslike. He claimed later[13] that he had supposed the loan to be 'an act of pure friendship', to afford immediate relief to a friend in distress. The understanding was that he would make over all his sources of income to Lowther and Mackreth, half to be returned to him and the other half to be used to pay off the loan; and that when this had been done, and an interest of 5 per cent charged, the matter would be finished. The deed to which he put his name can have said nothing of this gentleman's agreement, and whatever favourable gloss Lowther and Mackreth may have put on it at the time, it seems unlikely that Sir George would really have believed them.

The truth more probably is that it was a gamble on both sides. Sir George would have his debts paid for him and be relieved of all immediate worries. With credit restored he would be able to equip himself as befitted

---

* In the latter version the sum advanced was to have been £24,000 and the annuity from Sir George £1,600 for ninety-nine years. Perhaps this was the first offer which Sir George had the sense to reject for two pencilled corrections alter principal and interest to the sums finally agreed on.

a commander-in-chief and if, as was always possible, the climate or an enemy shot carried him off, he would not leave his lesser creditors unsatisfied. (Lowther and Mackreth were different: *they* had taken the risk with their eyes open and could well afford to lose their money.) All this, Sir George must have reckoned as worth the £800 a year he had agreed to pay. It was a substantial liability to be sure, but if all went well it could probably be met out of the emoluments a commander-in-chief might expect in a prosperous war with Spain. Nevertheless it *was* a gamble, for if there was no war and he returned empty-handed, his situation would hardly bear thinking about.

Looked at from the other side, through the eyes of Lowther and Mackreth, the arrangement was less a gamble than a very reasonable investment. Their victim was not likely to die in the West Indies: he had served there before without ill effect. If war came, their money could hardly be laid out better than in backing his fighting abilities and, war or no war, they could always squeeze him for the annuity as long as there was anything to squeeze. To make sure of this they persuaded him to make out a Power of Attorney entitling Lowther's banker, Mr Henry Boldero, to act as agent and draw his flag-pay and table-money. This, with the deed, made their position virtually unassailable. Provided Sir George did not die unexpectedly, they might count on an excellent return for their money for many years to come.

The fatal deed was signed on January 25, 1771, after which Sir George produced a long list of debts which he gave to Garforth to settle.* But so dilatory and negligent was the latter, that the new arrangement brought him no immediate relief. In this there may have been faults on both sides, for the list was incomplete. Kee's claims were omitted, and the old man was greatly incensed when he learnt this, although by the time he discovered what was going on, the mess was beyond even his powers to clear up. Meanwhile, the plaguing and pestering continued, to Sir George's great inconvenience, right up to the time he sailed.

Enough has been said for the moment on this distressing subject. But before the new Commander-in-Chief could proceed to Portsmouth and hoist his flag, there was one last involvement concerning the Hospital. Sir George had already quitted Greenwich, Admiral Holburne had not yet arrived, and during the interim period the secretary, backed by the directors, turned a number of pensioners out of two of the wards and

---

* The sum of these debts must have been substantial. By October Mackreth and Garforth claimed to have spent £4,809 17s 9½d in settling them.

converted them for the use of himself and his family. The Lieutenant-Governor was Captain Thomas Baillie. When he discovered what was going on he protested to the Admiralty in such terms that every sea-officer who heard about it seethed with indignation against the civilian branch. Sir George shared this feeling to the full. He had always suspected the directors (and Boys too for that matter), of wishing to turn the Governor into a cypher, and had taken good care in his day that they did not. Now he wrote to Holburne promising to support his authority 'against the Pride and Insolence of an upstart secretary'.[14] He also commended Baillie in the warmest terms. 'Keep a good lookout,' he adjured him, 'that the pen and ink men do not encroach on the rights of those for whom the hospital was intended, the Officers and Seamen who have faithfully served their King and Country; in that cause you must always be supported.' The matter was to be considered at the next General Court, the First Lord had desired him to delay his departure so as to be present, and every admiral in town was expected to attend to support the Governor's dignity.

The Court was held on April 23rd. Sir George recalled his own experiences as Governor and denounced the secretary's action as 'the most daring insolence'. Lord Sandwich agreed, and the directors received a very severe reprimand. Reporting the business in a second letter to his old captain Sir George concluded grimly: 'I fancy they will not attempt to interfere with the Governor's authority again.'[15] So Baillie carried his protest successfully. But this was not the end of the story.

By now the reinforcements for Jamaica were ready at Spithead. The ships were:

Princess Amelia (80)*	Captain S. Marshall
Boyne (70)	Captain Thos. Burnett
Modeste (64)	Captain Jno. Wheelock
Achilles (60)	Captain R. Collins
Diana (32)	Captain E. Onslow
Merlin (16)	Captain F. Fotheringham

Already on board the *Princess Amelia* were the faithful Pagett, who had thrown up his Greenwich chaplaincy to go again as Sir George's secretary, John Marr, a Compton dependant from Northampton who aspired to a

* It was waterside rumour that the *Princess Amelia* had been specially chosen for Sir George as a complimentary reminder of his affair with a royal princess twenty years before. The yarn, however improbable, would have done nothing to lessen his popularity with the seamen.

purser's warrant under Sir George's patronage, James Rodney, Jenny's second son, transferred from the *Antelope* to be under his father's eye, and a quite embarrassingly large number of volunteers, including Lord George Gordon, later notorious for his part in the Gordon riots. The Admiral's quarters were ready for him. But where was he? On April 19th he had received the orders to hoist his flag. Lord Sandwich had kept him in town until the 23rd for the General Court of Governors. But more than a week had passed since then, and still there was no sign of him. The faithful followers became increasingly apprehensive. Then, with a thousand rumours circulating as to his whereabouts, disaster threatened. The *Merlin*, with all his wine on board, of which more than £100 worth had paid no duty, was searched by the customs officers.

The customs house had no respect for flag-officers, and no intention of allowing any of them to have their liquor duty free. It had scored a notable success in 1755 when it obtained the confiscation of all Admiral Boscawen's liquor, at a time when Boscawen was a Lord of the Admiralty, and all the favour the latter could obtain was that the vessel was not confiscated too. Hoping for another distinguished victim, the master of the revenue cutter, a redoubtable individual called Styles had his men watching for days to catch Sir George's liquor being transferred to the flagship. All would have been well, however, but for five of the *Merlin*'s people who deserted and, for a consideration of five guineas, laid information. The faithful followers were beside themselves with anxiety. The only hope for the wine was a discharge order from the Treasury, if Sir George could obtain one. But where was he? On the first intimation that their liquor was in danger the Rev. Pagett leaped on a horse and rode as hard as he could ('Pagett rides like a post-boy', commented the admiring Marr) for London by way of Alresford. At the same time Marr wrote off to Lord Northampton at Castle Ashby in case Sir George was there. It was now May 5th.[16]

Four days later came reassuring news about the wine. Only fourteen cases had been seized. The rest were too well hidden. But still there was no news of Sir George, although his orders were waiting for him. As Pagett was still scouring the south of England, Marr, who seems to have lost hope of ever seeing his patron at Portsmouth, wrote again almost hysterically, to Lord Northampton.[17] 'I do, and I cannot help it, despair of for Sir George going the voyage . . .', he lamented. 'His creditors may tire and teaze him out of his life, but that's no way to be paid, and they will then repent of their harsh conduct when 'tis too late. I can't help accounting for his absence in any other manner than that he is too much pressed for what he can not pay. God send him down soon and safe at sea for we are losing every hour.'

It was so typical of Sir George to keep his confidence to himself. His followers need not have worried. He had not been held for debt or suffered any other misadventure. After finishing in London he had gone up to Northampton to make with his brother-in-law and former ward what both hoped would be the final settlement of their election expenses. After a series of complicated transactions involving a great many of those bonds and notes of hand which make his finances so baffling, a deed was signed on May 11th,[18] intended to clear him of all his liabilities to the Earl of Northampton, although as things turned out later it did nothing of the kind. Only when this was completed did he feel himself free to make his way south.

The story of shifts and expedients is nearly ended. Having completed his business on the 11th, Sir George drove swiftly down from Northampton, and was at the waterfront the following evening (May 12th). But it was not to the Sally Port, or Portsmouth hard, or Gosport, that he came. Thanks to Garforth's negligence in settling the debts there was still far too much danger of meeting some angry creditors at any of the places where he might be expected. Instead he probably hurried through Southampton as darkness was falling, to embark a few hours later from a lonely stretch of beach on the New Forest side of Southampton Water. The story has survived with the Drummond family who acquired the land a few years later, and however ignominious it may sound for a British admiral to do something of a moonlight flit in order to reach his flagship unmolested, it may well be true. Marr's letter shows that his creditors were still after him, and if the legend of a secret embarkation from the Cadland estate is to be accepted, this is most probably when it happened.*

Next day (May 13th), the flag of Vice-Admiral Sir George Rodney was flying once more from the masthead of a British warship, after an interval of nearly eight years, and on the 14th he wrote to advise the Admiralty of the Power of Attorney he had made out, entitling Boldero to claim his flag-pay and table-money.[19] The final touch had been added to the crazy settlement of his affairs, and he was at liberty to sail.

---

* There were two other times when Sir George might have embarked from the Cadland property, as a commander-in-chief. They were in December 1779 and in December 1781, but on neither of these occasions does there seem to have been any need for secrecy. It may be significant that an inn called The Jolly Sailor at Ashlett Creek used once to be The Admiral Rodney. I am indebted to M. C. Drummond, Esq., of Cadland for much interesting information on this topic.

Chapter 15

Commander-in-Chief, Jamaica

(1771–1774)

'It gives me particular pleasure that Sir George Rodney's behaviour is so agreeable to your colony as he is my intimate friend and chosen out by me as a person that I was in hopes would not give you any cause for complaint.'
(Lord Sandwich to Philip Pinnock, Esq., March 20, 1772.)[1]

ALMOST all the Rodney family were going to shake the dust of England from their feet for the next three years. Only George, the elder of Jenny's two sons, would remain behind to make his way in the Army. Once on board Sir George was eager to be off, but there was no hope of beating down channel while the wind blew so fresh from the westward and if he chafed, as no doubt he did, the others may have welcomed the opportunity of settling in properly while still comfortably inside the Wight. There was Henny of course and her three children, John aged six, Jane aged four and little Henrietta aged two; and with them gallant old Mrs Clies, ready if need be to leave her bones in foreign parts so she could still be with her daughter and grandchildren. So the great cabin would be noisy with the children's chatter, a distraction which never failed to delight Sir George, and the stern-gallery would make a pleasant retreat for Henny and her mother. As soon as six-year-old John came on board, the opportunity was taken to start him on his sea career by entering him on the ship's books as admiral's servant.[2]

At last the head of the family could brook the delay no longer and gave orders to sail, but the channel weather seemed as reluctant as his creditors to let him go. For three wet and miserable days the ships plunged backwards and forwards under what Sir George described as 'a greasy sky', until they were thankful to drop anchor in Torbay on the 22nd. A few days later they managed to beat down as far as the Lizard, before another south-westerly gale drove them back, helter-skelter into Plymouth. Here Sir George found the dockyard commissioner much concerned at the imminent prospect of an official visit by Lord Sandwich in the Admiralty yacht. Rear-Admiral Spry was uncertain how the First Lord would be received in the visiting squadron. Sir George was very ready to enlighten him.

'As no man whatever can have a greater regard and respect for Lord Sandwich than myself, you may be assured that I shall be glad of every opportunity of showing my attachment to him, and in case the Yacht . . . carrys the Admiralty flag I shall not only salute it with 19 guns but likewise give particular orders to all the captains of the squadron to do the same.

'But in case the Yacht comes in with a pendant only, I shall expect the captain of her to do his duty by saluting the King's flag entrusted to my charge, and should he neglect to do so I shall send a proper officer on board to put him in arrest for disrespect to the King's flag. I know my Lord Sandwich too well not to be sensible that he will approve of every officer who keeps up the dignity of the British flag.'[3]

On June 3rd the weather relented, and once the squadron was clear of the channel, day followed day of cloudless blue, across the Bay of Biscay, down the coast of Spain, and so to Madeira for water and wine. In the beautiful bay of Funchal they lay for five days while the boats worked to and fro, and Sir George sent a frigate to Tenerife, ostensibly with letters for the British Consul but actually to inspect the new fortifications at Santa Cruz. All across the Atlantic the halcyon weather continued. Week after week the ships dipped and swayed beneath a sun that grew ever warmer. The flying fish skittered hither and thither over the surface and, in Sir George's own words, it was 'so fine . . . that the smallest boat might have come with great safety'.[4] James Rodney, writing a dutiful letter to his uncle Lord Northampton in Marr's cabin, informed him that they had 'not had occasion to lash a table or chair since we left Plymouth'.[5] This young man had good reason to be pleased with himself for his father promoted him acting lieutenant twelve days before they reached St Kitt's. It was a useful step for a seventeen-year-old, just permissible provided he was sufficiently qualified, and there is no reason to suppose that James Rodney was not. So the pleasant voyage continued until, twenty-five days after leaving Madeira, the sharp outlines of Nevis and St Kitt's broke the western horizon. On July 16th they dropped anchor in Basseterre roads where, nine years before, a bitterly disappointed rear-admiral had learnt that he might not sail with his squadron to Jamaica. The notables came on board to plague him with their civilities, and we have a glimpse of Henny, well pleased the voyage was nearly over, and surrounded with magnificent pineapples at three for 6d. On July 24th the squadron dropped anchor at Port Royal, Jamaica.

Their first need was to water. Thirty years earlier Admiral Vernon had developed an excellent watering place at Rock Fort but this, Sir George discovered, had been neglected and abandoned. In its place, but at a considerable distance from the anchorage, were two private sources whose owners, in return for the hire of their pumps and gear, were pleased to charge 1s a ton for water, and were undoubtedly making a pretty penny. The situation, if a great fleet needed to water in a hurry, did not bear thinking about. Bombarded with complaints from his captains, and no less displeased himself, Sir George resolved to make the solution of the water problem his first task.

He enquired about Vernon's old watering place but was told that it was 'unwholesome'. A reservoir at Kingston was found to be 'ropey, thick, and of a disagreeable taste'. The river Cobra was choked and useless, while a promising well at Kingston was soon pumped dry. So in desperation he went to see Vernon's old watering place for himself, and found a rapid and clear run of water issuing with great force from a limestone rock about 500 yards from the shore. Mindful of the reports, he had it analysed and found it as soft and wholesome as could be wished. The owner of the site was prepared to accept a reasonable price, so plans were drawn up and estimates called for. With no more than a wharf on piles and 1,350 feet of stone guttering, it was reckoned a large fleet might water in five or six days, which before would have taken as many weeks. The estimated cost was under £1,000.

Still pleasantly occupied with this project, and with settling his family on shore, he was recalled to sterner matters by the return of one of his ships from a cruise, with a story of incompetence and failure. She was the *Sir Edward Hawke* (schooner). Although a naval vessel and commanded by a lieutenant, she had allowed herself to be seized by two Spanish *guarda-costas* who had carried her into Cartagena and then, after a few days, released her with a warning. Sir George was surprised and furious, and the wretched lieutenant who had submitted to these indignities received a formidable communication.

'*Princess Amelia*, Port
Royal Harbour,
'20 August 1771.

'*Sir*,

'I am extremely concerned to acquaint you, after perusing the orders you received from Commodore Mackenzie, your own journal, and your letter to Captain Hay of the *Carysfort* wherein you acknowledge your having submitted (to the dishonour of the British colours), to be carried in to Cartagena by two Spanish guarda-costas without making any resistance whatever, notwithstanding your orders were so very express to the contrary, I find myself under the necessity to examine into your conduct at a Court Martial which I shall order Commodore Mackenzie to assemble.

'You will please to let me know what time you will be ready to make your Defence, and I shall be very happy to find you clear yourself from the charges which my Duty obliges me to bring against you.

'*I am, Sir,*
'*Your most obedient, humble, Servant,*
'G. B. RODNEY.'[6]

Lieutenant Anthony Gibbs had sailed on his disastrous cruise before the new Commander-in-Chief arrived, but his order from Commodore Mackenzie are sufficiently unusual and curious to deserve attention. He had to deliver a letter to an individual called Pacheco on the island of Rosario on the Spanish Main. The mission was secret. Gibbs was to house his guns, disguise his ship as a merchantman, deliver the letter by night at a specified rendezvous, cruise off the land for a week, and return on the eighth day for an answer. Every line of his instructions emphasized the need for secrecy, the importance of finding the right Pacheco (for there were several), and the overriding importance of keeping clear of the Spanish authorities with whom, it will be remembered, Britain was on the verge of war.

But he was unlucky and inept. He managed to deliver the letter but then, instead of getting clear of the land he hung about trying to obtain water and was thus discovered by a powerful Spanish *guarda-costa* with his yards and topmasts on deck (part of his disguise), and no very clear explanation for his presence on the coast. The Spaniards were highly suspicious and invited him to accompany them to Cartagena where, at least, water might be obtained. Gibbs gave them the slip during the night, but next day the *guarda-costa* was on him again accompanied by a consort. Each mounted

12 guns with some fifty men, and could sail two feet to his one so, after clearing for action (but not offering even a token resistance) Gibbs tamely submitted. Only when a British frigate appeared off Cartagena some days later, was the *Sir Edward Hawke* released with the warning that if ever she appeared again within twelve leagues of the coast, she would be seized.

At his court martial Gibbs put up a very poor defence, and it is clear he should never have been sent on a mission of this kind. The charges against him were proved, he was dismissed the service, and Sir George sent the *Achilles* (60) and the *Guadeloupe* (28) to Cartagena to demand an apology from the Spaniards. But the matter did not end here.

Gibbs returned to England with an account of Sir George's proceedings which lost nothing in the telling. To the malicious and the ill-disposed it could all be explained in the simplest terms. The new Commander-in-Chief had gone out to restore his finances by a prosperous war; when he left England Spain had appeared to be climbing down and the war might be off; now, thanks to his deliberate provocation, it would certainly be on again. Before long the vapourings of one obscure, resentful individual were the talk of the town.

Certainly Sir George had been furious with Gibbs, and he may well have told him (as Gibbs said he did),[7] that if he had only fired a pistol over his vessel's side he would have sent out his cruisers and taken every Spanish vessel he met. The *Achilles* and the *Guadeloupe* had not returned before Gibbs sailed, but the latter predicted the damaging consequences of their visit. Custom prescribed that foreign warships anchored in the roads before entering any Spanish harbour. Gibbs was sure Sir George would send them straight in to provoke an incident, and most people seemed ready to believe him.

Lord Sandwich was particularly worried. These indiscretions, if indiscretions they were, were *his* responsibility. Since Sir George's departure he had been busy on his behalf and had obtained for him, as a partial compensation for losing the Hospital, the appointment of Rear-Admiral of England, worth £378 a year; indeed a very friendly letter[8] to inform Sir George of this was on its way to him when Gibbs arrived with his story. So the First Lord sat down to write again.

After quoting some of Gibbs's remarks, and some of those attributed to Sir George, he went on: 'These sorts of declarations are too indiscreet and too little founded on your instructions to allow me to give them the least credit, and therefore you may be assured that I shall discredit the idea of their being founded in fact till I have received your answer to this letter.'[9]

But he may have been more worried than he cared to admit for he ended with a warning: 'I will add one word more, and that is that upon a declaration of war larger squadrons must be sent and very probably senior officers to most of our stations in foreign parts. . . .' The hint would not be lost on Sir George.

Meanwhile the man on the spot, all unconscious of the pother in London, was handling the situation with the boldness and skill which never deserted him when commanding at sea. The *Achilles* and *Guadeloupe* delivered their protest without incident, but the Spanish apology was by no means to his satisfaction, being qualified (or so it appeared) by an insulting stipulation that 'if any other of H.M. ships were found within 12 leagues of the coast they would be taken, and their crews imprisoned'. No British admiral could be expected to swallow this, so the *Guadeloupe* was despatched again, to the renewed apprehensions of the politicians in London. 'Believe me,' wrote Lord Sandwich, 'you are got upon very delicate ground and I think you would have acted more judiciously if, instead of sending the *Guadeloupe* again . . . you had left us at home to judge the nature of the insult with the material we had in our possession. . . .'[10] But the man on the spot had everything under control. The later misunderstanding, as he explained after the *Guadeloupe* returned a second time, was the result of 'a malicious and faulty translation by a villainous Portuguese interpreter'.[11] After this final brush—carried out with full regard for international courtesy—the Spaniards knew where they were with the new Commander-in-Chief; and perhaps a few people in London learnt their lesson too.

So all was peace and tranquillity on the Jamaica station and Sir George, comfortably installed on shore in the bosom of his family, could forget his debts and his embarrassments as he gathered all the threads of command into his experienced and capable hands. Under his immediate observation was the dockyard, the new watering-place (which soon promised to be more expensive than anticipated), and the detailed survey of the harbour which he had ordered. Here lay his large ships, the *Princess Amelia* soon to be careened and refitted, while his frigates and smaller craft cruised on the station and brought back news from every quarter.

The Spaniards were now pursuing a good neighbour policy and the threat of war (however much this was to be regretted), had receded. All was quiet on the Musquito Shore whence Captain Carkett of the *Garland* brought the King of the Indians to pay his usual compliments. From the Bay of Honduras, however, reports were less satisfactory, for the English log-wood cutters (a settlement of indeterminate status, which cut mahogany on the strength of a treaty extracted from Spain in 1678), were complaining loudly that the Spaniards were poaching their slaves. Claims based on a value of £100 a slave were always met by counter-claims that the settlers had been stealing log-wood beyond their concession. This was a chronic irritant best left to the lawyers. Then, early in 1772, the Spanish guarda-costas seized an English ship from Jamaica which they caught red-handed stealing timber from the southern shore of Cuba. The case was quite different from that of the *Sir Edward Hawke*, and great was the surprise and indignation of certain clamorous gentlemen in Jamaica when the naval Commander-in-Chief refused to taken any action, on the grounds that it would be 'prostituting the dignity of the British flag to demand the restitution of vessels taken in the act of Piracy';[12] after which devastating retort the great body of unscrupulous and illicit traders also knew where they were with Sir George Rodney. Each case he treated on its merits without fear or favour. A letter from the Governor of South Carolina about the illegal seizure of a British ship resulted in the immediate despatch of a frigate to Vera Cruz; and on another occasion the murder of a British ship master resulted in the *Modeste* going to Porto Bello with a strong protest and demand for compensation.[13] From the first Sir George had the measure of the Spaniards; and others had now learnt their lesson, for these later incidents provoked no ripple of protest from London.

By the spring of 1772 the ridiculous fears in some quarters that he meant to start another war of Jenkins's ear were finally dispelled. 'I am glad to find the affair of the *Hawke* (schooner) terminated so well' wrote Augustus Hervey on February 25th.[14] 'We were all turned very sour here I assure you by it, and I hope the Spaniards will be more cautious for the future.' 'We are now got upon right ground', wrote Lord Sandwich on March 18th, after learning that the *Guadeloupe*'s second visit to Cartagena had not, after all, set the West Indies on fire.[15] Then a month later, after Sir George had expressed concern, as well he might, at the tone of some of the letters he had received from home, the First Lord went further. '. . . everything you have done is thoroughly approved . . .';[16] and with this, the absurd suspicions were forgotten.

Hervey was at this time a member of the Board of Admiralty. His letter to his old friend continues on a pleasantly familiar note. 'I beg you will not give yourself the trouble to send me any Madeira. . . . But if you will send me some fresh limes and chaddocks I shall thank you and readily accept them; or some Pine Apple roots, well done up, for my hot-house.

Naval news there is none, all goes on quietly—many suitors and little to bestow. Adieu. I envy you nothing but your Sun.'

That the Rodneys were enjoying Jamaica is clear from the bundle of letters which went off with the mail in March. Little Marr, reporting family news to Lord Northampton, said of Sir George: 'I never saw him look so well. His mind is at ease. He keeps little or no company and those not expensive, and everybody seems emulous who can oblige the whole family most. He does, and must, save money. . . .'[17] Marr's letter concludes with a reference to a young lady from London 'who lately arrived for the purpose of capturing some rich planter', but who very nearly captured the susceptible heart of James Rodney, much to his father's alarm. But James was a dutiful son, and the young lady had to look elsewhere.

The best picture of those early days comes from Sir George's own letter to Lord Northampton. 'I have lately been a long tour of the island, at least 70 miles, and better pleased with the Jamaica than ever. 'Tis certainly as fine a climate as any in the world, remarkably fruitfull, and so cold upon the mountains that I was glad to have two blankets. I propose to spend at least four months upon them from the beginning of June, by which I escape the hot weather, but I can not say that even that is disagreeable to me. . . . I intend sending you 8 Currasin birds who are very impudent here and attack the children, but I believe the climate of England will tame them. I have 10 now running about my yard and so tame that they will fly upon the table and make free with what's on your plate. I have three nests of mocking birds but fear they will not live. . . . Machoys and parrots without number. Now for business. . . .'[18]

The business related to a supply of mahogany for the great hall at Castle Ashby. This dealt with Sir George continued: 'My wife is in the mountains with Lady Trelawny and the Governor; I only came down to send despatches by the pacquet who is only detained while I write this letter. In May I shall send you several turtles and till September you may expect some every month as I have a Crawl of my own where there is at present at least 50, and I hope to have 100 soon, that I supply all my friends.'

1772 was indeed a happy year, and whatever may be thought of a commander-in-chief who proposed to spend 'at least four months' of every year in the mountains, no one can deny that Sir George in health was of more use on the station than Sir George sick on board his flagship in Port Royal harbour. Nor was he so detached as this letter might suggest. The picture of the sybarite taking his ease in the mountains should be balanced by another, equally valid, of the exasperated Commander-in-

Chief carrying on an acrid correspondence with the Commissioner for Sick and Hurt over conditions in the naval hospital. There were nearly 200 sick seamen there in August, and Sir George wanted the assistant-surgeon of the flagship (who could well be spared) to go along and help. But he found himself up against such jealous obstruction and departmental red tape, that even his authority was ineffectual.[19] Fresh turtle's meat in lieu of salt provisions was still his sovereign remedy for the sick and feeble. By sending small schooners far and wide to collect turtles, he could not only provide for his sick seamen and friends at home, but by sending several petty officers with each ship he was able to build up a body of much needed Caribbean pilots.

The only cloud on the horizon was the government's intention, as there was now no prospect of a war, to reduce his squadron. 'I must prepare you not to be surprised,' wrote Lord Sandwich, 'if this quiet should occasion the recall of some part of your squadron, which has been complained of in Parliament as too expensive.'[20] In June 1772 the *Boyne* and *Modeste* went home, and with them went an aggrieved and disappointed Marr. Sir George had satisfied his aspirations by making him purser of the *Modeste*, but Lord Sandwich had not confirmed this, and Marr wished to plead his case in person. Before the year ended the *Achilles* and *Lowestoft* were also ordered home.

As 1772 drew to its close Sir George, living as pleasantly and economically as he could ever hope to, began to worry about the future. From Jamaica he could keep the wolves at bay, although at the cost of nearly all his income.* But three years was the term of his appointment, and then what?

A way of escape from his predicament suggested itself in the autumn. Sir William Trelawny, the Governor, was in poor health and expected to resign. The Jamaica government was almost the best paid post overseas. Sir George consulted Lord Sandwich on his chances of succeeding him and received an encouraging reply. In November the Governor was sinking and on December 11th he died. Sir George was the first with the news, and with his own application. After waiting a week he wrote to the secretary of state for the colonies, Lord Dartmouth.

'Jamaica, December 19 1772.

'*My Lord,*

'Sir William Trelawny, H.M. Governor of this Island dying on the 11th

---

* Kee had discovered this by now and written a violent letter of protest. Sir George replied by sending him a turtle.

instant, I thought it my Duty to despatch one of H.M. ships with the news of that Event to the King's ministers, having previously given notice to the Lieutenant Governor and the legislature here of the time of her sailing and ordering the Captain to receive all such despatches as they should send.

'As the Government is thus become vacant, may I beg your Lordship will permit me to offer my most humble services and lay at His Majesty's feet my request to succeed the late Sir William Trelawny in the Government of his island of Jamaica.

'I have the honour to be, with the Greatest Respect, Your Lordship's most obedient and most Humble Servant,

'G. B. RODNEY.'[21]

For the next three months he was kept in suspense. On January 26, 1773, Lord Sandwich, unaware as yet of Sir William's death, was optimistic. 'I should be very glad to hear that Sir William Trelawny applied to quit his Government as I think you would stand very fair to succeed him. . . .'[22] But on February 12th things looked less promising. 'I yesterday communicated your last letter to Lord North and renewed my application concerning your succeeding the Government of Jamaica, but am sorry to tell you that matter does not bear so favourable an aspect. . . .'[23] He advised Sir George to write 'in as pressing a manner as possible' to Lord North and Lord Northampton. But twelve days later he wrote again with all hope gone. 'I do not meet with any encouragement that makes me flatter myself I shall succeed in procuring your appointment.'[24]

Sir George's hopes were finally killed by Lord Sandwich's letter of March 12th. 'By my last letter you will have perceived that there was little probability in your succeeding in your wish to be appointed Governor of Jamaica, and I now inform you that the successor is Sir Basil Keith; his father had particular connections with Lord Dartmouth and it was utterly out of my power to make any impression in your favour.'[25]

Sir Basil Keith! It was hardly credible. Ten years before, at Martinique, he had served under Sir George as a junior captain,* and he was quite undistinguished. The argument that his father had 'particular connections' with Lord Dartmouth was of course unanswerable, but others besides Sir George were surprised. Keppel for one. 'I don't mean to convey to you an ill impression of Captain Sir Basil Keith', he wrote at the time. 'He

---

* See Chapter 11, page 207.

is really a good and prudent man; but I don't think, Ambitious as he may be, he looked near so high as this Government.'[26]

Once again Fortune, after a brief, deceptive smile, had withdrawn her favours, and gloomy and apprehensive must Sir George's feelings have been as he entered his third and last year at Jamaica. All the bright promise had vanished and with it (one must suppose) much of the enchantment of his command. Even the happiness of his private life was no longer unalloyed. About this time old Mrs Clies died. Her son-in-law might have supported her loss with fortitude but Henny took it hard, and while she was worrying herself ill with grief she added to her husband's troubles by a series of unfortunate disagreements with some of the other ladies of the establishment. This was the situation when Marr returned in April 1773. Lord Sandwich had told him that there were many pursers at home worse off than himself and that his best prospect lay in returning to take his chance with Sir George. So back he had come, and was soon reporting to Lord Northampton.

'. . . on my arrival here I found Sir George and the family in perfect health, except Lady Rodney's reduced to a skeleton, so languid and pale that I scarcely knew her; all owing, or at least a great part, to the loss of her mother for whom she is in continual tears, and am afraid of the consequences. I am also of the opinion a part proceeds from the slight she feels at being neglected by several of her friends; that she feels herself entirely clear of the charges that have been brought against her is as true in my opinion as the Gospel; there seems to be a perfect attention paid to her upon Sir George's side and I must join in the opinion of the whole island that no Woman on Earth can behave in a more amiable manner than Lady Rodney.'[27]

Ill-natured talk flourishes on distant stations, and whatever the wretched business was it cannot have contributed to Sir George's peace of mind. Young James was still something of a worry too. There had been a Miss Parker since Marr left for England and Sir George, thoroughly apprehensive, had hurried the young man to sea, for salt water and absence to work their usual cure. But James Rodney, for all his susceptibility, was a dutiful and affectionate son. His engaging opening in reply to a parental rebuke—'Could I have thought that my going to dine at Mr. Pinnock's that day would have given my dear father a moment's uneasyness'[28]—is characteristic. The virtues of that happy home at Alresford are amply attested by the conduct of Jenny's sons towards their father in later years. Of George there was excellent news. His uncle had spoken to the Secretary at War who had spoken to the King, and an appointment in the Third Regiment of Guards had resulted. George at any rate was provided for, even if, on the Jamaica station, the glamour was fading, the ships going home, and a new Governor on the way out to whom Sir George would not enjoy paying his respects.

Work still brought its consolations. The watering-place at Rock Fort was a great success, with six spouts yielding 100 tons an hour. Six long-boats could fill up in ten minutes, and although the cost was more than double the original estimate, there would be no more gross profiteering in water. The survey of Port Royal harbour was complete too, and the channel buoyed with sections of the flagship's condemned mainmast, moored with old top-chains and worn-out anchors; so there would be no more extortionate pilot charges either. Much had been done to improve the dockyard, and the *Princess Amelia* had been completely refitted. But she was to fly Sir George's flag no longer, for on May 3, 1773, the *Portland* arrived to replace her. This was another depressing sign of the times. The new flagship was a fourth rate of only 50 guns.

With the Spaniards Sir George was now on the best of terms. When their register ship *Thetis* was wrecked in the Bay of Honduras, he sent a frigate to protect property for which he received a most grateful letter from the Governor of Yucatan. He was on good terms too with all the British authorities on shore, as well as the merchants. He sent a frigate to preserve order during a slave rising at Belize. Later in the year came a request from the civil powers in Jamaica for assistance to apprehend a dangerous murderer, and there followed an exciting man-hunt which resulted in Sir George receiving the Thanks of the Council, and one of his lieutenants a gold-hilted sword.

But although no one knew better the importance of these rich merchants, there were times when Sir George was vexed to the soul by them. The encouragement of trade was one thing, and the various customs regulations and navigation laws imposed from London were another. It was sometimes difficult, therefore, to reconcile the two against the background of selfishness, improvidence and greed, and the shameless chicanery habitually practised by the local courts. His chief concern was of course the safety of the island and its trade in time of war, but here again there was much that disturbed him.

There were, for example, the illicit traders (mostly Frenchmen and

Jews), who were allowed to take advantage of the freedom of the harbours and inlets round the coast to smuggle quantities of wine and brandy, soap, silks and stockings, and also hats. But it was useless to have these goods seized and handed over to the customs. Some venal lawyer would blandly argue that 'sea-officers were not authorized to make seizures', and much time and energy would have gone for nothing. Had it been only a matter of customs duties he might have shrugged it off. But what perturbed him (and loudly he complained), was the fact that the Jamaican authorities, by turning a blind eye to such commerce, were encouraging a dangerous increase in the number of French small craft and seamen, to provide our enemies with an enormous privateer fleet in time of war.

Equally pernicious was the recent legislation which allowed French merchantmen the use of three Jamaican ports, Kingston, St Lucia and Savannah-la-Mar. Before the Act, as he pointed out, Jamaica had nearly 100 sail of her own for carrying British goods to the Spanish main, and to the French and Spanish islands. But now, if he is to be believed, commerce in British bottoms had almost ceased, and hardly a pilot could be found for anywhere in the Caribbean.

In ways like these the legislators and the traders were laying up troubles for the future; but no amount of protesting from a mere sea-officer seemed to make one halfpenny worth of difference. When the merchants of Kingston raised a chorus of shocked protests at the way the Americans (in defiance of the navigation laws) were buying from the French islands instead of from themselves, he sent out and caught no fewer than thirteen of their merchantmen in one fell swoop as they cleared from Cape St Nicolas Mole, with sugar, molasses, and coffee. But this action, like all the others, was brought to nothing by the courts, and the ships were released. Sir George did not care for Americans, but by the end of his time at Jamaica he cared even less for the prosperous gentlemen on shore who grew fat on the seamen's toil but who could see no further than their own noses. The glories of flag-rank seemed to be as illusory as its material rewards, and each day the time was drawing nearer when he must return home and haul down his flag.

Whichever way he looked the horizon was empty. He had sounded Lord Sandwich on the chance of another naval command. 'You must be aware,' was the bleak reply, 'that the giving you a fresh command the moment your three years are expired in a former one, would draw so many enemies, both upon you and me, that common discretion would not allow me to think of such a measure.'[29] Sir George had suggested one of the other West

Indian governments. '. . . if they were in my gift,' Lord Sandwich continued, 'you would have a promise of one of them directly'; but unfortunately none was. None of Sir George's friends seemed able to do anything for him either, and the sands were running out. On March 20, 1774, came the official intimation that as his three years would soon be up he would shortly be relieved; and on June 27th the *Antelope* (50) arrived with his successor, Rear-Admiral Gayton. Well aware of his old friend's embarrassment, Lord Sandwich had enclosed a private letter with the official recall.

'*Dear Sir*,   'Admiralty, April 24 1774.

'I doubt not but that Lord Northampton and Mr. Henry Drummond, as well as the Duke of Chandos, with all of whom I have lately had much conversation upon your subject, will do me the justice to say that I am not indifferent to anything in which your welfare is concerned. I find by a letter from you to Lord Northampton that it will be inconvenient to you to return to England till your affairs are settled. You will therefore have leave to remain where you are, after you have resigned your command.

'I shall be very happy to hear that you are called out of your retreat, to which you may be assured I shall contribute to the utmost of my power, being at all times and on all occasions,

'*Your very sincere friend and humble*
servant,
'*SANDWICH*.'[30]

In the light of subsequent events it rather looks as if the First Lord saw more clearly than did Sir George how awkwardly he might be placed if he came home. But the latter was the last man to run away from difficulties. Besides, with Gayton commanding on the station (Gayton was something of a rough diamond), and with Sir Basil Keith as Governor, existence in Jamaica would be impossible. So the pleasant household broke up, and Henny and the children prepared to pack themselves on board the *Portland* with fifty tropical birds, some loads of mahogany for Castle Ashby, and who knows how many turtles and pineapples. Pagett, who had been pushing unsuccessfully for the chaplaincy of the 50th regiment, and little Marr, still disappointed of his purser's warrant, were returning home too. This crowding on board the little *Portland* was uncomfortably reminiscent of that other occasion when Pocock had taken the *Marlborough* and forced Sir George and all his followers into the 50-gun *Rochester*. Gloom and despondency there may well have been.

But there was one provision Sir George must make before his star set. James Rodney at twenty was still a lieutenant. Vacancies had been few in the squadron but Sir George had been able to promote Judd, his first lieutenant, into the 18-gun *Ferret* as Master and Commander, thereby clearing the way for James to step into Judd's shoes as first of the *Portland*. The next vacancy appeared unexpectedly with the *Antelope*. Captain Dickson of that ship was a sick man, and the doctors declared that he must go home at once. The temptation was irresistible. Sir George conferred with Gayton who made no objection, and James Rodney was posted to this 50-gun ship at the age of twenty. That done the *Portland* sailed.

Crowded together in the small two-decker the Rodney's and their followers could not have made a very cheerful company. For each of them the golden hopes of the outward voyage had become a mockery, and their homecoming, instead of being a matter for cheerful anticipation, was overshadowed by haunting fear. The *Portland* broke her voyage at Cape St Nicolas Mole, the French stronghold at the western end of St Domingo, where Sir George could for a while forget his troubles in a round of duty calls and a discreet appraisal of the port. Then she sailed again, and he had all the tedious voyage before him to ponder on his situation.

Round his neck like a millstone hung that fatal deed to Lowther and Mackreth. He had punctiliously fulfilled his own obligation. Over the last three years some £2,300, nearly half the original loan, had found its way back to them.[31] But now he realized how empty had been their assurances of partial repayment and generous treatment, for they had taken all and returned nothing. Again and again he must have asked himself how he could have put himself into the hands of such men. His great mistake had been his neglect to take advice. He had received plenty since from Kee, a whole bundle of whose letters, written over the last two years, he had kept. Kee's first knowledge of the arrangement had been when he went to collect the bills for his patron's flag-pay and table-money, and was confronted with Boldero's Power of Attorney and a copy of the deed. 'Had all the world told me you had done such a thing I would not have believed it', was his comment.[32]

He had every right to feel aggrieved. He was still, so far as he knew, Sir George's man of business. He was paying an allowance of £100 a year to George Rodney while his father was abroad, and he had even produced the necessary £90 for Sir George's patent as Rear-Admiral of England. Having expostulated with his patron he had ended with an urgent request for a Power of Attorney to receive at least the Rear-Admiral's salary and any freights. This Sir George had sent, but with small satisfaction to Kee, for the legal gentlemen, prompted no doubt by the vultures employing them, immediately invoked the original deed to invalidate it, so that until the opinion of the Attorney-General could be taken (a lengthy business and still undecided) not one penny of either could be touched. 'It's a Damn'd Deed I ever saw',[33] was the old man's explosive comment, at this new evidence of his patron's predicament. But there was nothing he could do until Sir George returned, and Sir George himself can hardly have seen clearly what his next move should be. He would have to discover, as soon as he arrived, how the creditors meant to treat him. If only his friends could find him some employment all might yet be well. In the meanwhile there was comfort in the thought that his parliamentary seat protected him from legal proceedings, and that Parliament still had some nine months of life. Much might be done in nine months.

In the last days of August the *Portland* was rolling up channel, past familiar marks that most of those on board had not seen for three years, and on the 31st she dropped anchor at Spithead. The Rodneys were home. Letters and newspapers came on board, all the news which exiles, after seven weeks at sea, absorb so eagerly, and with it one item of such appalling consequence as to send Sir George's hopes crashing to the ground. Parliament was to be dissolved almost at once. Sir George's last asset, his seat at Westminster, would be knocked from under him long before he could adjust his affairs; and with it would go his immunity. Fate could have devised no crueller blow. Had he known sooner he might have stayed in Jamaica. But here he was, back in England, and soon he would be in no condition at all to face his creditors.

In the face of this calamity, the Admiralty's refusal to confirm James Rodney's posting was a minor tribulation. Lord Sandwich wrote about it at once. After civilly expressing his satisfaction that his friend had felt able to return after all, he continued: 'I am sorry that I can not approve of your son's being made post captain from a lieutenant. I do assure you that if he were my own son I would not confirm his Commission. . . . You will not be surprised that I have written to the Board to desire that a Commission may be sent out for Captain Judd to be captain of the *Antelope* and for your son to be Master and Commander of the sloop.'[34] With his world falling in ruins about his ears Sir George made grateful acknowledgement. 'I am this moment favoured with your Lordship's letter of the 4th, the contents of which are so convincing that I should not desire the friendship you have so long honoured me with, were I not perfectly satisfied with the arrangement your Lordship has made. Far be it from me to desire your Lordship to break through so honoured and fixed a rule, even in favour of a son. . . .'[35]

With James Master and Commander of the *Ferret*, and at an age when his father was still a lieutenant, something at least had been saved from the wreck. But for the head of the family the issue was still in the balance. When he hauled down his flag there would be no more flag-pay and table-money for Lowther and Mackreth. All they might expect would be his half-pay, and the rents from his Hampshire property, to which might be added his salary as Rear-Admiral of England, if he chose to release it. If he made over everything he would be destitute while probably still falling short of his full obligation: but if he did not they would be able to proceed against him for debt, and Parliament was to be dissolved on September 30th.

Sir George hauled down his flag on the 4th and went on shore to learn his fate. For a day or two he lodged with Captain Marshall at Gosport. He proceeded to Bath, then to London. He visited the Admiralty (Lord Sandwich was away), and waited on Lord North who could not offer him the smallest hope of a government borough. After this he went to ground in Welbeck Street, giving out that he was too ill to venture abroad. What passed between him and the creditors can only be guessed, but Lowther, Mackreth and company were no longer the sympathetic, helpful friends they had appeared to be when their victim held great employment. The deed, the whole deed, and nothing but the deed was what they now insisted on. So Sir George went sick, or at any rate closed his doors to the world, and got down clearing up all the paper work outstanding from his recent command. He had much to do before Parliament dissolved.

Among other things he had to rebut a tremendous attack by the Navy Board over unauthorized and irregular expenditure. A severe hurricane in Jamaica in August 1772 had cleared the ground for many desirable improvements which he had lost no time in putting through. These had included an extension to the dockyard, a new wall, a new smithy, a new pitch-house, a new lookout post, some new piles along the quay, and much more, all of it clear evidence (to the Navy Board at least) that Sir George was as reckless with public money as with his own. They were now objecting to every item they had not authorized, as if the administrative convenience of the Navy Office was more important than health and efficiency in Port Royal dockyard. But the issue was desperately important for Sir George. He might have to pay for items not passed himself and such moneys as were due to him from the Navy might well be stopped until the account was squared.

Patiently, and (on the whole) convincingly, he answered the objections point by point. Only once, when the propriety of ordering a pump and a tank were questioned, did he allow himself a grumble. 'This article, I presume, was only inserted to increase the number of complaints.' Finally he concluded: 'I ever had, and ever Shall have, that respect for the Navy Board and their Orders which is justly their due. But while I have the honour of acting under the High Authority of the Board of Admiralty as their Commander-in-Chief in a very distant part of the World, and see contingencies arise which could not possibly be forseen. . . .' Here was the crux. An answer from England might take three months, and Sir George was not the man to wait while sailors and artificers died, quays tumbled down, and the service suffered. In those closely written pages, the fluent, polished sentences and the persuasive argument, he speaks for every man of action who ever found himself trammelled by official regulations and bureaucratic red tape.

But the Navy Board had a second barrel for him, in connection with his 'Imprest Account', money drawn on public funds for less tangible purposes. Sir George had not only drawn a great deal, but he had not drawn it through the correct channels. Much of it had gone on hiring small vessels, paying interpreters and pilots, and acquiring intelligence. Such disbursements, particularly the last, could be argued over interminably, and this the Board showed every intention of doing. Sir George was aggrieved. 'The rules of the Navy Board I don't pretend to understand . . . what difference could it make to the public service whether the Bills were drawn by the Admiral, or the officers acting in money matters under the Navy Board?'

Besides these replies, there was a report on Cape St Nicolas Mole, a more general one on the French and Spanish forces in the Caribbean, observations on the possibilities of Cape Antonio as a base (nine pages of this), a prospective view of the famous watering place at Rock Fort, and much more. Hour after hour in the house in Welbeck Street, pens scraped over the paper, pages were sanded down and stacked, corrected, re-written and the duplicates copied out. The results are impressive. But these might be Sir George's last official utterances and in justice to himself he could not produce anything less than his professional best.

September was nearly through. The paperwork was complete—or nearly, and certain other arrangements of a more private nature had been made as well. Finally, on the 30th, he wrote one more letter to the secretary.

'London, September 30th 1774.

'*Sir*,

'Having been in a very bad state of health ever since my return from Jamaica, I am advised by my Physicians to spend the Winter in a more temperate climate as the only chance I have of being restored to health.

'I must therefore desire you will please to lay this before their Lordships and beg their permission that I may have six months leave of absence.

'*I am, Sir, with great regard,*

'*Your most obedient and most humble servant,*

'*G. B. RODNEY.*'

It is almost inconceivable that so distinguished a man as Sir George Rodney could be subjected to the indignity of arrest for debt. But the fact remains that on the day he wrote this letter his Parliamentary immunity from that indignity ceased. Whatever the future might hold, life in England would be impossible in his altered circumstances, and to the Continent many a gentleman had withdrawn to economize.

He wasted no time. His last report bears the date October 1st. Three days later he was in France.

Chapter 16

Total Eclipse

(1774–1778)

'Oeconomy is what I hope to God you will pursue,
and you may do very well in France.'
(John Marr to Sir George Rodney, October 8, 1774.)[1]

ONE day, at the beginning of October 1774, an officer who only a few weeks before had flown his flag at sea, stepped unobtrusively on board the French packet at Dover. Sir George travelled without his family. Of his feelings as the shores of England faded from sight, as the low-lying coast of the Pas de Calais appeared ahead, as the unfamiliar harbour opened before him and the gabble of foreign voices broke in on his thoughts, there is one record. Shortly after landing he unburdened himself to Lord Sandwich.

'Calais, 4th October 1774.

'*My Lord,*

'Agreeable to your Lordship's advice I waited upon Lord North but found that I had no chance of a Government Borough as they had all been engaged before my application. I therefore took the advantage of the friendship you had shewn me in permitting me to repair to the Continent for the establishment of my health, in hopes that something may be done by my friends in the Spring towards my having some foreign employ.

'At Dover and since my being here, all the sea people belonging to that borough have been very solicitous that I should declare myself a candidate for that town as they much want an admiral to represent them, but as I have ever been a firm supporter of the measures of Government I have not given the least incouragement to that proposition tho' I have the greatest reason to imagine that a sea-officer would certainly carry that Borough as

269

most of the voters are seafaring men—but my Duty obliges me to submit to the determination of the King's Ministers.

'Your friendship, My Lord, has never forsaken me and I trust I shall still experience a continuance. The sudden blow of the dissolution of the Parliament has prevented my settling my affairs which I came home on purpose to do, and was the reason I did not avail myself of the real friendly orders you was so obliging as to sent to Jamaica.

'All I wanted to be in Parliament for was only to have time to settle my private affairs, and if employed abroad to have resigned my seat whenever the King's Ministers pleased. Surely, after so long and faithful attendance in Parliament, I might have been indulged in such a request.

'I shall not take up more of your Lordship's time than in assuring you that I shall ever bear a grateful remembrance of your Lordship's friend-ship and am, with real respect,

> '*Your most faithful and most obedient,*
> '*humble servant,*
> '*G. B. RODNEY.*'[2]

In this bitter moment he could not conceive his withdrawal as anything but temporary, and brief at that. All the same, the retreat must have been sufficiently humiliating. From Calais to Paris is 150 miles, across some of the dullest and poorest country in France. There can have been little in the passing scene to cheer his spirits as his conveyance rumbled and swayed along the dusty road to Paris.

However, his situation might have been much worse. Society in the eighteenth century was cosmopolitan. With suitable introductions an English gentleman, however much he might have to skimp and save in private, need not lack the sort of company to which he was accustomed. At the ambassador's there would be special opportunities for information and useful contacts, and there would be the post-bag and the English newspapers. On the surface, therefore, the same sophisticated appearance could be presented to the outside world, and its brilliant reflection (if not much else), still enjoyed. In any case, could it be doubted, with so many friends pressing on his behalf, that exile would be short?

A few days after arrival he received a letter from his son George. The little boy who had so adored his father in the old days at Alresford had lost nothing of his devotion. After expressing satisfaction that the hurry had not impaired his father's health or caused any inconvenience other than fatigue, this excellent young man continued: 'Can I, my dear Sir, be of any use to you here? Believe me, I should be very happy if I could take any trouble off your hands. I wish you would give me leave to inform myself concerning your private affairs and let me try if there is nothing to be done more for your advantage. Pardon me if what I ask seems impertinent. My love and affection lead me to endeavour to be of use to you.'[3]

George Rodney had been only seventeen when the family sailed for the West Indies, and it is clear that at no time had his father revealed to him the full depth of his commitments. The hasty withdrawal to France must have come as a shock. But he was shrewd and capable as well as devoted, and had reached man's estate. From now onwards he was to make it his business to straighten out, as best he could, his father's affairs; and before long Sir George, wayward and impulsive but learning by experience, was thankful to put everything into his hands.

These years of exile bring out the remarkable devotion which Sir George inspired. Strangers and acquaintances might see only the formidable sea-officer. But a warm and compelling personality lay beneath the surface. Kee had exploded when someone told him that when his patron lay on the road coming to London it had cost him four or five guineas. 'How', he exclaimed, 'can any man serve Sir George when he looks so lightly on a guinea than any other man would a single shilling?'[4] But he never wavered in his determination to save his patron if he could. Pagett had a scheme for concealing Sir George in Somerset,[5] and little Marr, 'ready and willing to offer my mite of service in the hour of adversity',[6] was a most faithful correspondent, only once referring to the money his patron owed him. His first budget of news followed closely on George Rodney's letter, and may be summarized thus: the imprest account was still held up, and Sir George's enemies were gleefully spreading the story that he had 'done for himself completely' by over-spending on intelligence.* Brother James (an exception to the united front of the family was showing), was taking no notice of Lady Rodney, for which Marr professed to despise him. But he concluded with the cheerful assurance that the ladies were only waiting for Mr George Rodney's escort to join the head of the family in Paris; and before the year ended, Henny and the little girls arrived, young John remaining under Pagett's care at Greenwich. So the first winter of the return from Jamaica closed in with the family in Paris but still unsettled, and Sir George complaining continuously of the cold.

---

* The facts appear to be these. Sir George had agreed to pay a certain source of information £365 per annum for three years. This, with a Spanish war still possible, was thought reasonable for the first year, but disallowed for the second and third.

Marr's letters help to explain the inveterate hostility of the Navy Board. 'A pique against you for not paying homage enough to their imaginary consequence', speaks volumes; and a little later he says outright that their refusal to pass the accounts proceeded 'from no other cause than that of a determined ill-will'.[7] His gossip is always diverting. Thus, on Sir George's predecessor at Jamaica: 'Commodore Mackenzie is mad. He went to the Admiralty with loaded pistols to demand why the promotion of flags stopped at him. . . .'[8] Sir George at his most exigeant had never carried things like this.

Exiles live on hopes and the Rodneys were no exception. A sea command being, for the time, impossible, Sir George revived two of the forlorn hopes which had failed him in the past. The first was the government of Jamaica, an encouraging report having reached him of Sir Basil Keith's ill-health. The other was his old claim to lands in the captured island of St Vincent, which Grenville had turned down thirteen years before. He could not get over the fact that General Monckton's grant had been confirmed while his had not, and he now deluded himself that a special memorial to the King might redress this injustice. So, for many months to come the devoted George Rodney, the Duke of Chandos (genuinely concerned at his kinsman's situation), and Henry Drummond, were busily collecting material and preparing a case.

While the family thus bestirred themselves, Sir George's humbler friends pestered the Navy Office to get his accounts passed, or at least to obtain the release of his salary as Rear-Admiral of England. The Admiralty Secretary had offered a ray of hope. 'Mr. Marr has shown me Mr. Stephens's private letter,' Kee wrote on March 17, 1775, 'by which I can not think but they must allow the intelligence, was it more than it is . . . am very ill and can not go about it, but as soon as I am able I will go about it and get the greater part allowed, if not the Whole. . . . I think', he concluded, 'you are used very ill by some people whom you have served greatly.'[9]

This last reference must be to Shuldham, whom Sir George had taken as his flag-captain at Martinique in 1762, and about whom Marr had received some confidential information which he passed on. 'Mr. Boldero told me two days ago he was more troublesome than all the rest; that he had employed a lawyer to a very great expense to foreclose the Mortgage and take possession of Your Estate, which he would have done at the hazard of ruining all your possessions to the destruction of yourself and family, but Mr Boldero has stopped him for the present. . . . What a pity you have nourished such a viper.'[10]

What of Sir George in Paris? He was suffering from the gout; he was sufficiently in pocket (or credit), in the autumn of 1775 to buy his son George some handsome embroidered waistcoats which were much admired when they arrived; and there is more than a suspicion that he was gambling again. His enemies in England believed this, and so did Marr who presumed to remonstrate. 'A report lately reached the Admiralty that you was every night at a public gaming-house . . . and that you played as much as ever.'[11] Whatever the truth, he was not, as yet, in actual want.

Meanwhile, on the other side of the Atlantic American rebels had opened fire at a place called Lexington and fought a battle on a hill above Boston; and in November, as a consequence of this, Lord George Germain became Secretary of State for the colonies. Here were exciting possibilities. An American war would certainly improve Sir George's chances of employment, and all the more perhaps as the new secretary, who would have the lion's share in its direction, had been a friend of Captain and Mrs Rodney in the old days at Hill Street. Lord George was a controversial figure. For disobedience of orders at the Battle of Minden he had been adjudged unfit to serve His Majesty in any military capacity whatever, and to most of his countrymen he was still the coward who had refused to charge at Minden. But whatever Sir George's feelings about the past, the new secretary was clearly a man to cultivate, so he lost no time in writing a fulsome letter of congratulation, with a tactful allusion to the 'gross, cruel, base, unjustifiable persecution' Lord George had undergone.[12] If Lord Sandwich was going to prove a broken reed, as now seemed likely, Lord George might usefully take his place.

So ended the year 1775 on a note of modified optimism. The memorial was taking shape, George Rodney found time to visit young John at school and reported well of him, Marr and Kee continued hopeful they might extract something from the wreck of Sir George's fortune, and the family remained well. For a while the rays of hope flickered more cheerfully over the exiles in Paris. There was even talk of Sir George having the Constantinople embassy or the government of New York.[13] But great sorrow was impending.

James Rodney, the younger son, had been left in the West Indies when the rest of the family came home. It will be remembered that the Admiralty had refused to confirm his posting to the *Antelope* but had confirmed him as Master and Commander of the 18-gun *Ferret*. For some time there had been no letters. Then, at the beginning of 1776, came rumours that the *Ferret* was overdue.

With sharpest forebodings the distracted father questioned every arrival from England who might have news. He wrote to the Admiralty, and in April the Admiralty replied.[14] Fears for the *Ferret's* safety were only too well founded. Commanded by James Rodney she had sailed from Pensacola on August 8, 1775. There had been a violent hurricane about that time and she had never been seen again.

It was a dreadful blow. Young James had always been so cheerful and spontaneous in his affection, and so promising in his profession. 'I flatter myself my dear father will be pleased to find that we got over a very hard gale of wind without meeting with any accident,' he had written, after bringing his ship through some bad weather, 'indeed I took every precaution I think that could be taken.' And on another occasion: 'I have been particularly careful to follow your advice in everything and be assured I always will continue to do so; therefore let me beg of you whenever you write to me, to give me as much of it as you can.'[15] There would be no more of such letters, and with poor James went one more link with those days of unforgettable happiness when Sir George was still only a captain, and Jenny was bringing up two small boys at Alresford. 'Such a droll, merry, little Monkey' was how she had described him. That had been twenty years ago but he had her letter still. Sir George looked out stonily on the alien world, his eyes as blue and piercing as ever. But the deepening lines on his face and the compressed lips began to tell their tale.

On May 7, 1776, Henny gave birth to her fourth child, another daughter whom they called Margaret Anne. The Rodneys were now living in the Hotel Bruxelles in the Rue Colombie. Several bills were paid towards the end of September,[16] but it seems that money was at last beginning to run short for only extreme necessity could have forced them to their next step. This was Henny's return to England to bring Sir George's situation home to some of his friends, and in particular to Lord Sandwich.

No doubt she did her best. It is said that she even attempted to have a subscription opened among the members of Whites' on her husband's behalf. But she did not see Lord Sandwich. The failure of her pathetic mission is recorded in her correspondence with that nobleman.[17]

Her approach was strictly formal and couched in the third person. Her only instructions from Sir George, she assured him, were for her to wait on him. But she hoped for his Lordship's indulgence to a distressed wife if she made it her particular request for her husband's appointment to the East India or other command, and that the imprest against him at the Navy Board could be taken off. On the large amount spent on intelligence, she emphasized that he had regular vouchers for all the money paid, and while not presuming to judge on the propriety of the mode of payment, humbly hoped that any impropriety (if such there were), would not be set against all his former services. She reminded him that at Martinique, where a large field was open to swell the contingent bill, Sir George's had been remarkably small. She concluded by hoping that on her return she would be able to assure Sir George that Lord Sandwich would still be his protector and friend.

All this must have made the First Lord acutely uncomfortable but he replied at once.

'Admiralty, 1 October 1776.

'*Madame*,

'I really can not describe the distress I feel in answering the Note which you sent me by my Secretary; the long acquaintance I have had with Sir George Rodney and the testimony I am always ready to give of the service he has done his Country as an Officer will always incline me to give him every support I can with any degree of propriety and I will appeal to the Duke of Chandos, Mr. Drummond, and others of Sir George's friends, whether I have not always done my utmost to serve him in some late objects he has had in view which, if he had succeeded in, might have given him some effectual assistance in his present difficulties; but the points that are the object of your note are what I can not by any means answer in a manner that will be satisfactory to you; the command in India is already given away and I am sure that if Sir George will consider the thing impartially he will see that tho' his merit as a Sea-Officer is undeniable, there are reasons that make it impossible for me to prevail on His Majesty to appoint him to the Command of a foreign Squadron.

'I have enquired at the Navy Office and I find that Sir George Rodney has now no Imprest against him, but what there is due to him must go to those who are legally empowered to receive it and the Admiralty can no way interfere in that business, especially as I understand there are more Claimants than one.

'As to the money expended at Jamaica and the mode of procuring it, it has been undoubtedly very irregular and unprecedented; and the Articles that have been disallowed at the Office are the same that have been refused to other Commanders-in-Chief upon the same and other Stations; and was Sir George to be indulged in that matter it would open a Door to many other Claimants and would, I apprehend, be of no use to him as whatever is due to him at the Navy Office must as I have already said go to those who are legally entitled to receive it.

'If it would give your Ladyship any satisfaction I will certainly wait on you before you leave London, but I think such an interview can have no other effect than giving much pain to us both, for as a Man in Office your husband had deprived me of the power of being useful to him, and as a private man, 'tho I have the warmest inclination to serve him to the utmost of my ability, unless his friends can point out to me some mode in which I may be useful to him, my offer of service is, I am sensible, little more than general professions of friendship.

'*I am, Madame,*
'*Your most obedient and most humble Servant,*
'*SANDWICH.*[18]
'Lady Rodney, No. 29 Percy Street.'

There is no reason to doubt the First Lord's sincerity. His hands were tied. Until the account with the Navy Office was cleared Sir George could not be employed, and precedent could not be broken to clear it without bringing a host of enemies on to the First Lord's back. As for releasing any money for Sir George's immediate needs (his half-pay or his pay as Rear-Admiral of England), all was frozen by the many conflicting powers of attorney which he had signed at different times. On this matter counsel's opinion, so long awaited, had proved singularly unhelpful. It was that the parties should reach some equitable agreement; that it was unreasonable to involve the Navy Commissioners in any contest; and that it was impossible to form any judgement from the contradictory instruments. All was true enough no doubt, but it only served to emphasize the unpalatable fact that so long as Lowther and Co. held out for their full due, nothing could be released.

Henny did not press matters. She thanked Lord Sandwich for his letter and his professions of friendship. She was extremely hurt to find all hopes of a command at an end and could not help saying she thought Sir George's case extremely unfortunate. She would transmit his Lordship's letter to him. Dignified and reproachful, but with nothing gained by her intervention, she withdrew.

Fortunately there was still Mr Richard Kee. She would almost certainly have seen him during her visit and Kee was prepared to fight Lowther and Co. to the last ditch. Still hopeful that his own power of attorney might prevail and determined, come what may, to prevent them touching the

Rear-Admiral's salary, he notified Sir George on October 18th that he might draw on him for £400. 'I have been ill these six months past,' he wrote, 'if I live I may get you clear'd of these embarrassments. I assure you I will do all I can. . . .'[19]

It was the brave old man's last letter. He died on November 3rd before Sir George's bill reached him. But when it did arrive a few days later it was accepted by Kee's daughter, Mrs Tyler, because of 'the great esteem' her father had always had for Sir George. It is possible that this £400 and nothing else kept the Rodneys in funds for the rest of their time in Paris.

The dreary winter months passed with Sir George long confined indoors, but in the spring of 1777 Henny again visited England. From Greenwich, where Sir Charles Hardy was now the Governor, she reported that he was 'much disliked', and that Lady Hardy and her daughters were 'the most vulgar, Disagreeable people I have ever seen'. But George Rodney met her there with news that some sort of settlement with the creditors seemed to be in sight.

'Stafford Street, April 11 1777.
'I received yesterday your letter and went immediately to Greenwich where I had the pleasure of seeing my mother in very good health.

'Before I left town I went to Mr. Mackreth's desiring he would have a meeting of the Creditors; he said it was necessary first to converse with Sir James Lowther, and would call upon me as soon as he had seen him. As I have never heard from him since I shall make it my business to see him tomorrow and hope, before the next post, some measure will be taken towards your returning to England.'[20]

There can be no doubt that Sir James Lowther, one of the wealthiest men in England and one of the most vindictive, was the chief obstacle to any settlement. Sublimely contemptuous of public opinion, he possessed both the means and the will to take extreme measures if his victim set foot in England, and George Rodney very much feared that he might, if given the chance. So, although his father's return was essential for a settlement—'I am assured by all friends, Mr. Drummond, etc., that it is absolutely necessary'—George Rodney was insistent that there must be no impetuous return without precautions taken. '. . . for God's sake, my dear Sir,' was his urgent conclusion, 'do not attempt it before some treaty is signed with the Creditors, and you have a lawyers opinion that you may come in safety.' It was a far cry from those friendly offers of assistance from Lowther and

Mackreth so recklessly accepted five years before. Sir George, in his reply, speaks from the heart.

'May 7 1777.

'*My Dear Son,*

'Amidst all my misfortunes and distresses nothing can give me a greater relief and satisfaction than hearing from a son whose affection is the only consolation that has enabled me to bear the weight of sorrow which has fallen to my lot. May God grant that you may never experience the same.

'Your letters, my dear Geo. are allways a cordial to my drooping spirits as they always convince me of that sincere affection which I ever have and ever shall prefer to that of every person whatever.'

Family matters rather than his unsettled business with the creditors filled the rest of his letter. His brother James, whom he had never forgiven for diverting so much of the Bridges inheritance, had at last made friendly overtures and this was no time to stand on injured dignity.

'I am glad your Uncle has not forgotten he has a nephew. Whatever may be his conduct give him no reason, My Dear George, to find fault. Tis for your dear sake alone that I keep any terms with him after the treatment I met with from his solemn promise of never parting with his House and lands at Alresford, and that he would never marry again.

'Twas from my affection to him that I suffered him and his first wife to enjoy what was in reality my just rights, for her fortune was paid of Mrs. Bridges personal Estate, the whole of which, after Mrs. Bridges death, was mine, with an almost assured certainty that it would one day come to you. I forebore prosecuting my full claims and little thought that a brother who owed me so much could have acted in the manner he has done. Weither or not he has any children I know not as I have not heard from him but once since he married.

'Adieu my dear Son, be assured that I am, and shall ever continue to keep you nearest my heart, while I am
'*Your most affectionate father,*
'*G. B. RODNEY.*'[21]

Hopes of a treaty with the creditors came to nothing. Sir James remained obdurate so Sir George stayed where he was. And now the shadow of events across the Atlantic obtruded more and more upon the Paris scene.

The Americans had declared their Independence, and French government circles made no secret of their satisfaction at England's embarrassment. An American ambassador was already installed in a house at Passy. He had appeared at Court without powder or sword. Anything American was all the rage, especially among the young, and whist, an English importation, had gone out completely to be replaced at every card-table by a new game called 'le Boston'. Sir George's feelings may be imagined. In desperation he wrote again to Lord Sandwich.

'Paris, October 15 1777.

'*My Lord,*

'Permit me once more to sollicit you that I may be named to His Majesty for a command. I have long waited in expectation that I should have received that favour at your Lordship's hands and have still hopes you do not intend entirely to deprive me of that expectation. . . .'[22]

The reply was disappointing.

'Admiralty, November 14 1777.

'*Dear Sir,*

'I wish I knew how to answer your letter that was yesterday delivered to me by your son in a manner that would give you comfort. But however painful it must be to me I can not avoid telling you that I do not think your object of obtaining a foreign command can be attended with success. . . .'[23]

He advised Sir George 'to procure from Government some annual income', and repeated his own professions of friendship and zeal to serve him. Sir George accepted defeat. Although by now he must have given up all hope of Lord Sandwich he would still maintain the courtesies.

'December 1st 1777.

'*My Lord,*

'I beg you will accept my sincere thanks for the letter you have honoured me with by the King's messenger, and your kind assurance of joining with my other friends towards obtaining an income from Government, till my affairs are put in such a condition as to enable me to serve in the profession I have always had most at heart. . . .'[24]

It was, after all, as a sea-officer that Sir George felt his situation most keenly. Chafing at his inaction he collected all the naval information he could and enclosed it with his letter. Maybe it would be of use. Maybe it would prevent them from forgetting him. At all events they could not say but he had offered his services, and some friend would let the King know he had done so.

The fourth winter was the worst of all. Henny was again in England and wrote that she was unwell. Sir George was on his own with the children. Money was short, with debts piling up and small prospect of being able to pay them, but overshadowing everything was the news from America. There was now every prospect of France coming to the help of the rebels; and if she did, what would be the position of a British admiral unable to leave the enemy capital because of the money he owed?

By the beginning of March 1778 Sir George was seriously alarmed. George Rodney had been looking for safe accommodation for him in London but without success, and his father grew impatient.

'Wednesday Eve, 11 March 1778.

'*My Dear Henny,*

'Not hearing from either you or my son by the last messenger gives me uneasyness inexpressible as the delay of finishing what has been promised obliges me to remain in the hotel where I am at an expense I could wish to avoid and daily adds to the sum I allready owe for Board and Lodging. I beg you will desire my Son to see Lord North again either at his House or Levee. Delays are worse than Death especially at this Critical time when every hour teems with momentary expectations of War.'

After a long digression on convoy and warship movements, of which more later, Sir George returned to family affairs. Admiral Byron was going out to command in American waters and there was the question of young John's future.

'In my last I did not answer what you proposed relative to my Boy Jno. He can not be better than with my friend Mr. Byron, especially as Geo. Byron I suppose will be a Captain and take him with him till he has served his time; but I owne my Dear, my Heart will not let me Determine in an affair of this Nature. The Blow I have experienced is allmost constantly in my thoughts and must ever prey upon my Heart. I leave it intirely my Dear to you, to do what you judge best. . . .

'I beg you will tell my friend Byron I wish him all the success possible.'[25]

The naval information which Sir George thought so important he passed on to the ambassador, Lord Stormont, and an interesting story it made.[26] He had been dining in company the day before, when the conversation turned on the report that a French admiral had returned the salute of two American warships. Many at the table had doubted this, but a gentleman whom Sir George afterwards learnt was the Secretary to the American Commissioners vouched for it. On two separate occasions, he said, the new American flag had been saluted by French warships as for a republic. The senior American captain, a certain Paul Jones, had well understood the importance of this. The Secretary had his report in his pocket and read out some of it to the company. 'I am the first person,' boasted Jones, 'who have occasioned France openly to avow the independence of America who, by returning the salute of her ships, has acknowledged them as free States.'

Shocked Sir George may well have been, but this was information of the highest importance, and he plied the communicative Secretary with questions. This Jones, it appeared, was a renegade Scot, and he had thirteen vessels for America under convoy. Sir George, well informed on the latest developments at home, pointed out that Great Britain had announced her intention of repealing all the laws the Americans complained of and was sending commissioners to reconcile all differences. Would this not, he asked, bring them back to their obedience? But the Secretary assured him that it was too late. Last October might have been different, but not now. Furthermore, he made no secret of the fact that his country had made a treaty with France and that Jamaica would not belong to Britain much longer. Whereupon Sir George hurried back to his hotel and wrote out a report of the whole conversation, as fast as his gouty fingers would let him.*

He also drew the ambassador's attention to his own situation.

'March 17 1778.
'*My Lord,*

'Nothing but the crisis which your Lordship's sudden departure from Paris seems to forebode would have induced me to take up your Thoughts and Time upon my private concerns. But the ungrateful necessity which will probably oblige me at all events to continue here ought perhaps to be known to your Excellency officially, as a justification of an English admiral's

---

* The Franco-American treaty was signed on February 6th and news of it was communicated to the British government by the French ambassador on March 13th, three days after Sir George's conversation with the Secretary.

conduct in an Enemy's Country in the time of war. My zeal for His Majesty's service upon every occasion, and my desire to be employed wherever my services may be thought useful, I flatter myself are not unknown to your Lordship. But as a gentleman and officer of high rank I can not quit a foreign country without discharging those necessary debts which my unfortunate situation has obliged me to incur during my residence here, for the Maintenance of myself and my family. They amount in all to about £600, and there are arrears due to me for my salary as Rear Admiral of Great Britain to the amount of £2000 and upwards, besides my half-pay as Vice Admiral which is detained by the Navy Board on account of a claim put in by Sir James Lowther. The favour I ask upon this subject is that your Excellency will be so good, upon your arrival in England, to make this my case known to the Secretary of State, and to use your endeavours that I may be permitted to draw for the sums above mentioned to enable me to quit this country with credit. . . .'[27]

The situation was much worse than he admitted to Lord Stormont. To Henny he wrote almost in despair.

'Thursday morn.

'*My Dear Henny*

'I have read over often your last letter and the more I peruse it the more it distresses me . . . the delay of sending a few hundred pounds makes my situation extreamly irksome to me, especially as a prosecution is begun against me for my note of hand to the amount of ninety odd pounds, as I told you in my former letter, and the second summons sent me yesterday. The people will wait no longer for them. What to do I really don't know. To speak to Lord Stormont I am unwilling, but I will talk to Mr. Janes upon the subject as he is a good man and feels the distress I am drove to. I am now at the ambassadors, writing this letter, as you may perceive by the pen and paper.

'I hope you will make yourself easy in regard to trustees and guardians for the children. If I have ever anything to leave you may depend upon being sole guardian and I will revoke the other Will immediately.

'. . . in all your letters you have not mentioned where I could be in safety, should I go to England. Lady Berkeley is going to leave Hampton Court soon and is expected in Paris. Do you think her appartments would be of service? Tis near Lord North's and I might have an opportunity of seeing him.

'Think for me, for I can scarce think for myself.'[28]

This was the lowest ebb. For more than three years Sir George had put a brave face on things, but every one of his distress signals had been ignored and his ship was almost on the rocks. 'Think for me, for I can scarce think for myself.' It was almost surrender.

But all was not yet lost. Friends in Paris were shocked by his situation. They made a point of waiting on him daily at his hotel to save him from annoyance and preserve what remained of his credit. Official word was spoken and an officer of the police was at hand to overawe any creditor who might seek to arrest him. Meanwhile, serious thought was given how to meet his commitments.

On March 20th he was able to inform Henny that M. Panchaud the eminent Swiss banker and one other friend had offered their assistance and assured him the money would be raised. 'Should this desirable event take place,' he wrote, 'you may expect me in London very shortly, a friend having offered me a bed in a place unsuspected till I can procure lodgings in the Verge of the Court. I propose to have the children and Evans to set out immediately after receiving the money, either for Boulogne or Ostend, as may be thought most advisable. . . . Tell my son to look out for a proper lodging but not to tell I am coming.'[29]

Eleven days passed. There was no word from England. The English in Paris were nearly all gone. Then, on the 31st, came a new development, best described by Sir George himself in his letter to Henny.

'I yesterday was to take my leave of Lady Dunmore who sets out for England this morning. The Marshal Byron came in and seeing me was extremely civil. He took Lady Dunmore, Mr. North, and Mr. Janes the Parson into another room and told them that he heard my stay in Paris was occasioned by the want of a remittance to discharge the Debts I must necessarily have contracted. That his purse was at my service, and begg'd that I would make use of it, that whatever sums, even to two thousand pounds might be necessary, he would immediately pay. . . .

'On the Marshal's return into the room they beckoned me out and made me acquainted with his Generous Offer, for which I begged they would make my acknowledgements, and how highly sensible I was of his friendship; but as I made no doubt but that I should soon receive proper remittances, I could not possibly avail myself of his generosity, but should ever retain it in my memory. Besides, my enemies would take advantage of my receiving pecuniary favours from Frenchmen of his high rank and instil insinuations to my disadvantage. Lady Dunmore and the two gentlemen were of my opinion and will report it to my advantage. Pray call upon her. She will be glad to see you. . . .'[30]

Louis Antoine de Gontaut, duc de Biron and Marshal of France, at this time an alert and active old man of seventy-six, represented all that was finest in the *ancien régime*. Bearer of an historic name, and a professional soldier of the highest distinction (he had been badly wounded at Dettingen thirty-five years before) he was universally respected as a man of the strictest honour and the most undeviating principles.* That he should go out of his way to smooth Sir George's path is a moving instance of disinterested generosity and chivalrous fellow feeling; but it is also a striking testimony to the impact made by Sir George's own personality upon the best society in Paris.

Eight more days passed, but still no word from England. However, M. Panchaud's offer remained open—to be accepted if war was declared suddenly. Moreover, the Marshal de Biron had renewed his own offer in the most charming and persuasive way, assuring Sir George that it had been no French gasconade at Lady Dunmore's but a genuine mark of friendship and regard. All France, he said, was sensible of the services Sir George Rodney had rendered his country, and that he had been treated disgracefully. What must have been a most agreeable conversation between a British admiral and a French nobleman was concluded by an invitation for Sir George's little girls to walk in the marshal's garden next day.

Still Sir George held out, hoping for some response from home. The end of the story he described to Henny in his letter of May 6th.

'I have this day accepted of the generous friendship of Marshall Duke Byron—who has advanced one thousand Louis in order that I may leave Paris without being reproached. Nothing but a total inattention to the distressed station I was in could have prevailed upon me to have availed myself of his voluntary proposal, but not having had, for more than a month past, a letter from any person but Mrs. Tatham and yourself, and my passport being expired, it was impossible for me to remain in this city at the risque of being sued by all my Creditors who grew so clamorous

---

* Madame de Genlis says of him: '*Il avait une taille majesteuse, une très belle figure, et l'air le plus imposant que j'ai vu. On dit de Brutus qu'il fut le dernier des Romains; on peut dire du maréchal de Biron qu'il fut en France le dernier fanatique de la royauté.*'

it was impossible to bear it, and had they not been overawed by the Lieutenant of the Police, would have carried the prosecutions to the greatest length. Their demands were all satisfied this day, and the few days I remain in this city will be taken up in visiting all those great families from whom I have received so many civilities—and whose attention, in paying me daily and constant visits, in a great measure kept my creditors from being so troublesome as they otherwise would have been.'

Sir George concluded: 'I propose the children should set out for Calais on Sunday where they may stay at Pain's with Evans till we can know how we are to be disposed of. I shall go myself by way of Dieppe that I may have an opportunity of being in London the shortest and least suspected way. I hope our friend Tatham will take care that I may have a lodging in a safe place—tis surely the Interest of my Creditors that I should not be disturbed. Nothing but my being employ'd can give them hopes of payment.'[31]

And so the uncomfortable sojourn abroad came to an end, and Sir George slipped back unheralded and unnoticed to an England embroiled in the most unhappy and least successful of all her wars.

NOTE

The intervention of the Marshal de Biron

There are several versions of this romantic episode. Of the principal figures only the Admiral has told the story, in his private correspondence with his wife where, one would suppose, he had no reason to conceal what really happened. However, French sources assert that he actually saw the inside of a French prison. A search for the origin of this legend (as I believe it to be), brings forward an interesting secondary figure in the story, the marshal's nephew, Armand Louis, duc de Lauzun (1747–93).

In 1792, after the outbreak of the Revolution, young Lauzun, who was well known in England, accompanied Talleyrand on his unpopular mission to London and before long, probably through the machinations of jealous French *emigrés*, he found himself in an English prison. Talleyrand and Hirsinger, the French *chargé d'affaires* in London, protested without effect and Hirsinger, writing home on February 12th, said: '*J'ai cru devoir me borner à compatir à son sort, et à rappeler aux Anglais qui me parlaient de lui que le maréchal de Biron, son oncle, tira des prisons de Paris en pareille occasion l'amiral Rodney.'* How some of Lord Rodney's friends, Lord Stormont and it is said the Prince of Wales and the Duke of York, started a subscription for de Lauzun's release and got him out of the country is not relevant here. But Hirsinger's seems to be the earliest suggestion (made fourteen years later) that Sir George was actually arrested.

To hark to the early months of 1778 when England and France were on the brink of war and Sir George's situation in Paris becoming increasingly difficult. Young Lauzun was in England until the first week of April when he returned to rejoin his regiment, and it is possible, although not certain, that he may have reported to his uncle the insinuations appearing in some English newspapers that Sir George was detained in France because the French feared his military talent. From this point legend and family tradition take over. Stung by this outrageous suggestion the chivalrous marshal proceeded to Versailles to obtain permission from his Sovereign to rescue the British admiral. *'Je vous envie d'avoir eu cette idée,'* replied Louis XVI, *'elle est française et digne de vous,'** whereupon the marshal drove in his carriage to the prison where Sir George was already incarcerated, and procured his release. Another agreeable story, first told by Wraxall, is of the French offering Sir George a command in their own navy, and of his freezing refusal.

But whatever the exact circumstances of the marshal's intervention, his chivalry and generosity are beyond dispute. It is even possible that although he may not have had to extract Sir George from a French prison, he was instrumental in saving him from being put inside one. The Lieutenant of Police, whose providential presence at the critical time overawed the more clamorous creditors and kept them at bay, must have been sent by someone: and the marshal was at that time colonel of the Gardes-françaises and Commander-in-Chief of all the troops in Paris.

* *Le duc de Lauzun* by Comte R. de Gontaut Biron, Librarie Plon, Paris, 1937.

Chapter 17

Suitor for Employment

(1778–1779)

'Ready at a moment's notice to go on any service.'
(Sir George Rodney to Lord Sandwich,
August 15, 1779.)[1]

SIR GEORGE'S first problem was a secure lodging where he would
be safe from legal proceedings. Although the law against debtors
was sharp and easily set in motion there were certain localities,
'liberties' they were called, where, by ancient prescriptive right,
or by the continuance of long tradition, or by some old statute of the realm,
no writ or warrant could be served. Some of these were too disreputable to
be considered, but there was one sort of 'liberty' particularly suitable.
'No arrest can be made in the King's presence nor within the Verge of his
Royal Palace.' So declared the learned Blackstone in his *Commentaries on
the Laws of England,* and many a gentleman in Sir George's situation had
been glad to take advantage of the fact. Sir George had hoped for apartments at Hampton Court, but his friends did better for him than this.
They found him lodgings in Cleveland Row, opposite St James's Palace.
No. 4 in the Row, where a Mrs Campbell was pleased to accommodate an
officer of high rank who had been unfortunate, was within 200 feet of the
palace entrance and therefore well within the prescribed limits of a verge.
It was not cheap.[2] But in its combination of security with ready access to
the Court and the ministers, it could not have been bettered. Here, in the
very centre of affairs, with all the world passing beneath his window, the
Secretary of State's office next door, and His Majesty just across the way,
Sir George went to earth.

The deadlock with the Navy Office and with the creditors continued,
but the debt of honour to the Marshal de Biron was settled at once. The
sum was substantial (something in the region of a thousand guineas in

English value), and Sir George was as hard up as ever. There is no knowing how he raised the money but raised it was, and within a day or two his note of hand came back with a charming letter addressed to '*Monsieur le Chevalier Rodney, Vice Admiral de la Grande Bretagne, à Londres*'.[3] Of the innumerable notes of hand with which Sir George's career was so unhappily strewn this, to the Marshal de Biron, is the only one that may be contemplated with some satisfaction (see Plate X). It will be noticed that the Marshal has drawn a line through Sir George's large and gouty signature to signify that the debt has been paid.*

Soon after his arrival Sir George went to make his bow, and was most graciously received by a monarch with whose views about a strong line with Americans he was so much in sympathy. Everything that he heard and learnt about the political situation must have encouraged the hope that before long his time would come.

A government with a fairly docile majority but by no means united was pursuing an increasingly unpopular policy under the compulsive influence of his Majesty himself and the Secretary for the Colonies, Lord George Germain. Seldom had there been a time when the clash of principals and personalities resounded more loudly, and with political cleavages striking so deep down into the services. The previous October there had been a most disconcerting military reverse when General Burgoyne was forced to surrender to the Americans at Saratoga. That summer saw the return of a succession of angry and frustrated generals, bursting with complaints and grievances, mostly directed against Lord George. Never a ripple on the political surface, never a variation in the winds which blew through Westminster or the Admiralty, would have been missed by the keen eyes or the sharp ears at No. 4, Cleveland Row.

Burgoyne arrived back in England at the same time as Sir George and the reception he received must have opened the latter's eyes to the intensity of political feeling. The government frowned and Burgoyne was forbidden the Court. But the opposition welcomed him effusively counting on his assistance in laying the responsibility for Saratoga squarely on the shoulders of Lord George—and Burgoyne was only too willing to oblige. A court martial was refused him, but there was to be an enquiry in camera. The opposition growled. He took his seat in the House of Commons, to the embarrassment of the ministers who did not dare to challenge him, and

---

* A livre Tournois was a franc minted at Tours, its value roughly equal to an English shilling. A Louis was a 20-franc piece. 24,000 livres Tournois might be taken as £1,200 or 1,000 guineas.

heard the motion for an enquiry into his orders defeated by 104 votes to 96. There could be no moving the government, but it could be shaken, and shaken it was when Burgoyne blandly announced his readiness to answer any questions on the recent disaster. Mr Charles James Fox followed this up with a motion to extend the enquiry to the whole expedition, tempers rose, and a deplorable scene developed with the two principals, Burgoyne and Lord George, bullying and scolding each other like a couple of oyster-women. A few days later the Lord Chancellor resigned in disapproval of the government's American policy. Then, as a last attempt to shut Burgoyne's mouth, the government ordered him back to his parole in America, and Burgoyne refused to go.

Sir William Howe and Sir Guy Carleton arrived in July. Carleton, with the successful defence of Canada to his credit, could hardly be made a government scapegoat, but Howe might usefully be loaded with part of the blame for Saratoga and it was Lord George's amiable intention that he should be. There was, however, one difficulty. His naval brother Admiral Lord Howe had commanded his squadron on the American coast with conspicuous ability, and it was Lord North's hope to strengthen the ministry by persuading him to join it. But Lord Howe made it quite clear that he had no intention of associating himself with the government so long as his brother remained under fire. Lord North therefore regretfully washed his hands of the whole matter, the Howe brothers were confirmed as irreconcilable opponents of the administration, and while disinterested observers were aghast that the country should be deprived of Lord Howe's services at such a critical time, Sir George Rodney, from his enforced seclusion, could not but mark with complacency the elimination of a dangerous professional rival.

Lord Howe was not the only flag-officer at odds with the government. Keppel, now commanding the channel fleet, was by no means happy about the state of his ships or the support he might expect from Lord Sandwich, and the sinister hints and warnings he received from his opposition friends did nothing to ease his mind. On July 27th he met the French fleet off Ushant and fought an indecisive and not conspicuously well managed action, the repercussions from which were to be loud and far reaching. But before these began to make themselves heard and felt, Sir George had an opportunity of being useful to the government, and at the same time obliging Lord Sandwich.

It will be remembered that shortly after Sir George gave up the Hospital but before he sailed for Jamaica, the Lieutenant-Governor, Captain Baillie, had protested against certain abuses which had recently crept into Greenwich. Sir George, preoccupied with his preparations for his new command, had commended Baillie for his vigilance, attended his last Court of Directors when the matter was discussed, and passed from the scene. Seven years went by, during which time the abuses had multiplied, and with them Baillie's complaints. How much credence should be given to these is less important than the fact that the opposition took them up with enthusiasm as a useful stick with which to attack the First Lord. This had now gone on long enough. The government could no longer tolerate active disloyalty. The time had come to settle Captain Baillie and Sir George Rodney, still a Director although he had attended no meeting since 1771, was invited from his retreat to assist in the process.

It put him in something of a quandary. Ostensibly Baillie was still the champion of the old sailors against the encroachments of 'the pen and ink men'. 'In that cause,' Sir George had once assured him, 'you must always be supported.' But this had been seven years ago. The affairs of the Hospital had long ceased to have much reality except as ammunition in the campaign conducted by the opposition. All the original charges and counter-charges had become subsidiary to this, and Baillie, whatever his merits, was now one of the enemy. So Sir George stifled any qualms he may have had. In the present ministers lay his only hope, and if he could make some political capital at Baillie's expense, so much the worse for Baillie. The Court met on August 12, 1778. Lord Sandwich was there and twelve other directors besides Sir George and Baillie. His charges were solemnly declared 'malicious and void of foundation', every director subscribing to this except of course Baillie himself.[4] On the following day he was dismissed.

So the ministers were left in no doubt at all that Sir George Rodney was firm for the government; and in the way things were going, with some admirals refusing service under the present administration, others squeamish about fighting the Americans, and others eliminating themselves by their own incompetence, the way might soon be clear for him to hoist his flag once more. But there was still the matter of the creditors. Without some treaty with them, no settlement was possible with the Navy Board; and until the Navy Board was satisfied Sir George could not be employed. Lord Sandwich made this quite clear. But before the year ended these last obstacles were removed.

Sir George had long been of opinion that by proceeding to extremes his creditors were depriving themselves of any prospect of getting anything out of him at all; whereas if they made it possible for him to be employed fortune might enable him to pay them something. This was probably the argument put forward to convince that arch-obstructionist Sir James Lowther; and the lesser creditors, Mrs Tyler included, must have been persuaded to agree. The exact details of the agreement have not come to light except that Mrs Tyler (still waiting for her £400), was prevailed on to give up her claim to Sir George's Navy bills in favour of Sir James Lowther, at the end of an affecting scene in which (if she is to be believed) Sir George with streaming eyes acknowledged the obligation he and his family owed her, and promised her his agency in the future.[5] The agreement was not a treaty and still less a final settlement, but rather a truce or armistice, intended to benefit all parties. A letter which Sir George wrote on December 1, 1778, bears witness to a great load lifted.

'As my Annuitants have made a proposal which I have reason to think will in great measure relieve me from my present situation, I flatter myself, from my long experience of your friendship, you will lend your assistance towards the finishing so desirable an object, more especially as it will be the means of all my Creditors being a . . . ly satisfied. Be so good, my Dear Sir, to favour me with any hour you may be at leisure that I may show you the proposal, as the sooner it takes place the sooner Lord Sandwich's reasons for not employing me will cease. . . .'[6]

The identity of Sir George's correspondent is unimportant: probably he was Paul Maylor, his new man of business. But the letter is momentous. It marks the end of the long financial winter during which all resources were frozen and even his personal liberty in jeopardy. Nor was the thaw slow in coming once agreement had been reached. A week or so later, in January 1779, the Navy Board received a direction from the Admiralty Office to allow Sir George's half-pay as Admiral of the White.[7] Furthermore, the existence of nineteen quarterly bills for his pay as Rear-Admiral of Great Britain, from December 25, 1772, to December 25, 1778, and totalling £1,749, suggests that the other arrears were also released. No doubt the Navy Office, with its long account going back to Sir George's expensive command at Jamaica, satisfied its own demands first, after which the creditors took most of what remained. But the deadlock was at last broken. Still residing in Cleveland Row but now a free man Sir George could direct all his energies to the great object of obtaining employment.

At this juncture the sensational quarrel between Keppel, the Commander-in-Chief of the channel fleet, and Sir Hugh Palliser his third in command, burst upon a startled public. For this distressing affair, which placed two brave and patriotic men in opposite camps, the intensity of political feeling must take most of the blame. Keppel, unfortunately for himself, was linked by every possible tie with the opposition while Palliser was not only a government supporter but a Lord of the Admiralty as well. Between them they made a mess of things when they met the French fleet off Ushant, which was regrettable, but need not have convulsed the country. But when at the end of the year the Admiralty ordered a court martial on Keppel, the ground was cleared for a battle royal in which nothing really mattered except whether one was for or against the administration and Lord Sandwich. The trial was followed with keen partisan interest from January 7th to February 11th, and when Keppel was acquitted the London mob showed its satisfaction by sacking Palliser's house in Pall Mall, and breaking Lord George Germain's windows. This was not the end of the matter because if Keppel was blameless (so argued the opposition), responsibility for the failure off Ushant must have been Palliser's. So the deplorable vendetta continued with another, but this time rather less publicized court martial on Palliser, at which he too was acquitted. The result of all this was to divide the corps of sea-officers into two camps, and to confer on Keppel an immortality which his qualities as an admiral would hardly have won him.

Although all Sir George's expectations rested on the government he took no part in the persecution of Keppel. One would like to think that he resisted all the blandishments of Lord Sandwich and Lord George Germain to be one of his judges, and it is quite possible he did. Nor had he any part in the trial of Palliser. In private he may well have remarked that his old friend had been a better captain than he was an admiral, but publicly, and throughout the whole bitter and extravagant squabble, he seems to have preserved a wise and discreet neutrality.

Nevertheless the squabble, and its effects on the higher ranks of the Navy, further improved his chances of employment, for now no opponent of the government would willingly hoist his flag at sea so long as Lord Sandwich remained First Lord. Keppel joined Howe on shore, protesting his satisfaction at hauling down his flag 'because it relieves me from further correspondence with the present Board of Admiralty'. At the top of the flag-list the field was thinning fast. Of the other rising stars of the last war Charles Saunders had died in 1775, Augustus Hervey suddenly in this same year, and Pocock, although still alive, was in angry retirement. For Keppel's successor the best choice the First Lord could make was old Sir

Charles Hardy from Greenwich Hospital, hoping (with unjustifiable optimism as it turned out) that his great seniority would compensate for his advanced years and poor health.

Meanwhile Sir George, watching events from Cleveland Row, lost no chance to build up his position with the men who mattered. In Lord Sandwich he may no longer have had much confidence, but there were others. To the King, whose say in the choice of men and measures was considerable, and to Lord George Germain, he could represent himself acceptably, and with perfect truth, as an able, active, and vehement supporter of the Royal authority, an inveterate opponent of American aspirations, and a forthright champion of the honour of England against all the world. Such a simple and straightforward point of view was refreshing and reassuring to those who felt the same way. Here, they must have argued, was a bright, sharp sword, unblunted by political misgivings, untarnished by past failures. Could the country afford much longer to forgo its services? At the Admiralty and the Navy Board some might still raise objections to Sir George Rodney, but these carried less and less weight as the country's danger increased and the field of choice narrowed.

Not that Sir George had given up hope of Lord Sandwich completely. He continued to send him any items of naval intelligence that came his way 'with his most respectful compliments'. But his chief hope now may well have been in the arrogant, unpopular, but powerful Secretary for the Colonies, whose views were so much in line with his own. Lord George was interested in naval matters and would have been happy to direct them, an aspiration which did not endear him to Lord Sandwich. He consulted Sir George about them and Sir George, never backward in airing his views, responded at length. In March 1779, just after Keppel's court martial had ended in a blaze of discomfiture for the government, Lord George asked him to put down on paper his thoughts on the disposition of our naval forces for the next campaign, and the very able paper he submitted is remarkable for its prescience, its precise knowledge of the ships available, and for certain strategic suggestions which later bore important fruit.[8]

Summer of 1779 saw the administration, and the Admiralty in particular, harried and perplexed more than ever. Spain declared war in June. In August a Franco-Spanish armada was able to anchor off Plymouth, while the local defences along the coast stood to arms, and poor Sir Charles Hardy fussed and misdirected the channel fleet leagues away to the westward. Further afield, in the West Indies, Sir George's friend Byron had disappointed expectations and would have to be replaced. In the Commons the opposition was still after Lord George's scalp over the orders to Sir William Howe before Saratoga, while in the Lords the Duke of Richmond (well briefed by Captain Baillie), was leading a new attack on Lord Sandwich to the ever popular battle cry of 'abuses in the Hospital'. It was against this unsettled and disturbing background that the decision was at last made to employ Sir George.

On August 15th, feeling perhaps that the time was ripe, he made one more application to Lord Sandwich. 'As it behoves every officer at this important crisis to devote himself to the service of his King and Country, permit me humbly to offer myself to go on any Enterprise whereby I may show my Attachment to His Majesty and the State. . . .'[9]

There was no immediate reply but the pause which followed was loaded with consequence. The chess-board was to be rearranged, new dispositions made, and a new impetus given to the war effort. On September 16th there was a meeting of the Cabinet, at which important strategic decisions were made about relieving Gibraltar and reinforcing the West Indies. Whoever commanded these operations might hold the destiny of the empire in his hands and certainly that of the ministry. It must have been at this momentous meeting that Sir George's appointment was discussed and provisionally decided on. But next day a carping voice was heard expressing doubts whether he could safely be employed in matters where large quantities of stores were involved. Such a niggling objection could have come only from the Navy Office, where enemies were never backward whispering things to Sir George's disadvantage. But it worried the King until Lord Sandwich, still confident in Sir George's abilities as a sea-commander (although less so perhaps in other matters), reassured him. '[I] omitted to mention to your Majesty that if Sir George Rodney should from his indigence have any temptation to make advantage of purchasing stores or anything else of that sort, he will have no means of doing it as at present there will be a Commissioner on the spot through whose hands all that business must be transacted.'[10]

Who was Sir George's advocate for this great appointment? At the time, and for some while afterwards, he was emphatic that it was the King and the King alone—and small thanks to Lord Sandwich; later, in the fulsome and exaggerated style to which too much attention need not be given, he was to allow all the credit to Lord George Germain: 'Tis to your friendship my Dear Lord, that I am indebted for my present situation in life';[11] and later still, when his relations with Lord Sandwich were once more fairly cordial, he said much the same sort of thing to him. Whoever it was, and it should be remembered that an appointment of this magnitude could not have been made *against* the opinion of the First Lord, the matter was officially settled on October 1st when his Commission was signed as 'Commander-in-Chief of H.M. ships and vessels at Barbados and the Leeward Islands and the seas adjoining'.[12] It was a wide and splendid commission giving all the scope for extended operations on the American coast which he had recommended in his paper to Lord George. With it, the last and greatest period of his career opens.

We can see him at this great moment through the eyes of Sir Nathaniel Wraxall[13]—incisive, forceful, and supremely confident, pressing his point, measuring out praise and blame (mostly the latter), regardless of who was present, and regrettably prone to talk overmuch about himself. 'I passed much of my time with him,' says Wraxall, 'at his residence in Cleveland Row, St. James, down to the very moment of his departure. Naturally sanguine and confident, he anticipated in his daily conversation with a sort of certainly, the future success which he should obtain over the enemy. . . .' This agrees well with the story, characteristic but probably apocryphical, of him demonstrating naval tactics with cherry stones at Lord George Germain's dinner table to show how he would beat the French if he got the chance. Sir George was now sixty-one, a ripe age. But the old fires were not extinct.

Chapter 18

The Relief of Gibraltar

(1779–1780)

'. . . the King is exceedingly pleased with you. He said
at the drawing room that he knew when Rodney was
out everything would go well.'
(Miss Jane Rodney to her father, March 4, 1780.)[1]

AND so once again, as in the great days, Sir George's chair was seen outside the Admiralty, while tailors, stationers, wine merchants, furniture makers, and the rest booked substantial orders and extended their credit for a commander-in-chief designate whose way of living had never been limited by his means. Remarkable indeed was the change of fortune. The fugitive debtor was now his country's man of destiny; the indigent suitor himself a dispenser of favours; and the unlucky gambler, by an odd paradox, almost the last throw of a harassed administration. Not that Sir George, in the glory of his new appointment, was forgetting the lessons of the past. In one rather unctious memorandum, he submitted that an officer from the Victualling Office might come out to save him the disagreeable task of drawing for public money 'which he wishes to avoid by all means.'[2] An imprest of £400 was still uncleared from 1774 and he wanted no more trouble of that kind.

Those who had not known him in his youth saw only a rather vain and talkative old man, too easily imposed upon by sycophants and flatterers, who had been on shore for the past five years and who had not commanded a squadron in wartime for seventeen. What they could not know was that he still possessed a keen and active brain; that he still revelled in business; and that whatever he might be in politics he was no reactionary where sea warfare was concerned. But no one who had heard him laying down the law at Lord George Germain's or elsewhere could have any doubts about his self-confidence.

296

Almost his first demand, only ten days after his Commission was made out, was for the new pattern locks from the Board of Ordnance, and for the improved type of cartridge for the carronades. The locks (like those on a flintlock pistol but larger) greatly improved the rate of cannon fire. He fully appreciated the importance of this and intended the fire to be hottest from his own flagship. So she must have the new locks without delay, and his other ships as soon as possible.

This vital matter settled, other demands followed in a steady stream through October and into November. There were the friends to be obliged and the dependants to be provided for, Pagett to be extracted from his Greenwich chaplaincy, young John Rodney, now fourteen, from the Royal Academy at Portsmouth, Erasmus Gower, formerly with Sir George in the *Princess Amelia* and *Portland*, who would be first lieutenant of the flagship, and many others, mostly with the disarming excuse: 'He being an old follower of mine and entitled to promotion.'* Sir George's old friends, and many new ones, positively inundated him with requests to provide for this or that deserving young man, requests which his natural good nature made it hard to refuse. He even took a young *protégé* of Sir James Lowther.

But, politics apart, there may have been misgivings in some quarters. Lord Sandwich knew him of old. So did Sir Charles Middleton, Comptroller of the Navy. Sir George might still be his old, brilliant self: on the other hand he might be a disaster. One safeguard would be to give him a reliable captain. There is no proof that the First Lord and Middleton put their heads together for this purpose. When Captain Walter Young was recommended to Sir George it was by Lord Sandwich. But Young's subsequent correspondence with Middleton[3] does suggest that he was expected to keep an eye on his Admiral and report back. Be this as it may, this comparatively obscure officer, at the beginning of the year an ageing lieutenant of fourteen years' seniority, was taken from the transport agent's office at Deptford and, on October 1st, posted to the 90-gun *Sandwich*, fitting out for the new Commander-in-Chief's flag. He served his Admiral well and Sir George esteemed him highly—but no more perhaps than Young esteemed himself. As will be seen, his private letters to Middleton are sharply pointed to give the impression that without his devoted captain, Admiral Sir George Rodney would hardly have been able to manage at all.

* The name Marr is missing. He was at this time Agent Victualler for the Navy at New York.

A more agreeable newcomer to his inner circle was at Sir George's own request. Three years earlier Dr Gilbert Blane, the fourth son of a small landowner in Ayrshire, had migrated to London, with good qualifications from Edinburgh in the humanities and in medicine and a recommendation to the great Dr Hunter. Hunter had recommended him to Lord Holdernesse and it was probably at the latter's house that Blane, now aged thirty, first met Sir George, whose health had not improved with the years. Gout, gravel, and their kindred complaints sometimes incapacitated him for days together, but so impressed was he with the Scottish doctor that he asked him to come as his private physician. Blane's admission as a supernumerary on board the *Sandwich* probably revived painful memories at the Navy Board of Sir George's addiction to expensive medical remedies; but by his appointment the Navy obtained much more than the services of a good personal physician to the Commander-in-Chief. For Blane was a man of ability. Before long his influence was to extend beyond Sir George's ailments to Sir George's whole fleet, and in the fullness of time to the entire Navy, as one of the great reformers and innovators in the science of medicine at sea.

October went by, and then the first week of November. The time was approaching when Sir George would be required at Portsmouth. But before he left London there was the ever-recurring nightmare of his private affairs. His friends were determined that this time there would be no rushing off at the last moment to make crazy, ill-advised arrangements, while all the world wondered where he was. November 13th was given over to business. On that day he made his son George his true and lawful attorney, transferring to him the absolute control of all his affairs at home. It was the wisest thing he ever did. At the same time he appointed Mr Paul Maylor of Broad Street as his London agent, in place of the late Mr Kee.[4] Mrs Tyler resented this bitterly. For years to come Sir George was to hear her voice complaining in shriller but fainter accents of debts dishonoured and promises unfulfilled. It is impossible to say whether he treated her shabbily or not, but when eventually she went to law it was to no purpose. There remained the creditors, still claiming their pound of flesh, and to satisfy them he insured his life against the arrears of the annuity. Three days later he was at Portsmouth.

At that momentous Cabinet meeting before Sir George's appointment, the urgent need to relieve Gibraltar had been discussed as well as the importance of reinforcing the West Indies. So precarious was the situation that the government was resolved on a supreme effort. It was their intention that the new Commander-in-Chief should first convoy supplies, food and reinforcements to Gibraltar, and that part of the convoy should continue on to Minorca, although this movement would not be under his direct control. At the same time another convoy with reinforcements for the West Indies and a new military commander-in-chief, Major-General the Hon. John Vaughan, would make the initial stage of its voyage in company with the Gibraltar ships.

To ensure success, most of the channel fleet would come temporarily under Sir George's orders. With this tremendous force he would escort the combined convoys until well past Ushant and into the Bay of Biscay. Then the West Indies ships, with a small ocean escort, would part company and head for Barbados while the main convoy, still heavily protected, would continue south to run the gauntlet of any opposition the enemy might send out until, all being well, Sir George brought it safely into Gibraltar Bay. The ships of the channel fleet would return home without delay, the Minorca ships would go on to their destination, and Sir George, with his flagship and three more of the line, would proceed to the West Indies.

It was most important to keep secret the extent of the operation planned. Sir George, who had strong views about security, had emphasized this in a recent paper to Lord George Germain, and it cannot be wholly coincidental that this need was re-emphasized at the Cabinet meeting on October 27th. It was impossible to conceal the store-ships, transports and victuallers at Portsmouth and Plymouth. But their orders made no mention of Gibraltar or Minorca. The clerks scribbled out copies of instructions for Jamaica, the Leeward Islands, and Pensacola, so that as far as anyone had any reason to suppose, they were all bound across the Atlantic. Only in Sir George's secret orders was an amended convoy list, allocating nearly half the vessels to Gibraltar and Minorca. Against the many muddles and mismanagements of the American war the success of this great operation stands out; and if one of the reasons is the secrecy which shrouded it, some of the credit belongs to the naval Commander-in-Chief.

Five years on shore had not cooled Sir George's ardour or lowered his old, exacting standards. The whole of Portsmouth soon knew that he had arrived. 'The delays that have been at this port,' he complained to Lord George Germain, 'and the almost total loss of naval discipline, is almost beyond comprehension.'[5] This was the voice Sir George's superiors had been hearing for more than thirty years. It was true that the Board of Ordnance had not yet provided the new locks, and the dockyard people got his flagship aground on the Spit sand (fortunately without damage) as they moved her out to Spithead. But at least she was ready, and most of his other ships too. Young, in a burst of efficiency, had just applied for the discharge of the gunner, the boatswain, and the carpenter, as quite unsuitable for the smart ship he intended the *Sandwich* to be. On November 21st Spithead resounded to a salute of seventeen guns as Sir George's flag, as Admiral of the White, climbed to the main-truck.

At Spithead were 15 of the line, one 44, and 7 frigates, waiting and ready; anchored at St Helen's were 8 transports with the 89th regiment on board, 4 victuallers and 6 storeships; the rest of the convoy was at Plymouth.[6] But the wind now settled down to blow fresh and steady from the westward. The delay decided Henny to come down to Portsmouth with twelve-year-old Jenny, who was old enough to remember coming home in the *Portland* five years before. Mother and daughter managed to get on board the *Sandwich,* and then on shore again before the weather broke in real earnest. 'I really did rejoice that we got so well on shore before it began,' wrote Henny, 'for I should have been sick as death; indeed, I am that on shore and very much fear in a way to be still sicker which is comfortable news both for you and me, but we are ever in ill luck.' A depressing letter for a husband loaded with responsibilities ended more cheerfully with good news of the children's health and a charming reference to little Anne Rodney (aged three), who 'never drinks her drop of wine after dinner without saying: "Papa and John's health".'[7]

On December 10th there arrived a curiously uncharacteristic letter from the First Lord.

'Admiralty, Dec. 8 1779.
'*Dear Sir,*
   'For God's sake go to sea without delay. You can not conceive of what importance it is to yourself, to me, and to the publick that you should not lose this fair wind. If you do, I shall not only hear of it in Parliament, but in places to which I pay more attention. . . . I must once more repeat to you that any delay in your sailing will have the most disagreeable consequences. . . .'[8]

Sir George may well have raised his eyebrows. Whatever the wind was doing at Whitehall it was still blowing hard from the west in Spithead. Clearly, someone's nerves were badly on edge. But the letter ended in the First Lord's more usual vein. 'There is another young man of fashion now in your squadron concerning whom I am tormented to death. I can not do anything for him at home, therefore if you could contrive while he remains with you by some means or other to give him rank you will infinitely oblige me. The person I mean is Lord Robert Manners who is now a lieutenant on board the *Alcide*. . . .'

A brother of the Duke of Rutland must certainly not be overlooked: nor was he. But still the wind continued contrary, and a few days later there was an explanation of the First Lord's nervous outburst. A rather disturbing report had come in, from a French source, of Spanish warships concentrating in the Straits.[9] Dated November 22nd it listed fourteen of them and hinted that they might be joined by fifteen or sixteen more. Every day increased the security risk.

But for another fortnight the boisterous westerlies pinned the fleet down to its anchorage, while ministers in London fumed and fretted. On December 11th George Rodney managed to get on board with another letter from Henny that cannot have contributed much to her husband's peace of mind. Another child was on the way (her fifth), and friends had been bothering her to forward more recommendations to him. George took back his father's reply. Henny was not to be uneasy and she was to keep up her spirits. About the recommendations he explained that admirals and captains were not schoolmasters to be responsible for every hopeful small boy with naval ambitions: but he added resignedly that he would take one more if the necessary conditions were complied with. Indulgent but sceptical he continued: 'Jenny's account of Loup knowing my purse when she dropped it shows what a sensible dog he is and must, as she says, endear him more to me; but she must pardon me if I say "Non credo".' Only at the end did he allow himself to comment on the great matter in hand. 'I wish I was once more at sea. You know there an Admiral has not a tenth part of the trouble and fatigue as when in port. . . .'

Letters and service papers of every kind poured in to overwhelm his labouring pen. Five days later he explained to Henny: '. . . every hour, day, and night, I am sending or receiving expresses. Even now, at 5 o'clock in the morning, I can scarce catch a moment to know how you and the dear girls are. . . .' For a man who professed to detest writing, Sir George's performance at this time, with nearly every letter as well as the duplicate written in his own hand, was prodigious.

At last, on December 23rd, the wind dropped to a flat calm with every sign of an easterly blow on the morrow. Sir George wrote his last letter to Henny. 'Health and happiness attend you and my sweet girls. Take care of them and take care of yourself—not forgetting my faithful friend Loup.'[10] Next day, as expected, the wind came fair and the ships were away. It was not possible to wait for the 300 sail expected from the Downs. They might catch up if they could. Off Plymouth the fleet lay to for twenty-four hours while the rest of the convoy and escort came out to join. When the great armada got under way once more, there were nearly 150 sail.*

Not even Sir George with his unshakable self-confidence could have foreseen the achievements which lay ahead. The picture has been too long clouded by his distressing embarrassments on shore. The time has come to look again at his qualifications for a great command.

As a junior officer he was active and resourceful. As a captain he showed the sort of leadership that made men wish to serve under him, and a tenacity in battle which commanded the admiration of all. At Le Havre and Martinique he demonstrated his ability to organize and handle a large number of units, and at Martinique a new accomplishment, that of being able to work with the military. His fighting career reached its peak when, at the age of forty-five, he prepared to sail to the succour of Jamaica with no more authority behind him than his own certainty that the island was in danger. But seventeen years had passed since he sailed the seas in wartime, and he had never commanded a fleet against the enemy.

Such fighting ideas as any sea-officer had at this time were shaped and guided (some would say curbed), by two very formidable sets of rules known as the Permanent and the Additional Fighting Instructions. They represented the accumulated experience of generations of sea-commanders, and the sea-officer disregarded them at his peril. But the effect of so much wisdom and precept had not been wholly good. Although the Instructions made it fairly easy to avoid defeat, they made it difficult, unless interpreted with an imagination and initiative not always found on the quarter-deck, to win a victory. Actions at sea became indecisive, and sometimes a commander's reputation stood or fell more by the respect he paid to the Instructions than to the damage he inflicted, or tried to inflict, on the enemy. Only on the happy occasions when a general chase was possible did their grip relax, to allow much liberty of action; and such occasions were few.

Sir George understood their drawbacks as clearly as anyone, and he was much too good an officer to let them tie his hands completely. Not that he would throw them overboard altogether—he was too good an

---

* Twenty-two of the line, one 44, and 7 frigates of the escort; 66 storeships, transports, and victuallers; see Appendix 6. Also many merchantmen.

officer for that also. But he was sure that within their sacred framework measures more likely to achieve results could be devised. The Instructions which he inherited when he hoisted his flag in 1779 had been re-shaped by Anson, modified by Boscawen, and brought up to date under the authority of Hawke, to embody the lessons of the Seven Years' War. They were thus the last word from the highest possible authorities. Nevertheless, to Sir George they were still capable of improvement, and if we wish to catch a glimpse of some of the things he had in mind we shall find them in the additions which he himself wrote and distributed to his captains during the waiting period at Spithead. The subject is too specialized to be discussed in detail, but two of his ideas are interesting and important. The latest Instructions had clarified the procedure for bringing a flying enemy to action when they laid down that the leading ship should engage the rearmost of the enemy, the next to pass on under cover of her fire and attack the next ahead, and so on until the rearmost engage the enemy's van. This probably derived from the second battle of Finisterre; but to Sir George, who had witnessed some discreditable incidents on that occasion, it was not enough. So he gave a sharper point to the article by adding: '. . . *each Ship, as they get up, are to engage their Opponents and on no Pretence to quit them until they are so disabled that they can not get away, or Submitt.*' He was strongly in favour of attacking from the leeward in certain circumstances, so he added a distinguishing pennant to the signal for a general chase, by which he could deliver the attack to windward or leeward at will.

But much more important than these alterations is the entirely new Article which he added to make a decisive result possible when fighting in line. Of all the dispositions prescribed by the Fighting Instructions the line held pride of place. Nothing could be attempted that might spoil it. Ships in line could support and cover each other; the admiral could (in theory) keep control until the last moment; and ships, if correctly disposed, could not be 'doubled on', that is have an enemy on either side. So the line in all its symmetrical perfection, must always be preserved. It was unfortunate that the perfectly disposed line never achieved a decisive result.

In Sir George's opinion the solution was, while holding the enemy if possible all along the line, to increase the fire-power and weight of the attack against one particular section of it, and smash through. This he hoped to ensure by closing up his line and massing his heavy ships. The Instructions already provided for the first, up to a point, but they made no provision for the second until he wrote an entirely new article which he distributed to his captains on the eve of sailing. 'If the Commander-in-Chief would have all the three-decked and heavy ships drawn out of their places in the line of battle, and form in the van of the fleet, he will hoist a white flag pierced with red at the fore top-gallant-mast head; but if he would have those ships draw out of the line and form in the rear of the fleet, he will put out the above flag and a red pennant under it; in both the above cases the ships who preceded and followed those ships, who have quitted the line to form in the van or rear, are immediately to close the line and fill up their places.' It was the sound military principle of concentration of attack, as old as the Macedonian phalanx, if not older. Indeed, its resemblance to the tactics of Alexander the Great makes one suspect that Sir George, an enthusiast for the works of Homer, may have extended his studies to the campaigns of the Macedonian hero. Here, at any rate, is why he was so determined on the new locks for his guns and some three deckers, with their extra weight of metal. There is nothing revolutionary in this: only a sensible return to basic military principles.[11]

By January 4th the great fleet was well down into the bay and sufficiently far out from the Biscay ports for the West India convoy to be detached. Sir George sent across a cordial farewell letter to his old friend General Vaughan. 'Depend upon it,' he wrote, 'I will be with you as soon as possible.'[12] Thirty-seven storeships, victuallers and transports, and some sixty merchantmen sorted themselves out from the main body. Captain Sir Hyde Parker* in the *Phoenix* (44) took them under his orders with a small escort. At sunset only a few were silhouetted against the evening glow. Next morning all were out of sight.

Evening fell on Friday, January 7th, some fifty leagues to the westward of Finisterre. The wind was light, the sea ran hollow and troublesome, and there was not a ship in sight. But by daybreak next morning some strangers had crept up over the north-eastern horizon. More than twenty of them could be seen against the dawn light, ploughing stolidly along to pass astern of Sir George's force. But not for long. At the British challenge they began to tack and Sir George signalled his men-of-war to do the same. Then the strangers began to crowd on all the sail they could at which Sir George, with who knows what feelings of incredulous joy, directed his convoy to lie to and hoisted the signal for general chase.

Luck like this had not come his way since he was a young captain. It was a Spanish convoy of sixteen merchantmen with a very small escort, and he

---

* Not to be confused with his father Vice-Admiral Sir Hyde Parker, Bart., in temporary command at the Leeward Islands and awaiting Sir George's arrival.

held them in the hollow of his hand. Led by the *Edgar* (74) and the *Pegasus* (28), his escort force shook out their reefs and were among the merchant-men before noon. 'They haul'd down their colours as fast as our ships came up with them' recorded Captain Pownoll of the *Apollo*. The largest escort, a two-decker, fired two or three shots before striking to the *Bien-faisant*. There were six smaller warships, the last of which struck to the *Ajax* at 2 p.m. The merchantmen were loaded with naval stores, provisions, and bale goods. The escorts all belonged to the Royal Company of the Caracas. They were the *Guipuzcoana* (64), *San Carlos* (32), *San Rafael* (30), *Santa Teresa* (28), *San Bruno* (26), *San Firmin* (16), and *San Vincente* (10). The unlucky force had sailed from San Sebastian on January 1st for Cadiz.

The twelve provision ships Sir George decided to take on with him to Gibraltar. The *Guipuzcoana*, beautifully built, brand new, and larger than the *Bienfaisant* to which she struck, he could not resist commissioning at once, and adding to his own escort force. The *San Firmin* and *San Vincente* he treated in the same way. Gower, first of the *Sandwich*, he promoted into the sixty-four which he renamed *Prince William* in honour of the third son of his Sovereign, then serving as a midshipman in the *Prince George*. There remained four merchantmen and four frigates. He put prize crews on board and detached the *America* (74) and *Pearl* (32) to escort them back to England.

For the next eight days the augmented convoy plodded down the coast of Spain and Portugal at five knots or less, lying to every night. On the 13th the *Dublin*, a ship which never brought Sir George much luck, lost her foretopmast, broke her foreyard, and had to be escorted into Lisbon by the *Shrewsbury*, thus reducing the escort to eighteen of the line and the *Prince William*. Repeated intelligence from passing ships gave warning of a Spanish squadron (some said fourteen of the line), cruising off Cape St Vincent. Captain Young wished to be sure of the latitude of the Cape before bearing up for the Straits but Sir George, who had probably rounded the promontory a good many more times than Young, pooh-poohed the idea. The fleet lay to as usual during the night of January 15th/16th to let the heavy sailers and stragglers catch up. Soon after daybreak land was sighted, and although Young complained later that they were very nearly embayed to the northward of the Cape, the ships began rounding it, most of them with a clear margin of ten to fifteen miles, shortly before noon. The wind blew fresh from the westward; the sky was overcast with occasional squalls of rain and visibility was poor.

Between 12.30 and 1 p.m., as the last stragglers were still rounding the Cape, the *Bedford* in the lead reported an enemy fleet to the south-east. She thought she saw '15 sail of large ships'. A little later, on board the *Sandwich*, they counted eleven. The situation was obscure. Until it was clearer it required careful handling, and at this important juncture the character and personality of Captain Young take possession of the scene— and of the ear of history. For Sir George, it must be admitted, was confined by his ailments, to his bed. The situation, as it developed, had to be reported to him by Young; and Young, in describing the business later, was not above raising his own credit with a picture (too partial to be wholly convincing), of an alert and purposeful captain guiding the decisions of an inept and vacillating Commander-in-Chief. But as this is the only picture we have, it cannot be ignored.[13]

On receiving the *Bedford*'s signal Young was for ordering a general chase at once 'as night was coming on'. This Sir George opposed, probably with good reason. Whatever Young might say later there were still five or six hours of daylight; the enemy strength was still uncertain; and he would have known, if his captain did not, that there might be strong opposition to bar his way. (It had been through over-eagerness in ordering a general chase that Byron lost his chance at Grenada.) So he suggested a line ahead for the time being. Young argued for a line abreast at one cable distance and the journals show that the signal for a line abreast at two cables distance was made soon afterwards. At 2 p.m. the hoisting of a red flag at the flagship's fore-topgallant mast head warned the fleet to prepare for battle. Meanwhile Young kept her under a press of sail.

At 2.30 p.m., when it was clear that the enemy was retreating, Sir George made up his mind. This was not the formidable force suggested by the intelligence report but a small squadron, probably unsupported, and almost within his grasp. He hesitated no longer and ordered a general chase.

This, as has already been explained, released his captains from the immediate control of the flagship. At once the fleet began to string out as the more ardent shook out reefs and hoisted top-gallant sails. Casks, barrels, and unwanted lumber went overboard to clear the guns; the battleships plunged forward, under their press of canvas; and the heavy sailing convoy began to drop astern. Sir George did not need to be on deck to realize that as things were, no ship would be able to fight her lower deck guns on the port side. It was the perfect occasion for the leeward position, for which he had so recently made provision in the signal book. Wedged in his bed as the *Sandwich* heeled to the gale he signalled his ships: 'Engage to leeward of the enemy.'

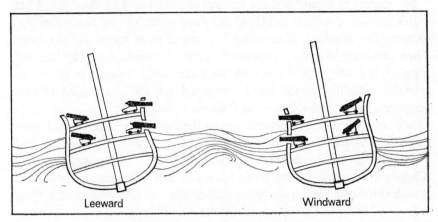

Advantage of the leeward position

The feeling of the Spanish Admiral, Don Juan de Langara, may be imagined. With nine of the line and two frigates he had been well placed to intercept any relief for Gibraltar. Confident that Sir George, with any heavy ships he might have, would already have parted company, he stood his ground as the leading British rounded Cape St Vincent. Then, as a seemingly endless succession of shapes materialized out of the grey emptiness beyond the Cape, confidence turned to uncertainty, and uncertainty to dismay. He thought he saw twenty-two of the line, three of great force, and in the beginning of Sir George's line abreast he imagined some perilous enveloping movement. He held on to the southward until the distance was down to three leagues. Then he fled incontinently. But it was too late.

At about 4 p.m. Captain J. Elliot in the *Edgar* was up with, and to leeward of the 70-gun *Santo Domingo*, limping along with a broken mainyard and no sails on her mainmast, and gave her his starboard broadside. Whatever reply the Spaniard made inflicted small damage on the *Edgar* which pressed on after the Spanish leaders. A few minutes later the 70-gun *Princesa*, to windward of the *Santo Domingo*, received the same treatment from the *Marlborough*, treatment which left her disabled in sails and rigging and apparently on fire. This, at any rate, was the impression on board the *Marlborough* whose ardour was temporarily damped by the great quantities of water she took in through her lower gunports. Other

British ships were coming up fast so Captain Penny decided to leave the Spaniard and press on.

But there was plenty of fight left in the *Princesa*. The *Ajax* raked her with a passing broadside and then bore away to engage the *Santo Domingo* to port. The *Montagu*, after giving her two or three more, did the same. Then came the *Bedford* (Captain E. Affleck), which stuck by her and engaged her hotly for more than an hour until, seeing the *Resolution* approach, she too passed on. It remained for the last named to take possession of the gallantly fought *Princesa* at about 5.30 p.m.

But long before the *Princesa* struck to the *Resolution*, disaster had overtaken the *Santo Domingo*. After her brief exchange with the *Edgar* she had been attacked by the *Marlborough* and the *Ajax*. Then the *Bienfaisant* (Captain J. MacBride) came up in her wake. She was thus engaging three British ships when her tragedy happened. She had just replied with three or four of her starboard guns to the *Ajax*'s second broadside, and was at the same time engaging the *Bienfaisant* with a few of her stern-chase guns, when she blew up at 5 p.m. The *Bienfaisant* was almost taken aback as she put up her helm and bore away to avoid the wreck. Some of the debris blew on board her and some fell near the *Marlborough*. Two hours later the frigate *Pegasus* saw two large fragments with men on them. She brought to and rescued one Spaniard on a piece of the ship's lower mast, the only survivor from a ship's company of 400.

By 6 p.m. daylight was fading from the sky, but now the pale light of

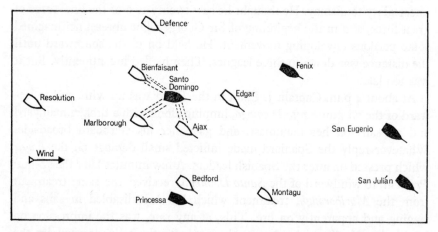

The Moonlight Battle, January 16–17, 1780; approximate situation at about 5.00 p.m. when the *Santo Domingo* blew up

the moon shone across the water to illuminate the next victim. This was Langara's flagship, the 80-gun *Fenix*. Between 7 and 7.30 the *Defence* (Captain J. Cranston), ranged up on her port quarter and fought her for one and a half hours as the two ships plunged through the night. Then the *Montagu* edged down from the windward. Her first broadside carried away the Spaniard's bowsprit. She gave her another and pressed on. The ponderous bulk of the *Royal George* appeared on her starboard quarter and one broadside from the three-decker shot away her mizen-mast. The Spanish flagship was now in a desperate state, without steerage way, her lower gun-deck awash, and rolling the water out through the gun-ports. Langara himself was wounded. Lastly came the *Bienfaisant* at about 8.30 with a few rounds from her upper and quarter-deck guns. The main topmast of the *Fenix* came crashing down, and she struck to the British sixty-four.

Meanwhile the *Montagu* was on the heels of the next ahead, the 70-gun *Diligente*. For forty-five minutes the Spaniard kept her distance, peppering her pursuer ineffectually with her stern-chasers. But the *Montagu* was a fast ship. Captain Houlton brought her within musket shot of the Spaniard's quarter; then at 9.15 p.m. he luffed up and fired his port broadside. No more was needed. The *Diligente*'s main topmast came down and she surrendered. The *Montagu* managed to put her first lieutenant and a prize crew on board and lay by her for the rest of the night.

Of Langara's unlucky squadron only five heavy ships remained and for the next half hour they fled together. But the pursuit was inexorable and the pitiless moonlight, gleaming fitfully through the cloud-wrack overhead, marked three more for destruction. Leading the British pursuit were the *Cumberland*, *Monarch*, and *Terrible*, followed by the *Culloden* and *Prince George*. The 70-gun *San Eugenio* gave a good account of herself in a running fight with the *Cumberland* and shot away her main topmast. But her end came at about 11 p.m. when all three of her own masts went over the side. Lieutenant Bowater, with a prize-crew from the *Terrible*, could not board her until daylight because of the heavy seas and the tangle of wreckage alongside.

Leaving the *Monarch* and the *Terrible* to look after the mastless *San Eugenio*, the *Culloden*, followed by the *Prince George*, hung grimly on to the next ahead which was the 70-gun *San Julián*. After half an hour of running fight the Spaniard luffed to give the *Culloden* her starboard broadside but lost her own main topmast in the exchange. The chase went on for a little longer until half an hour after midnight when the great bulk of the *Prince*

George interposed itself between the *Culloden* and the partly disabled *San Julián*. There could be no arguing with a three-decker. The Spanish colours came fluttering down and, despite the sea that was running, Lieutenant McWilliam, first of the *Prince George*, with a Marine officer, three petty officers, and thirty men, managed to scramble on board.

When Sir George ordered the general chase at 2.30, he summoned Mr Hiscutt, the master of the *Sandwich*. 'Master,' he said, 'this ship is not to pay any attention to the merchantmen or small ships of war. Lay me alongside the biggest ship you can, or the admiral, if there be one.'[14] Then, for eleven hours, the *Sandwich* plunged on after the fleet without firing a shot. As was usual when cleared for action, all the cabin bulkheads and partitions would have come down, so Sir George, from his bed at the after end of the ship, probably had a clear view of the whole length of the middle gun-deck, the swinging lanterns, the eternal see-saw as the bows rose and fell, and all the preparations for action. The hours passed with no means of knowing how his ships were doing, or what was happening. All he knew with certainty was that afternoon had given place to night, that the gale showed no sign of abating, and that every hour the Spanish coast was closer under his lee.

As the hours passed, with nothing to do except pound on, he would have been less than human if the occasional twinge of unease or apprehension did not pass through his mind. His captains were untrained: some of them he hardly knew. And with everything at stake on the dark, stormy waters, his accursed gout had laid him low. Small wonder if he was nervous, testy and irritable. But this is a far cry from Young's picture during these hours of a naturally irresolute admiral, only restrained on several occasions from calling off the chase by his cool and intrepid captain. This picture (which was for Middleton's private eye), cannot be confirmed or disproved, but it seems improbable. Sick or well Sir George was always the Commander-in-Chief, and in any case a signal of recall would not have been seen or heard in the conditions obtaining. However, before night ended, the *Sandwich* had the chance of firing her guns. At about 1.30 a.m. the occasional gun-flash ahead showed that fighting was still going on, and she steered for it. It was the 70-gun *Monarca*, engaged in a curiously unequal duel with the 36-gun *Apollo*.

The *Monarca* had been in the forefront of the Spanish retreat which is why she survived so long. She had been mauled in a running fight with a British seventy-four, probably the *Ajax*, and during this engagement had driven off the British *Alcide* with a lucky shot which brought down her main topmast. This was at about 1 a.m., after which she might have broken away altogether but for the little *Apollo* whose captain, Philemon Pownoll, had carried topgallants throughout the engagement when some of the battleships had not. Pownoll had a brilliant record as a frigate captain which he well sustained on this occasion. He claimed with justice that the *Monarca* struck to him, although whether she would have done so if the *Sandwich* had not come up may be doubted. What cannot be gainsaid is that the exchange between them brought the *Sandwich* on to the scene and gave her gunners their chance. It was not for them to know that the *Monarca* had already struck. The British flagship ranged up to within half a musket shot and fired her port broadside, volleys of small arms, and everything she had. Then, amid wailings and execrations from the unlucky Spaniards, she wore round with the intention of finishing her off. But before she could do so the situation became clear and she held her fire. Her one and only broadside, fired a little before 2 a.m., was also the last in the engagement.

Dawn found the British fleet in small groups round the prizes, with the gale still blowing and the water shoaling rapidly. Closest inshore were the three flagships, *Sandwich*, *Royal George*, and *Prince George*, with a handful of seventy-fours and the prizes *Monarca* and *San Julián*. Their situation was precarious. 'Strong gales and thick weather. No Sight of the Sun. 45 fathoms of water', was recorded that morning by the *Royal George*. Her prize crew were able to get the *Monarca* clear of shoal water, but for the partially dismasted *San Julián* it was more difficult. At about 7 p.m. she was observed to roll her main and mizen masts away, after which her rolling became too deep for any boat to board her. The *Invincible* stood by until 10 p.m. that night when, with only twenty-three fathoms under her keel, she hauled off. Soon afterwards the *San Julián* drove ashore, to be later salved by the Spaniards. Further down the coast the *Monarch* and *Terrible* stood by the mastless *San Eugenio*. For her there could be no hope either and before noon she was in the breakers. Further to seaward things were better. A little group, the *Edgar* and *Montagu*, with the *Alcide* and *Cumberland* (both lacking their main top-masts), stood by the *Diligente*. Further west were the *Bienfaisant* and the *Defence* with the disabled *Fenix*.* Further west still, and further to seaward was the *Princesa*, with the *Resolution* and *Pegasus*. Soon after dawn these were joined by half the convoy which had been plodding along unescorted all night. The rest were

* Only a lucky shift of wind saved the *Fenix* from going on the Accitera shoal the following night.

even further astern with the frigate *Porcupine*. Of all Langara's squadron which had cruised so confidently off Cape St Vincent, only two battleships and two small frigates escaped.

In the fortress of Gibraltar some 5,300 British and Hanoverian troops were beginning to feel themselves forgotten. On July 6, 1779, they had learnt officially that Great Britain and Spain were at war, and ten days after this a Spanish squadron appeared to blockade the port. They had been well provisioned in April, but nothing had come in since except the occasional shipload of bullocks and sheep from Tangier, and the occasional cargo of rice or barley. The defences were put in order and strengthened and, in view of the possibility of a prolonged siege with a consequent shortage of provisions, including flour, the troops were ordered to mount guard with their hair unpowdered.

The occasional cargo still crept through, but the weeks and the months passed with no material evidence whatever that the home government was not leaving the Rock to its fate. Captain John Drinkwater of the 72nd, who published an account of the siege soon after it was over, noted as early as November that '. . . bread, the great essential of life and health, was the article most wanted'. By the beginning of January 1780 the situation was critical. To quote the Captain again: 'Thistles, dandelions, wild leeks etc., were for some time the daily nourishment of numbers. Few supplies arriving from Barbary, and there appearing little prospect of relief from England, famine began to present itself with its attendant horrors.' On the 12th the commanding officers informed their corps that the governor was under the necessity of reducing their weekly allowance of provisions.

But within twenty-four hours of this dire announcement more cheerful rumours began to spread. Sir George's fleet was still 400 miles away, sailing down the coast of Portugal, but some sort of information must have reached somebody for on the 13th Vice-Admiral Duff, whose flagship the 50-gun *Panther* had lain under the guns of the Rock ever since the blockade began, ordered his small squadron to be ready to assist if a relief force appeared. Two days later his prescience was justified by the arrival of the first of Sir George's convoy, a fast brig which had parted company many weeks before in the Bay of Biscay. 'The Garrison are all on the wing,' wrote Mr Ancell of the 58th regiment, 'this morning flour sold for 6d per pound, which was some time past 2/– . . . spy glasses are mounted like cannon on the walls, directed towards the Gut.' Twenty-four hours passed before a second brig appeared. She was loaded with flour and was able to cheer the soldiers with an account of the capture of the Caraccas ships. The 17th was dull and hazy with no more ships arriving but with hopes and expectations mounting. Then, in the morning of the 18th there arrived a third ship, soon identified by the knowledgeable as one of the Caraccas prizes, bringing with her the electrifying report of an engagement off Cape St Vincent which she had witnessed at a distance, and of a large ship (nationality unknown), blowing up during the action. Hardly had this been digested when another Caraccas ship arrived, and then excited watchers reported the whole of Sir George's great convoy off Europa point.

There followed an anti-climax. The weather was dull and threatening. Great clouds lowered overhead. The wind puffed fitfully and died away altogether. Against the sombre background of sea and sky the distant ships wallowed impotently. Vivid flashes of lightning picked them out, their sails hanging limp from the yards. Under the eyes of the enthralled but power-less watchers they drifted helplessly past, until the current swept them out of sight behind the Rock. Only the frigate *Apollo* and one or two merchant-men managed to creep into the anchorage just before midnight.

Next day the flagship and most of the convoy were off Marbella, sixteen leagues to the eastward. A week would pass before they could beat back. But although the garrison could not immediately acclaim its rescuer, its relief was assured. Langara's flagship, with a spare topmast set up as a jury mizen and escorted by the *Edgar*, limped into the bay at 7 a.m. on the 19th, to be followed a little later by the *Defence, Invincible,* and *Prince George,* with eleven or twelve of the convoy. Each day saw the anchorage more crowded.

Sir George in the *Sandwich,* with five more of the line, managed to beat back to Tetuan roads by the 23rd. The oriental notables crowded on board to acclaim the victors and to protest, with gratifying unanimity, their desire to trade only with the British. Two days later, on the 25th, the flagship anchored in Gibraltar bay. An elderly gentleman, not yet recovered from the gout, was in no state to go down the side of a three-decker, so the ceremonies on shore had to be deferred. Indeed, Sir George arrived in pretty poor shape. Besides his gout he had caught a heavy cold. But so many matters demanded an immediate decision that a council of war was held at once in the great cabin of the *Sandwich.*

The problem of the Spanish sick and wounded was quickly settled. All were to be repatriated at once (a receipt being taken for each man) and they left next day. Sir George readily agreed to detail three fast sailing seventy-fours for the Minorca convoy, trusting they would be back in time to return with the rest of the channel fleet. But at the last moment the Governor could not bring himself to allow the transports with the 73rd regiment to go through. So the little convoy sailed with only the victuallers and the storeships, and so furious was General Murray to learn that General Eliott had kept his reinforcements that he refused to release 400 British sailors who were kicking their heels in Port Mahon, and the Navy suffered. But this was beyond Sir George's control.

However, the recovery of his lost prize-crews was not, or the release of British subjects detained in Spain, by a man for man exchange. Urbane but firm he made the Spaniards understand that he was not to be trifled with, and that he had enough ships to carry every Spanish prisoner to England unless his terms were accepted. At one stage he informed Langara, with whom he was on excellent terms personally, that because of his government's delay, accommodation was being prepared for him on board. This firmness had a wonderfully bracing effect on the Court of Madrid.

Scarcely less urgent was the need to inform the harassed administration in London of his success. Within forty-eight hours of his arrival his despatch went off, with the whole fleet commended in one sweeping tribute. 'The gallant behaviour of Admirals, Captains, Officers, and Men I had the honour to command was remarkably conspicuous. They all seemed activated by the same spirit and were anxiously eager to exert themselves with the utmost zeal to serve His Majesty.' Privately he had reservations. 'I have done them all like honour,' he confided to Henny, 'but it was because I would not have the world believe that there were officers slack in their Duty.'[15] One cause for his dissatisfaction must have been the flagrant disregard by many ships, of his signal to engage to leeward. But he would not spoil the general rejoicing with any note of discord. 'Keep this to yourself', he told her. With his despatch went a private letter to Lord Sandwich. It was time to get back on to his old footing with that nobleman.

'*Sandwich*, Gibraltar bay, 27 Jan. 1780.

'My Lord,

'I most sincerely congratulate you on the great success that has attended His Majesty's arms. I hope your enemies will now be confounded, and that you may long continue at the head of that Board you so ably direct, happy if by doing my Duty I can again possess that confidence that was my boast, and the loss of which I have most sincerely felt. I am truly sensible that the artful insinuations of designing men robbed me of that friendship I am sure your Lordship unwillingly withdrew; I am, and every will be, grateful for the favours and friendship you honoured me with in my youthful days, nor shall age or change of fortune ever make me deviate from my fixed resolution of ever proving myself a true and faithful friend to your Lordship. Receive me, my Lord, as such, and depend upon it I will never deceive you. The joy you may imagine I must receive on this happy occasion is greatly heightened when I consider it as the means of restoring me to your favour. . . .'[16]

Sir George was feeling a lot better. On the day his despatch went off he was able to get ashore. He landed at the Ragged Staff, paid his respects to his adversary Langara who was full of praise for the treatment he and his men were receiving, and dined with the Governor. He was at Gibraltar for nearly three weeks and although, as he told Henny later, his cold never left him all the time he was there, it does not seem to have affected his good humour, or his determination to give everyone his due. Pownoll of the *Apollo*, fearing a misapprehension, lost no time in making his Commander-in-Chief understand that the *Monarca* had struck to the *Apollo* before the *Sandwich* came up, and the great man took it very well. 'Well, Pownoll,' he replied, 'I have told them they may thank the *Apollo* for the *Monarca*'s being taken, for by firing at her and teasing her you led the *Sandwich* up.'[17] As for Captain Young, no praise could be too great. He was 'the very man I could have wished, excellent, diligent, brave, good officer endued with every quality necessary to assist a Commander-in-Chief'. He thanked Lord Sandwich for recommending him and concluded: 'I think myself much indebted to him for the late action and am not ashamed to acknowledge it.'[18]

The hero of the hour could afford to be generous. Flying his flag in the *Panther* was his old enemy of Martinique days, Vice-Admiral Robert Duff. Duff wished to go home to restore his health, and the courteous exchange between the two flag-officers on this subject was very different from their acrimonious correspondence fifteen years before. Sir George was anxious to oblige Duff but to do so would leave the station without a senior officer. So, in his spacious way, he authorized Captain Elliot of the *Edgar* to remain behind and hoist the broad pennant of a commodore, with a captain under him. So far so good. But he allowed Elliot to keep the *Edgar* which was not good at all, for although most of her complement had been transferred to the prizes, she belonged to the channel fleet. At

Gibraltar everyone was pleased, Duff because he could go home, Elliot because he was promoted, and Sir George because such patronage was very much to his taste. But at the Admiralty there was considerable annoyance. Evidently Sir George was still his old, independent, unpredictable self. After his successes only the mildest remonstrance was possible, but a frigate had to be sent out specially to order the *Edgar* and Captain Elliot home.

Sir George was no less urbane with his commander in the third post, Rear-Admiral Ross, a reputed supporter of the opposition. So flattered was Ross with his affability that he took the first opportunity after his return home, of writing to signify: 'my grateful sense of your polite conduct when under your command'.[19] But if the Commander-in-Chief left his politics on shore, others did not. By the time the fleet reached Gibraltar, and more and more while it was there, he was increasingly aware of a carping and censorious atmosphere, a nasty, backbiting spirit, which not even the recent successes could dispel. Officers had become political animals, criticizing each other's behaviour in the light of each other's politics with a freedom that shocked him. It was the unhappy aftermath of the quarrel between Keppel and Palliser, and the effect on discipline was enough to horrify an officer of the old Western Squadron. 'My brother officers still continue their absurd and illiberal custom of arraigning each other's conduct', he complained to Lord Sandwich.[20] His own ears had been assailed with fault-finding and scandal, all of which, in the mellow afterglow of their recent success he tried to disregard. 'In my opinion,' he continued, 'every Officer did his duty to his King and Country.' This should have been the last word on the subject and no doubt he hoped it would be. But the corrosion of party politics had gone too deep. By the time they were ready to leave Gibraltar he was seriously perturbed. Writing privately to George Jackson, assistant Secretary to the Admiralty, on January 28th he lamented the decay of 'the Old, Good, Necessary Discipline of the British Navy'. He went on ominously '. . . if the fleet I am going to command should be as negligent and disobedient as part of that which sailed from England with me, you will hear of Dismission upon Dismission'.[21] He named no names but plainly he foresaw trouble.

Chapter 19

First Exchanges: de Guichen

(February–August 1780)

'I wish everybody that calls Sir George Rodney's
temper and *judgment* in question had been in the fleet
these thirteen days to windward of Martinique. . . .'
(Lieutenant Sidney Smith to his father,
November 20, 1780.)[1]

GIBRALTAR had been relieved and fifteen of Sir George's fleet
and the Spanish prizes were on their way home. Sir George
himself in the *Sandwich*, with the *Ajax*, *Montagu* and *Terrible*,
all coppered* seventy-fours, the *Pegasus* (32), and the little *San
Vincente*, were now heading for the West Indies. It was not quite the
squadron the Admiralty had intended, but he took the *Terrible* because the
Shrewsbury had sprung a mast, and the *Pegasus* and *San Vincente* because
the two sloops meant for him had not turned up. He hoped never to see
Gibraltar again, and was at last beginning to shake off his cold and enjoy
the fine weather.[2] The only immediate worry was the lengthening sick-
lists in the squadron. Dr Blane recommended portable soup,† essence of
spruce, and extract of malt. A large demand for these was already on its
way home.

Seven times already had Sir George crossed the Atlantic in the service of
his country. First, to Newfoundland as a midshipman, and then on three
occasions as a captain and governor; then to Louisbourg with General
Amherst and three years after this to Martinique as a conqueror, in the
campaign that was snuffed out so ignominiously when Pocock came. Nine

---

* Sheathed with copper below the waterline, an essential protection against marine
growth, particularly in warm waters.

† Made by evaporation from the broth of lean meat. It was in the form of a greyish
white cake, stamped with the government broad arrow, and dissolved readily in cold
water.

317

years passed and then, from 1771 to 1774, he had commanded at Jamaica with every opportunity of acquainting himself with the western half of the Caribbean. Now, six years later still, all the West Indies were his and the North American seaboard too, if need be.

It would be exacting and specialized campaigning, in which the defence of the islands, the safe movement of convoys, and the maintenance of ships in some sort of seagoing condition would be an all-absorbing pre-occupation; in which every project and situation would probably depend on the arrival, or non-arrival of reinforcements from home; in which, between July and October, both sides cowered under the menace of the hurricane season; and in which, as often as not, professional soldiers and sailors would find every sort of obstruction placed in their way by the settlers and merchants for whom they supposed themselves to be fighting. He had seen it all before. But beyond all this was the battle which it was his avowed intention to force on the enemy, and when that took place much would depend on the quality of the captains awaiting him in the West Indies. From what he had seen since hoisting his flag, he may well have had misgivings.

In the Leeward group the French were still based on the fortress island of Martinique, and grimly must Sir George have reflected on the political considerations that had caused its return (with St Lucia), after the Seven Years War. Britain had Barbados with its favourable position to windward, and Antigua with its harbour and dockyard. Neither side had anywhere else of comparable strategic importance.

When the news of France's entry into the war reached the West Indies, both sides had struck quickly. The French from Martinique launched a successful attack against Dominica, while British from Barbados pounced on St Lucia and took it. As the latter was a great strategic prize (which Dominica was not) Britain had the best of the first exchange. But in 1779 things had not gone so well. A succession of French reinforcements had enabled Britain's enemies to take St Vincent and Grenada. The British reinforcements on the other hand had achieved next to nothing. Byron, who came out with thirteen of the line, failed to save Grenada, which was why he was being replaced. In the second exchange the French had won all along the line.

Both sides were now preparing for the third round. Awaiting Sir George on the station were seventeen of the line with Rear-Admirals Hyde Parker and Rowley. This would give the new Commander-in-Chief a total of twenty-one altogether, but that would be no guarantee of numerical superiority. Spain's entry into the war must sooner or later affect the balance; and there was the near certainty of French reinforcements too.

Indeed, although he could not have known it, the Comte de Guichen* with sixteen of the line, was not very far to the northward of him on a parallel course, shepherding a convoy of eighty-three transports and merchantmen towards Martinique. He had sailed from Brest on February 3rd, ten days before Sir George left Gibraltar but, because of the convoy, was making a slow passage. The two champions would arrive in the West Indies almost together.

On March 17th the little squadron arrived at Barbados and Sir George, always so punctilious about such matters, was displeased to find no letter or communication of any sort from Parker, nor any word of a rendezvous. For all he knew, land and sea forces might already have sailed to attack Porto Rico.[3] It was left to the local merchants to inform him that his second-in-command was at Gros Islet Bay, St Lucia. They also told him of a great French convoy expected hourly and escorted (here the report was erroneous) by only four men-of-war. So he sent to inform Parker of his arrival, directed his seventy-fours to cruise for five days to intercept the French if they could, and then had himself carried on shore '. . . much debilitated by the gout in both feet and my right hand and therefore rendered very low', as he described himself five days later.[4] On that same day (March 22nd), de Guichen, having eluded Sir George's screen, brought his great convoy triumphantly into Fort Royal Bay.

The French now acted with remarkable speed. They had twenty-three of the line, their troops were still on board the transports, and with no more delay than was needed for de Guichen to confer with the Governor of Martinique, the Marquis de Bouillé, they appeared in force before St Lucia. But when they saw the British defences their ardour cooled, and they returned to Fort Royal. Meanwhile Sir George, roused from his sick bed by an express from Parker, arrived with his whole squadron on the 27th.

Gros Islet Bay at the north-west end of St Lucia and only thirty miles from Fort Royal was, except for its lack of a dockyard and hospital, the most perfect advance base imaginable for operations against Martinique. Well sheltered from the prevailing easterlies and protected to seaward by the defences on Pigeon Island, a fleet could wait and watch in complete security. Later Sir George was to establish himself on shore with his own look-out post. But for the moment he was thirsting for action.

* Luc-Urbain du Bouexic, Comte de Guichen, 1712-1790.

Five days was all he allowed himself to take the measure of his new command. His force was almost equal to de Guichen's in numbers, but whereas nearly all the French ships were fresh from the dockyards of Europe, most of the British had been long on the station. Ships wore out rapidly in tropical waters. Few of Sir George's were coppered and five had fought under Byron at Grenada. Cordage, timber, canvas, and above all spare spars, were scarce; replacements from home had been meagre and infrequent, while successive squadrons had long emptied the storehouses at Barbados and Antigua. Remembering all this, captains tended to nurse their ships and wonder how much longer they would last.

But the new Commander-in-Chief was not the man for half measures. As the enemy had already paraded in force before St Lucia he was, in his own words, 'determined to return their visit and offer them battle'. So, on April 2nd he took his twenty-one battleships to sea. For two days they trailed their coats off Fort Royal, 'near enough to count all their guns and at times within random shot of some of their forts'. But de Guichen refused the challenge. This excursion opened Sir George's eyes to the condition of his ships. Those long on the station were so leaky and foul they could scarcely beat up against the lee-current, while the 74-gun *Fame* could scarcely keep afloat at all. So, leaving some of his coppered seventy-fours to watch the enemy, he took the rest of his fleet back to Gros Islet Bay.

Meanwhile, de Guichen and de Bouillé had concerted a plan. They would embark the Army on board the fleet and put to sea, thereby compelling Sir George to follow. Their hope was to lure him to leeward, away from the islands, then break back and land the troops on Barbados or St Lucia before the heavy sailing British ships, whose condition they could well guess, caught up with them. Accordingly, twenty-two of the line, five frigates, and three corvettes, having on board 3,000 troops under de Bouillé himself, sailed from Fort Royal on the night of April 13th/14th, their movement coinciding with and covering the sailing of the French trade for St Domingo.

Sir George's scouts did not fail him and he proceeded to sea at once. With twenty of the line (for the *Fame* was no longer seaworthy), one fifty and five frigates, he stood to the northward, past Fort Royal and St Pierre roads both of which were empty. At noon on the 16th the *Montagu* in the leading division made a signal for a fleet in the north-west. It was de Guichen, steering north under easy sail. Sir George at once signalled a general chase.

But this was no inferior force in headlong flight. It was commanded by

one of the best tacticians of his time, who had it well in hand. So at
3.47 p.m. Sir George called his own fleet to order by signalling a line of
battle abreast, and for the next two and a half hours ran down to leeward in
this formation. At 6.30 he swung back to the line ahead, steering north
once more. Before dark he turned his ships down wind again in line abreast
and finally, at 10 p.m., he swung them once more on to the northerly
course, throwing two frigates forward to maintain contact during the dark
hours. De Guichen, in the meanwhile, had watched the movements of his
opponent until dark, and all the while held on to the northward. At 1 a.m.
he formed his line of battle on the same course as the British, and at 5.30
he turned his fleet round by tacking together and stood to the south. The
two fleets were thus approaching each other on opposite courses as dawn
broke on April 17th.

At this point it should be remembered how slow and cumbersome were
the old fleets of sailing ships. Sir George and de Guichen had respectively
twenty-one and twenty-two battleships.* At the usual distance between
ships of two cables or 400 yards, each line could hardly be less than six
miles long, and Dr Blane has recorded that on this occasion de Guichen's
was nearer twelve.[5] With untrained or negligent captains, and some of Sir
George's would have cut a very poor figure in the old Western Squadron,
such unwieldy formations, unless carefully watched, might soon resemble
long, broken-backed snakes. However well handled, they would take more
than an hour to sail past each other.

There was also the problem of communication. A signal hung out by
the admiral from the centre of his own line could seldom be seen by more
than his next ahead and his next astern. To meet this difficulty frigates were
stationed at intervals down the line's disengaged side to repeat signals,
but it was a slow business. There were flags to cover all situations envisaged
in the Fighting Instructions, and an admiral could add any others he
thought might be useful, but his ability to communicate remained very
limited all the same. Nevertheless, the old Fighting Instructions, brought
up to date by Anson, Boscawen, and Hawke, were not so imperfect that
they could not be made to work, given a sufficiency of professional competence, fighting spirit, and loyalty.

The two Commanders-in-Chief still had a little time to perfect their
dispositions. At 5.30 Sir George signalled the *Stirling Castle*, leading the
van division, to make more sail. Six minutes later, in order to get all his
ships into their proper stations after the night, he repeated the general

* For details see Appendix 7.

signal for the line of battle ahead at two cables. His plan was to attack, with a concentration of force, the enemy's rear. At 6.45 he signalled this intention and every ship acknowledged. Action was to be close, 'and of course the admiral's ship to be the example', but the essence of the plan was concentration. That there should be no mistake about this he signalled at 7.0 to close the distance between ships to one cable.

As the two fleets approached each other, the French heading south and the British north, it became clear that the latter would hold the weather gauge. De Guichen seems to have considered trying to regain it by a tack to windward and hoisted a signal with this intention, but cancelled it.

For more than an hour the two long lines crawled past each other on opposite courses, and just beyond cannon range. At 8.30 Sir George judged that his moment had come. The leaders of the straggling French line were well away to the south, beyond the rearmost British ships; his own line had been brought together more compactly. Observers in the French ships saw each British battleship gradually become foreshortened as she put up her helm, squared her yards, and turned down wind. The line ahead suddenly became a line abreast. The distance between the fleets began to narrow.

The thrust, which should have been lethal, was defeated by the merest chance. Some time before it was launched, de Guichen had signalled his intention for his own fleet to wear (i.e. turn away before the wind and come round on the opposite course). The execution of this manœuvre coincided with that of Sir George to bear down. So it was that as the British attack was launched all de Guichen's ships swung away together and then came back on their old northerly course. Their threatened rear was once again the van which meant that should Sir George persist in his attack it could immediately be reinforced by the ships astern. This was not at all what he wanted. Baffled, as he supposed, by the French Admiral's divining his intention, he returned to his line ahead, still on a southerly course. He would carry on until opposite the new French rear, and try again.

For another hour the long line of French ships crawled past to the northward. Then he hoisted the signal to wear. The *Stirling Castle*, now the last in the line but as inattentive as ever, had to be signalled by name before she acknowledged. At 10 the whole British fleet wore round. When, at the conclusion of this manœuvre, the repeating frigates looked towards the *Sandwich*, they saw at her main topgallant masthead the red flag— 'Prepare for Battle'.

His ships were roughly as he wanted them, that is closed up opposite the French rear and about three miles from it, which was beyond effective range. But they were still more extended than he liked for his next signal was for the rear division (Rear-Admiral Rowley's), to close up. Once again Rear-Admiral Parker's division was leading with the *Stirling Castle* at its head, and as the prime essential was now to keep the fleet compact, that ship's reluctance to make sail was no disadvantage. At 11.50, when it looked as if his twenty ships were overlapping some fifteen of the enemy, he signalled for every ship to bear down and steer for her opponent. At 11.55 came the signal to engage, and a few minutes later that for close action.

The great moment had come. The British fleet began to edge down on the French line but still held their fire. Not so the enemy. Fifty-six years later an old gentleman of North Terrace, Mount Gardens, London, who had been a young gentleman in the *Intrepid* on this day, recalled how the action began. 'At about noon the French fleet began to attack as is their usual custom at a distance (what seamen term playing at long bowls), our fleet remaining quiet. Not even one Bull Dog opened its mouth till the proper time. Our captain, the Hon. Henry St John, said he would not fire a shot till we could see the buckles on the men's shoes, and on account of our near approximation we opened our fire with a hearty good will. We peppered away briskly, taking as much care as we could that our shot might tell; but we had not been long engaged before we discerned that some of the ships ahead of us were remiss in their duty. . . .'[6]

Mr Simpson, for this was the old gentleman's name, was correct in his observations although it may be doubted whether so much could have been clear to him at the time. In the van division under Parker there was certainly misunderstanding of Sir George's plan to concentrate on the French rear. He had made his intention clear at 6.45 in a signal which had been acknowledged by all ships; but it had been hauled down at 7.55 and may have passed from some captains' minds, if indeed it had ever registered at all. Now, after several hours of manoeuvring, the fleet was perfectly positioned to carry it into effect. The signal was 'For every ship to bear down and steer for her opponent'. All they had to do was to bear down on the enemy ship directly opposite them and overwhelm that part of the French line.

But to officers obsessed by the old idea that each ship must mark her opposite number, van, centre and rear, the signal had a very special (indeed almost sacred) but rather different significance. To these diehards

323

the ship to fight was always the enemy whose position in the line corresponded to their own, however far ahead she might be. Rear-Admiral Parker commanding the van division was just such an officer; and by a most unlucky chance Robert Carkett commanding the *Stirling Castle* at the head of the line was another.

Carkett's interpretation of the Fighting Instructions was rigid. As the fleets passed and re-passed each other he knew that when the time came his opponent would be the ship at the extreme end of the French line and none other. When he received the signal he bore down correctly enough. Indeed he was almost the first to engage. But then he pressed on up the French line, passing ship after ship to reach the French leader; and the *Ajax* and *Elizabeth*, confused by his example and that of the Rear-Admiral in the *Princess Royal*, fell into the same error and also pressed forward with the same misdirected zeal. At this supreme moment, with Sir George's weapon superbly poised, the blow began to go awry.

From the *Intrepid*, if Simpson is to be believed, and probably from the *Sandwich* in the centre, the ships of Parker's division could be seen pressing northward; and not only Parker's ships. The *Grafton*, leading the centre division, was pressing on too, widening the distance from her next astern, the *Yarmouth*; and the *Cornwall*, Sir George's next ahead, was misbehaving in the same way. Dr Blane reports a curious exchange between one of this ship's Marine officers and a lieutenant. As the smoke cleared, revealing the *Sandwich* a long way astern, the former remarked: 'We have made a great mistake here. There is a signal flying for close action at two cables length asunder, and we are a league ahead of the admiral. Pray tell the captain.' To which the lieutenant replied: 'No, damn him; let him find out for himself.'[7] It was a sad falling-off from old standards. But there was nothing Sir George could do. The *Sandwich* was approaching the French line. Two ships astern of the French Admiral singled her out, and in the roar of battle which followed, he had to digest his mortification and fury as best he could.

But his wish that his flagship should set an example was most nobly fulfilled. On that April 17th the *Sandwich* was probably the finest fighting unit in the British Navy. She opened fire at about 1.30 p.m., and with such devastating effect that in less than half an hour the third ship astern of the French Admiral, the 64-gun *Actionnaire*, bore away out of the line; her next astern, the 74-gun *Intrépide*, received the same treatment and did likewise. The British rear division under Rowley was tending to play at long bowls with the enemy, and it was soon impossible to see what was happening in the distant van. But in the centre the French were giving way and the credit belongs to the *Sandwich*.

Captain Young was on the lee gangway when Sir George came across to tell him that the French flagship was on their weather bow. It was surprising but true. The *Sandwich* had smashed her way through the line single-handed, and was now on the port quarter of de Guichen's 80-gun *Couronne*. The French Admiral, supported by the *Fendant* (74), and another ship, wore out of the line and came abreast of the *Sandwich* to rake her again and again, but when Sir George looked round for support from his own side, he looked in vain. The van was further away than ever and the rear division, which might have rallied to him, had worn round on the other tack without orders and was drawing away with their opponents to the southward. 'The English desert their commander', cried one of de Bouillé's aids on board the *Couronne*.[8] It was too true. And then, to windward of the reverberating mêlée round the *Sandwich*, there appeared, inexplicably, the British 64-gun *Yarmouth*.

She did not appear disabled, but lay about a quarter of a mile off with her main and mizen topsails backed as if hove to. It was certainly odd for she should have been away ahead beyond the *Cornwall*. Sir George's peremptory signal to make more sail she acknowledged but made no other response whatever. At this he desired Captain Young to order a shot to be fired into her to make her obey the signal, but no gun would bear. The *Yarmouth* continued her extraordinary behaviour for about an hour before she came down to support the flagship. Here was more material for enquiry later.

'3 ships on to the *Sandwich* at a time and Verry Ill supported by the Ships in her Division astern', was noted by the *Pegasus*, repeating frigate, at this time. Nevertheless so splendidly did the flagship fight that she kept her antagonists at bay for one and a half hours and set the *Couronne* on fire. It was hot work, close enough for sixty hand-grenades to be thrown, and close enough for a terrified dog to swim across from the *Couronne* to the *Sandwich*.* Eventually, with seventy shot in her hull and her masts tottering, she drew away to windward† having discharged 3,260 round-shot, sixty grape, and 100 of case and langridge. Three of her long

---

* The authority for this anecdote is Sir George himself, who took the animal under his special protection. Letter of May 27, 1780, to Lady Rodney, Mundy, Vol. 1, p. 299.

† According to Buor de la Charoulière, one of de Guichen's staff officers on board the French flagship, the *Sandwich* withdrew under fire from the *Fendant* (74), the *Couronne* (80), the *Palmier* (74), and the *Indien* (64). Lacour-Gayet refers to his many letters on the 1780 campaign. A.M. B⁴ 180.

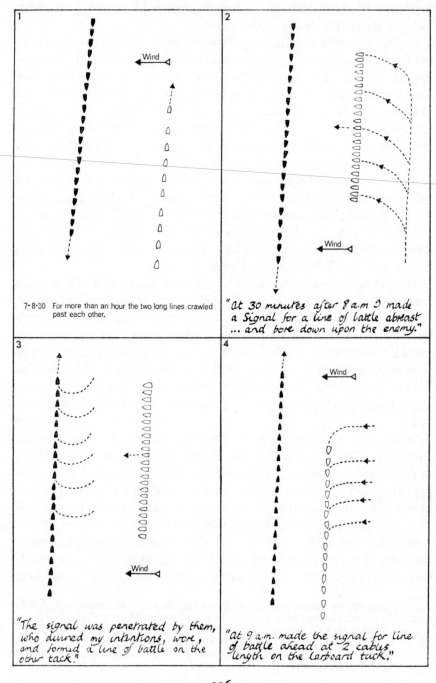

1

Wind ◁

7-8-30   For more than an hour the two long lines crawled past each other.

2

Wind ◁

"At 30 minutes after 8 a.m I made a Signal for a line of battle abreast ... and bore down upon the enemy."

3

Wind ◁

"The signal was penetrated by them, who divined my intentions, wore, and formed a line of battle on the other tack."

4

Wind ◁

"At 9 a.m. made the signal for line of battle ahead at 2 cables length on the larboard tack."

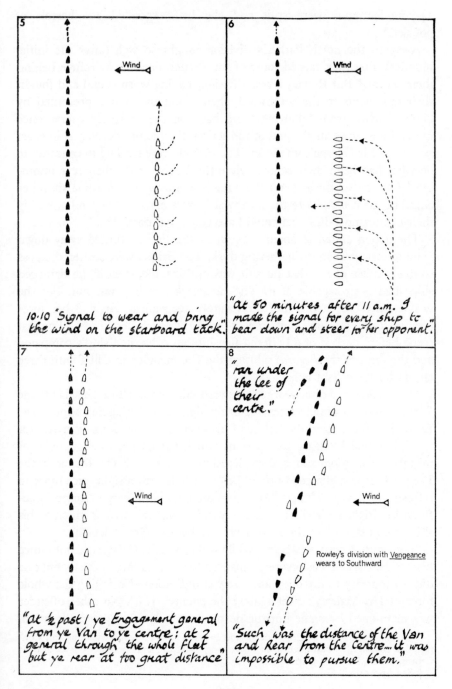

5

Wind ◁

10.10 "Signal to wear and bring the wind on the starboard tack."

6

Wind ◁

"at 50 minutes after 11 a.m. I made the signal for every ship to bear down and steer for her opponent."

7

Wind ◁

"at ½ past I ye Engagement general from ye Van to ye centre; at 2 general through the whole fleet but ye rear at too great distance"

8

"ran under the lee of their centre."

Wind ◁

Rowley's division with <u>Vengeance</u> wears to Southward

"Such was the distance of the Van and Rear from the Centre.... it was impossible to pursue them."

24-pounder guns were split and she had expended 160 barrels of powder.[9]

Away to the north Parker's division fought so well (after the initial blunder), that they caused some of the French line to take refuge behind their centre.* But Rowley's rear division, having worn round and fought their opponents to the southward, then found themselves prevented by battle damage from following them back on the northerly course once more. Thus, towards the end of the action, the picture developed in exact reverse of Sir George's intention. The French were tending to concentrate on what had been their centre, while the British, with their rear immobilized to the southward and the wretched *Stirling Castle* some six miles ahead of the *Sandwich* to the northward, were extended beyond anything their Commander-in-Chief could have conceived possible.

The action ended at about 4.15 when the French turned away down wind to disappear in the gathering dusk. The British were scattered across so many miles of sea that pursuit was unthinkable, even if the damaged ships had been capable of it. The *Sandwich* certainly was not. For the next twenty-four hours she could barely keep afloat. At 4.58 her fore-topmast came crashing down and the *Terrible* took her in tow. The last scene before dark is of a battered flagship, an exhausted ship's company, and the crew of the *Pegasus* saluting the Commander-in-Chief with three cheers for his gallant behaviour.

De Guichen had disappeared to leeward. Sir George shifted his flag to the *Terrible* and remained at sea repairing rigging and plugging shot holes. Revolving in his mind the failure of his attack he devised a new article for the Additional Fighting Instructions which left no possible loophole for mistake or evasion and had it distributed at once.† On the 20th the French fleet was glimpsed briefly before it faded from sight once more to refresh under Guadeloupe. For two more days Sir George cruised hopefully, his frigates distributed at every point, but this was as much as his ships could stand. On the 27th they were back at Gros Islet Bay.

In his public despatch, begun while still at sea, Sir George did not mince his words. Carkett was severely censured for '. . . leading in the manner he did, so contrary to my open and avowed indication of bringing the whole force of His Majesty's fleet against the enemy's rear'. No other offender was mentioned by name but the despatch ended with a grave allegation.

* '*Stirling Castle* and we Edg'd down and began with 3 of their Van Ships and Continu'd in Action till ½ past 3 when they bore away made sail and ran under the lee of their Centre.' (*Ajax*, Master's journal, Ad. 52/1543.)

† See Appendix 8.

'Tis with concern inexpressible, mixt with indignation that the Duty I owe my Sovereign and Country obliges me to acquaint their Lordships that during the Action with the French fleet . . . the British flag was not properly supported.'

True or false, the memories of Keppel and Palliser were much too raw and recent for anything like this to appear in the gazette, and the paragraph was suppressed. But Sir George, darkly suspecting that Lord Sandwich might do just this, made sure that Lord George Germain at least knew the full content of his despatch by sending him a copy privately, by the hand of the faithful George Rodney.[10] In his private letter to the First Lord he was even more outspoken.[11] He complained bitterly of 'barefaced disobedience to orders' and 'the entire want of discipline in the fleet'. Rowley was incompetent and Parker a dangerous knave. He even hinted that for political reasons 'the British flag was intended to be disgraced'. But what, he asked, could he do? 'The delinquents are too many and the public service too urgent for the matter to be investigated here.' Until discipline was restored the only remedy was to hoist his flag in a frigate, to ensure close supervision all along the line, and this was his intention. Captains Uvedale, late of the *Ajax*, and Bazely of the *Pegasus* went home with the despatch to explain things more fully.*

But in the smouldering atmosphere of recrimination which developed after the engagement Carkett was not the only culprit. The extraordinary behaviour of the *Yarmouth* called for enquiry, and Bateman her captain was put under arrest pending a court martial. This officer, who had been specially promoted for bravery at the battle of Toulon in 1744, seems to have been the victim of his own incapacity. The *Yarmouth* was a very poor sailer. Being unable to keep up with the *Grafton*, his next ahead, Bateman backed his main topsail to enable his next astern, the *Cornwall*, to catch up. But he could offer no satisfactory reasons why he waited as long as he did, or why he failed to support the *Sandwich*, and some of his defence is at variance with the evidence.[12] For his conduct on April 17th he was dismissed the service, a tragic end to a career which had started with such promise.

Of two captains in Parker's division (Bowyer of the *Albion* and Douglas of the *Terrible*), Sir George made the shattering comment that they 'really

---

* On reaching London Uvedale claimed complete forgetfulness of the whole action because, during it, something heavy fell on his head. Countess Cornwallis to Captain the Hon. W. Cornwallis, June 4, 1780.

meant well and would have done their Duty had they been permitted', which could only mean that their Divisional Admiral had prevented them. The latter was not known as 'Vinegar' Parker for nothing. What passed between him and Sir George will never be known but he went home in a state of fury and was with difficulty prevented from opening a pamphlet war against him. Rowley also had an exchange with his Commander-in-Chief over standing away from the centre, for which Sir George requested an explanation. Rowley replied smoothly that as the enemy rear wore round on the other tack he thought it his duty to follow them 'conceiving from the signal you made . . . that twas your intention to make your greatest impression on their Rear'. Sir George enclosed their correspondence with his despatch, much to Rowley's alarm, and warned him that his motion without orders had saved the enemy's fleet. He further admonished him that in future he had better confine himself to obedience to signals and orders, and added crushingly: 'the painful task of thinking belongs to me'.[13]

Rowley's unfortunate movement had been followed, but with much less excuse, by Commodore Hotham in the *Vengeance*, the last ship in Sir George's own division. The day after the battle, when Hotham sent one of his officers, Lord Winchelsea, to congratulate him, Sir George took the visitor into his gallery and demanded to know why the *Vengeance* wore round. 'To support Mr Rowley', was the unsuspecting reply, at which the Commander-in-Chief exploded. 'The British flag, my Lord, was on board the *Sandwich*; this, it was his duty to follow and support. He belonged to *my* squadron, not Mr Rowley's.' The startled junior then had the Fighting Instructions and the Articles of War thrust under his nose and was reminded that Sir George had the power to take Mr Hotham's head for his conduct, and that he would do so if he thought it proceeded from anything but mistake.[14] Hotham was probably loyal enough within his limitations, but it is hardly surprising that soon after this he applied (unofficially) to be transferred elsewhere. Then Carkett learnt that he had been singled out for special mention in the despatch and requested an explanation, at which Sir George really let himself go.

'*Sandwich*, at St Christopher's,

'30 July 1780.

'I have received your letter of yesterday acquainting me that you are credibly informed that in my public letter to the Admiralty relative to the action with the French fleet on 17 April last, your name was mentioned. It certainly was. . . .

'Your leading in the manner you did, induced others to follow so bad an example, and thereby forgetting that the signal for the line was only at two cables length distance from each other the van division was led by you to more than two leagues distance from the center division, which was thereby exposed to the greatest strength of the enemy and not properly supported.

'Could I have imagined your conduct and inattention to Signals had proceeded from anything but error in Judgment, I had certainly superceded you. But God forbid I should do so for error of judgement only. I only resolved, Sir, not to put it in your power to mistake again upon so important an occasion as the leading a British fleet to regular battle.

'You must now Sir (however painfull the Task), give me leave fairly to tell you that during the time you have been under my command you have given me more reason to find fault with your conduct as an officer than any other in the fleet (Captain Bateman excepted), by your inattention to signals and Sir by negligently performing your duty, and not exerting yourself as it behove the oldest captain in the fleet by setting the example of briskness, activity, and scrupulous attention to signals. . . .

'Judge yourself what I must have felt to observe that the two oldest captains of the fleet I had the honour to command were the only persons I had just reason to reprimand by public signal, and let them know *they had not obeyed*; your almost constantly keeping to windward of your station in sailing afterwards; the repeated signals made for the ship you commanded to get into her station; your being at an amazing distance from the fleet the night before the battle; my being obliged to send a frigate to order you down; your being out of your station at daybreak notwithstanding the line of battle was out all night; all this conduct indicated an inattention which ought not to have been shewn by an officer who had been bred in the good old discipline of the Western Squadron, and which nothing but the former service you had done your King and Country, and my firm belief in your being a brave man, could have induced me, as the Commander of a great fleet, to overlook.

'You may judge what pain it has given me to write this letter to an officer I have known so long and always had a regard for. But in great national Concerns, and where the service of my King and Country is entrusted to my care, it behoves me to do my duty and to take care that those under my command do theirs.

'Both of which, without favour or partiality, I shall strictly adhere to.[15]

How can the failure of April 17th be explained? Twenty-nine years later Dr Blane said he well remembered Sir George telling him that all the captains had been informed of the general plan, either orally or by letter.[16] Bowyer and Douglas and several others seem to have understood what was expected of them. It is hard to believe that Sir George failed to inform Parker or Carkett. Nevertheless it is on these two that the chief responsibility lies. No serious imputation can be laid against their courage or capacity. Parker was a famous fighter. Carkett had been specially promoted for bravery in 1758. They represented the hard core of experienced professionalism.

But such men do not always take kindly to new ideas. It is possible that Sir George's plan was perfectly clear to them but that, in a cross-grained, independent way, they deliberately mismanaged it, not for political reasons (Parker's subsequent employment by the government disproves this), but because it was unorthodox. There were some notorious precedents to support any subordinate who chose to follow the strict letter of the Fighting Instructions rather than the wishes of his Commander-in-Chief. An important contributory factor was that Sir George had little time to get to know his officers, let alone train them or exercise his fleet. Material and morale were poor, professional standards low, and loyalties sometimes divided, in spite of which some critics have blamed Sir George for not turning his command into a band of brothers in three weeks. 'Inattention to signals' was his final verdict on the matter, glossing over the more disturbing implications. He now resolved that his officers should learn their business properly.

Shipwrights, riggers, carpenters, and all their brawny perspiring underlings had less than a fortnight to prepare the ships before the next action. On May 6th de Guichen was again at sea, cruising to windward of Martinique. At once Sir George's fleet (leaving the *Fame* behind, and now the *Grafton* as well, with unserviceable masts) began to move out from Gros Islet Bay. For four laborious days they beat to the eastward out of the St Lucia channel. On May 10th the French were sighted, three leagues to windward.

De Guichen may have been disagreeably surprised to see the British. Whatever his intentions, nothing could be done until his tenacious adversary was shaken off. But his own ships were cleaner and faster, and he was well to windward. So, like a sprightly duellist, he paraded before his antagonist, always threatening but always just beyond reach, while the British plugged stolidly after him.

Now could be seen the salutary effect of Sir George's recent outbursts. He had declared that he expected implicit obedience to every signal, under the certain penalty of being instantly superseded, and the results were remarkable, particularly after he had carried out another threat and shifted his flag to a frigate.* The sharp blue eyes were everywhere. Admirals as well as captains were instantly reprimanded if out of station, and delinquent ships hurriedly regained their places as the Commander-in-Chief's flag bore down. A fleet of nineteen battleships was being drilled in the presence of a numerically superior enemy. It was a bracing experience and it went on for the next four days while the peaks of Martinique and St Lucia gradually sank below the horizon.

Nearly every day at about 2 p.m. (Captain Young used to say it was when their men had got their wine) the French would bear down threateningly in line abreast, at which the British would beat to quarters and prepare to engage. But it was never more than a French gasconade. After tantalizing their opponents with the prospect of a fight and evoking their admiration by the precision of their movements, they would haul their wind just out of range and draw away to windward.

It was a dangerous game to play with Sir George. On the 15th he contrived to lure them closer than usual by simulating a withdrawal. 'I suffered them to enjoy the deception', he wrote later, 'and their van ship to approach abreast of my centre when, by a lucky change of wind, perceiving I could weather the enemy, I made the signal for the third in command (who then led the van) to tack with his squadron. . . . The enemy's fleet wore instantly and fled with a crowd of sail.'

This time the leading British ship was Bowyer's *Albion*, and the divisional commander was Rowley. Had the wind continued from the new quarter the British line ahead would have covered the French line abreast, and no doubt a concentrated thrust down wind would have followed. But before this could happen both sides found it was heading them more and more. The British could only keep their sails full by bearing away onto a more northerly course. The French on the other hand did not bear away but tacked, thus bringing themselves neatly back to their original line ahead, and once more to windward. But they were not to escape without a mauling. The successive movements had brought the lines so close that the British van was able to engage the French centre and rear as the two fleets passed on opposite tacks. The *Albion*, too far ahead to get

---

* Sir George went on board the *Venus* (36), Captain J. Douglas, at 3 p.m. on May 13th and did not return to the *Sandwich* until the fleet arrived at Barbados on the 22nd.

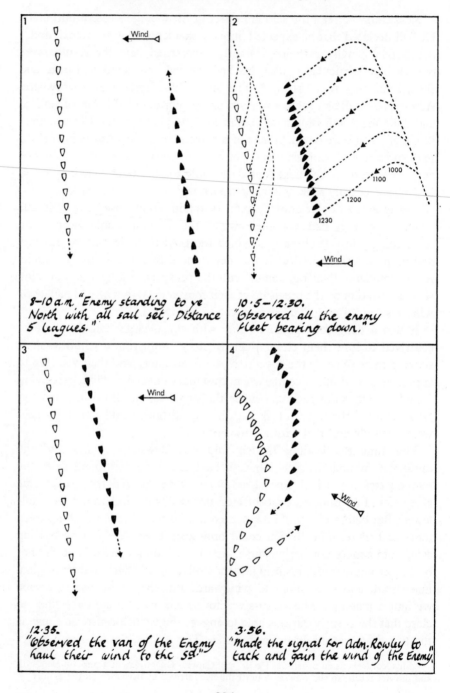

1

8-10 a.m. "Enemy standing to ye
North with all sail set. Distance
5 leagues."

2

10.5-12.30.
"Observed all the enemy
fleet bearing down."

3

12.35.
"Observed the van of the Enemy
haul their wind to the S.E."

4

3.56.
"Made the signal for Adm. Rowley to
tack and gain the wind of the Enemy."

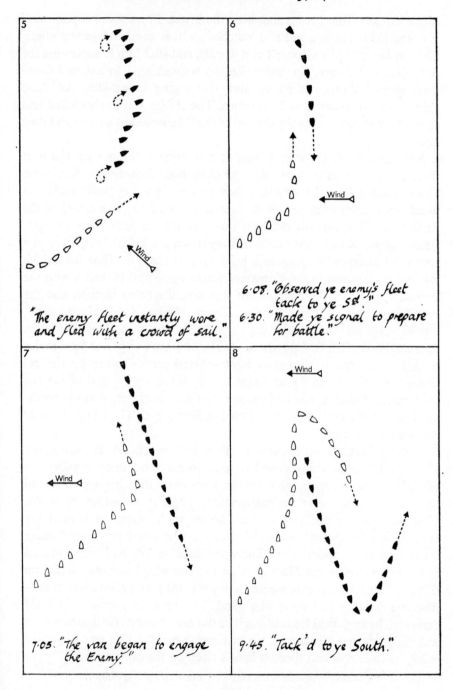

5

"The enemy fleet instantly wore
and fled with a crowd of sail."

6

6·08. "Observed ye enemy's fleet
        tack to ye S⁑."
6·30. "Made ye signal to prepare
        for battle."

Wind

7

7·05. "The van began to engage
        the Enemy."

Wind

8

9·45. "Tack'd to ye South."

Wind

much support from her second, bore the brunt. From about 6 p.m. until 7.30 the British centre and rear watched as 'that good and gallant officer Captain Bowyer' (Sir George's own words), and after him in succession the *Magnificent*, *Medway*, *Conqueror* (Rowley's flagship), *Vigilant*, and *Cornwall*, steered down the enemy line exchanging broadsides. All these ships sustained damage and casualties. The *Albion* had twelve killed and sixty-two wounded: Captain Watson of the *Conqueror* lost an arm and died later.

After this brush the enemy kept at a respectful distance for the next three days. Then on the 19th, after the chase had taken the two fleets some 120 miles out into the Atlantic, they met again on opposite tacks. As usual the French were to windward and managed to cross ahead of the British van, but on this occasion they showed an inclination to fight. After crossing ahead their van bore away down the British line, albeit at a respectful distance, keeping up a brisk fire. At the same time the British van, led by Hotham in the *Vengeance*, luffed up to deal faithfully with the French rear. Here the engagement was hot, the firing intense, and the casualties (most of them in the *Albion*, *Vigilant*, and *Marlborough*), roughly doubled those of four days earlier. But the French suffered more. In the opinion of Sir George 'the fire of His Majesty's ships was far superior to that of the enemy who must have suffered great damage by the re-encounter'. There can be no doubt he was right. By the end of the last exchange de Guichen had had enough. His fleet disappeared to the northward to seek the hospital and dockyard of Fort Royal. The series of classic encounters was over.

In these three actions French casualties had been heavy. Reports spoke of 1,400 killed in ships crowded with troops, and huge numbers of wounded.* De Guichen, who was six years older than his opponent and had lost a son in one of the engagements, broke down under the strain. 'The command of so large a fleet', he wrote, 'is infinitely beyond my capacity in all respects.' Not so Sir George, who positively thrived under the burden and responsibility. The valetudinarian who had been confined to his cabin during the Moonlight Battle, and who had been carried on shore at Barbados, wrote to assure Henny that the long periods of manoeuvring and fighting had done him good.[17] They were a tonic. To Lord Sandwich he explained that although he did not go to bed for fourteen days and nights during this period, yet at times, when the fleet was in perfect order, he stole now and then an hour's sleep on the cabin floor.[18]

* For British casualties on May 15th and 19th see Appendix 7.

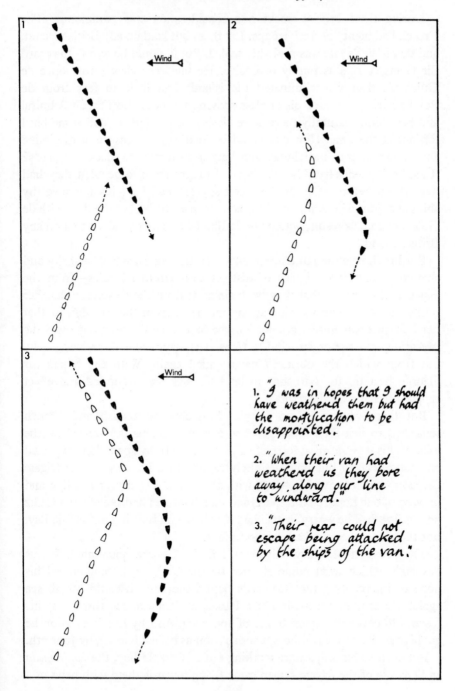

1. "I was in hopes that I should have weathered them but had the mortification to be disappointed."

2. "When their van had weathered us they bore away along our line to windward."

3. "Their rear could not escape being attacked by the ships of the van."

337

During these crucial weeks one consideration was paramount. The French had plenty of fresh troops. Let them but land on any British island, and that island's fate was probably sealed. But it would be wrong to regard Sir George's role as purely defensive. He saw very clearly that once de Guichen's fleet was eliminated the islands had little to fear from de Bouillé's troops. Hence his endless striving to get at the French Admiral and beat him. Naturally there were clashes of personality and some hard feelings at the time. How else could he instil some measure of discipline and efficiency into individuals too long accustomed to slack standards? 'In spite of themselves,' he said later, 'I taught them to be what they had never been before—Officers.' What else? He had kept his unseaworthy ships at sea for weeks, fought three actions, had the best of the duel with de Guichen, and, as result, not one of de Bouillé's soldiers had set foot on any British island.

But his fleet, although triumphant upon the ocean, was in a shaky and shattered condition. Signals of distress came from all sides—from the *Boyne* and *Cornwall* that they were sinking; from the *Conqueror* that her masts might go over the side at any moment; from the *Magnificent* that her bowsprit was unserviceable. For the first three the only hope was the precarious passage down wind to Gros Islet Bay where all arrived safely, but from which the *Cornwall* never sailed again. With the others Sir George beat up for Barbados to land his sick and wounded and effect repairs, arriving on the 22nd.

But there was to be no respite. Scarcely had British and French separated to lick their wounds when a new combatant advanced on the arena. This was the great force of ships and men from Spain, long expected and long delayed but now definitely reported on its way by the frigate *Cerberus*, which arrived hot-foot with the news. Twenty of the line and upward of one hundred transports and merchantmen had sailed from Cadiz on April 28th. The weary British had hardly begun refitting in Carlisle Bay, but thereafter they worked day and night.

The prospect of a new adversary left Sir George undaunted. In his despatch, which went home at once by the *Cerberus*, he announced his hope of intercepting the Spaniards before the French could put to sea again. He sent to warn Sir Peter Parker at Jamaica. He threw out his frigates to cover the Spanish line of approach. And by heroic exertion he got his own fleet to sea (although not so soon as he had hoped), by June 7th.

But even as his ships were working out of Carlisle Bay, the *Andromeda* and *Cyclops* of the frigate screen came flying towards them with news of a great mass of ships seen the previous day about 150 miles to windward of Martinique. Next morning Sir George himself was there, but too late. The ocean was empty except for three strange sail to the northward. In light airs and pouring rain two of these were taken before dark. Both were stragglers from the Spanish convoy. But the main body, twelve of the line and eighty-three transports, under Don José de Solano, had passed further north a few hours earlier to make their landfall at Guadeloupe.

The prospect now was that with only seventeen of the line (some of them very shaky), and two fifties, Sir George might soon be faced with a combined Franco-Spanish fleet of thirty-five. One seventy-four, the *Triumph*, had joined him on May 10th, but against this single addition, five of his battleships were now unfit for any operations at all. They were the *Fame* and *Boyne*, condemned by survey and barely capable of the voyage home; the *Grafton* with masts unserviceable; the *Conqueror* with no masts at all; and the *Cornwall* so leaky that she had to be beached. The odds were now almost exactly two to one and where in Heaven's name were the reinforcements promised by Lord Sandwich? Five or six of the line under Commodore Walsingham should have arrived long since. There had also been a promise of three more from Vice-Admiral Arbuthnot's squadron in North America, and where were they? He was not to know that Walsingham was still beating against headwinds, while the orders to Arbuthnot had gone astray. With what he had he passed round the southern tip of Martinique and up to Fort Royal in a last attempt to get between the two fleets. But again he was too late. Only two battleships were to be seen in the bay and three more in the carenage. De Guichen, with eighteen of the line, had slipped out two days before.

In this baffling game of hide-and-seek Sir George had twice been unlucky. He had missed de Solano by a matter of hours, and he had failed to prevent his enemies uniting. Over the first he had no cause to blame himself although he may have begun to doubt whether the position to windward of Martinique, where he had missed de Blénac eighteen years before, was the best for intercepting an enemy from Europe. But there was still a chance of catching de Guichen, for he was reported to be becalmed thirty miles to leeward of Dominica. It would be easy to run down to leeward and engage him, but less easy to beat back. Sir George resisted the temptation. There were still five French ships in Fort Royal, and he had too much respect for 'that enterprising general' the Marquis de Bouillé to leave the British islands exposed. So, for a week he cruised defiantly off Fort Royal. It was only a gesture, but one worth making.

Then, learning that French and Spanish had at last joined forces in Prince Rupert's Bay, Dominica, he returned to Gros Islet Bay on the 16th to hurry the repairs, stiffen the island's defences, and await whatever fortune might send.

The second half of June was tense. Hyde Parker with the homeward-bound convoy was stopped at Antigua. After a week of hesitation it was decided to sail the Tobago and St Lucia convoy home direct, without calling at St Kitt's. 'The Times are critical', he informed General Vaughan on the 14th. 'My maxim has always been, and ever shall be, to act offensively, but if the Circumstances of the Times render it absolutely necessary for His Majesty's Service to be on the Defensive, I trust I shall do my Duty in that disagreeable Situation in such a manner as to prevent the Public Enemy gaining any reputation.'[19] But on the 17th came a gleam of encouragement when the *Russell* (74) arrived from New York, to be followed a week later by the *Shrewsbury*. This brought Sir George's battleship strength to nineteen. Meanwhile the French and Spanish fleets moved to Fort Royal where, on the 29th, the *Ajax* counted thirty of the line in the bay and three more in the carenage. If an attack was coming, it would come soon. At St Lucia General Vaughan worked indefatigably to strengthen the shore defences. 'You may depend on my readiness ever to support the Measures You may think necessary',[20] wrote Sir George. At Martinique in 1762 Vaughan, then a colonel in the Grenadiers, had won Rodney's high esteem.[21] He had it still. Sir George also sent word to the other British islands that if they would but do their duty he would be on the back of the enemy attacking them the moment his reinforcements arrived. But the enemy remained curiously inactive, except for bitter dissentions among themselves. The Spaniards were not interested in French problems. Their only thought, after obtaining stores and provisions from their reluctant hosts, was for their own possessions in the Greater Antilles. There was much sickness in their ships. Tempers flared up between allies and duels were fought. Every day a concerted attack seemed less likely.

The crisis ended as quickly as it had arisen. On July 3rd and 4th three seventy-fours, the *Centaur*, *Culloden*, and *Egmont* arrived, with news that the rest of Walsingham's force was not far behind. Twenty-four hours later the combined fleets quitted the arena. They sailed from Fort Royal by night. Sir George's frigates shadowed them to Guadeloupe, thence to Santa Cruz, and last reported twenty-six of them steering west, conclusive proof that the danger was past. Finally, on the 12th, the rest of Walsingham's force arrived to swing the balance overwhelmingly in Sir George's favour. For four months, and with an inferior force of tired and worn-out ships, he had held a difficult position with great resolution and skill. As the odds increased, so had his activity and determination until, at the end, his enemies departed leaving him master of the islands. It was a most distinguished achievement.

So compelling has been the onward sweep of events that their impact at home has not yet been noted; and so infrequent were the packets that Sir George himself had been some time in the West Indies before the first congratulations on his earlier achievements reached him. The time-lag imposed by 3,000 miles of sea must, in the interest of consecutive narrative, be shared by the reader. But the arrival of great quantities of fleet-mail with Walsingham affords the best possible excuse for other matters to be dropped until the news from home has been digested.

The destruction of Langara's squadron and the relief of Gibraltar had certainly made their impact. The country, it appeared, was transported with delight—which was hardly surprising considering how the war had been going—and so, to judge from his letters, was Lord Sandwich. 'I scarcely know how to find words to congratulate you enough upon your late glorious successes and upon the eminent services you have done your country. The worst of my enemies now allows that I have pitched upon a man who knows his duty and is a brave, honest, and able officer.' This, from a nobleman whose smiles had for so long been withdrawn, was auspicious, even if the credit claimed for Sir George's appointment might appear a little strained. His Lordship continued: 'I have obtained you the Thanks of both Houses of Parliament; in the House of Lords I made the motion myself and mentioned what perhaps you yourself was not aware of, that you had captured more line of battleships than had been taken in any action in either of the two last preceding wars. I am also in hopes that before Captain Walsingham sails I shall be able to prevail upon His Majesty to give you some more substantial proof of his approbation. . . .' The First Lord's next letter (dated March 17th), contained the offer of a pension of £1,000 per annum, which was repeated three days later in the most flattering terms by Lord North himself.*[22]

Henny, writing from Portman Street, began with the safe arrival of the Caraccas prizes. Then she mentioned rumours and more rumours and

---

* As an alternative, the Lieutenant-Colonelcy of Marines with £1,500 per annum but less secure than the pension, was offered. Sir George chose the pension. The King thought the sum inadequate and ordered the grant to be made out for £2,000 per annum. (Lord North to Rodney, November 7, 1780. P.R.O. 30/20/21.)

herself 'absolutely worn out with expectations', until there arrived confirmation of the Moonlight victory. 'Everybody is beyond measure delighted as well as astonished,' she wrote, 'indeed it is impossible to describe the general applause that is bestowed upon you; or to mention the number of friends who have called to congratulate me on this happy event.' A few days later Captain Thompson of the *Hyaena*, who had repeated the flagship's signals during the action, came knocking at her door with letters for the family. '. . . if your curiosity leads you to hear the particulars of a sea battle,' her husband had written, 'he can better inform you than any other person.' So there followed a family dinner party, with Henny, George Rodney, and the little girls all ears for the captain's account of the first British victory at sea since Quiberon. There was a warm letter from Keppel: 'I can not help wishing most ardently for the success of my friends.' Miss Jane Rodney, as befitted a young lady of thirteen, had much to say about the illuminations, the firing of the Tower and Park guns, the verses in the *Morning Post*, and how they received the great news at her dancing academy. Even James Rodney took up the correspondence with his brother again: 'When you have a leisure moment I shall be very happy to have a line.'[23] It all made most agreeable reading, and if the bag contained any pressing reminders from Lowther, Mackreth and Co. they have not survived.

But time was short if the fleet was not to be caught by the hurricane season. 'In July stand by' was the old warning that no good seaman disregarded. There were thirty-one of the line, two fifties, and fourteen frigates to be dispersed, besides a host of smaller vessels, and it says much for the organization in the flagship's office that only five days after Walsingham's arrival the decisions were made, the orders distributed, and the ships under way.

Hotham remained at St Lucia for the protection of the islands, with seven of the line (of which three would go home with the September convoy), and most of the smaller vessels. With the rest of his fleet Sir George sailed for St Kitt's on the 17th, taking the trade with him. Here there was a further dispersal. Rowley and Walsingham carried on for Jamaica with ten of the line, to put themselves under Sir Peter Parker, while the *Boyne* and *Preston* sailed with seventy-four ships of the August convoy for home. Sir George in the *Sandwich* remained for the time being at St Kitt's with eight seventy-fours, the best available, and one sixty-four.*

Free at last from the immediate pressure of events he was now hoping

---

* For details of the dispersal see Appendix 9.

for a little rest. The usual reaction threatened. Writing to Henny at this time he expressed surprise that his health had stood up in the way it had, but admitted that he now felt 'much out of order and far from well'.[24] But for once the collapse did not happen. Instead, he was able to catch up on his correspondence—those long letters in a large, gouty scrawl, that took up so much of his time.

More than anything else his thoughts returned to his chances of a seat in the House. 'A man in our country is nothing without being in Parliament.'[25] He had written this to Henny from Barbados, after some bitter observations on the way the ministers were not supporting him. From St Kitt's he wrote on the same subject to Lord North, to Lord Sandwich whose sincerity (after the partial suppression of the Martinique despatch) he now greatly mistrusted, and to Lord George Germain. To the latter he waxed eloquent. 'I beg you will look upon me as a certain but humble supporter of your measures in Parliament should I obtain a seat there at the general election, which I hope will not be refused me. . . .' Not even the pension must be allowed to interfere with this. 'If it does,' he went on, 'I must beg your Lordship will be so good as to speak to Lord North upon the subject and beg that I may decline the pension; for in my opinion to be out of Parliament is to be out of the World, and my Heart is set on being in.'[26] There was more in this than a wish to assist in the councils of the nation. With a Parliamentary seat he could keep his creditors at bay. Without it the pension might well be forfeit to them anyway.

Taken all in all it was a more mellow Sir George that plied his pen so busily from St Kitt's. He was even prepared to bury the hatchet with James Rodney. 'I am glad my brother has become himself again', he confided to Henny. 'His wife is a good creature. I shall write to thank her for standing sponsor to my little girl.' This was an olive branch indeed, but the baby girl born the previous April and later the wife of Major-General Mundy, the Admiral's first biographer, was duly named Sarah after her sponsor. Still thinking of his new daughter the experienced father continued: 'Jenny says it has very good lungs; I fancy it disturbs her too early in the morning. Tell Anne I expect she knows me when I return. . . .'[27] So had he written a quarter of a century before, lest little Georgy should forget him.

As he reveals himself, the pattern is unchanged over the years, even to his invariable concern for his men's health and his expensive measures to safeguard it. Having ordered all the pernicious rum-stills round Gros Islet Bay to be destroyed, and rejected a shipload of the best Jamaica as immature, something else had to be found. Madeira wine was plentiful and (by Sir George's standards) cheap, so he cheerfully authorized the purchase of 200 pipes for the fleet, sending back twenty of them for the hospital at St Lucia. 'The unhealthy state of the ships under my command . . . which always occurs at this season of the year, is owing to the rawness of the rum.' This would be his answer if the Navy Board made their usual objection.

Chapter 20

American Interlude

(August–December 1780)

'I have the curses of the Congress and the
blessings of all the loyal Americans.'
(Sir George Rodney to George Jackson,
October 12, 1780.)[1]

THE onset of the hurricane season had partly cleared the board.
Along the great 600-mile sweep of the Leeward Islands, from
Tobago in the south to St Kitt's in the north, no forces
threatened save those of Nature. From friends on shore and
from ships at sea, from privateers, traders and island schooners, reassuring
reports confirmed one another. The Spaniards had departed in high
dudgeon to the Havannah; de Guichen and most of his fleet would soon be
returning to Europe, bringing the French trade with them; Jamaica could
be in no possible danger. Cruising to the north of Barbuda, for there was
some hope of catching de Guichen's convoy homeward bound, Sir George
had no doubt what he ought to do next.

The situation on the coast of North America was disquieting. Seven of
the line under the Chevalier de Ternay had arrived there in July, and
Rhode Island was already in French hands. Rear-Admiral Thomas Graves
had arrived at Sandy Hook at about the same time with six of the line.
The British Commander-in-Chief, Vice-Admiral Arbuthnot, had three
battleships, so Graves's reinforcements would bring his total to nine,
against de Ternay's seven. But if, as Sir George was now beginning to
think likely, de Guichen sent some of his ships up the coast to join de
Ternay, French superiority would be assured in a vital theatre.

In a very able memorandum from Cleveland Row, dated March 10,
1779,[2] he had recommended much greater flexibility in the West Indies
command, and in particular that during the hurricane months a strong
detachment from the West Indies should go to North America. Now, as the

345

man on the spot, he saw his arguments reinforced by the possibility of his French opponent doing just this. His Commission gave him virtually a free hand in the western hemisphere. His duty was therefore plain, even though it meant sacrificing a promising operation against Trinidad, and letting the French convoy go by unscathed. Explaining his action later to his old friend Whitshed Keene, he put it as a choice between 'Riches to myself with the loss of America, or a mediocrity of Fortune with the happiness of having saved so large a portion of the British Empire'.[3] 'And so,' he went on in the same exalted strain, 'I flew with the wings of National Enthusiasm to disappoint the Ambitious Designs of France, and to cut off all Hope from the Rebellious and Deluded Americans.'

It was the great line, the conception of duty that had sent him eighteen years before to save Jamaica. And although his expectations were, in some respects, to be disappointed, his strategic anticipation was absolutely sound. On August 16th, as the squadron headed north, the *Sandwich* was hailed by a small trader, the *Fair Rhodian*, with an express from Arbuthnot. Dated July 8th it reported the arrival of nine French battleships and five frigates, with transports totalling some forty sail, in the Delaware. This could hardly be de Guichen's ships which, although Sir George could not know it, were getting under way from St Domingo on that very day. Actually it was a belated and exaggerated report of de Ternay's arrival, but for all Sir George knew it might be more French reinforcements from Europe. So a reply was hastily penned. Arbuthnot might expect every assistance in Sir George's power: more he could not say in case the despatch was captured;[4] and the *Fair Rhodian* sped back to New York while the ten battleships lumbered after her into the cooler northern latitudes. One day a south-bound Bermudian spoke the *Centaur* with results to which we shall refer later. On September 14th the squadron anchored off Sandy Hook; and whatever concern may have been felt by the enemy, was more than shared by the Vice-Admiral who, for more than two years, had commanded on the station.

Marriott Arbuthnot was a prickly customer at the best of times. He was sixty-eight, six years older than Sir George, and advancing years had not sweetened his disposition. Orders for him to detach three of the line to the Leeward Islands had left England as early as October 1779, but they never reached Arbuthnot.* Later, when Sir George wrote to inquire

---

* They were on board the *Bonetta* (sloop) which met such bad weather that she took five months and ten days to reach New Providence in the Bahamas, by which time the despatches appear to have been lost or forgotten.

why no ships had been sent, his junior rebuked him. 'Your expression of surprise at not finding your squadron reinforced by the line of battleships from America would have been more properly suspended until you had known me to have received orders for that purpose. . . .'[5] Tart!

During the summer he had worked well enough with the Army in the operations against Charleston, but since that success he had directed his energies less against the enemy than against his military opposite number, Sir Henry Clinton, with whom he was now on the worst possible terms. Since the French occupation of Rhode Island, he had withdrawn his squadron to Gardner's Bay in Long Island sound, a secure anchorage some eighteen leagues to leeward, where he imagined himself to be blockading them. He was a jealous old man, quick to take offence, and much too set in his ways after fifty-four years at sea to be capable of adapting himself to a situation he did not like. It was impossible for him not to resent Sir George's coming.

As soon as he reached Sandy Hook Sir George detached four of the line to join Arbuthnot in Gardner's bay, and directed him officially to put himself under his command. Styling himself *'Commander-in-Chief of H.M. Ships and Vessels employed or to be employed at Barbados, the Leeward Islands, and on the seas adjacent, and superior officer of all H.M. ships and vessels employed on the coast of North America'*, he issued a general order for all commanders on the station to do the same. Then, as Arbuthnot remained resolutely unavailable for consultation, the *Sandwich* weighed and proceeded on her own up the North river, to drop anchor off the city of New York, so that Sir George might confer with Sir Henry Clinton.

Fortunately they were old friends, and the shortcomings of the absent Arbuthnot made further common ground between them. In two long and cordial discussions on September 16th and 17th, thirsting for action on Sir George's side, candid and realistic on Sir Henry's, they covered the whole of the war in North America.

Sir Henry rejoiced that Sir George had come, for more French ships were expected. In anticipation of this, Washington was increasing his forces by compelling the militia to incorporate in the regular regiments,* and there was talk of an attempt on New York. The arrival of Sir George's squadron could not but result in disillusionment and desertions.

Sir George, for his part, was loud in his complaints at the loss of Rhode

* By an odd coincidence Sir George's cousin Caesar Rodney of the Delaware Assembly was actively employed in this business at the time, on the orders of General Washington.

Island, the only harbour from which a blockade could be maintained against the three capital cities of America, Boston, New York, and Philadelphia; and when Sir Henry told him that the advice to evacuate had been given, and enforced, by Arbuthnot, he was aghast. 'What', he exclaimed, 'has not that man to answer for to his country.'[6] But Sir Henry, cautious and practical, could offer no hope of its recovery.

Thanks to Clinton's methodical habits (he put down a record of their conversation besides referring to it later in correspondence),[7] we can see something of Sir George in conference. He was at once aggressive and imaginative. Returning to the problem of dislodging de Ternay from Rhode Island, he seems to have come out with a wonderful scheme for luring him forth with a *ruse-de-guerre*. Let us assume, he argued, that another French squadron is on its way to North America, and that de Ternay is expecting it. Let some British ships under French colours appear off Block Island at a time when the wind is fair for de Ternay to emerge and let them be engaged in a sham fight with Arbuthnot's ships. The chivalrous de Ternay would almost certainly come out to assist his supposedly hard-pressed compatriots: and once out could be effectively annihilated by the combined force which had put on the entertainment for his benefit.

This ingenious project may have owed less to Sir George's originality than to his knowledge of the old classics.* But both commanders seem to have taken it seriously although they decided to shelve it for the time being. For Sir Henry had a project of his own, long prepared and of deadly secrecy, which he was about to spring on the American rebels. This was nothing less than the seizure of West Point, their main arsenal and principal fortress on the Hudson, through the connivance of one of their best generals.

Why Benedict Arnold turned traitor need not concern us here. But he was prepared to hand over his trust and change sides, and only the final details were waiting to be settled when Sir George arrived at Clinton's New York headquarters. A reference in Clinton's letter of the 17th to 'the plan I laid before you yesterday' may refer to this, and perhaps to the naval assistance Sir George was to give: for it is impossible to believe that he was not admitted into the secret and invited to co-operate. Also in the secret was Major John André, Clinton's adjutant-general, who was to meet Arnold in a day or two to settle the final details of the betrayal. Meanwhile

---

* We have it on the authority of Dr Blane himself that Sir George was 'an indefatigable reader of Homer'. (*Select Dissertations on Subjects of Medical Science.*)

the war at sea must go on. Captain Affleck was sent out to intercept some French provision ships, expected soon to sail from the Delaware.

Then Sir George professed himself indisposed, and no sooner had he done so than there came reports of another French squadron (twelve or fourteen of the line), on the coast. He must have been extremely ill or, as seems more probable, profoundly sceptical of the report and immersed in the plans against West Point, for he sent word to Arbuthnot to command the whole squadron and was prepared to turn everything over to him. Fortunately the alarm was false, the ships had been Sir George's own, and Arbuthnot stayed where he was. Before the scare died down, on September 21st to be exact, André was conveyed up the Hudson in the *Vulture* (sloop) for his appointment with Arnold.

The tragic sequel followed a few days later. Instead of the triumphant André with the plans of the rebel defences in his pocket, there came flying the fugitive Arnold, his name to be held up for all eternity to the execration of his countrymen. André had been caught on his way back to the British lines. For him there was no hope. As the days rolled on to the court martial and inevitable execution of this gallant and popular young officer, the atmosphere at Clinton's headquarters may be imagined. Then, to distract Sir George from the agonies of the military, two letters arrived from Arbuthnot.

In neither was there the least recognition of the purpose for which his superior had come. The four battleships had joined him but 'the only employment I can at present think of is to lose no time in supplying them with wood and water, and permitting them to put their sick on shore'. He expressed concern at Sir George's indisposition, 'but I must observe,' he added, 'if your health obliges you, Sir, to correspond at this distance, it can not be done by frigate at this season.' He would not come to New York. His second letter ended with a broad hint. 'Your ships call aloud for supplies but here we [have] none. The Winters are extremely severe that it is impossible to keep pace with the demand for Slops.' But he sent his secretary to pay his respects and Sir George responded courteously. 'I take the opportunity by Mr. Green your Secretary to congratulate on your glorious success in taking Charleston.'[8] Privately he considered Charleston a very poor exchange for Rhode Island, and Green 'a damned rascal'.[9]

But Sir George's arrival in North America raised a much more delicate issue than that of supplies and slops: it put him in a position to claim the commander-in-chief's share of any prize-money. Confronted with this unpalatable prospect Arbuthnot went into action. On October 2nd he issued a circular to all prize-agents claiming the commander-in-chief's share of all prizes taken on the station, and listing the ships to be regarded as under his command. To defeat Sir George's assumption of superiority, he defined himself as *'the Stationary Commander-in-Chief'*,[10] and if this did not cause derision on board the *Sandwich* his list of ships certainly did, for he included three of the four battleships Sir George had recently sent him, but for some inexplicable reason, perhaps haste, omitted the fourth, the *Shrewsbury*. The circular was his first move. Next day he wrote to Sir George.

'You are too good an officer,' he pleaded, 'not to know that if you supercede me as Commander-in-Chief I can not be reinstated but by that Authority who first honoured me with that appointment. The Confusion that this must create before it can be remedied from home is too obvious to be animadverted on. Do not then, I beseech you, Sir, let us cause any additional trouble to the King's Ministers, who have lately been sufficiently loaded without an added weight on our part. I hope therefore you will be pleased to suspend your power until a proper force of the enemy may make its appearance, to render the order unavoidable.'[11]

Lastly, on October 5th, he wrote to Lord Sandwich, protesting in the strongest possible terms at Sir George's 'very extraordinary' conduct. The burden of his complaint was uncomplicated and direct. All the carefully hoarded naval stores in North America would now be used up, and when Sir George departed he would certainly take with him the best of Arbuthnot's frigates. 'The Seniority of his Flag,' he concluded bitterly, 'is to confront and supercede wherever he chooses to be: if this be true it is too dangerous a power to trust long in such hands.'[12]

Sir George was more than a match for an opponent like this. Bland but inflexible he gave the Admiralty his own version of the dispute in a private letter to George Jackson on October 12th.

'. . . I am sorry to say that jealousy has arisen in the breast of Vice-Admiral Arbuthnot who has been absurd enough to write to me to give up my Authority and permit him to continue as Commander-in-Chief, using the most ridiculous arguments. You may be sure I answered him as I ought, and let him know I knew my Duty and did not come to America to be an Idle Spectator—but while I remained on the coast would Command-in-Chief, and take care the orders I gave were observed.

'. . . Mr Arbuthnot is governed by an artful fellow which makes him do things that will sully his reputation. 'Tis inconceivable the number of

Memorials I have against him, all of which I return, letting them know I do not come to enquire into Mr. Arbuthnot's conduct. Everything is in the greatest confusion, not the least order, and 'tis impossible but Sir H. Clinton or Mr. Arbuthnot must be recalled. I have had more trouble and fatigue in putting things in order and stationing ships properly than I had with the great fleet I commanded in the West Indies. . . .'[13]

It was absurd that the two admirals should not meet. Sir George did his best (writing on October 8th), to persuade Arbuthnot to join him at New York for a conference with Clinton, leaving Graves to watch de Ternay. As an olive branch he offered, in a private letter by the same packet, a lieutenant's vacancy to be at Arbuthnot's disposal. The reply, eight days later, was ungracious. 'My orders from the Board of Admiralty are positive, to attend in person the movements of the French squadron. . . . I have not lately heard from Sir Henry Clinton of any particular object to render my presence as Commissioner necessary at New York and therefore can not have any pretence for diverting from the execution of these orders. . . .'

The implication that only a message from Clinton could bring him to New York was bad enough, but Arbuthnot concluded on a note of defiance. 'Your partial Interference in the Conduct of the American War is certainly unaccountable upon principals of reason and precedents of service. . . .'[14]

Sir George was always polite. He replied at once. 'I am honoured with your letter of the 16th Instant and am sorry that my Conduct has given you Offence. None was intended on my part. Every respect due to you as an Officer and a Gentleman, my Inclination as well as my Duty led me to pay you in the strictest sense. If any designing men, by their insinuations, have led you to deviate from that good sense and politeness which Mr Arbuthnot was always known to have, I am sorry for it, and am convinced in your cooler moments, when you have reflected upon some of the paragraphs in your letter, you will wish they had been couch'd in more friendly terms. It was not Inclination or Choice that brought me to America. It was the Duty I owed my King and Country. I had flattered myself it would have met with your Approbation. I am sorry it has not. . . .'

But he was definitely nettled. 'Your anger at my partial interference (as you term it), with the American War not a little surprises me. I came to Interfere in the American War, to Command by Sea in it, and to do my best Endeavours towards the putting an End thereto. I know the Dignity of my own Rank, and the power invested in me by the Commission I bear intitled me to take the supreme Command, which I ever shall do on every Station where His Majesty's and the Public Service may make it necessary for me to go, unless I meet a Superior Officer, in which Case it will be my Duty to Obey his Orders.'[15]

He ended with some scathing comments on the way Arbuthnot was misusing his squadron, a severe reprimand for sending the *Raisonable* home without his superior's knowledge, 'unprecedented in the annals of the British navy', and some caustic observations on the way the coast had been allowed to swarm with privateers, 'not one single frigate from Charlestown bar to Sandy Hook'. The import of his message was clear. In not one instance had he the least intention of showing disrespect or giving offence. But the public interest must come before the susceptibilities of Vice-Admiral Arbuthnot.

A week later he sent copies of all their correspondence to the Admiralty. 'That I have been extremely tender in issuing orders to Vice Admiral Arbuthnot and have been attentive towards paying him every respect due to his rank, the Inclosed Letters I am sure will convince their Lordships. . . . I am assham'd to mention what appears to me the real cause and from whence Mr. Arbuthnot's Chagrene proceeds, but the Proofs are so plain, that Prize Money is the Occasion, that I am under the necessity to transmit them.' He also wrote by the same packet, but more succinctly, to Jackson. 'His proud spirit must submit. When I am convinced I am in the right on a point of discipline I will give way to no man.'[16]

Perhaps Arbuthnot got wind that Sir George was sending their correspondence home, for in his next letter (November 2nd) he made a recognizable attempt to be conciliatory. 'Be assured, Sir, that no designing men have interfered to influence my sentiments to your measures; they arise only from their novelty; I have referred their discussion to those under whose determination they must fall. I confess I am not qualified to decide as to the powers of a Superior Officer under your situation having quitted his Station by his own authority and endeavoured to supercede an Admiralty Commission, and in a great measure obstructing the execution of the powers the King had vested in me. For no precedent of the kind has ever occurred in the course of my service. I trust you will impute my conduct, as I have said, to the novelty of your measures, and arising from no disrespect to your rank.'

But it was beyond him to be conciliatory for long. His last paragraph recovered the old tart flavour. 'The four ships under the command of Commodore Drake arrived in want of every necessary store, and sickly;

and was so far from being of use that they detained me in port to put them in order—which indeed I judged was your principal object in sending them here.'[17]

So the correspondence ended. Arbuthnot and his secretary are not sympathetic characters. Captain Young, reporting confidentially to Middleton, is startingly outspoken about them. When the papers reached London the verdict went in favour of Sir George. His Majesty digested them and came out with the final word. 'Sir George Rodney's conduct seems, as usual, praiseworthy. I am sorry Vice Admiral Arbuthnot has lost his temper; the insinuation that prize-money has occasioned it seems founded.'[18]

To return to the main theme. By the second week in October Sir George had decided that de Guichen's ships would not be coming after all. But he remained convinced that eight of the line under de Monteil would have been detached to North America but for the unlucky chance meeting with 'that villain of a Bermudian' that spoke the Centaur as the squadron was on its way north, and then passed the news to the enemy. 'What a situation would Arbuthnot have been in,' he commented feelingly, 'had that squadron joined Ternay and I not have come.'[19]

So there was no battle in American waters that year. The winter closed in early with unusual severity, and Sir George, compelled by his health to live on shore, was soon complaining bitterly about the climate, and about the Army's failure to fight the war as he thought it should be fought. 'Slackness inconceivable in every branch of it,' was his considered opinion, 'Quartermasters and their deputies ad infinitum; barrack-masters and their deputies ad infinitum; Commisaries and their deputies ad infinitum; all of which make princely Fortunes and laugh in their sleeves at the General who permits it.'[20] Clinton's way was not Sir George's. He actually allowed his officers to perform in amateur theatricals! Nothing could induce Sir George to attend any of the performances. In his opinion the craggy-featured American general, until recently in command at West Point, would do more towards suppressing the rebellion than all the British generals put together. Clinton would have to pursue the war much more briskly if Sir George was to come again next year, and he had told him so.

Time was found during these weeks at New York to try Captain Bateman for his conduct on April 17th, an unpleasant business as the wretched man insulted his judges after receiving sentence. And Sir George at last overcame any scruples he may have had about promoting John

Rodney. By a few strokes of the pen he advanced him from lieutenant to post-captain at the age of fifteen and a half.

Making every allowance possible for an indulgent parent, it was a preposterous thing to do. The Age of Privilege permitted a commander-in-chief to drive a coach and six through most regulations, but young John had been at sea for less than a year. He had commanded a gun during the Moonlight Battle; he had witnessed the action of April 17th from a frigate; and he had risen from sixth to first lieutenant in the *Sandwich*. He was also a strapping lad of nearly six foot and already taller than his father. This appears to be the extent of his qualifications, apart from his being the son of the Commander-in-Chief. On October 4th Pagett made out the young man's commission as Master and Commander of the *Pacahunta* (sloop), and only ten days later he was posted to the *Fowey* (24), the guardship at Sandy Hook.[21] Contemporary comment is silent about all this. The outcome, however, was not entirely satisfactory.

The early onset of an exceptionally hard winter came as a most unpleasant surprise. By November 12th America had become 'this confoundedly cold country which pinches me so much that I never desire to see it again. Even now that I am writing,' so he informed Jackson, 'the pen freezes in my hand, and tis with no small pleasure that I am about to leave the command to Arbuthnot.'[22]

Nevertheless he had good reason to be satisfied with his New York visit. Whether or not his coming really averted that of de Monteil's eight battleships is an open question, but certain other gains, although some of them fortuitous, are beyond dispute. The men's health responded amazingly to the change of climate and to the fresh meat and the spruce beer they were able to get. Dr Blane, who managed to find a New York printer for his latest medical tract,* went so far as to say that health reasons alone justified going to North America. Then there was the taking of more than a dozen privateers, thanks to Sir George's measures. But the greatest benefit of all was that the squadron missed the appalling hurricane that swept the West Indies in October. Hotham's ships at St Lucia took the full blast. Of his smaller ships three foundered and three were wrecked.† Further to the westward the *Thunderer* (74) went down at sea with Commodore Walsingham and all her ship's company, and the *Stirling Castle*, still commanded by Carkett, was wrecked with only a handful of survivors on the Silver

---

* *An address to the Officers serving in H.M. Ships of War in the West Indies and America.*
† *Andromeda, Blanche* and *Chameleon* foundered. The *Laurel* was wrecked on Martinique, the *Deal Castle* on Porto Rico, and the *Beaver's Prize* on the back of St Lucia.

Keys. Three of Hotham's seventy-fours, the *Ajax*, *Egmont*, and *Montagu*, with the *Amazon* (32), were driven out to sea, dismasted, and escaped destruction by the narrowest of margins. 'How thankful we should be to Providence,' commented Commissioner Laforey at Antigua, 'that our fleet under Sir George Rodney were out of these seas.'[23]

Sir George was still unaware of his narrow escape but the hurricane danger was now past, the wind was fair, and the Caribbean, with its sunshine and its opportunities, was awaiting him. For some days the clerks in the Admiral's office had been busy. There would be a great exodus of shipping when the Admiral sailed, including the trade for home escorted by the *Yarmouth*, the trade and some troops for the Carolinas escorted by three frigates, and the ten battleships and seven smaller vessels for the Leeward Islands.* 'God bless you,' wrote Sir George to Clinton on the 13th, 'and send me from this cold country and from such men as Arbuthnot.' On the 16th they were all under way. There were no farewells from Arbuthnot, but Sir Henry Clinton wrote a letter after they had sailed.

'20 of November.

'*Dear Sir*,

'I understand from a certain signal that tis possible you may drop down at dusk to Staten Island this day. Should that happen tis probable I may not have it in my power once more to take you by the hand before you go, and thank you for *all* your goodness to us. I did intend to have paid my respects to you on board the *Sandwich*. By day the wind says No: by night I am told my boat is too small. If you leave us without my seeing you I heartily wish you health, happyness, and if possible still more Honour. I intreat that we may correspond and if practicable meet by 1st June at furthest, should you be appointed C. in C. here as well as West Indies.— for which God grant. Until you can come yourself let Hotham act for you. With every wish for your success in all you undertake, Believe me, Dear Sir,

'*Your Excellency's most faithfull,*
affectionate,
humble servant,
'*H. CLINTON.*'[24]

---

* With Sir George were the *Sandwich* (90), *Alcide, Centaur, Resolution, Russell, Shrewsbury, Terrible, Torbay* and *Triumph*, all seventy-fours, and *Intrepid* (64); also three 28-gun frigates the *Boreas, Cyclops* and *Triton*, and the smaller *Pacahunta, Shark, St Lucia*, and *Lizard*.

Chapter 21

St Eustatius

(December 1780–July 1781)

'. . . a fine nest of villains you have destroyed. I believe
a great many in England are concerned & equally
distressed with the Dutch at its being taken.'
(Lady Rodney to her husband, April 27, 1781.)[1]

TWENTY-FOUR hours out from Sandy Hook a violent gale
scattered Sir George's ships. The *Sandwich* reached Barbados
on December 6th after a stormy passage of twenty-one days.
All her consorts reported damage. The *Boreas*, incapably
commanded by John Rodney, put into Antigua. The *Shark* was missing.

The campaigning season could hardly have opened less promisingly
but worse was to come. Beyond reports of a violent gale at St Kitt's on
October 10th, no word had reached New York of the great hurricane that
had swept the Leeward Islands. Now, before their horrified eyes, was the
evidence—Carlisle Bay and Bridgetown almost unrecognizable; the storehouses not merely unroofed and empty but most of them not even standing.
It was the same at St Lucia. Of Hotham's ships, the *Ajax* and *Montagu*
were *hors de combat*, the fate of the *Egmont* was uncertain, and four
frigates and some smaller vessels had been lost. Until more masts and
stores arrived little could be done for any of the ships.

But waiting at Barbados were the packets from England with promises of
reinforcements. Seven of the line and a great convoy of stores might be
expected soon, with a new second in command. On this important appointment Lord Sandwich was disarmingly frank. 'It has been difficult, very
difficult,' he wrote, 'to find out proper flag-officers to serve under you.
Some are rendered unfit from their factious connections, others from
infirmity or insufficiency, and we have at last been obliged to make a

356

promotion to do the thing properly. Sir Samuel Hood is to have his flag and to bring out the next convoy to you.'[2]

This unexpected, and not wholly welcome, development will be discussed later. The First Lord continued with his news. Hyde Parker was back in England, grumbling a great deal and only with difficulty persuaded from opening a pamphlet war against his former chief. More agreeable was the intimation that his correspondent had been chosen as member for Westminster, 'without expense and with the almost unanimous concurrance of the most opulent city in the world'. Sir George would have preferred Hampshire: 'my partiality for my own County is, I trust, pardonable', he confided to Henny;[3] but Westminster it had to be as the Government hoped his glory might lessen the popularity of Charles James Fox.[4] There were family letters in plenty. Henny was so improved in her whist that she was confident she could play with Sir George when he came home 'without fear of being scolded'; the girls had been bathing at Brighthelmstone with the faithful Loup waiting outside their bathing-machine; and Jenny desired to learn the harpsichord.[5] And there were several communications in Mackreth's bold, upright handwriting, lauding the national hero to the skies but always concluding with a pointed reference to payments on the annuity.[6]

Meanwhile, opportunity beckoned, for the French, with only four of the line, were even weaker than the British. General Vaughan was on fire to embark his troops and pick up an island cheaply. Sir George agreed, and St Vincent was selected. Encouraging reports described it as devastated by the late hurricane, the fortifications ruinous, and the defenders few and sickly.

On December 9th Sir George was at Gros Islet Bay to embark the troops. For twenty-four hours all was bustle and anticipation. Then, to quote Captain Young, writing to Middleton, 'an unsteady fit seized the admiral and the whole was put a stop to. . . .' The hold-up lasted forty-eight hours. 'On the 12th we were found in a different mood,' Young continues, 'and the expedition was reassumed. . . .'[7] But by then it was too late. The delay at St Lucia had enabled the local French to warn their compatriots, and de Bouillé had time to supply the threatened island with stores and powder. The expedition sailed on the 14th and the troops landed unopposed two days later. Contrary to reports there was no hurricane damage and the mountain citadel, as Sir George was able to see for himself, was not only intact but full of French troops. General Vaughan led his men up to it, found no weakness anywhere, so led them down to the beach again. The soldiers re-embarked and the expedition was over.

What is to be made of this? Young is quite explicit that his Admiral's 'unsteady fit' caused the fatal delay, and one notices a repetition of the disparaging theme adopted in his report on the Moonlight Battle, when Sir George's 'natural irresolution' was only stiffened by the fortunate presence of his captain. Despite his unendearing propensity to report on his superiors (and Sir George was not his only target—Graves, Hyde Parker and Arbuthnot were also fair game) Young was a capable officer. Sir George thought highly of him. But his reports are too one-sided to command complete confidence. He is much too ready to parade his own virtues and indispensability. In a letter of September 22, 1780, he assures Middleton 'I have discharged the duty of a son to the admiral as well as that of his captain!'[8] Where, one wonders, were those other members of Sir George's intimate circle, Dr Blane his personal physician and Pagett his secretary for twenty years? But Young must be allowed to run on a little longer in his own peculiar way. 'I assure you I exert myself to the utmost of my power to keep our matters in order: at times they will get a little *outrée*, but in this I am obliged to you great men at home who have so poisoned my admiral that he really, and *ipso facto* thinks and believes himself to be the very man you have represented him. God help us, how much mistaken you and he are.'

Rightly or wrongly Sir George was no hero to his captain. But was this recently promoted officer really so important, and can his chief have been quite so dependent on him? There are refreshing indications that he was not, and that it was possible for Young to go too far. 'My captain has presumed to think for me instead of obeying', Sir George thundered on a later occasion. 'I have desired him never to do so again.'[9] This echo from a moment of irritation may help to correct the picture. And to close the subject of the failure before St Vincent, one would be more convinced of the naval Commander-in-Chief's responsibility for the delay if General Vaughan had made any allusion to it in his official report. But he does not.[10]

So ended a year of outstanding achievement, although Captain Young would deny Sir George most of the credit. If the island of St Vincent was a reverse, it is a small item in the balance sheet against the Moonlight Battle, Gibraltar, and the defence of the Leeward Islands, not to mention the possible saving of America. 1780 was, beyond dispute, Rodney's year, and such a year as Britain had not seen for a very long time.

January found the British in the Leeward Islands impatient for the arrival of Sir Samuel Hood, and on the 7th he reached Barbados. Flying his flag in the 90-gun *Barfleur* he brought with him the *Gibraltar* (80), *Invincible* (74), *Princessa* (70), *Panther* (50), *Sybil* (28), and *Swallow* (sloop).* He had pressed on ahead of his great convoy which arrived a week later. The reinforcements could not have been more welcome: but at the new second-in-command one pauses to wonder.

Hood at this time was far from having acquired the great reputation which he has since enjoyed. He had settled down as Commissioner at Portsmouth, and in the ordinary way could hardly have expected further promotion or another sea appointment. But he had long desired to return to active service and it is reasonable to suppose that the First Lord brought him forward because, as Sir George's old friend of thirty-five years' standing, he thought the appointment would be acceptable to both.

Hood, it will be remembered, had been with Rodney in the *Sheerness* and *Ludlow Castle*, and had commanded the *Vestal* at Havre in 1759. But when offered the second post under his old chief he acted very curiously. On the Saturday he wrote begging to refuse the appointment. On the following Monday he wrote again hoping he was not too late to change his mind.[11] Nor did Sir George show much enthusiasm. In a rather bleak acknowledgement he thanked the First Lord for sending him 'so good a man';[12] but although he wrote charmingly to Hood himself: 'I know of no one whatever that I should have wished in preference to my Old Friend Sir Samuel Hood,'[13] in private he is reported to have grumbled: 'They might as well send me an old apple-woman.'[14] Even at this early stage, both sides may have had reservations. Sir George was known to be exacting, while Hood may already have acquired a reputation for carping and censorious criticism. 'I wish you joy of Sir Samuel Hood', commiserated Keppel, on hearing of the appointment. 'It is impossible for me to say more than that. . . .'[15]

However, with his arrival everything seemed favourable for some great enterprise, and only thirteen days after his convoy dropped anchor at Barbados the opportunity presented itself. On January 27th the *Childers* (sloop) arrived hot-foot from England with the news that Great Britain had declared war against the States of Holland. Sir George was to consult with Major-General Vaughan upon the best means of attacking and subduing the possessions of the States General and the United Provinces, within his command; the islands of St Eustatius and St Martin were

---

* The *Gibraltar* (ex-*Fenix*), and *Princessa*, were two prizes from the Moonlight Battle. Hood's convoy of 120 sail included 9 storeships and 19 navy victuallers.

recommended as the first objects of attack.[16] Here was good fortune indeed. The Dutch in the West Indies could not know of the new situation for some time; and at least one of their possessions was of outstanding wealth and importance.

It is difficult to set down briefly all that might be said about St Eustatius. A rocky islet some ten miles or so to the north-west of St Kitt's and less than six miles long, it had been turned to the best possible use by the commercially-minded Dutch. Not for them the endless labours of the plantation, in competition with the larger British and French islands. There were a few sugar plantations it is true, but what made St Eustatius famous—or infamous—were the great stone warehouses, more than a mile of them along the beach, crammed with all the produce, raw and manu-factured, of the Old World and the New. For here the Dutch had set up a free-port which, under the stimulus of the American war, had developed into the great international market of the Caribbean. In its warehouses, or overflowing from them on to the beaches, were the bales of American cotton and tobacco which might still, in spite of the war, be traded to Europe and the mother country; American salt cod, bacon and maize, without which the West Indian planter could not feed his slaves; furs, lumber, and boxes of the best snuff. Sugar and rum, which might no longer reach the American market direct, reached it through the ware-houses of St Eustatius, and in reverse, manufactured goods from Europe could pass through the Dutch warehouses and so to any purchaser, what-ever his nationality. During 1780 the number of ships that officially entered the port was 3,217.[17] St Eustatius was a unique convenience for all who wished to evade the many tiresome restrictions imposed by warring nations on international trade.

Sir George regarded the island with particular loathing. Official opinion at home reckoned that two-thirds of the provisions sent out from England and Ireland under convoy were immediately shipped off to St Eustatius, whence they found their way to Martinique, and that without them the French could hardly keep their ships in a condition for sea.[18] That the Dutch should assist the King's enemies was bad enough, but he had good reason to believe that in their nefarious commerce they had the active co-operation of a great many British merchants, which was intolerable. For not only were provisions reaching the enemy in this way. Naval stores were too, and what was even worse, arms and ammunition. Such was the greed for gain that merchantmen would slip away from British convoys if they could, and putting profit before patriotism, proceed direct to the

Dutch roadstead where such tempting prices could be obtained.* On the subject of St Eustatius Sir George could scarcely contain himself. The Dutch were villains, the English merchants were traitors, and the island itself was a 'nest of vipers'[19] that preyed upon the vitals of Great Britain. He was half persuaded that but for its un-neutral commerce the American war would have long since ended.

And now the 'nest of vipers' was delivered into his hands. There would be no repetition of the St Vincent fiasco. The blow would be delivered 'like a clap of Thunder', swiftly, suddenly and with overwhelming strength. At the British islands an embargo was laid so successfully that the watchful de Bouillé, who guessed something must be in the wind, suspected an attempt to recover Grenada and hurried thither with 500 men. Every ship was to take part, including the bombs. Hood, with a strong force,† was to hover between Montserrat and Nevis until the moment to strike; Rear-Admiral Drake, with the six least seaworthy ships and two frigates, was to blockade the French in Fort Royal; the Admiral and General would sail from St Lucia with the main body as soon as the final preparations were complete. On the 29th the *Sandwich* arrived at Gros Islet Bay. On the 30th the Admiral and the General sailed with the main body‡ passing up the west side of Martinique to alarm St Pierre and Fort Royal. On February 2nd Hood sent word that there were 150 sail in the roadstead of St Eustatius and not 100 regular troops on the island. On the same day Sir George, making slow progress with his heavy sailing bombs, directed his second-in-command to proceed round the south side of the island and be in the roadstead 'before daylight tomorrow'.[20]

No shadow of presentiment or foreboding clouded the mind of trader or merchant when, on Saturday February 3rd, the great island mart of the Caribbean awoke to a new day. A Dutch frigate had just arrived from Europe with news that Holland was unlikely to become involved in hostilities. Reassured on this point, Dutch, French, English and Americans had turned again to their absorbing concerns. The warehouses were crammed, the beaches piled high with goods. A convoy of thirty ships had sailed for Europe thirty-six hours earlier but nearly 150 vessels still crowded the anchorage. When the British were sighted the general belief was that they had come to seize all French and American shipping.[21]

The island was at dinner (about 3 p.m.), when Sir George's fleet

---

* Twelve ships from Hood's convoy did this and were later found at St Eustatius.
† *Barfleur* (90), *Gibraltar* (80), *Alfred* (74), *Invincible* (74), *Monarch* (74), *Panther* (50).
‡ *Sandwich* (90), *Terrible* (74), *Torbay* (74), *Shrewsbury* (74), *Resolution* (74), *Belliqueux* (74), *Princessa* (70), *Prince William* (64), *Convert* (32), two fireships and two bombs.

dropped anchor. Powerful battleships took up their positions against the neglected fortifications, and in no more time than it took to send a boat ashore, the Governor found himself faced with a peremptory summons. Hardly a shot was fired. Only the *Gibraltar* and *Prince William* turned their guns for a few moments, and without orders, on an unfortunate Dutch frigate.* On shore 2,000 stout-hearted Americans begged to assist in the island's defences, but as the Governor had no thought of fighting they took to the hills.[23] Within an hour St Eustatius was in British hands, a small squadron was away after the convoy, and another to take possession of the smaller islands of St Martin and Saba. Meanwhile, in the roadstead, the rest of the fleet proceeded to secure nearly 150 prizes, many of them richly laden.

To the British commanders it was the occasion of a lifetime. 'The capture is beyond conception', Sir George informed Lord Sandwich on February 7th. To Henny on the same day it was 'the greatest blow . . . that Holland and America ever received'; to Lord Hillsborough 'a sudden clap of Thunder which had deprived them of their senses'; and again to Henny a few days later he exulted that 'there never was a more important stroke made against any state whatsoever'.[24] Clearly the duty of the two commanders called for their utmost vigilance to prevent such wealth being recovered by the enemy or reclaimed by the traitors. Its effective disposal demanded their unremitting attention and supervision. These considerations soon became almost an obsession. For the next three months all operations were affected by the importance of safeguarding St Eustatius and its immense treasure.

Sir Samuel Hood was the first to suffer (or so he complained) by this excessive concern. Within twenty-four hours of the capture Sir George had promised him the command of an expedition against Curaçao. 'You shall have five ships of the line,' he had said, 'and some frigates', and General Vaughan had seemed equally ready for the adventure. But Admiral and General soon lost all interest in Curaçao. Hood, bitterly disappointed, spoke his mind to the General who (he said) turned away in confusion. A few days later came a report (false as it turned out) that the Brest fleet was on its way to the West Indies, and this became Sir George's official reason for not attacking Curaçao although, according to the disgruntled Hood, the negative decision was made some time before the false report

---

* This was indiscipline. Nearly fifty years later an officer from the *Sandwich* remembered vividly a majestic figure in the red ribbon of the Bath walking the deck in anger and sending to put their captains under arrest.[22]

arrived. 'The Lares of St Eustatius', he commented, with questionable scholarship but unmistakable meaning, 'were so bewitching as not to be withstood by flesh and blood.'*

Whatever the enchantment, it must be conceded that St Eustatius presented a very complex problem. There were the warehouses, overflowing with goods, the anchorage, crowded with shipping, including the convoy so promptly hauled back; and besides all this a succession of vessels, mostly American which, deceived by the Dutch colours which Sir George kept flying, continued to sail unsuspectingly into the anchorage for weeks afterwards. All these had to be disposed of without delay, and if possible before a French fleet arrived from Europe. Finally, measures must be taken to ensure that the 'nest of vipers' could never again be a source of aid and comfort to the enemy.

Two days after the capture, Admiral and General signed a formal agreement that all vessels, merchandise, and public stores taken at the surrender of St Eustatius and its dependencies should be distributed according to the King's pleasure.[25] This was to bring everything into one account for the purpose of appraisal and distribution, otherwise the government might, according to custom, give the property captured on land to the Army and that seized afloat to the fleet. At a meeting of senior officers, it was decided to set up a commission with the two services equally represented. Sir George requested Hood to choose the naval representatives, and after some hours' deliberation Captain Young of the *Sandwich*, three other captains, Pagett, and Hood's own secretary, were selected. Hood thought it a 'solid, sensible and judicious arrangement'. The agent for the prisoners of war at St Kitt's, Mr Arietas Akers, was then suggested as the man best qualified to manage the sales, but there were objections. Young produced evidence that Akers had claims of some £40,000 to £50,000 on various people at St Eustatius, while Sir George took Hood aside to emphasize how very untrustworthy he was. So all agreed that he should have nothing to do with the business.[26]

This was to be the general policy:[27]

(*a*) All perishable goods to be disposed of without delay.

* Hood makes this damaging allegation in a letter to George Jackson, 'Barbados, 24 June 1781' (*Letters of Sir Samuel Hood*, N.R.S.) and made much the same complaint to Middleton on the same day (*Letters of Lord Barham*, N.R.S. Vol. 1). As Sir George has never had the chance to refute it, it might be pleaded on his behalf that he needed a few days to assess the situation before sending a powerful squadron 600 miles to leeward. St Eustatius fell on the 3rd. The false report, which settled the matter anyway, was received only eight days later, on the 11th.

(*b*) European goods found in Dutch and French stores and of use in the British islands, to be disposed of on the spot.

(*c*) All suspected British property to be locked up to await His Majesty's pleasure.

(*d*) American produce to be loaded into the shipping available and sent to England.

(*e*) All naval and military stores to be removed from the island, the naval stores going to St John's dockyard, Antigua.

(*f*) A faithful account of all the monies delivered in by the inhabitants to be counted, sealed up, marked etc., to await His Majesty's pleasure.

(*g*) French subjects, with their household goods, free to depart.

(*h*) Dutch merchants to be sent to England.

(*i*) Dutch planters to remain in peaceable possession of their estates.

Much of this was preposterously unrealistic. With a bench of learned judges to decide questions of ownership, a team of independent assessors

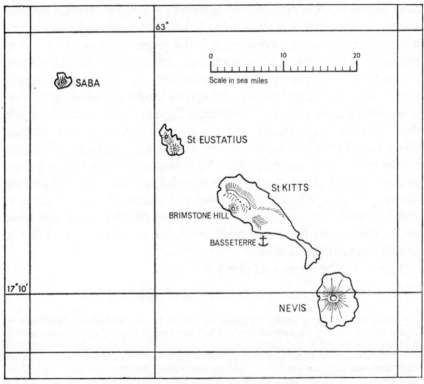

St Eustatius and St Kitt's (Admiralty Chart 2600)

and valuers, some capable accountants, and an efficient police force, the job *might* have been done. But as things were it is hardly surprising that the two commanders, unaided except for their committee and two secretaries, soon found themselves in deep water. In a matter of hours British merchants came flocking from neighbouring St Kitt's to claim property stored (for safety they said) on St Eustatius. Then came the false intelligence of the French fleet which necessitated the departure of Hood to cruise to windward of Martinique; and Sir George was left with the General, the committee, and the frenzied men of commerce.

For the next five weeks Hood's ships ploughed the seas with never a sight of a French topsail to break the monotony. Very different was the atmosphere at St Eustatius where his superior, deaf to prayers, threats, or expostulations, was making a series of sensational discoveries about the sort of trade that had been carried on from the island. The merchants, he was outraged to discover, had succoured de Guichen's battered fleet after the action of April 17th. Two heavily laden vessels, with cordage, naval stores and carpenters, joined it under Barbuda, without which several of the French battleships (Sir George believed as many as eight) would have had to run down to St Domingo. And after the October hurricane they had refused, although their warehouses were full, to supply the dockyard at Antigua with much-needed cordage.[28]

As the hectic weeks passed, Sir George's letters reiterate, on a rising note of indignation, his complaints against the commercial Dutch, and with even greater emphasis his accusations against 'the English burghers'. These gentlemen enjoyed an ambiguous position at St Eustatius. Any foreigner with a residence qualification of eighteen months might become a burgher and enjoy various commercial advantages. Many of the English merchants had greatly improved their trade by so doing, and to Sir George they were all traitors. For what conceivable purpose, he asked, could they have any reason for carrying on business on a Dutch island, except to trade with England's enemies? He could prove they were doing so from their books. The American rebellion, of this he was now positive, had long been crushed and the French islands starved into surrender, but for their pernicious activities.

To all of this the English merchants could only repeat that if their goods were warehoused on St Eustatius it was because its neutrality had afforded greater security than any of the British islands, an answer which did nothing to placate Sir George. Tempers rose as he remained adamant. The merchants' insistence that part of the St Eustatius property was quite legitimately theirs he dismissed as 'impudence', whereupon some of them from St Kitt's threatened the two commanders with arrest should either set foot on shore. They sent Sir George a long memorial drawn up by the Solicitor of St Kitt's but the Admiral, supported in his stand by Mr Georges, the Chief Justice of the island, returned a very short answer. All such documents, he informed them with sailorly directness, were put into a certain place called a quarter-gallery, as he could not afford time to peruse impertinent papers that presumed to teach him his duty.[29] So all through February and March the auctioneer's hammer rose and fell, disposing of the European and perishable goods at knock-down prices, while the West Indian produce was loaded into ships for England, and the naval stores went off to Antigua. As for the suspected English property, 'locked up to await His Majesty's pleasure', Sir George now meditated more drastic measures. He would persuade the General to agree to set the original Commission aside, so that the English traitors could be treated as they deserved.

- There is more here than the man of action, impatient of legal quibbles, and justly incensed against treachery and war-profiteering. Sir George was by this time a very sick man, and aware that his time might be short. Besides his old enemy the gout he was now suffering from a complaint so serious and so painful as to persuade him that he must soon return home. To Lord Sandwich he wrote in this sense on March 7th, and to Hood (confidentially) a week later.[30] The complaint, a severe stricture, sometimes yielding to treatment and sometimes not, coming as it did on top of his other disabilities, may help to explain the violence of some of his letters at this time. One in particular, written to his son George, is painfully revealing. He had just learnt that Lord Sandwich had, in spite of all his warnings, given another command to the detested Hyde Parker. At once all his old grievances against the First Lord boiled over in a furious tirade.

'What can I think of that man who, after receiving the most confidential letters from me as one of H.M. ministers, and where I had pointed out to him a Man who ought to have forfeited his Head for his treasonable behaviour in the battle of 17 April, and that I was ready to bring the charge, has since given that man the command at Plymouth, tho' he was well assured that Ministry had not a more bitter or more inveterate enemy. Can I trust that man with my Honour, or put the least Confidence in him? Tis impossible. I know him, and tho' I will ever be a most strenuous supporter of the present Ministry, if Lord S . . . h provokes me I will show to the World, and prove it too, that during his whole administration of Naval affairs he has been totally ignorant of the Duty of a First Lord of the Admiralty. . . .'[31]

There is much more in the same vein. It is the writing of a man tormented almost beyond endurance. We have Hood's word that Sir George's health varied. Had it not been so he could hardly have carried on. But woe betide any man—and most of all a merchant of St Eustatius—who crossed the Admiral when his maladies were upon him.

By the middle of March the loading of the West Indian and American produce was nearly finished. The convoy would be immensely valuable, and as sailing time approached its safety became a new preoccupation for Sir George. All he could spare for escort were the worn-out *Vengeance* (74), the *Alcmene* (32) also in poor condition, and the two Dutch men-of-war taken at St Eustatius.* Hotham would be in command. The Admiralty had been warned to expect it, and informed of its route, but Sir George was still uneasy. Too many people had been inquisitive about the sailing date, and the battleships in Fort Royal could make short work of the escort. So at the last moment he directed Hood to leave his weary beat to windward of Martinique and come round to blockade Fort Royal itself; and as soon as he was there the convoy sailed. With it went the Chief Justice of St Kitt's (purely out of friendship according to Sir George) to expose the treasonable activities of the English merchants, and taking with him him their ledgers and letter-books, for this purpose; and also, as prisoners, the two agents of the Continental Congress at St Eustatius, whose papers were expected to incriminate many more. In view of almost certain trouble from the business community Sir George requested George Jackson at the Admiralty to secure the services of the best Counsel available, and by the same packet sent word to his daughter Jenny that he would now be able to treat her 'with the best harpsichord money can purchase'.[32]

It seemed probable that he would. By the end of February the sale of a mere fourteen vessels and their cargoes had realized £100,529 10s 4¾d, and as the sales went on a prodigious quantity of money began to accumulate on board the *Sandwich*.[33] Meanwhile an unexampled profusion of naval stores were pouring into the dockyard at Antigua, to the consternation of Commissioner Laforey who found his storehouses overflowing and the

---

* These two ships of 62 and 38 guns, were both named *Mars* by the Dutch. Sir George renamed the larger ship *Prince Edward*.

avenues between them cluttered up, not all the material (or so he said) being suitable for His Majesty's ships. In vain he protested. Sir George, who had a pretty shrewd idea that the objections stemmed less from the unsuitability of the St Eustatius material than from the fact that it deprived the Commissioner and store-keepers of the 5 per cent they enjoyed if they bought at a higher price from the merchants, offered all the roofs, doors, and windows from the warehouses of St Eustatius lower town for extra storage; and with this the Commissioner had to profess himself content.[34]

Meanwhile Hood, struggling with the problems of maintaining a large squadron in the fluky conditions off Fort Royal, was becoming increasingly restive. He disliked his situation intensely. The substance of his complaint was that his ships were foul and leaky, that the light airs and currents under the land made it hard to keep as close in as he could wish, and that small French vessels could come and go without much difficulty under cover of darkness. Moreover, the French batteries made inshore work hazardous. To windward, he argued, was where he should be for intercepting any French reinforcements. He bombarded his superior with requests that he might go back to his former station, and his letters home at this time are full of complaints that Sir George would not let him.

But Sir George, with considerably more experience of the bay at Fort Royal than Hood, refused to be convinced that the inshore station was as difficult as his subordinate made out. The far-flung frigate screen to windward had not enabled him to intercept de Blénac in 1762, or de Solano in 1780. He was sure that with lookout frigates at the northern and southern ends of Martinique, Hood off Fort Royal could not fail to bring to action any enemy arriving from Europe. Furthermore if any ship needed stores, provisions, or water, Gros Islet Bay was handy and Hood had the opportunity (which, in Sir George's later opinion, he 'grossly neglected')[35] of sending them there. In any case, he may have argued, the sales were nearly finished, and soon he would be on the spot himself.

But Hood had more on his mind than the problems of his squadron. He was vexed and apprehensive at what was going on at St Eustatius. In mid-March he learnt that the original Commission had been replaced by another signed by Sir George and the General, empowering the untrustworthy Akers of all people to manage the sales. Captain Young, a member of the new Commission, was his informant. On behalf of all his officers Hood wrote back to protest. Young, in his reply, had the effontery to describe Hood's letter as 'extraordinary', and desired him to scratch his own (Young's) name from the original Commission, which Hood refused to do. Hood followed this up (April 1st) with a strong letter to Sir George, condemning Young for departing from the original agreement and deploring the appointment of Akers. He also professed himself 'much vexed and chagrined', as well he might be, at not being consulted. It does not appear that he received an answer.

He wrote again on the 9th, again without receiving an answer, and on the 28th he wrote for the third time, in rather stronger terms. 'From the friendship that has subsisted between us for so many years without the smallest interruption,' he began, 'I very much flattered myself you would have done me the honour to have been clear and explicit respecting the business at St Eustatius. . . .' Cooler and more detached than his chief he ventured no opinion on the treachery of the merchants or the island's part in sustaining the American rebellion, but clearly he foresaw trouble. 'The beaten path is allways the safest,' he went on, 'and when that is followed, supposing any error to have been committed by a stretch of power, it may find an excuse.' For Hood 'the beaten path' was the original Commission agreed on by all the officers. The other was 'no more than Power of Agency, and I very much fear,' he concluded ominously, 'it can not, upon any grounds of right and justice, be supported, and that it will bring both you and the General into more difficulty than you may be aware of.'[36]

Again Sir George seems to have made no reply. One can only recall how, almost exactly ten years before, and in a similar mood of reckless haste, he had put himself into the power of Lowther, Mackreth and Co. At St Eustatius it was not the vast wealth that clouded his judgement. Ill-health certainly played its part, but if his many letters are any guide, his resolve to take the law into his own hands sprang from his unshakable belief that the English merchants were traitors, and that unless he acted they would escape scot free. So all their goods must be sold too. '*Delenda est Carthago*', he wrote. 'What terms did Perjury—Treason—Rebels—Traytors deserve? None. And none they had.'[37]

But now events were to crowd so thick and fast as to drown the clamour of the merchants. The first was the sudden disappearance from the scene of that controversial officer Captain Walter Young. He had been ill for some time. On April 27th Dr Blane informed Sir George that there was little hope of his recovery, and on May 2nd he died. There is a note among Middleton's papers. 'The fleet has experienced a loss in Captain Young's death, for I believe there is not another man breathing, so calculated to control and guide to fame a character that Nature never intended could be either a hero or a man of business.'[38] The epitaph might have been written by Young himself. But whatever one may think of the Captain and his confidential reports he was a brave and capable officer, who won much glory on April 17th. For this at least he deserves to be remembered.

A little after noon, the day after Young died, a battle-damaged seventy-four from Hood's squadron dropped anchor in the roadstead of St Eustatius. Her pumps were working continuously to keep her afloat. She brought word that a French fleet had arrived in the Leeward Islands.

There had never been any doubt that sooner or later the French would come, but for once there had been no sloop or frigate flying ahead with warning of their approach. At 9 a.m. on April 28th, the day he wrote his candid letter to Sir George, the British second-in-command received word that two hours earlier the *Amazon*, cruising off Pt Salines, had sighted nineteen of the line and a large convoy to windward. With seventeen of the line he at once stood to the south-east. Progress was slow, but that evening, from the southern end of Martinique, some of the French could be seen from the masthead, still on the windward side of the island and apparently heading north. As there could be no certainty what they would do during the night, Hood brought to, with the unfortunate result that next morning his ships were widely scattered. While some like the *Gibraltar* had remained to windward in the St Lucia channel, tacking at intervals to clear the Diamond Rock, others handled less well drifted so far to leeward that dawn found them becalmed under the high land between St Pierre and Fort Royal.* He was still collecting them again in the early hours of Sunday, April 29th, when the enemy reappeared, standing boldly round the southern end of Martinique.

It was the Count de Grasse with twenty of the line and a huge convoy of 150 sail, who had slipped out from Brest on March 22nd. By 9 a.m. he was between Pt Salines and the Diamond, with the convoy well inshore and the battleships to seaward.

The operation which followed reflects great credit on the French Admiral. As his convoy hauled close under the land and pressed on for Fort Royal, he formed his line of battle on a southerly course to shield it, while the four ships in Fort Royal sailed out to join his rear. At the same time Hood was forming his line on a parallel course to leeward, to be joined before long by the *Prince William* from St Lucia, her crew augmented by

---

* This happened to the *Ajax*, *Alcide*, *Belliqueux*, *Invincible*, *Monarch*, *Terrible* and *Torbay*. (*Barfleur*—Master's journal, Ad. 52/2160.)

enthusiastic volunteers. At a range of never less than a mile the two long lines of ships (twenty-four French and eighteen British), drew slowly away to the southward exchanging broadsides. Behind them the huge, straggling convoy hauled in round the Diamond and crowded up the coast to Fort Royal.

De Grasse, to windward, kept his distance. His task was to lead his opponent away from the scene until the convoy was safe in port. But his shooting was effective. At the end of the day there were casualties in many of Hood's ships, including Captain Nott of the *Centaur* who died later. The *Intrepid* and *Centaur* were holed under water, the *Shrewsbury*, *Montagu* and *Torbay* had their lower masts badly wounded, and so dangerous was the condition of the *Russell*, with water over the magazine and gaining on the pumps, that Hood ordered her to St Eustatius, where she arrived on May 3rd with her news.

All next day (Monday April 30th) the light airs made it impossible for Hood to close. De Grasse's straggling line could be seen some four or five miles to the eastward, with his rear hull down. At noon they were some thirty miles south-west of St Lucia, and at dusk off the north end of St Vincent. But de Grasse still kept his distance. By this time the *Intrepid* and *Centaur*, which had been pumping continuously for twenty-four hours, could no longer keep their stations. Nor were the *Shrewsbury*, *Montagu* and *Torbay* in any state to fight. Before dark the main topmast of the *Intrepid* came crashing down. The fleets were now some seventy miles from Fort Royal and Hood decided to quit. Next morning (Tuesday May 1st) he was steering west, with the enemy six miles astern. By noon both fleets had re-formed on a northerly course, de Grasse heading for Fort Royal, and Hood to rejoin Sir George. By 6.30 that evening they lost sight of each other.

It is hard to understand how Hood could congratulate himself on his performance. But he did more. After declaring himself (possibly for the benefit of Lord Sandwich, Sir Charles Middleton, General Vaughan, George Jackson, and who knows how many other correspondents) 'perfectly conscious of no one omission in the whole of my conduct', he could not resist sneering at his opponent. 'Never', he assured his influential friends, 'was more powder and shot thrown away in one day before.' As de Grasse achieved his object while Hood's casualties were thirty-seven killed and 125 wounded, not to mention the *Russell* driven out of the line, the statement is certainly remarkable. Finally he dismissed his opponent with the breathtaking comment: 'He has, I thank God, nothing to boast (of).'[39]

Sir George has been blamed for Hood's lack of success. The British Commander-in-Chief, so runs the argument, obsessed with the importance of protecting St Eustatius, kept his gifted subordinate on an impossibly difficult station; and the fact that the gifted subordinate failed abysmally is taken as conclusive proof that the station was impossibly difficult. But Sir George was not ignorant of the conditions off Fort Royal. He had brought an invasion fleet there in 1762, and cruised off the port the previous year with ships very inferior to Hood's. Nor can it be assumed that Hood would have done better if Sir George had allowed him to cruise to windward. All that can be said with certainty is that de Grasse was brilliantly successful while Hood, with a respectable force and stationed on the French doorstep, allowed the local conditions to defeat him.

As he wrote his letters, the British second-in-command was pressing north with fifteen of the line. The situation was critical. The French now had twenty-four battleships in the Leeward Islands, and no one could say how many fresh troops. De Bouillé was still at Martinique, and if last year's campaign was anything to go by, would lose no time in attacking one of the British possessions, probably St Lucia or Barbados. Hood's retreat northwards was not because he feared for St Eustatius or St Kitt's, but because the wind and current made it difficult for him to reach either of the more important islands direct.

Meanwhile, Sir George, with a new captain, John Symons, had sailed from St Eustatius with the *Sandwich* and *Triumph*, to join Hood. As he passed St Kitt's the inhabitants, who had so recently threatened him with arrest, were firing their alarm guns, so he stood in for Basseterre roads to discover why. A large ship, also steering for the roads and apparently crippled, proved to be the *Centaur*, with the information that two more of Hood's ships, the *Torbay* and *Intrepid*, were also making for St Kitt's to repair shot-holes, and that the nervous inhabitants must have fired their guns on sighting the rest of the British squadron. By evening of the 9th the three cripples were patched up and under way with Sir George. Two days later they joined Hood between Antigua and Montserrat. Next day, (May 12th), the united force was storing and watering in St John's road in preparation for whatever lay ahead.

Two days were all Sir George would allow for this refreshment. On the 14th he sailed with twenty of the line.* Ailing and irritable, his flagship by

* *Sandwich* (90), *Barfleur* (90), *Gibraltar* (80), *Ajax, Alcide, Alfred, Belliqueux, Centaur, Invincible, Monarch, Montagu, Resolution, Russell, Terrible, Torbay, Triumph, Shrewsbury,* all seventy-fours, *Princessa* (70), *Intrepid* (64) and *Prince William* (64).

now in as bad a state as himself, he was ready to battle once more for the British islands although for all he knew some of them might already have fallen. It was known that de Bouillé had already struck at St Lucia. The *Pegasus* had brought this news before they left Antigua. But for the next nine days this was all that anybody did know. The wind was light. The heavy battleships crept towards Barbados at less than two knots. In the unbearable tension of this time it is small wonder that relations between the Commander-in-Chief and his second-in-command worsened.

There was a perceptible clash on the always delicate question of patronage. The action with de Grasse had created vacancies in Hood's squadron. In place of the late Captain Nott, Hood posted E. T. Smith, commander of the *Pacahunta* (sloop), into the *Centaur*, which Sir George confirmed, and appointed his own first lieutenant, John Burr, to command the *Pacahunta*, which Sir George disallowed. Hood was deeply aggrieved. 'Had I put Mr Burr into the very worst sloop of H.M. service,' he wrote, 'and you had assured me of giving him the *best*—three days hence, I think I owed it to you, as well as to myself, most respectfully to contend for his confirmation. You have been pleased to decree it otherwise and I shall never say another word about it.'

Nor did he. But never again after this letter did he subscribe himself as Sir George's 'very affectionate'. There was no breach. Sir George wrote next day, 'very politely' as Hood himself admitted, offering a battleship to one of Hood's brothers-in-law. But he stood firm over the *Pacahunta*. 'When my engagements are performed I shall be glad to obey any commands relative to preferment you can wish. But I must first comply with the promises I have made, many being to the first people in the kingdom. . . .'[40] The *Pacahunta* was required for the Hon. Alexander Cochrane, the twenty-three-year-old son of the Earl of Dundonald.

When at last Barbados crept over the horizon, everything was normal, with the British flag still flying over Bridgetown. Moreover, the attack on St Lucia had been repulsed. On the 10th 1,200 French troops had landed under the guns of their fleet. But when, two days later, de Grasse boldly anchored in Gros Islet Bay, the batteries soon drove him out again. There was luck as well as good management in this success. In the crisis the previous year many new batteries had been set up, using the guns of the dismantled *Cornwall*; but it was the chance arrival of three British frigates and a sloop a few hours before the French, that enabled them to be fully manned.

The enemy had withdrawn, but only to strike again. On the same day that Sir George reached Barbados (May 23rd), French troops were going ashore at Tobago, 200 miles further south. This news reached Barbados just before midnight on the 26th. Sir George was sleeping on shore and could not be informed until next morning, when the situation was examined. Most of the ships were still desperately short of water and in need of fresh vegetables. Could he afford the time to make good this deficiency? The report spoke of only two of the line and 900 French troops. The natural defences of Tobago were strong, and its troops and militia, recently reinforced by some of General Vaughan's engineers, should be able to hold out for some while. A slight delay was therefore an acceptable risk. In any case there was also Barbados to consider. What if the new threat was just a feint to lure the British fleet away before an enemy descent here? So reassurances were sent to Tobago that a relief force would sail next day, and by evening on the 28th Rear-Admiral Drake with no more than six of the line and three frigates* was on his way with the 69th regiment, a flank company of the 60th, and a company of volunteers.

Nevertheless, Tobago was the French objective. Drake sighted the main body of the enemy fleet at the same time as he made his landfall (May 30th), and withdrew as quickly as he could. He was back at Barbados on June 2nd and Sir George sailed early next morning with the whole fleet, determined, as he told everybody, to give battle whenever he should meet the enemy.

But Tobago disappointed expectations by surrendering as soon as Drake turned back. The belief that de Bouillé had issued orders to burn four plantations every four hours until the inhabitants surrendered broke the spirit of the militia.[41] When Sir George's fleet approached the island, fourteen strange sail were sighted to the south-west, and soon afterwards some thirty more, standing out from Great Courland Bay. It was de Grasse. At 4 that afternoon (June 5th), the whole French fleet could be seen heading north. At 6 p.m. they were nine or ten miles directly to leeward in a very irregular line between Grenada and the Grenadines. Sir George had only to hoist the signal to bear down, and he would be among them before dark. Again he resisted the temptation. With Barbados defenceless he must not be lured to leeward. Instead he ordered lights to be shown during the night in the hope that de Grasse would keep up with him and fight next day. But a fleet action was no part of the French Admiral's plan. He turned back to Tobago, and on the 9th the discomforted British fleet anchored once more at Barbados.

* *Gibraltar, Alfred, Belliqueux, Invincible, Princessa, Resolution, Amazon, Cyclops* and *Triton.*

There could be no disguising the setback. Under the shadow of failure, although Tobago was not of the first importance, the atmosphere grew heavy with recrimination. Hood, with whom his chief's shortcomings were now something of an obsession, blamed him for not taking the whole fleet to Tobago at once. 'I laboured much to effect it,' he informed Jackson, 'but all in vain. . . . Nay, had he even gone when Mr Drake did, the island would have been saved.'[42] One might share Hood's indignation if one could be sure that the whole fleet was in any condition to proceed at once. Sir George made it very clear in his despatch that it was not. As the fleet lay inactive at Barbados, feelings grew bitter. Only four days after his return, while still smarting over Tobago, Sir George turned his resentment once more against the disloyal merchants of St Eustatius.

Instructions from London, when they arrived, had been reasonably clear about the goods seized. By a Royal Decree the Crown relinquished its claims to everything except 'the Provisions and the Ordnance, Arms and Ammunition, and Military stores'. Everything else, which meant in effect the produce of all the sales and the whole of Hotham's valuable convoy was, by Royal bounty, conferred on the victors, but with one proviso. Not included in what might be distributed were *'such effects as shall be proved to be the Property of British subjects, lawfully exported thither'.*[43] One need not be a lawyer to see the loopholes here.

The wording of the Royal Decree should have warned Sir George to hold his hand, but it is not certain that he had yet received it.* Throwing caution to the winds, and directly counter to the intentions of London, he now instructed Akers to arrange for the final disposal of the stores belonging to 'the people calling themselves British merchants'. The letter, apparently dated June 13th, is not extant, but enough can be deduced from Akers's reply[44] to understand Hood's virtuous horror when he heard about it. Sir George's action, emotional and vindictive, cannot be defended. His enemies, and they were many, attributed it to greed and 'wicked rapacity', the old story, while disloyal merchants and most of the legal profession joined in the disapproving chorus so loudly that the echoes may still be heard today. But his friends, while deploring his unwisdom, may see in it no more than the final outcome of his implacable resentment against the 'nest of vipers', and his impatience with what he called legal chicanery. He had borne much, and the strain was telling.

* Vaughan at St Lucia had it on May 30th but Sir George, at Barbados on that date and subsequently absorbed in the abortive operations to save Tobago, may not have done so. Or he may have suspected what was coming and resolved to act before he could be stopped.

He was now a very sick man indeed, but he had not the least desire to go home and face the music over St Eustatius and answer questions about Tobago unless he must. Tormented by doubts and racked by ill-health, he went on hoping desperately for his complaint to improve, and his condition provoked no sympathy at all from his second-in-command. 'It is quite impossible,' wrote Hood on June 24th, 'from the unsteadyness of the Commander-in-Chief, to know what he means three days together. One hour he says his complaints are of such nature that he can not possibly remain in this country, and is determined to leave the command with me; the next day he says he has no thought of going home.'[45]

The ailing Commander-in-Chief, with his biting tongue and his uncertain temper, pouring out his wrath on disloyal merchants and uneasily conscious that his days might be numbered, is a distressing figure. And now, with the Royal Proclamation known to all, Nemesis threatened. The merchants and lawyers became so clamorous that by the beginning of July Admiral and General were on the defensive. The tone of exultation is gone. In a joint letter to Germain dated July 3rd, they poured out their woes. 'Persecutions', they declared, '[are] already commenced by these disappointed miscreants who pursue every means to harass us and who, we are assured, will employ every engine of litigation against us.'[46] They expressed the hope that crown lawyers would be directed to defend them.

Nevertheless—uneasy, exasperated and overwrought as he may well have been, Sir George never forgot his duty to acknowledge merit and reward the deserving—even among the humblest.

'*Sandwich*, Carlisle bay, Barbados, 29 June 1781.

'*Sir*,

'Be pleased to represent to their Lordships that during the time the French fleet made its appearance off St. Lucia a number of seamen to about 80 belonging to the transports and victuallers, actuated by the generous motive of serving their country, voluntarily entered themselves on board the *Prince William*, then lying at Gros Islet incapable of joining the fleet for want of hands, which she was, by their assistance, enabled to do (in) Time enough to get into action.

'The bare discharge of them to their respective ships would be but a bad encouragement for them or others in like circumstances to act in so noble a manner. I have therefore ordered them to be discharged by Pay List back to their vessels; and have given them each a Guinea a man to buy them necessaries which they are very bare of, and shall direct a Bill to be drawn on the Navy Board for the amount, which I hope will meet with their Lordships approval.'[47]

It was the old, understanding leadership that always won him devotion wherever he commanded. Nevertheless, in a private letter to Lord Sandwich, written on the same day, he admitted 'I am really very much out of order'.[48]

Fortunately, the game was nearly played out. The hurricane season was at hand. On July 5th de Grasse sailed from Fort Royal with twenty-seven of the line and near 200 merchantmen. His destination would first be Cape François in St Domingo, whence the merchantmen would proceed home. But most of his warships, Sir George judged, would go to reinforce the French in North America, and to North America, as in 1780, he meant his own ships to go as well. But whether his health would permit him to go with them was now more than doubtful. At Antigua, towards the end of July, the leaky *Sandwich* was found to be in no condition to proceed: only Jamaica dockyard could put her right. About himself, too, Sir George now made up his mind. On the 25th he signed the order for Hood to proceed to North America with fourteen of the line and five frigates, returning after the first full moon in October. Three days later he shifted his flag to the *Gibraltar*, Langara's former flagship, which was due to go home with the trade.

On the 30th the *Gibraltar* was once more at St Eustatius. From her decks Sir George could survey the empty roadstead, the roofless warehouses, and the deserted beaches. It is unlikely that he felt any remorse, but twinges of apprehension there may well have been, for before he sailed he amended his instructions to his agents in a curious document dated July 31st. After once more enumerating the iniquities of the merchants he grudgingly conceded that 'a few, a very few may have been less guilty', and went on: 'As it is far from my intention or desire that the innocent should suffer with the guilty, and though the whole is forfeit by the Laws of War, I shall be glad, as far as lies in my power, to mitigate its rigours; and as far as my consent can possibly go I sincerely give it my opinion that attention should be shown to those merchants or factors who have legally imported their goods, and that you, as my agents, consent to their being restored.'[49] This belated recognition of his orders from London meant little. Most of the goods were by this time scattered to the four winds.

Chapter 22

'Determined to Serve Again'

(August–December 1781)

'. . . not less than 80 actions commenced against
Sir George Rodney over the St. Eustatius affair.'
(*Hampshire Chronicle*, September 28, 1781.)

'. . . no man with British feelings would join in the
condemnation of the Hon. Admiral.'
(Lord North in the House of Commons,
December 4, 1781.)[1]

I T was not merely his weakness for captured enemy ships that decided
Sir George to make his passage in the *Gibraltar*. She too needed
skilled attention at home, and in any case she drew too much water
for the Hudson River. Returning with him were Captain Symons,
Pagett, tired at last of the sea (or his employer), and now pushing for a
comfortable living on shore, and Dr Blane. Also in his large retinue were
Benedict, Richard and Henry Arnold,[2] children of the only general on
either side who, in Sir George's opinion, really understood the business of
war. The inventory of Sir George's furniture and personal effects sent
across from the *Sandwich* included one large and one small mahogany
bedstead, two cots and a field bedstead, two mahogany dining-tables and a
card-table, four escritoires, two sophas, a mahogany dressing-glass, and a
set of curtains for the large bed with mosquito nettings; his plate included
as many as thirty silver table-spoons.[3]

With him sailed another invalid ship, the 74-gun *Triumph*. There was a
huge, crawling convoy of close on 150 sail, with the frigate *Pegasus* in
attendance to waft Sir George over to North America if, at the last moment,
his condition improved. But it did not. In the latitude of Bermuda he
submitted to the inevitable and sent her off to New York, with a final
word to Hood to put himself under Arbuthnot, or whoever he might find
commanding there. Whatever was going to happen in North America that
autumn, the responsibility would not be his.

For him there would be other battles on the home front. It was a bitter thought that any applause for what he had achieved would certainly be drowned by the clamour over St Eustatius. This wretched island promised to betray all the rosy prospects of its first capture. At first the news had been received in England with enthusiasm. The guns of the Tower were fired and government stocks rose $1\frac{1}{2}$ per cent.[4] His Majesty had been particularly impressed by the richness of the booty and noticeably gracious to Henny at the drawing-room. There had been talk of a peerage, and Sir George had let it be known that if this went as high as an earldom he wished to style himself Earl Rodney of Rodney Stoke, in consequence of which his ducal kinsman had offered to sell back the old family lands at a fair valuation, and only Henny had voiced her reluctance to live in a county as damp and dull as Somerset.[5] She need not worry now. The earldom had receded, probably for ever, before the clamour of the merchants and the opposition.

The government, he could be fairly sure, would back him over St Eustatius. They could hardly do otherwise. But this was no guarantee of a satisfactory decision in the courts. True, there was a huge sum in Drummond's Bank to the joint account of Vaughan and Rodney, but until the legal situation was cleared up this could not be touched. His finances had not benefited by one sixpence from his prodigious capture. As for the Royal grant of £2,000 a year—it would not go far with Lowther and Mackreth pressing their claims. The government again, he could be fairly sure, would make no difficulty about his returning to the West Indies. But could he himself be sure that the medical treatment he sought would restore him sufficiently? On all sides there were doubts and uncertainties. Sitting in Langara's great cabin Sir George may well have given way to gloomy thoughts.

But, as always, he could find comfort and consolation in his family. His dear girls would be two years older, or nearly, and there was little Sarah whom he had not yet seen. Best of all was the fact that his beloved George had found himself just the sort of wife his father most approved, and was now happily married.

This was quite the best thing to come out of the otherwise unlucky year 1781. The young lady was Miss Anne Harley, only daughter of the immensely wealthy Alderman Harley. Sir George, urging the match from New York, had encouraged his son to disclose his affections, and Mr Harley, recognizing that young people could not live upon love alone, had promised a generous settlement to which Sir George, in the first flush of anticipated affluence after St Eustatius, had intended to add £800 a year. 'I am ready to sign any writing whatever,' he had written on February 6th, 'that may contribute to the Happyness of the person who is, and allways will be, Dearer to me than my own life. May you, my Dear Son, experience that happyness that was once the lot of your Father, and may the young lady be but like your Mother, and felicity must attend you. . . .'[6]

George, much less easily carried away, had hinted that it might be necessary to defer his own bliss until remittances could be sent from the West Indies, and that in any case the settlement of his father's 'encumbrances' ought to come first. He had also begged his father to be perfectly explicit over his own affairs when communicating with Mr Harley. Nevertheless, the marriage had gone through. St Eustatius should have put the Rodneys on equal terms with the wealthy Harleys, and perhaps it still would. But whatever happened, George was now as well settled as any fond father could wish.

It was a pity that John continued to disappoint, but his advancement to post-captain at the age of fifteen and a half had startled even his mother. 'So you have made John a captain,' wrote Henny when she heard of it, 'I hope he will do you honour. I trust he will, but I wish to God he would be more attentive in his letters which absolutely are not common Grammar. Tell him this when you are alone, but not before anybody I intreat. . . .'[7] John's illiteracy might have mattered less if his seamanship had been good, but it was not. The *Boreas* had been badly handled returning to the West Indies from New York and had to refit at Antigua; after St Eustatius he had chased the sloop carrying his father's despatches for a whole night under the impression that she was an enemy;[8] and the only item on the credit side was when, with three other ships, he arrived at St Lucia just in time to send men on shore to man the batteries and thus save the island. By this time he had exchanged into the *Sybille* (32), and he was still commanding her when Sir George went home. He was extravagant too. One hundred guineas from his father, when in New York, to equip himself for his first command had gone nowhere, so the young man had borrowed more from his agent on the expectation of prizes not yet taken. The indulgent father may well have pursed his lips.*

The convoy was intolerably slow. The *Gibraltar*, with her important

---

* John Rodney also appears to have inherited his father's taste for play. Lieut. George Cookson of the artillery, visiting the *Boreas* in Carlisle Bay on January 15, 1781, was surprised to find her very juvenile captain throwing dice with two of his midshipmen for £5 a throw! (From the unpublished memoirs of Lieut.-General Cookson, by kind permission of his descendant, P. G. Whicher, Esq.)

passenger, forged ahead. She had a fire on board (extinguished without much difficulty), and one Sunday Pagett conducted Divine Service, an event sufficiently unusual to be recorded in the captain's journal. At Cork, where she put in for water, there were speeches and an exchange of polite messages with the Viceroy, and on September 19th she dropped anchor in Cawsand Bay. The sailors in Plymouth dockyard (good judges of a sea-officer one may suppose) gathered to cheer the victor of the Moonlight Battle as he came ashore, but Sir George did not linger. With so much in the balance, including his own reputation and future, he was off with the least possible delay to Windsor, to present his case before His Majesty himself.

So it came about that on September 24th an astonished Sovereign just returned from hunting, was informed that Admiral Sir George Rodney had arrived that morning at the castle and was seeking audience. His Majesty was embarrassed. His favourite Admiral might, or might not be, under a cloud. Until he had consulted his ministers he could not be sure, and in any case he now disapproved of the goings on at St Eustatius. So, with prudent caution, he pleaded fatigue. Sir George might expect to be received properly in a day or two in London. But while the official voice remained silent, all the newspapers speculated wildly on his reception, his health, and his future. One most unfortunate development had already darkened the horizon. Hotham's convoy, with the cream of the West Indian produce from St Eustatius had, in spite of warnings, been taken in the channel approaches. The chorus of abuse from some quarters would be louder than ever. But there could be no doubt about Sir George's popularity with the masses. A large crowd awaited him on the pavement outside the house in Albemarle Street where he was to lodge, and as he made his gouty descent from his carriage women were before him to strew his path with flowers and garlands.[9]

It may be doubted if the ministers gave him a similar welcome. They had not wished his return at all. But here he was, and thanks to him the Parliamentary opposition, which had never lacked ammunition in this wretched war, now had a lot more. However, he was much too valuable to be thrown to the wolves. The government majority would be large enough to have the St Eustatius business approved, despite the outcry, and in the meanwhile he needed medical attention. So, to a chorus of charges and countercharges Sir George, protesting vehemently that he had done the right thing and would do so again, that the British merchants were traitors and most of the opposition as well, shook the dust of London from his feet and betook himself to Bath.

He put himself into the hands of Sir Caesar Hawkins, but into the horrid details of eighteenth-century surgery, or the methods of that eminent practitioner, there is no need to enter here. Hawkins did a good job, however. He cured his patient and he won his friendship and esteem. However, Sir George's recovery from an extremely trying ordeal was not helped by the news from America and London.

De Grasse had gone to America as expected, and Hood's reinforcements to that station might have been invaluable but for the incompetence of Arbuthnot's successor, Sir Thomas Graves. For here any cause for gratification ended. Graves met de Grasse off the Chesapeake with all the advantages, but so mishandled his ships as to throw away almost certain victory. Hood, whose own performance in the action had been less than distinguished, spared nothing of his bitterness in his letters home. His dissatisfaction with his old chief was forgotten in his deep disappointment over Graves. How different if Sir George had been in command! 'I am persuaded,' he wrote to Middleton, 'had that admiral led His Majesty's squadron from the West Indies to this coast, the 5th of September would, I think, have been a most glorious day for Great Britain.'[10] This was a tribute indeed. News of the engagement reached England quickly, to retard the recovery of the invalid at Bath, who saw only too clearly what had gone wrong. Had Graves only attended to the intelligence sent him, and united his forces off the Capes of Virginia, de Grasse would never have landed his troops.* As for his bungling at the Chesapeake, enough was clear for Sir George to burst out explosively: '. . . his mode of fighting I will never follow'. Fortunately for his peace of mind the ultimate consequence of that miserable business, the surrender at Yorktown, would not be known for some time. But the signs were plain enough. 'In my poor opinion,' he concluded, 'the French have gained a most important victory, and nothing can save America. . . .'[11]

But there were still more troubles on the home front before he could return to the fray. In London the Treasury Solicitor and the Counsel briefed by Jackson were preparing the best defence they could, in their principal's absence, against the merchants of St Eustatius. There were affidavits to be signed and accounts and books to be produced. The unfortunate Pagett, acting as the link between Jackson in London and his irascible chief in Bath, found his way beset with thorns. Sir George entrusted him with the key of his escritoire (the first time he had ever done so) and despatched him to London to make a copy of the St Eustatius

* Sir George was not to know that this intelligence reached Graves too late.

accounts. There was some muddle over this, and a very confused and incomplete set of papers reached Jackson, who complained. Sir George was furious and persuaded himself that Pagett had 'confused the accounts on purpose'. A few extracts from his reply to Jackson—'. . . convinced that he minds nothing but his own dirty interest . . . too angry at the jealous fellow to write to him. . . .'—throw some light on the temper of a fractious convalescent, when the mood took him. He concluded: 'Writing this long letter in a damned angry mood for the insolent manner the account has been given you, will put me back two days at least, but as the waters begin to agree with me my return to London will be in a fortnight when all matters must be settled before I sail. . . .'[12]

Plainly he was on the mend although still far from well. But three weeks later he was still at Bath, and friends in London began to worry. There was never any question in the government's mind that he must go out again. Large French reinforcements were expected to sail from Brest in mid-November (reports spoke of 10,000 or 12,000 troops for an attack on Jamaica), and the convalescent at Bath was still the best admiral available— if he *was* available. Cabinet ministers vied with each other in their blandishments. The breath was scarcely out of Lord Hawke's body before the post of Vice-Admiral of Great Britain was offered and, it need hardly be said, accepted. The 90-gun *Formidable*, the only three-decker fit for foreign service, would be fitted for his flag. 'Our loss will be great,' wrote Lord Sandwich on November 6th, 'if we are deprived of your assistance.'[13] Not that Sir George needed any persuasion. Friends at Bath were amazed at the ardent spirit in the emaciated frame. '. . . lean and ill, but hearty', was how Lord Pembroke described him on November 8th, adding that he 'talks of nothing but serving'. Next day he found him 'in high spirits but by no means in high vigour', but 'determined to serve again'.[14] Sir George's spirit was unquenchable. Patriotism, dedicated professionalism, supreme self-confidence and ambition, all the sources of energy and resilience which had driven him and sustained him and made him the man he was, were welling up anew. His glittering command with its opportunities of service and so much else—how could he possibly relinquish it? But he was still exhausted by his treatment. '. . . may your Lordship never endure the pain and torture I have undergone' he had written to Lord Sandwich on the 4th. To Jackson he was specific. 'My complaint has been, and still continues, A Stricture, which my old friend Sir Caesar Hawkins assures me must have killed me if I had stay'd on a month longer in the West Indies.'[15]

At last the doctors were satisfied, and in mid-November he set off. There was an abundance of good inns on the Bath road for the traveller who desired comfort and had to go by easy stages. Inn-keepers, ostlers, and chamber-maids bestirred themselves on learning that the small, spare gentleman with the pinched features and the incisive manner was Sir George Rodney, who had taken more enemy ships than any other admiral in this war or the last. Great personages were common enough on that road but a national hero was a rarity. And so, to London.

Hardly had he brought his weary body to rest in Albemarle Street once more when there was a portent. The Common Chamberlain of the City of London, John Wilkes, Esq., with certain others, waited on him with the Freedom of the City in a gold box.[16] Coming as it did when so many suits were being filed against him, and when the Parliamentary opposition was preparing its attack, this was most heartening. Fortified by the City's approval Sir George returned with renewed energy to professional matters. He could not leave for Portsmouth until Parliament had debated St Eustatius. There would be time to make sure that his ships were in the best possible shape.

From his heavy correspondence over the next fortnight we may glimpse what Sir George, at the summit of his career and convinced that he would soon be at grips with the enemy, considered of the first importance. The new signal books of some of his contemporaries had never much interested him, and he could get along well enough with the old Sailing and Fighting Instructions, when modified to meet his requirements. But if the stream of paper which poured from Albemarle Street is any guide, his two priorities were, as ever, seamen's health and gunnery. Day after day he plagued the Admiralty and the various departments with requests and recommendations. He was uncertain which of six preventives against scurvy was the best, but he must have them all; rupture, far too common among seamen, was the subject of a long and informed memoranda; and he was determined that the authority of Dr Blane, who was going out with him again, should extend beyond the fleet to the hospitals on shore. The flint-lock mechanism for firing the great guns had more than proved its worth against de Guichen. The guns of his new flagship must be so fitted without fail, and with the ingenious arrangement (also devised by Sir Charles Douglas) by which they could be worked at extreme traverse. That gifted officer had consented to come as his First Captain, so the gunnery of the fleet would be as well cared for as its health. Sick or well Sir George never lost his firm grasp of essentials.[17]

Not that the smaller, personal matters, were neglected. Captain Symons returned his best thanks for his appointment as captain of the *Formidable*, acknowledging Sir George's kindness as the means of eventually finding him something better; little Marr, who had been turned out of his job at New York by the vengeful Arbuthnot, was to be accommodated on board the *Formidable* until something could be found for him in the West Indies; these were followers so Sir George could do no less. By the same token the pathetic memorial of Midshipman Skey, who lost a leg on April 17th, to have his lieutenant's commission confirmed, was warmly and sympathetically endorsed by his old Commander-in-Chief.

The Parliamentary attack, when it came, proved something of a damp squib. On November 30th the censorious and opinionated Member for Malton, Mr Edmund Burke, gave notice that he intended to move, at some convenient day, for copies of the instructions sent to Sir George Rodney, relative to the disposal of the property found on the island of St Eustatius. Sir George was ready for him, and desired the Hon. gentleman would choose his day and the sooner the better, as he was ordered for foreign service. But then, instead of sitting down, he announced that as he was on his legs he would say a few words upon Lord Cornwallis's surrender, and was well away on this subject before he could be called to order by the Speaker. Lord North interposed smoothly to say that the business might be taken up at an early date. Mr Burke then intimated ominously that *if* the General and Admiral had orders from the government to do what they did, then the King's ministers would alone be criminal, at which Sir George was on his feet again. 'Whether I had instructions or not,' he burst out defiantly, 'my conduct would have been just what it was at St Eustatius.' December 4th was fixed for the motion.

Some echoes of this debate have come down in the pages of Debrett's *Parliamentary Register*. Sir George and General Vaughan were both in their places when Burke reopened his motion, but before he had fairly started Lord George Germain objected that the question of the confiscations was already at issue in the courts. Did the Hon. gentleman wish to interfere? Burke brushed this aside as too ridiculous to be considered and swept into his stride. He poured scorn on the immense force unleashed on St Eustatius, contrasting it with the inadequate one sent against St Vincent. St Eustatius had no choice but to surrender at discretion—'discretion' he scoffed, a word which the captors appeared to have misinterpreted as 'destruction'. He then went on to condemn the illegality of the whole affair. The captors had no excuse whatever for neglecting to take advice. The Attorney-General and the Solicitor-General of St Kitt's were both available. Why had they not been consulted? With curious partiality he ignored the Chief Justice of the island, who had been Sir George's active supporter.

He then turned to what he called 'the glorious business of the sales', which had occupied the two commanders from the beginning of February to the beginning of May. Twenty-one ships of the line and 3,000 veteran troops might, in his opinion, have been more usefully employed elsewhere. If they had been, then Tobago would not have been lost, and de Grasse would never have been left at liberty to bring upon us the dreadful disaster of the Chesapeake. Tobago, he averred, bending his words to the most damaging interpretation possible, had been taken under Sir George's very eyes. The French Admiral had said so himself, and that he had several times offered the British battle. . . . But this one-sided version of the facts, followed by aspersions on Sir George's courage, seems to have been too much for some members. The word 'odious' may have been thrown back at the speaker for at this point he brought his speech to an end with the sharp reminder that it was *not* odious to accuse 'Guilt in stars and ribbons, Guilt rewarded and countenanced by the Official and the Opulent'.

Sir George replied in detail. The Dutch were enemies. He had resolved to show no favour to the English inhabitants because they deserved none. The property he seized was on behalf of the King, and the stores and provisions were all sent to the dockyard at Antigua. As to the charge of inactivity—he had expeditions planned against Curaçoa and Surinam, but they had to be cancelled when he received word of an enemy fleet approaching, intelligence which, unfortunately, proved to be false. The fleet had not been inactive. Under Sir Samuel Hood, 'as good an officer as himself', it had been blockading Martinique, and it was no crime to send it on that service. Only the *Sandwich* and the *Triumph*, both unseaworthy, had remained at St Eustatius. As for Tobago, he had sent ships and men immediately, and more were on the way when the island fell. To sail down wind to fight de Grasse would have been to risk Barbados. Finally, had the Commander-in-Chief in North America acted on the intelligence he sent him, de Grasse would never have reached the Chesapeake but instead have been intercepted off the Capes of Virginia.

General Vaughan took up the story, protesting that his troops on the island were less than a third of the number claimed by the Hon. Member. As to the charges of rapacity and greed, he had not made a single shilling by the capture. Indeed it was quite otherwise. He then revealed to an interested

House that the Jews of St Eustatius were so captivated by their generous treatment that their synagogue had presented him with an address, expressing their happiness at being under the mild government of King George III. He was sorry that, in point of order, he could not lay this document upon the table. The members were sorry too, and desired him to read it as part of his speech. This the General attempted, but so poor was the lighting that he could not see to do so, whereupon Sir George, whose eyesight was excellent, obligingly read it out to the Members himself. When the House divided at midnight only eighty-nine members supported Burke's motion. Against it were 163.[18]

Four days later Sir George was at Portsmouth. He hoisted his flag in the *Arrogant*, a small seventy-four, for passage to Plymouth where the *Formidable* was still in dock. After the usual delays imposed by the weather she dropped anchor in Cawsand Bay on December 17th. Then gale followed gale from the westward, all his ships were unready, and the delays and frustrations so exasperated him that the gout returned to both hands and feet with such severity as to compel him to take up his residence on shore and to employ an amanuensis, even for his signature. Fifty years later Commissioner Ourry's son remembered Sir George and his father, both crippled with gout, sitting on either side of the fire in the Commissioner's house, and the Admiral, the least reticent of men when his own affairs were concerned, barking out: 'Damme, Paul, if I get near that rascal de Grasse, I'll break his line.' This was his formula for victory—close action and overwhelming gunfire from a concentration of heavy ships round his own flag, in fact the tactics of April 17th, but without the mistakes. 'Break the line and every man take his bird' was another favourite saying long remembered by his hosts.[19]

On New Year's Day 1782 he managed to write a long letter to Henny, but some of his comments: 'my shagreen at being detained in this horrid port . . . neglect, unwillingness, and disobedience . . . faction and party',[20] speak volumes. From the beginning of his career to the end, dockyard inefficiency and slackness always roused particular ire in him. A week later he was making much the same complaints to Lord Sandwich, but by this time from more comfortable quarters on board the *Formidable*.[21] At last, on January 8th, the wind came round to the north-west and without a moment's delay the squadron came to sail.* But once clear of the Sound the

---

* *Formidable* (90), *Namur* (90), *Arrogant* (74), *Conqueror* (74), *Fame* (74), *Hercules* (74), *Marlborough* (74), *Anson* (64), *Nonsuch* (64), *Prothee* (64), *Repulse* (64), *Yarmouth* (64), *Flora* (36) and *Alert* (sloop).

Chapter 23

The Saints

(January–August 1782)

'Your Excellency will have observed that whatever
efforts are made by the land armies, the Navy must
have the casting vote in the present contest.'
(General Washington to the Comte de Grasse,
October 1781.)[1]

FOR more than six years Britain had been fighting alone. Graves's
failure at the Chesapeake had sounded the knell of her hopes in
North America. The Navies of France, Spain, and Holland,
better than they ever were in the later conflict, were stretching her
resources to the limit. On all sides the bastions were falling. In November
de Grasse quitted the scene of his American triumph and swept south once
more. The capture of Jamaica was confidently anticipated. As an appetiser
before the main course, St Eustatius, well prepared but ineptly defended,
was snapped up almost in passing.* On the 26th he was back at Fort
Royal with thirty of the line. Hood, furious that Digby, Arbuthnot's
successor in North America, would not allow him more than three ships
from his own squadron, followed him back to the Leeward Islands with a
mere eighteen. On December 5th he reached Barbados, and although
subsequent reinforcements raised his number to twenty-two, the dice were
loaded against him.

Sir George, as we have already noted, sailed from England on January 9,
1782, with twelve of the line to restore the situation. He wasted no time,
not even putting in for wine and water at Madeira; but weeks must pass
before he arrived, and indeed the game had begun even before he sailed
from Plymouth. In mid-December the entire French armament put to sea

* With the island was lost £250,000 of the money which was intended for the payment
of the troops in North America.

to attack Barbados. But the ships could make no headway against the St Lucia current and after a week of struggle they returned to Fort Royal. They tried again at the end of the month with no better success, after which the commanders decided to attempt St Kitt's instead and sailed for that island on January 5th. Hood hastened north to interrupt their operations if he could. After collecting 500 troops from Antigua he bore down on St Kitt's, neatly out-manœuvred de Grasse in Basseterre roads on the 25th, anchored his twenty-two ships in a strong defensive position and opened communications with the military who had withdrawn to Brimstone Hill. Here he was to remain for the next three weeks while the soldiers fought it out.

On February 19th, in the evening, the *Formidable* dropped anchor at Barbados. Governor Cunningham and General Christie came on board at once with the latest news, which was that the St Kitt's garrison was still holding out, but by the last advice was hard pressed. On the naval side there was a shortage of stores of every description, and of provisions. Hood's ships were making do with yams instead of bread,[2] on hearing which Sir George at once put his own ships on two-thirds allowance. Most disturbing of all was the news that the settlements of Demerara and Essequibo, with the fort and six ships of war, had submitted to the French on January 3rd without offering any resistance at all, for which, as Sir George grimly remarked, the lives of the commanding officers were certainly in danger.[3]

The speedy relief of St Kitt's was the first consideration. Anticipating the squadron's needs, some patriotic merchant captains in Carlisle Bay had 100 tons of water ready, so that the ships were able to water all night and sail next morning. But when, after three days of baffling northerly winds, they were approaching Antigua, the news came out that Brimstone Hill had capitulated on the 13th and that by that time in all probability the islands of Nevis and Montserrat had gone as well. On the 25th Hood's ships hove in sight, having cut their cables and stolen away as soon as the last defences fell, and Sir George brought the united fleet back to Gros Islet Bay. Nothing had been achieved and the reverses were mounting.

There followed a loaded pause. It was the high-water mark of French success. De Grasse lay safe in Fort Royal with his thirty of the line awaiting reinforcements and planning his next *coup*. Barbados, St Lucia, and Antigua (greater prizes than any secured so far) were still in British hands, but no one had much doubt that the next French objective would be Jamaica, in concert with their Spanish allies. Sir George was quite sure of this. The Leeward group had quite lost its old importance. 'Oh, damn these islands!' he exclaimed testily, when reminded of them, 'Jamaica is of ten times more consequence than all of them put together.'⁴ And to make sure of Jamaica's safety he would have to give de Grasse 'a drubbing'. A curious conviction seems to have possessed him that he would do this, and soon.

Meanwhile there were the expected French reinforcements. Hood, liverish, irritable, and holding himself in with difficulty, fretted himself ill over his chief's airy refusal to believe that they would sail before March. There were a number of administrative projects such as dockyard and hospital reorganization, a redistribution of provisions, and the defences of Antigua, which Sir George wanted to settle first. Not until March 9th did he find time for his first letter to Henny, a spirited composition when he came to write it, with the dramatic opening: 'Through storms and tempests and contrary winds we forced our way in five weeks to Barbados.' Sir George always had a pretty taste in rhetoric, and the fact that the gout had at last left his hands may have stimulated his powers. After reviewing the situation in the West Indies he returned to the epic story of the outward passage. 'None but an English squadron and copper-bottomed could have forced their way to the West Indies as we have done. . . . Ushant we weathered in a storm but two leagues, the sea mountains high which made a fair breach over the *Formidable* and the *Namur*.' His satisfaction over his speedy passage is justified. The *Formidable*'s journal confirms that a calculated risk was taken in clearing Ushant, and that with less resolute leadership the squadron might have been delayed a very long time. He continued in the same exalted vein. 'Persist and Conquer is a Maxim that I hold good in War, even against the elements, and it has answered, for till I got the length of Madeira nothing but violent gales prevailed which you are sea-woman enough to know were directly contrary; yet notwithstanding this we made a passage in five weeks which is scarcely credible.'

One may picture him as his pen scratches over the paper, and the bright West Indian light reflects upwards from the water into the cabin. At this point perhaps he looks up, to be reminded of pleasanter things than the weary grind of responsibility. 'I would not for the world have left the portraits of my dear girls behind me. They are the joy of my life and converse with me daily. By looking at them they calm my mind and even ease the torment of the gout when it is upon me. . . .'

Then came four pages on that well-worn theme, the villainies of the merchants, with some tart observations on the loss of St Eustatius, before he approached his conclusion. 'I am of opinion', he wrote, 'that the great events which must decide the empire of the ocean will be either off Jamaica or St Domingo; and as I know you are a great politician I make you thus mistress of this affair, that you may inform our Jamaica friends at home that I have their preservation entirely at heart. Tell my dear girls that I write too long a letter to their mother to write to them too by this oppertunity, but they may depend upon hearing from me very soon. . . . Converse with them I have daily and they both seemed pleased as if they wished to answer.'[5]

From such pleasant avenues of escape Sir George was dragged back to reality by Hood's reiterated insistence that something must be done about intercepting the French reinforcements. But when at last the relentless junior persuaded his chief to send him out, his cruising ground was limited from five to ten leagues directly to windward of Pt Salines, in other words only to guard the St Lucia channel south of Martinique, which left no provision in case the French came in between Dominica and the northern end of the island. Hood urged the importance of guarding both approaches. But Sir George was adamant against dividing his force.

On March 16th Hood sailed with eleven of the line. Next day he received sure intelligence that the French reinforcements might arrive at any moment, on learning which Sir George joined him at once with the rest of the fleet. But nothing could persuade the Commander-in-Chief to divide his force. There were 100 miles of ocean to be guarded between Marie Galante to the northward and the St Lucia channel. From the 20th to the 27th the fleet patrolled an eighty-mile stretch to windward of Dominica and Martinique but saw nothing. On the 25th Sir George modified his disposition by stationing three of the line off Marie Galante. But the task was too hard. On the 28th it was learnt that three enemy battleships and three frigates, bringing with them some 6,000 troops, had slipped through somehow and were now lying safe in Fort Royal. The British fleet returned to Gros Islet Bay.

De Grasse had now thirty-six of the line and sufficient troops under de Bouillé for the conquest of Jamaica. He could sail when it suited him. Forty miles to the southward lay Sir George with thirty-seven. The pieces were all in place for the last moves of the game. In the British fleet no one might go on shore except on duty; frigates patrolled continuously off Fort Royal; and from his watch-post on Pigeon Island Sir George, more confident than ever, maintained unceasing vigilance. His ailments had miraculously left him, and for once he had no complaints about his officers, 'not but I am obliged,' he wrote on the 31st, '(notwithstanding my old age), to be at times twenty-five and set them all an example.'[6] Remarkable words for the usually testy and capricious invalid. Indeed, at this time it was Hood who was laid up, and in a more than usually apprehensive state of mind at what his unpredictable chief might do next. But on April 3rd Sir George paid him a visit on board the *Barfleur*, staying with him two hours. 'I never found him more rational,' wrote the gratified junior immediately afterwards, 'and he gave me very great pleasure by his manner of receiving what I said respecting the future operations.' But Hood could never be happy with any superior for long and this letter ends on the usual sour note: '. . . no great reliance to be placed in a man who is so much governed in matters of the greatest moment by Whims and Caprice'.[7]

Nevertheless, sick or well, an unsteady, capricious invalid or his alert, rational self, Sir George's great day was approaching. In America the war was lost; at home the government had fallen. All his friends were out of office and the whole political background which sustained him was receding into a discredited past. But no word of this had yet reached the Leeward Islands. Here at any rate, in this golden month of April 1782, Fortune was to make amends for so much frustration and disappointment. From the moment the French put to sea, three days after his cordial interview with Hood, events moved unfalteringly to their triumphant conclusion.

De Grasse planned to embark de Bouillé's troops and the siege equipment for Jamaica and sail with all the French trade for St Domingo in one massive and complicated operation. During the night of April 6th/7th part of the French convoy came out from Fort Royal, but it put back on sighting the British cruisers. One of these, the *Endymion*, hurried back to Gros Islet Bay to report. Sir George was dining ashore that evening with little Marr, now the agent victualler for the island; other guests included Rear-Admiral Drake, Captains Cornwallis and Gardner, and some lesser lights from the hospital and the victualling office. The *Endymion*'s captain made the mistake of coming ashore to deliver his message in person. He was admitted to the presence, only to be violently abused from the dinner table for daring to quit his station. When moved to anger Sir George did not mince his words. So trenchant was he on this occasion that the lesser lights at the bottom of the table thought it high time for them to go. Captain Cornwallis (he tells us) could scarcely contain his surprise and indignation at Sir George's outburst, while the poor captain, who could hardly be asked to sit down after such a reception, made some excuse about a sprung bowsprit and escaped as quickly as he could. In the painful pause that followed, Sir George, who may have noticed Cornwallis's expression, came across to explain. 'He is one of my own making,' he said; 'I never spare them, by God.'[8]

The episode, as described by Cornwallis, leaves behind it a feeling of unpleasantness. But Smith of the *Endymion* had no business on shore so long as the signal station on Pigeon Island (set up for the purpose) was working; and Cornwallis, by sympathizing with Smith, reveals laxer standards than those of his Commander-in-Chief. All this shows something of Sir George's difficulties, even with good men like Cornwallis. The latter, without entering further into the matter and expecting that the fleet would sail at once, then reminded the Admiral that his ship was caulking and coppering, only to be sharply corrected. 'I shall sail in the morning', he was told. And so it turned out. The whole French force emerged on the 8th and steered north to collect more of their trade from Guadeloupe. But before noon on the same day every one of the thirty-seven British battleships was also at sea, and stretching to the northward in pursuit.

Tuesday, April 9th, was a day of drifting ships and sporadic gunfire along the coast of Dominica. More than 100 warships, British and French, strained to catch the faint catspaws of wind coming off the land. Groups separated and came together again in their respective squadrons, and between the squadrons and the shore crept the heavy sailing French merchantmen. Between 9 and 10 a.m. eight ships of Hood's division were close enough to engage fifteen of the French van and centre. The *Royal Oak*, *Montagu*, and *Alfred* suffered considerably, and Captain Bayne of the *Alfred* was killed. More ships came up as they caught the breeze. The *Formidable* was in action for a quarter of an hour, long enough to lose a lieutenant and four men. Altogether some twenty ships from each side were engaged at one time or another before the freshening breeze at about 2 p.m. enabled the French to haul their wind and disengage. As a result of this action the French *Caton* (64) had to be detached to Guadeloupe for repairs.

All next day (the 10th) Sir George crept up on de Grasse. Both fleets tacked occasionally to avoid falling away to leeward, which made progress extremely slow. In the evening a signalling error by Sir Charles Douglas brought the British van to a halt for a while, but later that night there was a collision in the French fleet when the *Zélé* (74) ran on board the *Jason* (64), damaging her so badly that she had to follow the *Caton* and make for Guadeloupe. Next morning (the 11th) the damaged *Zélé* and a French 80-gun ship disabled aloft could be seen straggling to leeward of their consorts, and Sir George signalled a general chase. By afternoon some half-dozen British ships were close enough to the two lame ducks to induce de Grasse to bear down to their assistance. There was no fighting for Sir George at once recalled his headmost ships; but de Grasse thus lost much of his ground to windward. That night the *Zélé* had another collision, this time damaging herself so severely that she too had to be detached. The misadventures of this unlucky ship, and the French Admiral's chivalrous reluctance to abandon her, set the scene for the events which followed.

Dawn on Friday April 12th found both fleets still only a few miles from each other, between the northern end of Dominica and the little group of islets known as the Saints. At 5 a.m. the lookouts from the British ships could just discern the mass of the enemy fleet to the north-eastward, while a little further round at north a solitary seventy-four with her foremast gone and her bowsprit snapped off short was proceeding under tow in the direction of Guadeloupe. This was the *Zélé*, the cause of the French Admiral's predicament. For de Grasse had lost so much precious ground by coming down to cover his lame ducks that on this Friday morning his northerly progress was effectually blocked by the Saints. There were only two things he could do. He could either run down to leeward into the arms of the British, or turn to the southward and probably keep his windward position, but at the expense of some sort of brush with his opponent. Sir Charles Douglas, after reviewing the situation at first light, entered the Admiral's cabin with the dramatic announcement that God had given him his enemy on the lee bow, but his appreciation was faulty. De Grasse had already decided to claw his way to the southward. But whatever the French Admiral intended, the correct course for Sir George was to form his line as quickly as possible and make what ground he could to windward. Whether he gained the weather gauge or not, he would at any rate come within range provided he acted at once. There was one further consideration. Hood's van division had suffered casualties on the 9th, while Rear-Admiral Drake's rear division was virtually undamaged. They must therefore change places. So, before 6 o'clock, the signal went out for the line ahead at two cables distance: the Admiral in the third post to make sail and lead. That there were no collisions or misunderstandings in this rather complicated operation speaks well for the discipline and seamanship displayed. From the mass of warships in close order, all with their heads to the southward, the ships of Drake's division began to lead out in the prescribed order in the direction of the enemy. Dr Blane records that 'the line of battle was formed in an incredibly short time'.[9] Four of Hood's ships, which were already heading purposefully northward towards the disabled *Zélé*, were recalled. These decisions made, Sir George went below to have breakfast with Sir Charles Douglas, Captain Symons, Pagett, and Dr Blane. Lord Cranston remained on deck to watch the enemy.

Meanwhile the French were forming their own line on a southerly course. The leaders of Drake's division could see their van hauling out from under the Saints, and their centre and rear forming between the Saints and Guadeloupe. The heads of the two lines began to creep towards each other, and as the distance closed it became clear that although Drake's ships were sailing as close to the wind as possible, the French would still keep the weather gauge. At about 7.30 the leaders of the French van, *Hercule*, *Neptune*, *Souverain*, *Palmier*, *Northumberland*, began to pass ahead of Drake's division, firing at extreme range. Captain Taylor Penny of the *Marlborough*, who had the honour of leading the British line, held on for another ten minutes until the distance was down to about 400 yards, when he bore away slightly to lead along the French line and opened fire. After him, in majestic succession, each under three topsails and fore-staysail, came the rest of his division—*Arrogant*, *Alcide*, *Nonsuch*, *Conqueror*, *Princessa* (taken in the Moonlight Battle and now flying Drake's flag), *Prince George*, *Torbay*, *Anson*, *Fame*, and *Russell*—backing and filling occasionally to keep station, and passing slowly along the French line at about two cables distance. The *Marlborough* opened fire at 7.40 a.m. It was 7.50 when the *Russell*, the last ship in Drake's division, came into action.*

The centre followed. At eight minutes past eight the *Formidable*, in the middle of Sir George's own division, began to engage. There was little that anyone could see beyond the next ahead and astern, and the French ships slipping past to starboard. Beyond this the cannon smoke obscured everything. Nevertheless, there can be no doubt about what was uppermost in Sir George's mind as he sailed into action. It was *to contract his line still further and to close the range*. His signals make this quite clear. At first he had ordered a distance of two cables between ships. But before action was joined this was amended to one, and further reminders came with his repeated signals for the divisions to close. Then, shortly after eight o'clock, the signal for close action was reinforced by an order for the leading ships to alter course to starboard—that is, towards the enemy. Not that there was any flinching. On the contrary every British ship was constantly luffing up to close the range. Captain Savage of the *Hercules*, wounded in the right

* For British and French fleets on April 12th and casualties, see Appendix 10.

foot early in the day, sat in his chair on the gangway shaking his fist at each enemy ship as she passed and exhorting his gunners to aim between wind and water 'to sink the French rascals'.[10] Dr Blane, his pockets full of tourniquets, had obtained Sir George's permission to attend on deck, in case there should be any sudden call for his assistance. Throughout the fleet the spirit was very different from two years earlier.

At 8.30 a round-shot killed Captain Blair of the *Anson*. By 8.40 the *Marlborough*, having passed twenty-two of the enemy, had reached the end of the French line and hove to in order to repair damages. At 9 o'clock the carpenter of the *Fame* came up to report that the ship had made 4 ft 8 in of water in the last quarter of an hour, and that it was still coming in very fast and gaining in the powder-room. At the same time the *Russell*, the last ship in the van division, luffed up to rake the sternmost enemy, having passed all their line. But so long were the lines and so slow the progress in the light airs, that some of Hood's division had still to come into action after most of the van had disengaged. The *Barfleur*, for instance, did not open fire until 9.25.

But now interest shifts to the centre where the *Formidable*, having backed her topsails in the approved fashion to prolong her exchanges with de Grasse's *Ville de Paris*, was approaching the last ships of the French centre. Some of these, and the leaders of the French rear, were in trouble. A shift of wind was heading them so that they could no longer hold their places in the line. Caught by this cruel trick of fate the *Glorieux, Diadème, Destin, Magnanime,* and *Réfléchi* were forced to bear away more and more, or be taken aback. There was confusion, ships fouled each other and fell away to leeward, and before the advancing *Formidable* a gap opened in the French line.

But this was not yet apparent on board the British flagship. Here the first intimation that all was not well with the French was the appearance of the next adversary, already so far to leeward as to be bearing down on her almost bow to bow. It was the 74-gun *Glorieux*, the first victim of that disastrous shift of wind, trying desperately to keep her sails full and at the same time to keep clear of the British flagship. Sir George, accompanied by Dr Blane, stepped out onto the starboard gangway to obtain a better view. The Frenchman was going to pass so close they would have to depress their guns to hit her between wind and water. Sir George turned to the Physician of the Fleet. 'Run down,' he said, 'and tell them to elevate their metal.' Perplexed, Blane proceeded on his errand, which was of course to direct the gunners to raise the breeches and thus depress the muzzles.

Thanks to Sir Charles Douglas the guns of the *Formidable* could not only bear for much longer on the target but they could also get off more rounds in that time. Terrible indeed was the succession of broadsides now fired into the unlucky Frenchman. The *Glorieux* passed within pistol shot, so close that Blane could see her gunners throwing away their sponges and handspikes in order to save themselves below. The 90-gun *Namur* astern of the flagship continued the work. Further down the line Captain Cornwallis in the *Canada* watched her approach, her masts already tottering. He baulked her attempt to cross his bow and gave her a broadside at point-blank range. Not a gun replied. One head looked out from a gun-port. Then, through the smoke, he saw her main and mizzen topple slowly backwards to come crashing down over her stern; a moment later the foremast went in the opposite direction, demolishing the bowsprit as it fell. She gave one last, convulsive roll which brought the sea in through her lower gun-ports, then lay still on the water.

In each ship astern of the *Formidable* the hot starboard guns fell silent as the last Frenchman passed out of range. But now ahead of the flagship appeared the confused mass of French ships sagging to leeward. Sir Charles Douglas, looking ahead from the hammock nettings at the forward end of the quarter-deck, saw them; he also saw the large gap after the ship the *Formidable* had just trounced, and he perceived that the wind would permit the *Formidable*, by luffing a little perhaps, to sail through it. Here, he felt, was an opportunity not to be missed.

What followed has been the subject of much discussion and some misrepresentation. Attendant on Douglas was a thirteen-year-old midshipman who, forty-seven years later as a retired admiral, wrote an account of what passed.[11] The recollections of Admiral Sir Charles Dashwood are the impressions of a child of thirteen, set down after the lapse of nearly half a century. But as Dr Blane was still below, they are almost the only source of information on the most controversial episode of the battle.

'Dash,' exclaimed Douglas, coming down from his view-point, 'where's Sir George?' 'In the after-cabin, Sir,' was the reply. As both turned aft the Admiral appeared and Douglas took off his hat. 'Sir George,' he said, 'I give you joy of victory.' 'Pooh!' replied the Admiral, 'the day is not half won yet.' 'Break the line, Sir George,' insisted Douglas, 'the day is your own and I will insure you the victory.' At this point there probably followed more persuasion and argument than Midshipman Dashwood managed to remember for posterity, but Sir George was unconvinced. Probably he disliked having anything sprung on him; in any case the matter required thought. 'No,' he replied, 'I will not break my line.' Still Douglas urged that the helm be put a-port. Sir George would not have it. The two then separated, the Admiral going aft and the captain forward. The minutes were passing. To Sir George, judging by his hesitation, the advantage of cutting through to windward may have seemed as doubtful as it did to some informed opinion at the time and later.* Furthermore, if he cut through, could he be sure that his captains would follow him? He had been isolated in battle before. Above all there were the Fighting Instructions, with their insistence on the sanctity of the line. It was easy for Douglas to give advice: Douglas did not bear the responsibility.

After their short turn in opposite directions the two came together again in the same spot. Quietly and coolly Douglas repeated his request. 'Only break the line, Sir George, and the day is your own.' By now the Admiral had made up his mind. 'Well, well!' he replied, in a quick and hurried way, 'do as you like.' Immediately afterwards he turned round and walked into the cabin.

As the helm went over and the bows of the *Formidable* swung slowly to starboard, Dashwood went flying below to warn the gunners to be ready to fire from the other side, and a few moments later they opened on four Frenchmen, foul of each other to port. Meanwhile Sir George, it may be supposed, was proceeding through his own quarters to his stern-gallery, to reassure himself that the rest of his division was following. Thirty-five years before, at the battle of Finisterre, Captain Rodney of the *Eagle* had looked out in just the same way for support which had been slow in coming. Only two years before, off Martinique, Sir George Rodney in the *Sandwich* had fought his way through the enemy line with no support at all. But this was April 12, 1782. With undeviating precision the next five ships, *Namur*, *St Albans*, *Canada*, *Repulse*, and *Ajax*, followed their admiral through the gap. The time was just 9.15.

Ahead of the *Formidable* was the 90-gun *Duke*, 'the tremendous Duke' as she was called from her figurehead of Butcher Cumberland in his red coat. Douglas, her former captain, had already fitted his improvements to her artillery. At about the same time as Sir George and Douglas were conferring on the flagship's quarter-deck, Gardner, the *Duke*'s captain, was startled to discover enemy ships to port, for the Frenchmen bearing down on him had already conformed to the shift of wind. Before he realized it he also was sailing through the enemy line (if it can still be

---

* See in particular Captain Thomas White's 'Naval Researches'. White was a lieutenant in the *Barfleur*.

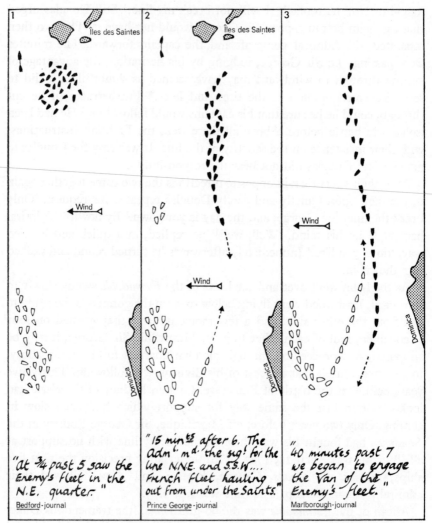

1

Îles des Saintes

Wind

Dominica

"at ¾ past 5 saw the Enemy's fleet in the N.E. quarter."

Bedford-journal

2

Îles des Saintes

Wind

Wind

Dominica

"15 minᵗˢ after 6. The Admᵗ. mᵈ. the sigᵗ for the line N.N.E. and S.S.W.... French Fleet hauling out from under the Saints."

Prince George-journal

3

Wind

Dominica

"40 minutes past 7 we began to engage the Van of the Enemy's fleet."

Marlborough-journal

BATTLE OF THE SAINTS, APRIL 12, 1782

called a line), and, as he confessed later, his first horrified thought was that he might, like Byng, be shot on his own quarter-deck for his appalling transgression. Then, looking astern, he was relieved to see his Commander-in-Chief in the *Formidable*, followed by other ships, doing exactly the same thing.[12]

Six ships astern of the *Formidable*, Commodore Affleck in the *Bedford* was faced with the same situation. After passing ten ships to starboard he

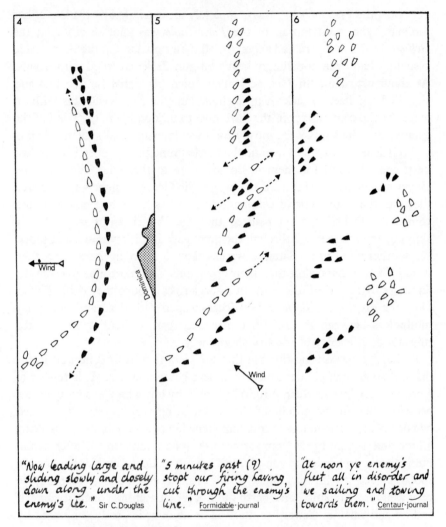

"Now leading large and sliding slowly and closely down along under the enemy's lee." Sir C. Douglas

"5 minutes past (9) stopt our firing having cut through the enemy's line." Formidable-journal

"at noon ye enemy's fleet all in disorder and we sailing and towing towards them." Centaur-journal

BATTLE OF THE SAINTS, APRIL 12, 1782

saw the Frenchmen ahead of him moving across his bow in line of bearing as the shift of wind took them. With all Hood's division astern he led on to the northward to inflict a third break in the French line.

The pattern of the battle had been made—and broken. A lull now descended as the wind, killed for the moment by so much gunfire, dropped almost completely. On the British side there was a sorry story of topmasts and topsail-yards shot away. The *Fame* was still making three feet of water per hour; the *Prince George* was completely incapacitated by the loss of her foremast; the main topsail of the *Formidable* was shot to ribbons; the *Belliqueux* and *Monarch* had expended all their powder. On the French side casualties had been appallingly heavy on gun-decks crowded with troops. At about 9.30 a.m. Sir George hauled down his signal for the line and signalled the fleet to tack. Half an hour later he reinforced this with an order for the commander in the third post to tack and gain the wind of the enemy. But the ships were mostly too busy knotting and splicing rigging and repairing damages to resume the battle immediately, even if there had been enough wind for them to do so; more to the point, there was no longer an enemy to windward to engage. Sir George's signals to tack well illustrate the limitations of command once a battle became extended and confused. He had not yet realized that the French ships were already slipping away to leeward through the great gaps in his own line, and round the southern end of it. Battered wrecks though many of them were, they were in better shape aloft than their opponents, and more able to catch the faint airs that came off the land. In disorganized groups they drifted clear. Only the dismasted *Glorieux*, her decks heaped with dead and dying, lay motionless between the British centre and rear, a silent witness to the murderous efficiency of the British gunnery.

Perhaps it was during this lull that Sir George refreshed himself in the manner so engagingly described by a near contemporary. 'It is related of Lord Rodney,' wrote Rear-Admiral Ekins,* 'by one who was a party on the occasion, that in the middle of the battle, being very thirsty, he directed one of his little attendants to mix him some lemonade. The boy, observing a lime and a knife black from former use upon a table in the after cabin, immediately proceeded to comply, and having made it, but being without a spoon, stirred it with his knife. "Child", said Lord Rodney, "that may do very well for a midshipman's berth but not for an admiral; drink it yourself and go and call my steward to me."' The account is partly confirmed by Lord Cranston's picture of a Commander-in-Chief, too preoccupied to quit the quarter-deck for any sort of refreshment, but with a lemon constantly in his hand and frequently at his lips.[13]

Slowly the breeze returned and the sails began to fill. Hood dropped his boats into the water to pull the *Barfleur*'s head round. So did Inglefield of the *Centaur*. A French frigate managed to pass a tow line across to the *Glorieux*. Ships began to move again. Soon the head of every British ship still in the fight was pointing to the south or to the south-west, as the

* *Naval Battles,* 1824.

respective captains began to understand what had happened. Sir George, looking across the water, saw the *Glorieux* in the midst of his own fleet and remembered his Homer: now, he remarked, was to be the contest for the body of Patroclus.* But there was no contest here. The tow was cast off as the British ships approached and in the afternoon the *Royal Oak* quietly took possession. At half past one the *Fame*, although far from having mastered her leaks, recorded in her journal: 'Made all the sail we could to come up with the flying enemy.' And so it was with all the British fleet except the *Royal Oak* and the disabled *Prince George*.

All afternoon and until dusk, the British ships with their damaged masts and yards followed the shattered French fleet. Sir George's cautious insistence that they should pursue 'in a body' provoked the usual scathing criticism from Hood who would have preferred a general chase with more sail carried. Affleck of the *Bedford* also thought that had the pursuit been keener 'many more must have been taken'.[14] This is as may be, but an equally respectable witness, Sir Charles Douglas, has recorded that 'the victors stuck so close to their flying (late) antagonists as to leave them no time to rally or repair any part of their damages'.[15] And close they certainly were, for at 3 p.m. the British van and centre were so hotly engaged with the enemy rear that the French leaders were obliged to form and put about to support them. During this phase of the action the *César* and *Hector* (both seventy-fours), which with the *Glorieux* had borne the brunt when the British broke through, fell astern. At half past three the sorely tried *César* struck to the *Centaur*. An hour later the *Hector* lowered her colours to the *Canada*. Cornwallis pressed on but the *Alcide*, coming up after her, fired another broadside into the now silent Frenchman, killing her captain, and took possession.

Another straggler in the French retreat was the old 64-gun *Ardent*, formerly British, which had been taken off Plymouth in 1779. Shortly before six the *Belliqueux* and *Prince William* engaged her. A few shots were exchanged and she struck. Then, with surprising promptness, she hoisted British colours (the explanation is that she had some British prisoners on board) and within five minutes was standing in to the British fleet. She was a prize worth taking, having on board all de Bouillé's siege artillery for Jamaica.

But the noblest prize of all was still labouring on under no more than a foresail, lower steering-sail, and mizen-topsail, although the pursuers had

* This is the earliest version of this anecdote, as told by Dr Blane in a letter of April 22, 1782.

been snapping at her heels for some time. The Comte de Grasse may not have been a great admiral, but he was a great gentleman, and when all seemed lost he had striven to rally his flying divisions. But Bougainville, with the van almost intact, pressed on into the gathering dusk. So did the 80-gun *Couronne*, ignoring appeals shouted across the water. At 6 p.m. the mighty *Ville de Paris*, deserted by all her consorts, was exchanging shots with the *Marlborough* and *Barfleur*. The *Russell* bore down under her stern and raked her. De Grasse, unwilling to strike to any two-decker, sheered over towards Hood's flagship. The *Barfleur* fired one last, tremendous broadside at point-blank range, and down came the flag of de Grasse from the main topmast-head, and the flag of France from the ensign staff, and all the signal flags together. The time was just 6.30 p.m. Immediately afterwards Sir George, to the consternation of his Second-in-Command, made the signal for the fleet to break off the action and lie to.

This decision to end the action as soon as the French flagship struck, brings Sir George's professional judgement into conflict with Hood's, whose violent condemnation of his chief, in a number of extremely outspoken letters to eminent personages, has shaped opinion on the subject ever since. Hood, who would have pursued with much more vigour during the afternoon, would also have carried on through the night to finish the business next morning. By so doing, he assured his correspondents, he would have secured 'full twenty sail of the enemy's line of battle before dark' and 'almost every ship' of the remainder next day, an assertion which can be neither proved nor disproved but which certainly does not err on the side of modesty.[16] Sir George was more concerned with his own fleet's damage aloft, the shortage of powder, the safety of the prizes, and above all the dangers of a night action: for there would be no moon this time to save his ships from firing into each other. He may have credited the retreating French with more order and unity than they possessed; and he later admitted that he had some fear of being lured by false lights to leeward.[17] Almost certainly he erred on the side of caution. But this is not to admit that Hood's vauntings can be wholly accepted. During the night the French showed a very clean pair of heels. Commodore Affleck, who collected six ships and continued the pursuit until 3 a.m., found the western horizon bare at daylight. All he could see from the masthead were Sir George's ships to the south-east. Nevertheless, one cannot imagine Captain Rodney of the *Eagle* neglecting to press home an advantage. Time takes its toll. For the previous four nights (since making contact with the enemy) Sir George had not slept at all;[18] and twelve hours of intense, nervous strain had passed since he made his decision to attack. Some allowances must be made for age and exhaustion.

The aftermath of the battle appears as a series of sharply defined vignettes against a darkening background of sea and sky. Lord Cranston, 'over his shoes in blood',[19] boards the *Ville de Paris*; de Grasse, dignified in defeat but bitter against Bougainville and the captains who deserted him,[20] consents to go on board the *Formidable* next day; Sir George in his armchair on the quarterdeck, cannot take his eyes from the enormous bulk of the *Ville de Paris*. In every ship boatswains and carpenters labour with exhausted men to repair battle damage, while around them and beneath cruise a ghastly attendance of hungry sharks; and before midnight, away in the darkness, a sudden flame appears, followed by an explosion, as someone in search of liquor on board the captured *César* upsets his candle with catastrophic consequence. Upwards of 400 Frenchmen, with Lieutenant Hayes and fifty-eight of the *Centaur's* people, perished in this last tragic event.

Next morning Hood came on board the *Formidable* to urge a hot pursuit, only to be silenced by his chief's 'Come, we have done very handsomely as it is'. This was final. One did not argue with Sir George. So the disgruntled Second-in-Command had to work off his bad temper on Sir Charles Douglas, which he did before returning to the *Barfleur*,[21] leaving the Commander-in-Chief to direct the fleet *his* way, and to make a start on his correspondence.

He must have enjoyed this. Family letters came first (with Sir George at his most eloquent) before even the official despatch or the private communication to Lord Sandwich. Henny's letter was the longer, but George Rodney's the more revealing.

'April 13th at Sea, 1782.

'Joy to my dearest Son. His Majesty's arms have proved victorious over his Enemys, and the French fleet have met with a total defeat. De Grasse in the *Ville de Paris* has graced our Victory, and four more of the line. He is at this moment setting in my stern gallery and declares that his fleet was superior in force to mine tho' mine more in number. The Battle was long and very bloody on the Enemy's side and miraculously otherways on ours considering that the Action continued more than ten hours without one moment's interval. Jamaica will be saved by it. Every ship had troops and military stores on board. They are now so much shattered that it will be impossible for them to repair their losses, and I believe will not give us Battle again this war. I am at this moment persuing them. The shattered condition of my ships would not permit me to do it last night and my fleet are not used to night actions. I am sure, had I permitted it, half my fleet had destroyed the other and done more harm than good. . . .'[22]

The excellent George could be relied on to spread this information in the right quarters and in particular to deal with any awkward questions about why the French fleet got away. The official despatch—'It has pleased God, out of his Divine Providence, to grant to His Majesty's arms a most complete Victory'—was written next day, as was the private letter to Lord Sandwich. In these Sir George was full of praise for everyone, particularly for Hood, Drake, Affleck, and Douglas. From him at any rate there would be no recriminations. Everything had been for the best and Jamaica was safe. Nor, in any of his other letters, and he wrote a great many, was there one hint of criticism or complaint. On the 15th the *Andromeda*, commanded by Captain Byron, sailed for England with Lord Cranston and the official despatches. She had on board also the gallant Lord Robert Manners, late of the *Resolution* and badly wounded in the action, who would not survive the voyage. The victorious fleet, with all but one of its prizes in tow, pursued its leisurely course for Jamaica, reconnoitring the islands as it passed, and slowly putting itself to rights.

De Grasse remained two days on board the *Formidable* where everything was made as agreeable for him as possible. Cornwallis saw him absorbed in the capture of a shark from the captain's stern gallery and apparently without a care in the world. The huge Frenchman, he was 6 ft 2 in tall, pleased his host immensely by professing to fall in love with the portraits of the Misses Rodney, restored to the cabin bulkhead after their refuge during the battle in the Admiral's wine store. But Sir George, despite his long exile in Paris, was no linguist, so most of the conversation fell to that excellent French scholar Sir Charles Douglas. Dr Blane was presented as '*le médecin de nos armées navales qui est presque assez habile pour faire revivre les morts*', to which the Count, humouring the badinage, replied '*et peut-être pour faire mourir les vivants*'. Blane found him most affable and communicative, exceedingly critical of the politicians in Paris, and of opinion that the British Navy was at least 100 years ahead of the French.[23] Discipline had broken down on board the *Ville de Paris*, as in the other prizes, after she struck, and there had been drunkenness and looting. De Grasse was worried about £5,000 of his private fortune that had been on board her. He was at once reassured, and his captors were even better than their word, for before long money chests, many more than his own, were arriving in his cabin.

But the record of successes was not yet complete. The two sixty-fours *Caton* and *Jason*, having completed their repairs at Guadeloupe, were on their way to rejoin de Grasse, knowing nothing of his defeat. Off Porto Rico on the 20th they had the misfortune to fall in with the ships of Hood's division, cruising ahead of the main fleet. With them were taken the 32-gun frigate *Aimable* and the former British sloop *Ceres*.

On the 29th the *Formidable* dropped anchor in Port Royal harbour, Jamaica. Flying their flags in the crowded anchorage were Sir Peter Parker in the *Sandwich*, Thomas Graves in the *London*, and Joshua Rowley in the *Ramillies*. It may be doubted whether any of these distinguished officers were particularly pleased to see Sir George, but the good folk of Port Royal and Kingston had been under no delusion as to their danger, and were jubilant at their deliverance. However, Sir George was in no mood to be pestered with addresses. The *Formidable*'s side was hauled to the wind to keep her cool and the victorious Commander-in-Chief resolutely remained on board.

Undoubtedly Jamaica had been saved, but with so many enemy troops at St Domingo, and so many French and Spanish warships at Cape François and Port-au-Prince, the danger had not passed completely. But all of May went by and then June with nothing but the routine of fleet administration, most of which Sir George turned over to Hood, and not one word from the authorities at home. This was disquieting. Soon Sir George took up his residence on shore. Observers noted his preoccupation and some ascribed it to misgivings about his conduct of the battle, and fears as to how the news might be received in England. Cornwallis saw him as a man 'uncertain whether he was to be rewarded or punished', and goes on to hint that the censorious voice of Hood was only silenced by his chief's compliance in advancing so many of Hood's followers,[24] a hypothesis sufficiently improbable to shake one's faith in Cornwallis as a wholly reliable witness. But this is how tongues wagged in the weeks which followed.

It is true enough, however, that the battle made many vacancies for the Commander-in-Chief to fill. Hood's deserving young cousin and Keppel's less deserving nephew both became captains, while John Rodney, the object of so many misdirected favours and not even present at the battle, moved from his frigate to the 64-gun *Anson*. But many other officers of very different quality moved up with him in the promotions which followed the battle. Alexander Ball and Davidge Gould might never have commanded ships at the Nile, Sidney Smith have defended Acre, or Lord Northesk have flown his flag at Trafalgar, without Sir George's patronage at this time. Ben Hallowell, another Nile captain, was also under his protection. The future was well cared for.[25]

July came, with the hurricane season soon to be expected, and Sir George was again considering taking his ships to North America. But still authority at home remained strangely silent.

On March 20, 1782, unable any longer to withstand the mounting tide of hostility at home and disaster abroad, Lord North resigned. The opposition, the men who had supported Keppel against Palliser, Baillie against Lord Sandwich, and the merchants of St Eustatius against Sir George, took office under Lord Rockingham. It was hardly to be expected that so staunch a supporter of the late administration as Sir George Rodney, with St Eustatius against his name, would be allowed to fly his flag much longer. It is perhaps surprising that he was allowed to continue as long as he did.

The new First Lord was Keppel, and bitterly must he have cursed the situation in which his political friends had landed him. For Keppel, it was whispered, was aghast at being expected to pole-axe his old friend, and held out against it as long as he could. But the men who had placed him at the head of the Admiralty were very much his masters in politics. On May 2nd the unhappy First Lord, unaware of course of the recent victory, one result of which had been the posting of his own nephew, sat down to compose a difficult letter.

'May 2 1782.

'Dear Sir George Rodney,

'The task of writing disagreeable information to you falls unpleasantly to my lot. The situation I am placed in makes it on course my duty to trouble you with this letter. Reasoning upon the subject I am sure you will think un-necessary. It is enough for me to inform you as shortly as I am able that the King's servants have judged it for reasons of State that Admiral Pigot should immediately proceed to the West Indies and there take upon him the chief command of the fleet at present under your direction, and that you should, upon Admiral Pigot's arrival, give him every information in your power, resigning the command to him and returning with as little loss of time as possible to England.'[26]

Four copies did he write with his own hand in case of mishap. Pigot's qualifications to supersede Sir George were his high position on the flag-list and his firm attachment to the new government. He had never before hoisted his flag at sea.

In due course the new Commander-in-Chief left London to embark on board the *Jupiter* (50) at Plymouth. Meanwhile the *Andromeda*, with Sir George's despatches, had struck soundings at 8 p.m. on May 15th, and picked up her pilot off Lundy next morning. As soon as Lord Cranston and Captain Byron landed they wasted no time on the road, reaching London at 2 a.m. on the 18th. The Admiralty day started early. The despatches were opened by Stephens and digested by Keppel well before 8 a.m. because at that hour notes of congratulation from both gentlemen reached Henny in Portman Street. By 10 o'clock Sir George's family letters had been sorted from the bag and delivered to the delighted household. Captain Byron called a little later.[27]

To recall a national hero was unthinkable. A hasty consultation took place among the men in power, as result of which a King's messenger left for Plymouth that same morning to stop Pigot before he sailed. The despatch was in the *Gazette* the same day. The thanks of both Houses of Parliament were voted at the earliest possible moment, Keppel in the Lords being seconded by Lord Sandwich who could not resist quizzing his successor about the rumours of Sir George's recall. Uncertain whether Pigot would be stopped or not Keppel fenced awkwardly. 'What was thrown out by the noble Earl on that head', he protested, 'proceeded upon the vague report and fable of the day. There was no official evidence of the existence of such a thing before the House, and it was therefore improper to dwell upon it.'[28] But although the King's messenger was only twenty-eight hours on the road, he was exactly twenty-eight hours too late. Pigot had sailed on the morning Sir George's despatches reached London, and a fast cutter sent out after the *Jupiter* failed to catch her. So Keppel had to write again.

'May 29th 1782.

'*Dear Sir George Rodney,*

'I am sure no one friend you have in the world could have rejoiced more than I have done at your glorious success in defeating the French off

Dominique. Admiral Pigot was sailed before your despatches giving the account of it reached London so that no letters could be wrote to you by him. I trust the measures relating to Admiral Pigot's being sent to the command in the West Indies will remain for your quiet reasoning till we meet, (and I hope amicably), in this country. Secrets of government can not, with propriety, be divulged, and therefore I am sure you will not expect explanations from me upon this subject. . . .'[29]

Pigot made a fast passage but rumour flew ahead faster still. As early as June 10th Marr at St Lucia wrote to warn his patron of the alarming report 'that Admiral Pigot has kissed hands on his being appointed Commander-in-Chief in these seas'. The unhappy agent-victualler, so recently installed and now fearful of another turn of Fortune's wheel, thought it 'hardly possible', but all the same he was so low-spirited he could scarcely write. He begged Sir George to remember the aspirations of a nephew in his secretary's office to be purser of a frigate.[30]

So when the *Jupiter* dropped anchor in Port Royal on July 10th, Pigot's appearance did not come as a complete surprise. For the new Commander-in-Chief the situation cannot at first have been easy. Nor can his arrival have done anything to allay the gnawing doubts (if doubts there were) in Sir George's mind, as to how the news of the battle would be received at home. But after a few more days of suspense there arrived a second packet bulging with comforting assurances that all was well. There was a communication from one of the new Secretaries of State, Lord Shelburne, beginning auspiciously 'My Lord',[31] so the peerage was safe at last, whatever disgruntled individuals in the West Indies might be saying. It was only a British barony and Henny, while congratulating her 'dear Lord' on his title, confessed that she was not quite satisfied with the degree of it 'because the Nation is not'.[32] But in Parliament all Sir George's enemies were in retreat. Charles Fox had been forced to admit that if the Admiral wished for an earldom he would not oppose it, while Burke had trimmed his sails to the wind by dropping his motion and conceding in the House that if there was a bald spot on the head of a Rodney he had no objections to covering it with laurels.[33] It was clear that there were to be no recriminations and that the new government would make what amends it could. Hood was to receive an Irish barony, Drake and Affleck would become baronets. Best of all perhaps, a certain Sir Francis Bassett had already given notice that he would shortly move for an income to be settled on the new peer. Upon his supercession Sir George has left no comment. Lord

Sandwich, in his own congratulatory letter, put forward the common-sense view. 'I am sure that your being recalled in the height of your glory will be the most fortunate event that ever happened to anyone.'[34] Probably Lord Rodney, as he must now be called, agreed. His work was done, and he could now anticipate his homecoming with complacency.

And so the board was cleared for the last time. Pigot, seconded by Hood, took the main fleet to North America; Graves in the *Ramillies*, with the French prizes and such ships as needed repair, sailed for England with the trade; and the late Commander-in-Chief transferred himself, his retinue, and his belongings to the *Montagu*. A storm in a tea-cup marred his departure. On the eve of sailing, in a last exercise of that flag-officer's patronage which was so dear to him, he appointed three worthy but unqualified midshipmen as lieutenants on board the *Shrewsbury* whose captain, himself posted only a few weeks before and probably driven beyond endurance by the crazy state of his new command, refused to accept them. He was ordered into arrest. Captain Isaac Coffin was no plaster saint but on this occasion right was on his side. But long before he faced his court martial (and was acquitted) Lord Rodney was far away, with other things to think about. His farewell letter to Hood is almost in holiday mood.

'*Montagu* off Burmuda, Aug. 8 1782.

'*My Dear Lord,*

'I was too ill during my continuance at Port Royal to write to you and to congratulate you on the great approbation of your Sovereign and both Houses of Parliament. Give me leave now to do it which I most sincerely do, and Hope it will not end in an Irish Peerage. Depend upon it you will have an English one. I will not be violent but will speak out and say it ought to be. I am told that if I insist upon it they will give me an Earldome. I certainly will demand it and at the same time say they ought to give you an English barony. You may be sure, my Dear Friend, I will look about me before I act, and know the ground I tread on. Our most gracious Sovereign will grant us anything I am well assured of.

'Thank God I allready experience the difference of Climate, but tis with real concern that I say poor Captain Marshall still continues extreamly ill. I wanted to take him on board the *Montagu* and send his ship to joyn Mr Pigot, but it would have broken his heart as he had set it upon the *Flora*. I am sure Mr Pigot has too great a regard for him not to wish to save his life, which nothing but a speedy passage to England can do.

'On my arrival at Portsmouth I will pay my respects to Lady Hood if its but for a moment, and to kiss the hand of your sweet girl, tho' Lady Rodney may be present.

'Adieu, my Dear Friend. May health and happiness attend you is the sincere wish of him who is with truth,

'Yours most faithfully,
'RODNEY.'[35]

Chapter 24

Bleak Glory

(1782–1792)

'Without disparaging any of the other brave sea-officers
that have lately and in former times augmented the lustre
of the British flag, I can safely say that your Lordship
has surpassed all their glorious achievements, as no one
before you can boast of having taken or destroyed
16 ships of the line in the space of two years & a half, &
captured the commanding admiral of each of the nations
with which we are at war.'
(Speech by Lord Sandwich, on Lord Rodney receiving
the Freedom of the borough of Huntingdon,
December 1782.)[1]

O N Wednesday September 15, 1782, the inhabitants of Bristol
learnt with surprise and pleasure that Lord Rodney's flagship
had arrived off the Flatholm. The equinoctial gales had
forced this diversion on the *Montagu*, but the London road
was as good as any in the kingdom, and the Admiral would be able to get to
town with little loss of time. Thus it was that a seagoing career which had
started fifty years before, came to an end at 5 p.m. that afternoon when
Lord Rodney stepped ashore to take up his night's lodgings at the house
of Mr Tindall at the fort.

Bristol of all places would not lose an opportunity like this. That
evening an enormous number of citizens turned out with torches to pay
their respects. Their repeated 'Huzzas' compelled the opening of the fort's
inner gate, and there was the national hero with a group of officers on the
steps outside Mr Tindall's front door. Not all of the invaders could see him.
Would Lord Rodney be pleased to stand on a chair ? His Lordship declined
but condescended to show himself from an upper window, to be greeted
with renewed applause after which the satisfied crowd withdrew to the
Bush Inn where there was arrack punch for the quality, and two barrels of

beer for the populace. For the next fortnight every newspaper in England entertained its readers with stories of the hero's return. How, next morning, when his account was requested from Mr Weeks of the Bush Inn, that sturdy patriot replied: 'Your Lordship forgets that you paid it beforehand on 12 April'; and how, after this, when the Admiral expressed his wish to reach Bath as quickly as possible, it was again the irrepressible Mr Weeks, dressed as a postillion on the box, who drew out his watch with the memorable words: 'As your Lordship said to the Governor of St Eustatius on demanding his capitulation, "in an hour, my Lord, and not a moment longer"'. And in an hour it was, if the newspapers are to be believed, and then, after the briefest of halts, on to London.[2]

Lord Rodney derived no satisfaction at all from popular applause, and inept allusions to April 12th. At sixty-four he had achieved glory enough. More to the point would be his reception by his Sovereign and by the new ministers, and the details of the new settlement approved by Parliament. Upon matters like these, and the sums to be paid by the government for the French prizes, would depend the style in which he would be able to support his new dignity. Henny was already installed at Purbrook Park near Portsmouth, on a short lease fortunately, for the spacious prospects anticipated immediately after St Eustatius could no longer be hoped for. Her husband, with so much to discuss in town, settled for the time being in Hertford Street. He was disappointed to learn that Lord Sandwich had just gone into the country, vexed that the Admiralty would not pay a penny on the prizes until they were safely at Spithead, but reassured over the ministry's attitude towards the pension.[3]

For a while the public claimed him. Before Lord Sandwich returned he was away to Hampshire for the entertainment prepared by the Duke of Chandos and the Corporation of Winchester. From Avington he drove with the Duke into the city. The Militia fired a *feu-de-joie*, the populace took the horses from the carriage and drew it up the High Street to the Guildhall, and the Corporation presented him with the Freedom of the City in a box made of the Heart of Oak, after which there was a superb entertainment, with illuminations, bonfires, and four hogsheads of beer. Something very similar had to be endured at Bristol a few weeks later, with dinner at the Merchant's Hall, followed by a ball, after which he had to return to town to be entertained by the City at the London Tavern. The toast of the evening was of course 'Lord Rodney, with three times three'. The honoured guest then did what was expected of him by proposing 'Prosperity to the City of London and its Trade and Commerce', and then, after nearly every other commander on April 12th had been toasted, he rose once more to confound the politicians by proposing the health of Lord Keppel.[4] 'I left the London at 9 o'clock,' he wrote afterwards to Henny, 'and was in hopes of going privately home, but that was not allowed. The horses were forceably taken up, and the coach drawn by the Mob to Hertford Street. In the City the mob behaved very peaceably but in Westminster many windows destroy'd* because they had not eluminated in time. In short, about 11 I got home, heartyly tired of their affection. So much for my City treat.'[5]

Meanwhile his flag was at last hauled down. The ministers handled a prickly subject with velvet gloves. Once again Keppel was the spokesman. 'My Dear Lord,' he wrote privately on October 21st: 'Since seeing your Lordship, the Board has judged it proper to dismantle the *Montagu* at Portsmouth. She will therefore be ordered into harbour . . . the Board judging it respectful to your waiting till I had privately informed you of it, that you may rest satisfied with their attention. No object at present pointing itself for the services of a flag-officer so high in rank as yourself being wanted, your Lordship will in common form be directed to strike your flag and come on shore as soon as you honour me with a line.'[6] And so, while his Lordship nursed his gout and worried about the French prizes and fussed over the details of the pension, a great chapter of naval history finally closed.

Money was still his main preoccupation. The Admiral had suffered too much not to be anxious. But his warm and generous sympathy to those whose misfortune he could understand was as strong as ever. 'I have been out,' he informed Henny at this time, 'and visited poor Mrs Burnett who, 'tho' recovered, has been very much pulled down. She talks of going to Bath in a day or two—and as I fear her finances are low I propose begging her acceptance of a small Bill to pay her expenses upon the road. Much I can not afford, and hope a twenty pound Bill will not be taken amiss. . . .'[7]

In December there were alarming rumours of gales in the Atlantic. Graves' convoy had been scattered. The *Ville de Paris* had been reported with her main and mizen masts gone, her upper and middle deck guns jettisoned, and her stern burst in by a sea. When last seen she was bearing away for the Azores with her stern canvassed over and jury masts going up, but this had been as long ago as September 23rd. Her fate was still uncertain when, just before Christmas, the indomitable hero mastered his gout and

---

* Horace Walpole suffered in this way. His letter of November 29th to the Countess of Ossory is very scathing.

went off to fulfil a long-standing engagement with Lord Sandwich, and to receive the Freedom of the Borough of Huntingdon. Once again there were the toasts, the parades, the speeches (the principal one by Lord Sandwich himself) and the illuminations. But such junketings, on top of a winter journey from London, were too much. A few days later the public learnt that the brave Admiral Rodney was lying dangerously ill at Huntingdon, and that a London physician had been summoned in haste.

This was the end of the public entertainments, although not the end of Lord Rodney's capacity to draw a crowd; for when, the following March, he appeared as a witness at the Court of King's Bench, people so thronged to see him that proceedings in court had to be discontinued.[8] But a sick man he remained for most of 1783. Henny and the children stayed on at Purbrook—'keep it we must,' he told her, 'until the time runs out'[9]—while her lord attended such functions in town as he considered sufficiently important and endeavoured to restore his health. At Bath he developed a close friendship with John Wilkes. 'Lord Rodney has been here 3 hours this morning', Wilkes informed his daughter on April 21st. 'He has given me a variety of interesting particulars which I dare not transcribe. He has a whole house in Gay street and presses me much to accept apartments and live with him. He pressed cordially. He is alone except a physician, visits very few, and goes to no balls etc.' To Wilkes the Admiral seems to have unburdened himself in his usual way. 'He neither loves nor commends Howe,' Wilkes went on, 'and thinks he is highly culpable for not destroying the whole fleet of France and Spain off Gibraltar, as he says Howe might have done.' Wilkes was a sympathetic and understanding crony. The two old gentlemen were much together after this and their friendship endured.[10]

The semi-truce with Lowther, Mackreth and Co. continued, and it at last became possible to get some idea of how the Admiral's finances stood. There would not be much from the French prizes, for hope had been abandoned for most of them. One survivor from the *Ville de Paris* had been picked up from a piece of wreckage and landed at Havre, but all he could remember was that his name was James Wilson and that he had seen the *Glorieux* go down the day before. The *Hector* had foundered in bad weather off Newfoundland after an action with two French frigates. The *César* had blown up. From the others the Admiral's sixteenth brought in a mere £5,016 13s 5½d,[11] which was disappointing. But since George Rodney had taken over his father's affairs they had been transformed. George was methodical and conscientious. Every claim was carefully examined, every receipt safely filed. Between 1780 and 1782 he paid out the staggering sum of £32,700 from old notes of hand (often with huge accumulation of interest), arrears on annuities, and tradesmen's accounts (some going back nearly twenty years).[12] These disbursements swallowed up every penny of the prize-money and other benefits since 1779. But with the slate now clean (or almost), it was possible to see ahead much more clearly.

On the credit side there was the salary of £430 per annum as Vice-Admiral of England, the English pension bringing in a clear £2,000 a year, and the second pension which, because it was on the Irish establishment, would bring in no more than £1,300 unless the recipient went to live in Ireland which was not to be thought of. There should also have been the Admiral's half-pay, but this was still going to Lowther, Mackreth and Co. At a rough estimate, £3,700 a year might reasonably be hoped for.

On the debit side there was a settlement of £800 a year on George Rodney and £300 a year on John. Seven annuities arising from old debts and impossible to recover accounted for another £600 a year, and later there was a settlement of £500 a year on Lady Rodney. This left only £1,500 a year, provided that Lowther, Mackreth and Co. remained quiescent. It was adequate for a gentlemanly existence, and if the St Eustatius decision went the right way there might one day be a great deal more. But for the time being there could be no question of buying a country seat. This sad truth was at last brought home in August 1783 when the Admiral discovered the property which, above all others, might have suited him. Less splendid than Avington but more elegant than Alresford, Cams Hall in Hampshire, with its handsome park and plantations at the top of Portsmouth harbour, its great oval reception rooms, and its marble chimney pieces, represented an ideal. Moreover, the country about it was all gravel, an important consideration for a sufferer from the gout. 'I own I like it much,' he informed Henny on the 23rd, 'and could it be taken for a year or two with the park and the farm, I own I should prefer it to any place in this Country and wish I had the money ready. . . .'[13] But here, as always, was the crux. Eventually a small house was acquired at Kensington Gore[14] where he could entertain his friends in a very modest way, and whence he could drive pleasantly through the parks to the House of Lords.* For the great world was still an absorbing interest. He had his visits to Court, and the debates in the Lords, besides his circle at Bath.

* With characteristic disregard for regulations Lord Rodney neglected to acquire an official pass for crossing the Green Park and the Horse Guards on his way to Parliament until a complaint was made, when he was obliged to apply in proper form. It can hardly be a coincidence that the complainant was Mackreth. (H.O. 42/8.)

And it was well that he had these distractions, for the next few years were to bring their full measure of disappointment and sorrow.

He had been married to Henny twenty years. She had borne him six children, the last, whom they named Edward, appearing in 1783. Often they had been difficult years, but the picture is always of a united family. Adversity had never shaken them. But when at last port was reached and the shades of illustrious retirement beckoned alluringly, the family broke up. George Rodney remained, as ever, his father's stay and consolation; and with the other children there was no lasting breach. But between Lady Rodney and her husband some sort of agreement was reached that they should live apart. The separation was final, and nowhere is there any indication why it happened.

That there was a very serious crisis in the family at this time, however, is revealed by John Wilkes in a letter to his daughter dated July 27, 1784. 'Lord Rodney is in great affliction that his eldest daughter run to the blacksmiths at Gretna Green last Thursday with Sir William Chambers son. One of Lord Rodney's sons played the same game with I know not whom the week before and is said to have contrived it for his sister. . . .'[15] Whatever the truth about Gretna Green, Jane Rodney certainly married George Chambers about this time. As for John Rodney, for it was indeed this spoilt young man, now aged nineteen, to whom Wilkes was referring, he eloped with Lady Catherine Nugent, daughter of Lord Westmeath, and married her that July.

Henny's feelings about all this are not recorded. Perhaps she sympathized with the young people. She may even have sided with them. But to a man like Lord Rodney such a double blow cannot be measured in words. Jenny was his favourite daughter, the image of himself, and only seventeen. And as for John! How could he ever hold up his head again?

Perhaps because of this appalling blow, perhaps because his physician really did advise wintering in the south of France, the Admiral withdrew to the Continent before the year ended. News had reached England that the Comte de Grasse was to face an enquiry into his conduct on April 12th. Society retained sympathetic memories of the melancholy, dignified Frenchman. Lord Rodney considered him 'a brave but unfortunate man', and hoped to pay his respects. Writing to Lord Temple before his departure he delivered himself of a curiously flavoured tribute. 'On what a pinnacle does the Character and Honour of a Commander-in-Chief of either Navy or Army stand when, after every fatigue of Mind and Body, and Conducting with Diligence, Activity and Resolution the Forces entrusted to his

Care to the field of Battle . . . the tongues of Envy, Malice and Detraction are let loose; and those who merited the least Honour claim the Greatest, and slander the Character of that Officer whose misfortune was owing maybe to their wilful mistaking his signals and Orders.' The misbehaviour of April 17th off Martinique still rankled; but as his pen scratched on, it seems that later grievances did too. 'But Grant success attends his Conduct,' he continued, 'and Victory triumphant crowns his Toylls, is the Commander-in-Chief less obnoxious to the minds of Envy who pine at his Success and with Malicious Wisper endeavour to steal from him the Honours justly due to him alone? Such, My Dear Lord, is the penalty paid by those who aspire to command Fleets and Armys, and by what has befallen the Great and Gallant Officer Count de Grasse I am convinced that Faction and Party were not confined to the Fleets of Britain. . . .'[16] It would be pleasant to know that the two admirals met again, to grumble together over the effects of politics on discipline, and to lament the days when standards were different.

Lord Rodney travelled far. In an hotel in Florence a lieutenant who had served in the *Barfleur* on April 12th was presented, and received a warm shake of the hand.[17] The waters of Spa were tried. But before the end of 1785 he was home again, for the long drawn-out process of law relating to St Eustatius was at last coming to an end in Westminster Hall.

Over the disposal of the goods it will be remembered that Sir George and General Vaughan, with the ready connivance of the late Captain Walter Young, had disregarded the committee of officers and managed things very much by themselves. Hood never forgot or forgave this. As the possibility began to dawn on him that the capture might yield nothing at all, he wrote to his old chief, scarcely bothering to conceal the venom.

'*Barfleur*, off C. Tiburon, Feb. 7 1783.

'. . . It is to your Lordship and Gen. Vaughan we must look in this sad business, as everything was transacted by your joint orders, in direct opposition to a solid, sensible, and judicious plan, unanimously fixed by your own particular desire and which, had it not been departed from, the principal inconveniences and distresses would have been prevented. I took the liberty of warning you in time against what you were about, and your Lordship has acknowledged the receipt of my letters. It is become a very serious concern to me. I have had a great deal of Fagging my Lord with scarce any advantage, and if the Courts of Justice do not relieve us, which I have full confidence they will do, I shall, after all my fatigue and trouble, return home as poor as I came out.'[18] Hood liked prize-money as much as anyone.

Sir George's case had been, and still was, that any British merchant with property on the island must have been trading with the enemy and must therefore be a traitor—and in most cases he was probably right. So he had confiscated ruthlessly. But to guard against any possible claims in the courts he had seized every commercial letter-book and ledger he could lay hands on. With special care because, as he averred, they proved his case against the merchants up to the hilt, they were all put on board Commodore Hotham's ship for England and safely lodged in the Secretary of State's office. If he had been ruthless, he had also been circumspect.

But as the tedious battle fought itself out in the courts, it was discovered that these damning documents were missing. Soon after Lord George Germain ceased to be Secretary of State they had been removed from the office, and try as they would the representatives of Rodney and Vaughan were unable to trace them. This is all that can be stated with certainty. But too many people were interested in their disappearance to make their fate a matter of much doubt. Lord Shelburne had been the Secretary of State when the papers disappeared but his Lordship, now out of office, kept well clear of the affair. Mr Knox, Under Secretary to the Colonial Department at the time, was able to produce a Mr Pollock, still first clerk in the office, who remembered delivering them on his Lordship's orders. And from Dublin came a hint, from a not very respectable individual, Thomas Digges, agent for the American prisoners during the war, that the papers were still in existence and might yet be produced—for a consideration.[19]

But from that day to this no further word has been heard of them, so the case of Rodney and Vaughan failed. When the last appeal had been heard and dismissed the judgement was: 'Restitution to the Claimants, not to the amount of the Sales, but according to the full, original value of Prime Cost, with charges, freights, and insurance.'[20] This was in 1786. There was more than £100,000 of St Eustatius money in the joint account, but with more than ninety actions already threatening, and claims amounting to upwards of £300,000, the outlook for the captors was grim. Lord Rodney might still enjoy his title and his glory, but he would be left with precious little else.*

* As examples of the demands now made there is the claim of Mr Elias Lindo for £6,700, judgement in his favour by Lord Camden in March 1789, and an order for payment on the joint-account signed by Rodney and Vaughan in January 1790. Claim No. 49 from a Mr Hoelein amounted to £1,137 11s 10d, but the plaintiff was prepared to accept £1,000; the goods in question had been sold for a mere £154 13s 9d. More complicated

'Cruel and unjust'[21] was how the Admiral described the verdict. He vowed he would have Lord Lansdowne (Shelburne that was) impeached; he also wanted to sue him for £500,000. To his friends he admitted that he would soon be '£200,000 worse than nothing'.[22] Wilkes, sympathetic but perplexed, thought that only an Act of Parliament in the next session could save him. Nothing could be done about the former Secretary of State, whose reputation for straightforwardness had never been of the best, but a Memorial was presented to the King, and a pamphlet entitled *A Plain State of Facts relative to the Capture of St. Eustatius* was printed in 1787, and copies despatched to everyone interested from His Majesty downwards. It cost the Admiral £110 which he could ill afford.

For the captors of St Eustatius were now in a perilous situation themselves. As the Admiral pointed out in his Memorial, there was a very real danger of his private fortune being attached, and all his emoluments and rewards being 'wrested from him by those very men whose treasonable practises he once had the means of proving'.[23] It were tedious to pursue the shifts and expedients adopted to extend the processes of the law to avert this danger; but they went on until the Admiral's death. Sufficient to conclude this last incursion into Lord Rodney's finances by saying that at this time of all times, when things were at their worst, the egregious John Rodney had the effrontery to approach his father for further pecuniary aid, using his half-brother as intermediary. George kept his temper, but his reply was unanswerable. '. . . the last time my father was here I mentioned to him the request you made him relative to money matters and I told you, if I mistake not, that it was not profitable for me to say *much* upon that subject, because I was sure he had it not in his power to be very generous. And I must again repeat that from my knowleged of his affairs I fear he has not sufficient to make himself comfortable. . . .'[24] The long-suffering George concluded: '. . . I give you my word neither my father or myself are in the situation that, from the general tenor of your letter, you suppose us to be. . . .'*

But thanks to his eldest son, and no doubt to the Harleys and other connections, it was possible for the old man to live out his life in comfort, and at the same time to make the occasional incursion (generally wrong-

than most was the case of the Swiss-owned *Helvetia* which anchored off St Eustatius the day before the capture. Besides her cargo of cloth she had 180,000 florins on board. Ship and cargo were sold in one lot, without inventory, and before official condemnation, for £15,000. (P.R.O. 30/20/23, 21, and 18 respectively.)

* Wraxall describes Lord Rodney's hospitality at Kensington Gore as 'very far from splendid'.

headed and violent) into public affairs. In 1788 the government's anti-slavery bill stirred up the old fires. To him, as a Freeman of Bristol and Liverpool, it was nothing less than 'an Act of Suicide' against the commerce of Great Britain, and its effects he was quite sure, would be the drain of indentured labour from our own island to the plantations. There was not a slave, he protested, that did not live better than many poor, honest day-labourers in England, and the Bill could only work to the advantage of our enemies among whom he included 'the ungrateful Americans'. Day after day he hobbled into the House of Lords to rally the diehards, and when at last the Bill was dropped he claimed the chief credit.[25]

Later that year the King's mental condition raised grave constitutional issues. Pitt, tenacious of office, brought in a Bill establishing the Prince of Wales as Regent with restricted powers. Partisan feeling, whipped up by the Dukes of York and Clarence, was strong against the proposed limitations. Fox and his colleagues, who might expect office if the new Regent was unfettered, fanned the flames, and Pitt felt the ground slipping beneath him. Lord Rodney, with his genius for political miscalculation, ardently espoused the cause of the Prince of Wales.[26] Apparently the unfettered prerogative meant more to him than the near certainty of his old enemy Fox in office unless, as is possible, some post or sinecure had been promised. However, in the beginning of 1789 the King recovered, Pitt remained in power, and the result of Lord Rodney's intemperate opposition was brought sharply home to him in March when a guard-ship promised to John Rodney went to someone else.

The First Lord was the Earl of Chatham, whose naval brother Sir George had himself promoted in 1779, even though he and all his family were in opposition to the government. The outraged father now launched a devastating reproof by reminding Lord Chatham of this, and to complete his discomfiture he enclosed Lady Chatham's grateful letter of acknowledgement, received just before he sailed.[27] There could be no answer to this. Lord Rodney might be a tiresome survival from the past but he was still a national figure. So when next year some of the fleet had to be commissioned, John Rodney was not forgotten.

As the years went by, more and more of the old Admiral's days were passed under his son George's roof, either at Hanover Square or at Alresford, with occasional visits to Mr Harley's splendid new seat in Herefordshire. George now had a family of his own and the Admiral adored his grandchildren. Already he was thinking of their careers. 'The young rogues must learn figures soon. In a few years it will prove which of them will take to business, or being idle military men not worth a sixpence but with a red or blew coat and a sword dangling to their side.' To which he added, for he was writing to the daughter of Mr Thomas Harley, 'But I hope they will turn to the former.' And again that same autumn of 1788, when Mrs Rodney was expecting her fourth, he urged that George and his friends should remain at Alresford killing partridges, while their wives joined him at Bath for the waters bringing the little boys with them. 'Remember, the children never plague me but contribute to my health.'[28]

One of the obligations that falls on heroes in retirement is to have their portraits painted. Sir Joshua Reynolds who, thirty years before had painted a rear-admiral fresh from bombarding Havre, was in 1787 called on for a full length in the grand manner for the royal palace at St James; and about the same time something rather similar was commissioned (almost certainly by Mr Harley), from Mr Thomas Gainsborough, to hang at Berrington. Gainsborough, never at home with heroics, rather lost sight of the Admiral in his concern for the dramatic presentation of a victorious commander. But Sir Joshua, who was painting the last great portrait of his working life and may have known it, marked all that time had done to a once handsome and engaging young officer, and produced a grim master-piece, more eloquent than words. A few years later the old man, too tired perhaps to stand for another full length, was not too tired to deck himself out extravagantly in a new uniform, and sit for the talented Mr Mosnier.

And so the fires died down at last. Lowther, Mackreth and Co. had ceased to plague him since he began an action against them.[29] The St Eustatius money in the bank trickled away as claim succeeded claim, but these things mattered less now than family affairs, children and grand-children. The last years were passed almost entirely in the domestic tranquillity of George Rodney's London home or at Alresford. With more than seventy years behind him Lord Rodney was still an alert and polished gentleman with the grand manner. 'Bear it ever in mind', he would warn his daughters, 'that a lady or gentleman can not be too polite. Politeness is due, even to a begger. Never neglect it, even to your own servants.'[30] The old man was on good terms with John and Lady Catherine, while of Henny's other children, Anne and Sarah were still within the family circle and dearly loved. Of Henny herself and Edward her youngest, who was the contemporary of the Admiral's grandsons, it is not possible to speak with certainty, nor of Jane who had been his favourite. But something of the spirit of these last years may be caught in two letters written on the same day to a former secretary.

'Old Alresford, Feb. 7 1791.

'*Dear Gerrard,*

'As I have promised my good old nurse Betty Payne a chance in the lottery of a sixteenth part of a tickett, you will much oblige me if you will purchase the 1/16 part of a tickett for her, and enter it in her name, and as I shall soon be in Town I will repay you the purchasing money. Adieu, and be assured I am, '*Your sincere friend, etc.,*
'*RODNEY.*[31]

From the second letter it appears that as soon as the young ladies of the household heard of the favour shown to Betty Payne they lost no time in pressing the indulgent old gentleman to go shares with them in a second ticket, and to write for it at once—which he did.

As his end approached he viewed it with dignified resignation. 'I have at last been able to get down stairs,' he wrote to a friend, 'but I find myself so very weak after the severe fit of sickness I have lately undergone, and my spirits so low, as to convince me that my hour-glass is almost run out. But it is what I must expect from my years and infirmities. However, I have no cause to complain on that score as my days have been multiplied beyond what I imagined, or my constitution promised. I am therefore content, and must bear with patience and resignation the lot of human nature.'[32]

Three weeks before his death he wrote to Lord Amherst, once his passenger in the *Dublin* and now the Commander-in-Chief, with a request that his son George might be allowed to remain on the list of lieutenant-colonels in the army, and flattering himself that 'from our old acquaintance he will meet with your kind assistance'.[33] It was the last of those urbane solicitations which, all his life, he penned with such practised skill. Even with the shadows closing upon him he copied out the duplicate in his own hand—a careful and methodical old gentleman to the end.

On the night of May 23, 1792, while at his son's London home in Hanover Square, Lord Rodney's pain became so severe as to render him insensible. His physician, Sir Walter Farquhar, was immediately summoned. After some little time consciousness returned and Sir Walter said to him: 'I hope, my dear Lord, you feel yourself better.' 'I am very ill indeed', replied the Admiral, and a few moments later he expired.[34] It was 5 o'clock in the morning of May 24th.

Chapter 25

Afterwards

'I grieve exceedingly for the death of Lord Rodney.
We have lost an amiable friend and the country its
bravest and most successful hero.'
(John Wilkes to his daughter, May 31, 1792.)[1]

LORD RODNEY'S lifelong connection with Hampshire made Alresford the only possible resting place for his remains. They brought him back to the old home and on June 1st laid him beneath the aisle of the church, close by Jenny's monument.* Public tributes followed at once and were substantial. The Council of Jamaica had already set up their splendid marble monument in the Roman manner. Now the City of London followed suit with the Admiral in naval uniform for St Paul's. In the House of Lords the Duke of Clarence made a speech. A ship of the line, the first of several to bear his name, was launched in 1809.

Three weeks before Lord Rodney's death, Lord Sandwich died at Hinchingbrooke. It was fitting that these two should quit the stage together. Within a few months the worst excesses of the French Revolution startled and horrified the world and a new age began. The stress of events raised some curious echoes from the past. Henny, who had withdrawn to France, found herself stranded at Fontainebleau as the revolutionary government prepared to fight all Europe. In a pathetic appeal to Pitt dated October 1, 1792, she described her situation[2]—utterly destitute, her pension precarious and all the English gone except herself. It seems her cries were heard, for the Dowager Lady Rodney was not left to face the Terror but brought home at the eleventh hour, to survive for many years. At the same time a French nobleman, the duc de Lauzun, visiting England to buy horses for his government, was thrown into jail—until someone

* Information given to the Hon. Simon Rodney by the sexton of Old Alresford church.

o*

remembered that he was the nephew of the late Marshal de Biron, who had befriended Sir George Rodney in 1778. Then some of the Admiral's friends, headed it was said by the Prince of Wales, opened a subscription for de Lauzun's release.[3]

George, second Lord Rodney, survived his father only ten years. Old debts, long forgotten from the Northampton connection, reappeared to plague him. The drain on the St Eustatius account continued. In December 1801 he was at Penzance to avoid the worst of the English winter and stricken with a mortal illness.[4] On Christmas Day he made his will. As his own family would inherit Berrington and the Harley fortune George, ever thoughtful for others, made his main provisions for Henny and his father's younger children—'knowing I can not more essentially serve every part of the family than by putting their Dear Mother in a situation that will enable her best to serve and assist them.'[5] He died on January 2, 1802.

For a sea-officer with a command the year 1793 should have been the gateway to opportunity and distinction. John Rodney was appointed to the 50-gun *America* and then to the 74-gun *Vengeance*, but in August 1795, before she was ready for sea, he broke his leg. It had to be amputated and he was superseded. This was the end of his career. In 1799, on being passed over in the flag promotion, his name was removed from the list of captains and there followed many obscure years as Chief Secretary to the government of Ceylon. All that his father's preferential treatment brought him was the doubtful distinction of holding the rank of captain longer than any other officer in the history of the Royal Navy. He married three times, had sixteen children, and died at Boulogne in 1847, within two months of his eighty-second birthday.[6]

Edward, youngest of the Admiral's children, also joined the Navy, first appearing on the books of his brother John's ship in May 1793. As lieutenant of the *Magicienne* in 1800 he distinguished himself in a very gallant boat action. Advanced to post rank in 1806 he commanded first in the Mediterranean and then on the East Indies station. The end of the war, and the long peace which followed, cut short a career of promise.[7]

Of the Admiral's service contemporaries, Charles Saunders had died in 1775, Keppel and Byron in 1786, and Pocock on April 3, 1792. When his own time came Lord Rodney was fourth in the list of Admirals of the White and fifth in the whole flag-list. Arbuthnot, his old opponent in North America, survived him by two years. When the war broke out in 1793 Hood went to command in the Mediterranean. With no superior to criticize he fell foul of the Army commanders and of the Board of Admiralty itself, as result of which he was recalled and no further use made of his talents. After many years as Governor of Greenwich Hospital he died in 1816 aged ninety-two, having outlived by many years every other high commander of the American war.

Henny too outlived nearly all her contemporaries, and survived to extreme old age. For many years she resided at 19, Southampton Street, off Fitzroy Square. Latterly she seems to have been a difficult and exacting old lady and something of a character. She died on February 28, 1829, in her ninety-first year.

By this time the long war against France was far enough away for interest to revive in events of an earlier age. *The life and correspondence of Lord Rodney* by the Admiral's son-in-law Major-General Mundy had appeared in 1826 and was reprinted in 1830. Mundy, who married Sarah Rodney in 1801, is unlikely to have known his father-in-law well, if at all, but from Henny he probably received the misleading and inaccurate information about the Admiral's early life which mars his opening chapters. She also put at his disposal a great quantity of her husband's papers, mostly relating to the later years, and these, with much else of an official nature, he selected and arranged, not always in the correct sequence, cutting out paragraphs where family feeling or the Admiral's reputation might suffer and adding his own explanatory comments.

The appearance of Mundy's work stirred up the embers of the old controversy about whose mind had inspired the famous manœuvre of 'breaking the line'. For there were several schools of thought about this and considerable interest both inside and outside the service. So there developed, over the next few years, a correspondence in a number of seriously-minded journals, echoes from which are sometimes heard even today.

First in the field were the supporters of a Scottish writer on naval tactics, John Clerk of Eldin whose work, in the opinion of the *Edinburgh Review*, Sir Walter Scott and many landsmen north of the Tweed, must have put the idea into Sir George Rodney's head. When it was learnt that the Admiral had actually possessed a copy of Clerk's work and annotated it, the case seemed as good as proved; and to confirm it, several gentlemen came forward to relate how, on various occasions before sailing to fight de Grasse, Sir George Rodney had revealed that if he got the chance, 'break his line' was just what he intended to do. No one suggested that these words might point equally well to a repetition of what he had done to de Guichen's line on April 17, 1780.

Clerk's supporters were inflexibly opposed by Sir Gilbert Blane, Sir George's former physician (writing under the name of Scrutator), and by Major-General Sir Howard Douglas, son of Sir George's First Captain, Sir Charles Douglas. Sir Howard, who was Inspector of Artillery and author of a standard work on gunnery, wrote an article in the *Quarterly Review* in 1829, giving the entire credit for the manœuvre to his late father, on the strength of what young Dashwood said he overheard on the quarter-deck. And a few weeks after this Dashwood himself, by this time a retired admiral living at Torquay, sent to the *London Courier* his own very circumstantial account of the exchanges between Sir George and Sir Charles. In the same number the *Courier* also printed a letter from Admiral Sir James Saumarez who had commanded the *Ramillies* on the great day, and who wrote from Guernsey to say that in all his service career he had never heard it suggested that the famous manœuvre had been anything but 'unpremeditated and accidental'. This settled Clerk of Eldin.

But the Douglas challenge, besides infuriating the Rodney family, brought a host of retired veterans into the fray. Of these the most formidable was a certain Captain Thomas White, formerly lieutenant in the *Barfleur*, whose *Naval Researches* (London, 1830) is the best informed and most objective account of the engagements in the American war. White scouted the claims of Clerk of Eldin, and was sure he never heard of the altercation between Sir George and Sir Charles on the quarter-deck until he read about it in an account published in 1824. Other informed opinions besides those of White tended to play down Dashwood's colourful story, partly because it was felt that Sir George would never have tolerated, or Sir Charles have ventured such interference; and partly because, at no time since the battle, in any of Sir Charles's letters to his old chief, was there the slightest hint of the claims his son now made for him.

Sir Howard was not convinced. Having quarrelled with the *United Services Gazette* for printing some of Hood's scathing remarks about his father, he brought out a pamphlet of his own in 1832—*Naval Evolutions*—which contributed nothing new.

Meanwhile the Rodney family engaged themselves in detailed correspondence with their new champion, and the editor of the *United Services Gazette* opened its columns to him, this last with results not wholly to the satisfaction of any of the other controversialists. For Captain White's researches concluded by asking whether the famous manœuvre had really been such a good thing after all, and deciding that it had not. This extinguished the flames of controversy like a douche of cold water, for

White was far too well informed and articulate to be argued with. All the other combatants tip-toed from the field, glad to leave the obscure heretic in possession so long as his disturbing suggestion was aired no more in public. Nor has it been since, which may explain why 'breaking the line' on April 12, 1782, has for so long been accepted as a pinnacle of naval achievement.

It may be doubted whether all who fought in the battle shared this opinion. Certainly the Commander-in-Chief did not.* As a naval commander Rodney was, from first to last, an experienced professional, bred in traditional practices, capable indeed of improving on them, but too much a man of his time to have any use for inspiration or originality in naval matters. But he possessed to the highest degree the eternal virtues of the fighting commander throughout the ages, the aggressive spirit, and powers of leadership based on firm discipline coupled with unremitting concern for his men's well being. This, and a professional judgement rarely if ever at fault, make up his claim to greatness.

And so, if he ever, in a mood of candid reminiscence, surveyed those four great battle pictures which adorn Mr Harley's dining-room at Berrington, he would probably have dismissed the two of the Saints rather quickly. From the professional point of view there was not much to commend in his last victory except the fleet discipline and the gunnery. He might have dwelt with some complacency on the Moonlight Battle. His nerve had not failed as the fleet drove on into shoal water, and the leeward position had proved its worth. But Luny's great picture of the *Sandwich* on April 17, 1780, commemorates, in the writer's opinion, the peak of a great sea-officer's career; and it would be surprising if the old Admiral, fighting his battles over again, did not recall that day with special pride. For if ever a fleet was superbly directed and (one ship at least) magnificently fought, it was on this occasion off Martinique when Sir George Rodney, unsupported and alone, broke through the French line to show how victory might be won. And if the memory of his delinquent subordinates still rankled, he could have taken grim comfort from the thought that without the unpleasantness afterwards, and the examples he was forced to make, the corps of sea-officers might never have returned to anything approaching the old professional standards before the war ended.

Berrington still has its great pictures, but not much else of the Admiral will be found there. It was never his home. The houses in Hill Street and

* 'On his victory on April 12, 1782, I know he thought little.' Sir Gilbert Blane to the editor of the *Athenaeum*, February 19, 1809.

Hertford Street where he lived, and at the corner of Hanover Square where he died, have long since disappeared, along with No. 4 Cleveland Row. Avington saw little of him after his boyhood there and has other ghosts.

But Old Alresford today is much as Captain Rodney knew it when he and Jenny first made their home there. The plain Georgian church, Mr Hoadley's vast rectory, and the road across the bishop's great dyke, make its character still. One may still stand at the corner where the London Road comes across from Preston Candover where a zealous sea-officer once recommended a press be stationed to catch the sailors coming up from Portsmouth;[8] or look across the fields to the great pond where Captain Rodney promised his wife we shall always have what fish we please and 'an opportunity of showing our Mercy in not suffering the poor birds to be shot at'. The farms he owned when money was plentiful still work the land, and the great beech trees planted to hide his brother James's house now beautify both properties, in lofty disregard of an old family quarrel long forgotten.

Here then is where memories crowd thickest, and where the shade of the Admiral, if it ever chose to repair again to the scenes of his earthly pilgrimage, might most readily wander. Least changed of all is that plain, substantial mansion, which the successful young captain of the *Eagle* built from the proceeds of two days' furious activity in the Atlantic more than 200 years ago.

Appendix 1

A list of the fleet sent to Lisbon under the command of Admiral Sir John Norris in 1735. (Ad. 1/379)

Britannia (100)	Royal Oak (70)
Princess Amelia (80)	Sunderland (60)
Namur (90)	Dreadnaught (60)
Torbay (80)	Defiance (60)
Norfolk (80)	York (60)
Princess Caroline (80)	Swallow (50)
Hampton Court (70)	Deptford (50)
Buckingham (70)	Pembroke (50)
Burford (70)	Lichfield (50)
Grafton (70)	Warwick (50)
Captain (70)	Leopard (50)
Berwick (70)	Greyhound (20)
Orford (70)	Pool (fireship)
Kent (70)	Griffin (fireship)

Appendix 2

British and French squadrons at Second Battle of Finisterre, October 14, 1747

		Killed	Wounded
Devonshire (66)	Rear-Admiral Hawke		
	J. Moore	12	52
Kent (64)	T. Fox	1	10
Edinburgh (64)	T. Cotes	6	19
Yarmouth (64)	C. Saunders	22	70
Monmouth (64)	H. Harrison	18	70
Princess Louisa (60)	C. Watson	12	62
Windsor (60)	T. Hanway	8	59
Lyon (60)	A. Scott	20	79
Tilbury (60)	R. Harland	6	13
Nottingham (60)	P. Saumarez	13	25
Defiance (60)	J. Bentley	11	42
Eagle (60)	G. B. Rodney	16	54
Gloucester (50)	P. Durell	6	15
Portland (50)	C. Steevens	7	12
Hector (44)	T. Stanhope	1	1
Vulcan (fireship)	Lieutenant Lockhart	—	—
	TOTAL	159	573

French squadron, as in order of battle (Schomberg)

l'Intrépide (74)	Comte de Vaudreuil
Le Trident (64)	M. d'Amblement
Le Terrible (74)	Comte du Guay
Le Tonnant (80)	M. de l'Etanduère, Chef d'escadre
	M. du Chaffaut
Le Monarque (74)	M. de Bedoyerre
Le Severn (56)	M. du Rouret
Le Fougueux (64)	M. de Vigneau
Le Neptune (70)	M. de Fromentière

432

Appendix 3

THE AMERICAN RODNEYS

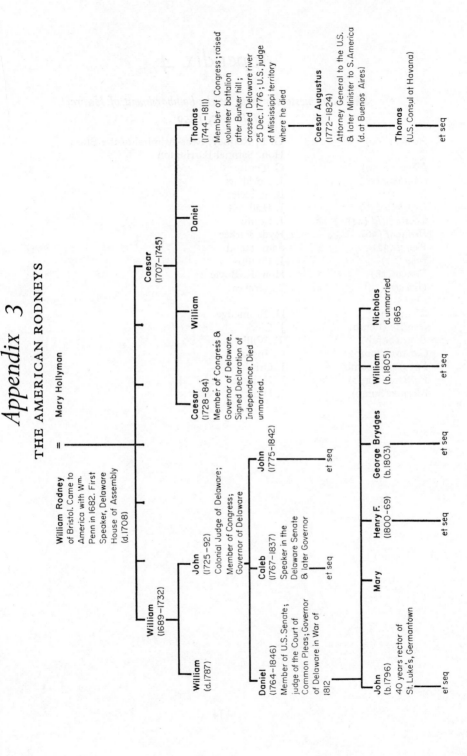

William Rodney of Bristol. Came to America with Wm. Penn in 1682. First Speaker, Delaware House of Assembly (d.1708) = **Mary Hollyman**

William (1689–1732)

William (d.1787)

John (1725–92) Colonial Judge of Delaware; Member of Congress; Governor of Delaware

Caesar (1707–1745)

Caesar (1728–84) Member of Congress & Governor of Delaware. Signed Declaration of Independence. Died unmarried.

William

Daniel

Thomas (1744–1811) Member of Congress; raised volunteer battalion after Bunker hill; crossed Delaware river 25 Dec. 1776; U.S. judge of Mississippi territory where he died

Caesar Augustus (1772–1824) Attorney General to the U.S. & later Minister to S. America (d. at Buenos Aires)

Thomas (U.S. Consul at Havana)

et seq

Daniel (1764–1846) Member of U.S. Senate; judge of the Court of Common Pleas; Governor of Delaware in War of 1812

Caleb (1767–1837) Speaker in the Delaware Senate & later Governor

et seq

John (1775–1842)

et seq

John (b.1796) 40 years rector of St. Luke's, Germantown

et seq

Mary

Henry F. (1800–69)

et seq

George Brydges (b.1803)

et seq

William (b.1805)

et seq

Nicholas d. unmarried 1865

Appendix 4

Ships and vessels present at the bombardment of Havre,
July 4–5, 1759

Achilles (60)	G. B. Rodney, Rear-Admiral of the Blue; Hon. Samuel Barrington
Norwich (50)	G. Darby
Chatham (50)	J. Lockhart
Isis (50)	E. Wheeler
Deptford (50)	J. Hollwall
Chesterfield (44)	J. Scaife
Brilliant (36)	Hyde Parker
Vestal (32)	Sam. Hood
Juno (32)	J. Phillips
Boreas (28)	Hon. R. Boyle
Unicorn (28)	T. Graves
Fly (8)	
Wolfe (8)	H. Bromedge
Basilisk (bomb)	J. Clerk
Blast (bomb)	T. Willis
Carcass (bomb)	C. Inglis
Firedrake (bomb)	J. Orrok
Furnace (bomb)	J. Faulkner
Mortar (bomb)	J. Hunt

Appendix 5

Ships under the command of Rear-Admiral Rodney
at the taking of Martinique, 1762

Original Leeward Islands squadron, formerly under Commodore Sir James Douglas

★Dublin (74)	Sir J. Douglas	*Stag* (32)	H. Angel
	Ed. Gascoigne	*Crescent* (28)	T. Collingwood
★Culloden (74)	Jno. Barker	*Levant* (28)	W. Tucker
★Temple (70)	Lucius O'Brien	*†Echo* (24)	J. Laforey
Raisonable (64)	M. Shuldham	*Nightingale* (20)	J. Campbell
Belliqueux (64)	T. Saumarez	*★Fowey* (20)	J. Mead
Bienfaisant (64)	G. Balfour	*†Rose* (20)	F. Banks
Montagu (60)	W. Parry	*Arundel* (20)	Alex. Innes
Danae (40)	H. Martin	*†Barbados* (14)	Staire Douglas
Woolwich (44)	W. Bayne	*Antigua* (12)	J. N. P. Nott
		Virgin (12)	J. Brisbane

From England with Rear-Admiral Rodney

†Marlborough (68)	Rear-Adm. Rodney	*†Basilisk* (bomb)	R. Brice
	W. Hollwall	*★Granado* (bomb)	J. Hawker
Vanguard (70)	R. Swanton	*★Thunder* (bomb)	Boteler
Foudroyant (84)	R. Duff		
★Dragon (74)	A. Hervey		
Modeste (64)	Hon. R. B. Walsingham		
★Nottingham (60)	S. Marshall		

From Dominica, with Brigadier-General Lord Rollo's troops

★Sutherland (50)	J. Legge	*★Penzance* (40)	J. Boyd
★Stirling Castle (64)	M. Everitt	*Repulse* (32)	J. C. Allen
Falkland (50)	F. S. Drake	*★Lizard* (28)	J. Doak

From Belleisle, with four regiments of foot.

Temeraire (74)	Matt. Barton	*Actaeon* (28)	P. H. Ourry

From New York, with Major-General Monckton's troops

★Devonshire (64)	G. Darby	*★Dover* (40)	Hon. P. T.
★Alcide (64)	T. Hankerson		Percival
Norwich (50)	W. MacCleverty	*Greyhound* (20)	T. Francis
(*Rochester* (50)	T. Burnett, arrived on February 12th with army victuallers.)		

★ Sent with Douglas to Jamaica (April 1762).
† Added by Pocock to his own force (May 1762).

Ships detailed for the bombardment before disembarcation on January 16, 1762. (Rear-Admiral's Order Book.)

Culloden and *Temple*—as close as possible to the Point Negro, to silence that battery.

Sutherland—a little to the westward of *Culloden* and *Temple* to scour the country between Negro Point and Cas Navires.

Devonshire—against the first battery at Cas Navires.

Alcide and *Norwich*—against the 2nd and 3rd batteries at Cas Navires, to westward of *Devonshire*.

Penzance—between *Devonshire* and *Alcide*, to scour that part of the country.

Nottingham and *Woolwich*—against the battery at Cas Pilotte.

Repulse—as close as possible to the Green Gully between Cas Navires and Cas Pilotte.

Appendix 6

The great convoy which sailed under the command of
Sir George Rodney, December 1779

Escort force sailing from Spithead

Sandwich (90)	Adm. Sir G. B. Rodney		
	W. Young		
Prince George (98)	Rear-Adm. R. Digby		
	P. Patton		
Royal George (100)	Rear-Adm. J. L. Ross		
	J. Bourmaster		
Ajax (74)	S. Uvedale	*Terrible* (74)	J. Douglas
Alcide (74)	J. Brisbane	America (64)	S. Thompson
Alfred (74)	W. Bayne	†Phoenix (44)	Sir Hyde Parker
Bedford (74)	E. Affleck	Pearl (32)	G. Montagu
Culloden (74)	G. Balfour	†Greyhound (28)	Dickson
Cumberland (74)	J. Peyton	*Pegasus* (28)	J. Bazeley
Edgar (74)	J. Elliot	*Triton* (28)	S. Lutwidge
Monarch (74)	A. Duncan	*Hyaena* (24)	E. Thompson
Montagu (74)	J. Houlton	*Porcupine* (24)	Hon. H. S. Conway
Shrewsbury (74)	M. Robinson	†Tapageur	Ld. Chas.
		(cutter)	Fitzgerald

Escort force sailing from Plymouth

Defence (74)	J. Cranston	*Marlborough* (74)	T. Penny
Dublin (74)	S. Wallis	*Resolution* (74)	Sir C. Ogle
†Hector (74)	Sir J. Hamilton	*Bienfaisant* (64)	J. MacBride
Invincible (74)	S. Cornish	*Apollo* (36)	P. Pownoll

Convoy for Gibraltar and Minorca

9 transports with 2nd Bat. 73rd Foot, for Minorca.
1 transport with Hanoverian recruits and stores for Gibraltar.
11 victuallers with provisions for Gibraltar.
2 victuallers with provisions for Minorca.
4 storeships with ordnance stores for Gibraltar.
2 storeships with ordnance stores for Minorca.

Convoy for the West Indies

8 transports with the 89th Foot for the Leeward Islands.
10 transports with the 88th Foot and about 400 recruits for Jamaica.
7 victuallers with naval provisions for the Leeward Islands and Jamaica.
5 victuallers with army provisions for St Lucia and Pensacola.
6 storeships with naval stores for the Leeward Islands and Jamaica.
1 storeship with army stores for Pensacola.

* Present at the Moonlight Battle.
† Detached under Sir Hyde Parker with the West Indies convoy.

Appendix 7

British order of battle and casualties on April 17, 1780

Ship	Commander	Killed	Wounded	
Stirling Castle (64)	R. Carkett	4	34	
Ajax (74)	S. Uvedale	4	13	
Elizabeth (74)	Hon. F. Maitland	9	15	
Princess Royal (90)	H. Harmood	5	14	Van
	(Rear-Adm. Hyde Parker)			
Albion (74)	C. Bowyer	3	2	
Terrible (74)	J. Douglas	14	26	
Trident (64)	A. J. P. Molloy	7	35	
Grafton (74)	T. Newnham	3	15	
	(Commodore T. Collingwood)			
Yarmouth (64)	N. Bateman	5	15	
Cornwall (74)	T. Edwards	21	48	
Sandwich (90)	W. Young	20	37	
	(Admiral Sir Geo. Rodney)			Centre
Suffolk (74)	A. Crespin	2	12	
Boyne (68)	C. Cotton	2	2	
Vigilant (64)	Sir G. Home, Bart.	14	2	
Vengeance (74)	J. Holloway	1	6	
	(Commodore W. Hotham)			
Medway (60)	W. Affleck	2	3	
Montagu (74)	J. Houlton	9	26	
Conqueror (74)	T. Watson	13	36	Rear
	(Rear-Adm. J. Rowley)			
Intrepid (64)	Hon. H. St John	7	9	
Magnificent (74)	J. Elphinston	1	10	
Centurion (50) to assist the rear	TOTAL	146	360	

French order of battle on April 17, 1780
(From Chevalier)

Van	Centre	Rear
Destin (74)	Citoyen (74)	Intrépide (74)
Vengeur (64)	Caton (64)	Triton (64)
Saint-Michel (60)	Victoire (74)	Magnifique (74)
Pluton (74)	Fendant (74)	Robuste (74)
Triomphant (80)	Couronne (80)	Sphinx (74)
Souverain (74)	Palmier (74)	Artésien (74)
Solitaire (64)	Indien (64)	Hercule (74)
	Actionnaire (64)	

British casualties on 15–19 May, 1780

Ship	May 15th Killed	May 15th Wounded	May 19th Killed	May 19th Wounded
Vigilant	3	10	9	15
Medway	1	10	2	11
Conqueror	2	13	3	10
Albion	12	64	12	61
Cornwall	3	5	4	10
Intrepid			1	—
Suffolk			1	21
Triumph			4	14
Vengeance			3	16
Magnificent			5	23
Terrible			3	9
Preston			—	3
TOTAL	21	100	47	193

Total of British casualties for April 17th, May 15th, and May 19th amounts to 214 killed and 653 wounded.

Chevalier gives the French casualties for the 3 days' fighting as 158 killed and 820 wounded.

Appendix 8

The Admiral presents his compliments to Rear-Admiral Hyde Parker and desires he will order the following articles to be inserted in the Signal Books of the ships in His Division in addition to the Additional Fighting Instructions by day.

35.

When the Commander-in-Chief thinks the Van of the Fleet are at too great a distance from the Center he will hoist a red flag pierced with white at the Fore-topgallant Masthead when the Van are immediately to close and upon no account to be more than 2 cables length from each other or the distance prescribed by the Signal for the line; and when he thinks the Rear of the Fleet are at too great a distance from the Center he will hoist the above mentioned flag at the Mizen topmasthead when they are immediately to close with all despatch possible and no ship whatever to chace from the Fleet during action before the main body of the enemy's fleet are beat or a particular signal or order for that purpose.

Sandwich, at Sea, April 22, 1780.
(From the MSS copy at Brizes Park)

Appendix 9

The dispersal of the fleet (July–August 1780)

Remaining at St Lucia under Commodore Hotham for the protection of the Leeward Islands

Vengeance (74)			*Venus (36)	Rover (16)
Montagu (74)			*Alcmene (32)	San Vincente (10)
Ajax (74)			*Amazon (32)	Drake
Egmont (74)			*Blanche (32)	Hornet
Fame (74)		To go	*Brune (32)	Reynard
Suffolk (74)		home with	*Convert (32)	Surprise
Vigilant (64)		September	Albemarle (28)	Aetna (bomb)
		convoy	*Andromeda (28)	Carcass (bomb)
			*Laurel (28)	Vesuvius (bomb)
			Deal Castle (24)	Salamander } fireships
				Blast

To St Kitt's with the Commander-in-Chief and the convoy, sailing July 17th

Princess Royal (90)
Albion (74)
Berwick (74)
Conqueror (74)
Elizabeth (74)   Sailed from St Kitt's July 24th for Jamaica with
Grafton (74)   Rear-Admiral Rowley and Commodore Walsing-
Magnificent (74) ham. To put themselves under Sir Peter Parker
Thunderer (74)
Stirling Castle (64)
Trident (64)
Barbados (sloop)

Boyne (68)
Preston (50)   Home with the August convoy from St Kitt's

*Sandwich (90)
*Alcide (74)
*Centaur (74)
*Culloden (74)
*Russell (74)   Cruising with the Commander-in-Chief. Arrived
*Shrewsbury (74) with him at Sandy Hook September 14th
*Terrible (74)
*Torbay (74)
*Triumph (74)
*Yarmouth (64)
*Fortunee (38)

*Intrepid (64)
*Boreas (28)   From Barbados and Antigua

* Coppered.

441

Cyclops (28)   Arrived Sandy Hook September 23rd and 25th
Greyhound (28)

Medway (60)   With convoy to Antigua and St Kitt's and thence
Centurion (50)   home, June–July
Cornwall (74)   Condemned after the action of May 19th. Incapable
of the voyage home and broken up at St Lucia

   * Coppered.

Appendix 10

British and French fleets on April 12, 1782

British order of battle and casualties

		Killed	Wounded	
Marlborough (74)	T. Penny	3	17	
Arrogant (74)	S. Cornish	0	0	
Alcide (74)	C. Thompson	No return		
Nonsuch (64)	W. Truscott	3	3	
Conqueror (74)	G. Balfour	7	23	
Princessa (70)	Rear-Adm. F. S. Drake			
	C. Knatchbull	3	22	
Prince George (98)	J. Williams	9	24	Foremast shot away
Torbay (74)	J. L. Gidoin	10	25	
Anson (64)	W. Blair	3	13	Cross-jack shot away
Fame (74)	R. Barbor	3	12	Main topsail-yard shot away
Russell (74)	J. Saumarez	12	27	Fore and mizen masts dangerously wounded
America (64)	S. Thompson	1	1	3 topsail-yards and 3 topmasts unserviceable
Hercules (74)	H. Savage	7	19	3 topmasts, fore topsail-yard and jib-boom unserviceable
Prothee (64)	C. Buckner	5	25	Main topmast shot away
Resolution (74)	Ld. R. Manners	5	34	7 shots in foremast
Agamemnon (64)	B. Caldwell	14	14	2 topmasts shot away
Duke (98)	A. Gardner	13	61	Main topmast shot away
Formidable (98)	Adm. Sir G. B. Rodney			
	J. Symons	15	39	
Namur (90)	R. Fanshaw	6	23	
St Albans (64)	C. Inglis	0	6	Main topmast badly damaged
Canada (74)	W. Cornwallis	2	23	3 shots in foremast and 4 in mainmast
Repulse (64)	T. Dumaresq	4	11	
Ajax (74)	N. Charrington	9	10	Main topsail-yard badly wounded
Bedford (74)	Cdre E. Affleck	0	17	Foremast and foreyard fit only for fair weather
	T. Graves			
Prince William (64)	A. Wilkinson	0	0	
Magnificent (74)	R. Linzee	6	11	

		Killed	Wounded	
Centaur (74)	J. H. Inglefield	No return		Main topsail-yard and jib-boom shot away
Belliqueux (74)	A. Sutherland	4	10	Bowsprit and main top-mast badly wounded
Warrior (74)	Sir J. Wallace	5	21	Fore topsail-yard shot away
Barfleur (98)	Rear-Adm. Sir S. Hood J. Knight	10	37	
*Monarch (74)	F. Reynolds	16	33	
Valiant (74)	S. C. Goodall	10	28	
Yarmouth (64)	A. Parry	14	33	
Montagu (74)	G. Bowen	12	31	Fore topmast dangerously wounded
Alfred (74)	W. Bayne	12	40	
Royal Oak (74)	T. Burnet	8	30	Main topmast lost on April 9th

N.B. Casualty figures are taken from Schomberg but amended, when a return is available, from damage reports in P.R.O. 30/20/22, and from ships' journals. Dr Blane gives the British casualties for April 9th and 12th as 261 killed and 837 wounded.

French order of battle

3me *escadre (bleu). Bougainville*

Hercule (74)
Souverain (74)
Palmier (74)
Northumberland (74)
Neptune (74)
Auguste (80). Flag
†Ardent (64)
Scipion (74)
Brave (74)
Citoyen (74)

1re *escadre (blanche). De Grasse*

†Hector (74)
†César (74)
Dauphin Royal (80)
Languedoc (80)
†Ville de Paris (104). Flag
Couronne (80)
Eveillé (64)
Sceptre (74)
†Glorieux (74)

* The *Monarch*'s correct station was ahead of the *Barfleur*, but as she could not reach it in time on the morning of April 12th, Hood directed her to take station astern of his flagship.
† Taken during the battle.

2me escadre (blanche et bleu). De Vaudreuil

Diadème (74)
Destin (74)
Magnanime (74)
Réfléchi (74)
Conquerant (74)
Magnifique (74)
Triomphant (80). Flag
Bourgogne (74)
Duc de Bourgogne (80)
Marseillais (74)
Pluton (74)

N.B. This is the line as given by Chevalier—*Histoire de la Marine Française pendant la guerre de l'Independence Americaine*, Paris 1877. Troude confirms this order except that he places the *Neptune* between the *Hercule* and the *Souverain*.

Appendix 11

Some of the honours conferred on Admiral Lord Rodney

1762,	May,	Thanks of both Houses of Parliament. Capture of Martinique
1764,	January,	Baronet of the United Kingdom
1768,	March,	Freedom of borough of Northampton
1771,	August,	Rear-Admiral of Great Britain
1780,	March,	Freedom of Edinburgh. Taking Spanish convoy.
	March,	Freedom of City of London in a gold box, and Thanks of both Houses of Parliament. Victory over Langara
	August,	Freedom of Liverpool
	November,	Order of the Bath, and Thanks of the Council of Jamaica
1781,	August,	Freedom of Exeter
	November,	Vice-Admiral of Great Britain
1782,	May,	Thanks of both Houses of Parliament. Victory over de Grasse
	June,	English peerage
	June,	Freedom of Poole, Great Yarmouth, and Huntingdon
	September,	Freedom of Leicester
	October,	Thanks of Irish Parliament
	October,	Freedom of Winchester
	November,	Freedom of Cork (in a gold box), Bristol and Dundee
	November,	Thanks of the City of London
	December,	Freedom of Southampton
1783,	January,	Thanks of Linlithgow
	February,	A £1,000 statue voted by the Jamaica Assembly. Thanks of the Corporation of Shipmasters of Leith
1789,		Elected Member of the Free Economical Society by order of Catherine of Russia

Sources

My principal sources have been the Admiralty records in the Public Record Office, and the *Rodney Papers*, also in the Public Record Office. Of the first, the following classes have contributed most:

Ad. 1. Admiralty in-letters. Captains' letters and letters from Commanders-in-Chief, covering forty years of Rodney's official life.
Ad. 2. Admiralty Order-books and Out-letter books, ranging from Secret Orders sent out by the Board, to unimportant communications from the secretary.
Ad. 36. Ships' muster rolls.
Ad. 51. Captains' journals.
Ad. 52. Masters' journals.

The *Rodney Papers* comprise 26 bundles, catalogued as P.R.O. 30/20/1–26. They were presented to the Public Record Office by Harley Rodney Esq. in 1906 and 1916 and are only partly classified. Order-books, journals, and letter-books are easily located and have, as a rule, their official counterparts in the Admiralty records. But besides these there are vast quantities of miscellaneous letters, papers, accounts and receipts, mostly of a private nature, which are hardly classified at all. This applies particularly to bundles 20 to 26. There is also a small amount of material in the possession of the Hon. Simon Rodney, which I indicate as *Rodney Papers (Brizes Park)*. Finally there are two printed volumes, *Letter Books and Order Books of Admiral Lord Rodney, 1780–1782*, printed for the Naval History Society, New York 1932. They include the order-book from November 1781 to September 1782, which has no counterpart in the Public Record Office in London.

Two other sources deserve special mention. They are the papers of the 4th Earl of Sandwich, which I designate simply as *Sandwich Papers*, followed by the volume number if the material is included in one of the volumes printed by the Navy Records Society, or *Sandwich Papers (unpublished)*, if it is not; and the papers at Castle Ashby in Northamptonshire, all unpublished, the *Compton Papers*.

The following printed works I have found particularly useful:

BAUGH D. A. *British Naval Administration in the Age of Walpole*, Princeton, New Jersey, 1965.
CORBETT J. S. *England in the Seven Years War*, 2 vols., Longmans, London, 1907.
CORBETT J. S. *Signals and Instructions, 1776–1794*, Navy Records Society, London, 1908.
ERSKINE D. *Augustus Hervey's Journal*, William Kimber, London, 1953.
HANNAY D. *Letters of Sir Samuel Hood*, Navy Records Society, London, 1895.
KEPPEL, Rev. T. *Life of Viscount Keppel*, 2 vols., London, 1842.
LAUGHTON J. K. *Letters and Papers of Charles, Lord Barham*, vol. 1, Navy Records Society, London, 1907.
LEWIS M. *England's Sea-officers*, Allen and Unwin, London, 1939.
MUNDY G. B. M. *Life and Correspondence of the late Admiral Lord Rodney*, 2 vols., Murray, London, 1830.
NAMIER L. B. *The Structure of Politics at the accession of George III*, Macmillan, London, 1957.
NORTHAMPTON, Marquess of, *The Comptons of Compton Winyates*, John Lane, London, 1930.

PARES R. *War and Trade in the West Indies (1739–1763)*, Oxford, Clarendon Press, 1936.

RICHMOND H. W. *The Navy in the War of 1739–48*, 3 vols., Cambridge University Press, 1920.

SCHOMBERG I. *Naval Chronology*, 5 vols., 1815.

TOYNBEE P. *Letters of Horace Walpole*, 16 vols., Oxford, Clarendon Press, 1902–5.

WRAXALL N. W. *Historical Memoirs of my own Time (1772–1784)*, Kegan Paul, London, 1904.

Other sources are more conveniently indicated in relation to the chapters to which they contribute.

CHAPTER I

RODNEYS AND BRIDGES

IN MANUSCRIPT

History of the Rodney Family by Sir Edward Rodeney. (*Rodney Papers (Brizes Park).*)
Colonel Rodney's memoirs of his father. P.R.O. 30/20/26.
History of Alresford and its Environs by Robert Boyes, *c.* 1774. Winchester Public Library.

PRINTED

Dalton's *English Army Lists* and *Commission Registers.*
Cal. of State Papers, Domestic from 1670 onwards.
The Princely Chandos by J. R. Robinson, Sampson Low, London, 1893.

p. 18, n.   1.   Petition of Colonel Caesar Rodney. B.M. Add.MSS. 5853.
p. 20, n.   2.   Court of Chancery 11/1042/30. *Rodney* v. *Handasyde, 1734*; 11/1037/31. *Rodney* v. *Samwell.*
p. 21, n.   3.   Mrs Constantia Nethercott to Lord Bute, November 4, 1760. Transcribed from the *Bute Papers,* formerly in the possession of Sir Lewis Namier.
p. 23, n.   4.   *Hampshire, a short survey of the County of Southampton.* MS. by Thomas Gatehouse, *c.* 1778. Winchester Public Library.
p. 23, n.   5.   Prerogative Court of Canterbury, Wills at Somerset House. 1751 (Busby) George Bridges Esq., Southampton, June, fo. 165.
p. 25, n.   6.   Rodney to Whitshed Keene, December 20, 1780. Greenwich MS. 81/066/2.
p. 26, n.   7.   Ad. 36/4053.
p. 27, n.   8.   Schomberg, vol. 1, p. 165.

CHAPTER 2

YOUNG MR RODNEY

IN MANUSCRIPT

Captain's journal *Dreadnaught*, 1733–37. Ad. 51/273.
Captain's journal *Romney*, 1738. Ad. 51/797.

Captain's journal *Dolphin*, 1739–40. Ad. 51/255, 256.
Muster roll *Dreadnaught*, 1733–37. Ad. 36/811, 814, 817.
Muster roll *Romney*, 1738. Ad. 36/2985, 2986.
Muster roll *Dolphin*, 1739–40. Ad. 36/862.

p. 29, n.	1.	P.R.O. 30/20/22.
p. 29, n.	2.	Ad. 36/811, 814. Also *Dreadnaught*'s pay-books, Ad. 33/345, 353.
p. 29, n.	3.	Ned Ward, *The Wooden World*, 1707.
p. 33, n.	4.	Norris to Admiralty, May 22, 1735. Ad. 1/379.
p. 33, n.	5.	Letter of August 3, 1755, to Mrs Rodney, P.R.O. 30/20/20.
p. 36, n.	6.	Letter of September 8, 1755, to the Hon. Charles Compton. P.RO. 30/20/25.
p. 36, n.	7.	Norris to Admiralty, March 21, 1736–37. Ad. 1/379.
p. 36, n.	8.	Administration (Prerogative Court of Canterbury), Somerset House. December 1739 (Farrant), Harry Rodney.
p. 36, n.	9.	Ad. 36/286.
p. 38, n.	10.	Rodney to Admiralty, April 30, 1755. Ad. 1/2384.
p. 39, n.	11.	Ad. 36/3850.
p. 40, n.	12.	Ad. 36/862.

CHAPTER 3

THE FORTUNATE LIEUTENANT

IN MANUSCRIPT

Captain's journal *Dolphin*, 1740–41. Ad. 51/256.
Captain's journal *Namur*, 1741–42. Ad. 51/620.
Muster roll *Essex*, 1741. Ad. 36/1048.
Muster roll *Namur*, 1741–42. Ad. 36/2098.
Pay-book *Namur*, 1741–42. Ad. 33/379.
Captain's letters, 'H' (Holburne), 1740–41. Ad. 1/1881, 1882.
Captain's letters, 'R' (Robinson), 1741. Ad. 1/2380.
Admiralty out-letters, 1740. Ad. 2/56.
Vice-Admiral Mathews to Secretary of State, 1742. S.P. 42/91.
Vice-Admiral Mathews to Admiralty, 1741–42. Ad. 1/381.

PRINTED

Current numbers of the *London Evening Post, London and Country Journal* and *Daily Gazetteer*.

p. 45, n.	1.	Schomberg. Vol. 1, p. 177.
p. 48, n.	2.	Ad. 3/45 (Board minutes), records 'List of officers appointed to *Namur* at desire of V. Adm. Mathews . . . George Bridges Rodney, 5th lieutenant.'
p. 53, n.	3.	Copy in S.P. 42/91.
p. 53, n.	4.	Copy in S.P. 42/91.
p. 54, n.	5.	Mathews to the Duke of Newcastle, August 18, 1742. S.P. 42/91.
p. 54, n.	6.	State of ships. S.P. 42/91.

CHAPTER 4

JUNIOR CAPTAIN

IN MANUSCRIPT

Captain's journal *Plymouth*, 1742–43. Ad. 51/699.
Captain's journal *Sheerness*, 1744. Ad. 51/899.
Muster roll *Plymouth*, 1742–43. Ad. 36/2781.
Muster roll *Sheerness*, 1743–44. Ad. 36/3599.
Muster roll *Ludlow Castle*, 1744–45. Ad. 36/1858, 1859, 1860.
Captain's letters 'R' (Rodney), 1743–45. Ad. 1/2380, 2381.

p. 55, n.   1.   Wraxall, p. 190.
p. 60, n.   2.   Admiralty to Rodney, December 2, 1743. Ad. 2/481.
p. 64, n.   3.   *Daily Advertiser*, September 21–24, 1744.
p. 67, n.   4.   Account with Francis Magnus, P.R.O. 30/20/26.

CHAPTER 5

THE *EAGLE*

IN MANUSCRIPT

Captain's journal *Eagle*, 1746–48. Ad. 51/326.
Muster roll *Eagle*, 1746–48. Ad. 36/971, 972.
Captain's letters 'R' (Rodney), 1746–48. Ad. 1/2381, 2382.
Anson and Hawke to Admiralty, 1746–47. Ad. 1/87, 88.

PRINTED

Admiral Hawke by R. F. Mackay, Oxford, Clarendon Press, 1965.

p. 70, n.   1.   'Eagle at Harwich, Jan. 10th 1745/46.' Ad. 1/2381.
p. 76, n.   2.   Captain's journal *Kent*. Ad. 51/501.
p. 80, n.   3.   Account with Francis Magnus, P.R.O. 30/20/26. See also the *Drakeford Papers* (H.M. Drakeford 12c), in the Staffordshire County Record Office. Drakeford was the agent who handled many of the prizes.
p. 80, n.   4.   Admiralty to Rodney, July 13, 1747. Ad. 2/692.
p. 80, n.   5.   Fox to Admiralty, July 1, 1747. Ad. 1/1782.
p. 82, n.   6.   Evidence at Captain Fox's court martial, which provides many details of the engagement. Ad. 1/5291.
p. 85, n.   7.   P.R.O. 30/20/20.
p. 86, n.   8.   Rodney to Anson, November 19, 1747. (*Rodney Papers, Brizes Park.*)
p. 86, n.   9.   Letter of August 1, 1747. P.R.O. 30/20/26.
p. 86, n.   10.   Account with Francis Magnus. P.R.O. 30/20/26.
p. 87, n.   11.   ibid.
p. 88, n.   12.   Keppel to Anson, December 17, 1747. *Life of Keppel*, vol. 1, p. 120.
p. 88, n.   13.   'You know I abhor court martials.' Rodney to Mrs Rodney, July 30, 1756. P.R.O. 30/20/20.
p. 89, n.   14.   *Life of Keppel*, vol. 1, p. 133.
p. 89, n.   15.   Anson to Sandwich, May 10, 1748. *Sandwich Papers* (unpublished).

CHAPTER 6

THE *RAINBOW*

IN MANUSCRIPT

Captain's journal *Rainbow*, 1751–52. P.R.O. 30/20/4.
Master's journal *Rainbow*, July–December 1749 and June–December 1750. P.R.O. 30/20/4.
Muster roll *Rainbow*, 1749–52. Ad. 36/2811.
Captain's letters, 'R' (Rodney), 1749–52. Ad. 1/2382, 2383.
Letter-book, 1749–58. P.R.O. 30/20/6.

PRINTED

An account of Newfoundland, etc., by Captain Griffith Williams, Royal Regiment of Artillery, London, 1765.
Journal of the Commissioners for Trade and Plantations, 1749–53.
Cambridge History of the British Empire, vol. 6, chapter 5, Newfoundland.

p. 91, n. 1.   P.R.O. 30/20/13.
p. 91, n. 2.   Wraxall, p. 191.
p. 92, n. 3.   Principal sources for subsequent events are the minutes of the Sea Club (later the Amicable Marine Society) at Greenwich, and Hervey's journal.
p. 94, n. 4.   Ad. 1/597.
p. 94, n. 5.   Ad. 3/60.
p. 96, n. 6.   P.R.O. 30/20/18.
p. 99, n. 7.   Ad. 1/2382.
p. 101, n. 8.   Anson to Rodney, April 30, 1750. P.R.O. 30/20/20.
p. 101, n. 9.   Bedford to Rodney, May 15, 1750. P.R.O. 30/20/20.
p. 101, n. 10.   P.R.O. 30/20/26.
p. 102, n. 11.   Cornwallis to Rodney, June 25, 1750. P.R.O. 30/20/13.
p. 102, n. 12.   Rodney to Admiral Smith, May 22, 1750. Printed in *Chronicles of the 18th Century* by M. Wyndham, vol. 1, Hodder and Stoughton, London, 1924.
p. 102, n. 13.   Rodney to Anson, October 27, 1750. B.M. Add. MSS. 15,956 fo. 323.
p. 103, n. 14.   Disbursements and accounts, P.R.O. 30/20/16.
p. 104, n. 15.   Orders and instructions, Ad. 2/73. Also P.R.O. 30/20/6.
p. 105, n. 16.   Lady Aubrey Beauclerck to Rodney, May 26, 1751. P.R.O. 30/20/23.
p. 105, n. 17.   Prerogative Court of Canterbury, Wills at Somerset House. 1751 (Busby) George Bridges Esq., Southampton, June, fo. 165.
p. 105, n. 18.   P.R.O. 30/20/23.
p. 106, n. 19.   P.R.O. 30/20/25.
p. 108, n. 20.   Lord Holdernesse to Rodney, February 1752. P.R.O. 30/20/12.

CHAPTER 7

JENNY

IN MANUSCRIPT

All the letters between Rodney and Mrs Rodney are from P.R.O. 30/20/20.
Captain's journal *Prince George*, 1755–56. Ad. 51/726.
Captain's letters 'R' (Rodney), 1753–56. Ad. 1/2384, 2385.
Letter-book, 1749–58. P.R.O. 30/20/6.

p. 110, n. 1. *Bath Journal* (arrivals), August 29, 1752.
p. 110, n. 2. Marriages of Oxford Chapel, Vere Street, St Marylebone (1736–54). *Harleian Soc.*, Vol. 47.
p. 110, n. 3. P.R.O. 30/20/26.
p. 111, n. 4. Edmondson's *Baronagium Genealogicum* (1784), vol. 6.
p. 111, n. 5. Hon. Charles Compton's accounts, P.R.O. 30/20/25.
p. 112, n. 6. B.M. Add. MSS. 32,995, fo. 104 and folios 110–113.
p. 112, n. 7. B.M. Add. MSS. 32,735, fo. 102 and fo. 104.
p. 120, n. 8. P.R.O. 30/20/25.
p. 121, n. 9. Andrews to Rodney, November 19, 1755. P.R.O. 30/20/25.
p. 121, n. 10. Prerogative Court of Canterbury, Wills at Somerset House. 1755 (Paul) The Hon. Charles Compton Esq., Middlesex, December, fo. 308.
p. 121, n. 11. Admiral Osborn to Rodney, November 29 and December 3, 1755; Wm. Mildmay to Rodney, December 8, 1755. P.R.O. 30/20/13.
p. 126, n. 12. P.R.O. 30/20/20.

CHAPTER 8

THE *DUBLIN*

IN MANUSCRIPT

Captain's journal *Dublin*, 1757–58. Ad. 51/278.
Captain's letters 'R' (Rodney), 1757–58. Ad. 1/2385, 2386.
Letter-book, 1749–58. P.R.O. 30/20/6.
Hawke to Admiralty. Ad. 1/89.

PRINTED

Grenville Papers, 4 vols, 1852–53 (ed. Smith).

p. 130, n. 1. Colonial Office, C.O. 5/53.
p. 130, n. 2. Lady Egmont to Rodney, January 29, 1757. P.R.O. 30/20/25.
p. 131, n. 3. *Augustus Hervey's Journal*, chapter XIV.
p. 135, n. 4. Rodney to Grenville, September 23, 1757.
p. 135, n. 5. Hawke to Admiralty. Ad. 1/89.
p. 136, n. 6. Rodney to Grenville, October 19, 1757.
p. 137, n. 7. ibid.
p. 137, n. 8. Horace Walpole: quoted in *The Comptons of Compton Winyates*.

p. 138, n. 9. Rodney to Grenville, October 21, 1757.
p. 139, n. 10. Rodney to Navy Board, December 31, 1757.
p. 139, n. 11. Rodney to Navy Board, June 17, 1757.
p. 140, n. 12. Colonial Office, C.O. 5/53.
p. 141, n. 13. Rodney to Grenville, March 15, 1758.
p. 142, n. 14. Letter of March 30, 1758. C.O. 5/53.
p. 144, n. 15. Captain Parry of the *Kingston* to Admiralty, October 11, 1758. Ad. 1/2295.

CHAPTER 9

CHANNEL COMMAND

IN MANUSCRIPT

Captain's journal (1759)

Achilles Ad. 51/3747	*Firedrake* Ad. 51/3833
Basilisk Ad. 51/83	*Furnace* Ad. 51/3852
Blast Ad. 51/116	*Mortar* Ad. 51/4267
Carcass Ad. 51/162	*Vestal* Ad. 51/4000

Master's journal (1759)

Carcass Ad. 52/556	*Furnace* Ad. 52/596
Firedrake Ad. 52/854	*Mortar* Ad. 52/661

Letter-book, 1759–61. P.R.O. 30/20/7.
Order-book, 1759–61. P.R.O. 30/20/1.
Admiral's journal, August 26–December 31, 1759. Ad. 50/21.
Admiralty Secret Orders, 1759. Ad. 2/1331.
Rodney to Admiralty, 1759–60. Ad. 1/93.
Intelligence reports, 1759. Ad. 1/3945; 1760. Ad. 1/1746.

PRINTED

Grenville Papers, 4 vols, 1852–53 (ed. Smith).
Barrington Papers, vol. 1, Navy Records Society.

p. 151, n. 1. Rodney to Admiralty, June 6, 1759. Ad. 1/93.
p. 151, n. 2. Rodney to Admiralty, June 10, 1759. Ad. 1/93.
p. 152, n. 3. Intelligence report 'du Havre le 20 Juin 1759'. Ad. 1/3945.
p. 153, n. 4. Ad. 2/525.
p. 160, n. 5. P.R.O. 30/20/20.
p. 161, n. 6. B.M. Add. MSS. 32,893 fo. 269.
p. 164, n. 7. Rodney to Admiralty, June 18, 1759. Ad. 1/93.
p. 164, n. 8. Newcastle to Anson and Anson to Newcastle, June 15, 1759. B.M. Add. MSS. 32,892 folios 94–96.
p. 165, n. 9. Newcastle to Luxmore, November 15, 1759. B.M. Add. MSS. 32,898 fo. 273.
p. 165, n. 10. B.M. Add. MSS. 32,899 folios 266–7.
p. 167, n. 11. Captain's journal *Aquilon*. Ad. 51/76.
p. 168, n. 12. P.R.O. 30/20/7 and Ad. 1/93.
p. 170, n. 13. B.M. Add. MSS. 32,916 fo. 255.

CHAPTER 10

MARTINIQUE

IN MANUSCRIPT

Captain's journal 1761–62.

Basilisk Ad. 51/83	*Marlborough* Ad. 51/576
Dublin (*Douglas Papers*, Greenwich).	*Thunder* Ad. 51/4368
Foudroyant (*Duff Papers*, Greenwich).	

Master's Journal 1761–62.

Basilisk Ad. 52/543	*Marlborough* Ad. 52/1350
Granado Ad. 52/874	*Thunder* Ad. 52/1478

Letter-book 1761–63. P.R.O. 30/20/8.
Order-book 1761–63. P.R.O. 30/20/2.
Admiral's journal 1761–63. Ad. 50/23.
Admiralty Secret Orders 1761. Ad. 2/1331.
Rodney to Admiralty, 1761–62. Ad. 1/307.
Memorandum book, orders 1762. P.R.O. 30/20/16.
Anson Papers, Staffordshire Record Office. U/10/1.

p. 172, n.	1.	*Rodney Papers* (*Brizes Park*).
p. 172, n.	2.	B.M. Add. MSS. 32,915 fo. 111.
p. 173, n.	3.	B.M. Add. MSS. 32,916 fo. 257.
p. 173, n.	4.	B.M. Add. MSS. 32,919 fo. 324.
p. 174, n.	5.	B.M. Add. MSS. 32,921 folios 51–52.
p. 176, n.	6.	P.R.O. 30/20/14.
p. 179, n.	7.	Legge to Rodney, December 14, 1761. P.R.O. 30/20/8.
p. 183, n.	8.	Admiral's journal, January 15, 1762. Ad. 50/23.
p. 183, n.	9.	P.R.O. 30/20/19. Reproduced in *Signals and Instructions*.
p. 186, n.	10.	B.M. Add. MSS. 32,933 fo. 430.
p. 186, n.	11.	B.M. Add. MSS. 32,934 fo. 267.
p. 187, n.	12.	Letter of February 10, 1762, from an officer of Colonel Scott's light infantry. Quoted by Mundy.
p. 187, n.	13.	Monckton to Lord Egremont. Quoted by Mundy.
p. 187, n.	14.	Report of Commandant de Ligneris, February 11, 1762. C8 A64 Arch. Nat. (Col.) Paris.
p. 188, n.	15.	*War and Trade in the West Indies*, pp. 187–8.
p. 189, n.	16.	B.M. Add. MSS. 32,934 fo. 255.
p. 189, n.	17.	B.M. Add. MSS. 32,935 fo. 95.
p. 190, n.	18.	See in particular Marr to Rodney, October 20, 1775, P.R.O. 30/20/20. Also Captain Hollwall to Captain Duff, June 5, 1762, in the *Duff Papers* at Greenwich.
p. 190, n.	19.	Rodney to Amherst, February 23, 1762. P.R.O. 30/20/8.

CHAPTER 11

THE COMING OF POCOCK

IN MANUSCRIPT

Captain's journal *Foudroyant* 1762–63. Ad. 51/3843.
Letter-book 1761–63. P.R.O. 30/20/8.

Order-book 1761–63. P.R.O. 30/20/2.
Admiral's journal 1761–63. Ad. 50/23.
Admiralty Secret Orders, 1762. Ad. 2/1331.
Rodney to Admiralty, 1762–63. Ad. 1/307.
Memorandum book, orders, 1762–63. P.R.O. 30/20/16.

PRINTED

Grenville Papers, 4 vols, 1852–53 (ed. Smith).

p. 191, n. 1. Master's journal *Aquilon*, March 1762. Ad. 52/1152.
p. 192, n. 2. Lacour-Gayet, '*La Marine Militaire sous Louis XV*', 1910, p. 393.
p. 192, n. 3. Admiral's journal, Ad. 50/23.
p. 194, n. 4. Rodney's two letters to Monckton are March 9 and 14, 1762. P.R.O. 30/20/8.
p. 196, n. 5. '*Marlborough*, St John's roads, Antigua. March 24, 1762.' Ad. 1/307.
p. 200, n. 6. Pocock to Rodney, April 21, 1762.
p. 200, n. 7. Rodney to Pocock, April 27, 1762.
p. 201, n. 8. Pocock to Rodney, April 28, 1762.
p. 205, n. 9. Duff to Admiralty, August 28, 1762. Ad. 1/1704.
p. 205, n. 10. Rodney to Anson, July 22, 1762. P.R.O. 30/20/26.
p. 206, n. 11. ibid.
p. 206, n. 12. Rodney to General Rufane, June 19, 1762. P.R.O. 30/20/14.
p. 208, n. 13. Plan of St Pierre from the survey made by Captain Stott R.N. in 1763. At Greenwich.
p. 208, n. 14. Rodney to Grenville, December 4, 1762.
p. 208, n. 15. Rodney to Grenville, February 1, 1763.
p. 209, n. 16. Some of the Martinique accounts have survived in P.R.O. 30/20/20.
p. 209, n. 17. Rodney to Grenville, February 1, 1763.
p. 211, n. 18. Holburne to Rodney, May 12, 1763. P.R.O. 30/20/14.
p. 211, n. 19. P.R.O. 30/20/26.
p. 212, n. 20. P.R.O. 30/20/14.

CHAPTER 12

HIS MAJESTY'S BOUNTY

IN MANUSCRIPT

Minutes of the General Court of Governors of Greenwich Hospital, 1764–68. Ad. 67/10, 11.
Minutes of the Council of Directors of Greenwich Hospital, 1766–69. Ad. 67/135.

PRINTED

Grenville Papers, 4 vols, 1852–53 (ed. Smith).
The Palace and the Hospital, or Chronicles of Greenwich by the Rev. A. G. l'Estrange, 1886.

p. 214, n. 1. See twelve-page memorial submitted to Pitt in 1787. *Chatham Papers*. P.R.O. 30/8/172.

p. 214, n. 2. P.R.O. 30/20/26.
p. 217, n. 3. Webb's account in P.R.O. 30/20/16.
p. 219, n. 4. Account book P.R.O. 30/20/16.
p. 222, n. 5. Account books P.R.O. 30/20/16 and 20.
p. 222, n. 6. *Compton Papers* 1119.
p. 223, n. 7. *Compton Papers* 1125.
p. 224, n. 8. Namier and Brooke, *The History of Parliament: The House of Commons, 1754–1790.*
p. 224, n. 9. P.R.O. 30/20/20.
p. 225, n. 10. Rodney to Chatham, December 3, 1766. *Rodney Papers (Brizes Park).*
p. 225, n. 11. P.R.O. 30/20/25.

CHAPTER 13

THE NORTHAMPTON ELECTION

IN MANUSCRIPT

MSS. of Joseph Hall of 1785, original now lost. Copy in the Northamptonshire Record Office.

Minutes taken during the 1768 election. Northamptonshire Record Office.

Depositions and testimonies of the Parliamentary enquiry. Northamptonshire Record Office.

PRINTED

The Records of the Borough of Northampton (ed. C. A. Markham and J. C. Cox), Northampton 1898.

Current numbers of *Northampton Mercury.*

p. 227, n. 1. Lady Egmont to Lord Northampton, September 8 and 13, 1767. *Compton Papers* 1121.
p. 230, n. 2. Board minutes, Ad. 3/75.
p. 236, n. 3. Joseph Hall.
p. 236, n. 4. *The Comptons of Compton Winyates.*

CHAPTER 14

THE QUICKSANDS

p. 238, n. 1. P.R.O. 30/20/20.
p. 239, n. 2. See p. 101.
p. 239, n. 3. P.R.O. 30/20/22.
p. 239, n. 4. Rigby to Lowther, August 20, 1761. Lonsdale papers at Lowther.
p. 239, n. 5. P.R.O. 30/20/20.
p. 241, n. 6. Debts listed in Chancery 12/601/21. *Rodney v. Mackreth, Lonsdale and Garforth,* 1785.
p. 241, n. 7. Ad. 67/11.
p. 241, n. 8. *Rodney Papers (Brizes Park).*

p. 243, n. 9. Barrington to Hawke, August 6, 1770. *Mariner's Mirror*, XIX, 281–284.

p. 243, n. 10. Rodney to Sandwich, January 15, 1771. P.R.O. 30/20/26.

p. 244, n. 11. P.R.O. 30/20/20.

p. 245, n. 12. Chancery 12/601/21.

p. 245, n. 13. Memorandum written *c.* 1792. P.R.O. 30/20/22.

p. 247, n. 14. Rodney to Holburne n.d. Royal United Services Institute, NM 91. H2/69.

p. 247, n. 15. Rodney to Holburne, April 29, 1771. Royal United Services Institute, NM 91. H2/70.

p. 248, n. 16. Marr to Lord Northampton, May 5, 1771. *Compton Papers* 1123.

p. 248, n. 17. Marr to Lord Northampton, May 9, 1771. ibid.

p. 249, n. 18. *Compton Papers* 1135B.

p. 249, n. 19. P.R.O. 30/20/20.

CHAPTER 15

COMMANDER-IN-CHIEF, JAMAICA

IN MANUSCRIPT

Muster roll *Princess Amelia*, 1771. Ad. 36/7273.
Muster roll *Portland*, 1774. Ad. 36/8047.
Rodney to Admiralty, 1771–74. Ad. 1/239.

p. 250, n. 1. *Sandwich Papers*, vol. 1, p. 383.

p. 250, n. 2. Ad. 36/7273.

p. 251, n. 3. Rodney to Rear-Admiral Spry, May 27, 1771. P.R.O. 30/20/26.

p. 251, n. 4. Rodney to Lord Northampton, July 16, 1771. *Compton Papers* 1125.

p. 251, n. 5. James Rodney to Lord Northampton, July 15, 1771. *Compton Papers* 1126.

p. 253, n. 6. Minutes of Gibbs Court Martial. Ad. 1/5305.

p. 254, n. 7. *Sandwich Papers*, vol. 1, p. 380 n.

p. 254, n. 8. Sandwich to Rodney, August 15, 1771. P.R.O. 30/20/20.

p. 254, n. 9. Sandwich to Rodney, November 27, 1771. P.R.O. 30/20/21.

p. 255, n. 10. Sandwich to Rodney, December 30, 1771. P.R.O. 30/20/26.

p. 255, n. 11. Rodney to Admiralty, December 4, 1771. Ad. 1/239.

p. 256, n. 12. *Cal. of Home Office Papers*, February 24, 1772. Extract of a letter from Sir George Rodney dated 'Jamaica, Jan. 29 1772'.

p. 256, n. 13. P.R.O. 30/20/14.

p. 256, n. 14. P.R.O. 30/20/20.

p. 256, n. 15. P.R.O. 30/20/21.

p. 256, n. 16. Sandwich to Rodney, April 20, 1772. P.R.O. 30/20/21.

p. 257, n. 17. Marr to Lord Northampton, March 23, 1772. *Compton Papers* 1123.

p. 257, n. 18. Rodney to Lord Northampton, March 23, 1772. *Compton Papers* 1125.

p. 258, n. 19. See in particular Rodney to Admiralty, August 23, 1772. Ad. 1/239.

p. 258, n. 20. Sandwich to Rodney, March 18, 1772. P.R.O. 30/20/21.

p. 259, n. 21. Colonial Office, C.O. 5/154.

p. 259, n. 22. P.R.O. 30/20/20.
p. 259, n. 23. ibid.
p. 259, n. 24. ibid.
p. 259, n. 25. ibid.
p. 260, n. 26. Keppel to Rockingham, March 15, 1773. Printed in *Life of Viscount Keppel.*
p. 260, n. 27. Marr to Lord Northampton, April 6, 1773. *Compton Papers* 1123.
p. 260, n. 28. *Compton Papers* 1126.
p. 262, n. 29. Sandwich to Rodney, September 6, 1773. P.R.O. 30/20/20.
p. 263, n. 30. ibid.
p. 264, n. 31. Accounts. P.R.O. 30/20/20.
p. 264, n. 32. Kee to Rodney, July 3, 1772. P.R.O. 30/20/20.
p. 265, n. 33. Kee to Rodney, November 10, 1773. ibid.
p. 265, n. 34. Sandwich to Rodney, September 4, 1774. P.R.O. 30/20/20.
p. 266, n. 35. Rodney to Sandwich, September 7, 1774. *Sandwich Papers*, vol. I, pp. 388–9.

CHAPTER 16

TOTAL ECLIPSE

p. 269, n. 1. P.R.O. 30/20/20.
p. 270, n. 2. *Sandwich Papers* (unpublished).
p. 271, n. 3. George Rodney to his father, October 11, 1774. P.R.O. 30/20/20.
p. 271, n. 4. Marr to Rodney, October 8, 1774. ibid.
p. 271, n. 5. Pagett to Rodney, October 9, 1774. P.R.O. 30/20/14.
p. 271, n. 6. Marr to Rodney, October 23, 1774. P.R.O. 30/20/20.
p. 272, n. 7. Marr to Rodney, November 30, 1775. ibid.
p. 272, n. 8. Marr to Rodney, May 9, 1775. ibid.
p. 272, n. 9. Kee to Rodney, March 17, 1775, ibid.
p. 272, n. 10. Marr to Rodney, March 17, 1775. ibid.
p. 273, n. 11. Marr to Rodney, October 20, 1775. ibid.
p. 273, n. 12. Rodney to Germain, November 12, 1775. *H.M.C. Stopford Sackville MSS.*
p. 273, n. 13. George Rodney to his father, January 30, 1775, March 28, 1775, May 11, 1775. P.R.O. 30/20/20.
p. 274, n. 14. P.R.O. 30/20/14.
p. 274, n. 15. James Rodney to his father, October 24, 1773, August 26, 1774. P.R.O. 30/20/20.
p. 274, n. 16. P.R.O. 30/20/16.
p. 274, n. 17. *Sandwich Papers* (unpublished).
p. 276, n. 18. *Sandwich Papers* (unpublished).
p. 277, n. 19. P.R.O. 30/20/20.
p. 277, n. 20. ibid.
p. 278, n. 21. P.R.O. 30/20/26.
p. 279, n. 22. *Sandwich Papers* (unpublished).
p. 279, n. 23. P.R.O. 30/20/20.
p. 279, n. 24. *Sandwich Papers* (unpublished).

p. 280, n. 25. B.M. Add. MSS. 39,779 fo. 71.
p. 281, n. 26. Rodney to Stormont, March 13, 1778. *H.M.C. Stopford Sackville MSS.*
p. 282, n. 27. P.R.O. 30/20/22.
p. 283, n. 28. Greenwich 35. MS. 0288.
p. 283, n. 29. B.M. Add. MSS. 39,779 fo. 73.
p. 284, n. 30. Greenwich 35. MS. 0287.
p. 285, n. 31. Greenwich 35. MS. 0289.

CHAPTER 17

SUITOR FOR EMPLOYMENT

PRINTED

Lord George Germain by Alan Valentine. Clarendon Press 1962.

p. 287, n. 1. P.R.O. 30/20/26.
p. 287, n. 2. Some of Mrs Campbell's charges are in P.R.O. 30/20/16.
p. 288, n. 3. The note of hand and its covering letter are in P.R.O. 30/20/16.
p. 290, n. 4. Ad. 67/11.
p. 291, n. 5. Mrs Tyler to Rodney, May 20, 1783. P.R.O. 30/20/22.
p. 291, n. 6. *Rodney Papers (Brizes Park).*
p. 291, n. 7. Copy in P.R.O. 30/20/15.
p. 293, n. 8. Rodney to Germain, March 10, 1779. P.R.O. 30/20/21. Also in *Stopford Sackville MSS.*
p. 294, n. 9. P.R.O. 30/20/26.
p. 294, n. 10. *Sandwich Papers, vol. 3.* Cabinet minutes, September 16, 1779, pp. 181–182; Lord Sandwich's reassurances, p. 155.
p. 294, n. 11. Rodney to Germain, August 2, 1780. *Stopford Sackville MSS.*
p. 295, n. 12. P.R.O. 30/20/26.
p. 295, n. 13. Wraxall, p. 192.

CHAPTER 18

THE RELIEF OF GIBRALTAR

IN MANUSCRIPT

Captain's journals (1779–80). Ad. 51 series.
Ajax, Alcide, Alfred, Apollo, Bedford, Bienfaisant, Culloden, Cumberland, Defence, Edgar, Hyaena, Invincible, Marlborough, Prince George, Resolution, Sandwich, Terrible.
Master's journals (1779–80). Ad. 52 series.
Ajax, Alfred, Bedford, Cumberland, Defence, Invincible, Monarch, Montagu, Pegasus, Porcupine, Royal George, Sandwich, Triton.
Muster roll *Sandwich* (1779–80). Ad. 36/8863.
Rodney to Admiralty, 1779–80. Ad. 1/311.
Admiralty Secret Orders, 1779. Ad. 2/1336.

PRINTED

A History of the Siege of Gibraltar by Captain J. Drinkwater, late of the 72nd, *c.* 1785.

A Circumstantial Journal of the long and tedious blockade and Siege of Gibraltar by S. Ancell of the 58th Regt. Liverpool 1784.

Armada Espanola by C. F. Duro, Madrid 1901. Vol. 7.

p. 296, n. 1. Mundy, vol. 1, p. 263.
p. 296, n. 2. *Sandwich Papers, vol. 3*, pp. 188–189.
p. 297, n. 3. *Letters of Lord Barham, vol 1.*
p. 298, n. 4. *Rodney Papers (Brizes Park).*
p. 299, n. 5. Rodney to Germain, December 25, 1779. *H.M.C. Stopford Sackville MSS.*
p. 300, n. 6. Lists in P.R.O. 30/20/12 and 30/20/15.
p. 300, n. 7. P.R.O. 30/20/21.
p. 300, n. 8. ibid.
p. 301, n. 9. P.R.O. 30/20/15.
p. 302, n. 10. Rodney to Lady Rodney, December 11, 1779. Greenwich 35. MS. 029; December 16th and 23rd, Mundy, vol. 1, pp. 209–211.
p. 304, n. 11. *Signals and Instructions, 1779–1794*, pp. 180–234. Two sets of the Sailing and Fighting Instructions, one Captain Young's and the other apparently from Rodney's secretary's office are in P.R.O. 30/20/19.
p. 304, n. 12. Rodney to Vaughan, January 3, 1780. *Sir John Vaughan Papers*, William L. Clements Library, Michigan.
p. 306, n. 13. Young to Middleton, July 24, 1780, *Letters of Lord Barham*, vol. 1, pp. 64–66.
p. 310, n. 14. Mundy, vol. 1, pp. 221–222 n.
p. 314, n. 15. Rodney to Lady Rodney, February 7, 1780. ibid. p. 230.
p. 315, n. 16. *Sandwich Papers*, vol. 3, p. 193.
p. 315, n. 17. Pownoll to Sandwich, January 19, 1780. ibid, p. 192.
p. 315, n. 18. Rodney to Sandwich, February 4, 1780. ibid, p. 195.
p. 316, n. 19. Ross to Rodney, March 6, 1780.
p. 316, n. 20. Rodney to Sandwich, February 16, 1780. *Sandwich Papers*, vol. 3, pp. 201–202.
p. 316, n. 21. Rodney to Jackson, January 28, 1780. P.R.O. 30/20/10 and B.M. Add. MSS. 9344/42.

CHAPTER 19

FIRST EXCHANGES: DE GUICHEN

IN MANUSCRIPT

Captain's journals (1780). Ad. 51 series.
Alcide, Sandwich, Trident, Vengeance, Venus.
Master's journals (1780). Ad. 52 series.
Ajax, Albion, Montagu, Pegasus.
Rodney to Admiralty, 1780. Ad. 1/311.
Admiralty Secret Orders, 1779. Ad. 2/1336.

The Expedition of Major-General John Vaughan to the Lesser Antilles, 1779–1781, by R. N. McLarty. University of Michigan, doctoral dissertation, 1951.

p. 317, n. 1. *Life and Correspondence of Admiral Sir Sidney Smith* by J. Barrow, 1848. Vol. 1, p. 12.
p. 317, n. 2. Rodney to Lady Rodney, February 15, 1780. Greenwich 35. MS. 0291.
p. 319, n. 3. Secret Orders, December 8, 1779. Ad. 2/1336.
p. 319, n. 4. Letter of March 22, 1780. *Rodney Papers (Brizes Park).*
p. 321, n. 5. Letter to the editor of the *Athenaeum*, February 19, 1809.
p. 323, n. 6. Greenwich, 35. MS. 0237.
p. 324, n. 7. Letter to the editor of the *Athenaeum*, February 19, 1809.
p. 325, n. 8. According to Mundy (vol. 1, pp. 293–294 n.) de Bouillé related this anecdote to Rodney on a visit to England after the war.
p. 328, n. 9. Report by the gunner of the *Sandwich*, Ad. 1/311.
p. 329, n. 10. Rodney to George Rodney, April 26, 1780. P.R.O. 30/20/10.
p. 329, n. 11. Letter of April 26, 1780. *Sandwich Papers*, vol. 3.
p. 329, n. 12. Court Martial minutes in P.R.O. 30/20/18; also in *Letters of Lord Barham*, vol. 1.
p. 330, n. 13. Rodney to Sandwich, May 31, 1780. *Sandwich Papers*, vol. 3.
p. 330, n. 14. ibid, pp. 217–218.
p. 331, n. 15. P.R.O. 30/20/12. Also in Mundy, vol. 1.
p. 332, n. 16. Letter to the editor of the *Athenaeum*, February 19, 1809.
p. 336, n. 17. Letter of May 27, 1780. Mundy, vol. 1.
p. 336, n. 18. Letter of May 31, 1780. *Sandwich Papers*, vol. 3.
p. 340, n. 19. *Sir John Vaughan Papers*, William L. Clements Library, Michigan.
p. 340, n. 20. ibid. Letter of July 2, 1780.
p. 340, n. 21. Rodney to Anson, February 28, 1762. *Anson Papers*, U/10/1. Staffordshire Record Office.
p. 341, n. 22. Sandwich to Rodney, March 8 and 17, 1780, *Sandwich Papers*, vol. 3; North to Rodney, March 20, 1780, P.R.O. 30/20/21.
p. 342, n. 23. Lady Rodney to Rodney, February 23, 1780, and Miss Jane Rodney to Rodney, March 4, 1780, Mundy, vol. 1; Keppel to Rodney, March 6, 1780, P.R.O. 30/20/26; James Rodney to Rodney, March 2, 1780, P.R.O. 30/20/20.
p. 343, n. 24. Letter of July 30, 1780. Mundy, vol. 1.
p. 343, n. 25. Letter of May 27, 1780. ibid.
p. 343, n. 26. Letter of August 2, 1780. *H.M.C. Stopford Sackville MSS.*
p. 343, n. 27. Letter of July 30, 1780. Mundy, vol. 1.

CHAPTER 20

AMERICAN INTERLUDE

IN MANUSCRIPT

Captain's journal (1780) *Sandwich*. Ad. 51/840.
Rodney to Admiralty (1780). Ad. 1/311.
Letter-book (1780–1781). P.R.O. 30/20/9.
Arbuthnot to Admiralty (1780). Ad. 1/486.

PRINTED

Letter-books and Order-books of Admiral Lord Rodney, 1780–82, ed. Barck. Naval History Society, New York, 1932, vol. 1.

p. 345, n. 1. P.R.O. 30/20/12.
p. 345, n. 2. Rodney to Lord George Germain, March 10, 1779. P.R.O. 30/20/21. Also in *H.M.C. Stopford Sackville MSS.*
p. 346, n. 3. Letter of October 1, 1780. Greenwich 51. MS. 066/1.
p. 346, n. 4. Arbuthnot to Rodney, July 8, 1780; Rodney to Arbuthnot, August 16, 1780. Ad. 1/486.
p. 347, n. 5. Letter of April 20, 1780. P.R.O. 30/20/12.
p. 348, n. 6. Rodney to Vaughan, November 1, 1780. P.R.O. 30/20/21.
p. 348, n. 7. Clinton to Rodney, September 18, 1780. P.R.O. 30/20/12.
p. 349, n. 8. Arbuthnot to Rodney, September 20, 1780. P.R.O. 30/20/12; Rodney to Arbuthnot, September 25, 1780. Ad. 1/486.
p. 349, n. 9. Rodney to Jackson, November 12, 1780. B.M. Add. MSS. 9344/52.
p. 350, n. 10. *Letter-book and Order-book (Barck)*, vol. 1, p. 22.
p. 350, n. 11. Letter of October 3, 1780. P.R.O. 30/20/12.
p. 350, n. 12. Letter of October 5, 1780. *Sandwich Papers*, vol. 3.
p. 351, n. 13. B.M. Add. MSS. 9344/47.
p. 351, n. 14. Letter of October 16, 1780. P.R.O. 30/20/12. Also in Barck, vol. 1.
p. 352, n. 15. Letter of October 19, 1780. Ad. 1/311. Also in Barck, vol. 1, and Mundy, vol. 1.
p. 352, n. 16. Letter of October 30, 1780. P.R.O. 30/20/10.
p. 353, n. 17. P.R.O. 30/20/12.
p. 353, n. 18. The King to Sandwich, December 1, 1780. *Sandwich Papers*, vol. 3.
p. 353, n. 19. Rodney to Jackson, October 30, 1780. P.R.O. 30/20/10; Rodney to Admiralty, October 20, 1780. Mundy, vol. 1.
p. 353, n. 20. Rodney to Germain, December 22, 1780. *H.M.C. Stopford Sackville MSS.*
p. 354, n. 21. Muster roll *Sandwich* (1780), Ad. 36/8863 and *Pacahunta* (1780), Ad. 36/10400. Commissions in P.R.O. 30/20/20.
p. 354, n. 22. B.M. Add. MSS. 9344/52.
p. 355, n. 23. Laforey to Middleton, November 2, 1780. *Letters of Lord Barham*, vol. 2.
p. 355, n. 24. P.R.O. 30/20/12.

CHAPTER 21

ST EUSTATIUS

IN MANUSCRIPT

Captain's journals (1780). Ad. 51 series: *Gibraltar, Russell.*
Master's journals (1780). Ad. 52 series: *Barfleur.*
Rodney to Admiralty, 1780–1781. Ad. 1/314.
Letter-book (July 1780–April 1781). P.R.O. 30/20/9.
The Expedition of Major-General John Vaughan to the Lesser Antilles, 1779–1781, by R. N. McLarty. University of Michigan, doctoral dissertation, 1951.

PRINTED

A Plain State of Facts relative to the Capture of St Eustatius, c. 1787.

Letters from Sir George Bridges, now Lord Rodney to H.M. Ministers relative to the Capture of St Eustatius. 1789.

Letter-books and Order-books of Admiral Lord Rodney, 1780–82, ed. Barck. Naval History Society, New York, 1932.

p. 356, n. 1. Greenwich 35. MS. 0292.

p. 357, n. 2. Letter of September 25, 1780. P.R.O. 30/20/26 and *Sandwich Papers*, vol. 3.

p. 357, n. 3. Letter of December 10, 1780. Mundy, vol. 1.

p. 357, n. 4. Maylor to Rodney, September 5, 1780. P.R.O. 30/20/21.

p. 357, n. 5. Lady Rodney to Rodney, October 22, and November 13, 1780. P.R.O. 30/20/21.

p. 357, n. 6. P.R.O. 30/20/14.

p. 357, n. 7. Letter of December 26, 1780. *Letters of Lord Barham*, vol. 1.

p. 358, n. 8. ibid.

p. 358, n. 9. Rodney to Hood, February 5, 1781. Greenwich 50. MS. 0096.

p. 358, n. 10. Vaughan to Germain, December 22, 1780. C.O. 318/8.

p. 359, n. 11. Hood to Sandwich, September 16 and 18, 1780. *Sandwich Papers*, vol. 3.

p. 359, n. 12. Rodney to Sandwich, December 25, 1780. *Sandwich Papers*, vol. 4.

p. 359, n. 13. Rodney to Hood, January 4, 1781. Greenwich 50. MS. 0096.

p. 359, n. 14. *Journals and Letters of Sir T. Byam Martin*, Navy Records Society, 1902.

p. 359, n. 15. Keppel to Rodney, November 10, 1780. P.R.O. 30/20/26.

p. 360, n. 16. Most Secret Orders, December 20, 1780. Mundy, vol. 2.

p. 360, n. 17. Vaughan to Charles Jenkinson, President of the Board of Trade, February 13, 1781. C.O. 1/51.

p. 360, n. 18. Paper read to the Cabinet by Lord Sandwich, September 1779. *Sandwich Papers*, vol. 3.

p. 361, n. 19. Rodney to Whitshed Keene, April 26, 1781. Greenwich 51. MS. 066.

p. 361, n. 20. Barck, vol. 1.

p. 361, n. 21. Rodney to Lord Hillsborough, February 7, 1781. P.R.O. 30/20/21.

p. 362, n. 22. Pamphlet *c.* 1830 by 'An Old Naval Officer', in P.R.O. 30/20/21.

p. 362, n. 23. Rodney to Admiralty, February 10, 1781. P.R.O. 30/20/9.

p. 362, n. 24. Rodney to Sandwich, February 7, 1781. *Sandwich Papers*, vol. 4.
Rodney to Hillsborough, February 7, 1781. P.R.O. 30/20/21.
Rodney to Lady Rodney, February 7 and 12, 1781. Mundy, vol. 2.

p. 363, n. 25. A copy of the agreement is enclosed in Vaughan to Germain, February 7, 1781. C.O. 5/238.

p. 363, n. 26. Hood to Young, April 9, 1781. Greenwich 50. MS. 0096.
Hood to Rodney, February 7, 1783. P.R.O. 30/20/22.

p. 363, n. 27. *A Plain State of Facts* etc.

p. 365, n. 28. Rodney to Commissioner Laforey, February 27, 1781. P.R.O. 30/20/9.
Rodney to Admiralty, March 26, 1781. Ad. 1/314.

p. 366, n. 29. Rodney to Lady Rodney, March 18, 1781. Greenwich 35. MS. 0292.

p. 366, n. 30. Rodney to Sandwich, March 7, 1781. Mundy, vol. 2.

Rodney to Hood, March 15, 1781. Greenwich 50. MS. 0096 and P.R.O. 30/20/12.

p. 367, n. 31. Rodney to George Rodney, March 7, 1781. P.R.O. 30/20/21.

p. 367, n. 32. Rodney to Jackson, March 19, 1781, P.R.O. 30/20/9, and April 27, 1781, P.R.O. 30/20/22. Rodney to Lady Rodney, March 18, 1781. Greenwich 35. MS. 0292.

p. 367, n. 33. P.R.O. 30/20/21.

p. 368, n. 34. Laforey to Rodney, April 6, 1781. P.R.O. 30/20/9. Rodney to Laforey, April 14, 1781. Mundy, vol. 2. See also *Letters of Lord Barham*, vol. 2, pp. 123–126.

p. 368, n. 35. Later insertion by Sir George against his letter to Hood of March 15, 1781. Letter-book (1780–1781). P.R.O. 30/20/9.

p. 369, n. 36. Hood to Rodney, April 1, 9 and 28, 1781, P.R.O. 30/20/22. Hood to Young, April 9, 1781, Greenwich 50. MS. 0096.

p. 369, n. 37. Rodney to Colonel Bayard, March 29, 1781. P.R.O. 30/20/22.

p. 370, n. 38. *Letters of Lord Barham*, vol. 1, p. 97.

p. 371, n. 39. Hood to Middleton, May 4, 1781 (with Hood to Rodney of same date enclosed), ibid. Hood to Sandwich, May 4, 1781, *Sandwich Papers*, vol. 4. Hood to Jackson, May 21, 1781, *Letters of Sir Samuel Hood*.

p. 373, n. 40. Hood to Rodney, May 12, 1781, P.R.O. 30/20/12. Muster roll *Pacahunta* (1781) Ad. 36/10400. Rodney to Hood, May 13, 1781, Greenwich 50. MS. 0096.

p. 374, n. 41. Governor Ferguson to Germain, June 5, 1781, and the inhabitants of Tobago to Governor Ferguson, June 6, 1781. C.O. 101/24.

p. 375, n. 42. Letter of June 24, 1781. *Letters of Sir Samuel Hood*.

p. 375, n. 43. *Letters to H.M. Ministers* etc.

p. 375, n. 44. Akers to Rodney, June 30, 1781. P.R.O. 30/20/22.

p. 376, n. 45. Letter to Jackson, *Letters of Sir Samuel Hood*.

p. 376, n. 46. C.O. 318/7.

p. 377, n. 47. Ad. 1/314.

p. 377, n. 48. *Sandwich Papers*, vol. 4.

p. 377, n. 49. Mundy, vol. 2.

CHAPTER 22

DETERMINED TO SERVE AGAIN

IN MANUSCRIPT

Captain's journal *Gibraltar* (1781). Ad. 51/395.
Rodney to Admiralty, 1781–82. Ad. 1/314.

PRINTED

Letter-books and Order-books of Admiral Lord Rodney, 1780–82 (ed. Barck), Naval History Society, New York, 1932.
Debrett's *Parliamentary Register*, vol. 22.
Current files of *Hampshire Chronicle* and *Northampton Mercury*.

p. 378, n. 1. Debrett's *Parliamentary Register*, vol. 22.
p. 378, n. 2. *Gibraltar* muster roll (1781). Ad. 36/9454.
p. 378, n. 3. P.R.O. 30/20/17.
p. 379, n. 4. J. F. Jameson, *American Historical Review*, VIII, pp. 701–702.
p. 379, n. 5. Lady Rodney to Rodney, March 22, 1781, P.R.O. 30/20/21 Duke; of Chandos to Rodney, March 24, 1781, ibid.
p. 380, n. 6. George Rodney to Rodney, December 6, 1780, P.R.O. 30/20/20; Mr Thomas Harley to Rodney, December 6, 1780, P.R.O. 30/20/24; Rodney to George Rodney, February 6, 1781, *Rodney Papers (Brizes Park)*.
p. 380, n. 7. Lady Rodney to Rodney, November 13, 1780. P.R.O. 30/20/21.
p. 380, n. 8. Lady Rodney to Rodney, March 17, 1781, Mundy, vol. 2.
p. 381, n. 9. Mundy, vol. 2, p. 156. *Hampshire Chronicle*, October 1, 1781.
p. 382, n. 10. Letter of September 30, 1781. *Letters of Lord Barham*, vol. 1.
p. 382, n. 11. Rodney to Jackson, October 19, 1781. B.M. Add. MSS. 9344/59.
p. 383, n. 12. Letter of October 19, 1781. P.R.O. 30/20/10.
p. 383, n. 13. P.R.O. 30/20/21.
p. 383, n. 14. *Pembroke Papers* (ed. Lord Herbert), Cape, London, 1950.
p. 383, n. 15. Rodney to Sandwich, November 4, 1781, *Sandwich Papers*, vol. 4; Rodney to Jackson, November 8, 1781, P.R.O. 30/20/10.
p. 384, n. 16. *Northampton Mercury*, October 15, 1781.
p. 384, n. 17. Rodney to Admiralty, November 20, 24, 28, and December 5, 6, 7, 1781. Ad. 1/314.
p. 387, n. 18. Debrett's *Parliamentary Register*, vol. 22.
p. 387, n. 19. P.R.O. 30/20/21.
p. 387, n. 20. Greenwich 35. MS. 0295.
p. 387, n. 21. Letter of January 6, 1782. *Sandwich Papers*, vol. 4.

CHAPTER 23

THE SAINTS

IN MANUSCRIPT

Admiral's journal (1781–82). P.R.O. 30/20/3.
Captain's journals (1782). Ad. 51 series:
Alcide, Andromeda, Andromache, Anson, Bedford, Belliqueux, Fame, Formidable, Jupiter, Marlborough, Monarch, Montagu, Prince George, Russell, Torbay.
Master's journal (1782). Ad. 52 series: *Centaur.*

PRINTED

Letter-books and Order-books of Admiral Lord Rodney, 1780–82 (ed. Barck). Naval History Society, New York, 1932.
Histoire de la Marine Française pendant la guerre de l'Independence Americain, by E. Chevalier. Paris, 1877.
Naval Researches by Captain Thomas White, London, 1830.

Naval Battles by Rear-Admiral Ekins, 1824.
Select Dissertations on Subjects of Medical Science by Doctor Gilbert Blane.
Account of the Battle . . . in a letter to Lord Dalrymple, by Doctor Gilbert Blane, 1782.
Life and letters of Admiral Cornwallis by G. Cornwallis West, Robert Holden, 1927.

p. 389, n. 1.   *Correspondence of General Washington and the Comte de Grasse,* Washington, 1931.

p. 390, n. 2.   Rodney to the Commissioner of Victualling, March 16, 1782. Barck, vol. 1, p. 299.

p. 390, n. 3.   Rodney to George Rodney, March 15, 1782. P.R.O. 30/20/24.

p. 391, n. 4.   Hood to Sandwich, April 3, 1782. *Sandwich Papers,* vol. 4.

p. 392, n. 5.   Mundy, vol. 2.

p. 393, n. 6.   Letter to Robert Udney, March 31, 1782. P.R.O. 30/20/21.

p. 393, n. 7.   Hood to Middleton, April 3, 1782. *Letters of Lord Barham,* vol. 1.

p. 394, n. 8.   *Life and letters of Admiral Cornwallis.*

p. 395, n. 9.   Blane. *Letter to Lord Dalrymple.*

p. 397, n. 10.   *Breaking the Line* by 'An Old Naval Officer', ('G.C.', a lieutenant in the *Hercules*), Cheltenham, 1830.

p. 398, n. 11.   Letters to *London Courier,* July 8, September 19, and November 13, 1829. Also Ekin's *Naval Battles,* 1824.

p. 400, n. 12.   P.R.O. 30/20/21 which contains most of the controversial writing relating to the battle.

p. 402, n. 13.   Wraxall, p. 466.

p. 403, n. 14.   Affleck to Sandwich, April 25, 1782. *Sandwich Papers,* vol. 4.

p. 403, n. 15.   Douglas to Middleton, April 28, 1782. *Letters of Lord Barham,* vol. 1.

p. 404, n. 16.   Hood to Sandwich, April 13, 1782, *Sandwich Papers,* vol. 4; Hood to Middleton, April 13, 1782, *Letters of Lord Barham,* vol. 1; Hood to Jackson, April 16, 1782, *Letters of Sir Samuel Hood.*

p. 404, n. 17.   'Reasons for not pursuing the enemy after the victory', Mundy, vol. 2, pp. 248–250 and P.R.O. 30/20/26.

p. 404, n. 18.   Rodney to Lady Rodney, April 13, 1782. Mundy, vol. 2.

p. 405, n. 19.   Wraxall, p. 463.

p. 405, n. 20.   Blane, *Letter to Lord Dalrymple.*

p. 405, n. 21.   Hood to Middleton, April 13, 1782, *Letters of Lord Barham,* vol. 1; Hood to Jackson, April 16, 1782, *Letters of Sir Samuel Hood.*

p. 406, n. 22.   *Rodney Papers (Brizes Park).*

p. 406, n. 23.   Blain, *Letter to Lord Dalrymple.*

p. 407, n. 24.   *Life and letters of Admiral Cornwallis.*

p. 408, n. 25.   Warrants etc., April–June 1782. P.R.O. 30/20/17.

p. 409, n. 26.   P.R.O. 30/20/26.

p. 409, n. 27.   Miss Rodney to Rodney, May 27, 1782. Mundy, vol. 2.

p. 409, n. 28.   *Hampshire Chronicle,* June 3, 1782.

p. 410, n. 29.   P.R.O. 30/20/26.

p. 410, n. 30.   ibid.

p. 410, n. 31.   Shelburne to Rodney, May 30, 1782. ibid.

p. 410, n. 32.   Lady Rodney to Rodney, n.d., P.R.O. 30/20/21.

p. 410, n. 33.   Cobbett's *Parliamentary History, 1782–83,* XXIII, p. 78.

p. 411, n. 34.   Sandwich to Rodney, May 26, 1782. P.R.O. 30/20/21.

p. 412, n. 35.   *Rodney Papers (Brizes Park).*

CHAPTER 24

BLEAK GLORY

PRINTED

Letters of John Wilkes to his daughter (1774–1796), pub. 1804.
Current files of *Hampshire Chronicle* and *Northampton Mercury*.

p. 413, n. 1.   *Sandwich Papers* (unpublished).

p. 414, n. 2.   *Hampshire Chronicle* and *Northampton Mercury*, September–October 1782.

p. 414, n. 3.   Rodney to Lady Rodney n.d. Greenwich 38. MS. 0297–0299.

p. 415, n. 4.   *Hampshire Chronicle*, Dec. 1782.

p. 415, n. 5.   Letter n.d., B.M. Add. MSS. 39,779 fo. 146.

p. 415, n. 6.   P.R.O. 30/20/26.

p. 415, n. 7.   Greenwich 38. MS. 0300.

p. 416, n. 8.   *Northampton Mercury*, January–March 1783.

p. 416, n. 9.   Greenwich 38. MS. 0297.

p. 416, n. 10.   Wilkes to his daughter, vol. 2, letters CVIII, CXII, CXIII.

p. 416, n. 11.   Account from Paul Maylor, P.R.O. 30/20/21.

p. 417, n. 12.   P.R.O. 30/20/22.

p. 417, n. 13.   Greenwich 36. MS. 0946.

p. 417, n. 14.   Charges for work done between March and December 1785. P.R.O. 30/20/18.

p. 418, n. 15.   Wilkes to his daughter, vol. 3, letter XXI.

p. 419, n. 16.   Letter of September 24, 1784, formerly in possession of Maldwin Drummond, Esq.

p. 419, n. 17.   Captain Thomas White to 3rd Lord Rodney, *c.* 1832, P.R.O. 30/20/21.

p. 420, n. 18.   P.R.O. 30/20/22.

p. 420, n. 19.   William Knox to General Vaughan, *c.* April 1786; Rodney to Knox, July 1, 1786; letter from Thomas Digges, August 2, 1786. *Shelburne Papers*, W. L. Clements Library, University of Michigan.

p. 420, n. 20.   Petition to the King, May 1787. P.R.O. 30/20/21.

p. 421, n. 21.   Rodney to Vaughan, September 7, 1788. *Egerton MSS.* B.M. 2137 fo. 45.

p. 421, n. 22.   Wilkes to his daughter, vol. 3, letter XLIV.

p. 421, n. 23.   P.R.O. 30/20/21.

p. 421, n. 24.   P.R.O. 30/20/24.

p. 422, n. 25.   'Paper received from Lord Rodney, March 1788', *Liverpool Papers*, B.M. Add. MSS. 38,416 fo. 71; Rodney to Mrs Rodney, July 4, 1788, P.R.O. 30/20/21.

p. 422, n. 26.   Rodney to Captain John Willett Payne, November 18, 1788. 38258–9 Royal Archives, Windsor Castle. Wilkes to his daughter, January 20, 1789, vol. 3, letter LXXVIII.

p. 422, n. 27.   Rodney to Chatham, March 18, 1789. P.R.O. 30/20/21.

p. 423, n. 28.   Rodney to Mrs Rodney, July 4 and September 21, 1788; to George Rodney, October 13, 1788. ibid.

p. 423, n. 29.   *Rodney v. Mackreth, Lonsdale and Garforth, 1785.* C.12/601/21.

p. 423, n. 30. Rodney to Miss Anne Rodney, n.d., Mundy, vol. 2, p. 371.
p. 424, n. 31. P.R.O. 30/20/26.
p. 424, n. 32. Mundy, vol. 2, pp. 361–2.
p. 424, n. 33. Letter of April 30, 1792. P.R.O. 30/20/26.
p. 424, n. 34. Mundy, vol. 2, pp. 362–363.

CHAPTER 25

AFTERWARDS

p. 425, n. 1. volume 4, letter XLII.
p. 425, n. 2. P.R.O. 30/8/172.
p. 426, n. 3. *Le duc de Lauzun* by Comte R. de Gontaut Biron, Librarie Plon, Paris, 1937.
p. 426, n. 4. George, 2nd Lord Rodney, to A. B. Drummond, December 8, 1801. Letter in possession of Maldwin Drummond, Esq.
p. 426, n. 5. P.R.O. 30/20/23.
p. 426, n. 6. O'Byrne's *Naval Biographical Dictionary*, 1849. *The Complete Peerage* (1895), vol. 6.
p. 426, n. 7. James's *Naval History* (1878 ed.), vol. 3, pp. 36–37.
p. 430, n. 8. Rodney to Admiralty, September 26, 1756. Ad. 1/2385.

Index

469

Rodney, Catherine, John's wife 216
Rodney, Edward (sixth child) 216, 418;
naval career 426
Rodney, George, captain of marines 17, 20,
22
Rodney, George (son) (later 2nd Lord
Rodney), Pl. XVIII, 111, 118, 119,
120, 123, 145, 222, 261, 380, 417, 421,
423, 426; affection for father 270,
271; and Rodney's creditors 277;
warns Rodney not to return to
England 277; Rodney's attorney 298;
marries 379; Rodney with 423;
transforms father's affairs 416; writes
to Lord Sandwich 270-1
Rodney, Mrs George 423
RODNEY, Admiral Lord George Bridges 21,
22, 23, 39, 123, 217, 432, 434, 435, 437,
438, 443; Pls. I, XVI, XVII; able
seaman 30; accepts Biron's help 284;
accepts Jamaica command 244; and
Admiralty 58; admiral of the White
300; Admiralty seat 224; allowed half
pay 291; at Alresford 111, 145, 423;
and ambassador on debts 282; and
Americans 262; and anti-slavery 422;
applies for land in West Indies 208,
213-14; and Arbuthnot 346 ff.; arguments over the dealing 427 ff.; attacks
Spain 306; a baronet 214, 410; at Bath
38 ff.; blamed for Hood failure 372;
on blockade 170; on books of Berwick
36; and H.M.S. Bounty 213 ff.;
buried at Alresford 425; buys farms
125; and Cadiz merchants 102; and
card sharper 239 n; captain of the
Plymouth 54, 55; captures French
merchantmen 262; captures Spanish
ships 305; censures officers 328-30;
and Channel Fleet 299; chosen to
counter invasion 149; to Clinton 355;
command, hope of 272; commands
Dublin 132-46; commands Eagle
70 ff.; commands Fougueux 113;
commands Kent 110; commands
Ludlow Castle 64 ff.; commands
Monarch 122; commands Marlborough
176; commands Prince George 115 ff.;
commands Rainbow 94 ff.; commands
Sheerness 59; commended 46, 54;
complains about inefficiency 151-2;
complains against Dutch 363; and the
Comptons 103-4; to Charles Compton
120; conflict with Hood 404; congratulated 341; to Continent 418;
convalesces at Barbados 209; Council
of War 135, 154-5; acts counter to
Royal decree 375; and court martials
87 f., 121, 126; creditors of 298; and
customs 248; daughters born 127, 225,
274; daughter goes to Gretna Green
to marry 418; death of 424; debts of
225, 238 ff., 266; and deserters 127;

RODNEY, Admiral Lord George Bridges—
continued
detains French officers 168; on disobedience of officers 331; on dissolving
Parliament 265; and dispute with
Arbuthnot 350-1; joins Dolphin 40;
on Dreadnaught 29 ff.; dreads return-
int to debts 264; at Dublin 61, 62;
and Duff 203; and Dutch in West
Indies 361; early Naval life 30 ff.,
38 ff.; eclipse of 269 ff.; in England
again 286; to H.M.S. Essex 46;
executor of Compton will 121; faces
the enemy 320; family return in
Portland 263 f.; and family 379;
finances of 86 f., 416, 417; to First
Lord on Hyde Parker 366-7; and
Fox's order 76; a freeman 291; freeman of Northampton 229, 233; freeman of the City 384, 414; freeman of
Huntingdon 416; and freight money
67; on French incident 118-19; and
French ships in West Indies 192 ff.;
furniture on Sandwich 378; on future
258; gambling debts of 238 ff.; in
Garner Bay 347; and George (brother)
242; to son George 278; with son
George 423; to Lord Germain 273;
and the Gibbs affair 254; in Gibraltar
Bay 313; Governor of Jamaica 258-9;
Governor of Newfoundland 94; and
grandchildren 423; to Grenville 208;
Governor of Greenwich Hospital
218 ff.; handwriting, Pl. X; and
Harrow 25; and health of men
343-4; to Henry on debts 282; to
Henrietta on victory 362; to Henrietta
387; house built 102-3; honours of
446; and Hood's complaining 368;
to Hood 378; and House of Hanover
67; ill-health of 108-9, 128, 144,
210, 222, 266, 366, 376, 387, 416;
informs King of victory 406; impatient of return 280; instructions to
attack Havre 153; interests of 222;
Jamaica C.-in-C. 250, 257; Jamaica,
relieved of 267; farewell letter to
Jane (wife) 117; to Jane 113, 114, 115,
116, 120; to Jane (daughter) 367;
leadership of 377; life as lieutenant
40 ff.; at Lisbon 38, 57; loans offered
245; loses flagship 200; loses Saltash
seat 112; loses Okehampton seat 173;
loss of parents 36; married life of
111 f.; marries Henrietta Clies 217;
marriis Jane Compton 110; M.P. for
Saltash 104; M.P. for Okehampton
164; and merchants 206; 365-6, 377,
381, 420; mixed reception 381; and
money worries 343, 415; death of
mother 36; 5th Lieutenant of Namur
48; and new command 319; at Newfoundland 92, 107; and New York 354;